D0520206

Using MS-DOS® 5

Que® Development Group

Using MS-DOS® 5

Library of Congress Catalog No.: 90-63254

ISBN: 0-88022-668-4

93 92   9 8 7 6 5

Interpretation of the printing code: the rightmost double-digit number is the year of the book's printing; the rightmost single-digit number, the number of the book's printing. For example, a printing code of 91-1 shows that the first printing of the book occurred in 1991.

Some of the art in this book was created by Hartman Publishing.

This book is based on MS-DOS Version 5.0 and earlier versions.

Publisher: Lloyd J. Short

Associate Publisher: Karen A. Bluestein

Acquisitions Manager: Terrie Lynn Solomon

Product Development Manager: Mary Bednarek

Managing Editor: Paul Boger

Book Designer: Scott Cook

Production Team: Martin Coleman, Sandy Grieshop, Betty Kish, Bob LaRoche, Kimberly Leslie, Howard Peirce, Tad Ringo, Bruce Steed, Suzanne Tully, Susan VandeWalle, Mary Beth Wakefield, Lisa Wilson

Product Director
Walter R. Bruce III

Senior Editor
Jeannine Freudenberger

Editors
Sara Allaei
Gail S. Burlakoff
Barbara K. Koenig

Technical Editor
Greg Schultz

Composed in Garamond and Macmillan
by Que Corporation

TRADEMARK
ACKNOWLEDGMENTS

Q ue Corporation has made every effort to supply trademark information about company names, products, and services mentioned in
this book. Trademarks indicated below were derived from various sources.
Que Corporation cannot attest to the accuracy of this information.

Apple and ProDOS are registered trademarks of Apple Computer, Inc.

AutoCAD is a registered trademark of Autodesk, Inc.

COMPAQ is a registered trademark of COMPAQ Computer Corporation.

CP/M is a registered trademark of DRI and Crosstalk is a registered trademark of Digital
Communications Associates, Inc.

dBASE III PLUS is a trademark and dBASE IV is a registered trademark of Ashton-Tate
Corporation.

DESKMATE is a trademark of Radio Shack.

First Publisher and Harvard Graphics are trademarks of Software Publishing Corporation.

IBM, IBM PC XT, and Quietwriter are registered trademarks and IBM ProPrinter and PS/2 are
trademarks of International Business Machines Corporation.

Lotus, 1-2-3, Freelance, and Symphony are registered trademarks of Lotus Development
Corporation.

Managing Your Money is a registered trademark of Micro Education Corporation of America
(MECA).

MS-DOS, Microsoft, and XENIX are registered trademarks of Microsoft Corporation.

Norton Utilities is a trademark of Symantec Corporation.

PageMaker is a registered trademark of Aldus Corporation.

Paradox is a registered trademark of Ansa Corporation.

PC TOOLS Deluxe is a trademark of Central Point Software.

PROCOMM PLUS is a registered trademark of DATASTORM Technologies.

Q&A is a registered trademark of Symantec Corporation.

Quattro is a registered trademark of Borland International, Inc.

Quicken is a registered trademark of Intuit.

Reflex: The Analyst is a trademark of Borland-Analytica, Inc.

SideKick is a registered trademark of Borland International, Inc.

Smart is a copyright of Innovative Software.

SpinRite II is a trademark of Gibson Research Corporation.

SuperCalc is a registered trademark of Computer Associates International, Inc.

UNIX is a registered trademark of AT&T.

Ventura Publisher is a registered trademark of Software, Inc.

WordPerfect is a registered trademark of WordPerfect Corporation.

WordStar is a registered trademark of WordStar International.

XTreePro is a trademark of Executive Systems, Inc.

Zenith is a registered trademark of Zenith Electronics Corp.

Trademarks of other products mentioned in this book are held by the
companies producing them.

Walter R. Bruce III is the author of Que's *Using Enable/OA; Using Paradox 3; Using DataEase; Using PROCOMM PLUS*, Second Edition; *Using PC Tools Deluxe*; and *Using Carbon Copy Plus*. He has written several instructional texts for use in intermediate and advanced workshops on using popular microcomputer software packages. He also has led workshops for government and private industry clients.

Donald R. Eamon is a production editor for Que Corporation. He also served as a columnist for *Computer Shopper Magazine* and is author of over 60 articles that cover such diverse computer-related subjects as software-piracy prevention, hardware problem-solving techniques, and graphical interface philosophy.

Phil Feldman has written many articles in engineering journals and personal computer magazines. He is the author of Using *QBASIC* and was a contributing author to *Que's MS-DOS 5 User's Guide*, Special Edition. With Tom Rugg, he has coauthored more than a dozen books, including *Using QuickBASIC 4* and *QuickBASIC Programmer's Toolkit*. Feldman is chairman of 32 Plus, Inc., a software development and consulting firm.

David W. Solomon is product development director for New Riders Publishing and specializes in operating systems, database management, and programming. He has developed custom software for scientific and business applications. Solomon is author of *MS-DOS QuickStart* and *Using UNIX* and a coauthor of *Que's MS-DOS 5 User's Guide*, Special Edition; *Using dBASE IV*; and *Using Turbo Prolog*, all published by Que Corporation.

Timothy S. Stanley, a product development specialist for Que Corporation, also has served as technical editor and author for several of Que's titles. Specializing in operating systems and environments and in spreadsheet and database applications, Stanley has contributed to *Que's MS-DOS 5 User's Guide*, Special Edition; *Using 1-2-3 Release 3.1*, Second Edition; *Using dBASE IV*; *Upgrading to DOS 5*; *Windows 3 Quick Reference*; and *Batch Files and Macros Quick Reference*.

Rich Ward writes and works in the software industry. His projects have included work on teams developing Lotus 1-2-3 Release 3, SunOS, SCO UNIX/XENIX, and 1-2-3 Release 2.3. He works as a software engineer for the start-up company Beyond, Inc., Cambridge, MA.

Contents at a Glance

TABLE OF CONTENTS ▼

I   The Role of DOS in Personal Computers

III Getting the Most from DOS

13 Understanding Batch Files, DOSKey, and Macros 401

IV   Command Reference

V   Appendixes

Introduction

Since its introduction in 1981, MS-DOS has grown to be the most widely used operating system in the world. Thousands of applications programs have been written for the MS-DOS operating system. With over 10 million users, MS-DOS affects more people than any other software product ever written.

As MS-DOS has evolved, Que Corporation has helped hundreds of thousands of personal computer users get the most from MS-DOS. *Using MS-DOS 5* represents Que's continuing commitment to provide the best microcomputer books in the industry.

MS-DOS is the operating system of choice for most personal computer users and will remain so for the foreseeable future. *Using MS-DOS 5* offers DOS users a source of information to help them organize their work with the PC more effectively, make their hardware respond more efficiently, and provide a resource of answers to questions about the capabilities of DOS.

Who Should Read This Book?

Using MS-DOS 5 is written for PC users who need a tutorial reference to DOS. The book explains the key concepts of DOS without being technical and intimidating. Developed to address the majority of your DOS needs, *Using MS-DOS 5* also recognizes that your learning time is limited. Whether you are just beginning to use DOS or you have been using MS-DOS 5 and need a better understanding of it, *Using MS-DOS 5* is for you.

What Hardware Is Needed?

This book applies to the family of IBM personal computers and their close compatibles. This list of computers includes the IBM Personal Computer, the IBM Personal Computer XT, the IBM Personal Computer AT, and the IBM PS/2 series. Dozens of other computers that use MS-DOS and are manufactured or sold by COMPAQ, Zenith Data Systems, EPSON, Leading Edge, Tandy, Dell, Northgate, CompuAdd, and other companies also are covered by this book. If your computer runs the MS-DOS operating system, you have the necessary hardware.

What Versions of DOS Are Covered?

This book specifically covers MS-DOS and IBM DOS Versions 3 and later. Special attention is given to Version 5.0 and to the DOS Shell. Users of DOS 2 also will find their version covered to their satisfaction. If you use DOS 2, you can generalize much of the book to that version, but many useful DOS features and commands included in the newer DOS versions are not available to you.

What Is Not Covered?

Some of the more esoteric DOS commands and less frequently used switches and parameters are not covered in the text but are included in the Command Reference. *Using MS-DOS 5* does not include coverage of the DEBUG or LINK commands, for example, nor does this book include a technical reference to the DOS applications programming interface. If you are interested in programming at the operating system level, you will find that Que offers a complete line of books that cover DOS programming.

Also not included in this book are computer-specific setup or configuration commands, such as IBM's SETUP for the PS/2 and Toshiba's CHAD for laptop displays. Although these commands are often distributed with the same disks as MS-DOS, the commands vary too much from one manufacturer to another to be covered adequately here. Your computer-supplied manuals and your PC dealer are the best sources of information about machine-specific features.

The Details of This Book

You can flip quickly through this book to get a feeling for its organization. *Using MS-DOS 5* begins with fundamentals and builds your DOS capabilities to a practical level. The Command Reference provides a resource to commands as well as an information base to complete your DOS expertise. The book also includes a set of useful appendixes. The book is divided into four parts.

Part I: The Role of DOS in Personal Computers

Part I is an introductory tutorial on the PC and DOS. If you are a DOS beginner, Part I lays a foundation of understanding on which you will draw while reading the rest of the book.

Chapter 1, "Understanding the Personal Computer," takes a look at today's PCs. The chapter explores the major components of the PC and addresses the use of system and peripheral hardware. In this chapter, you get a feel not only for your system but also for systems with different keyboards, displays, and peripherals.

Chapter 2, "Understanding the Role of DOS," introduces DOS as the PC's operating system. This chapter examines DOS from both a product-oriented and a software-oriented point of view. Chapter 2's explanations of the parts of DOS and how they interact clears up any confusion about what DOS does on your PC.

Chapter 3, "Starting DOS," steps through the process of booting DOS, explaining important concepts along the way. You also are introduced to the DOS Shell, the visually oriented user interface provided with DOS 5.

Chapter 4, "Using the DOS Shell," gets you up and running with the DOS Shell. This chapter explores the DOS Shell screen and discusses the aspects of the Shell common to all its commands.

Chapter 5, "Using DOS Commands," introduces DOS commands and tells you how to use them. You learn the concepts behind issuing commands at the DOS command line. The chapter explains syntax, parameters, and switches in an easy-to-learn fashion. Important keys and various examples of the DIR command also are covered.

Chapter 6, "Understanding Disks and Files," recognizes the important job DOS performs in managing disks and files. This chapter defines files and clearly explains file-naming conventions. Also explored are the uses of hard disks and floppy disks and the common disk capacities available with DOS, as well as the disk-level DOS commands that copy and compare floppy disks and analyze disks for damage.

Part II: Putting DOS To Work for You

This part of the book covers the DOS commands and concepts that make up the core of DOS's utility. With your knowledge of Part II, you will be able to use DOS effectively to manage your PC work.

Chapter 7, "Understanding Disk Preparation and Management," examines the process of formatting disks. You learn what formatting does and how DOS uses formatted disks to store your files. You also learn how to partition a hard disk into sections that DOS can use as logical disks. Also presented is the disk-level DOS command, CHKDSK, which analyzes disks for damage.

Chapter 8, "Understanding Hierarchical Directories," explains fully the important concept of DOS tree-structured directories. This inside look at DOS's file-management strategy prepares you to manage the DOS file system.

Chapter 9, "Managing Directories," picks up where Chapter 8 leaves off. In this chapter, you use DOS Shell and DOS command-line directory-level commands to customize a multilevel file system on your PC. You learn how to create, change, and remove DOS directories. Included are commands that enable you to view your directory structure.

Chapter 10, "Keeping Files in Order," illuminates the file-level DOS Shell and DOS command-line commands. Because you are likely to spend most of your time with DOS working with files, this chapter offers an in-depth view of these commands. The text explains each command with examples that will help you appreciate the full power of the important file-level commands.

Chapter 11, "Understanding Backups and the Care of Data," offers some important considerations for protecting your data. DOS provides several important commands that enable users to maintain disk backup sets of a hard disk's contents. These commands and the concept of developing a backup policy are discussed in this chapter.

Part III: Getting the Most from DOS

Part III provides the information you need to tap the expanded power available with DOS. This part of the book helps you use the many features provided with DOS and helps you customize your computer system.

Chapter 12, "Using the DOS Editor," provides a tutorial approach to DOS's built-in, full-screen, text-file editor. The examples developed in this chapter show you how to use the MS-DOS Editor as a day-to-day utility. With the careful attention given to the Editor's practical use, you learn the skills needed to compose a text file. Practical examples of using the Editor to create memos and batch files also are presented.

Chapter 13, "Understanding Batch Files, DOSKey, and Macros," guides you through the process by creating batch files and keystroke macros. The commands related to batch files are explained in a tutorial style. Useful examples help make mastering the basics of batch files easier. The important concept of the AUTOEXEC.BAT file also is explored. The new keystroke-recording utility DOSKey is introduced. You learn how to use DOSKey to make entering DOS commands easier and faster, as well as how to record commonly used commands as macros.

Chapter 14, "Configuring the DOS Shell," discusses how you can customize your use of the DOS Shell. In this chapter, you learn how to set various options that determine how you interact with the Shell. You also learn how to add and remove program items and program groups from the program list area of the DOS Shell window and how to associate particular file name extensions with a specific application program listed in the program list.

Chapter 15, "Configuring Your Computer and Managing Devices," is a comprehensive collection of DOS commands that helps you get the best performance from your PC. By using these commands, you can control the way DOS sees your system's drives and directories and controls your peripheral devices. You also learn several useful techniques—from creating a CONFIG.SYS file to using disk-caching software with extended memory.

Part IV: Command Reference

Part IV contains the comprehensive Command Reference. The commands, which are arranged in alphabetical order, are shown with syntax, applicable rules, and examples where needed. When a command is also covered elsewhere in the book, a chapter reference is provided. You can use the section both as a reference when you have problems and as a source of practical advice and tips during "browsing sessions." In all, the Command Reference is a complete, easy-to-use, quickly accessed resource on the proper use of DOS commands.

Part V: Appendixes

Using MS-DOS 5 includes four appendixes containing useful summary information. Appendix A is a list of the most common messages displayed by DOS with explanations for each message. Appendix B summarizes the changes and additions of commands between version changes. Appendix C explains the DOS control and editing keys. Appendix D tells you how to use Edlin.

Finally, printed inside the front and back covers, you will find the "DOS Survival Guide." This handy chart lists the main commands and keystroke sequences you need to know to navigate successfully in DOS.

Learning More about DOS

If *Using MS-DOS 5* whets your appetite for more information about DOS, you are in good company. Thousands of Que's readers have gone on to purchase one or more additional Que books about DOS.

No one book can fill all your DOS and personal computer needs. Que Corporation publishes a full line of microcomputer books that complement this book.

If you are a corporate trainer, need to teach beginners and intermediates about DOS, or feel that you need a more visual approach to DOS, you may be interested in purchasing Que's *MS-DOS 5 QuickStart*. This book features a graphics approach to learning DOS and is geared to the beginner. Que also offers the *MS-DOS 5 PC Tutor*—an interactive learning tool for the classroom environment or motivated self-starters.

Que's MS-DOS 5 User's Guide, Special Edition, is a comprehensive learning tool and reference volume for users of MS-DOS and PC DOS. This book is especially suitable for readers who are proficient with applications programs but who have grown beyond elementary tutorials and could benefit from a more in-depth understanding of DOS.

You are probably using MS-DOS 5 on a PC equipped with a hard disk drive. The key to efficient computer use is effective hard disk management. *Using Your Hard Disk* provides the in-depth information you need to get the most from your hard disk.

Newer versions of DOS support powerful equipment to help your programs run quickly and efficiently. If your current hardware is not up to the task of running the extensive new software packages, examine Que's *Upgrading and Repairing PCs*. This informative text shows you how to get the most from your hardware and how to upgrade your system to handle the new breed of high-powered software, such as Lotus 1-2-3 Release 3.1, dBASE IV 1.1, Microsoft Windows 3.0, and WordPerfect. According to Mark Brownstein of *InfoWorld*, *Upgrading and Repairing PCs* is "one of the best books about the workings of personal computers I've ever seen; it will be a useful, easy-to-read, and interesting addition to most anyone's library."

Other reference tools for the DOS user include *DOS Programmer's Reference*, 2nd Edition; *DOS Tips, Tricks, and Traps*, 2nd Edition; *MS-DOS Quick Reference* and *MS-DOS 5 QueCards*. *DOS Programmer's Reference* offers comprehensive coverage of the programming aspects of MS-DOS. Que's *MS-DOS 5 QueCards* is a desktop reference tool that DOS users of any experience level will find invaluable. *DOS Tips, Tricks, and Traps*, 2nd Edition, provides a topical collection of in-depth DOS tidbits.

All these books can be found in better bookstores worldwide. In the United States, you can call Que at 1-800-428-5331 to order books or obtain further information.

Using MS-DOS 5 follows the Que tradition of providing quality text that is targeted appropriately for the DOS user. Because of the dedication to this goal, Que ultimately has only one way of getting better—by hearing from you. Let Que know how you feel about this book or any other Que title. Que wants to keep improving its books, and you are the best source of information.

Conventions Used in This Book

Certain conventions are followed in this edition to help you more easily understand the discussions. The conventions are explained again at appropriate places in the book.

Uppercase letters are used for file names and DOS commands. In most cases, the keys on the keyboard are represented as they appear on your keyboard. Key combinations are connected by hyphens. For example, Ctrl-Break indicates that you press the Ctrl key and hold it down while you also press the Break key.

Words or phrases that are defined for the first time appear in *italic* characters. Words or phrases you are to type appear in **boldface** characters. Uppercase letters are usually used in the examples for what you type, but you can type commands in either upper- or lowercase letters. All on-screen messages appear in a `special typeface`.

The notation for issuing commands and running programs appears, in fullest form, in lines like the following:

dc:pathc\CHKDSK *filename.ext* /*switches*

In any syntax line, not all elements of the syntax can be represented in a literal manner. For example, *filename.ext* can represent any file name with any extension. It also can represent any file name with no extension at all. However, command names and switches are represented in a literal way. To activate the command **CHKDSK.COM**, you must type the word **CHKDSK**. Any literal text you type in a syntax line is shown in uppercase letters. Any text you replace with other text (variable text) is shown in lowercase letters.

Not all parts of a syntax line are essential. Any portion of a syntax line that you see in **boldface** letters is mandatory; you must always give this part of a command. In a previous example, to issue the CHKDSK command, you must type the word **CHKDSK** as it appears.

Portions of a syntax line that you see in *italic characters* are optional; you supply these items only when needed. If you do not type an optional item, DOS uses the item's default value or setting for the item.

Part I

The Role of DOS in Personal Computers

Includes

Understanding the Personal Computer

Understanding the Role of DOS

Starting DOS

Using the DOS Shell

Using DOS Commands

Understanding Disks and Files

Understanding the Personal Computer

Your personal computer is a convenient tool that can increase your productivity. When you use it in an informed manner, the personal computer can provide indispensable benefits. You're not alone in relying on this revolutionary machine. Just read the Sunday paper—the ads offer an array of personal computers. Yet the proliferation of personal computers is a relatively new phenomenon.

Until a few years ago, computers were large, expensive machines that were not available to individual users. Early computers were room-sized cabinets filled with thousands of tubes and transistors. The few users who knew anything about computers had to share with other users the resources of these early machines.

As recently as the early 1970s, computers were filled with thousands of discrete electronic parts and integrated circuits called *chips*. Circuitry based on thousands of chips is expensive to manufacture and maintain. During that decade, however, advances in computer technology produced complex chips that incorporated the jobs of hundreds of these discrete components. Most of the essential electronic building blocks a computer needs now can be contained on one of these miniature chips, or *microprocessors*.

Computers that use these chips are called *microcomputers*. By the end of the 1970s, several companies had begun to sell microcomputers. Microcomputers were small enough and inexpensive enough for individual users to purchase for use in their businesses or homes. And through the notion of having a microcomputer dedicated to a single user, the term *personal computer* developed.

Reading about those old personal computers now is like reading about the first automobiles. By today's standards, both were slow and temperamental. To maintain these early machines, the owner needed to be somewhat of a scientist. Without those pioneering automobiles, however, your driving experience might be far less routine today. Likewise, without the early microcomputers, you might still be doing all your automated work by hand. While automobiles took nearly 40 years to become practical personal transportation, microcomputers have taken less than 10 years to revolutionize the way people approach their work.

In the early 1980s, International Business Machines (IBM) introduced the IBM Personal Computer, which was an immediate success. Before long, the IBM PC captured the infant microcomputer industry and shaped its formative years. The IBM microcomputer was so popular that it became a de facto standard for personal computers.

Today, many manufacturers sell computers that are functionally equivalent to the IBM Personal Computer. Nearly all programs developed for the IBM microcomputers also run on these so-called *compatible* personal computers offered by other manufacturers. The primary software that IBM's personal computers and the compatibles have in common is the MS-DOS disk operating system introduced by Microsoft for the original IBM PC.

In this chapter, you learn about system elements that can be generalized to any IBM PC or compatible. If you have never used a personal computer, reading this chapter will give you a good start. If you're an old hand at using computers, you may want to skim the chapter to refresh your basic knowledge.

Key Terms Used in This Chapter

Display	The screen or monitor
DOS	An acronym for Disk Operating System. In IBM PC, XT, AT, PS/2, and functional compatibles, DOS refers to both IBM DOS and MS-DOS.

Peripheral	Any device (aside from the main components) that is connected to the computer to help it perform tasks
Disk	A plastic or metal platter coated with magnetic material and used to store files. A disk drive records and plays back information on disks.
Modem	A device for exchanging data between computers through telephone lines
Input	Any data a computer reads
Output	Any data a computer puts out
Bit	A binary digit; the smallest discrete representation of a value that a computer can manipulate
Byte	A collection of eight bits that a computer usually stores and manipulates as a unit
K (kilobyte)	1,024 bytes, used to show size or capacity in computer systems
M (megabyte)	1,024 kilobytes, used to measure values or capacities of millions of bytes
Data	A catch-all term that refers to words, numbers, symbols, graphics, photos, sounds—any information stored in bytes in computer form
File	A named group of data in electronic form

Exploring the Components of Computer Systems

Note: To read this chapter, you don't need to switch on your PC. Having your PC nearby, however, may be handy. The topics covered here discuss what the computer is all about.

Personal computer systems based on the IBM PC come in a wide variety of configurations. For example, you can find equally powerful machines in the traditional desktop configuration, in portable laptop models, in compact lunchbox-sized computers, and even in hand-held models.

Hardware and software are the two main segments of a computer system. Both must be present for a computer to do useful work for its operator. Hardware and software work together in a manner similar to a VCR and a videocassette. The VCR unit itself is like the hardware because it is electro-mechanical. The videocassette is like the software because it contains the information and control signals necessary for the VCR to display pictures on the TV screen.

Understanding Computer Software

At one time, you may use your VCR to view a videocassette that contains cartoons. At another time, you may watch a taped public television special on the crisis in education. Even though you use the same hardware (VCR) at both viewing sessions, the software (the videocassettes) stores different pictures and sounds. Likewise, the PC can be a word processor during one work session and a database manager during the next. The software program you use is designed to work in a specific way.

Your computer has the potential to do useful work. By using different software packages, or applications programs, you determine what kind of utility you get from your computer. Software enables a PC to be a flexible tool. You can program (instruct) a computer to perform a wide variety of operations. Almost anything you can reduce to calculations can be made into a program and then entered into the computer.

You probably use many small "computers" that have been programmed. Calculators, telephones with number memories, VCRs that automatically record television programs, and arcade games are examples of small computer-assisted devices that use a form of software. These devices have built-in software, so their usefulness is limited to their built-in capabilities. Because personal computers are designed to accept outside software, they are far more versatile than programmed devices.

You can teach your computer to perform chores much as these everyday devices do. With the proper software, the computer can serve as a word processor, a spreadsheet, a project manager, a mailing-list generator, or even a wily chess opponent! Table 1.1 illustrates some of the variety of software you can buy for your computer.

Table 1.1
Computer Software

Type of Software	Example
Operating systems	MS-DOS, UNIX
Databases	dBASE IV, Reflex, Q&A, Paradox 3.5
Spreadsheets	Lotus 1-2-3, Quattro
Word processors	WordPerfect, WordStar, Microsoft Word
Sales management	Act!
Utilities	PC Tools Deluxe, Norton Utilities, SideKick
Graphics	AutoCAD, CorelDRAW!, Freelance Plus, Harvard Graphics
Integrated programs	Smart, Symphony, Microsoft Works
Games	Flight Simulator, Jeopardy!
Home finance	Managing Your Money, Quicken
Desktop publishing	First Publisher, Ventura Publisher, Aldus PageMaker
Communications	ProCOMM Plus, Crosstalk

The operating system, such as MS-DOS, is the most important type of software for the PC. Operating systems provide a foundation of services for other programs. These services provide a uniform means for programs to gain access to the full resources of the hardware. Operating systems that help programs access disk resources are called *disk operating systems*. (Chapter 2 introduces you to disk operating systems.)

This book shows you how to use the most common operating system for the IBM PC and compatibles. The IBM versions of DOS (also called PC DOS) and the different versions of Microsoft Corporation's DOS (MS-DOS) are highly compatible. For this reason, the generic term *DOS* is used to refer to both.

Understanding Computer Hardware

A PC's *configuration* is based on the PC's components and its overall outward appearance. The PC sitting on your desk is a configuration of components, or hardware.

Hardware is the collection of electro-mechanical components that make up the PC. In general, the term *hardware* refers to the system unit, the keyboard, the screen display, the disk drives, and printers. The components exist in a wide variety of configurations, but the computers all operate in essentially the same manner. Figure 1.1 presents three common PC configurations. Notice that in all three cases, the PCs have system units, keyboards, displays, and disk drives. Internally, the PCs have many common components that make up the microprocessor support circuits.

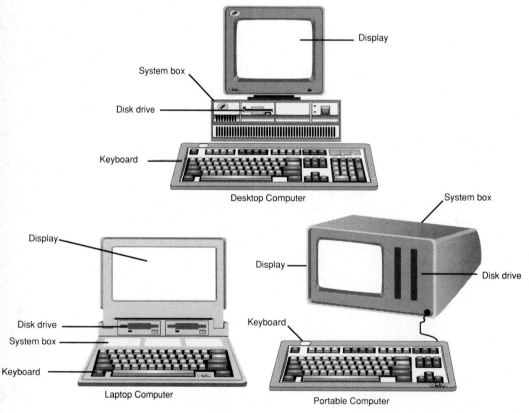

Fig. 1.1. Common PC configurations.

Hardware falls into two main categories: system hardware and peripheral hardware. *System hardware* is directly associated with processing or computing activity. The microprocessor is the system-hardware component that is central to the computer's capability to function. Because of the microprocessor's central role, it is also called the *central processing unit*, or *CPU*.

Technically, any device used by a computer for input or output of data is a *peripheral*. Displays, printers, modems, keyboards, and disk drives are all items of peripheral hardware. Peripheral hardware supports the system hardware's computing activity.

System Hardware

A PC's system hardware consists of the microprocessor and its support components and circuits. The microprocessor is a chip that does the computing in the computer. System hardware is often soldered or socketed to circuit boards in the computer.

The computer's random-access memory, or RAM, performs a system-hardware function by storing programs and data while the PC is turned on. System read-only memory, or ROM, also is considered system-level hardware. ROM contains program pieces that are stored permanently. The PC's microprocessor can retrieve information from ROM but cannot store any new information in ROM. Because the contents of ROM are not very flexible, ROM is often called *firmware*.

The microprocessor steps through a program in order to execute it. To coordinate the complex interactions between the microprocessor and the rest of the electronic parts, such as RAM and ROM, the microprocessor relies on a constantly timed set of pulses. These pulses are produced by a clock-timing generating circuit. Don't confuse this clock-timing generating circuit with the clock-calendar that keeps the time of day and date. The timing generator is more like a metronome that ticks at a determined speed to provide a beat for musicians to follow.

Peripheral Hardware

System hardware must have outside input in order to compute. The input comes from various devices called *input devices*. The keyboard is an example of an input device.

When the system hardware has completed some aspect of its work, it must output the result for you to see or store in order for the work to be useful. The system hardware's output goes to *output devices*. Your PC's display monitor is an example of an output device.

A great deal of your interaction with the PC takes place between you, the keyboard, and the display. Fortunately, the basic concepts of using a keyboard or viewing a display are simple. Some differences do exist, however, between different keyboards or different displays. The next two sections discuss some of the principles that control keyboards and displays. Understanding these principles may help you avoid confusion when working with this book, DOS, and your applications programs.

Exploring the Computer Display

The *display*, also called the *monitor* or the *screen*, is the part of the computer's peripheral hardware that produces visual output. The display is the normal, or *default*, location for output for the PC; the display is the PC's primary output device.

Most displays offered with PCs work on the same principle as a television set. Like televisions, most PC displays use a *cathode ray tube* (CRT) as the means to display output. (Some PC users refer to the PC's display as the CRT.) Manufacturers also incorporate other types of technology into computer displays. For example, to produce flatter (and thinner) displays, manufacturers use a technology known as a *gas plasma* display. Gas plasma displays produce an orange color against a dark background.

Another technology adapted to computer displays is liquid crystal. *Liquid crystal displays* (LCDs) work on the same principle as many digital watch displays. Most LCDs produce dark characters against a lighter background. Older LCD screens work well only in brightly lighted rooms because the light striking the display increases the contrast of the display output. Most newer LCDs employ a backlight that increases display contrast.

Regardless of the display type, all displays have one function in common. They take electrical signals and translate them into patterns of tiny picture-element dots, or *pixels*, that you can recognize as characters or figures. Not all displays produce the same total number of pixels. Some displays are noticeably sharper than others. The more pixels available with a display, the sharper the visual image. The sharpness, or *resolution*, of the visual image is a function of both the display and the display adapter.

The *display adapter* is a collection of circuits that interface with the system hardware. The display adapter controls the computer display. In some PCs, the display circuitry can be part of the *motherboard*, which is the main circuit board that contains the majority of the PC's system components. The display circuitry also can be on a separate board, which fits into a slot in the computer. The display adapter can be a Monochrome Display Adapter (MDA), Color Graphics Adapter (CGA), Enhanced Graphics Adapter (EGA), Video Graphics Array Adapter (VGA), or some less-common type of special display adapter. All these display adapters fall into one of two main categories: adapters that display *text only* or adapters that display *text* and *graphics*.

Text Displays

The letters, numbers, and punctuation you see on-screen are produced as patterns of dots, or pixels. Each pattern is stored in the computer's memory in a code known as the American Standard Code for Information Interchange (ASCII).

Most programs use a display operating mode called *text mode*. In text mode, ASCII-coded characters compose the visual display. Each ASCII code represents a letter or a symbol. When a program instructs the display adapter to display a letter or symbol, the adapter "consults" an electronic table containing ASCII codes. The display adapter uses the electronic table like a set of stencils.

The principle is similar to the principle used to display scores on a lighted sports scoreboard. Instead of lighting a pattern of bulbs, the display adapter illuminates a pattern of pixels. Each number on the scoreboard is a different arrangement of illuminated bulbs. Each letter on your screen is a different arrangement of pixels.

The standard ASCII character set contains 128 characters—a sufficient number to represent all the letters, numbers, and punctuation commonly used in English. When IBM introduced the PC, however, the company added another 128 codes to the standard ASCII set. The additional codes, referred to as *extended ASCII codes*, represent pixel patterns that display lines, corners, and special images like musical notes.

Programs can use combinations of these extended ASCII characters to produce boxes and other graphics-like characters. In text mode, display adapters can produce only predetermined characters and special shapes. The extended codes enable a text display to incorporate a wide variety of borders, boxes, and icons. The original IBM PC had a display adapter—the

Monochrome Display Adapter—that could operate only in text mode. Nearly all currently available monochrome adapters also operate in graphics mode.

Graphics Displays

In graphics mode, the display adapter can control and light up any pixel on the screen. Thus, complex figures with curves and fine details can be displayed. Graphics-based screens are perhaps the most pleasing to view. Charts, drawings, digitized pictures, animated game characters, and what-you-see-is-what-you-get (WYSIWYG) word processing text are all graphics-based outputs.

The computer must work harder to create a graphics image than to create a text image, however. A graphics screen does not have an electronic stencil. In order to light the correct pixels on the display, the display adapter must find the screen-coordinate points for each pixel. No table of pixel patterns exists, as in text mode.

Not all monitors and display adapters have the same number of pixels available. The greater the number of pixels, the finer the detail (and the greater the cost) of the display. Each computed pixel has characteristics that tell the graphics adapter what the color or intensity of the pixel should be. The greater the number of colors and intensities, the more storage space in memory is required. Graphics adapters offer varying combinations of pixel densities, colors, and intensities. Table 1.2 lists the various display types, including the colors available and the pixel resolution.

Figure 1.2 demonstrates the principle of resolution that affects the quality of a graphics display. The higher-resolution image (left) uses four times as many pixels as the low-resolution image (right).

Fig. 1.2. Resolution in a graphics display.

Your applications programs may use text mode or one of the graphics modes. Before you decide to buy software that uses a graphics mode, let your dealer help you determine whether the package is suitable for your display.

Table 1.2
Resolution and Colors for Display Adapters

Adapter Type	Graphics Mode	Pixel Resolution	Colors Available
CGA	Medium resolution	320 × 200	4
CGA	High resolution	640 × 200	2
EGA	All CGA modes		
EGA	CGA high resolution	640 × 200	16
EGA	EGA high resolution	640 × 350	16
MGA	Monochrome graphics	720 × 348	2
MDA	Text only	N/A	N/A
VGA	All CGA and EGA modes		
VGA	Monochrome	640 × 480	2
VGA	VGA high resolution	640 × 480	16
VGA	VGA medium resolution	320 × 200	256

TIP

Tip: Most CGA or EGA display-system users can upgrade their display adapters and displays to the newer VGA display system by installing new hardware. Check with your dealer to determine whether you can take advantage of the higher-resolution VGA display system.

Exploring the Computer Keyboard

Keyboards, like displays, can vary from PC to PC. The effect of one keyboard's variation from others is not as critical as the differences among displays and display adapters. Programs normally don't require that you use a specific type of keyboard; but you need to understand how DOS and other programs use the keys on your keyboard. Like displays, keyboards have certain common characteristics. This section familiarizes you with the keyboard.

The computer keyboard has the familiar QWERTY layout. (The name QWERTY comes from the letters found on the left side of the top row of letters on a standard typewriter.) But a computer keyboard is different from a typewriter keyboard in several important ways.

The most notable difference is the presence of the "extra" keys—the keys that do not appear on a typewriter. These special keys are described in table 1.3. The keyboard also includes 10 or 12 special function keys.

Table 1.3
Special Keys on the Computer Keyboard

Key	Function
Enter	Signals the computer to respond to the commands you type; also functions as a carriage return in programs that simulate the operation of a typewriter
Cursor keys	Change your location on-screen; include the left arrow, right arrow, up arrow, and down arrow
PgUp/PgDn	Scroll the screen display up or down one page
Home/End	Home moves the cursor to the screen's upper left corner; End moves the cursor to the lower right corner.
Backspace	Moves the cursor backward one space at a time, deleting any character in that space
Del	Deletes, or erases, any character at the location of the cursor
Insert (Ins)	Inserts any character at the location of the cursor
Shift	Creates uppercase letters and other special characters; when pressed in combination with another key, can change the standard function of that key

Key	Function
Caps Lock	When pressed to the lock position, causes all letters to be typed in uppercase. To release, press the key again.
Ctrl	Control key; when pressed in combination with another key, changes the standard function of that key
Alt	Alternate key; when pressed in combination with another key, changes the standard function of that key. Not all programs use Alt.
Esc	In some situations, pressing Esc enables you to "escape" from the current operation to an earlier one. Sometimes Esc has no effect on the current operation. Not all programs respond to Esc.
Num Lock	Changes the numeric keypad from cursor-movement to numeric-function mode
PrtSc	Used with Shift to send the characters on the display to the printer
Print Screen	Found on Enhanced Keyboards; same as Shift-PrtSc
Scroll Lock	Locks the scrolling function to the cursor-control keys. Instead of the cursor moving, the screen scrolls.
Pause	Suspends display output until another key is pressed (not provided with standard keyboards)
Break	Stops some programs in progress
Numeric Keypad	A cluster of keys to the right of the standard keyboard. The keypad includes numbered keys from 0 through 9 as well as cursor-control keys and other special keys.

Many of the special keys are designed to be used in combination with other keys. For example, pressing Shift and PrtSc in combination causes DOS to print the contents of the current screen through an attached printer.

Simultaneously pressing Ctrl and PrtSc causes DOS to print continuously what you type. Pressing Ctrl and PrtSc a second time turns off the continuous printing. Table 1.4 describes the more common key combinations used in DOS.

Table 1.4
DOS Key Combinations

Keys	Function
Ctrl-Num Lock	Freezes the display; pressing Ctrl-S or any other key restarts the display.
Shift-PrtSc	Prints the contents of the video display (print-screen feature)
Print Screen	Found on Enhanced Keyboards, same as Shift-PrtSc
Ctrl-PrtSc	Sends lines to both the screen and the printer; giving this sequence a second time turns off this function.
Ctrl-C Ctrl-Break	Stops execution of most programs
Ctrl-Alt-Del	Restarts MS-DOS (system reboot)

The function keys are shortcuts. Not all programs use these keys, and some programs use only a few of the function keys. When used, however, they automatically carry out repetitious operations for you. For example, F1 is often used for on-line help.

On-line help displays instructions from the computer's memory to help you understand a particular operation. The DOS 5 Shell uses F3 to back out of one operation and move into another. In a DOS Shell session, F10 moves the cursor to the menu line, where you select actions. These and other keys recognized by DOS 5's Shell are explained in later parts of this book. The action provided by a function key is determined by the program you are using. Always check the program's documentation to determine the result of pressing any function key.

The keyboard is the way you put information into the computer. Each character you type is converted into code the computer can process. The keyboard therefore is considered an input device. DOS expects commands to be input through the keyboard as you work at the DOS level.

AT Keyboards and Enhanced Keyboards

Many early PC-compatible computers use a keyboard like that of the IBM PC. Other machines use keyboards patterned after IBM's Personal Computer AT keyboards. IBM's PS/2 computers use the 101-key Enhanced Keyboard. Some users prefer the keyboard arrangement of the original PC keyboard, whereas others prefer the AT-style keyboard or the Enhanced Keyboard.

You can determine whether your computer has a PC-style keyboard, a Personal Computer AT-style keyboard, or an enhanced-style keyboard. For example, you find the Print Screen and Pause keys only on the Enhanced Keyboard.

The 102-Key Keyboard

Some keyboards enable you to change key caps and switch key definitions for the Caps Lock, Ctrl, Esc, and ~ (tilde) keys. Northgate Computer Systems, for example, offers these options as well as an enhanced-style keyboard.

Northgate's enhanced-style keyboard locates the first 10 functions keys to the left instead of across the top of the alphabet and number keys. Because this arrangement requires one more key than the 101-key Enhanced Keyboards, this type of keyboard is called the 102-key keyboard.

Nonstandard Keyboards

Small computers, such as "lunchboxes" and laptops, use nonstandard keyboards, usually to conserve space. On some computers, space is so restricted that you need an external numeric keypad for use with software that performs advanced calculations. Most laptop computers don't have room for a dedicated numeric keypad. A group of the letter keys also serve as numeric keys when you press a special function key (often labeled *Fn*) on the laptop's keyboard.

Your computer manuals explain how to use the special functions of the nonstandard keyboard. Usually, the "missing" keys are functionally available to you through multiple-key sequences. Normally, however, a nonstandard keyboard does not affect your work with DOS.

Exploring the System Unit

In a typical desktop PC, a box-shaped cabinet contains all other parts of the PC. This box is called the *system unit*. The devices connected to it are the *peripherals*. The system unit and peripherals make up the complete computer system. Peripherals such as the display and the keyboard are connected to the system unit.

The system unit houses all but a few parts of a PC. Included are circuit boards, a power supply, and a small speaker. System units vary in appearance, but a horizontal box shape is the most common. A vertical "tower" shape is also popular because it frees desk or table space.

The system unit houses the computer's main circuit board, called the motherboard. The motherboard contains the microprocessor and the circuits and chips that support it.

Normally, the motherboard has electrical sockets into which users can plug various adapter circuit boards for additional peripherals. The electrical sockets are often referred to as *expansion slots* because of their slot-like appearance.

Electronic components known as chips provide the computer with its memory and are located on the motherboard. In some cases, an additional memory adapter is plugged into an expansion slot to increase the system's memory. The number of expansion slots available varies from model to model. Most motherboards have a socket for a math coprocessor. Math coprocessors improve the speed and precision of calculations in number-intensive programs.

In addition to standard system-level components, most system units house other hardware devices or their associated adapter boards. A great variety of devices can be included in a PC, but a few types are common. Figure 1.3 shows the parts of a typical system unit, and the following sections discuss these parts in more detail.

Hard disk platters are sealed inside the hard disk drive.

Floppy disks are encased in either a flexible 5 1/4-inch jacket or a rigid 3 1/2-inch jacket.

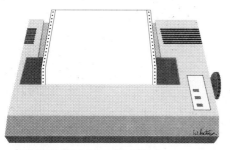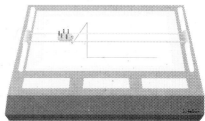

A printer is like a typewriter without a keyboard. It accepts input from the computer and renders the input as characters on paper.

A plotter lets you draw with the computer.

Fig. 1.3. A hypothetical system unit and related peripheral devices.

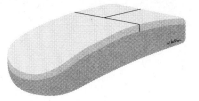

A mouse is a computer input device whose shape is vaguely reminiscent of a real mouse.

A modem enables you to transfer signals between computers by using telephone lines.

A digitizer tablet provides a work surface that many users find more natural than using a mouse. The "puck" display shows the position of the puck on the tablet.

Fig. 1.3. Continued.

Understanding Disk Drives and Disks

Disks and disk drives work together to store and retrieve information and programs. Disk drives are complex mechanisms, but they carry out a basically simple function. They read and write information from and to disks. You don't have to know about the mechanical aspects of disk drives to use them, but some insight into drive mechanics helps you appreciate the drives' role. *Disks* are circular platters or pieces of plastic that have magnetized surfaces. The disk drive rotates the disk in much the same way a phonograph rotates a record. Within the drive, one or more read/write heads convert electrical signals (computer data) into magnetic fields on the disk's magnetic surface. This process is called *writing data to the disk*. Disk-drive heads also recover, or *read,* the magnetically stored data and present it to the computer as electrical signals that the PC can use.

Computers don't store data on disks in a disorganized fashion. Computers rely on the operating system (MS-DOS, for example) to provide a template for disk organization. When a computer writes to a disk, DOS ensures that the data is stored as a named collection of information called a *file*. You (or the program) refer to files by name. DOS supervises the translation of the file's name into a set of physical coordinates, which the disk drive uses to read the correct data. A disk's primary job, therefore, is to act as a storage medium for files, much as a VCR tape stores a movie or television program. Unlike data stored in silicon memory chips, magnetically stored disk data is not lost when the computer's power is turned off.

You know that a drive is reading from or writing to the disk when the small light on the front of the disk drive or on a front panel of your computer comes on. The light is the drive's signal that the drive is in use. Generally, you should not open a floppy disk drive door or eject a disk until the light goes out. If you open the door or eject a disk while the light is on, an error message probably will be displayed. In rare cases, the program may stall or you may lose disk data.

Two types of disks (and their drives) are available in a variety of sizes. Disks are either *floppy* or *hard*. Floppy disks, also called *diskettes*, are removable, flexible, and have a lower capacity (store less data) than hard disks. A floppy disk's primary advantage is that it is portable. You can use floppy disks to move data from one computer to another. DOS, as well as other software, is supplied on floppy disks. Hard disks, also called *fixed disks*, are nonremovable, high-capacity rigid platters. To increase storage capacity, several platters can be stacked within a single hard disk drive. Both sides of each platter are available for data storage. Most DOS-based disk drives operate in this two-sided manner and thus are called double-sided disk drives.

The components of a disk drive are roughly similar to those of a phonograph. The disk, like a record, rotates. A positioner arm, like a phonograph's tone arm, moves across the radius of the disk. A head, like a pickup cartridge, translates the encoded information to electrical signals. Unlike phonographs, however, disk drives do not have spiral tracks on the disk's surface.

The disk's surface is recorded in concentric rings or tracks. Track arrangement on each platter surface resembles a rings-within-rings geometry. The closer the adjacent tracks are packed on the disk, the greater the storage capacity of the disk. Chapter 7 explains in more detail how DOS uses the drives and disks on a PC.

Floppy Disks

Floppy disks store from 360K to 2.88M of data and come in two standard sizes. (Other sizes of floppy disks are available but are not widely used.) *Minifloppies* are 5 1/4-inch disks, and *microfloppies* are 3 1/2-inch disks. The mini- or micro- prefix refers to a floppy's physical size, the size of the disk's jacket. Floppy disks generally are referred to as *floppies* or *diskettes*. In this book, the term *floppy disk* refers to both 5 1/4-inch and 3 1/2-inch disks.

Although floppies come in two sizes, each size has more than one storage capacity. For example, 5 1/4-inch floppies generally are either 360K double-sided double-density, or 1.2M double-sided high-density. 3 1/2-inch disks are either 720K double-sided double-density, 1.44M double-sided high-density, or 2.88M double-sided ultra-high-density. Make sure that you know your drive's specification before you buy or interchange floppies. Floppies of the same size but with different capacities can be incompatible with a particular disk drive.

Fixed Disks

In 1973, IBM developed a hard-disk technology and code-named it *Winchester*. Winchester is sometimes used to refer to any hard disk.

Hard disks often consist of multiple, rigid-disk platters. The platters spin at approximately 3,600 RPM, which is much faster than a floppy disk drive spins. As the platters spin in the drive, the head positioners make small, precise movements above the tracks of the disk. Because of this precision, hard disks can store enormous quantities of data—from 10M to more than 100M.

Despite their precision, hard disks are reasonably rugged devices. Factory sealing prevents contamination of the housing. With proper care, hard disks should give years of service.

Hard disks range from 3 1/2 to 8 inches in diameter. The most common size, 5 1/4-inch, holds between 2.5M and 10M of information per platter side. A hard disk capacity of 40M to 65M is typical.

Understanding Peripheral Devices

In addition to the display and the keyboard, several other peripherals can be useful. Many state-of-the-art computer programs require that you use a mouse to take the greatest advantage of the program's features. Other peripherals, such as printers and modems, enable you to use your computer's output as you want.

The Mouse

The mouse is a device you move on the surface of your desk. The computer correlates the movement of the mouse to the movement of some object on the display. The mouse is contoured to fit comfortably under your hand. The contoured shape and the cable tailing from the unit gives the vague appearance of a mouse sitting on the table. The mouse's switch buttons (it has two or three) are positioned so that they lie beneath your fingers.

Not all software supports mouse input, but many popular programs do. Generally, mouse-based programs enable you to use the mouse to point to options on-screen and click one of the buttons on the mouse in order to carry out a task.

Printers

Printers accept signals (input) from the CPU and convert those signals to characters (output), which usually are imprinted on paper. You can classify printers in two ways: by the manner in which they receive input from the computer and by the manner in which they produce output.

The way a printer receives input from the PC is important in determining the type of printer assignments you make with DOS and other software. The type of output a printer produces is a matter of print quality, graphics capability, and speed.

The terms *parallel* and *serial* describe the two methods by which printers receive input from personal computers. The terms *dot-matrix*, *daisywheel*, *laser*, and *inkjet* name the generic categories of printer output.

TIP

> ***Tip:*** Serial printers operate at longer cable lengths than parallel printers. A serial printer can be 50 feet or more from the PC, whereas a parallel printer may have trouble getting its input from a cable more than 15 feet long. Having a printer nearby is convenient but can be noisy. When buying a printer, ask your dealer to demonstrate both serial and parallel printers before you decide.

Printers usually are rated by their printing speed and the quality of the finished print. Some printers print by using all the addressable points on the screen, much as a graphics display adapter does. Some printers offer color printing.

Parallel and Serial Printers

You connect printers to the system unit through a *port*, a connector on the back of the system unit. A port is an electrical doorway through which data can flow between the system unit and an outside peripheral. A port can have its own expansion adapter or can share an expansion adapter with other ports or circuits. Color Graphics Adapters (CGA) often contain a port for connecting a printer.

The terms *parallel* and *serial* relate to the way the electrical data is delivered from the port to the printer. A serial port delivers the bits of the data byte one after another in a single-file manner. Sending one complete byte (character) using serial communications takes longer, but communications require fewer wires in the cable. Serial printers can communicate with the port over longer distances than parallel printers. (In other words, you can put a serial printer farther away from the computer.)

With a parallel port, all the bits of a data byte are sent at the same time through separate wires in the parallel cable one complete byte (character) at a time. Parallel printer connections are more common than serial connections.

Dot-Matrix, Daisywheel, Laser, and Inkjet Printers

All printers have the job of putting their output on paper. Most of the time, this output is text, but output also may be a graphics image. The four classifications of printers are distinguished by the mechanical method of getting output on the page.

The most common printer is the dot matrix. Dot-matrix printers use a print head that contains a row of pins, or wires, which produce the characters. A motor moves the print head horizontally across the paper. As the print head moves, a vertical slice of each character forms as the printer's controlling circuits fire the proper pins. The pins press corresponding small dots of the ribbon against the paper, leaving an inked-dot impression. After several tiny horizontal steps, the print head leaves the dot image of a complete character. The process continues for each character on the line.

The daisywheel printer also steps the print head across the page but strikes the page with a complete character for each step. All the characters of the alphabet are arranged at the ends of holders that resemble spokes on a wheel. The visual effect of this wheel is similar to a daisy's petals arranged around the flower head. Because the characters are fully formed, rather than made of dots, the quality of daisywheel printing is high.

Laser printers use a technology similar to photocopying. Instead of a light-sensitive drum picking up the image of a photocopied document, the drum is painted with the light of a laser diode. The image from the drum is coated with toner (usually a black powder), and the toner is then transferred to the paper in a high dot-density output. The output characters look fully formed. Laser printers can also produce graphics image output. The combination of high-quality text and graphics can be extremely useful for desktop publishing.

Inkjet printers are similar to dot-matrix printers in that a head mechanism moves horizontally across the paper and produces a line of characters. The inkjet head shoots fine jets of ink onto the paper to form characters. The quality and speed of inkjet printer output approach those of laser printers, although inkjet characters are not quite as crisp.

Modems

Modems are peripherals that enable a PC to communicate over standard telephone lines. Modems are serial-communications peripherals. They send or receive characters or data one bit at a time. Modems can communicate with other modems at speeds of from 30 to 960 or more bytes per second. Modems require communications software to coordinate their communications with other modems.

Some modems can be installed within the system unit in an expansion slot. A modem that is built into the system unit is called an *internal* modem. Most modems attach to the system unit through a serial-communications connector. The modem is contained in its own stand-alone case. This stand-alone type of modem is called an *external* modem.

Modems differ in the speed with which they communicate information. Some modems can communicate at about 30 characters per second. Most popular modems communicate between 120 and 240 characters per second. Some special modems are capable of 1,920 characters per second. As a rule of thumb, faster modems cost more than slower ones.

Some modems incorporate facsimile (FAX) circuitry so that they can be used for FAX transmission and reception. Modems that communicate 960 characters, or more, per second are becoming increasingly popular. As FAX use becomes more widespread, FAX-modem combinations may become more prevalent.

Understanding How Computers Work with Data

Now that you have been introduced to the essential parts of a computer system, you are ready for a general overview of how these parts carry out the job of computing. Fortunately, you do not have to know the details of a computer's operation to use a computer effectively in your work. But if you do undertake some exploration, you may adjust more quickly to using a computer. The fundamentals of computing are easier to understand than many people think.

Computers perform many useful tasks by accepting data as input, processing it, and releasing it as output. Data is any information. It can be a set of numbers, a memo, an arrow key to move a game symbol. Input comes from you and is translated into electrical signals that move through a set of electronic controls. Output can be grouped into three categories:

- Characters or graphics the computer displays on-screen or on some form of hard copy

- Signals the computer holds in its memory

- Signals stored magnetically on disk

Computers receive and send output in the form of electrical signals. These signals are stable in two states: on and off. Think of these states as you think of the power in the wire from a light switch you can turn on and off. Computers contain millions of electronic switches that can be either on or off. All forms of input and output follow this two-state principle.

The term used to describe the two-state principle is *binary*, which refers to something made of two parts. Computers represent data with binary digits, or *bits*—0 and 1. For convenience, computers group eight bits together. This eight-bit grouping is called a *byte*. Bytes are sometimes packaged in two-, four-, or eight-byte packages when the computer moves information internally.

Computers move bits and bytes across electrical highways called *buses*. Normally, the computer contains three buses. The *control bus* manages the devices attached to the PC. The *data bus* is the highway for information transfer. The *address bus* routes signals so that data goes to the correct location within the computer. The microprocessor is connected to all three buses and supervises their activity.

The microprocessor can address certain portions of its memory in any order. This portion of the computer's memory is called *random-access memory*, or *RAM*. Some portions of a computer's memory are permanent. This portion of memory is called *read-only memory*, or *ROM*. ROM is useful for holding unalterable instructions in the computer system.

The microprocessor relies on you to give it instructions in the form of a program. A *program* is a set of binary-coded instructions that produce a desired result. The microprocessor decodes the binary information and carries out the instruction from the program.

You can begin from scratch and type programs or data into the computer each time you turn on the power. But of course, you don't want to do that if you don't have to. Luckily, the computer can store both instructions and start-up data, usually on a disk. Disks store data in binary form in files.

As far as the computer is concerned, a file is just a collection of bytes identified by a unique name. These bytes can be a memo, a word processing program, or some other program. The job of the file is to hold binary data or programs safely until the microprocessor calls for that data or program. When the call comes, the drive reads the file and writes the contents into RAM.

Displaying a word on a computer screen seems to be a simple matter of pressing keys on the keyboard. But each time you press a key to enter a character, the computer carries out a series of complex steps.

A personal computer is busy on the inside. Program instructions held in random-access memory (RAM) are called up and executed by the CPU. Resulting computations are stored in RAM. The CPU uses the data bus to determine *what* the data should be, the control bus to determine *how* the electrical operations should proceed, and the address bus to determine *where* the data or instructions are located in RAM.

Summary

This chapter provides a quick overview of personal computers. DOS is much easier to learn when you are familiar with the PC and its components. In this chapter, you learned the following important points:

- IBM and compatible computers operate basically in the same way.

- A computer's hardware works with software to do useful work.

- System hardware does the "computing" in the PC.

- Peripheral hardware provides the PC with input and output capability so that the PC can work with you.

- PCs have text displays or graphics displays. Text displays cannot show the output of many graphics-based software programs. Graphics displays can show both text and graphics.

- The PC's keyboard offers standard typewriter keys as well as special keys, such as the function keys. Programs like DOS and the DOS Shell determine how the special keys work.

- The PC's main box is the system unit. The system unit houses the disk drive(s) and the motherboard, where the system hardware resides.

- Disk drives are either hard disk drives or floppy disk drives.

- Many PC systems include a printer, modem, or mouse. PCs accommodate these outside peripherals as well as other attachments.

- Computers "compute" by operating on binary representations of information. The source of the information is called input. The destination of the resulting computational result is called output. PCs store information in eight-bit bytes.

You will gain insight into computers as you progress through this book. The next chapter introduces the role of DOS in the personal computer. Because DOS was designed around the system hardware and peripherals discussed in this chapter, you may want to move directly to Chapter 2 while the information in this chapter is fresh in your mind.

Understanding the Role of DOS

2

Chapter 1 introduces personal computer systems and their components. That chapter describes software and shows how data moves in the computer. This chapter introduces DOS, the disk operating system, which serves as an important link between the hardware, the software, and you.

> *Tip:* As with Chapter 1, you can read this chapter without being at your computer.

An *operating system* is a collection of computer programs that provides recurring services to other programs or to computer users. These services include disk and file management, memory management, and device management. Computers need software to provide these services. If the computer's operating system software did not provide these services, the user or the user's applications program would have to deal directly with the details of the PC's hardware, file system, and memory use.

Without a disk operating system, every computer program would have to contain instructions telling the hardware each step it should take to do its job, giving step-by-step instructions for storing a file on a disk, for example. Because an operating system already contains these instructions, any program can call on the operating system when a service is needed. The operating systems are called *disk operating systems* because most of the commands are kept on the disk (floppy or hard) rather than in memory. As a result, the operating system requires less memory to run.

37

IBM-compatible personal computers use MS-DOS or its close relative, IBM DOS. MS-DOS is the disk operating system developed by Microsoft Corporation to provide a foundation of services for operating an IBM PC or compatible computer. Manufacturers of personal computers, such as Zenith, IBM, and COMPAQ, tailor MS-DOS for use on their computers. In fact, hundreds of brands and models of PCs use some form of MS-DOS. The manufacturers may put their own names on the disks and include different manuals with the DOS packages they provide. But all types of DOS are similar when they operate on a PC. When you read about DOS in this book, you can safely assume that what you read applies to the version of DOS used by most manufacturers. In special cases, differences are noted.

Key Terms Used in This Chapter

Program	Instructions that tell a computer how to carry out tasks
BIOS	Basic Input/Output System; the software that provides the basic functional link between DOS and the peripheral hardware in a PC
Redirection	A change in the source or destination of a command's normal input or output
Application	A program; a set of instructions that tell the computer to perform a program-specific task, such as word processing
Interface	A connection between parts of the computer, especially between hardware devices; also refers to the interaction between a user and an applications program
Batch file	A series of DOS commands placed in a disk file. DOS executes batch-file commands one at a time.

What Is DOS?

DOS is an acronym for Disk Operating System. Nearly every computer has some sort of disk operating system. Computers that do not have disk operating systems are severely limited in reliable data storage. Disk operating systems manage many of the technical details of computers besides disk-file storage. From the user's perspective, however, disk management is perhaps the most important service these operating systems provide.

Many computers, including personal computers and large multiuser computers, use these three letters—DOS—as part of their operating system's name. Microsoft's MS-DOS and IBM's version of MS-DOS, IBM DOS, are examples, as are Apple's DOS 3.3 and ProDOS.

Although various operating systems are all called DOS, more people associate the term *DOS* with MS-DOS than with any other disk operating system in the world. In this book, the term *DOS* refers to MS-DOS, a single-user, single-tasking disk operating system that provides the framework of operation for millions of today's personal computers.

Examining the Variations of MS-DOS

MS-DOS is an operating system that accommodates variation in its exact makeup while retaining its core characteristics. Just as a car model can have differences in style, color, and standard equipment, DOS can have variations. The basic framework for the car (and DOS) enables differences to be introduced as the final tailoring of the finished product. This capability for variation enables various computer manufacturers to adapt MS-DOS to their computers. Both IBM DOS and COMPAQ DOS, for example, are variations of MS-DOS. As DOS has matured as a product, it has been enhanced, and these enhancements have been released as new versions of DOS. Each new version has built on its predecessor while retaining the original version's primary design features.

Product-Specific Variations of DOS

Today, all commonly available variations of MS-DOS are similar in design and operation—with good reason. MS-DOS works with computers designed around Intel's 8086 microprocessor family. This family includes the 8088, 8086, 80286, 80386, and 80486 microprocessors. When conceiving the original IBM Personal Computer, IBM designers selected the Intel 8088 microprocessor to be the "brains" of their computer.

IBM's Personal Computer was a grand success. The enormity of the original IBM PC's influence on the PC market convinced other PC manufacturers using the 8086 family to follow closely IBM's personal computer design. Because IBM used an open approach to designing the IBM PC, other companies could configure their computers to use programs and hardware designed for the IBM PC. From a DOS perspective, these computers are virtually alike, even though the PCs may be more advanced than the original IBM PC.

The closeness of a PC's design to the IBM PC and to other IBM personal computers, such as the IBM PC/AT, determines to what degree a PC is said to be *IBM-compatible*. No industry standard concerning compatibility has been established formally. Instead, a de facto standard has emerged through the principle of supply and demand. The buying public has demanded a high degree of IBM compatibility in PCs. Most PCs (and their respective variations of MS-DOS) that were not designed to be compatible with the IBM PC have been discontinued, sell in specialty markets, or are available only in countries other than the United States. Because of this "shaking out" of the market, most PCs are capable of successfully operating using a version of IBM DOS, even though most compatible manufacturers offer their own variation of MS-DOS.

Users see the variations in MS-DOS implementations among PC manufacturers as subtle differences, usually limited to the names of a few commands or the manner in which parameters are given. Some manufacturers include in their MS-DOS packages additional utilities that work with a feature of that manufacturer's PC model. Yet as a general rule, if you are proficient at using one variation of MS-DOS, you are proficient with all variations of MS-DOS. In a practical sense, the terms MS-DOS, IBM DOS, and DOS are interchangeable. You can use just about any compatible computer that runs DOS as its operating system by applying what you have learned about DOS from working with another PC.

Changes among Versions of DOS

Another type of variation involves the evolution of the product itself. As MS-DOS has evolved, the core product has been enhanced several times. Each release of enhancements is a distinct version of the program. Since its appearance in the summer of 1981, DOS has evolved through five major versions. Table 2.1 lists the important differences among versions of DOS, beginning in 1981. (Appendix B provides more detailed coverage of these changes.)

Table 2.1
Quick Reference to Versions of DOS

MS-DOS Version	Significant Change
1.0	Original version of DOS
1.25	Accommodates double-sided disks
2.0	Includes multiple directories needed to organize hard disks
3.0	Uses high-capacity floppy disks, the RAM disk, volume names, and the ATTRIB command
3.1	Includes provisions for networking
3.2	Accommodates 3 1/2-inch drives
3.3	Accommodates high-capacity 3 1/2-inch drives; includes new commands
4.0	Introduces the DOS Shell and the MEM command; accommodates larger files and disk capacities
5.0	Includes enhanced memory management, task swapping, an improved DOS Shell, a full-screen text editor, and support for even larger disk capacities

Even with the introduction of Microsoft's OS/2 and the presence of several versions of the UNIX operating system, DOS remains strong. You can expect your investment in learning DOS to continue paying dividends; most industry experts predict that DOS will have a presence in the PC picture for years to come.

TIP

Tip: Operating systems such as OS/2 and UNIX are getting a great deal of media attention. One of these systems eventually may emerge as the replacement for DOS in everyday personal computing. Even if you move to OS/2 or UNIX at some point, however, you will find that you can use much of your DOS expertise with these operating systems.

Examining the DOS Package

Your purchase of a computer probably included a DOS package. You may have purchased DOS as a separate item if your computer did not include DOS. Most dealers and manufacturers either supply DOS with each new PC or sell DOS as an accessory package to a PC. Most often the DOS package includes one or more manuals and two or more disks. The DOS software itself is on the disks.

MS-DOS Version 5.0, for example, comes packaged with three or six disks depending on the computer model for which the software is intended. DOS packages supplied by particular computer manufacturers may have more or fewer disks. The disks may contain supplemental programs for the PC, such as programs that control unique hardware features in particular PC models. These supplemental programs often are considered part of DOS because the manufacturer includes them in the physical DOS package. Depending on the context, supplemental programs may be associated with the term *DOS package*, but for the purpose of this book, you should consider such supplemental programs to be outside of DOS.

Normally, the DOS package contains a DOS reference manual, which is an important supplement because it contains specific information about your version of DOS. The DOS reference manual included in the DOS package must attempt to supply an accurate description of that version of DOS for new and advanced users alike. Therefore, many PC users prefer to consult another book, such as this book or other books about DOS published by Que Corporation. DOS users can select a book that fits their needs closely, whether they are beginning, intermediate, or advanced DOS users.

Many manufacturers include in the package other manuals that look similar to the DOS reference manual and contain information specific to the computer model or its auxiliary software. COMPAQ, for example, supplies a manual describing the operation of the tape unit included in some COMPAQ models. Although the discussion of the tape unit includes references to DOS, this manual is not considered a standard part of DOS for all PCs. The topics in these specialty manuals are not covered in this book, so keep such additional manuals at hand for reference.

Understanding the Purpose of DOS Disks

DOS disks that come in the DOS package are special disks because they contain DOS files—the files needed to start your PC and subsequently support your commands and applications. These DOS files contain the computer-level instructions that provide the functional aspects of DOS. The PC doesn't have these computer-level functions built in. In a way, the DOS disks serve as the key that unlocks the potential of the computer. When the operating system information stored on these disks is loaded into your PC, programs can take advantage of the PC's computing potential.

> *Note:* If you are fairly new to DOS, here's a word of wisdom. Don't use the master DOS disks that come in your DOS package for everyday work. The manufacturers intend for you to make copies of these master DOS disks and use the copies when you need to use DOS. (Indeed, with DOS 5.0, you have to install the operating system on your hard disk or on other floppy disks before you can use it.) Be sure to store your masters in a safe place. You should have at least one known, good (tested) set of working DOS floppies even if your computer has a hard disk that contains the DOS files.
>
> Even after you have installed DOS on your hard disk, keep floppy disk copies of your DOS package disks. You may need them if your hardware experiences problems or some software holds your hard disk hostage.

You can hold the DOS disks in your hand because the disks are physical. The instructions that the disks contain, however, are logical—not physical. In the world of computers, you view something in a logical way by understanding the concept of its operation.

This conceptual view includes the steps that make the computer "compute." Each time you turn on your PC, it must refresh itself by reading the DOS instructions from the DOS system files on the PC's start-up disk into the PC's working memory before the computer is ready to run your favorite software. DOS, your PC, and your favorite software work together to produce the computing result. If you remove any ingredient, you cannot compute.

In a similar way, when you mow your lawn, you count on the operation of the mower and the application of your mowing technique to get the job done. Mowing the lawn is conceptually the interplay between you, the mower, and the lawn. If you simply push a dead mower over the grass, you are going through the motions, but the grass is not mowed. If you start your mower but let it sit in one spot, the potential of the spinning blades is available, but the grass is still not mowed. Only when you start the mower and push it correctly across your lawn is the lawn mowed.

Likewise, you can start DOS on your computer and let it sit, but you are not doing any useful computing. You can attempt to use your computer without starting DOS, but nothing happens. Conceptually, DOS is the go-between that links you with the computer's capability of doing useful work. You have to know how to start DOS from the files on the DOS disks or on a hard disk. After DOS is started, you can mow through a memo or a spreadsheet.

Tip: You must prepare all disks with DOS before DOS can use them; only disks prepared with the DOS system files can start your PC. Disks that contain the DOS system files are DOS boot disks.

Note: Some laptop computers include the DOS 5.0 system files and command interpreter in permanent read-only memory (ROM). If your laptop PC is configured in this way, you can turn on your computer and start DOS without inserting a disk.

Examining the Files on the DOS Disks

Like the files on other disks, the files on the DOS disks have specific purposes. Every file available to DOS has a *file name*. The file name can have two parts, with a period separating the parts. The first part, called the *root file name*, can include up to eight characters. The optional second part of the file name, called the *file name extension*, can be up to three characters long. On the DOS disks, a file name extension helps describe the general purpose of the file. Each version or variation of DOS has an individual assortment of file names on the DOS disks. Even with the variations, you can benefit by looking at the file names of one particular DOS disk. The following list shows the names of the DOS files on the MS-DOS Version 5.0 disks.

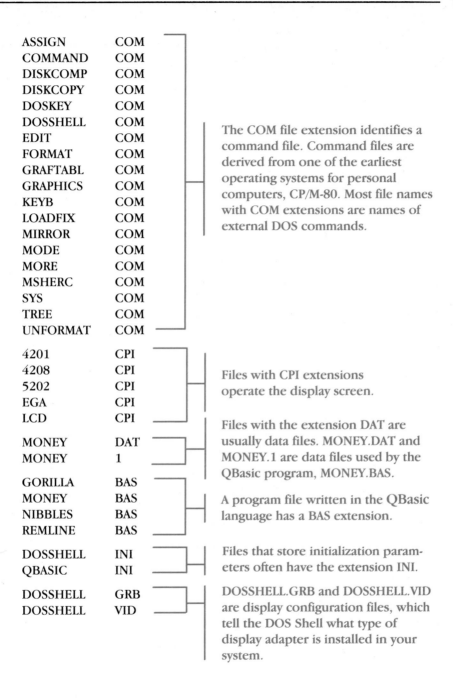

ASSIGN	COM
COMMAND	COM
DISKCOMP	COM
DISKCOPY	COM
DOSKEY	COM
DOSSHELL	COM
EDIT	COM
FORMAT	COM
GRAFTABL	COM
GRAPHICS	COM
KEYB	COM
LOADFIX	COM
MIRROR	COM
MODE	COM
MORE	COM
MSHERC	COM
SYS	COM
TREE	COM
UNFORMAT	COM

The COM file extension identifies a command file. Command files are derived from one of the earliest operating systems for personal computers, CP/M-80. Most file names with COM extensions are names of external DOS commands.

4201	CPI
4208	CPI
5202	CPI
EGA	CPI
LCD	CPI

Files with CPI extensions operate the display screen.

MONEY	DAT
MONEY	1

Files with the extension DAT are usually data files. MONEY.DAT and MONEY.1 are data files used by the QBasic program, MONEY.BAS.

GORILLA	BAS
MONEY	BAS
NIBBLES	BAS
REMLINE	BAS

A program file written in the QBasic language has a BAS extension.

DOSSHELL	INI
QBASIC	INI

Files that store initialization parameters often have the extension INI.

DOSSHELL	GRB
DOSSHELL	VID

DOSSHELL.GRB and DOSSHELL.VID are display configuration files, which tell the DOS Shell what type of display adapter is installed in your system.

README	TXT	

Files with the TXT extension are text files that contain supplemental information. For example, the README.TXT file provides special instructions for installing DOS 5.0.

PACKING	LST	

PACKING.LST contains a list of all files on the MS-DOS 5.0 distribution disks and a list of DOS files found on a set of 360K floppy disks on which you have installed MS-DOS 5.0.

APPEND	EXE
ATTRIB	EXE
BACKUP	EXE
CHKDSK	EXE
COMP	EXE
DEBUG	EXE
DELOLDOS	EXE
DOSSHELL	EXE
DOSSWAP	EXE
EDLIN	EXE
EMM386	EXE
EXE2BIN	EXE
EXPAND	EXE
FASTOPEN	EXE
FC	EXE
FDISK	EXE
FIND	EXE
HELP	EXE
JOIN	EXE
LABEL	EXE
MEM	EXE
NLSFUNC	EXE
PRINT	EXE
QBASIC	EXE
RECOVER	EXE
REPLACE	EXE
RESTORE	EXE
SETVER	EXE
SHARE	EXE
SORT	EXE
SUBST	EXE
UNDELETE	EXE
XCOPY	EXE

EXE files are executable program files. Except for technical details of their internal structure, they are much like COM files. By entering the root name of an EXE file, you cause a program to run.

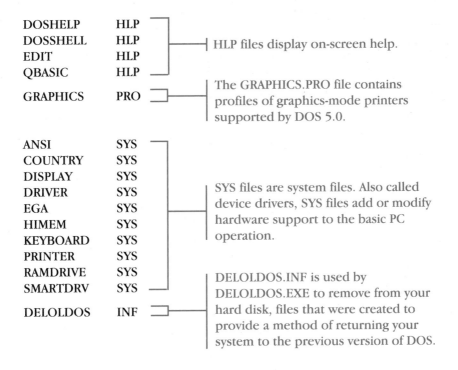

DOSHELP	HLP	
DOSSHELL	HLP	HLP files display on-screen help.
EDIT	HLP	
QBASIC	HLP	
GRAPHICS	PRO	The GRAPHICS.PRO file contains profiles of graphics-mode printers supported by DOS 5.0.

ANSI	SYS	
COUNTRY	SYS	
DISPLAY	SYS	
DRIVER	SYS	SYS files are system files. Also called
EGA	SYS	device drivers, SYS files add or modify
HIMEM	SYS	hardware support to the basic PC
KEYBOARD	SYS	operation.
PRINTER	SYS	
RAMDRIVE	SYS	
SMARTDRV	SYS	DELOLDOS.INF is used by
DELOLDOS	INF	DELOLDOS.EXE to remove from your hard disk, files that were created to provide a method of returning your system to the previous version of DOS.

Understanding the Parts of DOS

Remember that the DOS disks contain the files necessary for DOS to do its job. When DOS is loaded, it acts as a go-between so that you and the PC can do useful computing. You also can look at DOS as an entity divided into modules. This modularity enables DOS to "divide and conquer" the various operating system requirements placed on DOS by users and programs.

DOS has four main functional components:

- The command interpreter (COMMAND.COM)
- The DOS Shell
- The basic input/output system (BIOS)
- The DOS utilities

All four components are contained in files that come with the disks in your DOS package. In the following sections, you learn about these components and their duties.

Note: Don't worry if you haven't completely grasped the significance of a computer's operating system at this point. An operating system is a multifaceted software creation, and some facets are easier to master than others. You may benefit from reading this chapter again after you have read through the rest of the chapters in Part I. Many ideas presented in this chapter are touched on again in later chapters. Rest assured that after you start using DOS, you quickly will develop your own personal definition for this versatile operating system.

The Command Interpreter

The command interpreter is DOS's "friendly host." It interacts with you through the keyboard and screen when you operate your computer. The command interpreter is also known as the *command processor* and often is referred to simply as COMMAND.COM (pronounced "command dot com" or just "command com"). COMMAND.COM accepts your DOS commands and sees that they are carried out.

COMMAND.COM displays the *DOS prompt* (C>, A>, and so on), also known as the *command prompt* or the *command line*. The DOS command prompt is a request for input. When you enter a command, you are communicating with COMMAND.COM, which then interprets what you type and processes your input so that DOS can take the appropriate action. COMMAND.COM, through DOS commands, handles the technical details of such common tasks as displaying a list of the contents of a disk, copying files, and starting your programs.

You can compare COMMAND.COM to a waiter. When you go to a restaurant, you may be attended by a waiter whose job is to see to your needs. You communicate your dining requests to the waiter as you communicate your command requests to COMMAND.COM. When you are ordering, for example, the waiter may inform you that an entree is not available or that a combination of additional side dishes isn't included with a certain dinner. Similarly, COMMAND.COM communicates to you when a command is not available or when an additional part of a command is not allowed.

Your waiter doesn't prepare your meal. The waiter communicates your instructions to the personnel in the kitchen in a way that the cooks understand. Likewise, COMMAND.COM itself doesn't carry out most DOS commands; instead, it communicates to other modules of DOS that specialize in the requested service. Your waiter may provide some simple services, such as pouring more water or offering condiments. These simple services are built into the waiter's job. COMMAND.COM also has some simple DOS commands built in. These built-in commands are available whenever you are using DOS. COMMAND.COM does not have to rely on the presence of other DOS modules to carry out the work of these *internal commands*.

COMMAND.COM is an important part of DOS. Many PC users may think of COMMAND.COM's operation as being the essence of DOS because COMMAND.COM is so visible. DOS does many things behind the scenes, but COMMAND.COM is up front (see fig. 2.1). Thus, PC users equate issuing commands with performing DOS-level PC-management work because issuing DOS commands is the primary area of their DOS activities. Because you instruct COMMAND.COM rather than the hardware directly, you never need to know the details of how the hardware operates.

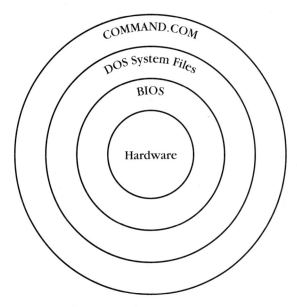

Fig. 2.1. *The relationship of COMMAND.COM with other DOS modules and your hardware.*

Chapter 5 discusses DOS commands more fully, and Part II of this book is devoted to the DOS commands users most often issue. Issuing commands, however, is only a part of using DOS to manage a PC. Many of the commands you issue at the DOS prompt work with the file system. Chapter 6 provides an inside view of the file system and makes using disk- and file-related DOS commands more meaningful.

The DOS Shell

The DOS Shell, available in DOS 4.0 and much improved in MS-DOS 5.0, is a visually oriented interface between you and the command interpreter. The DOS Shell provides an alternative to typing commands at the DOS command prompt. By using the DOS Shell, you can perform DOS functions without having to memorize all the available DOS commands. You can think of the DOS Shell as a protective layer between you and the command interpreter (COMMAND.COM), as depicted in figure 2.2. The DOS Shell is a final layer that insulates you from having to control details of the computer's hardware electronically.

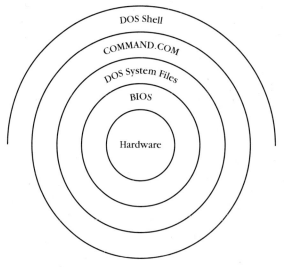

Fig. 2.2. The DOS Shell in relation to other DOS modules and hardware.

Instead of giving you the command prompt, the DOS Shell lists directories and file names on your screen, helping you keep track of the programs and data on your disks (see fig. 2.3). Through menus and helpful screen prompts, the Shell enables you to manipulate the listed file and directory names to perform disk- and file-related tasks easily.

Using the DOS Shell, you also are able to start applications programs by selecting from a list on-screen. When you first install MS-DOS 5.0, the DOS Shell lists four options in the program list, the lower half of the screen, as shown in figure 2.3. You easily can add more programs to the list, turning the DOS Shell into a command center from which you can control any session with your computer.

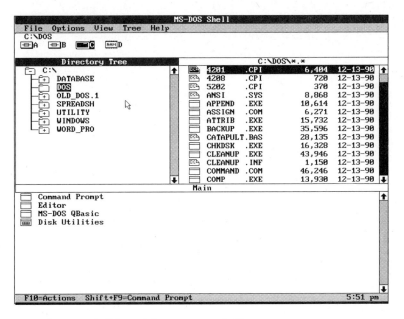

Fig. 2.3. The DOS Shell list of directories and files.

The Shell even enables you to switch quickly between several programs on your PC, a procedure sometimes referred to as *task swapping*. For example, you may be working on your monthly budget in a spreadsheet program and decide that you need to consult travel expense data, which is stored in a database file. Without forcing you first to leave the spreadsheet program, the DOS Shell's Task Swapper enables you to start the database program, retrieve the desired information, and then switch back to the spreadsheet. Indeed, with the Shell, you can switch back and forth among several programs at the touch of a keystroke.

Chapter 4 introduces you to the DOS Shell, explaining how to get around on the DOS Shell screen and how to control the screen display. You also learn how to use the DOS Shell as a platform from which to run all other programs on your computer's hard disk. Specific capabilities of the DOS Shell are covered in Part II of this book. Chapter 14 also describes how to configure the DOS Shell to fit your needs.

The Basic Input/Output System

The so-called *hidden*, or *system*, files are another part of the operating system. These special files define the hardware to the software. When you start a computer, the DOS system files are loaded into RAM. Combined, the files provide a unified set of routines for controlling and directing the computer's operations and are known as the *input/output system*.

The hidden files interact with special read-only memory (ROM) on the motherboard. The special ROM is called the *Basic Input Output System*, or simply *BIOS*. Responding to a program's request for service, the system files translate the request and pass it to the ROM BIOS. The BIOS provides a further translation of the request that links the request to the hardware (see fig. 2.4).

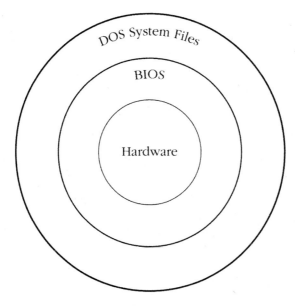

Fig. 2.4. *The DOS system files as they relate to BIOS and the hardware.*

DOS provides uniform service to the hardware by getting assistance from the permanent ROM BIOS in the computer. ROM BIOS can vary among computer makers, but the computers are highly compatible when the design of the ROM BIOS is integrated with DOS. In large part, the DOS input/output system, through the special BIOS, determines the degree to which a PC is IBM compatible.

The Hidden Core of DOS

Inside a working PC, DOS is the collection of services that DOS offers in the form of built-in groups of related instructions, or *software routines*. These routines are the core of the services DOS provides to your applications programs. The extensive file-system management provided by DOS, for example, is made up of these routines. Programmers can access these software routines to perform a variety of internal operations with the PC. These functions are common repetitive actions that operating system designers have included in DOS to make life easier (and programs more uniform) for PC programmers. DOS commands themselves rely on these service routines to do standard low-level computer work. By accessing the built-in DOS service routines, a program doesn't need the details of how DOS works with the PC. With the interface to DOS service built in, computer languages and the programs they produce can use DOS uniformly.

The internal file system and input/output aspects of DOS are often as invisible to DOS users as interaction with the DOS Shell or COMMAND.COM is obvious. When you order from a waiter, you don't need to know the details of how your meal is prepared. You just want timely service and satisfaction with your food. Similarly, you (or your program) want timely and appropriate services to be conducted by the internal parts of DOS. You don't care how DOS goes about doing its internal job, detailed though the procedure may be.

Fortunately, you do not have to know much about these internal DOS programming concerns to operate your PC. Having some idea of what goes on at the internal level, however, may give you more insight into how a DOS command or your word processing program works. Programming at the DOS level is fascinating and rewarding to many, but this book does not attempt to teach you the programming aspects of DOS. If you want to know more about programming at the DOS level for additional insight or to write actual programs, you can refer to books published by Que Corporation on this topic. *DOS Programmer's Reference,* 2nd Edition, by Terry Dettmann, and *Using Assembly Language,* 2nd Edition, by Allen Wyatt, are suggested.

If the programming aspects of DOS do not interest you, you are not alone. Most DOS users are generally uninformed about "what goes on in there," and they do just fine. As your DOS skills increase, however, you may find that having a general layman's notion of "what goes on in there" enables you to become a more self-reliant PC user. Throughout this book, you get simple explanations of internal operations, helping you learn about this invisible but essential part of DOS.

The DOS Utilities

The DOS utilities carry out useful housekeeping tasks, such as preparing disks, comparing files, finding the free space on a disk, and printing in the background. Some utilities provide statistics on disk size and available memory and compare disks and files. The utility programs are files that reside on disk and are loaded into memory by COMMAND.COM when you type the command name. They are called *external commands* because they are not loaded into memory with COMMAND.COM every time you turn on your computer. An example of an external command is the FORMAT command, which is used to prepare disks for use with DOS.

Disk operating systems insulate you and your programs from the need to know exactly how to make the hardware work. For example, to list the contents of a disk in a disk drive, you don't need to know the capacity or recording format of the disk or how to get the computer to direct the output to the screen. An applications program that needs to store data on disk does not have to reserve space on the disk, keep track of where the data is stored on disk, or know how the data was encoded. DOS takes care of all these tasks.

Understanding the Functions of DOS

By now, you no doubt suspect that DOS does many "technical" tasks that are not easy to comprehend. Certainly, much of DOS's activity is technical. But most of the DOS activities you need to understand in order to make DOS work effectively are not difficult. This section briefly describes the common DOS functions you use again and again as your computing expertise grows. Later sections treat each topic in detail.

Managing Files

One of DOS's primary functions is to help you organize the files you store on your disks. Organized files are a sign of good computer housekeeping, and good housekeeping is crucial when you want to take advantage of the storage capacity available on today's disks.

Consider, for example, that the smallest capacity floppy disk can hold the equivalent of 100 letter-sized pages of information. Now imagine that each sheet of information makes up one file: you have 100 files to keep track of. If you use disks that can hold more information than a standard floppy disk (such as a hard disk), file organization becomes even more crucial.

Fortunately, DOS gives you the tools to be a good computer housekeeper. DOS lists files for you, tells you their names and sizes, and gives you the dates when they were created. You can use this information for many organizational purposes. In addition to organizing files, DOS can duplicate files, discard files that are no longer useful, and replace files with matching file names.

Managing Disks

Certain DOS functions are essential to all computer users. For example, all disks must be prepared before they can be used in your computer. This preparation is called *formatting*, which includes checking disks for available space. Other DOS disk-management functions include the following:

- Labeling disks electronically

- Making restorable backup copies of files for security purposes

- Restoring damaged files on disk

- Copying disks

- Viewing the contents of files on a disk

Redirecting Input and Output

DOS expects its input to come from a standard place, such as the keyboard. DOS sends its output to a standard place, such as the display screen. DOS designers recognized that sending output to another device, such as a printer, may sometimes be necessary. Therefore, they provided DOS with the capability of *redirecting*, or sending in another direction, the output that normally goes to the standard output. Through redirection, a list of files that usually appears on-screen can be sent to the printer. You see useful examples of the redirection of common commands when these commands are discussed.

DOS also contains commands that enable you to tailor your PC's hardware environment to your specific needs. In fact, DOS provides much versatility in its configuration capabilities. Fortunately for users just starting with DOS, the standard configuration of the PC works fine. In this book, however, you do learn how to make simple alterations of the PC's DOS configuration.

Adding configuration control to your DOS activities isn't an everyday activity. Usually, a user establishes a tailored configuration using the CONFIG.SYS file. When established, the CONFIG.SYS file remains relatively unchanged. Chapters 14 and 15 cover the topic of configuration. Don't worry about configuration for now. You will be ready to understand it later.

Running Applications Programs

Computers require complex and exact instructions—programs—to provide you with useful output. Computing would be impractical if you had to write a program every time you had a job to do. Happily, that condition is not the case. Programmers spend months doing the specialized work that enables a computer to function in many different ways: as a word processor, database manipulator, spreadsheet, or generator of graphics. Through a program, the computer's capabilities are applied to a task—thus the term *applications programs*.

Applications programs, like DOS, are distributed on disks. DOS is the go-between that gives you access to these programs through the computer. By simply inserting a disk into your computer's disk drive and pressing a few keys, you have an astonishingly wide variety of easy-to-use applications at your disposal.

Applications constantly need to read data from or write data to disk files. You need to see what you have typed by viewing text information sent to the screen or printer. The program you are using needs you to enter information by typing from the keyboard or moving the mouse in a certain way. These input and output tasks are common repetitive computer tasks, but electronically they are not trivial. Thanks to DOS, you can take the repetitive tasks for granted. DOS takes responsibility for the technical details of input and output, providing applications with an easy-to-use connection, or program interface, that sees to the details of these repetitive activities. As a computer user, you want easy-to-understand information about disk files, memory size, and computer configuration. DOS provides these services.

You can compare DOS to a soft-drink dispenser. When you walk up to a soft-drink machine, you concern yourself with having the right coins and making a selection. You probably don't think of the wires, motors, refrigeration equipment, or the mechanism that calculates change. You know to put the coins into the slot, press the correct button, and pick up your drink from the dispenser. The maker of the soft-drink machine has provided you with an easy-to-use interface that has relatively simple input and provides straight-forward output. You have a need, and through your actions, the machine carries out many detailed steps internally to provide you with a service that fills your need. DOS's service provisions are not unlike those of the soft-drink machine. DOS is perhaps a bit more complicated, but the concept of internal details you don't see is the same for DOS as it is for the soft-drink machine.

Running Macros and Batch Files

Most of your interaction with DOS takes place through the keyboard or with a mouse. You type commands for the DOS Shell or COMMAND.COM to carry out or use the mouse to select options from menus. Commands, however, also can be stored in memory as a *macro* or placed in a disk file called a *batch file* and "played back" to COMMAND.COM. Chapter 13 covers macros and batch files and explains how to create them.

COMMAND.COM responds to these batches of commands from the computer's memory or from a file, just as COMMAND.COM responds to commands typed from the keyboard. Macros and batch files can automate frequently used command sequences, making keyboard operation simpler.

Difficult-to-remember command sequences are ideal candidates for macro or batch-file treatment.

Handling Miscellaneous Tasks

Some DOS functions, such as setting the computer's clock and calendar so that files and applications programs can have access to dates and times, fall into a "miscellaneous" category. You also may need to use DOS's text editor to create text files such as memos, notes, or batch files. You even can see the amount of RAM available for applications programs through DOS.

Developing a Working Knowledge of DOS

Anyone who intends to use a personal computer can benefit from a working knowledge of DOS. You cannot use your computer to run most popular programs unless you start the program with DOS. Although someone you know may be willing to do DOS-related work for you, you will become more proficient at computing if you learn a little DOS. Besides, the results greatly exceed the effort you spend learning DOS.

Summary

In this chapter, you have learned some facts about the role of DOS in personal computing. The following are some important points to remember:

- The term *DOS* is an acronym for Disk Operating System. Many computer operating systems have the term *DOS* in their names.

- MS-DOS is the name of an operating system for IBM PCs and close compatibles. To most PC users, DOS means MS-DOS.

- When PC users use the term *DOS*, they may be referring to only one contextual part of DOS.

- DOS works with the Intel 8086 family of microprocessors.

- The DOS package includes a number of disks that contain the files necessary for DOS to do its job.

- The file names on the DOS disks include extensions that indicate the purpose of each file.

- The BIOS layer of a PC is contained in permanent ROM and works with the hardware to provide a foundation of services for DOS.

- COMMAND.COM is the DOS command processor. COMMAND.COM executes DOS commands.

- The DOS Shell program, available with DOS 4.0 and DOS 5.0, provides a visually oriented environment that enables the user to execute DOS commands by selecting them from a menu and to start and switch between several application programs easily.

- DOS has many functions, including managing files and disks, redirecting input and output, running applications programs and batch files, and handling miscellaneous tasks such as setting the computer's date and time.

As you read the following chapters, you will find that DOS can be useful in a variety of ways. More than one hundred DOS commands and functions are available. This book emphasizes those that are essential to using a personal computer for running off-the-shelf programs. You quickly become familiar with the essentials of DOS through this approach.

Starting DOS

3

N ow that you have an overview of the PC and of DOS, you are ready to start your PC and learn more about the practical operation of DOS. This chapter is an overview of the start-up process. The first time you start your computer, you may not know what to expect. After you learn a few computer terms and perform the basic start-up procedure, however, you begin to feel at ease. Before you flip the switch on your PC, take time to understand some preliminary information about the start-up process.

The operators of early computers started their computers by entering a short binary program and then instructing the computer to run the program. This binary program was called the "bootstrap loader" because the computer, through the bootstrap program, figuratively pulled itself up by the bootstraps to perform tasks. The early computer operators shortened the name of the start-up process to *booting*. The term stuck. Today, *booting the computer* still refers to the start-up procedure. Fortunately, the process of booting is now relatively automatic.

Note: This chapter assumes that you do not know how to boot or know the process behind booting. A few commands are necessary to show you the start-up process, but don't worry if you do not know them. Just type the examples; later chapters cover these commands in detail.

Key Terms Used in This Chapter

Cold boot	The process of starting a PC from a power-off condition
Warm boot	The process of restarting a PC while the power is on
Cursor	The blinking line or solid block that marks where the next keyboard entry will appear
Pointer	The arrow- or block-shaped on-screen object that you move by moving a mouse input device across the surface of your desk
Default	A condition or value that the computer, the program, or DOS assumes when you choose not to supply your own
Prompt	A symbol, character, or group of characters indicating that you must enter information
DOS prompt	The characters that COMMAND.COM displays to inform you that you can enter a DOS command. C> is an example of a DOS prompt.
Command	A text directive to COMMAND.COM, issued at the DOS prompt, that instructs DOS to provide an operating system service
Parameter	Additional instructions given with a command to let DOS know how to carry out the command
Syntax	The way commands and parameters should be put together at the DOS command prompt. COMMAND.COM interprets the syntax of your instructions to DOS.
Logged drive	The current default disk drive that DOS uses to carry out commands that involve disk services. Unless you change the prompt with a command, the letter of the default drive is the DOS prompt.

Performing a Cold Boot

The term *cold boot* is derived from the fact that the computer's power is off and that the unit is not yet warm. If the booting process is new to you, you should make a few preliminary checks part of your booting routine.

Making Preliminary Checks

If you travel by airplane, you may have noticed that before taking off, a pilot checks to make sure that all equipment is in working order. Just as this preliminary check of the airplane is important, so is your check of your computer's equipment. Your PC isn't as complicated as an aircraft, but a few preliminary checks help you avoid "crashes."

Computers like clean, steady power sources. Choose a good electrical outlet that does not serve devices such as copy machines, hair dryers, or other electrical gadgets. Ask your computer dealer about a line conditioner, or surge suppressor, if you must share an outlet.

Make sure that the switch is off before you plug in your computer. Some computers have switches marked with 0 and 1. The switch side marked 0 is the off switch position. Many PCs keep themselves turned off after a electrical "drop out" even when the PC's switch is in the on position. This feature ensures that unsettled power conditions have passed before you can turn on the unit again after switching it off.

Ventilation is important to computers. Make sure that your PC has room to breathe. Computers must dissipate the heat generated by their internal electronic components. Keep paper, books, beverages, and other clutter away from the system unit's case.

TIP

> ***Tip:*** If you stand your computer's system unit on end on the floor, make sure that the cooling fan is not obstructed by the back of a desk or some other furniture. Use one of the commercially available vertical floor stands to make the system unit more stable. Watch out for dust accumulation in the fan area from extra dust on the floor.

Keep this book, your DOS manual, DOS disks, and your PC system manual nearby for reference. The disk you use to boot your computer can be labeled "Start-up," "System," "Main," or "DOS." Check your DOS manual if you are not sure which disk is bootable, or ask your computer specialist to provide a bootable DOS system disk. The DOS 5.0 Setup program, for example, instructs you to label the bootable disk "Start-up." From this point on, this chapter refers to the bootable disk(s) supplied in your DOS package as the *DOS Master disk(s)*.

Inserting the Disk

For the initial cold boot, use your DOS Master disk. To ensure that the DOS disk (or any other disk for that matter) does not get erased accidentally, you should *write-protect* the disk. To write-protect a 3 1/2-inch microfloppy disk, locate the plastic write-protect shutter and slide it so that the window is open (see fig. 3.1). To write-protect a 5 1/4-inch floppy disk, locate the write-protect notch and cover the notch with a write-protect tab so that the notch is covered (see fig. 3.2). When a disk is write-protected, the drive cannot write new information on the disk even if you inadvertently issue a command that attempts to write data to the disk.

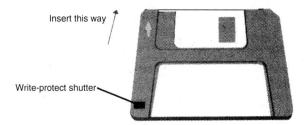

Fig. 3.1. *Microfloppy (3 1/2-inch) disk showing built-in write-protect shutter.*

Insert the write-protected bootable DOS Master disk into drive A. Check your PC's system manual for the location of drive A and for disk-insertion instructions. When you have inserted a disk properly, the label usually faces the top on horizontal drives and the left on vertical drives (see fig. 3.3). To complete the insertion of a 5 1/4-inch disk, close the drive door or turn the latch clockwise. If the disk does not go in, make sure that the drive doesn't contain another disk. Never jam or buckle a disk during insertion; you could cause permanent damage to the disk. Insert 3 1/2-inch disks gently, pushing until you hear a click. The drive closes by itself (see fig. 3.4).

Fig. 3.2. Minifloppy (5 1/4-inch) disk showing write-protect notch.

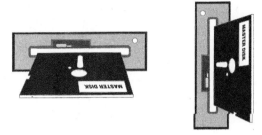

Fig. 3.3. Inserting 5 1/4-inch disks into horizontal and vertical drives.

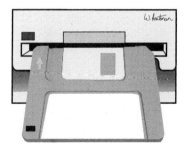

Fig. 3.4. Inserting a 3 1/2-inch disk.

> *Note:* For this exercise, you boot from a floppy disk. Even if you have a hard disk with DOS installed, learn how to boot from a floppy disk in case your hard disk becomes unbootable. Booting from a prepared hard disk is the same as booting from a floppy, except that you do not insert a disk into the floppy drive.

After you insert the disk, close the drive door. (Microfloppy drives close themselves.) If you have a key lock on the front of the system unit, unlock the unit.

Finally, turn on the display switch, if necessary, and give your screen a few seconds to warm up. (Some displays are powered from the system unit and do not have a switch.) Locate the computer's power switch. It is often on the right side toward the rear of the system unit. Snap on the switch. At this point, the cold boot has begun.

TIP

> *Tip:* Always let the spring action of the PC's power switch snap the switch on or off. If you hold the switch arm between your fingers and ease the switch on, the switch doesn't make immediate and decisive electrical contact. Easing the switch on may cause fluttering power, and the PC may fail to turn on.

If you or your computer supplier installed DOS on your hard disk, you can boot from the hard disk simply by turning on the computer.

Watching the Progress of the Boot

The instant you snap on the switch, the computer's electronics do a *power-on reset* (POR). The RAM, the microprocessor, and other electronics are zeroed out, similar to cleaning the slate. The system then begins a *power-on self-test* (POST). The POST ensures that your PC can deal responsibly with your valuable data. The POST can take from a few seconds to a couple of minutes. During the POST, you may see a description of the test or a blinking cursor on the display, similar to the following:

```
ABC Computer Co.

Turbo

RAM check

640K

OK
```

When the POST finishes, you hear one beep, and drive A starts activity. The bootstrap loader then loads DOS from the Master DOS disk into the computer's *random-access memory* (RAM).

Technical Note: The term *booting* is derived from the old concept that with no external help, you can "pull yourself up by your boot-straps." In other words, you can start with nothing and turn it into something useful. Needless to say, the act of creating something from nothing requires some wide interpretation of what "nothing" is. When you boot your PC, the PC is nothing on a scale of computing output. The potential is there, but you cannot compute with it.

Much of this computing potential resides on the DOS boot disk in three disk files. The file that contains the core of DOS, the file that contains the basic input and output additions for ROM BIOS, and COMMAND.COM are all waiting on disk to be loaded into the PC. Before the PC can load these files and make DOS available, the PC must test itself, initialize external hardware, and load the three DOS files from disk into random-access memory (RAM).

Special instructions built into the PC enable the PC to access a predetermined part of the boot disk and read the boot sector into RAM. The boot sector contains a short machine-language program that finds and loads two DOS hidden system files. The boot program then looks for the CONFIG.SYS file in the root directory of the boot disk. (CONFIG.SYS is discussed in Chapter 15.) If CONFIG.SYS is found, the boot program opens the file and installs into memory any device drivers to which CONFIG.SYS refers.

By loading device drivers at the time of booting, the boot program gives the PC the provision to operate in a configuration tailored to the specific needs of the PC's individual hardware and running requirements. Most device drivers are built into DOS's BIOS extensions, but CONFIG.SYS device drivers are selectable and included under your control.

The boot program locates the COMMAND.COM file and loads it. When COMMAND.COM is found, it is loaded into memory. The boot program turns control of the PC's resources over to COMMAND.COM. COMMAND.COM searches the root directory of the boot disk for a file named AUTOEXEC.BAT. If the AUTOEXEC.BAT file is found, its contents are executed as a series of DOS commands. (Chapter 15 discusses AUTOEXEC.BAT.) By providing for this special batch file to be executed at boot time, DOS can tailor the start-up of every PC to meet the specific needs of the user.

When AUTOEXEC.BAT has been executed by COMMAND.COM, you see the DOS prompt, or *system prompt* (assuming that one of the commands does not start a program such as the DOS Shell). COMMAND.COM is then ready to receive your command.

Viewing DOS

When the cold boot completes its preliminary loading of DOS, a DOS screen appears, ready to accept your commands. The screen you see depends on the version of DOS running on your computer and on the view of DOS you have chosen. With DOS 4.0 and later, you have two view options:

- The command line (DOS's only view prior to 4.0)

- The DOS Shell

The command line is the traditional look of DOS. The command line appears on a plain screen with one letter of the alphabet representing the current, or active, drive, followed by a greater-than symbol (see fig. 3.5).

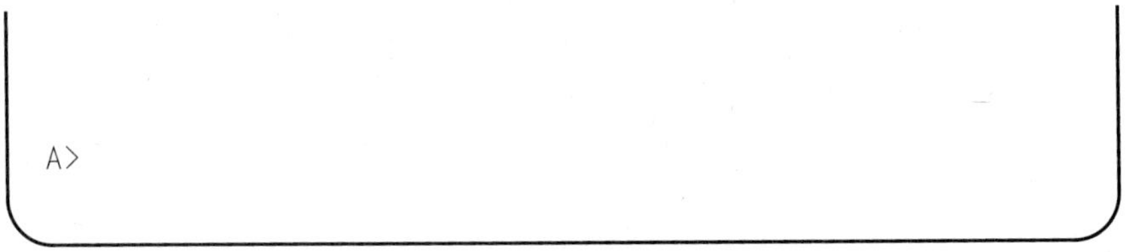

```
A>
```

Fig. 3.5. The traditional DOS command line.

The combination of this drive letter and greater-than symbol is referred to as the *command prompt* or *DOS prompt*. The most common command prompts are A> for floppy disk systems and C> for hard disk systems. If you are using Version 3.3 or an earlier version, or if you or your dealer has enabled the command line view, the plain command prompt is your view.

> *Note:* The DOS 5.0 Setup program that installed the DOS system files on your Master disks probably created a special start-up file named AUTOEXEC.BAT. When your boot disk contains this file, DOS reads it every time you boot your computer. Setup places in AUTOEXEC.BAT a command that causes the command prompt to appear in one of the following forms (depending on whether you are booting from the floppy disk drive—drive A—or from the hard disk drive—drive C):
>
> ```
> A:\>
> ```
>
> ```
> C:\>
> ```
>
> These command prompts are equivalent, respectively, to the prompts A> and C>, but they provide a bit more information. The colon (:) and back slash (\) represent the *directory path*, which is discussed fully in Chapter 8.

Note: If you are using DOS 5.0 and you boot from a master DOS disk, you may see the DOS 5.0 installation program, Setup. You can stop Setup by pressing Esc; you then see the DOS prompt.

The DOS Shell is a relatively new look for DOS, first available in DOS 4.0 and significantly enhanced in DOS 5.0. The DOS Shell provides a full-screen visually oriented "window" with menus, screen areas, pop-up help screens, and graphic representation of directories and files (see fig. 3.6). You can issue many standard DOS commands by pointing and selecting with a mouse.

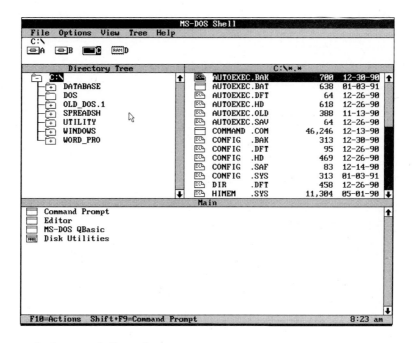

Fig. 3.6. The DOS Shell window.

The DOS Shell provides the friendliest way to use DOS, but you should also learn the basic commands from the command line. Working with the DOS prompt is the traditional way to use DOS. Even though using the Shell is easy, you still need to know something about DOS commands and terminology because they remain substantially unchanged from previous versions of DOS. If you have DOS 4.0 or 5.0, refer to Chapter 4 for details on using the DOS Shell. For now, press the F3 key to exit the DOS Shell. You see the DOS prompt appear. When the prompt appears, you are operating your computer from the DOS command line.

> *Note:* The DOS Shell that comes with DOS 5.0 isn't the only visually oriented user interface to DOS. Many independent companies sell add-on software that performs many of the same functions as the DOS Shell. In fact, the term *shell* is often used to describe any program that adds a layer of user friendliness to an existing program.
>
> Programs like PC Tools Deluxe, XTreePro, and Lotus Magellan give you a DOS user interface similar to that of the DOS Shell. Many users find that shell programs enable them to use the features of DOS more competently. Others discover that without some knowledge of the DOS command line, they are at a disadvantage when they must operate a PC other than their own. This book encourages you to learn both the DOS Shell and command line.

Entering the Date and Time

DOS uses the date and time to indicate, or *stamp*, the time and date of a file's creation or last change. Most contemporary computers come with a built-in, battery-powered calendar and clock. The clock keeps correct time even when the unit's power is off so that the correct time and date are always the default values. Many older PCs, or PCs based on the original IBM PC, do not have built-in clocks. These PCs keep time when the power is on, but you must set the correct time as a follow-up of the boot process to ensure proper time and date stamping.

When a computer boots, it automatically reads the time and date from the system clock but may ask you to enter each manually. If your computer's boot disk contains an AUTOEXEC.BAT file, DOS does not prompt you for the time and date during the boot process unless the AUTOEXEC.BAT file contains the two commands, DATE and TIME. When no AUTOEXEC.BAT file is present, DOS always prompts you to enter the correct time and date. Some configurations of DOS offer the date prompt first and then offer the time prompt; others offer the time prompt first.

The prompt for the current date is as follows:

```
Current date is Thu 10-31-1991

Enter new date (mm-dd-yy):
```

Unless you have a battery-powered system clock, you need to enter the current date at the prompt. Even if you have a battery-powered clock, the date may be incorrect.

To accept the default (suggested) date, press Enter. If the date is not correct, you should change it now. Look at the date template, which DOS shows in parentheses. Enter the calendar month as a number (1 through 12) in place of *mm*. Likewise, enter the day between 1 and 31 in the place of *dd*. When you enter *yy*, you do not have to include the century. DOS assumes the twentieth century and accepts *91* for 1991, *92* for 1992, and so on.

> *Note:* A *default* value is a suggested response that DOS or an application program uses unless you suggest another value. When you are working with the DOS Shell or the DOS command line, DOS accepts the default if you make no specific choice when the computer prompts you. You usually press Enter to accept the default. You learn more about defaults when you read about commands in later chapters.

If you enter a value that DOS is programmed to reject, DOS lets you know with an error message. Don't worry about making a mistake; DOS prompts you again for the date, and you can reenter the date correctly.

> *Note:* DOS is programmed to issue on-screen error messages when you provide an incorrect response. Different mistakes produce different error messages. Appendix A is a useful guide to the error messages that DOS is programmed to provide. Reviewing the various error messages helps you understand DOS's handling of the mistakes it detects.

The DOS prompt for the current time is as follows:

```
Current time is 11:17:00.75a

Enter new time:
```

When prompted, enter the current time. The template for time is *hh:mm:ss*. The hours are in 24-hour (military) clock format for DOS 3.3 and earlier versions. With these versions, you don't see the *a* or the *p* in the DOS time prompt. DOS 4.0 and later versions accept 12-hour time with a trailing *a* or *p* for A.M. or P.M. You can include the seconds, but they aren't required. Again, if you enter a time format that DOS isn't programmed to accept, DOS prompts you again.

> *Note:* Often called *Return* or *New Line*, Enter is an important key to
> DOS. You press Enter to activate a command you type at the com-
> mand line. You can type a command at the DOS prompt or a re-
> sponse to a command's prompt, but DOS does not act on your entry
> until you press Enter. In a sense, Enter is like a "Go" key, which
> instructs DOS to execute a command or accept a response. You
> always can correct a line while you are typing by using Backspace.
> After you press Enter, however, you cannot correct the line. If you
> press Enter without a command at the prompt, DOS simply scrolls
> up a new command line.

If your PC prompts you for the time and date and you respond, the boot
operation is complete. If your AUTOEXEC.BAT file bypasses the time and
date steps, the boot operation is completed without a time and date step.

Using the Booted PC

After the boot is complete, the system prompt indicates the *logged drive*,
which is the active drive that responds to commands. For example, an A>
prompt and a blinking cursor tell you that DOS is logged onto drive A,
usually a floppy disk drive. A C> prompt and a blinking cursor indicate that
DOS is logged onto the C drive, usually a hard disk drive.

You can change the logged drive simply by entering the drive letter followed
by a colon(:) and then pressing Enter. DOS reads the drive letter and colon
as the disk drive's name. For example, you can change from drive A to C by
typing **C:** at the prompt and pressing Enter. The sequence on-screen is as
follows:

```
A>C:
C>
```

Understanding the Logged Drive

DOS remembers the logged drive as its *current* drive. Many commands use
the current drive and other current information without your having to
specify the information in the command.

You need not specify the drive if you are requesting information from the logged drive. (If you are using two floppy drives, substitute B: for C: in the examples and exercises.) This special attention to the logged drive, however, doesn't mean that the other drives in your system are out of reach. You can use any drive on your system at any time by using a drive specifier in a command. You learn later how to include the drive name when you request information from a drive that is not current.

Stopping the Computer's Action

You occasionally may want to stop the computer from carrying out the action you requested through a DOS command. You may, for example, want to stop a command that produces long output or takes a long time to complete. You also may want to stop a command that you issued in error. Besides switching the power off (the last resort), three key sequences are available to stop a command in DOS:

Sequence	Action
Ctrl-C	Stops commands in which DOS pauses for you to type more information. DOS carries out many commands too quickly for you to intervene with Ctrl-C.
Ctrl-Break	Performs the equivalent of Ctrl-C. The Break key is located next to the Reset key on some keyboards. On some keyboards, Break shares the same key with Scroll Lock or Pause.
Ctrl-Alt-Del	The warm-boot key sequence. Ctrl-Alt-Del should not be your first choice to stop a command, but sometimes Ctrl-C or Ctrl-Break does not work. If this approach fails, turning off the power is the last resort.

You can think of these key sequences as the "panic" buttons to stop DOS. They are handy if you need to use them.

Performing a Warm Boot

The warm boot restarts the computer as the cold boot does, but you perform a warm boot when the PC's power is on. A warm boot restarts DOS without your touching the power switch; the warm boot is easier on the electronic components of your computer than turning the power off and then back on.

You may need to warm boot your PC for several reasons. If you change your system's start-up configuration (described in Chapter 15), you have to restart the PC. If your system becomes "hung" or unresponsive to keyboard input, you often can perform a warm boot. You even can start a different version of DOS from another disk by performing a warm boot.

For the cold boot, you insert the DOS system disk and then switch on the computer. For the warm boot, your PC is already switched on. For the purpose of this exercise, make sure that you have the DOS system disk in drive A. (For normal everyday situations, insert the DOS disk into drive A only if you don't have a hard disk.) You then simultaneously press three keys: Ctrl, Alt, and Del.

Look at the keyboard and locate the Ctrl, Alt, and Del keys. Hold down both Ctrl and Alt and then press Del. The PC skips the preliminary POST operation and immediately loads DOS.

Whether you have cold booted through a power-up or warm booted using Ctrl-Alt-Del, your PC is reset, refreshed, and ready for a computing session.

> ***Note:*** Warm booting a running computer is generally preferable to turning its power off and then back on. Each time you turn on your computer, electricity surges through its electronics, and your hard disk has to lurch into action. Although this start-up procedure is normal, performing a cold boot when you could do a warm boot places an unnecessary strain on the system's components.
>
> The Ctrl-Alt-Del keystroke usually is effective to perform a warm boot, but occasionally you may be forced to use your computer's Reset button, if your computer has one. Sometimes your computer's keyboard may be so "frozen" that your PC doesn't recognize that you have pressed Ctrl-Alt-Del. In such a case, you should press the Reset button. Your computer restarts without "powering down" but otherwise acts as if you had performed a cold boot, performing the POST operation and then loading DOS.
>
> Many PCs, however, do not have a Reset button. If you don't have a Reset button and the Ctrl-Alt-Del command doesn't work, you have to perform a cold boot. Turn off the power switch, count to 10 to give the hard disk time to stop completely, and turn the power back on.

Summary

This chapter presents the boot process that starts your PC. As part of the boot process, you are introduced to the following key points:

- The boot process resets your computer for a fresh DOS session.

- You must insert the DOS disk into the A drive in order to boot unless you have a hard disk with DOS installed.

- When you perform a cold boot, the PC performs a POST test before prompting for time and date.

- Systems without an AUTOEXEC.BAT file prompt for time and date as part of the boot operation.

- In the command line view, DOS shows a prompt that indicates the logged drive.

- In the DOS Shell view, DOS presents a visually oriented user interface through which you select actions you want to carry out.

The next chapter introduces the fundamentals of using the DOS Shell. Chapter 5 then discusses the concept of DOS commands. Now that you know how to boot your PC, you are ready to use the Shell and the command line to get the feel of managing your computer through DOS.

Using the DOS Shell

The DOS Shell program, available in DOS 4.0 and much enhanced in DOS 5.0, is a visually oriented user interface. The DOS Shell replaces the DOS command line with easy-to-use and easy-to-understand menus and enables you to use a mouse to perform many common DOS tasks. Managing your computer is easier from the DOS Shell because you select commands from a menu instead of typing them on the DOS command line.

More significantly, with the DOS Shell, you can easily perform operations that are impossible to perform simply through the command line. For example, you can start one applications program and then switch to a second application without exiting from the first. You can search quickly through directories or even an entire hard disk for a specific file name (or file names). Using a mouse, you can select and copy files between directories or between disks without having to type a file name. The Shell also enables you to view the contents of disk files in ASCII or hexadecimal (base 16, a numeric code in which non-ASCII file contents can be represented). Using the DOS Shell, you even can associate specific file-name extensions with a particular applications program so that selecting a file causes DOS to start the associated program.

This book presents the basics of DOS from the perspectives of both the DOS Shell and the command line. The Shell, however, may become your preferred interface to DOS. This chapter introduces you to the DOS Shell, guiding you around the DOS Shell screen and describing how to control the display. The text discusses the aspects of the Shell common to all the program's commands. The material also explains how to use the program list area to start a program.

After you become familiar with the information in this chapter, turn to Chapter 5 for a basic introduction to using the DOS command line. You then will be ready to examine the other chapters in the book. Part II, in particular, explains how to perform DOS tasks from either the DOS Shell or the command line.

When you understand the information presented here and in Part II of this book, you may want to learn how you can customize the Shell. Turn then to Chapter 14, "Configuring the DOS Shell," to learn how to fine-tune the DOS Shell to fit your needs best. Chapter 14 also explains how to use the Shell's impressive task-swapping capability.

Key Terms Used in This Chapter

Shell	A program that acts as a user interface to the features and capabilities of an operating system
Mouse pointer	The block- or arrow-shaped screen icon that indicates where the mouse action will occur
Selection cursor	An area of highlighted text that shows where selected action will occur
Scroll bar	An area of the screen containing arrows and icons that serve to move the items through the window
Pull-down menu	Additional selection items that drop down when an item from a horizontal list is selected
Text mode	Screen mode available to all PC users. In text mode, all screen presentation is composed of ASCII characters.
Graphics mode	Screen mode available to users of PCs equipped with graphics adapters. In graphics mode, screen presentation uses bit-mapped graphics.

> *Note*: To reap the greatest benefit from the Shell's modern design, you should use a mouse. For the mouse to be available, the *mouse device driver* must be loaded into memory before you run the DOS Shell. This chapter and remaining chapters often recommend the mouse method of performing a task but also explain the equivalent keyboard methods.

Getting Started with the DOS Shell

When you install DOS 5.0, you are asked whether you want the DOS Shell to start every time you turn on your computer. If you select this option, you need merely to turn on your computer to reach the DOS Shell screen.

 If your computer does not display the DOS Shell automatically when you turn on your computer, type **DOSSHELL** at the DOS prompt to load the DOS Shell into memory. The DOS Shell first displays a copyright notice and then displays the full-screen DOS Shell window. When the Shell first loads, it also displays a smaller window in the center of the screen containing the message Reading Disk Information. After the Shell scans the file information on your boot disk, which may take a few seconds, the Shell removes the small window and displays a listing similar to figure 4.1.

Understanding the DOS Shell Window

When you start the DOS Shell for the first time, the DOS Shell window looks similar to figure 4.1. The top line of the screen, the *title bar*, displays the program name, MS-DOS Shell. The second line of the screen, called the *menu bar*, lists the names of available menus. You can select all DOS Shell commands from menus that pull down from the menu bar.

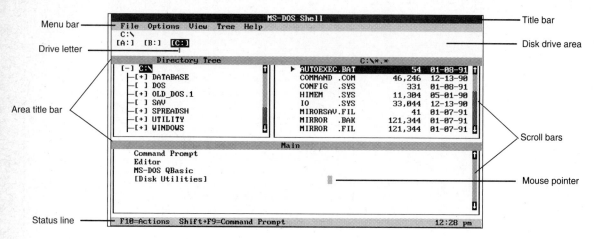

Menu bar — File Options View Tree Help

Title bar — MS-DOS Shell

Drive letter — C:\ [A:] [B:] [C:]

Disk drive area

Area title bar — Directory Tree / C:*.*

Scroll bars

Mouse pointer

Status line — F10=Actions Shift+F9=Command Prompt 12:28 pm

Fig. 4.1. The Initial DOS Shell window.

Just below the menu bar, the DOS Shell window lists the current drive and directory and the available disk drives. This book refers to this portion of the screen as the *disk drive area*. The first time you display the Shell, the drive area lists the current drive and directory and the available drives in the following manner:

```
C:\
[A:] [B:] [C:]
```

If your computer doesn't have a hard (fixed) disk drive, [C:] is not listed. If your system has more than one hard disk drive, you also may see [D:], [E:], and so on (refer to Chapter 6 for a complete discussion of disk drives).

Initially, the DOS Shell window displays in text mode, as shown in figure 4.1. "Understanding the Shell Screen Modes" in this chapter discusses how to switch the display to a graphics mode. Figure 4.2 shows the 34-line graphics mode available for VGA displays.

In graphics mode, the drive area depicts your disk drives area as follows:

The icons that depict drives A and B represent floppy disk drives. Drive C's icon indicates that this drive is a hard disk drive. Refer to Chapter 6 for a full discussion of disks and drives.

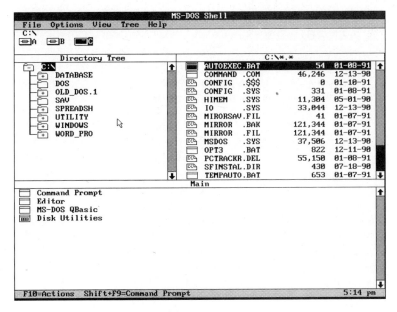

Fig. 4.2. The DOS Shell window displayed in graphics screen mode.

The last line of the DOS Shell window is the *status line*. The status line usually displays two messages: `F10=Actions` and `Shift+F9=Command Prompt`. At the right end of the status line, the Shell displays the current time. Occasionally, the status line also displays other messages related to the command you are executing.

Between the drive area and the status line, the DOS Shell divides the window into rectangular *areas*, each of which is headed by an *area title bar*. On the right side of each area is a *scroll bar*, with which you use a mouse to move around within an area.

When you start the Shell for the first time, the window is divided into the drive area and three larger areas (again see fig. 4.1). The *directory tree area* is in the upper left quadrant of the window—below the drive area. This portion of the screen lists the directories of the current disk drive in a tree-like format. Use of the directory tree area of the DOS Shell window is covered extensively in Chapter 9, "Managing Directories."

The *file list area*, in the upper right quadrant of the Shell window, lists the names, file size, and file date (when last changed) of files in the current directory (refer to Chapter 8 for a complete discussion of directories). The name of the current directory appears in the area title bar. Refer to Chapter 10, "Keeping Files in Order," for more about using the file list area.

The bottom half of the DOS Shell window is called the *program list area*. This area of the screen serves as a menu for starting DOS applications and for accessing DOS disk-related utility programs. This area lists a group of programs, referred to as a *program group*. The name of the currently listed program group appears in the area title bar. "Using the Program List" in this chapter discusses how to use this portion of the DOS Shell screen.

Occasionally, you may want to remove one or more areas from the Shell screen to provide more room for the other areas. Refer to "Modifying the View" in this chapter for more about turning window areas on and off.

At times, a fourth area, the *active task list area*, also may be displayed in the DOS Shell window. The active task list area displays the names of DOS applications you have activated through the DOS 5.0 task swapper. Figure 4.3 shows the DOS Shell window with the active task list displayed.

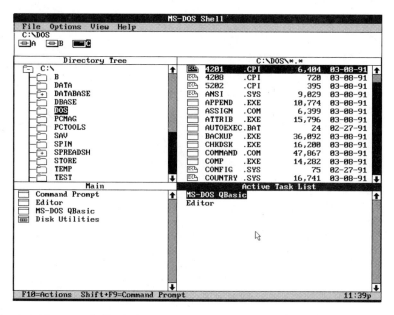

Fig. 4.3. The DOS Shell window with the active task list displayed.

Selecting an Area

Even though you can have as many as five areas displayed in the DOS Shell window—disk drive, directory tree, file list, program list, and active task list—only one area is *selected* (active) at a time. The selected area is indicated by a highlighted area title bar. An area must be selected before you can perform any operation in that area.

When you first start a DOS Shell session, the drive letter of the current disk drive is highlighted, indicating that the disk drive area is selected. The area title bars shown in figures 4.1 and 4.2, for example, are not highlighted. Contrast these figures with figure 4.3, which shows a highlighted area title bar above the active task list.

You have two methods by which to select an area in the Shell window:

- Move the mouse pointer into the area you want to activate and click the left button. The Shell highlights the area's title bar.

- Press the Tab key to cycle through the areas that are currently displayed in the window.

Moving Around in an Area

After you have selected an area, the Shell highlights one of the items listed in the area. This highlight is called the *selection cursor*. To move the selection cursor within the selected area, use one of the following methods:

- Use the cursor-movement keys on the keyboard. Press the up- or down-arrow key to move, respectively, up or down one item at a time. Press PgUp or PgDn to move, respectively, up or down a page at a time. Press Home or End to go, respectively, to the beginning or end of the list.

- Use the mouse and the scroll bar to scroll up or down (see fig. 4.4).

The scroll bar has the following components:

- A *scroll arrow* at the top and bottom of the bar. Clicking the mouse pointer on the scroll arrow scrolls text up or down one line at a time. Click the scroll arrow and hold down the right mouse button to scroll continuously in the direction of the arrow.

- A *scroll box*, located on the scroll bar between the up-scroll arrow and the down-scroll arrow. The position of the box on the scroll bar indicates the relative position of the selection cursor with respect to the entire list of items in the selected area.

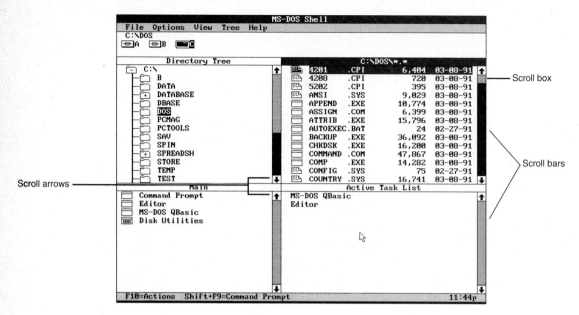

Fig. 4.4. Scroll bars located on the right side of each area of the Shell window.

Click the scroll bar above the scroll box to move the selection cursor up one page at a time. Click below the scroll box to move down one page at a time.

You can scroll quickly through the list in either direction by clicking the scroll box, holding down the left mouse button, and dragging the box in the direction you want the selection cursor to move.

Using the DOS Shell Menus

You can initiate virtually every DOS Shell operation by choosing options from menus. These DOS Shell menus fall into two categories: the menu bar and pull-down menus.

Using the Menu Bar

When the disk drive area, directory tree area, or file list area is active, the menu bar lists five menu names: File, Options, View, Tree, and Help. The Tree menu name does not appear when the program list is the active area. Selecting a menu name displays a pull-down menu.

You can select a menu option from the menu bar in one of three ways:

- Move the mouse pointer to an option and click the left button.

- Press the F10 key or the Alt key to activate the menu bar. Shell underlines one letter in each menu name and places a selection cursor on the menu name File at the left end of the menu bar. Press the key that corresponds to the underlined letter in the menu name you want to select. To select View from the menu bar in figure 4.1, for example, press F10 or Alt and then press V.

- Press F10 or Alt to activate the menu bar, use the right- or left-arrow key to move the selection cursor to your choice, and press Enter. This method is sometimes called the *point-and-shoot method*.

Even after you have selected a menu name, you still can select another menu name by clicking with the mouse or by using the left- or right-arrow key.

Using Pull-Down Menus

When you select a menu name from the menu bar, the Shell displays a pull-down menu, which displays a list of items below the menu bar. If you select File, for example, while the file list is the active area, the Shell displays the File pull-down menu shown in figure 4.5. The items listed in the menu depend on which area is active.

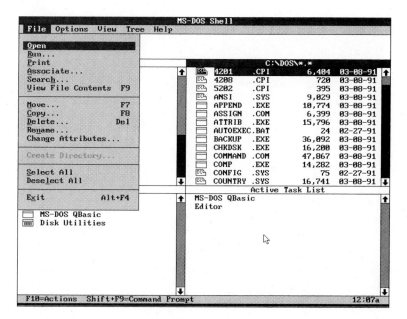

Fig. 4.5. *The File pull-down menu displayed when the file list area is active.*

To select an item from a pull-down menu, use one of the following methods:

- Move the mouse pointer to a menu item, and click the left button.

- The Shell underlines one letter in each menu item. Press the key that corresponds to the underlined letter in the item you want to select. To select View File Contents from the File menu in figure 4.5, for example, press V.

- The Shell places the selection cursor on the first item at the top of the pull-down menu. Use the down- or up-arrow key to move the selection cursor to your choice, and press Enter.

When a menu is pulled down, you can display an adjacent menu by pressing the left- or right-arrow key. To cancel a pulled-down menu without making a selection, click the mouse on the menu name or anywhere outside the menu, or press Esc. The Shell returns to the preceding window display. You also can press Alt or F10 to cancel a pulled-down menu while maintaining an active menu bar so that you can select another menu name.

The DOS Shell uses the following conventions when it lists menu items:

- A menu item that displays a dialog box (discussed later in this chapter) ends with an ellipsis (…).

- A menu item that is dimmed, such as the Create Directory item shown in figure 4.5, is not a valid option in the current context.

- Some menu items toggle between two states—on or off. A menu item that is toggled on displays a small diamond (♦) to the left of the item name. The diamond is absent when the item is turned off.

- Some commands that can be selected through menu items have shortcuts in the form of *key combinations*, or *keystroke commands*. When a keystroke command shortcut is available for a command, the Shell lists the keystroke in the menu, to the right of the equivalent command. Five of the commands in the File menu, for example, list shortcut keystroke commands (again see fig. 4.5).

Using Keystroke Commands

The DOS Shell provides many keystroke command shortcuts. Many of these commands are listed in pull-down menus. Two such commands, F10 and Shift-F9, are listed in the Shell window status line.

Table 4.1 lists all DOS Shell keystroke commands for DOS 5.0. After you have learned these keystroke commands, you may find them quicker to use than any equivalent menu items. To perform each command, you have to press a single keystroke or keystroke combination. Using menus always requires that you use multiple keystrokes or that you take one hand from the keyboard to use the mouse. Each command in the following table is discussed later in the book.

Table 4.1
DOS Shell Keystroke Commands

Key	Function
F1	Displays context-sensitive help
F3	Exits the DOS Shell, returns to the command line, and removes the DOS Shell from memory (same as Alt-F4)
Alt-F4	Exits the DOS Shell and returns to the command line and removes the Shell from memory (same as F3)
F5	Refreshes the file list(s)
Shift-F5	Repaints the screen
F7	Moves selected file(s)
F8	Copies selected file(s)
Shift-F8	Extends selection in add mode
F9	Views file contents
Shift-F9	Accesses the command line without removing the DOS Shell from memory
F10	Activates the menu bar (same as Alt)
Alt	Activates the menu bar (same as F10)
Del	Deletes selected file(s)
+	Expands one level of the current branch in the directory tree
*	Expands all levels of the current branch in the directory tree
Ctrl-*	Expands all branches in the directory tree
- (hyphen)	Collapses the current branch in the directory tree
Alt-Tab	Switches between active task and the DOS Shell
Alt-Esc	Cycles through active tasks

continues

Table 4.1 (*continued*)

Key	Function
Shift-↑	Extends selection up
Shift-↓	Extends selection down
Esc	Cancels current function
Tab	Cycles through areas
Ctrl-/	Selects all files in the selected directory
Ctrl-F5	Refreshes the selected directory

Using Dialog Boxes

As you work with the DOS Shell, the program routinely displays messages and prompts in pop-up boxes, called *dialog boxes*, on the screen. Any menu item that ends with an ellipsis (…) displays a dialog box when you select the item. For example, selecting Copy from the File menu displays the Copy File dialog box, shown in figure 4.6.

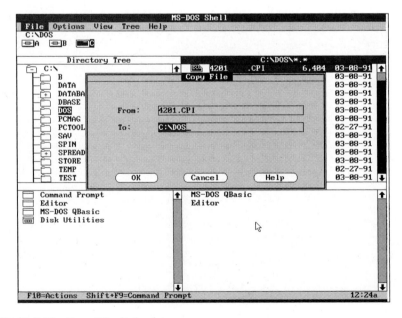

Fig. 4.6. *The Copy File dialog box.*

Dialog boxes fall into two general categories: those that request information and those that provide information. The Copy File dialog box in figure 4.6 is an example of a dialog box that requests information. Pressing F1, by contrast, displays a dialog box that provides information and is entitled MS-DOS Shell Help. This help screen, shown in figure 4.7, assists you in learning the Shell.

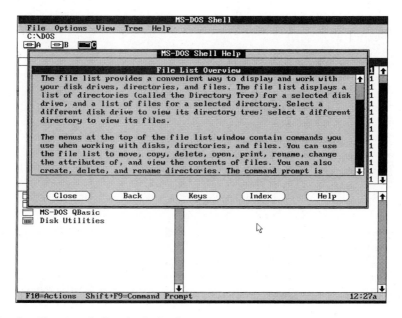

Fig. 4.7. *The DOS Shell Help dialog box.*

All dialog boxes are built from a standard set of elements: text boxes, list boxes, option buttons, option check boxes, and command buttons. The following sections explain how to use each element.

Using a Text Box

When you need to type information in a dialog box, the Shell includes one or more rectangular boxes known as *text boxes*. The Copy File dialog box shown in figure 4.6 contains two text boxes, one labeled From and one labeled To.

To make an entry in a text box, you first highlight the box. Using the mouse, move the mouse pointer to the box, and click the left button. Alternatively, you can press Tab or Shift-Tab repeatedly until the text box is highlighted.

Often the Shell provides a default value in each text box. The text boxes in figure 4.6, for example, include the default values 4201.CPI and C:\DOS. When you select a text box, the Shell highlights any default contained in that text box. Typing new text in the text box replaces the default value.

Sometimes you don't want to replace the entire default value in a text box. When you want to edit the value, press the right- or left-arrow key to cause the Shell to remove the highlighting. You then can edit the existing entry.

After you have made the desired entry or changed the value in the text box, press Enter to accept the value that is displayed in the text box.

Using a List Box

Some dialog boxes contain information or a list of choices displayed in a rectangular area, referred to in this book as a *list box*. A title bar appears at the top of each list box, as well as a scroll bar on the right side of the list box. Figure 4.7 shows a help dialog box containing a list box entitled File List Overview.

Often the text or list is too long to fit in the list box, so the Shell enables you to scroll vertically through the contents of the box. To scroll through a list box, use your mouse and the scroll bar, or use the cursor-movement keys.

Using Option Buttons

Some dialog boxes use *option buttons* for selecting command settings. Each option button is a circle (a pair of parentheses if your screen is in text mode) followed by a command setting. Option buttons always occur in groups—never alone. The buttons in each group are mutually exclusive.

The File Display Options dialog box shown in figure 4.8, for example, contains option buttons listed on the right side of the dialog box, beneath the label Sort By. Displayed file names can be sorted by name, extension, date, size, or disk order, but the Shell does not sort files by more than one of these parameters at a time.

Option buttons operate in a way similar to the buttons on a car radio. When you select a button from the group, any button that was already selected "pops out," or is canceled. Only one button is active at any particular time. The active button is indicated by a dot in the circle (or between the parentheses). The Name option button in figure 4.8 is selected, indicated by the dot in the circle.

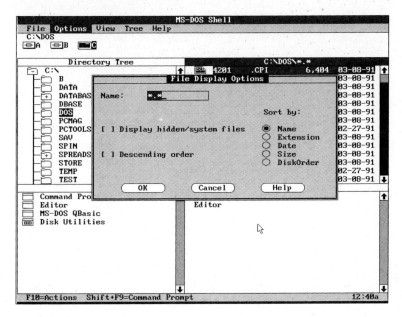

Fig. 4.8. *The Sort By option buttons listed on the right side of the File Display Options dialog box.*

To select a different option button, use the mouse to click the desired option button. Alternatively, use the Tab or Shift-Tab key to move the underscore (cursor) to the group of option buttons. Then use the up- or down-arrow key to move the dot to the desired button. Press Enter to select the new option.

 # Using Option Check Boxes

Some Shell dialog boxes enable you to select the desired command settings by "checking" the appropriate *option check boxes*. An option check box is a pair of brackets followed by a command setting. The File Display Options dialog box in figure 4.8, for example, contains the following check boxes:

    [ ] Display hidden/system files

    [ ] Descending order

An option check box turns a command setting on or off. The setting is checked (or on) when an X appears between the brackets. The setting is off when the space between the brackets is blank. To toggle the setting on or off, use the mouse to click between the brackets. Alternatively, use the Tab or Shift-Tab key to move the cursor to the option check box, and press the space bar. Each time you click the box or press the space bar, the option toggles on or off.

Using Command Buttons

After making any desired entries in text boxes, selecting appropriate option buttons, and checking the correct check boxes, you are ready to execute the DOS Shell command. To do so, select one of the *command buttons*—the rounded-rectangular buttons near the bottom edge of the dialog box.

Most dialog boxes in the DOS Shell contain three command buttons labeled OK, Cancel, and Help (again see fig. 4.8). The OK command button activates the choices you have made in the dialog box and executes the command, if any, with which the dialog box is associated. The Cancel command button aborts any changes you may have made in the dialog box and returns to the DOS Shell window. The Help command button accesses the Shell's on-line help facility.

To execute a command button, use one of the following methods:

- Move the mouse pointer to the desired command button, and click the left mouse button.

- Press Tab or Shift-Tab to move the cursor to the desired command button, and press Enter.

Tip: You can execute the command associated with a dialog box by pressing Enter, even though the cursor is not in the OK command button (as long as the cursor is not on one of the other command buttons).

Modifying the View

The DOS Shell is quite flexible. In the directory tree area and file list area, you can display directories and file names from any of your computer's disk drives, including directories and file names from two disks at once. You also can display just the program list, and you can change the entire screen to a graphics mode and can show as many as 60 lines of information on a single screen (depending on the capability of your computer's monitor).

The following sections describe how to modify the display to list directories and files from other disks, to display files from two disks at once, and to change the amount of information displayed about each file. In addition, the following sections show you how to display the program list full-screen and how to change the number of lines that display on-screen.

Logging On to a Different Disk and Refreshing the Directory Tree

As you learned in Chapter 3, each time you turn on your computer, the operating system (DOS) is loaded from one of your computer's disks. This disk is the boot disk. If your system is configured to start the DOS Shell immediately after your computer boots up, the Shell window lists directories and file names found on the boot disk.

Often, you may need to display the directories and file names on a disk other than the boot disk. Figure 4.8, for example, shows three drive letters: A, B, and C. Drive C is the boot disk; therefore, the directories found in the C drive are shown in the directory tree. Drive C's icon is highlighted, indicating that C is the currently selected disk drive.

To display in the directory tree the directories found on another disk, move the mouse pointer to the drive icon of the desired disk and click the left mouse button. Alternatively, press the left- or right-arrow key until the Shell highlights the drive letter you want, and then press Enter. The Shell displays a message that the Shell is reading the disk information and then displays in the directory tree and file list areas of the DOS Shell window the directories and file names from the target disk. Figure 4.9, for example, shows file names from a disk in drive B.

Because the DOS Shell enables you to start other programs that may create, modify, or delete files on your disk, the list of files in the DOS Shell window may at times be inaccurate. If you suspect that the directory tree area or file list area does not reflect the actual contents of the disk, you should use the Shell's Refresh command. To refresh the file list, press F5 or perform the following steps:

1. Select <u>V</u>iew from the menu bar to display the View menu, shown in figure 4.10.

2. Choose <u>R</u>efresh.

The Shell displays the message `Reading Disk Information` and then returns to the DOS Shell window and displays the updated list of directories and files in the directory tree and file list areas.

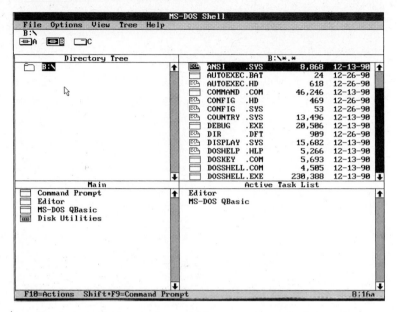

Fig. 4.9. *Displaying the directories and file names from the disk in drive B.*

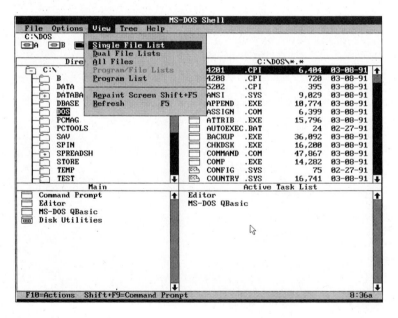

Fig. 4.10. *The View menu.*

Switching between Dual and Single File Lists

From time to time, you may want the convenience of seeing lists of directories and files from two disks at once. Perhaps you want to copy a file from one disk to another, or maybe you want to compare the list of files on one disk to the list of files on another disk.

The DOS Shell enables you easily to display two file lists on the same screen. Follow these steps:

1. Select <u>V</u>iew from the menu bar to display the View menu (again see fig. 4.10).

2. Choose <u>D</u>ual File Lists from the View menu.

The Shell replaces the program list area, at the bottom of the window, with a second disk drive area, directory tree area, and file list area showing the directory tree and file list from the current disk drive (see fig. 4.11). This view is called a *dual file list*.

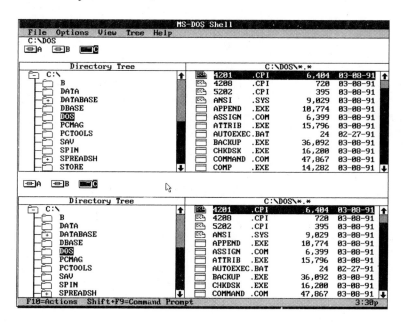

Fig. 4.11. *A dual file list.*

3. To select a second disk drive in the bottom portion of the window, use the mouse to click the icon in the bottom disk drive area for the drive for which you want to list directories and files.

Alternatively, use Tab or Alt-Tab to cycle the selection cursor until it highlights the drive icon of the currently selected drive in the bottom disk drive area. Then use the left- or right-arrow key to highlight the desired drive icon, and press Enter.

The Shell lists directories and file names from the second disk in the lower set of directory tree and file list areas (see fig. 4.12). You can switch between the two lists by using the mouse or the Tab key.

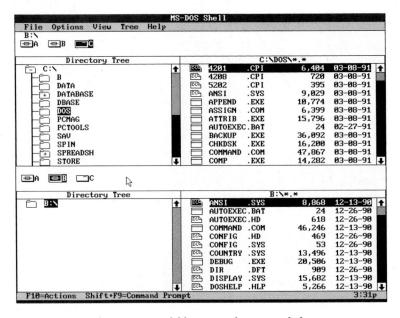

Fig. 4.12. Viewing directories and file names from two disks at once.

Sometimes you want to display a single set of disk drive, directory tree, and file list areas. In addition, you do not want to display the program list area at the bottom of the screen. Use the following procedure to turn on a single list:

1. Select Underline_View from the menu bar to display the View menu.

2. Choose Single File List from the View menu.

The window displays a screen similar to figure 4.13, referred to as a *single file list*.

> *Note*: When you exit from the DOS Shell, it remembers the changes you have made using the View menu. The next time you start the Shell, it will have the same appearance.

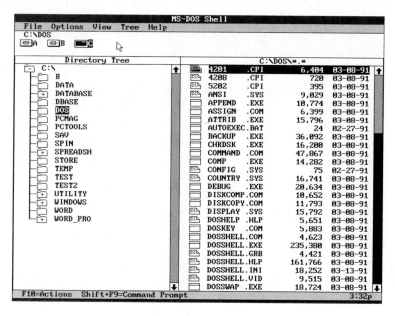

Fig. 4.13. Viewing a single file list.

Displaying All Files

Occasionally, you may want the Shell window to display all files on a disk, regardless of the directory. To display all files in a single list, complete the following steps:

1. Select <u>V</u>iew from the menu bar to display the View menu (again see fig. 4.10).

2. Choose <u>A</u>ll Files.

On the right side of the screen, the DOS Shell displays an alphabetical list of the file names of all files on the current disk (see fig. 4.14). The Shell also lists on the left side of the screen information about the file at which the selection cursor is located and about the currently selected file(s).

Switching between the Program List and the Program/File Lists

The first time you start the DOS Shell, the DOS Shell window displays the directory tree area, the file list area, and the program list area. Some users prefer to use the Shell primarily as a menu for starting applications programs and so don't want to view the directory tree and file list every time. The Shell, therefore, provides a view that displays only the program list.

```
                              MS-DOS Shell
 File  Options  View  Tree  Help
 C:\WORD_PRO\ENDATA
 ⊟A  ⊟B  ▇C
                                        *.*
                            ▣  $(0)      .MCM        512   09-05-90   8:32a  ↑
 File                       ▣  04FIG01 .TIF      154,270   03-06-91   4:18p
   Name  : $(0).MCM         ▣  04FIG02 .TIF      154,270   03-06-91   4:23p
   Attr  : ....             ▣  04FIG03 .TIF      154,270   03-06-91   4:19p
 Selected      B     C      ▣  1-README.CLP          968   10-05-90   2:00a
   Number:     1     1      ▣  1099_A   .WK1        3,679   02-16-90   2:42p
   Size  :     9,380        ▣  10FIG03 .TIF      112,190   01-02-91   5:14p
 Directory                  ▣  10FIG03B.TIF      112,190   01-02-91   5:03p
   Name  : ENDATA           ▣  123      .MU      222,685   10-05-90   2:00a
   Size  :     5,601,452    ▣  123      .RF        3,403   10-05-90   2:00a
   Files :           350    ▣  123IMP   .FLT      69,136   10-17-90  12:46p
 Disk                       ▣  127002   .BAK      46,592   12-28-90   5:18p
   Name  : QUE BRUCE        ▣  127002   .DOC      46,592   12-29-90   1:12p
   Size  : 104,515,584      ▣  127003   .DOC      35,393   01-07-91   3:48p
   Avail :   4,411,392      ▣  127004   .DOC      56,832   01-14-91   1:52p
   Files :       3,101      ▣  127004   .DOC      56,832   01-14-91   1:52p
   Dirs  :         109      ▣  3        .DOC       1,536   12-13-90   3:31p
                            ▣  3270     .TXT       9,058   05-01-90   3:00a
                            ▭  3D       .BAT          74   11-23-88  11:27a
                            ▭  3DN      .BAT          70   10-07-88  12:43p
                            ▣  3DN      .TXT           6   10-07-88  11:03a
                            ▣  3_BY_7   .INF         512   03-24-86  10:06a
                            ▣  3_BY_7   .INF         512   03-24-86  10:06a
                            ▣  4-1      .TIF     307,362   11-22-90   1:29p
                            ▣  4-10     .TIF     307,362   11-22-90   1:40p
                            ▣  4-11     .TIF     307,362   11-22-90   1:41p
                            ▣  4-12     .TIF     307,362   11-22-90   1:42p  ↓
 F10=Actions  Shift+F9=Command Prompt                               9:36a
```

Fig. 4.14. The All Files list.

To turn off the directory tree and file list areas and display the program list full-screen, execute the following steps:

1. Select Ⅴiew from the menu bar to display the View menu.

2. Choose Ⲣrogram List.

The Shell uses nearly the entire screen to display the program list area, as shown in figure 4.15.

If you decide later that you want to display the directory tree and file list areas on the screen along with the program list area, complete the following steps:

1. Select Ⅴiew from the menu bar to display the View menu.

2. Choose Program/Ⲃile Lists.

The Shell returns to the original view, with the disk drive area, directory tree area, and file list area in the top half of the screen and program list area in the bottom half of the screen.

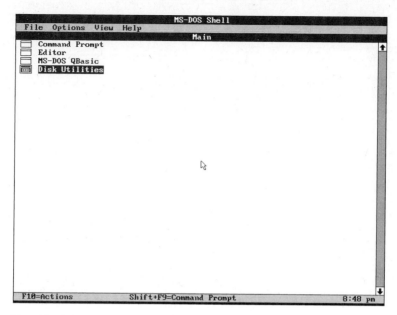

Fig. 4.15. The full-screen program list area.

Understanding the Shell Screen Modes

The Shell window can be displayed in one of several *screen modes*; the number of available screen modes depends on the type of display adapter and monitor you have. Figure 4.1 shows the DOS Shell window in 25-line low-resolution text mode. This setting is the default start-up screen mode when DOS 5.0 is first installed. This mode is one of three screen mode options available to DOS 5.0 users who have a Color Graphics Adapter (CGA).

If you have an Enhanced Graphics Adapter (EGA) or Video Graphics Array adapter (VGA), you can take advantage of additional screen modes that squeeze more lines of text on the screen—up to 43 lines with an EGA adapter and monitor and up to 60 lines with a VGA adapter and monitor. Figures 4.2 through 4.15 show the Shell window in 34-line medium-resolution graphics mode.

To change the screen mode, follow these directions:

1. Choose Options from the menu bar to display the Options menu, shown in figure 4.16.

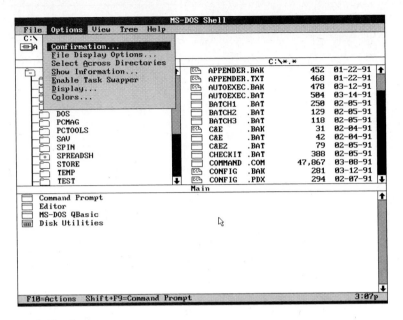

Fig. 4.16. *The Options menu.*

2. Select Display from the Options menu to display the Screen Mode dialog box, shown in figure 4.17.

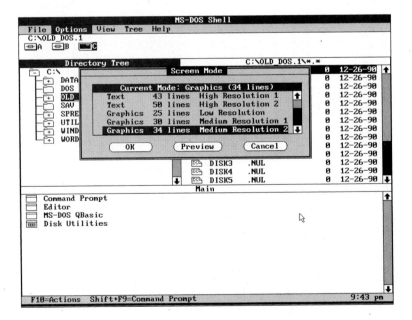

Fig. 4.17. *The Screen Mode dialog box.*

3. Choose the desired screen mode from the list box.

   Use the mouse and scroll bar or the cursor-movement keys to scroll the list. Click the desired screen mode with the mouse, or highlight the screen mode with the selection cursor and press Enter.

4. Choose the OK command button.

The Shell returns to the DOS Shell window and repaints the screen in the new screen mode.

Using the Help System

At any time during a DOS Shell session, pressing F1 causes a help window to appear. On-line help assists you with the current selection or action so that you can make an informed selection.

The Shell's help system is *contextual*. That is, DOS looks at the menu item currently highlighted and provides information about that selection. You can go from that help screen to other help screens to get help on additional topics. Figure 4.18 shows a typical help screen.

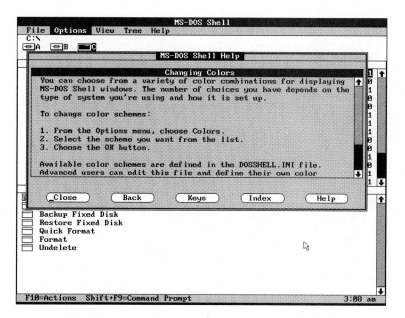

Fig. 4.18. The Changing Colors help screen.

Five command buttons appear at the bottom of a help screen:

• Close returns you to the screen from which you pressed F1.

- Back returns you to the preceding help screen.

- Keys displays an index of help information on keystroke commands.

- Index displays the DOS Shell help index, a list of topics on which you can receive help.

- Help displays information on how to use the help system.

Use the mouse and scroll bar or the cursor-movement keys to display the information in which you are interested. Additional related topics are listed in a different color on the help screen. Use the Tab key to highlight the related topic and press Enter, or use the mouse to click the topic. The Shell displays another help screen.

Choose the Close command button, or press Esc to return to the screen from which you pressed F1.

Using the Program List

In addition to providing an alternative DOS interface to the command line, the DOS Shell also provides a convenient method for running all the other programs stored in your computer. A program that performs this function is sometimes called a *menuing program*. The Shell's program list area provides menuing capability.

Items listed in the program area of the DOS Shell window fall into two categories: program items and program groups. A *program item* starts a specific software application on your hard disk; a *program group* is a collection of program items or other program groups.

Program groups enable you to group your applications programs by category. For example, you may create a Word Processing group, a Database group, and a Spreadsheet group. By default, the initial list of program items, which you see when you first start the DOS Shell, are in the Main program group. The Main group includes another program group named Disk Utilities, which includes program items that perform disk-related DOS commands.

You can tell easily whether an option listed in the program list area is a program item or a program group. When the DOS Shell window is in text screen mode, program group names are enclosed in brackets. For example, the Disk Utilities program group is listed as follows when the screen is in text mode:

```
[Disk Utilities]
```

If you have chosen a graphics screen mode, the Shell uses special icons to distinguish between program items and program groups. The following icon appears to the left of program item names:

The following icon appears to the left of program group names:

When you first install DOS 5.0, the program list area lists the program group Main. This group includes the program items Command Prompt, Editor, and MS-DOS QBasic. Selecting a program item starts the selected program. Also included in the main program group is the program group Disk Utilities. Selecting Disk Utilities causes the Shell to display another group of program items, the Disk Utilities group, which consists of DOS utility programs that enable you to copy, back up, restore, format, and undelete disks. You can press Esc to return to the preceding program group.

The title bar of the program list area displays the name of the current program group. When you first start the DOS Shell, the program list title bar displays the label `Main`.

Accessing the DOS Command Line

You can move temporarily from the Shell to the DOS prompt, keeping the Shell in memory. Use one of the following methods:

- Position the mouse pointer on the Command Prompt item, in the program list area, and *double-click*—press twice in rapid succession—the left mouse button.

- Press Tab or Shift-Tab until the program list area is the selected area. If the Command Prompt item is not already highlighted, use the arrow keys to move the selection cursor to this item. Press Enter.

- Press Shift-F9.

The DOS prompt appears. You now can enter DOS commands. To return to the Shell, type **EXIT**, and press Enter.

Note: Both the Command Prompt item in the program list and the Shift-F9 keystroke command start a secondary command processor. The same action occurs when you issue the DOS COMMAND command. When you start a secondary command processor, typing the EXIT command is the signal to DOS that you want to return to the primary command processor. When you are in the DOS Shell, COMMAND.COM has loaded and executed DOSSHELL.EXE; typing EXIT after accessing the DOS prompt returns control to DOSSHELL.EXE.

The other way to get to the DOS command prompt is to exit from the DOS Shell. This method, however, causes DOS to remove the Shell from the computer's memory. To exit the Shell, press F3, press Alt-F4, or follow these steps:

1. Select File from the menu bar to display the File menu.

2. Choose Exit from the File menu.

The Shell returns you to the DOS prompt. Remember, you have exited the Shell, so to restart the Shell, type **DOSSHELL**, and press Enter.

Starting a Program

When you want to start or run an application listed in the program list, use one of the following methods:

- Position the mouse pointer on the program item in the program list area and double-click the left mouse button.

- Alternatively, press Tab or Shift-Tab repeatedly until the program list area is the selected area. Use the up- and down-arrow keys to move the selection cursor to the desired program item. Press Enter.

- Move the selection cursor to the program item. Select File from the menu bar to display the File menu. Choose Open.

For example, to start the DOS Editor, use one of the preceding methods to select the Editor program item in the Main program group. Similarly, you can start the programming environment MS-DOS QBasic by selecting the MS-DOS QBasic program item in the program list area of the Shell window.

Other methods of starting programs are described in Chapter 10.

Accessing the Disk Utilities Program Group

The Disk Utilities program group in the program list area enables you to access several standard DOS commands. When you select a command, a panel appears in which you can type the standard parameters DOS requires for the command. In all respects, these commands behave exactly the same as if you had typed them at the DOS prompt. Refer to the following chapters for descriptions of these commands and ways to use them from both the DOS Shell and the command line:

Disk Utilities Item	DOS Command	Chapter Reference
Disk Copy	DISKCOPY	6
Backup Fixed Disk	BACKUP	11
Restore Fixed Disk	RESTORE	11
Quick Format	FORMAT /Q	7
Format	FORMAT	7
Undelete	UNDELETE	10

Summary

As you can see, the DOS Shell adds a new dimension to using DOS. Even if you are comfortable using DOS at the DOS prompt, you will want to explore the DOS Shell. Important points covered in this chapter include the following:

- The DOS Shell is a program that acts as a user interface to the features and capabilities of the MS-DOS operating system.

- You can scroll quickly through a DOS Shell area in either direction by clicking the scroll box, holding down the left mouse button, and dragging the box in the direction you want the selection cursor to move.

- When you select a menu name from the menu bar, the Shell displays a pull-down menu.

- You can modify the view of the DOS Shell window to display more or less information.

- The DOS Shell provides many keystroke command shortcuts. Many of these commands are listed in pull-down menus.

- The Shell window can be displayed in one of several screen modes, depending on the type of display you have.

- At any time during a DOS Shell session, pressing F1 causes a help window to appear.

- You can view the directories of more than one disk at a time by using the dual file lists feature.

- In addition to providing an alternative DOS interface to the command line, the DOS Shell also provides a convenient method for running all the other programs stored on your computer.

- Several DOS commands, such as DISKCOPY and FORMAT, are available in the Disk Utilities program item.

Using DOS Commands

Now that you have learned your way around the DOS Shell, you need to become familiar also with the DOS command line. This chapter introduces you to the elements that make up DOS commands and teaches you how to issue commands correctly at the DOS prompt.

Key Terms Used in This Chapter

Command	A group of characters that tell the computer what action to take
Syntax	A specific set of rules you follow when issuing commands
Parameter	An additional instruction that defines specifically what you want the DOS command to do
Switch	A part of the command syntax that turns on an optional function of a command
Delimiter	A character that separates the "words" in a command. Common delimiters are the space and the slash.

Wild card   A character in a command that represents one or
                   more characters. In DOS the **?** wild card represents
                   any single character. The * wild card represents any
                   remaining characters in a "word" in the command.

Understanding DOS Commands

To communicate your need for service to DOS, you enter DOS commands
at the DOS command line. Commands are made up of groups of characters
that are separated, or *delimited*, by certain other characters. A command
you give to DOS is similar to a written instruction you may give to a work
associate. Both the DOS command and the written instruction must communicate your intentions using proper form, or syntax. Both must communicate what action you want carried out and what the objects of that action
are.

For example, if you need to duplicate a sign on a bulletin board so that you
can post it on another bulletin board, you may tell a work associate: "Copy
sign A to sign B. Be sure to verify that you have made no mistakes." Similarly,
if you want DOS to copy the contents of disk A to disk B, you give DOS the
following instruction:

DISKCOPY A: B:

To verify that the copy is the same as the original, you instruct DOS to
compare the two disks:

DISKCOMP A: B:

DISKCOPY and DISKCOMP are the DOS commands that determine what
action is to be carried out. The drive letters A: and B: indicate where the
action is to be carried out. Although the instructions to duplicate a sign look
more natural than the DOS DISKCOPY command, the two are quite similar.

DOS recognizes and responds to more than 100 commands. The most
useful commands are built into the command processor and are immediately available at the command line. Because of the built-in availability of
these commands, they are called *internal commands*.

Other commands are stored as utility programs on your DOS disk(s) or in
a hard disk directory. Because these commands are not built into the
command processor, they are called *external commands*. You execute
external commands by typing the command at the command line the same
way you execute internal commands.

Learning the "ins and outs" of issuing DOS commands takes some practice. Fortunately, DOS commands have a familiar structure, and you soon will branch out from the examples in this book to your own forms of the DOS commands.

Understanding the Elements of a DOS Command

You issue commands to tell DOS that you need its operating-system services. Although each DOS command provides an individual service, all DOS commands conform to standard rules. Using DOS is easier when you understand the concepts behind the commands. With that understanding, you can generalize many of these rules to different commands.

To begin to understand DOS commands, you need to know two fundamental facts:

- DOS requires that you use a specific set of rules, or syntax, when you issue commands.

- Parameters, which are a part of a command's syntax, can change the way a command is executed.

Syntax is the order in which you type the elements of the DOS command. Using proper syntax when you enter a DOS command is like using proper English when you speak. DOS must understand clearly what you are typing in order to carry out the command.

You can think of the command name as the action part of a DOS command. In addition to the name, many commands require or allow further directions. Any such additions are called *parameters*. Parameters tell DOS what action to take or how to apply the action. Using DOS commands is really easy as long as you follow the rules of order and use the correct parameters.

> *Note:* Most applications software incorporates the issuing of commands as part of the software's operation. The commands discussed in this book are DOS commands. Be sure that you know the difference between DOS commands, which are issued at the DOS command line, and the commands you learn to use with your applications software.

The Command Syntax

Command syntax can be compared to the phrasing of a spoken or written sentence. The order of the words, the punctuation, and the vocabulary are important ingredients for good communication. When you communicate with DOS, you need to use the proper ingredients so that DOS can interpret your intentions correctly. Like most PC programs, DOS cannot decide to ignore what you "say" but do what you mean. Unfortunately, PCs don't have the capacity for intelligence that people do. If you use improper syntax in a DOS command, DOS objects with an error message—even if the mistake is minor.

This book uses a symbolic form to describe a command's syntax. With this symbolic form, the parts of the command are given names you can relate to. When you actually enter the command, however, you substitute real values for the symbolic names. In other cases, the examples are commands you can enter exactly as shown. Don't worry that you won't be able to tell the symbolic form of a command from a literal example. They are clearly marked in both cases. If you make a mistake and enter a symbolic word in the command line, DOS simply objects with an error message. You won't damage anything.

Because many DOS commands have several parameters, switches, and defaults, different forms of these commands may be correct. Even though the simple versions of DOS syntax work effectively, most DOS manuals show the complete syntax for a command, which makes the command look complex. For example, the complete symbolic syntax for the DIR command can look like the following:

DIR *d:path\filename.ext /P/W/S/B/L/O:sortorder/A:attributes*

You use the DIR command to display a directory of one or more files stored on a disk. This command may look formidable, but don't worry. Command syntax is much easier to understand if you look at the elements on the command line one at a time.

Some parts of a DOS command are mandatory. These parts represent information that must be included for the command to work correctly. Mandatory parts of a command are the minimum that DOS can understand. When you read that an element of syntax is required, or mandatory, be sure to include a proper value for that element when you enter the command. In this book, mandatory elements are signaled by **boldface type.**

When you enter only the mandatory command elements, DOS in many cases uses default parameters for other elements. Thanks to defaults, many commands are simple to issue. DOS recognizes the default values either because the values are programmed into DOS or because you established the value in an earlier command. Recall the discussion of the logged drive in Chapter 3. When you log onto another drive, that drive becomes the *current* drive. If you omit from a command the drive's command-line specifier, DOS uses the current drive.

Syntax elements for which DOS maintains default values are considered *optional*. You do not have to enter optional elements. If you intend for DOS to use a default value, you can save keystrokes by omitting the optional syntax element. DOS accepts commands with all syntax elements present, even though some elements are optional. By including all syntax elements, however, you assert full control over what DOS will do. In this book, optional elements are signaled by *italic type*.

When you enter all syntax elements, DOS uses the exact instructions in place of default values. In the DIR command example, the **DIR** is mandatory. The rest of the command, *d:path\filename.ext /P/W/S/B/L/O:sortorder /A:attributes*, is optional.

The Command-Line Parameters

In addition to the command's name, a DOS command contains syntax elements known as *parameters*. Parameters (sometimes called *arguments*) are the parts of a command line that provide DOS with the objects of the command's action. The objects may be files, system settings, or hardware devices.

In the DIR example, *d:* identifies which disk drive the command will use for its action. *d:* represents the drive parameter in the command. When you give the command, you substitute for *d:* the drive letter of your choice (A:, B:, or C:).

path, a parameter that is introduced in Chapter 8, refers to the directory path leading to the command. For now, don't worry about *path*.

filename.ext stands for the name of a file, including its extension. In DOS, file names can include up to eight letters. The name also can contain an extension, which consists of a period and up to three more letters. For instance, you may type the file name **MYFILE.123**.

If you pay close attention to the sample syntax and commands, you will note that spaces separate, or *delimit*, the command name and some parameters. Other commands use the slash (/) character to separate parameters. Delimiters are important to DOS because they help DOS break apart (or *parse*) the command. For example, the command **DIR A:** is correct; **DIRA:** is not.

The Optional Switches

A *switch* is a parameter that turns on an optional function of a command. Switches are special parameters because they usually are not the objects of a command's action; rather, switches modify the command's action. Switches can make a basic command more versatile. In the DIR example, /P, /W, /S, /B, /L, /O, and /A are switches. Note that each switch is a character preceded by a forward slash (/)—not a backslash (\). Not all DOS commands have switches. In addition, switches consisting of the same letter may have different meanings for different commands. For example, you can use the /W switch with the DIR command to display a *wide* directory of files.

Getting Command-Line Help

One of the most convenient features inaugurated in DOS 5 is an on-line help facility. In earlier versions you had to memorize command syntax. In DOS 5, an on-screen command summary for each DOS command is available at any time from the command line.

To access on-line help for the use of a particular command, use one of the following procedures:

- Type the DOS command, followed by the switch /?
- Type **help**, followed by the DOS command

For example, to get a command summary of the DIR command, type either of the following commands, and press Enter:

DIR /?

HELP DIR

DOS displays the help screen shown in figure 5.1.

Issuing DOS Commands

Take a moment to become familiar with the instructions used in this book for entering commands. The notation helps you distinguish between what you type and what the computer displays. If you feel that issuing commands is going to be difficult, relax. You don't have to memorize commands instantly; instead, you will learn by doing. If you get lost, just back up a few sections and reread the text. Millions of people use DOS commands—we all had to start from scratch and learn how.

```
C:\>dir /?
Displays a list of files in a directory.

DIR [pathname] [/P] [/W] [/O[:sortorder]] [/A[:attributes]] [/S] [/B] [/L]

    pathname      The directory and/or files to list.
    /P            Pause after each screenful of information.
    /W            Use wide list format.
    /S            Display files in the specified directory and all subdirectories.
    /B            Use bare format (filenames only).
    /L            Use lower case.
    /O            List files in sorted order.
    sortorder     N  name              S  size
                  E  extension         D  date and time
                  G  group subdirectories  -  prefix to reverse order
    /A            Display files with specified attributes.
    attributes    D  subdirectories    R  read-only files
                  H  hidden files      A  files ready for archive
                  S  system files      -  prefix meaning "not"

Switches may be preset in DIRCMD environment variable.  Override
preset options by prefixing any switch with -, e.g., /-W.

C:\>
```

Fig. 5.1. Using the DOS on-line help facility.

Figure 5.2 breaks down the different elements that make up a typical DOS command—the DIR command. As you can see, only two of the switches (/P and /W) are illustrated.

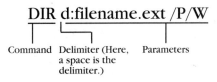

Fig. 5.2. The syntax of the DIR command.

Figure 5.3 is a diagram of the DIR command explained in the preceding sections. This diagram illustrates the steps needed to issue a DOS command, steps covered in detail in the following sections.

Typing the Command Name

You enter a command when the command line displays the DOS prompt. This prompt usually consists of the drive letter followed by the greater-than character >. Notice that immediately following the > is the blinking cursor.

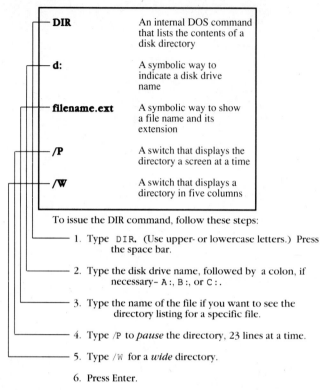

DIR	An internal DOS command that lists the contents of a disk directory
d:	A symbolic way to indicate a disk drive name
filename.ext	A symbolic way to show a file name and its extension
/P	A switch that displays the directory a screen at a time
/W	A switch that displays a directory in five columns

To issue the DIR command, follow these steps:

1. Type DIR. (Use upper- or lowercase letters.) Press the space bar.

2. Type the disk drive name, followed by a colon, if necessary— A:, B:, or C:.

3. Type the name of the file if you want to see the directory listing for a specific file.

4. Type /P to *pause* the directory, 23 lines at a time.

5. Type /W for a *wide* directory.

6. Press Enter.

Fig. 5.3. *Issuing the DIR command.*

As you may recall, the cursor marks the point at which your keystrokes will be displayed as you enter them.

The command name is like a key to the DOS operating system. A command's name identifies the action the command is programmed to perform. COMMAND.COM is the DOS command processor that reads the command you type. COMMAND.COM can carry out several built-in (*internal*) commands. It also knows how to load and run the *external* utility command programs whose names you enter at the DOS prompt.

When you type a command at the DOS prompt, make sure that you leave no space between the > and the first letter of the command name. Enter all DOS command names immediately following the prompt. If the command has no parameters or switches, press the Enter key after you type the last letter of the command name.

You can take advantage of default parameters when you enter a command line. For example, if you type the directory command at the prompt as follows:

DIR

and then press Enter, DOS supplies the drive parameter (even though you didn't type it). DOS uses the logged (current) drive, which in this case is drive C.

Adding Parameters

When you are instructed to enter parameters other than switches, this book shows them in one of two ways—lowercase or uppercase. If a parameter is shown as lowercase text, you are to supply the value for that text (substitute the appropriate information for the symbolic notation in the book). The lowercase letters are shorthand for the full names of the parts of a command. As in the command name, uppercase letters indicate that you enter letter-for-letter what you see—the literal meaning of the command.

To add a file-name parameter to the DIR command, you can type the following:

    DIR C:MYFILE.TXT

In symbolic notation, MYFILE.TXT would be shown as *filename.ext*.

Remember that you separate parameters from the rest of the command. Most of the time the delimiter is a space, but other delimiters, such as the period (.), the backslash (\), the slash (/), and the colon (:) are available. Look at the examples in this book to see which delimiter to use.

You can recognize any switches in the sample text by the leading slash character (/). Always enter the switch letter as shown. Do not forget to type the slash. Suppose that you enter the DIR command with a switch character, as follows:

    DIR/W

The / serves as the delimiter and tells DOS that a switch is about to follow.

Ignoring a Command Line (Esc)

You occasionally may make a mistake when you are entering a command. Remember that DOS does not act on the command until you press Enter. You can correct a mistake by using the arrow keys or the Backspace key to reposition the cursor. Press the Esc key, however, if you want to type an entirely new command. The Esc key cancels the entry and gives you a new line. Just remember that these line-editing and canceling tips work only *before* you press the Enter key. Some commands can be successfully stopped with the Ctrl-C or Ctrl-Break sequence, however. To restore the system prompt, press Esc.

Executing a Command

The Enter key is the action key for DOS commands. Make a habit of stopping and reading what you have typed before you press the Enter key. After you press Enter, the computer gets busy and carries out your command. During the processing of the command, DOS does not display your keystrokes. DOS does remember your keystrokes, however, so be aware that the characters you type could end up in your next command.

DOS stores keystrokes that have not yet been displayed in a *type ahead buffer*. DOS's type ahead buffer, a temporary storage area in RAM, can fill with keystrokes, especially when your PC is hung. When the type ahead buffer fills, your PC beeps when you press an additional key. DOS's use of buffer storage areas also gives DOS some special editing capabilities.

Using the DOS Editing Keys

When you type a command and press the Enter key, DOS copies the line into an input *buffer*—a storage area for command-line keystrokes. You can pull the preceding command line from the buffer and use it again. This feature is helpful when you want to issue a command that is similar to the last command you used. Table 5.1 lists the keys you use to edit the input buffer.

TIP

Tip: DOS 5 includes a new utility program called DOSKey. Among other things, DOSKey enables you to reuse DOS commands more easily at the command line. See Chapter 13, "Understanding Batch Files, DOSKey, and Macros," for a discussion of this valuable program.

Using DIR To Look at Files

The DIR command is one of the first commands most DOS users learn. The command quickly provides a list of files, along with the date and time of creation, and the file sizes.

Knowing which files are on your disks and when you created the files can be important. You can keep a list of files manually—quite a task—or use the DOS DIR command to get a list of the files on each of your floppy disks or your hard disk.

Table 5.1
DOS Command-Line Editing Keys

Key	Action
⊢← →⊣	Moves the cursor to the next tab stop
Esc	Cancels the current line and does not change the buffer
Ins	Enables you to insert characters into the line
Del	Deletes a character from the line
F1 or →	Copies one character from the preceding command line
F2	Copies all characters from the preceding command line up to, but not including, the next character you type
F3	Copies all remaining characters from the preceding command line
F4	Deletes all characters from the preceding command line up to, but not including, the next character typed (opposite of F2)
F5	Moves the current line into the buffer, but does not allow DOS to execute the line
F6	Produces an end-of-file marker ($^\wedge$Z) when you copy from the console to a disk file

Issuing the DIR Command

DIR stands for DIRectory. A directory is a list of files. The DIR command displays a volume label, five columns of information about the files, and the amount of unused space on the disk.

Try the DIR command now. Type the following:

DIR

Then press Enter so that DOS can execute the command. You have just told DOS to display a list of files from the logged drive. You can also type **DIR A:** to specify drive A or **DIR C:** to list the files on drive C. The A or C is the optional drive parameter. If you don't specify a drive, DOS uses the logged drive by default.

You can change the logged drive by typing the drive letter followed by a colon, and then pressing Enter. For example, typing **A:** at the DOS prompt changes the logged drive to drive A. A disk must be in a drive before DOS can make it the logged drive. Remember that you can log only to a drive your system contains. By changing the logged drive, you can switch between a hard disk and a floppy disk.

Using Scroll Control

The term *scrolling* describes what happens as a DOS screen fills with information. When DOS displays in response to your typing or as a result of a DOS command, the text fills in from left to right and top to bottom. As the screen fills, information scrolls off the top of the display. To stop a scrolling screen, you press the key combination Ctrl-S (hold down the Ctrl key and then press S). Press any key to restart the scrolling. On Enhanced Keyboards, press the Pause key to stop scrolling.

With the DIR command, you can use the /P switch and the /W switch for scroll control.

If you want to see more file names on a single screen, you can use the /W switch. The command **DIR /W** displays only the file names in a wide multicolumn format, in which many files fit on a single screen (see fig. 5.4). This wide format does not include the additional information about each file that a directory listing usually provides.

For a complete and convenient listing of the directory, use the /P switch. The command **DIR /P** pauses the display so that the listing is presented page-by-page. Press any key to display the next page of information.

> *Note:* When you see the message `Press any key to continue`, DOS really means that you should press *almost* any key. If you press the Shift, Alt, Caps Lock, Num Lock, or Scroll Lock key, DOS won't respond. The easiest keys to press are the space bar and the Enter key.

```
A:\>dir /w

 Volume in drive A is STARTUP
 Volume Serial Number is 159A-AD78
 Directory of A:\

COMMAND.COM    EGA.SYS        DISPLAY.SYS    FORMAT.COM     PACKING.LST
WINA20.386     ANSI.SYS       COUNTRY.SYS    HIMEM.SYS      KEYB.COM
KEYBOARD.SYS   MODE.COM       SETVER.EXE     SYS.COM        UNFORMAT.COM
AUTOEXEC.DFT   CONFIG.SYS     DIR.DFT        CONFIG.HD      AUTOEXEC.HD
        20 file(s)     250004 bytes
                        30720 bytes free

A:\>
```

Fig. 5.4. The display produced by the command DIR /W.

For example, if your DOS 5 Startup disk is in drive A and you type **DIR /P**, the following directory listing is displayed:

```
Volume in drive A is STARTUP
Volume Serial Number is 159A-AD78
Directory of A:\

COMMAND    COM    46246    12-13-90    4:09a
EGA        SYS     4885    12-13-90    4:09a
DISPLAY    SYS    15682    12-13-90    4:09a
FORMAT     COM    32285    12-13-90    4:09a
PACKING    LST     3610    12-13-90    4:09a
WINA20     386     9349    12-13-90    4:09a
ANSI       SYS     8868    12-13-90    4:09a
COUNTRY    SYS    13496    12-13-90    4:09a
HIMEM      SYS    11120    12-13-90    4:09a
KEYB       COM    14699    12-13-90    4:09a
KEYBOARD   SYS    24336    12-13-90    4:09a
MODE       COM    23313    12-13-90    4:09a
SETVER     EXE     9162    12-13-90    4:09a
SYS        COM    13200    12-13-90    4:09a
UNFORMAT   COM    17680    12-13-90    4:09a
AUTOEXEC   DFT       24    12-26-90    9:45p
CONFIG     SYS       53    12-26-90    9:45p
```

```
DIR          DFT      909    12-26-90      10:13p
CONFIG       HD       469    12-26-905:29p
Press any key to continue . . .

(continuing A:\)
AUTOEXEC     HD       618    12-26-90       5:29p
        20 file(s)      250004 bytes
                         30720 bytes free
```

Examining the Directory Listing

Look at the directory listing in the preceding section. The first line in the listing is the *volume label*, an identification you specify when you prepare the disk. The volume label is optional, but including it can simplify the job of organizing your disks.

Below the volume label is the *volume serial number*. This number is assigned automatically by DOS (Versions 4.0 and later) when the disk is formatted. DOS uses this number to identify the disk you have inserted into a particular drive.

The next lines in the directory listing contain file information. Each line in the directory describes one file: its name, extension, size (in bytes), and the date and time you created or last changed the file (assuming that you entered the time and date when you booted your computer). The next sections look more closely at this information.

The last line of the directory tells you the total number of files a disk contains and the amount of free space available. Free space is measured in bytes. This information is useful when you want to determine how many more files a disk can hold.

File Names and Extensions

A file name has two parts—the name and the extension—separated by a period. In the directory listing, however, spaces separate the file name from the extension.

In any single directory, each file must have a unique full name. DOS treats the file name and the extension together as the entire name. The file names MYFILE.123 and MYFILE.ABC are unique because each file has a different extension. The file names MYFILE.123 and YOURFILE.123 are also unique. Many DOS commands make use of the two parts of the file name separately. For this reason, giving each file both a file name and an extension is a good idea.

File names should help you identify the contents of a file. A file name can contain only eight alphanumeric characters; the extension, only three. You may need some ingenuity to come up with unique names with meaning.

DOS is particular about which characters you use in a file name or an extension. To be on the safe side, use only letters of the alphabet and numbers—not spaces or a period. DOS truncates excess characters in a file name.

File Size and the Date/Time Stamp

The directory listing's third column shows the size of the file in bytes. This measurement is only an approximation of the size of your file. Your file may use more bytes than indicated. Because computers reserve blocks of data storage for files, files with slightly different data amounts may have identical file-size listings. This factor explains why a word processing memo with only five words can occupy 2K of file space.

The last two columns in the directory listing display a date and a time. These entries show when you created the file or, in the case of an established file, when you last altered it. Your computer's internal date and time are the basis for the date and time "stamp" in the directory. As you create more files, the date and time stamp become invaluable tools in determining which version of a file is the most recent.

Using Wild-Card Characters with DIR

Perhaps you have seen a Western movie in which a poker-playing cowboy says, "Deuces are wild!" You know that this sentence means that the number two cards can take on a value other than their own. Computerists have borrowed this wild-card concept and applied it to file-name operations on computers. You can use wild-card characters in file names to copy, rename, delete, list, or otherwise manipulate file names.

DOS recognizes two wild-card characters: the question mark (?) and the asterisk (*). You can place the ? character in any full file name. The ? matches any one character in that position. The * in a file name or in an extension matches all characters in that part of the full file name.

If you type **DIR** followed by the file name, the selected list of files is displayed. The long form of the DIR command looks like this:

DIR *d:filename.ext*

Remember to type your actual drive letter instead of the *d:*. In place of *filename.ext*, you can type something like **MYFILE.123**. The DIR command you just typed tells DOS to list a directory of all files that match MYFILE.123. The directory listing would list only one file, MYFILE.123. When you use DIR alone, DOS lists all files in the directory. When you use DIR with a file name and extension parameter, DOS lists only files that match that parameter.

Used with wild cards, the DIR command becomes more powerful. If you want to see a listing of all files that have an extension of 123, you can use the * wild-card character. The * replaces every character from the asterisk to the end of the part of the command in which it is located.

For example, suppose that you type the following:

    DIR *.123

DOS lists any file with the 123 extension, including both MYFILE.123 and YOURFILE.123. If you issue the command **DIR MYFILE.***, you may get a listing of MYFILE.123 and MYFILE.XYZ.

> *Tip:* You can give your letter files an LET extension and your memo files an extension of MEM. With this technique, you can use the DIR command with a wild card to get separate listings of the two types of files.

The **?** wild card differs from the * wild card. Only the character in the same position as the **?** is a match. If you issue the command **DIR MYFILE?.123**, files like MYFILE1.123, MYFILE2.123 are displayed, but MYFILE10.123 is not. The same rules apply to any other command that allows wild cards.

The wild-card designation *.* replaces every character in the root file name and every character in the extension. *.* selects *all* the files in a directory.

> *Caution:* The *.* specification is a powerful tool; be sure to use it with caution. When used with commands such as DEL, the specification can be dangerous. For example, the command **DEL *.*** will delete *all* files in the directory.

Other examples of wild-card uses with the DIR command are shown in the following list:

Command	Result
DIR MYFILE.123	Presents directory information for the file MYFILE.123
DIR *.123	Lists every file with the extension 123 in the directory
DIR M*.*	Lists each file whose name begins with the letter M
DIR *.*	Lists all files in the directory; the same as typing just **DIR**
DIR *.	Lists all files that have no extension
DIR ???.BAT	Lists all three-letter files that have a BAT extension
DIR MYFILE.???	Lists all the files named MYFILE that have three-letter extensions

Reviewing the DIR Command

The DIR command displays more than a list of file names. As your computing expertise grows, you will find many uses for the information provided by the full directory listing (see fig. 5.5).

APPEND EXE 10614 12-13-90 4:09a

| APPEND is the file name; it can be up to eight characters long | EXE is the extension. | 10614 is the file size in bytes. | The file was created or last modified on December 13, 1990. | Time of creation or modification was 4:09 a.m. |

```
Volume in drive A is UTILITY
Volume Serial Number is 159A-B085
Directory of A:\

APPEND    EXE     10614 12-13-90    4:09a
ATTRIB    EXE     15732 12-13-90    4:09a
BACKUP    EXE     35596 12-13-90    4:09a
CHKDSK    EXE     16328 12-13-90    4:09a
COMP      EXE     13930 12-13-90    4:09a
DISKCOMP  COM     10428 12-13-90    4:09a
DISKCOPY  COM     11393 12-13-90    4:09a
FIND      EXE      6642 12-13-90    4:09a
LABEL     EXE      8954 12-13-90    4:09a
RESTORE   EXE     38054 12-13-90    4:09a
SORT      EXE      6618 12-13-90    4:09a
4201      CPI      6404 12-13-90    4:09a
4208      CPI       720 12-13-90    4:09a
5202      CPI       370 12-13-90    4:09a
ASSIGN    COM      6271 12-13-90    4:09a
DRIVER    SYS      5384 12-13-90    4:09a
EGA       CPI     49068 12-13-90    4:09a
        17 file(s)     242506 bytes
                       110592 bytes free

A:\>
```

Fig. 5.5. The elements of a directory listing.

Summary

As you can tell, there is an underlying logic to issuing DOS commands. Even though each DOS command has its own characteristics, each command has a defined syntax, which can include parameters and switches. The basic knowledge of how to issue DOS commands is an important ingredient in your mastery of DOS. Following are the key points covered in this chapter:

- You issue commands to DOS for operating system services.

- The proper phrasing of each DOS command is called the command's syntax.

- In addition to the name of the command, a syntax line can contain parameters and switches.

- The DIR command, like many other DOS commands, uses optional parameters. When the optional parameters are omitted, the values are supplied as DOS defaults.

- You can edit a DOS command line by using special DOS editing keys.

- Some commands allow wild-card characters (? and *) as substitutes for position-matching in file-name parameters.

The next chapter completes your introduction to DOS by covering the important subject of disks and files. Although you are moving on from this chapter, you will want to review the ideas presented here when you begin to use DOS commands.

Understanding Disks and Files

6

O ne of the primary roles of a disk operating system is to provide the service of storing and retrieving data to and from disks. This chapter introduces you to the fundamentals of how DOS handles this role.

To provide data storage and retrieval, the operating system not only must oversee the many technical details of the disk hardware but also must provide a bookkeeping method for file storage and retrieval on disks. The disk operating system should provide these services without your needing to know the internal details of the operations. This chapter introduces you to DOS's file-bookkeeping methodology.

DOS generally insulates you from the technical details involved in storing and retrieving data on your computer. At times, however, you must handle and prepare for use the magnetic media—typically disks—that actually store the data. This chapter gives you a brief overview of the types of disks that may be used in your system and demonstrates several frequently used disk-related commands.

Key Terms Used in This Chapter

File system	The predefined organization used by a disk operating system to get data, in the form of files, to and from a disk
File	A variable-length collection of related information that is referenced by a name
Name	The first portion of a file name, consisting of up to eight characters; usually describes the contents of a file
Extension	A file-name suffix, which can include a period and up to three characters; usually describes the type of file
Disk	A magnetic storage medium and the predominant means of file storage for DOS
Disk drive	The electro-mechanical components that record and play back data to and from the magnetic surfaces of a disk
Hard disk	A built-in, fixed disk drive
Floppy disk	Any lower-capacity disk that you can remove from your PC's drive
Minifloppy	5 1/4-inch disk
Microfloppy	3 1/2-inch disk
Diskette	Another term for 5 1/4- and 3 1/2-inch disks
Platter	A disk contained in a hard disk drive
Track	A circular section of a disk's surface that holds data
Cylinder	The conceptual alignment of heads on the same track position on different sides (and platters) of the same disk
Sectors	Fixed-size components of a track
Format	The specification for a disk's use of its physical space

Introducing the DOS File System

A file system is an organized collection of files. As a user, you see the DOS file system at work in the files you organize into directories and subdirectories on your disks. Each file is a named group of data that DOS seems to manipulate as one continuous unit. Behind the scenes, however, DOS uses a complex structured management strategy. The DOS file system reflects this strategy. A file system includes not only the files but also the internal tables that record the file organization, as well as built-in rules that ensure the consistency of file organization.

Understanding Files

A *file* is a variable-length collection of related information that is referenced by a name. Picture a file cabinet full of file folders, each with a name on the tab. Neither the cabinet nor the individual pieces of paper in the folders are files. Only the named collection in one folder is considered a file. Think about the file cabinet, the folders, and the papers for a moment to understand the relationship (see fig. 6.1). Electronic files can be compared to a traditional file cabinet. The drawers are like floppy disks or hard disks. The file folders are like files.

File names are helpful for locating the information in the correct file. Yet the file name itself is not the memo, spreadsheet, or other information you use. Think again of a file cabinet. The information stored on individual papers in the folders is the source of records for the subject named on the file folder. Without properly named folders to group the related papers, access to the information is greatly hindered. Likewise, DOS enables you to group related information in the form of files. DOS and DOS-based applications software let you open named files whenever you want to store information on a disk.

In a computer setting, a file can contain data (information), programs (instructions that guide computer tasks), or both. A file can exist on a disk, on magnetic tape, on punch cards—even in a computer's memory. Files are made up of elements of data or programs. The individual elements can be stored as patterns of holes in a paper tape, as patterns of magnetic fields on the surface of a disk, or in many other ways. Physical storage techniques for files vary greatly. In all likelihood, however, your computer stores files on a disk. Disks are the predominant means of file storage for DOS. When you see the term *file* in this book, you can count on it to mean *disk file*.

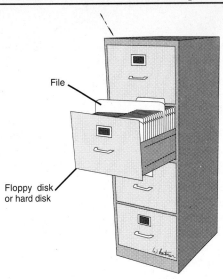

File

Floppy disk
or hard disk

Fig. 6.1. *Electronic files compared to a file cabinet.*

DOS uses file names to identify files. A full *file name* consists of up to eight characters followed by a period (.) and up to three characters called the extension. The period and extension are optional.

The first, or *name*, portion of a file name (before the period) often describes the *contents* of the file. Extensions, on the other hand, are traditionally used to describe the *type* of file.

Someone using a word processor, for example, may use as the name portion of a file name the name (or a close approximation) of a person who will receive a memo. The extension MEM may then safely be used. A memo to Mr. Duncan can be called DUNCAN.MEM. Similarly, the extension .DOC is commonly used for office policy document files. A monthly policy statement may be named JAN.DOC. DOS enables you to use a wide variety of file names. You are free to develop your own file-naming conventions provided that you stay within the character limits imposed by DOS.

> *Note:* Differentiating between people is much easier if they have both first and last names. The same is true of files. DOS provides for a name (first name) and an extension (last name). When you name your files, use both parts of the file name so that you can better identify the file later. Many applications programs add their own file extensions, however; with these programs, you simply supply the first portion of a file's name.

Selecting File Names

DOS ensures that every one of your files has a name. In fact, DOS does not provide a way to put file data on a disk without a file name. When a file is created, either by your applications software or a DOS file-service routine, DOS places the name of that file in one of DOS's directories. A directory is DOS's equivalent to a library card file. You will learn more about directories later. For now, just think of a directory as a table for holding file names and locations.

DOS provides room in each directory entry for an eight-character name and a three-character extension. When you include a file name in a command, you place a period (.) between the file name and extension.

> *Note:* DOS uses the file-naming convention of the once dominant CP/M operating system. DOS designers felt that using the CP/M file-naming convention would make the transition from CP/M-based computers to DOS-based computers easier for users. The DIR command that shows a listing of the file names in a directory is used also in the CP/M operating system. Many file-related concepts were adapted for DOS from the CP/M operating system. As DOS has matured, the DOS file system has been enhanced well beyond the capabilities of the original CP/M file system.

The characters you see on your computer screen are the ASCII-code representations of bytes of data. One character is stored in one byte. The name field of a directory entry is 11 bytes long (8 for the first part of the file name plus 3 for the extension). DOS accepts for file names most characters you would use for "everyday" names. You can use in file names the upper- and lowercase letters *a* through *z*; DOS automatically stores letters in uppercase in a directory entry. The numeric characters *0* through *9* also can be used. Many punctuation characters also are allowed in file names.

Following are the rules for file names.

1. A file name consists of the following:

    a. A name of one to eight characters

    b. An optional extension of one to three characters

    c. A period between the name and the extension if an extension is used

2. The following characters are *allowed* in a file name:

    a. The letters *A* through *Z*. (Lowercase letters are transformed automatically into uppercase.)

    b. The numbers *0* through *9*

    c. The following special characters and punctuation marks:

    $ \# \& @ ! ( ) - \{ \} ' _ \sim \char94 \char96

3. The following characters are *not allowed* in a file name:

    a. Any control character, including Escape (27d or 1Bh) and Delete (127d or 7Fh)

    b. The space character

    c. The following special characters and punctuation symbols:

    $ + = / [ ] " : ; , ? * \backslash < > | $

4. If DOS finds an illegal character in a file name, DOS usually stops at the character preceding the illegal one and uses the legal part of the name. (There are a few exceptions to this rule.)

5. A device name can be part of a name but cannot be the entire name. For example, CONT.DAT or AUXI.TXT are acceptable; CON.DAT or AUX.TXT are not.

6. Each file name in a directory must be unique.

7. A drive name and a path name usually precede a file name. (Path names are discussed in Chapter 8.)

To understand why DOS "objects" to the use of some characters in file names, you must look below the surface of DOS. Certain characters are not allowed because DOS will not pass those characters from the keyboard to the command or external command program that controls a file's name. You cannot, for example, use the Ctrl-G ($\char94$G) character in a file name. Ctrl-G tells an input device to sound the computer's bell or beep signal. The Escape character produced by the Esc key is another character DOS does not accept as part of a file name. DOS interprets the Esc key as your request to cancel the command line and start again.

Another example of an unacceptable (disallowed) character is Ctrl-S ($\char94$S). DOS and other operating systems use Ctrl-S to stop the flow of characters from the input device to the output device. Ctrl-S stops a scrolling screen, for example. If you press Ctrl-S while entering a file name, DOS assumes that you are entering an input-stopping character—not part of a file name.

You cannot use in a file name any characters that COMMAND.COM and external command programs use to divide the parameters and switches from the command in a command line. Because DOS must break out, or *parse*—be capable of distinguishing the various components of—the command line, certain characters are seen by DOS as delimiters of parameters or parts of a parameter. The backslash character (\), for example, separates directory names in a path specifier. DOS always reads the backslash on the command line to indicate part of a path.

Avoiding Reserved Names

DOS reserves names for its built-in input and output devices. You may recall that DOS can treat some devices in a PC in a high-level way by accepting their names as input or output parameters in a command line. Before using the file-name parameters from a command line to look for a file, DOS checks whether the name is a device name. Table 6.1 lists the built-in DOS input and output device names and their purposes.

Table 6.1
DOS Device Names

Device Name	Purpose
COM*x* or AUX	Identifies the serial communication port(s)
LPT*x* or PRN	Identifies the parallel printer port(s)
CON	Identifies the screen and keyboard
NUL	Identifies the "throw away" or "do nothing" device

Never attempt to write a disk file with a name that is the same as one of the device names listed in table 6.1. DOS will intercept the device name, even if you add an extension, and try to use the device—not the file you intend— to complete the command. Use a device name only as a device parameter in a command.

Observing File-Naming Conventions

A convention is an informal rule that is not explicitly enforced. DOS file names often follow certain conventions. Although you can use any file name that follows DOS's character and device-name rules, you will want to observe file-naming conventions whenever possible. You can, for example, name a memo file and give it a BAT extension; but this extension has a special meaning to DOS because all batch files have the extension BAT. (Batch files are covered in Chapter 13.) As long as you do not try to execute the memo as a batch file, DOS is happy. If you try to execute the memo file, however, DOS sees the BAT extension and tries to execute it. Of course, the memo cannot be executed.

You can name an EXE file with a COM extension. Although both files are executable, they have internal differences. DOS does not take the extension's name to mean that the file is indeed an EXE or COM file. DOS inspects a key part of the file before deciding how to load and execute the program file. If you name a spreadsheet file as an EXE or COM file, for example, DOS is not fooled into executing the nonprogram file. In all likelihood, your system will simply "lock up," and you will have to warm boot to begin again.

Many software manufacturers use certain extensions for special files in their applications programs. To avoid confusion about the contents of a file, avoid using certain extensions. Table 6.2 lists some conventional file-name extensions and their meanings. The program names listed in the table are examples only. More than one program may, and often does, use the same extension in its file-naming conventions.

Table 6.2
Common File-Name Extensions

Extension	Common Use	Extension	Common Use
ARC	Archive (compressed file)	CNF	Program configuration information
ASC	ASCII text file	CHP	Chapter file (Ventura Publisher)
ASM	Assembler source file		
BAK	Backup file	COM	Program file
BAS	BASIC program file	CPI	Code page information file (DOS)
BAT	Batch file	DAT	Data file
BIN	Binary program file	DBF	Database file (dBASE)
C	C source file	DCT	Dictionary file
CBL	COBOL source file	DEV	Program device driver file
CFG	Program configuration information		

Extension	Common Use	Extension	Common Use
DIF	Data Interchange Format file	PIF	Program Information File (TopView/Windows)
DOC	Document (text) file		
DRV	Program device driver file	PRO	Profile (configuration file)
DTA	Data file	PRN	Program listing for printing
EXE	Executable program file	PS	PostScript program file
FNT	Font file		
IDX	Index file (Q&A)	RFT	Revisable Form Text (Document Content Architecture)
IMG	GEM image (graphics) file		
HLP	Help file		
KEY	Keyboard macro file (ProKey)	SAV	Backup file
LET	Letter	SYS	System or device driver file
LST	Listing of a program (in a file)	STY	Style sheet (Ventura Publisher; Microsoft Word)
LIB	Program library file		
MAC	Keyboard macro file (Superkey)		
MAP	Linker map file	TIF	Picture file in tag image format
MSG	Program message file	TMP	Temporary file
NDX	Index file (dBASE III)	TST	Test file
OBJ	Intermediate object code (program) file	TXT	Text file
		WK1	Worksheet file (1-2-3, Release 2)
OLD	Backup file		
OVL	Program overlay file	WK3	Worksheet file (1-2-3, Release 3)
OVR	Program overlay file		
PAK	Packed (archive) file	WKQ	Quattro spreadsheet file
PAS	Pascal source file		
PCX	Picture file for PC Paintbrush	WKS	Worksheet file (1-2-3 Release 1 and 1A)
		ZIP	Compressed file (PKZIP)

> *Tip:* You don't have to memorize all these file-naming conventions. The documentation supplied with your applications programs will alert you to the file-naming conventions used by that program.

Avoiding Bad File Names

When you enter file names in a command, DOS may not simply reject a bad file name. In certain cases, DOS takes some unusual actions. The following example uses the COPY command to show what can happen. (Don't worry about learning all about COPY from this example; the command is covered in detail in Chapter 10). The general form of COPY takes a source-file parameter and copies the file to the destination-file parameter. If the destination file doesn't exist, DOS creates the file. The example assumes that the source file, TEST.TXT, already exists on the default drive. To create a new file from the file TEST.TXT, you can, for example, enter the COPY command as follows:

COPY TEST.TXT 123456789.1234

Notice that both the file name and the extension given for the destination file name have an extra character. The file name has the extra character *9* and the extension has the extra character *4*. You might predict that DOS will issue a message warning that the file name and extension are both too long. No such luck! Without issuing a warning, DOS silently chops off (*truncates*) the file name to eight characters and the extension to three characters. DOS then completes the COPY operation by creating a new file. The resulting file, named by DOS, is 12345678.123. DOS always discards excess characters in the file name and extension and uses the remaining characters as the file parameter.

Illegal characters in a file name can stop DOS from carrying out a command. The following interaction with DOS is an example. Again, the example assumes that the source file exists.

```
COPY 12345678.123 1[3.123
     File creation error
        0 File(s) copied
```

As you might expect, the illegal character / in the target file's extension stopped DOS from completing the copy operation. If you use the same / character in a reporting command, such as DIR, DOS issues another error message. The following sequence shows the error message issued.

```
DIR [

   Parameter format not correct -  [
```

Not every character that is illegal in a file name stops DOS from carrying out a command. In the following example, the semicolon character is at the end of the destination file's extension.

```
COPY 12345678.123 12345678.12;

   1 file(s) copied
```

DOS carries out the COPY command and creates a new file from the destination parameter. To see the new file's name, issue the DIR command and view the listing:

```
Volume in drive C is LAP TOP
Volume Serial Number is 1628-BA9A
Directory of C:\DATA
.     <DIR>     01-16-91  12:06a
..    <DIR>     01-16-91  12:06a
TEST TXT  6     08-25-91   9:25a
12345678  123  6    08-25-91   9:32a
12345678  12   6    08-25-91   9:35a
5 file(s) 18 bytes
1978368 bytes free
```

DOS adds the 12345678.12 file. DOS reads the semicolon in the command as a closing delimiter. The remaining part of the target-file parameter becomes the new file's name.

Not many DOS users with any experience would purposely use illegal characters in a file name. But typos easily can creep into your DOS commands and introduce illegal characters into file-name parameters. Just remember that DOS's reaction to an illegal file name isn't always predictable.

Examining Disks and Drives

Being able to store named collections of data in files is of little use unless you have a convenient medium on which to store the files. PC designers chose disks as this medium. Disks, both removable and fixed, have a virtual monopoly on file storage in PCs. Tape and CD ROM (Compact Disk Read-Only Memory) finish a distant second and third. Disk drives, DOS's warehouse for file storage, offer convenience, reliability, reusability, and rapid access to files. Because disks play the primary role as the storage medium for files, you should have some understanding of how disks perform this storage job.

Understanding the Disk's Magnetic Storage Technique

Disk drives are electro-mechanical components that record and play back data that is stored on the magnetic surfaces of a disk. Normally, the data is in the form of a file. During the recording, or *writing*, of a file, an electronic circuit translates the PC's electrical data into a series of magnetic fields. These magnetic fields are mirrored (weakly) by the oxide coating of the disk in the drive. In effect, the original data is imprinted magnetically on a disk. The information has changed its state. Electrical information is changed to magnetic information.

During the playback, or *reading*, of data from the disk's surface, an electronic circuit translates the magnetic fields back into electrical signals, and the data is once again in electrical form. The disk's original magnetic imprint, the file, is not destroyed by the reading operation. The file is still on the disk after it is read. Under normal use, only recording over the old imprint, called *overwriting* the disk, will change the imprint. Many file-related commands overwrite the previous contents of files. Commands that overwrite must be used with respect.

Unless you overwrite a file, the file is permanent. The recorded magnetic imprint on the disk is resistant to weakening and, with proper care, will last for years. Other magnetic fields, however, such as those produced by motors, magnetic paper clip holders, ringing telephones, and televisions, can weaken the magnetic imprint on a disk; and the disk's files can become unreadable in a short time. If the data being translated magnetically from a disk has some loss of integrity, your computer will not be able to fill in what is missing or wrong. The result is a *read error*. Read errors can end a work session unpleasantly because DOS will stop your computing when it detects a critical error. Disk drive designers must strive for perfect data reproduction from computer disks. One bad spot on a disk can result in a message similar to the following:

```
General failure error reading drive A:
```

This message sometimes signals the unrecoverable loss of all data on a disk.

TIP

Tip: Probably the most frequent cause of this General failure message is accidental use of an unformatted disk.

Looking into Disk Drives

The mechanical parts and electrical circuits of disk drives are complex. Although disk drives are parts of PC systems, the drives are machines in their own right. DOS relies on the driver programs of the BIOS to signal a drive's electronic circuitry to control the actions of the drive's mechanical components. You don't have to be concerned with the drive's complexity.

All disk drives have in common certain components: read/write heads, head-positioner mechanisms, and disk-spinning motors. All disk drives record on disks. Some disks are removable; some are built into the drive. Both fixed disks and removable disks are spun on a center spindle within the disk drive.

Many of today's PCs have both fixed disks and removable disks installed in their system units. DOS includes provisions in its BIOS extensions for both types of drives. Even with their common features, fixed and floppy disk drives have some important distinctions. Knowing these distinctions will help you understand how each type of drive operates in your system.

Hard Disk Drives

Drives with built-in disks are called *fixed disk drives* or, because their disks are made of a hard, rigid metal, *hard disk drives*. These terms may be shortened to *fixed disk* or *hard disk*. In this book, the term *hard disk* is used to describe the built-in, fixed disk drive. A hard disk drive can contain more than one hard disk, or *platter*. Multiple platters are arranged in a stack with space between the individual platters. Hard disk drives have large storage capacities, sometimes holding millions of bytes.

Figure 6.2 shows a cut-away view of a typical hard disk. The circular platters in the figure are the drive's magnetic disks. A head-positioner arm holds the read/write heads above and below each surface of each platter. When the drive leaves the factory, the inside components are not open; the drive is sealed closed. The seal keeps dust, hair, dirt, smoke, and other contaminants out of the delicate mechanical parts within the drive.

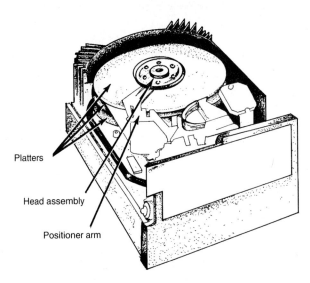

Platters

Head assembly

Positioner arm

Fig. 6.2. An inside view of the main components of a hard disk.

Some seasoned PC users refer to hard disks as *Winchester* disks. Winchester is a name derived from an IBM code name for the sealed disk-drive technology developed by IBM. Hard disks have the advantages of quick operation, high reliability, and large storage capacities. Hard disks have the disadvantage of tying the data stored on the disk to the PC in which the drive has been installed. Because the hard disk's platters cannot be removed, the data is tied to the drive. Hard disks are installed in a PC with mounting hardware and interconnecting power and data cables. To move an entire hard disk to another computer just to use the hard disk's data is impractical. When you need to move data between the hard disks of two computers, you can use the XCOPY command, or the BACKUP and RESTORE commands. These commands are covered in Part II of this book.

Floppy Disk Drives

In a PC system, the disadvantage of tying data to the hard disk is counterbalanced by the PC's floppy disk drive. Floppy disks are protected by a permanent jacket, which covers the flexible mylar disk and is coated with a magnetic sensitive film. The first floppy disks were 8 inches in diameter. By today's standards, the early 8-inch floppy disks didn't store much data, considering their size. Some 8-inch floppies could store only 320K of data. Today, floppy disks store from hundreds of thousands of bytes to nearly 1.5 million bytes.

Some early microcomputers used 8-inch floppies as their standard. For several years, the pioneering microcomputer makers offered 8-inch floppy drives as the alternative to such primitive off-line file storage as paper tape and cassette recording.

A smaller version of the 8-inch floppy, the 5 1/4-inch *minifloppy*, quickly became the floppy of choice for PC designers because of its size. The 3 1/2-inch *microfloppy* is yet another departure from its larger, older cousins because it incorporates a rigid plastic case (its jacket) as a protective cover. The 3 1/2-inch mylar circular medium inside a microfloppy disk is flexible, like the media in 8-inch and 5 1/4-inch floppies.

Figure 6.3 shows a microfloppy disk being inserted into a drive. It is not possible to interchange disks between size (diameter) classes of floppy drives.

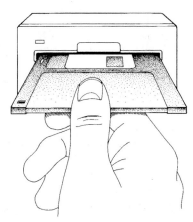

Fig. 6.3. *Inserting a microfloppy (3 1/2-inch) disk into a drive.*

Officially, the smaller two sizes of floppy disks are called *diskettes*; the 8-inch version is called a *disk*. The term *floppy disk* (or just *floppy*) refers to any jacket-enclosed disk that you can remove from a PC's drive. If identifying the type of floppy is important, the size qualifier (as in "3 1/2-inch floppy") is often used to make a distinction. *Minifloppy* always refers to 5 1/4-inch floppy disks; *microfloppy* always refers to 3 1/2-inch floppy disks. You probably will read or hear the term *disk* used to mean any floppy or hard disk when the disk type is clear in context. In other contexts, the term *diskette* is used to refer to both 3 1/2-inch and 5 1/4-inch disks.

Understanding the Dynamics of the Disk Drive

The dynamics of the disk drive are a function of the drive's electronics. The drive contains many components that interact with each other. These components are covered in the next sections.

Disk Drive Heads

Disk drives use one or more record/pickup or read/write *heads*. The heads of a disk drive are analogous to the pickup cartridge of a phonograph. The cartridge "picks up" vibrations from the stylus riding in the track and converts them to electrical energy. Disk heads convert magnetic energy to electrical data. Although several heads can be used in a disk drive, the electronics of the disk drive accept data from one head at a time.

Disk drive heads come in different shapes. Figure 6.4 illustrates two common head configurations. The heads are held in position by flexible metal head-holder assemblies. A set of wires carrying electrical signals connects to the head and passes through the head-holder assembly, where the set connects to a flexible ribbon cable. The ribbon cable absorbs wire movements when the head assembly moves. The hard-disk head assembly is low in mass to allow for start-stop control during high-speed head positioning.

On most floppy disks, data is recorded by a head on each of their two sides, or surfaces. Floppy drives that use a head on each side of the floppy disk are called *double-sided* drives. Hard disk drives can accommodate more than one double-sided platter because the drives incorporate heads on both sides of each platter. Using both sides of a disk or platter doubles its capacity. Incorporating multiple platters in a hard disk further multiplies its capacity by the number of heads employed.

Disk Tracks

Regardless of the type of disk drive, all disks spin on a center axis like a record spinning on a phonograph. A floppy disk spins at 360 revolutions per minute. The rotational speed of a hard disk is 10 times higher (approximately 3,600 RPM). The heads, which are positioned above the spinning surface of the disk, are held and moved in distinct steps by an actuator arm and head positioner. The heads of a floppy disk drive touch the medium's surface; the heads of a hard disk drive ride above the surface of the medium on a cushion of air. At each step position, the alignment of the head and the spinning disk produces a circular track.

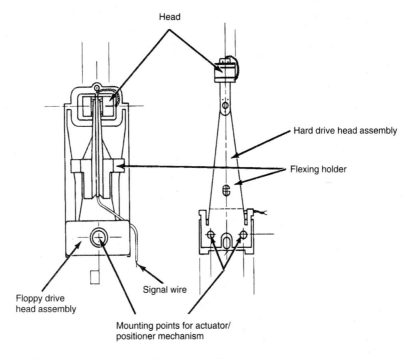

Fig. 6.4. Typical disk drive head assemblies.

The track is not a physical track like the groove in a record, but rather a ring of magnetically recorded data. Unlike the phonograph, which plays a record's contents by following a single, spiraling track, the disk drive steps from track to track to retrieve data. Figure 6.5 gives some idea of the position of the tracks. Notice that the tracks are not depicted as a spiral. All the tracks on a disk's surface are perfect concentric circles. The number of concentric tracks available on one disk's surface is determined by the head positioner's mechanical movements, the density of the magnetic medium, and the gap between the head and disk.

Disk Cylinders

A disk drive's multiple heads are affixed to a single positioner mechanism. When one head moves one track on its side of a platter (or floppy), the other heads all move one track on their respective sides of their respective platters.

Picture a top head riding over track 10 of side 1 of a platter, while the bottom head is riding under track 10 of side 2. If the disk has more than one platter, all the heads of that disk are positioned on track 10 of their associated side and platter. This conceptual alignment of heads on the same track position on different sides (and platters) of the same disk is called a *cylinder* (see fig. 6.6). The term *cylinder* is derived from the imaginary shape of the stacked circular tracks at any one stopping point of the positioner mechanism.

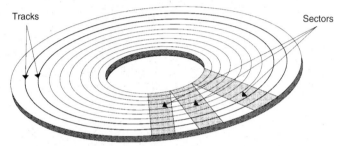

Fig. 6.5. *Concentric tracks on a disk's surface.*

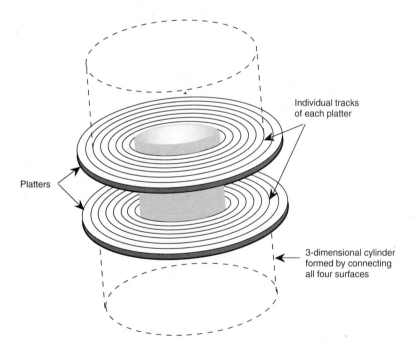

Fig. 6.6. *Tracks, platters, and cylinder.*

Because only one head can be active at one time, the drive must activate all its heads in sequence to write (or read) all tracks at the cylinder position. Head activation starts at the top head. To fill a cylinder, a four-head drive writes a track with head 1, then head 2, then head 3, and finally head 4. The head positioner moves one cylinder, and the sequence repeats. Processing all tracks of a cylinder before moving to the next cylinder is efficient because all heads are already at new track positions.

Disk Sectors

When a disk is blank, as it is when it comes from the factory, the disk contains no tracks and therefore no information. DOS has to prepare the disk to accept data. This preparation process is known as *formatting*. Formatting, as the name implies, places a uniform pattern of format information in all tracks of the disk. This format information in each track enables DOS to slice each track into smaller, more manageable, fixed-size components. These components are called *sectors*. Figure 6.7 shows the sectors of a floppy disk represented as slices of the disk's surface. The figure shows the boundaries for every other sector. The concentric arcs between the indicated sectors are the disk's tracks. Notice that each track has the same number of sector boundaries (and therefore sectors).

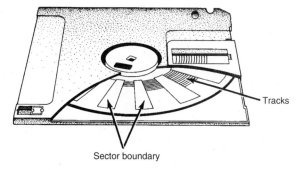

Fig. 6.7. A visual representation of sectors.

DOS reads and writes disk data one sector at a time. Some of DOS's internal file-system bookkeeping is done by sectors. To DOS, a sector is the disk's most manageable block of data. DOS uses 512-byte sectors by default.

The number of sectors formatted into each track is tied to the data density the drive uses when reading or writing data. The more dense the recording in a track, the greater the number of sectors that can be formatted. The more tracks, the greater the number of sectors per disk.

Designers select the number of tracks and the number of sectors per track with reliability in mind. Floppy disk drives are designed with more margin for error than hard disk drives. You easily can see why some margin for error is desirable for a drive that must ensure the mechanical alignment of each disk a user shoves in the door. Floppy disk drives must read disks that may have been stored in a place where the disk's magnetic information has been weakened. Even with the protective jacket, the magnetic-coated surfaces of many floppy disks become contaminated with smoke, dust, or fingerprints. The drive must be able to tolerate some contamination on a disk and still perform its function without numerous errors. Clearly, no disk drive can avoid errors if the disks it uses are abused. Drive heads can't read through liquid spills or dents made by a ballpoint pen.

Hard disk drives have higher capacities than their floppy cousins. Most typical PCs contain a hard disk that can contain at least ten million bytes of information. The higher capacity is due in large part to the precision of the drive's critical components working with the special oxides used to magnetically coat the platters. In addition, the working parts of the drive are sealed at the factory in a way that protects the platters, positioners, and heads from particles and contamination. With outside influence over these critical components sealed out, the hard disk drive can offer more tracks and sectors in the same physical space. When you consider that most hard disks have more than one platter, each capable of two-sided operation with more tracks than floppy disks, you can begin to see how hard disks get their large storage capacities.

Understanding Disk Formats

Disk drives have a universal way to divide a disk's available physical space. The number of platters, the number of sides, the number of tracks, the number of bytes per sector, and the number of sectors per track are the specific details that allow this logical division of a disk's physical space. The specification for a disk's use of its physical space is called the disk's *format*. PCs use a variety of disk-drive sizes and formats. Some PCs can handle both 5 1/4-inch and 3 1/2-inch floppies. Most PC users and software manuals differentiate one format from other formats by using the byte-capacity figure for the desired format. Each new version of DOS has maintained support for disk formats supported by its predecessors. This support ensures that disks made with older drive formats can be used with current versions of DOS.

Floppy Disk Formats

The first DOS-supported disk drives allowed for double the number of tracks on a 5 1/4-inch floppy disk than the standard 5 1/4-inch disk formats of the time. These DOS formats were called *double-density* formats. The original PC disk size and format was 5 1/4-inch, single-sided, 40 tracks, with 8 sectors per track and 512 bytes per sector. These disks are called *single-sided, double-density* (*SSDD*) disks. The capacity of this 8-sector, single-sided format is 160K (K equals 1,024 bytes).

Technical Note: Computers generally store data in groups of 8 bits. The 9-bit group of data is called a *byte*. By design, digital computers are most efficient when working with numbers as some power of 2. Numbers that are powers of 2 can be represented directly in binary notation.

Computer programmers and designers apply this power-of-2 convention to the expression of a quantity of bytes. A kilobyte, for example, is 2^{10} or 1,024 bytes. 2 kilobytes = 2,048 bytes or 2K. A megabyte, or 1M, equals 1,024K. It's not important for you to know about numbers in the power of 2 except to note that capacity in kilobytes or megabytes has this 1,024 rather than 1,000 multiplier. For scaling purposes, you can think of 1K as approximately 1,000 bytes.

The capacity of disk drives is stated in bytes as either kilobytes or megabytes. The storage capacity of a hard disk is in the order of millions of bytes; megabyte is the usual capacity descriptor. The capacity of floppies is in the order of hundreds of thousands to slightly more than a million bytes. Both kilobyte (K) and megabyte (M) can be used as a multiplier to describe the capacity of a floppy.

The early single-sided format was extended by making the disk format double-sided in DOS 1.1. All floppies are double-sided in the sense that they have two sides. The term *double-sided* in the formatting sense means that data is recorded on both sides of the disk. Only drives equipped with a second head can accommodate double-sided recording. To differentiate these two-sided disks from disks that used only one side for storage, disk makers called them *double-sided, double-density* (*DSDD*) disks. Clearly, by using both sides for storing data, the format capacity doubled—to 320K. Today a PC with a single-sided disk drive is rare. Most 5 1/4-inch floppy drives are equipped with two heads.

As disk drives became more sophisticated in design and great improvements were made to magnetic materials, the number of sectors per track was increased from 8 to 9 in DOS 2, with no reliability problems. Both DSDD and SSDD formats were given the extra sector per track. This new format, which could store more data than the earlier DSDD and SSDD formats, quickly became popular with users. The single-sided, 9-sector version has a capacity of 180K; the double-sided version has a capacity of 360K. To differentiate between the DSDD and SSDD 8-sector formats and these DSDD and SSDD 9-sector formats, think of the former as DSDD-8 and SSDD-8 and the latter as DSDD-9 and SSDD-9.

The evolution of DOS to Version 3.0 provided for disks with four times (quadruple) the number of tracks of those early standard disks. These 80-track *quad-density* formats were applied to 5 1/4-inch disks as well as to the newer 3 1/2-inch disks. DOS provided one quad-density format of 9 sectors per track, used primarily on 3 1/2-inch disks. This quad-density, 9-sector format is called QD-9. The QD-9 disk capacity is 720K. Another quad-density, high-capacity quad format of 15 sectors per track, is used primarily on 5 1/4-inch drives. The quad-density, 15-sector format is called *HC* (for high capacity), even though it can be referred to just as properly as *QD-15*. The QD-15 format, with a capacity of 1.2M, was popularized by the IBM PC/AT.

For 3 1/2-inch disks, DOS 3.3 added a high-capacity format that supports the 80-track quad density but provides 18 sectors per track. This high-capacity format offers 1.44M of storage space from a microfloppy. This QD-18 format is sometimes called 3 1/2-inch HC. Boxes of disks intended for formatting to 18 sectors per track are usually labeled HD, for high density.

In DOS 5, the latest version of DOS, a still higher-capacity format for 3 1/2-inch disks, offers 2.88M of storage. This newest format provides 36 sectors per track on 80-track quad-density microfloppies. To use this new format, however, you must have a floppy disk drive, as well as disks manufactured specifically to achieve the 2.88M storage capacity.

Table 6.3 summarizes the common floppy disk formats. Chapter 7 explains the details of the FORMAT command.

Raw Capacity and Usable Capacity

The process of formatting a blank disk places on the disk some data that is not part of the disk's total capacity. A 1.44M disk, for example, holds more than 1.44M bytes of information. You cannot use this extra space, however;

it's the space used by the sector-identification and error-checking information. If you buy disks for a 1.44M drive, the disk's identification label may say that the disk has a 2M capacity. Disks for a 720K drive may indicate a 1M capacity.

Table 6.3
DOS Floppy Disk Formats

Format	Tracks	Sectors/Track	Total Sectors	Usable Capacity
SSDD	40	8	320	160K
DSDD	40	8	640	320K
SSDD-9	40	9	360	180K
DSDD-9	40	9	720	360K
QD-9	80	9	1420	720K
QD-15	80	15	2400	1.2M
QD-18	80	18	2880	1.44M
QD-36	80	36	5760	2.88M

To understand this apparent discrepancy, you need to understand the difference between total, or raw, capacity and usable, or formatted, capacity. The larger of the two numbers for the same disk is considered the *raw capacity* of the disk. Raw capacity includes the space the formatting information will use at format time. The smaller of the two numbers for the same disk is the *usable capacity* of the disk. This number of bytes is available for storing files after the formatting information has been put on the disk.

Fortunately, most hard disk manufacturers state the capacity of their drives as the formatted capacity. Hard disks also lose some overhead space. If you have any doubt as to the meaning of a hard disk's stated capacity, ask the dealer whether the capacity is determined before or after formatting. In this book, disk capacity refers to usable capacity after formatting.

Hard Disk Drive Formats

Formats for hard disks nearly always employ 512-byte sectors, usually with 17 sectors per track. *Run-length limited* (RLL) drives employ 26 sectors per track, and *enhanced small device interface* (ESDI) drives ordinarily use 34,

35, or 36 sectors per track. You can understand the concept of hard disk capacity by remembering the concept of cylinders. Hard disks, you may recall, have two or more heads. Remember that a cylinder is the alignment of all the heads on the same track on both sides of each platter. A disk with 306 tracks on one side of one platter has 306 cylinders. The total number of tracks on the disk is the number of cylinders times the number of heads. The disk's capacity in bytes is the number of tracks times the number of sectors per track, times the number of bytes per sector. To obtain the capacity in kilobytes, divide the result by 1,024. To obtain the capacity in megabytes, divide the kilobyte total by 1,024. For approximations of capacity in megabytes, you can divide by a rounded 1,000.

DOS does not provide the low-level format data for a hard disk as it does for a floppy disk. Hard disks normally are given a low-level format at the factory. End users seldom need to initiate a low-level format on a hard disk. DOS uses the low-level format as a base upon which to perform its high-level format. In a discussion of hard disk formatting, the term *format* refers to the high-level format initiated by the DOS FORMAT command. During the formatting of a hard disk, DOS initializes its bookkeeping tables and then writes "dummy" data into the disk's tracks. From your point of view, formatting a hard disk is the same basic operation as formatting a floppy. DOS keeps the details of the low-level format hidden and out of your way.

TIP

Tip: Sometimes the alignment of a hard disk's read/write heads can drift slightly after continual use. This drifting does not affect the information that has been written to the disk, but can make it difficult for the heads to locate the information because the low-level format identification information, which is needed to find the data, is no longer aligned beneath the heads. This problem can be eliminated by doing a low-level format of the disk to align the low-level disk tracks with the current location of the heads.

Normally, performing a low-level format of your hard disk erases all existing data. But third-party software is available to do a low-level format without losing data. The best known product of this type is SpinRite II, from Gibson Research Corporation, Laguna Hills, CA.

Table 6.4 shows some typical hard disk formats. An increasing number of hard disk capacities are being used in PCs.

Table 6.4
Hard Disk Formats

Typical Disk	Sectors/Track	Heads	Cylinders	Capacity
IBM PC/XT	17	4	306	10M
IBM AT	17	4	615	20M
IBM AT (Late Model)	17	5	733	30M
IBM PS/2 Model 60	36	7	583	70M

Trying Some Disk Commands

To get some hands-on practice with disks, try the commands in the following sections. You will learn a few disk commands and some other common DOS commands. The exercises will build on your knowledge of commands from the last chapter and help reinforce the information about disks and files presented in this chapter.

Determining Your DOS Version with VER

Not all PCs run the same version of DOS. DOS has evolved through five major versions with minor version changes along the way. Not all commands are available in all versions, nor do all commands work exactly the same in all versions. Being able to determine exactly which version you have is useful. DOS includes the VER command to help you to do just that.

VER, one of the DOS commands with no parameters or switches, is easy to learn and use. VER is an internal command built into COMMAND.COM. Because VER is internal, COMMAND.COM does not have to find the VER program on the DOS disk (or in the DOS subdirectory).

Clearly, you need to boot DOS on your PC before you can issue any commands. If you haven't started your PC, do so now. If you are uncertain about how to boot, check back to Chapter 3. If you want to perform a warm boot (reboot) using a floppy disk system, remember to put the working DOS disk into drive A and press Ctrl-Alt-Del.

Issuing VER is easy. When you see the DOS prompt, simply enter the command as follows:

VER

Don't forget to press Enter to send the command line to DOS. DOS will report which version of DOS you used to boot the PC. What you see on the screen will look something like this:

```
IBM DOS Version 5.00
```

If you have a PC manufactured by a company other than IBM, DOS is referred to as MS-DOS. For example, if you have a Toshiba brand PC, you may see something like the following:

```
Toshiba MS-DOS Version 5.00
```

In both of these VER reports, you see a manufacturer's name and the DOS version number. The VER report, like the output of many DOS commands, may vary slightly.

> *Note:* When you boot with one version of DOS and then, later in the session, use the external commands from another version, DOS may object with an error message. Implementations and versions of DOS often don't mix because of slight differences. If you get a `Wrong DOS Version` message, chances are good that you've booted one version and used an external command from another version.

Clearing the Screen with CLS

When you issue a series of DOS commands, your screen soon can become cluttered with output text. You occasionally may want to clear the screen before issuing the next command. Just use the internal CLS command to do the job.

Like VER, CLS command line has no parameters or switches. Simply type the following command and press Enter:

CLS

DOS clears the screen and places the command prompt and cursor in the upper left corner of the screen.

Copying an Entire Disk with DISKCOPY

Copying one disk (a source disk) to another disk (the target or destination disk) is a practical and useful exercise. DISKCOPY is the external DOS command that carries out the exercise. DISKCOPY makes an exact copy of a source disk. DISKCOPY is an ideal command to use when you need to make a copy of a disk, such as a master applications program disk. DOS provides other commands to copy the contents of one disk to another (you learn more about these commands in Part II), but DISKCOPY is the only disk-level copy command offered by DOS.

When you use DISKCOPY, you copy the format and content of the source disk. DISKCOPY uses the formatted capacity of a source disk to determine whether the destination disk is the same format. If you have a 360K-source disk, you must copy it to a 360K-destination disk. A 1.2M floppy will DISKCOPY only to a 1.2M floppy.

DISKCOPY is a floppy-disk-only command—it won't copy a hard disk. Don't worry about harming your hard disk with DISKCOPY in an errant command line. DISKCOPY issues an error message if the disks involved in the operation aren't compatible, but the command won't hurt a hard disk.

DISKCOPY is an external command that you load from disk. You must have the disk that contains DISKCOPY in your current drive or set the correct path with the PATH command (see Chapter 8 for information about PATH). Use the DISKCOPY command to copy floppies only.

The complete correct syntax for DISKCOPY is as follows:

DISKCOPY *sd: dd:* */1 /V*

sd: represents the optional name for the drive that holds the disk you want to copy; this drive is called the *source* drive. *dd:* is the optional name of the drive that holds the disk to receive the copy. This *destination* drive is sometimes called the *target* drive (see fig. 6.8). If you don't specify any drive name, DOS assumes that you want to use the current drive. DOS prompts you to insert and remove source and destination disks as necessary.

The */1* switch causes DOS to copy only the first side of a double-sided disk. The */V* switch instructs DOS to verify that the copy and the original are identical.

As always, type a colon (:) after the drive name. COMMAND.COM needs the colon as an indicator that you are naming a drive as a specifier. Insert a space between the source and destination drive names. The space delimits the source and destination drive parameters. If you use a blank, unformatted disk as the destination disk, DOS first formats it. An example of the DISKCOPY command follows:

DISKCOPY A: B:

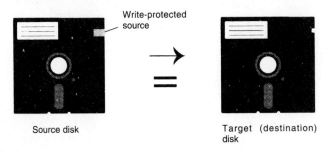

Source disk   Target (destination) disk

Fig. 6.8. The DISKCOPY command makes an exact copy of another disk.

After you issue the DISKCOPY command, DOS prompts you to put the disk(s) into the proper drives (see fig. 6.9). Make sure that you put the disks into the correct drives. Write-protect the source disk (by placing a tab over the write-protect notch on a 5 1/4-inch disk or by opening the write-protect slide on a 3 1/2-inch disk) to safeguard its contents in case of a disk mix-up.

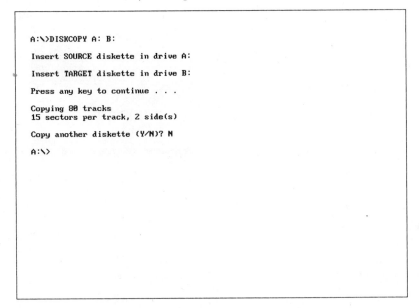

```
A:\>DISKCOPY A: B:

Insert SOURCE diskette in drive A:

Insert TARGET diskette in drive B:

Press any key to continue . . .

Copying 80 tracks
15 sectors per track, 2 side(s)

Copy another diskette (Y/N)? N

A:\>
```

Fig. 6.9. A typical DISKCOPY command sequence and messages from DOS.

When the disks are in place, you are ready to continue. Press a key to start the disk-copy process. When the process finishes, DOS asks whether you want to make another copy. Press Y to copy another disk or N to exit the command.

If you leave out the drive names in the DISKCOPY command line, DOS uses the current drive as the specifier. To avoid confusion, you always can provide both the source and destination drive names.

If the drives or disks are not compatible, you get an error message, and nothing is copied (see fig. 6.10).

```
A:\>DISKCOPY A: B:

Insert SOURCE diskette in drive A

Insert TARGET diskette in drive B

Press any key to continue . . .

Copying 80 tracks
15 sectors per track, 2 side(s)

Formatting while copying

Drive types or diskette types
not compatible

Copy process ended

Copy another diskette (Y/N)? N

A:\>
```

Fig. 6.10. An error message produced by the DISKCOPY command.

If you issue the DISKCOPY command with no drive parameters, DOS uses the current drive to do the copying. DOS prompts you to insert the source and destination disks alternately. Depending on your system's memory, you will swap disks once or several time. Make sure that you don't get the disks confused as you swap them. Be sure to write-protect the source disk to ensure that you don't accidentally overwrite the original data.

Note: The designers of DOS provided a way for PCs with only one floppy drive to work with source and destination disks. Many DOS commands, such as DISKCOPY, COPY, and DISKCOMP, treat the single drive as though it were two—these commands divide their operation into two phases. If you have one floppy drive (even if you have a hard disk) and you issue the command **DISKCOPY A: B:**, DOS reads the source disk from the floppy drive as drive A and then asks you to insert the destination disk for drive B. On a single floppy drive system, drive B is really drive A. Even though you have one physical drive, DOS treats it logically as two. DOS can use the drive name B: for some commands by viewing the single drive logically. Your part in the one-drive-as-two operation is to ensure that you insert the correct disk into the drive when DOS prompts you. DOS keeps the identity of the drive straight internally.

Comparing Disks with DISKCOMP

You can confirm that two disks are identical by using the external command DISKCOMP. DISKCOMP compares each track of one disk to each track of another disk, sector by sector. Like DISKCOPY, DISKCOMP is a floppy-only command. You cannot use DISKCOMP to compare two hard disks. The disks and capacities must be the same for both disks in the comparison. Any difference in disks made with DISKCOPY is a sign of a problem disk. One practical use of DISKCOMP is to compare a master disk included with an applications software package to a working copy; DISKCOMP will confirm whether the working copy is good.

The DISKCOMP command compares two disks of equal size and capacity to confirm that both are the same. Normally, you use DISKCOMP to test disks that were made from originals using the DISKCOPY command. Because DISKCOMP doesn't write any information to either disk, both disks can be write-protected. If the disks are identical, DOS displays the message Compare OK.

The syntax for DISKCOMP is similar to that of DISKCOPY. Just as with DISKCOPY, one drive can act logically as two. Issue the command in the following form:

DISKCOMP *d1: d2:* /1 /8

Because the disks are being compared, not copied, they are referred to as *d1:* and *d2:* rather than source and destination. The drive specifiers *d1:* and *d2:* are optional. Load the two disks at the DOS prompt; DOS confirms the comparison or points out the differences. The /1 switch causes DOS to compare only the first sides of the disks. The /8 switch compares only the first 8 sectors of each track on the disks. As with DISKCOPY, when the first compare operation is completed, DOS asks whether you want to compare another disk.

An example of the DISKCOMP command is as follows:

DISKCOMP A: B:

Again, if you omit a drive designator, DOS uses the current drive.

In the sequence shown in figure 6.11, a working copy of a master disk is compared to the original master. Notice the compare errors. The working copy is no longer reliable, or other files have been added to the disk since DISKCOPY was first used to make a working copy from the master. The best way to solve the problem is to make a new working copy.

```
A:\>DISKCOMP A: B:

Insert FIRST diskette in drive A:

Insert SECOND diskette in drive B:

Press any key to continue . . .

Comparing 80 tracks
15 sectors per track, 2 side(s)

Compare error on
side 0, track 0

Compare error on
side 0, track 3

Compare another diskette (Y/N)? N

A:\>
```

Fig. 6.11. Comparing a working copy of a master disk to the original disk.

If you issue the DISKCOMP command with no drive parameters, DOS carries out the comparison using just one drive. DOS prompts you to insert the first and second disks alternately. Depending on your system's memory, you will swap disks once or several time. By entering DISKCOMP alone, without parameters, you tell DOS to use the current floppy drive even if your system has two. Make sure that you don't mix up the disks when you're swapping them. If you don't keep track of which disk DOS wants in the drive, you may end up comparing part of a disk to itself.

Summary

In this chapter, you have read about drives, disks, and files. You have learned about the internal DOS commands VER and CLS and the external disk-level commands DISKCOPY and DISKCOMP. Following are the key points covered in this chapter:

- DOS organizes files into a file system that DOS manages.

- Disks are the main storage media of a DOS-based PC.

- Files are the storage units of disks.

- All files have names of up to eight characters to the left of a period and up to three characters to the right of the period. File-name characters must be "legal" to DOS.

- DOS tracks file names in a disk directory. Each file name in a directory must be unique.

- By convention, certain file names refer to specific types of files. You can override file-naming conventions, but observing these conventions helps keep file names more meaningful.

- DOS uses one of its standard devices when you use a file name that contains the device name. You should avoid using the names PRN, CON, NUL, LPT, and COM in file names.

- During formatting, DOS divides disks into tracks, cylinders, and sectors. A disk's storage capacity is governed by the total number of sectors on the disk.

- Typical floppy-disk storage capacities are 360K, 720K, 1.2M, 1.44M, and 2.88M. Each floppy drive is designed to work optimally at one of these capacities.

- The VER command reports which DOS version you are using.

- The CLS command clears the screen.

- The DISKCOPY command is an external command that makes a mirror-image copy of a source disk.

- The DISKCOMP command is an external command that compares two disks for equality and reports any comparison errors.

The next chapter begins Part II of this book, which introduces many DOS commands and some additional file-system concepts. Part I has given you a foundation. You may want to review some of the concepts and rules presented in Part I as you work through Part II.

Part II

Putting DOS To Work for You

Includes

Understanding Disk Preparation and Management

Understanding Hierarchical Directories

Managing Directories

Keeping Files in Order

Understanding Backups and the Care of Data

Understanding Disk Preparation and Management

I n Chapter 6, you learned the basics of using disks and files in DOS. This chapter builds on that knowledge and introduces useful disk-related DOS commands from both the DOS Shell and the command line. You learn about preparing blank floppy disks and hard disks, assigning volume labels, transferring the system files, and analyzing disks for problems.

Key Terms Used in This Chapter

Format	Initial preparation of a disk for data storage
Volume label	A name that identifies a particular disk
Track	A circular section of a disk's surface that holds data
Sector	A section of a track that acts as the disk's smallest storage unit
Disk partition	A division of a hard disk that DOS sees as an individual area of access

Logical drive	A partitioned section of a hard disk that DOS views as an additional hard disk
Boot sector	A special area in track 0 of each DOS disk. DOS uses the boot sector to record important information about a disk's format. DOS later uses this information when working with the disk.
Internal command	A DOS command that is built into COMMAND.COM
External command	A DOS command whose instructions are stored in a separate file (that is, a file other than COMMAND.COM)

Understanding Disk Preparation

Even though floppy disks and audio cassette tapes both use magnetic media to store information, in some ways, disk and tapes are not alike. You can't just drop a disk into a disk drive and use it. You must prepare disks electronically before you can store information on them. This electronic preparation process is called *formatting*.

DOS's FORMAT command performs this preparation process for disks. You do nothing more than enter the command. FORMAT analyzes a disk for defects, generates a root directory, sets up a storage table, and makes other technical modifications.

Think of unformatted and formatted disks as being comparable to unlined and lined sheets of paper (see fig. 7.1). The lines on a sheet of paper provide you with an orderly way to record written information. The lines also act as a guide for whoever reads the information. New (unformatted) disks are like unlined sheets of paper to DOS.

When you format a disk, DOS *encodes*, or programs, data-storage divisions on the disk's surface. As you learned in Chapter 6, these divisions are concentric circles called *tracks* (see fig. 7.2). DOS decides what type of drive you have and then positions the tracks accordingly. DOS also writes on the disk's first track—track 0—data that records the vital information about the disk's format. Later, DOS can quickly read this information to determine how to work with the disk.

Fig. 7.1. Formatted disks are comparable to lined paper.

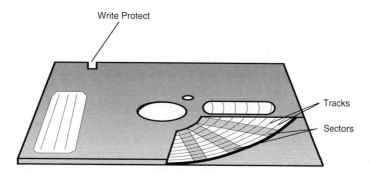

Fig. 7.2. Anatomy of a microfloppy disk.

As you can see from figure 7.2, each track is divided into segments called *sectors*. DOS stores data in the sectors and uses the track number and sector number to retrieve the data. DOS commands use tracks and sectors as road maps to carry out their operations. DOS tracks the use of the sectors in a special disk table called the *file allocation table (FAT)*. The FAT logs every sector on a disk. One of FORMAT's primary responsibilities is to set up the disk's FAT in track 0. Based on the capacity of the disk (and the version of DOS), the FAT may track a disk's sectors in units of multiple sectors called *clusters*. A cluster is DOS's minimum file allocation unit.

A standard 5 1/4-inch double-density floppy disk (one that holds 360K of data) has 40 tracks per side. Quad-density 5 1/4-inch disks (1.2M) and both double-density and high-density microfloppy disks (720K and 1.44M) have 80 tracks per side. DOS provides for FATs and directories to accommodate the relative capacities of disks.

Formatting disks will become a routine job for you, but always be careful during the process. Formatting potentially erases all information from a disk. As a general rule, if you format a disk you have already used, everything stored on that disk disappears. Be careful not to format a disk that contains files you want to keep.

 DOS 5 introduces a new, more forgiving FORMAT command. In most cases, a disk formatted with DOS 5 can be unformatted (using the UNFORMAT command), but only if you unformat before creating or copying files onto the disk you inadvertently formatted.

One way to avoid formatting a disk by accident is to label your disks, using the paper labels supplied with the disks. Another precaution is to write-protect 5 1/4-inch disks with a tab or to open the write-protect slide window on 3 1/2-inch disks. In any case, before you try to format a previously used disk, use the DIR command to see which files are on the disk and determine whether you want to lose them.

Understanding the FORMAT Command

Note: With some external commands, like FORMAT, DOS prompts you to place the proper disk into the drive before the command is carried out. If you have a floppy disk system, you can remove the DOS working copy that contains the FORMAT program, insert the disk to be formatted, and press any key. Hard disk systems normally are set up to search for and load an external command from a directory on the hard disk. Chapter 8 explains this process.

The FORMAT command prepares disks for use as external data storage media. Neither floppy disks nor hard disks can be used until they have been formatted. You also can format disks that have already been formatted.

Before DOS 5, reformatting a disk effectively erased the data stored on the disk. In DOS 5, the FORMAT command first determines whether the disk contains data. If the disk contains data, FORMAT saves the file information to a safe place on the disk where UNFORMAT can find the information if you need to unformat the disk. You can unformat a disk formatted with DOS 5, but only if you have not created or copied other files onto the disk.

The DOS 5 FORMAT command clears the disk's file allocation table (FAT) and the first character from each file name in the root directory but does not erase any data. (The program does scan the entire disk for bad sectors.) FORMAT then saves the first letter of each file name to a safe place on the disk.

Caution: FORMAT is one of the DOS commands that quickly can wipe out the entire contents of a disk. Even though FORMAT is safer in DOS 5 than in earlier versions, before you use the FORMAT command, make sure that you are familiar with its syntax. FORMAT issues warning messages on-screen and prompts you for verification before formatting a hard disk. Get in the habit of exercising extreme care when you use FORMAT, especially if your version of DOS is earlier than DOS 5. Read the screen prompts, and keep backups of your data.

Formatting Floppy Disks

The process of formatting floppy disks from the DOS Shell is different from that of formatting them from the command line. Both methods are described in the sections that follow.

DOS also provides several formatting options through command-line switches. See "Using FORMAT's Switches," later in this chapter, for a discussion of formatting disks using the switches.

Before you begin, you should have a floppy disk you can format. Mixing formatted disks with unformatted disks is easy when you are working with a fresh box of disks. To avoid a mix-up, place an indicator on the label of each disk you format. The indicator may be as simple as a dot, a check mark, or the letter *F* for "Formatted." For these exercises, the indicator is the literal identifier—the word *Formatted*.

To format a floppy disk, write *Formatted* on the label, and follow the directions for your system. Boot from the hard disk, or insert the DOS Startup disk into drive A, boot your computer, and follow the subsequent directions for your system.

Formatting a Disk through the DOS Shell

Perhaps the easiest way to use the FORMAT command is through the DOS Shell. Follow these steps:

1. If the Shell is not already loaded, type **DOSSHELL** at the command prompt, and press Enter. The DOS Shell window appears on your screen.

2. Select Disk Utilities from the program list area. The Shell displays the Disk Utilities program group list, shown in figure 7.3

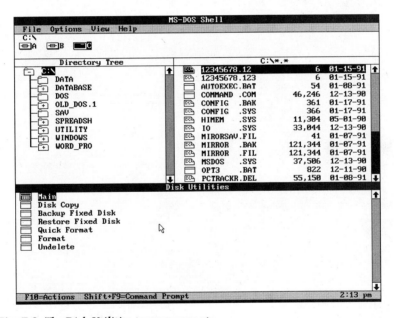

Fig. 7.3. The Disk Utilities program group.

3. Select Format from the program list area, to display the Format dialog box shown in figure 7.4.

   Notice that the Parameters text box contains the default entry a:.

4. To format a disk in your A drive, click the mouse pointer on the OK command button, or press Enter. (To format a disk in a drive other than drive A or to use one or more of the FORMAT command switches, see this chapter's "Using FORMAT's Switches" section. Type the appropriate FORMAT command parameters in the Parameters text box.)

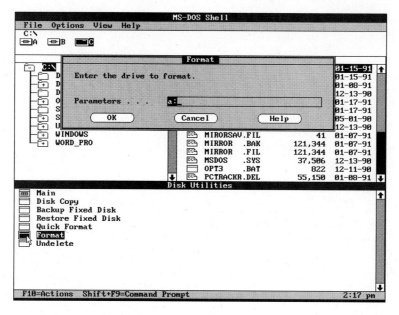

Fig. 7.4. *The Format dialog box.*

> **Tip:** To display a help screen that lists all available parameters for the FORMAT command, type /? in the Parameters text box, and then press Enter.

After you click OK or press Enter at the Format dialog box, the Shell clears the screen and then displays the following prompt at the top of the screen:

```
Insert new diskette for drive A:
and press ENTER when ready...
```

5. Remove any disk that may be in drive A and insert the disk labeled *Formatted*. Press Enter to cause DOS to format the disk.

The messages displayed during the formatting process vary a bit, depending on whether you are formatting a new disk or a previously formatted one. When you press Enter at the prompt, the program displays the message `Checking existing disk format`. If the disk has not yet been formatted, a message similar to the following appears on the next line of the screen:

```
Formatting 1.44M
```

If you are formatting a previously formatted disk, DOS displays messages similar to the following as the formatting process begins:

```
Checking existing disk format
Saving UNFORMAT information
Verifying 1.44M
```

DOS is performing a "safe" format so that you can unformat the disk later (by using the UNFORMAT command). The disk capacity stated depends on the capacity of the disk drive you are using and the density of the media (topics discussed in Chapter 6).

As DOS begins to format the disk, the indicator on the drive glows, and DOS indicates progress as a percentage. When 100 percent of the disk is formatted, DOS displays the message

```
Format complete
Volume label (11 characters, ENTER for none)?
```

You can give the disk a volume name of up to 11 characters, or you can press Enter to omit the volume name.

Finally, by displaying messages similar to the following, DOS tells you about the disk's formatted capacity:

```
1457664    bytes total disk space
1457664    bytes available on disk

    512    bytes in each allocation unit
   2047    allocation units available on disk

Volume Serial Number is 2628-13FD

Format another (Y/N)?
```

Press Y and then Enter to format another disk, or press N and then Enter to quit. DOS then displays the message

```
Press any key to return to MS-DOS Shell...
```

Pressing a key on the keyboard causes DOS to display the DOS Shell window. To return to the Main program list, press Esc or click the Main program list icon.

Note: The DOS 5 FORMAT command differs significantly from earlier versions of the command. Previous versions of FORMAT write the hexadecimal value F6 to every data byte in a floppy disk, erasing all existing data. The DOS 5 FORMAT command, on the other hand, performs a "safe" format of both hard and floppy disks. The program first determines whether a disk has already been formatted. If the disk has been formatted, FORMAT clears the FAT, root directory, and boot record but does not erase any data. Then, after scanning the entire disk for bad sectors, FORMAT saves a copy of the FAT, root directory, and boot record to a safe place on the disk where the UNFORMAT command can find them. The file that contains this information is called the *MIRROR-image file*.

If the disk has not yet been formatted, FORMAT overwrites every data byte with the hexadecimal value F6. If you want FORMAT to overwrite all data on a previously formatted disk, use the /U switch, discussed in this chapter's "Performing an Unconditional Format."

Performing a Quick Format from the DOS Shell

Sometimes you want to clear all data from a disk without having to wait for the standard formatting procedure to run. DOS 5 provides a new formatting option—Quick Format—that enables you to reformat a disk quickly. This option is available from both the DOS Shell and the command line.

To quick-format a disk from the DOS Shell, use the following procedure:

1. If the Shell is not already loaded, type **DOSSHELL** at the command prompt and press Enter. The DOS Shell window appears on your screen.

2. Select Disk Utilities from the program list area. The Shell displays the Disk Utilities program group list (again see fig. 7.3).

3. Select Quick Format from the program list area to display the Quick Format dialog box shown in figure 7.5.

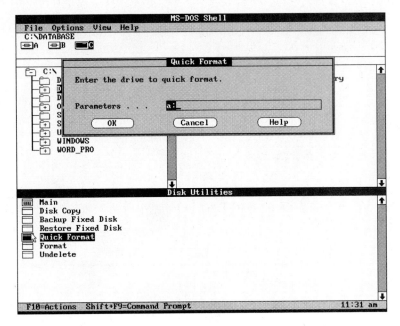

Fig. 7.5. The Quick Format dialog box.

Here, as in the Format dialog box, the Shell displays a Parameters text box that contains the default entry a:.

4. To quick-format a disk in the A drive, click the mouse pointer on the OK command button, or press Enter. To quick-format a disk in another drive, type the drive letter, followed by a colon (:), and press Enter.

The Shell first clears the screen and then displays the following prompt at the top of the screen:

```
Insert new diskette for drive A:
and press ENTER when ready...
```

5. Remove any disk that may be in drive A, and insert the disk you want DOS to quick-format. Press Enter.

DOS displays the following series of messages:

```
Checking existing disk format
Saving UNFORMAT information
QuickFormatting 1.44M
```

DOS performs a "safe" quick format, like the one discussed in the preceding section. The disk capacity stated depends on the capacity of the disk drive you are using and the density of the media (refer to Chapter 6).

After the disk has been formatted, DOS displays the series of messages discussed in the preceding section. DOS then asks whether you want to

```
QuickFormat another (Y/N)?
```

Press Y and then Enter to format another disk, or press N and then Enter to quit. DOS then displays the following message:

```
Press any key to return to MS-DOS Shell...
```

Pressing a key on the keyboard causes DOS to return to the DOS Shell window. To return to the Main program list, press Esc or click the Main icon.

> *Note:* The DOS Shell's Quick Format and Format options, listed in the Disk Utilities program group, both perform a "safe" format. Quick Format is faster than Format because Quick Format does not scan the entire disk for bad sectors.

Formatting a Disk from the Command Line

FORMAT is an external command—a program that is not loaded automatically each time you start your computer. COMMAND.COM must load FORMAT from one of your system's disk drives. Therefore, before you can use FORMAT from the command line, the current disk and directory must contain the program FORMAT.COM, or the directory that contains your DOS program files (including FORMAT.COM) must be in your system's path. (See Chapter 8 for a discussion of PATH).

> *Note:* The DOS 5 Setup program inserts into your system's AUTOEXEC.BAT file a command that ensures that all DOS external commands are in the system's path.

The complete syntax for the FORMAT command is as follows:

FORMAT d: */Q/V:label/F:size/S/B/U/1/4/8/N:sectors/T:tracks*

All the FORMAT switches are discussed in this chapter's "Using FORMAT's Switches."

To format a floppy disk from the command line (without using any switches), display the DOS command prompt and perform the following steps:

1. To format a disk that is in drive A, type **FORMAT A:** and press Enter. To format a disk in another drive, type the appropriate drive letter in place of *A*.

   After you type the command to format the disk, you see a message similar to the following:

   ```
   Insert new diskette for drive A:
   and press ENTER when ready
   ```

2. Remove any disk that may be in drive A, insert the disk labeled *Formatted*, and press Enter to begin the formatting process.

The messages displayed during the formatting process are the same as those described in "Formatting a Disk through the DOS Shell."

> *Caution:* Versions of DOS earlier than Version 3.0 do not require you to specify the drive that holds the disk you want to format. In these early versions, if you issue the FORMAT command with no drive parameter, DOS formats the current disk (which may be the working copy of DOS). If you have write-protected the DOS working copy, FORMAT cannot format the DOS disk.

Looking at FORMAT's Reports

The primary purpose of FORMAT is to divide the disk into logical storage sectors, but this task is not the command's only purpose. Both during and after the formatting process, FORMAT issues several reports. Versions of DOS earlier than DOS 4.0 show the track and sector numbers as formatting takes place. With DOS 4.0 or later versions, the FORMAT command provides a continual update of what percentage of the disk has been formatted.

When 100 percent of the disk is formatted, DOS displays the message:

```
Format complete
Volume label (11 characters, ENTER for none)?
```

You can give the disk a volume name of as many as 11 characters, or press Enter to omit the volume name.

Then FORMAT reports the disk's capacity. The report shows, in bytes, the total disk space available. If FORMAT finds *bad sectors*—spots on the disk that may not hold data reliably—FORMAT marks these sectors as unusable, and displays how many bytes are unavailable because of the bad sectors.

DOS displays the number of bytes each *allocation unit* (or *cluster*—the smallest group of sectors DOS will allocate to a file) can contain, and how many allocation units are available on the disk for storage.

The report also indicates the unique serial number—a random hexadecimal (base 16) number—DOS has assigned to the disk. DOS uses this number at different times to determine whether you have removed a disk from the disk drive and replaced it with another. The report for a 1.44M formatted disk may look like this:

```
1457664    bytes total disk space
1457664    bytes available on disk

    512    bytes in each allocation unit
   2047    allocation units available on disk

Volume Serial Number is 2628-13FD
```

The next part of the report asks:

```
Format another (Y/N)?
```

To format another disk, press Y and then press Enter. Press N to return to the DOS prompt.

Using FORMAT's Switches

To modify and add versatility to FORMAT (and many other DOS commands), you can add switch parameters. Be sure to type a slash (/) followed by the switch letter. The Command Reference section provides more details on valid switch combinations.

 DOS 5 provides an on-line help facility to help you learn the proper syntax when you enter commands at the command line. For example, if you type **FORMAT /?** or **HELP FORMAT** and press Enter, DOS displays the help screen shown in figure 7.6.

```
C:\>FORMAT /?
Formats a disk for use with MS-DOS.

FORMAT drive: [/Q] [/V:label] [/S] [/B]
FORMAT drive: [F:size] [/U] [/V:label] [/S] [/B]
FORMAT drive: [/1] [/4] [/U] [/V:label] [/S] [/B]
FORMAT drive: [/8] [/U] [/S] [/B]
FORMAT drive: [/N:sectors] [/T:tracks] [/U] [/V:label] [/S] [/B]

    /Q          Performs a quick format.
    /U          Performs an unconditional format.

    /V:label    Labels the disk as specified.
    /S          Copies operating system files to the formatted disk.
    /B          Allocates space on the formatted disk for operating system.

    /F:size     Formats specified floppy disk size (e.g., 360, 720, 1.2, 1.44).
    /N:sectors  Formats specified number of sectors per track.
    /T:tracks   Formats specified number of tracks per disk side.
    /1          Formats a single side of a floppy disk.
    /4          Formats a 360K floppy disk in a high-capacity drive.
    /8          Formats eight sectors per track.

C:\>
```

Fig. 7.6. *The FORMAT help screen.*

Most of the FORMAT commands you need to issue are simple. The average DOS user needs only a few of the command's switches. (The remaining switches provide advanced features or provide compatibility with older versions of DOS.) Table 7.1 lists the switches available with the FORMAT command.

Table 7.1
FORMAT Switches

Switch	Action
Q	Performs a quick format on a previously formatted disk; new in DOS 5
/U	Formats a disk so that it cannot be unformatted with the UNFORMAT command; new in DOS 5
/V:*label*	Causes FORMAT to label the disk being formatted with the volume label specified by the *label* parameter
/S	Produces a bootable DOS *system* disk that contains the hidden DOS system files and COMMAND.COM
/B	Reserves space on formatted disk for hidden DOS system files; creates on the formatted disk hidden files with the same names and approximately the same file size as the real system files

Switch	Action
/F:*size*	Formats a disk to the capacity specified by *size*. The possible values for *size* include the following:

160,	160K,	160KB
180,	180K,	180KB
320,	320K,	320KB
360,	360K,	360KB
720,	720K,	720KB
1200,	1200K,	1200KB, 1.2, 1.2M, 1.2MB
1440,	1440K,	1440KB,1.44, 1.44M, 1.44MB
2880,	2880K,	2880KB, 2.88, 2.88M, 2.88MB

Switch	Action
/N:*sectors*	Formats a disk with the number of sectors specified by the *sectors* parameter (number can range from 1 through 99). The disk drive, controller electronics, and the disk driver must support the specified number of sectors.
/T:*tracks*	Formats a disk to the number of tracks (per side) you specify in *tracks* (number can range from 1 through 999)
/1	Formats a disk as single-sided; ordinarily, used with the /8 switch to format 8-sector-per-track disks to be compatible with DOS 1.0 and 1.1 systems
/4	Formats a 5 1/4-inch disk with 40 tracks per side (360K) in a high-capacity (1.2M) drive; resulting disk may be unreadable by a standard 360K (double-sided, double-density) drive
/8	Formats a disk with 8 sectors per track rather than 9 or 15

The next sections describe some of the ways to use FORMAT's switches.

Performing a Quick Format

One way to clear all data from a disk is to format the disk. Because the formatting procedure can be relatively slow, DOS 5 introduces a *quick format* capability, available only when you reformat a disk that has already been formatted.

To clear data from a particular disk, type the command **FORMAT /Q** and press Enter. (For more about the Quick Format option of the FORMAT command, refer to this chapter's "Performing a Quick Format from the DOS Shell" section.)

Performing an Unconditional Format

Unless you use the /U switch, the DOS 5 FORMAT command performs a "safe" format of previously formatted disks. FORMAT first determines whether the disk has been formatted. If it has been formatted, FORMAT clears the FAT, boot record, and root directory but does not erase any data. FORMAT then scans the entire disk for bad sectors, after which FORMAT saves a copy of the FAT, boot record, and root directory to a safe place on the disk (in the MIRROR-image file) where the UNFORMAT command can find them. If the disk has not been formatted previously, FORMAT over-writes every data byte with the hexadecimal value F6.

To cause DOS to overwrite all data on a previously formatted floppy disk (called *unconditional* formatting), use the /U switch. For example, use the following command to format unconditionally a disk in the A drive:

    FORMAT A: /U

DOS then writes the hexadecimal value F6 to every sector in the disk, erasing all existing data.

> ***Note:*** All versions of DOS earlier than 5.0 *always* perform unconditional formatting on floppy disks. Most earlier versions of DOS do not overwrite all data when formatting a hard disk but do erase the FAT, root directory, and boot record. COMPAQ DOS 3.2 and earlier versions, AT&T DOS 3.1 and earlier versions, and some Burroughs DOS versions do overwrite all data, even when formatting a hard disk. All DOS versions earlier than 5.0 provide no way to unformat a disk—hard or floppy. DOS 5's FORMAT command never overwrites all data on a hard disk. Use the /U switch to overwrite all data when formatting a floppy disk.

Adding a Volume Label

DOS reserves a few bytes of data space on disks so that you can place an electronic identification—a *volume label*—on each disk. A volume label is simply a name to help you identify the disk. The function of a disk's volume label is not unlike that of a book's title.

The /V:*label* switch transfers the volume label to a formatted disk. (You substitute an 11-character name for the new disk for *label*.) As you see in this chapter, the DOS LABEL command can do the same disk-naming job.

> *Note:* DOS 4 and DOS 5 also assign a volume serial number to each formatted disk. DOS uses this number to determine whether you have changed floppy disks.

DOS 5 prompts you for a volume name when you format a disk. If you have DOS 4.0 or earlier, you must use the /V switch to assign a volume label to a floppy disk during formatting. Each time you format a disk with DOS 5, DOS prompts you for an 11-character volume name, as follows:

```
Volume label (11 characters, ENTER for none)?
```

To skip a volume name, press Enter. If you decide to type a name, comply with the following rules:

1. You can use any of the following characters in any order as a volume label:

   a. The letters *A* through *Z* and *a* through *z*

   b. The numerals 0 to 9

   c. The following special characters and punctuation symbols:

      $ # & @ ! ( ) - { } ' _ ~ ^ `

   d. A space character (DOS 3.3 and later versions)

2. Do *not* use any of the following characters in a volume label. They are *not allowed*.

   a. Any control character (ASCII 31 and lower), and the DEL character (ASCII 127)

   b. The following special characters and punctuation:

      + = / [ ] " : ; , ? * \ < > |

When you enter an illegal character in the volume label, DOS 5 displays the message `Invalid characters in volume label` and asks you to enter the volume label again. If you try to type more than 11 characters, DOS causes your computer to beep. After you type the volume name, press Enter.

Adding System Files

If you want to be able to use a disk to start your computer, the disk must contain hidden DOS system files as well as the command processor (COMMAND.COM). One way to install these system files on a disk is to use the /S switch during the formatting procedure. The /S switch reduces the disk's available storage capacity by as much as 114K.

> *Note:* Don't use the /S switch with FORMAT unless you plan to boot from the disk. Hard disk users rarely use the /S switch to format disks because a hard disk rarely needs to be reformatted.

When formatting with /S is complete, a report similar to the following report for 1.44M disk is displayed:

```
System transferred.

Volume label (11 characters, ENTER for none)?
```

Type a volume name or press Enter. DOS displays the following messages:

```
1457664   bytes total disk space
 117760   bytes used by system
1339904   bytes available on disk.

    512   bytes in each allocation unit
   2617   allocation units available on disk

Volume Serial Number is 2A50-1CD2

Format another (Y/N)?
```

If you need more than one disk that can be used to boot your computer, press Y to begin formatting another disk; press N to return to the DOS prompt. You can use the formatted disk(s) to start your computer.

To format a disk without making it bootable, reserving the option of making it bootable later, use the /B switch. This switch, in effect, reserves space for the hidden system files but does not copy COMMAND.COM to the disk.

Formatting Disks of Different Capacities

DOS provides several FORMAT switches that enable you to format floppy disks to any storage capacity supported by the operating system and your hardware.

Each floppy disk drive in your system has a maximum storage capacity. By default, DOS expects all disks formatted in a particular drive to be formatted to the drive's maximum capacity. On occasion, however, you may want to format a lower-capacity disk. For example, you may need to format a box of double-density 3 1/2-inch disks (720K) in a high-density (1.44M) 3 1/2-inch drive.

The most useful switch for formatting disks of a different capacity is the /F:size switch, available with DOS 4.0 and later versions. For example, to format a 720K disk in a 1.44M drive (the A drive), you can use the following command:

FORMAT A: /F:720

The /1 switch tells DOS to prepare a single-sided disk for use in a single-sided disk drive.

The /4 switch enables you to format a disk in a high-capacity disk drive for use in a double-sided, double-density disk drive. Use this switch to prepare a disk in your 1.2M 5 1/4-inch drive for use in a 360K drive. You need to use the /4 switch if you are formatting a disk on a 1.2M drive system, such as an AT, but are using the disk in a 360K system, such as an IBM PC-XT. If you use the /4 switch, be sure that the disk you are formatting is designed for the 360K capacity (double-density rather than high density).

> *Note:* Even though the /4 switch is provided for downward compatibility, disks prepared in this way frequently cannot be read on the 360K drive. Drive electronics are optimized for the drive's highest capacity.

/8 prepares a disk with 8 sectors per track (seldom used).

The /N and /T switches enable you to vary the *number* of *tracks* and sectors on high-capacity floppy disk drives. These switches are useful when you are preparing 720K microfloppies on a 1.44M drive with DOS 3.2 or 3.3. (DOS versions earlier than 3.2 generally do not support 3 1/2-inch drives; for DOS 4.0 and higher, use the /F:size switch instead).

The Command Reference section includes syntax for using these switches with the FORMAT command. If you need to use the less common switches, consult the Command Reference for more information.

Unformatting a Disk

Sooner or later, virtually all PC users format a disk accidentally. DOS 5's UNFORMAT command is your best hope for undoing the damage. UNFORMAT is designed to unformat hard and floppy disks. To unformat, a floppy disk must have been formatted with the DOS 5 FORMAT command. UNFORMAT does not work on floppy disks formatted with earlier versions of DOS. UNFORMAT also can help you recover from accidental change or damage to a hard disk's partition table.

Ideally, you never will need to use the UNFORMAT command. Because UNFORMAT completely rebuilds a disk's file allocation table (FAT), root directory, and boot record, you should use this command only as a last resort. If you accidentally delete a file, use the DOS 5 UNDELETE command to recover the file. If you accidentally format an entire disk, you must use UNFORMAT to try to recover the data that was on the disk. The degree of success you will have in completely recovering all files depends partly on whether and how recently you ran the MIRROR command, discussed in Chapter 15, "Configuring Your Computer and Managing Devices." Successful recovery of an accidentally formatted floppy disk also depends on which version of DOS you used when you accidentally formatted the disk.

> *Caution: Do not* install DOS on the problem hard disk—the DOS files would overwrite files you want to recover. *Do not* copy or save files of any kind to the reformatted hard disk. If you have to reboot the computer, use a bootable floppy disk.

UNFORMAT has two primary uses:

- To recover files after an accidental format
- To rebuild a damaged partition table on your hard disk

If you want to use UNFORMAT after an accidental format, the syntax is as follows:

UNFORMAT d: */J /L /P /TEST /U*

Note: The discussions that follow assume, in some cases, that you have run the MIRROR command. The MIRROR command copies your hard disk's FAT, root directory, and boot record and saves this information in a safe place on the disk. MIRROR gives this file (referred to as the *MIRROR-image file*) the name MIRROR.FIL. After MIRROR creates this file on a disk, running MIRROR again on that disk causes MIRROR to rename the existing MIRROR.FIL (calling it MIRROR.BAK) and create a new MIRROR.FIL. This change occurs every time (after the first) you run the command on that disk. MIRROR also creates a hidden file (named MIRORSAV.FIL) that contains information needed to rebuild the root directory. For a complete discussion of MIRROR, including instructions for adding the command to your AUTOEXEC.BAT file so that a MIRROR-image file is created automatically whenever you boot your computer, see Chapter 15, "Configuring Your Computer and Managing Devices."

The DOS 5 FORMAT command also creates a MIRROR-image file during the "safe" format procedure. (This file is "visible" only to the UNFORMAT command and cannot be listed by the DIR command.) If you use the /U switch with FORMAT, however, no MIRROR-image file is created.

d: is the drive that contains the disk to be unformatted.

/J causes UNFORMAT to verify that MIRROR.FIL, created by MIRROR, accurately reflects the current disk information.

/L searches a formatted disk and lists the file and directory names found.

/P sends all output to a printer.

/TEST provides a test run to indicate whether UNFORMAT can unformat a disk successfully.

/U attempts to unformat a disk without the benefit of a MIRROR-image file.

If you want to use UNFORMAT to rebuild a hard disk partition table, the syntax is as follows:

    UNFORMAT /PARTN */L /P*

/PARTN causes the command to try to rebuild the hard disk partition.

/L displays the current partition table.

/P sends all output to a printer.

The commands UNFORMAT /? and HELP UNFORMAT display a short help screen summarizing the parameters available in UNFORMAT (see fig. 7.7). Each parameter listed is explained in one of the following sections.

```
C:\>UNFORMAT /?
Rebuilds disk structure, using information saved by FORMAT or MIRROR.

UNFORMAT drive: [/J] [/L] [/P] [/TEST] [/U]
UNFORMAT /PARTN [/L] [/P]

   drive:   Drive to unformat.
   /PARTN   Restore disk partition table.
   /J       Verify that the Mirror files agree with information on disk.
   /L       List all file and directory names found, or display current
            partition table, when used with /PARTN.
   /P       Echo messages to print on LPT1:.
   /TEST    Do not write changes to disk.
   /U       Unformat without using Mirror file.

MIRROR, UNDELETE, and UNFORMAT (C) 1987-1991 Central Point Software Inc.

C:\>
```

Fig. 7.7. The UNFORMAT help screen.

Verifying the MIRROR-Image File

After running MIRROR and creating the file MIRROR.FIL, you may want to make sure that the command made a valid copy of the system information. You can use the /J switch for this purpose. For example, to verify that the MIRROR-image file created by MIRROR on drive C contains the current FAT, root directory, and boot-record information, type the following command and press Enter:

UNFORMAT A: /J

UNFORMAT first tells you to insert a disk into the specified drive and press Enter. When you follow these instructions, the computer beeps and displays the following warning message:

```
Restores the system area of your disk with
the image file created by MIRROR

    WARNING!!    WARNING!!

This should be used ONLY to recover from the inadvertent use
of the DOS FORMAT command or the DOS RECOVER command.
Any other use of UNFORMAT may cause you to lose data!
   Files modified since the last use of MIRROR may be lost.
```

Then the message `Just checking this time` is displayed. This message assures you that you are performing a test and that you can ignore the warning this time. Nothing will be written to the disk.

Next, UNFORMAT displays the following messages:

```
The LAST time MIRROR was used was at hh:mm on mm-dd-yy.
The PRIOR time MIRROR was used was at hh:mm on mm-dd-yy.

If you wish to use the LAST file as indicated
above, press 'L.' If you wish to use the PRIOR
file as indicated above, press 'P.' Press ESCAPE
to terminate UNFORMAT.
```

(For the *hh:mm* and *mm-dd-yy* in these messages, UNFORMAT substitutes the times and dates when MIRROR.FIL and MIRROR.BAK were created.) These files are the files created the last time you used MIRROR and the time before that, respectively. Type the letter **l** to cause UNFORMAT to compare the contents of MIRROR.FIL to the actual FAT and root directory on the specified disk. Type **p** to cause UNFORMAT to compare the previous MIRROR-image file to the actual system area of the disk. UNFORMAT then displays the message `The MIRROR image file has been validated.`

Finally, if UNFORMAT finds that the contents of MIRROR.FIL match the hard disk's FAT and root directory, you see the following message:

```
The SYSTEM area of drive d has been verified
to agree with the image file.
```

Otherwise, UNFORMAT displays the following message:

```
The SYSTEM area does NOT agree with the
image file.
```

When the image file, MIRROR.FIL, does not agree with the system area (the FAT, root directory, and boot record), one or more files have been changed or added since you last used the MIRROR command. If you had to use UNFORMAT now to recover from an accidental format, the files that have been changed or added would be lost.

Using the MIRROR-Image File To Recover from an Accidental Format

Suppose that you just formatted a hard disk accidentally (or used the DOS RECOVER command incorrectly—see the Command Reference for a discussion of RECOVER). You need to use UNFORMAT. Assuming that you have been using MIRROR routinely on the disk, UNFORMAT uses the information stored in the file MIRROR.FIL to restore the FAT, root directory, and boot record to the way they were when you last ran MIRROR. Files created or changed since you last ran MIRROR cannot be recovered by UNFORMAT (unless you are trying to recover from an accidental FORMAT command where you used the DOS 5 safe-format option—DOS 5's safe format also creates a MIRROR-image file).

To use the UNFORMAT command to unformat an accidentally formatted disk on which you recently have run MIRROR, type the following at the DOS prompt:

    UNFORMAT d:

(Remember that this **d** stands for *drive*.) Be sure to type the appropriate drive letter.

UNFORMAT first tells you to insert a disk into the specified drive and press Enter. When you follow these instructions, the computer beeps and displays the following warning message:

```
Restores the system area of your disk with
the image file created by MIRROR

   WARNING!              WARNING!

This should be used ONLY to recover from the inadvertent use
of the DOS FORMAT command or the DOS RECOVER command.
Any other use of UNFORMAT may cause you to lose data!
   Files modified since the last use of MIRROR may be lost.
```

Next, UNFORMAT displays the following messages:

```
The LAST time MIRROR was used was at hh:mm on mm-dd-yy.
The PRIOR time MIRROR was used was at hh:mm on mm-dd-yy.
```

```
If you wish to use the LAST file as indicated
above, press 'L.' If you wish to use the PRIOR
file as indicated above, press 'P.' Press ESCAPE
to terminate UNFORMAT.
```

For the *hh:mm* and *mm-dd-yy* in these messages, UNFORMAT substitutes the times and dates when MIRROR.FIL and MIRROR.BAK were created. These files are the files created the last time you ran MIRROR and the time before that, respectively. Type the letter **l** to cause UNFORMAT to use MIRROR.FIL to rebuild the formatted disk. If you inadvertently issued MIRROR after you accidentally formatted the disk, type **p** to use MIRROR.BAK instead (because MIRROR.FIL will contain the newly formatted system area rather than the system area as it existed before the format).

After you type **l** or **p**, UNFORMAT again causes your computer to beep and then displays the following messages:

```
The MIRROR image file has been validated.

Are you SURE you want to update the SYSTEM area
of your drive d (Y/N)?
```

UNFORMAT substitutes the correct drive letter for *d*.

Press Y to indicate that you want to continue updating the system area of the formatted disk, or press N to quit UNFORMAT and return to the command prompt.

If you choose to update the system area, UNFORMAT writes to the disk's system area the FAT, root directory, and boot record that have been stored in MIRROR.FIL (or MIRROR.BAK). This operation unformats the disk and recovers all files except those added or changed since the last time you used MIRROR.

For example, suppose that someone in your office accidentally formats drive C, a hard disk that has been protected by MIRROR. You can use UNFORMAT to restore the disk to the way it was when MIRROR was last issued. Type the following command at the DOS prompt:

UNFORMAT C:

At the prompt, type the letter **l** to cause UNFORMAT to use MIRROR.FIL to restore drive C. Then, when UNFORMAT asks whether you are sure you want to do this, type **Y**. UNFORMAT uses MIRROR.FIL to rewrite the FAT and root directory, restoring the hard disk to the way it was the last time you issued the MIRROR command.

Recovering from an Accidental Format without a MIRROR-Image File

Even if a MIRROR-image file is not available for a formatted disk, the UNFORMAT command may be able to recover most of the data. This process takes more time than if a MIRROR-image file were available, however.

If you use UNFORMAT to try to unformat an accidentally formatted hard disk on which there is no current MIRROR-image file, the syntax is as follows:

UNFORMAT d: /U /L /TEST /P

Replace the **d:** with the drive designator of the accidentally formatted hard disk. The /U parameter stands for "unformat" and tells UNFORMAT that you are not using a MIRROR-image file created by MIRROR or FORMAT. The optional /L parameter causes UNFORMAT to list on the screen all files and directories found during the UNFORMAT operation. Similarly, /P causes UNFORMAT to send the entire UNFORMAT process to your printer. Use the /TEST option to run a simulation of the process so that you can see which files UNFORMAT can recover before you cause any changes to be written to the hard disk.

After you execute the command, UNFORMAT displays the following messages:

```
CAUTION !!

This attempts to recover all files lost after a
FORMAT, assuming you've NOT been using MIRROR. This
method cannot guarantee complete recovery of your
files.

The search-phase is safe: nothing is altered on the
disk.
You'll be prompted again before changes are written to
the Disk.

Using drive d:

Are you SURE you want to do this?
If so, type in 'Y'; anything else cancels.
```

To continue with the unformat operation, press Y and then press Enter. Press any other key to cancel the process.

While searching the disk, UNFORMAT displays the following message:

```
Examined nn root entries
Files found in the root: x
Subdirectories found in the root: y
Searching disk...
pp% searched, mm subdirs found.
```

UNFORMAT substitutes the number of root-level entries it finds for *nn*, the number of root-level files it finds for *x*, and the number of root-level subdirectories it finds for *y* (*nn=x+y*). (See Chapter 6 for a discussion of files, and see Chapter 8 for a discussion of the root directory.) As UNFORMAT searches the disk, the command continually updates the last message, substituting the percentage of the disk read for *pp* and the number of subdirectories found for *mm*.

After UNFORMAT completes its search of the hard disk data, the command lists the subdirectories found. Because the DOS FORMAT command erased root-level directory names, UNFORMAT gives each root-level directory the name SUBDIR.*nnn* (*nnn* represents a number from 1 through 999). The first subdirectory is SUBDIR.1, the second subdirectory is SUBDIR.2, and so on. UNFORMAT also indicates the number of files found on the disk.

UNFORMAT next displays the warning:

```
Warning! The next step writes changes to disk.
Are you SURE you want to do this?
If so, type in 'Y'; anything else cancels
```

To proceed with the unformat operation, press Y and then press Enter. UNFORMAT starts checking for file fragmentation. If you have not used a program, such as the PC Tools Compress program, to unfragment the files on your hard disk, individual files may be broken into fragments on the hard disk. When UNFORMAT locates a fragmented file, the command has no way to find the next segment of the file; therefore, UNFORMAT asks whether you want to truncate or delete the file. UNFORMAT tells you the total size of the file as well as the number of bytes in the first fragment. To recover this fragment of the file, press T and then press Enter. Press D and then Enter to cause UNFORMAT to omit this file from the new directory.

After UNFORMAT deletes or truncates all fragmented files, it rebuilds the FAT, root directory, and boot record by using the information found during the search. Finally, UNFORMAT indicates how many files were recovered and displays the following message:

```
Operation completed.
```

At the end of the process, most files that were neither truncated nor deleted are intact. UNFORMAT may include in a file, however, data that doesn't belong to that file. This error can happen if a file is fragmented into two blocks of data that at some point are separated on the disk by data from another file. If the other file is later deleted, leaving an unallocated space, this space may seem to UNFORMAT to be part of the file. The only way to discover this type of error is to use the file—run the file if it is a program, or display the file's contents if it is not a program.

Rebuilding a Partition Table

UNFORMAT also enables you to recover from a corrupted hard disk partition table. Such an error normally generates the DOS message `Invalid drive specification`. To recover from this problem, you first must issue the UNFORMAT command with the /PARTN switch, and then use UNFORMAT without this parameter to restore the FAT, root directory, and boot sector.

To recover from a corrupted hard disk partition table, boot your computer (with a floppy disk if necessary) and display the DOS prompt. Change to a disk drive that contains the UNFORMAT file, UNFORMAT.COM. If your only hard disk is inaccessible because of partition table corruption, use a copy of the program on a floppy disk. (UNFORMAT.COM is contained on the Startup disk, one of the disks used during DOS 5 installation.) Type the following command at the DOS prompt:

UNFORMAT /PARTN

UNFORMAT prompts you to insert the disk containing the file PARTNSAV.FIL and to enter the name of that disk drive. Place in a drive the disk that contains the copy of the partition table created by MIRROR (see "Saving the Partition Table" in Chapter 15). Type the letter of this drive, and press Enter. MIRROR rebuilds the partition table from the file PARTNSAV.FIL found on the floppy disk.

After UNFORMAT has rebuilt the partition table, the program prompts you to insert a Master DOS disk into drive A and to press Enter. Place a bootable DOS disk in the A drive and press the Enter key. UNFORMAT causes your computer to reboot. Finally, use the copy of UNFORMAT to restore the FAT, root directories, and boot record, following the steps described in "Using the MIRROR-Image File To Recover from an Accidental Format" in this chapter.

Reviewing the Concept of Defaults

A *default* value is the value DOS uses for a parameter if you don't specify otherwise. In Part I, you used the DIR command without the drive parameter. In this case, DOS assumes that you want the directory for the logged drive, the current drive, to serve as the *default* value for the drive parameter in the DIR command.

The concept of defaults is important if you want to be effective with DOS commands. DOS uses certain default values to carry out its services. You can override many of these values through commands or switches.

For example, when you boot your computer, DOS automatically logs to the drive that holds the bootable disk. This drive is the current drive. DOS normally displays the current drive name in the DOS prompt and uses this drive to execute commands.

With most DOS commands, DOS uses the current drive as the default disk drive parameter if you don't specify otherwise. In other words, if the drive parameter you want to use for a DOS command is the same as the current drive, you do not have to enter the drive letter. If you want to issue a command to affect another disk drive, you must include the drive parameter for that disk in the command line. DOS commands often are shorter and cleaner if you leave out the defaults. Many command examples in this book assume some default values. The logged drive is a frequently used default.

Using FORMAT on Another Drive

In Chapter 5, you learned that COMMAND.COM contains certain built-in DOS commands, called *internal* commands. Commands that reside in separate files on disk are called *external* commands. COMMAND.COM must find and load external commands before executing them. If the external commands are not on the logged disk, you must enter a drive specifier before the command name.

The drive specifier is the name of the drive that contains the command's program file. You learn in Chapter 8 how to give DOS the correct path to the external commands.

Suppose that your computer has a hard disk and two floppy drives. You want to format a disk in drive B. You have FORMAT.COM on a disk in drive A and a blank disk in drive B.

Type **A:** and press Enter to make the drive holding the DOS working disk your default drive. Then type **FORMAT B:** to format the unformatted disk in drive B.

If you had changed to drive B, the command **FORMAT B:** would produce an error message. Because drive B is not the default drive, DOS cannot find FORMAT.COM.

One solution to this dilemma is to issue the command **A:FORMAT B:**. DOS finds the FORMAT command on the DOS disk in drive A as specified in the command. The formatting is done on the unformatted disk in drive B as specified in the command.

Preparing the Hard Disk

The next sections deal with dividing and formatting the hard disk. Be sure to heed all warnings and read all explanations carefully.

> *Caution:* Many computer dealers install the operating system on a computer's hard disk before you receive it. If your dealer has installed an applications program, such as a word processor, *DO NOT FORMAT THE HARD DISK*. If you reformat your hard disk, all programs and data will be erased.

Dividing a Hard Disk with FDISK

The hard disks used by today's PCs can be divided logically into partitions. Before you can format a hard disk, you must partition it. A partition is simply a section of the storage area of a hard disk. Many operating systems, including DOS, can use disk partitions, and most systems have some utility program that creates and manages partitions. DOS's utility program for partition creation and management is the external command FDISK.

> **Note:** Many dealers have already used FDISK on a system's hard disk before the system is delivered to the end user. FDISK also is executed automatically by the DOS 5 Setup command during installation. If your hard disk contains files, it has already been partitioned with FDISK and formatted. If you have any questions about the state of your hard disk's preparation, consult your dealer.

Most hard disk users choose a DOS partition size that includes the entire hard disk. In other words, the one physical hard disk appears to DOS as one logical hard disk. FDISK enters into a hard disk partition table information indicating that the entire disk is available to DOS and that the disk is bootable.

Some PC users want another operating system to reside on a hard disk with DOS. Different operating systems use file systems that are not compatible with each other. FDISK provides a means to divide the hard disk into separate sections isolated from each other. DOS can use one partition section while another operating system, such as UNIX, uses another. Through separation, each operating system sees its partition as its own hard disk. At any particular time, only one operating system is active, called the *active partition*. FDISK controls which partition is active in a multipartition situation.

Hard disk capacities have increased during the last few years. FDISK enables DOS users to divide these larger hard disks into a *primary DOS partition* and additional *extended partitions*. To DOS, the primary and extended partitions look like distinct disk drives. The extended DOS partition consists of fixed-size logical disks. A *logical drive* is not a separate physical disk; but DOS treats each logical drive as if it were a separate disk. Through logical disks, one hard disk drive can have, for instance, logical drives C, D, and E.

Until DOS 4.0, the largest drive DOS could manage as one partition was 32M. Drives with capacities of more than 32M have been available for some time. FDISK and DOS's extended-partition capability give users of large-capacity drives a means to put to work these capacities greater than 32M. DOS 4 and DOS 5 enable you to use your entire hard disk as a single partition.

> *Caution:* The FDISK command has provisions to delete an existing partition from the disk partition table. If you delete an existing partition, all data in the files contained in that partition is lost. Be sure that you have backed up or copied any data from a partition you are about to delete. FDISK is not a command to experiment with unless your hard disk contains no data. Be cautious when you use FDISK.

The syntax for FDISK is as follows:

FDISK

Notice that FDISK has no parameters.

With DOS 3.3 and later, you can use FDISK to create more than one DOS partition. After you define a primary DOS partition with FDISK, you can define an extended DOS partition, which you divide into one or more logical drives. All primary DOS partitions and logical drives must be formatted using the FORMAT command before they can be used. When DOS is the active operating system, as reflected in the partition table, DOS boots from the active DOS partition. You then can log onto one of the logical drives. The primary DOS partition normally is assigned the drive name C.

After you partition the hard disk(s), DOS respects the logical drives and creates a file system for each drive when the drive is formatted.

Formatting a Hard Disk

Like floppy disks, hard disks must be formatted before use. The DOS 5 installation program (Setup) formats the hard disk as part of the DOS installation process.

Assume that the hard disk (or logical disk) you are going to format is drive C. If you are formatting another drive, use its drive name (letter) in place of *C*. Note that if your drive is not the primary DOS partition, you do not need the /S switch because DOS boots only from the primary DOS partition. Put your working copy of the DOS Startup disk into drive A, log onto that drive by typing **A:**, and then type the following command and press Enter:

FORMAT C:/S

FORMAT issues the following warning message and confirmation prompt:

```
WARNING, ALL DATA ON NON-REMOVABLE DISK
DRIVE C: WILL BE LOST!

Proceed with Format (Y/N)?
```

This prompt is extremely important. When the prompt appears on-screen, examine it carefully to confirm the disk drive name (letter) before you answer **Y**. If you make a habit of pressing Y to the confirmation prompts of less dangerous commands, you may make a serious mistake with this final FORMAT confirmation prompt. If the drive is the one you intend to format, press Y. If not, press N to terminate FORMAT.

If you answer **Y**, FORMAT updates the display with progress reports on its operation. DOS 4.0 and later versions report the percentage of formatting completed. Other versions report the head and cylinder count. Depending on the capacity of the disk being formatted, the process can take from a few minutes to more than a half hour. The greater a disk's capacity, the longer the process. When the disk has been formatted, FORMAT issues the following message:

```
Format complete
```

FORMAT may not be finished, however. If you used the /S switch, you will see the following message:

```
System Transferred
```

FORMAT next prompts for the volume label with the following message:

```
Volume label (11 characters, ENTER for none)?
```

Enter the volume label and press Enter. The discussion of the /V switch in the preceding discussion of FORMAT's switches includes a list of allowable volume label characters. If you decide later to change this label, you can use the LABEL command (available in MS-DOS 3.1, or PC DOS 3.0, and later versions).

Finally, FORMAT displays a report showing the disk space formatted, the bytes used by the system files, defective sectors marked (if any), and the number of bytes available on the disk. Don't be surprised if the report shows some bad sectors in your hard disk. Hard disks, especially those whose formatted capacity exceeds 21M, frequently have a few bad sectors. These bad sectors are marked as unusable in the FAT and are not allocated to a file.

Note: If you boot your PC with a version of DOS earlier than 4.0, you cannot expect to find everything you stored on a disk greater than 32M in size. Versions of DOS earlier than 4.0 are not designed for extensions that accommodate disks greater than 32M. Furthermore, some third-party disk-utility applications programs cannot handle the DOS 4.0 and 5.0 extensions to the boot sector. If you have DOS 4.0 or later and you want to use a disk optimizer such as the Norton Utilities or a rapid backup program such as FASTBACK, make sure, before you use the application, that the version you have can handle DOS 4.0/5.0 partitions larger than 32M.

Naming Disks with LABEL

The external command LABEL adds, modifies, or changes a disk's volume label. In DOS, a volume label is a name given to a physical or logical disk (the volume). The LABEL command is available with PC DOS 3.0 and later versions and MS-DOS 3.1 and later versions. If a disk's volume label is blank (if the user pressed Enter when FORMAT or LABEL prompted for the label), you can use the LABEL command to add a volume label.

DOS displays the volume label when you issue commands such as VOL, CHKDSK, DIR, and TREE. In DOS 3.2 through DOS 4.0, FORMAT asks for a hard disk's volume label before reformatting the disk. Giving each disk (physical and logical) a volume label is a good idea. A disk with a unique volume label is easier to identify than one that doesn't have a label.

The syntax for the LABEL command is as follows:

LABEL *d:label*

d: is the name of the drive that holds the disk to be labeled. *label*, the optional label text you supply as the new volume label, can include from 1 through 11 characters. (The allowable characters for a volume label are discussed in "Adding a Volume Label" in this chapter.) If you do not supply the *label* parameter, LABEL automatically prompts for a new label.

The command sequence for the LABEL command looks like the following:

LABEL

DOS responds:

```
Volume label in C is BOOT DISK
Volume serial number is AB02-07E8
Volume label (11 characters, ENTER for none)?
```

You enter the text for the volume label; DOS assigns the new label. If you simply press Enter in response to the prompt, you are telling DOS to delete the current label and leave it blank. DOS confirms your decision by prompting as follows:

```
Delete current volume label (Y/N)?
```

When you press Y and then Enter, DOS deletes the current label. If you press Enter only, or any character other than Y or N, DOS repeats the prompt.

When you issue a LABEL command with the optional *volume_label* parameter of from 1 through 11 characters, DOS immediately updates the specified or default drive's label with no warning prompt. Some special restrictions affect your use of LABEL:

- You cannot use the LABEL command on a networked drive.

- With DOS 3.2 and later versions, you cannot use LABEL on a disk in a drive that is affected by the SUBST or ASSIGN command.

> *Note:* Some third-party programs can edit the volume label of a hard disk formatted with a version of DOS earlier than DOS 3.1. Ask your dealer to recommend one of these third-party programs, or upgrade your DOS version to 5.0.

Examining Volume Labels with VOL

The internal command VOL is convenient when you want to view a disk's volume label or verify that a label exists. VOL is a display-only command; it does not modify the current volume label. VOL shows the volume label created during the disk's formatting or modified by a subsequent LABEL command.

VOL accesses the disk's volume label from the root directory and then displays the label. You can use VOL freely because it does not change any files or the label name. The command accommodates an optional drive parameter and uses the default drive if no drive parameter is given.

The syntax of the VOL command is simple:

VOL *d:*

d: is the optional name of the drive whose volume label you want to see. If you omit a value for *d:*, DOS displays the label for the default drive.

To see the volume label of the disk in drive A, enter the following command:

VOL A:

DOS responds with the following (or similar) message for your disk:

```
Volume in drive A: is WORK_DISK1
```

CHKDSK, TREE, and DIR include the volume-label display as part of their output.

Transferring the DOS System Using SYS

All DOS disks have a DOS file system, but only disks with the DOS system files and COMMAND.COM can be used to boot DOS. The external command SYS transfers (copies) the hidden system files from a bootable system disk. Some versions of SYS (prior to 3.3) do not transfer COMMAND.COM and thus require you to use COPY to transfer COMMAND.COM to the target disk. DOS 3.3 and later versions transfer COMMAND.COM as a part of the operation of SYS.

You learned in a previous section that you can make a disk bootable by using the /S switch with the FORMAT command. Normally, users know in advance that they want a bootable disk and use this command sequence. The SYS command is provided for use when a formatted disk must be made bootable. The disk must have room for the system files SYS intends to transfer, and those system files must be compatible with the version of DOS being used.

To use SYS successfully, you need to observe the following rules:

- SYS requires that the destination disk be formatted.

- The destination disk must contain sufficient free space for the two hidden system files and COMMAND.COM (116,796 bytes for DOS 5 system files), or the disk must already contain earlier versions of the system files or have been formatted with the /B switch.

- With DOS 3.3 or earlier versions, system files had to be contiguous. If a disk contains user files and does not contain the two system files, DOS issues the following error message:

```
No room for system on destination disk
```

- You cannot use SYS on a networked drive. If you want to use SYS on a networked drive, you must either log off the network or pause your drive to perform the SYS command. For exact restrictions, consult your system's network documentation.

- You must give the destination-drive parameter for the SYS command. SYS does not use the current drive for the destination parameter. The source drive for the system files is always the current drive. With DOS 4.0 or later, you also can specify a source-drive parameter.

Note: If you are in doubt about which DOS version is on the boot disk, you can issue the VER command; DOS displays the version. Remember that one of the hidden files is the input-output (IO) system, which contains device drivers for the implementation of DOS on a particular computer. Although many implementations of the IO system file are compatible with one another, some may not be. For this reason, you should not mix DOS versions or implementations when using the SYS command. Indeed, you should never mix versions of DOS on one computer.

The syntax for the SYS command is as follows:

SYS d:

If you are using DOS 4.0 or later, you can also provide the source drive for the system files, as in the following:

SYS ds: dd:

The drive specified by **dd:** is the target, or *destination*, drive for the system files. You must include a drive name (letter) for drive **dd:**. The drive specified by **ds:** is the drive that is used for the *source* of the system files.

Suppose that you are using DOS 5 with a hard disk and that you have an empty disk you want to make bootable to use with another computer. Put the formatted disk into drive A and make sure that your current PATH setting includes the directory which contains SYS (see Chapter 8 for information on the DOS path). Then enter the following command:

SYS C: A:

The C: is optional; if you are logged to drive C, C: is already the default source for the system files. SYS replies with the following message:

```
System transferred
```

The system files are now on the disk in drive A. If you want, you now can use this disk to boot your computer.

Analyzing a Disk with CHKDSK

The external command CHKDSK analyzes a floppy or hard disk. CHKDSK checks a disk's FAT, directories, and, if you want, the fragmentation (the spreading out of parts of a file) of the files on the disk. Optionally, CHKDSK repairs problems in the FAT due to lost clusters and writes the contents of the lost clusters to files. CHKDSK also provides an option to display all files and their paths (paths are discussed in Chapter 8). Upon completion, CHKDSK displays a screen report of its findings.

> *Note:* Running CHKDSK periodically on your hard disk and important floppies is good practice. Because the FAT and the hierarchical directory system work together to track file names and locations, a problem in either the FAT or one of the directories is always a serious problem. In all likelihood, CHKDSK will find and fix most problems it finds in a disk's internal bookkeeping tables.

You issue the CHKDSK command with the following syntax:

CHKDSK *d:path\filename.ext /F/V*

d: is the optional drive name to be checked. If the drive name is omitted, the current drive is assumed.

path is the optional path to the directory containing the files to be analyzed for fragmentation. If a path is omitted and a file specifier is given in the command line, the current directory is assumed.

filename.ext is the optional file name and extension for the file(s) to be analyzed for fragmentation. If a file-name parameter is not present on the command line, CHKDSK does not check for fragmentation.

/F is the optional *fix* switch, which instructs CHKDSK to repair any problems encountered.

/V is the *verbose* switch, which instructs CHKDSK to provide file names to the screen as the files are being analyzed.

CHKDSK is DOS's self-test command. CHKDSK makes sure that the internal tables which keep files in control are in order. Although the technical details of how CHKDSK does its analysis are beyond the scope of most casual DOS users, the better you understand CHKDSK, the more comfortable you will be when the command uncovers problems. Just because you don't understand exactly how CHKDSK works doesn't mean that you should avoid using it. CHKDSK checks for the following problems in the FAT:

- Unlinked cluster chains (lost clusters)

- Multiple linked clusters (cross-linked files)

- Invalid next-cluster-in-chain values (invalid cluster numbers)

- Defective sectors where the FAT is stored

CHKDSK checks for the following problems in the directory system:

- Invalid cluster numbers (out of range)

- Invalid file attributes in entries (attribute values DOS does not recognize)

- Damage to subdirectory entries (CHKDSK cannot process them)

- Damage to a directory's integrity (its files cannot be accessed)

CHKDSK then produces a screen report that summarizes disk and system memory usage. Figures 7.8 and 7.9 show typical CHKDSK reports.

> *Note:* Take advantage of the CHKDSK command's capability to make a "dry run" of its checking routines. You can use this capability to assess reported problems. For example, before issuing CHKDSK with the /F switch, issue the command without the switch. CHKDSK without /F prompts you if the command finds a problem (as though you had used the /F switch). After you have assessed the findings of CHKDSK and have taken remedial actions (such as those that follow), you can issue CHKDSK with the /F switch so that the command can fix the problems it finds.

DOS stores every file as a chain of clusters. (Each cluster is a group of sections; clusters are referred to as *allocation units* in DOS 4 and later.) Each entry in the disk's directory points to the entry in the file allocation table (FAT) that contains the list of clusters allocated to a file.

```
C:\>CHKDSK

Volume QUE BRUCE   created 02-28-1991 1:04p
Volume Serial Number is 166C-83D3
Errors found, F parameter not specified
Corrections will not be written to disk


    168 lost allocation units found in 6 chains.
    344064 bytes disk space would be freed

104515584 bytes total disk space
    75776 bytes in 3 hidden files
   272384 bytes in 111 directories
 97984512 bytes in 2960 user files
  5838848 bytes available on disk

     2048 bytes in each allocation unit
    51033 total allocation units on disk
     2851 available allocation units on disk

   655360 total bytes memory
   477936 bytes free

C:\>
```

Fig. 7.8. A typical report produced by CHKDSK issued with no parameters.

```
C:\>CHKDSK \DOS\*.*

Volume QUE BRUCE   created 02-28-1991 1:04p
Volume Serial Number is 166C-83D3

104515584 bytes total disk space
    75776 bytes in 3 hidden files
   272384 bytes in 111 directories
 98099200 bytes in 2962 user files
  6068224 bytes available on disk

     2048 bytes in each allocation unit
    51033 total allocation units on disk
     2963 available allocation units on disk

   655360 total bytes memory
   477936 bytes free

C:\DOS\FORMAT.COM Contains 2 non-contiguous blocks
C:\DOS\KEYB.COM Contains 2 non-contiguous blocks
C:\DOS\KEYBOARD.SYS Contains 2 non-contiguous blocks

C:\>
```

Fig. 7.9. Report produced when CHKDSK is issued with a path.

CHKDSK processes each directory, starting at the root and following each subdirectory. The indicated cluster chain is checked using the directory entry's FAT pointer. The size of the file in bytes is compared to the size of the FAT's allocation in clusters.

CHKDSK expects to find enough chained clusters in the FAT to accommodate the file but not more than are necessary. If CHKDSK finds too many clusters, it issues the following message:

```
Allocation error,
size adjusted
```

The file is truncated (excess clusters are deallocated) if the /F switch is in effect.

CHKDSK makes sure that each of the FAT's clusters is allocated only once. In rare circumstances, such as power problems or hardware failures, DOS can give two different files the same cluster. By checking each cluster chain for cross-linked files, CHKDSK can report "mixed-up" files. Each time you see the message `filename is cross-linked on cluster X`, copy the file reported in *filename* to another disk. CHKDSK will report another file with the same message. Copy the second file to another disk also. Chances are good that the contents of the two files will be mixed up, but you have a better chance of recovering the files if you save them to another disk before CHKDSK "fixes" the problem.

CHKDSK expects every cluster in the FAT to be available for allocation, part of a legitimate directory-based cluster chain, or a marked bad cluster. If CHKDSK encounters any clusters or cluster chains that are not pointed to by a directory entry, CHKDSK issues the following message:

```
x lost clusters in Y chains
```

CHKDSK then prompts as follows:

```
Convert lost chains to files (Y/N)?
```

If the /F switch is active, CHKDSK turns each cluster chain into a file in the root directory. Each file created will have the name *FILEnnnn.CHK*. (*nnnn* is a number, starting with 0000, that increments by 1 for each file created by CHKDSK.)

You can use the DOS TYPE command to examine the contents of a text file, and you may be able to use a word processor to put the text back into its original file. With a binary (program or data) file, the TYPE command won't do you any good. If the problem is with a program file, you may need to use the DOS COMP or FC command to compare your disk's binary files with their counterparts from your master disks.

The disk does not lose any sectors physically. A lost cluster report does not indicate that the clusters are bad. Lost clusters indicate only that DOS made a bookkeeping error in the FAT, which makes some cluster(s) appear to be lost to DOS. The clusters are not tied to a directory entry, yet they are marked as being in use. The lost cluster problem is most likely to occur when you are running disk-intensive programs such as dBASE IV or WordPerfect. Although they are not to blame for lost clusters, the programs increase DOS's exposure to bookkeeping errors. Programs that use disk files to swap sections of program and data too large for memory may ask DOS to read and write work files hundreds of times in an afternoon of computing. Power glitches or interruptions, heated hardware components, and electrical interference can turn a cluster chain number into a different number at the critical moment that DOS is writing the number into the FAT. Still, when you consider the millions of bytes for which DOS is responsible in a typical PC, DOS's reliability record is superb. CHKDSK recovers most clusters that DOS bookkeeping errors lose.

When you use CHKDSK, the following rules apply:

- CHKDSK begins execution immediately after you enter the command. If you use a one-disk system, use the drive B: parameter to allow for changing from the disk containing CHKDSK to the disk to be analyzed.

- CHKDSK reports problems found during operation but does not repair them unless you include the /F switch in the command line.

- You should run CHKDSK at least weekly. Run CHKDSK daily during periods of extreme file activity.

- CHKDSK converts lost clusters to files if you answer **Y** to the `Convert lost chains to files (Y/N)?` prompt. CHKDSK places the files in the disk's root directory, with the name *FILEnnnn.CHK*.

- If CHKDSK terminates because the root directory has no more entries available for converted chain files, clear the current *FILEnnnn.CHK* files by erasing them or copying them to another disk. After the files are cleared from the root, reissue CHKDSK.

For this sample CHKDSK exercise, suppose that you are copying a group of files from your hard disk to a floppy. During the copy, the lights flicker and then go out completely. In a few seconds, power is restored to normal. Your computer reboots DOS and awaits your input.

Power problems during file operations such as COPY can cause DOS's bookkeeping job to be interrupted. The directory and the FAT can contain errors. To ensure that no errors go undetected, you issue the CHKDSK command on the floppy disk, as follows:

CHKDSK A:

CHKDSK begins to analyze the floppy disk in drive A and then displays the following report:

```
Volume SCRATCH DISK created 09-12-1989  11:23a
Errors found, F parameter not specified
Corrections will not be written to disk

A:\DBASE1.OVL
Allocation error, size adjusted

  730112 bytes in total disk space
  415744 bytes in 4 user files
  314368 bytes available on disk

    1024 bytes in each allocation unit
     713 total allocation units on disk
     307 available allocation units on disk

  655360 total bytes memory
  409856 bytes free
```

Because you did not specify the /F switch, CHKDSK did not repair the problem. You can examine the problem further before reissuing CHKDSK with the /F switch. You look at a directory listing of the files on drive A to see whether you can determine the nature of the allocation problem. The directory listing shows the following:

```
Volume in drive A is SCRATCH DISK
Volume Serial Number is 1982-BA9A
Directory of  A:\
DBSETUP  OVL     147968 10-21-88  12:22a
DBASE3   OVL      85024 12-28-88   9:04p
DBASE6   OVL     114832 10-20-88  11:22p
DBASE1   OVL          0 09-12-89   1:46a
        4 File(s)     314368 bytes free
```

The last directory entry, DBASE1.OVL, shows a file size of 0 bytes. A 0-byte file size should never result from a COPY operation. The file's directory size entry is suspicious. To further clarify the nature of the allocation error, compare the CHKDSK report with the directory listing generated by the DIR command.

The CHKDSK report shows 415,744 bytes in the 4 files. When you total the bytes in the directory listing, you can account for only 347,824 bytes in the

4 files. Both CHKDSK and the directory listing show 314,368 bytes available on the disk. CHKDSK and DIR both report available disk bytes as the number of bytes in unallocated disk clusters—not the difference between the capacity of the disk and the number of bytes in the disk's files. Both commands get the disk's remaining capacity indirectly from the FAT.

Because both commands agree on the FAT's calculation, you must assume that the directory entry for DBASE1.OVL is incorrect in its reflection of the file's size. CHKDSK can repair the directory entry. Issue the CHKDSK command again, this time using the /F switch, as follows:

CHKDSK A: /F

CHKDSK then reports the following:

```
Volume SCRATCH DISK created 09-12-1989  11:23a

A:\DBASE1.OVL
Allocation error, size adjusted

 730112 bytes in total disk space
 415744 bytes in 4 user files
 314368 bytes available on disk

   1024 bytes in each allocation unit
    713 total allocation units on disk
    307 available allocation units on disk

 655360 total bytes memory
 409856 bytes free
```

To confirm that the problem you suspect in the directory is repaired, list the directory of the disk again. You see the following:

```
Volume in drive A is SCRATCH DISK
Volume Serial Number is 1982-BA9A
Directory of  A:\
DBSETUP  OVL    147968 10-21-88  12:22a
DBASE3   OVL     85024 12-28-88   9:04p
DBASE6   OVL    114832 10-20-88  11:22p
DBASE1   OVL     65536 09-12-89   1:46a
        4 File(s)      314368 bytes free
```

Notice that DBASE1.OVL shows 65,536 bytes instead of 0. The available capacity of the disk remains unchanged. Now the total bytes shown in the directory listing are within a few thousand of the difference between the disk's capacity and the total bytes free. You can account for this small difference by considering that some of the files do not completely fill their last allocated cluster. The error in the directory is corrected, and the disk is ready for use again.

Summary

This chapter presents the important FORMAT command and other disk-level DOS commands. The chapter covers the following key points:

- Hard disks and floppies must be formatted before they can be used to store files.

- Formatting sets up a directory for file-name and status information and a file allocation table (FAT) for tracking the availability of storage space on the disk.

- FORMAT accepts several switches, including the /S switch, which makes the disk bootable; the /F switch, which enables you to specify disk capacity; and the /Q switch, which performs a quick format.

- Before a hard disk can be formatted, it must be partitioned by FDISK.

- Disk partitions can be DOS partitions or partitions of another operating system.

- DOS partitions are either a *primary* (bootable) partition or an *extended* partition divided into one or more logical drives.

- DOS views logical drives as being the same as physical disks and assigns each logical drive its own drive-name letter.

- The UNFORMAT command restores a disk that has been inadvertently formatted.

- The LABEL command adds or changes a disk's volume label.

- The VOL command displays a disk's volume label.

- The SYS command transfers the DOS system files from a bootable disk to another disk. SYS can be used to upgrade a disk's DOS version.

- CHKDSK is a disk-level command that finds and fixes problems. CHKDSK analyzes a disk's FAT and directory system.

- When you include the /F switch, CHKDSK can repair most problems it encounters.

The next chapter introduces you to DOS's hierarchical directory system. With knowledge of the hierarchical directory system, you will be able to use DOS commands in a multilevel directory system.

Understanding Hierarchical Directories

T his chapter covers the DOS file-management strategy, teaching you the role of directories and explaining their hierarchical structure. The chapter explains in detail how to understand and navigate the path to each file and program on your disks. You also learn how to change special file attributes that determine such characteristics as whether a file can be erased, listed in the directory, or accessed as a read-only file.

Key Terms Used in This Chapter

Directory	A disk-based table of file names and other file-related information, that DOS uses with the file allocation table (FAT) to access a file's data content
Root directory	A master directory created on each disk by FORMAT
Subdirectory	An additional named directory created by a user
Attribute	A directory-based indicator of a file's status. Attributes include read-only, archive, system, hidden, and volume label.

Reviewing Disks

To set the stage for learning about directories, you should review some of the concepts that help you understand DOS disks. As you recall, DOS uses a drive name or parameter to reference each disk drive on your system; DOS uses letters, such as A, B, and C, as names for the drives. Before DOS can use a disk in a drive, the disk must be formatted. The FORMAT operation establishes key tables on each disk along with vital information about the disk's format. DOS uses the tables and disk information as a template for managing the disk's storage capabilities. When you format a disk, DOS creates a root directory and file allocation table on the disk.

Because each disk has the tables necessary to stand on its own as a storage medium, DOS enables you to use multiple disks. DOS keeps track of the logged drive and uses the drive as the current drive. Internally, DOS stores the current drive's name. When you issue a command without an optional drive parameter, DOS uses the stored drive letter. For example, if you type the command **DIR** without specifying a drive letter, DOS produces a directory listing from the current drive. In this case, DOS seems to approach its file system as a single set of files.

If you use a drive parameter with a command, DOS accesses the file-system tables from the specified disk. When you type the command **DIR B:**, DOS produces a listing of the contents of the disk in drive B even if drive A is the current logged drive. DOS commands can access files on all types of disks. If DOS can format a disk on your system, DOS can use that disk. With a drive parameter, you have immediate access to any disk on your system, and you access the files on any disk by using commands that work with any other disk.

Understanding the Role of Directories

The *directory* is an important table, created by the FORMAT command on each disk. Each DOS-prepared disk has one directory, called the *root directory* because it is the root of the disk's file system. DOS uses the directory as a kind of index system for finding desired files. Individual members of this index system are called *directory entries*. DOS provides for a fixed number of directory entries in the root directory. This number is the same for the same types of disk formats but varies with different formats. Disks with larger capacities have more root directory entries.

By using DOS commands, you can see much of the makeup of a directory. The DIR command, you remember, accesses and displays selected parts of directory entries:

```
Volume in drive A is QUE BRUCE
Volume Serial Number is 0773-09E8
Directory of  A:\
DBSETUP  OVL     147968 10-21-88      12:22a
DBASE3   OVL     85024  12-28-88      9:04p
DBASE6   OVL     114832 10-20-88      11:22p
DBASE1   OVL     65536  09-12-89      1:46a
        4 File(s) 413360 bytes
    314368 bytes free
```

The DIR command does not display all the elements of a directory entry, however. Table 8.1 lists the components of a directory entry.

Table 8.1
The Main Features of DOS Directories

Feature	Example	What is Stored
File name	THANKYOU	Eight-character file prefix
File-name extension	DOC	Three-character file suffix
File attributes	R (read-only)	Special status information about this file used by DOS
Time	10:22	The time of creation or last modification
Date	11-14-91	The date of creation or last modification
Starting cluster	576	The number of the first cluster allocated to this file by DOS in the FAT
File size	1024 bytes	The number of bytes in this file

You undoubtedly recognize the file name, extension, time, and date components of a directory entry as being displayed by the DIR command. DIR also displays the file size. These components, or *fields*, of a directory entry contain information useful to you as well as to DOS (see fig. 8.1). DIR displays this information because it is helpful for your file management activities.

| File Name | Extension | Attributes | Reserved | Time | Date | Starting Cluster | Size |

Fig. 8.1. The fields of a directory entry.

> *Note:* DOS also stores volume labels in directory entries, using the combined file name and extension fields to form an 11-byte (character) field (see Chapter 7). The FORMAT and LABEL commands write your choice of a volume name into the root directory entry for a disk. DOS knows that the directory entry is a volume label because the volume label attribute for the entry is set.

The starting cluster and file attribute fields, shown in table 8.1 and in figure 8.1, are not included in the DIR command's displayed output. The *starting cluster* field contains the cluster number of the first cluster DOS has allocated for a particular file's storage. The *file attribute* field contains special status information that DOS uses to determine how the file is to be managed internally. Because these two fields are not as visible or as self-explanatory as the fields displayed in the DIR listing, the next two sections look at them in more detail.

Chaining through a File

The starting cluster field of a file's directory entry is the key to the file's storage allocation as tracked in the FAT (file allocation table). You recall that DOS creates a FAT for each disk during formatting. For each cluster (allocation unit) on the disk, the FAT indicates whether the cluster is allocated to a file. Much as a restaurant hostess looks at a table chart for a place to seat you, DOS looks at the FAT for available clusters when a file is created or enlarged. When you arrive early at a restaurant, it is nearly empty, and the hostess seats you in the general vicinity of other guests, leaving other sections of the restaurant unused. When DOS allocates files on a freshly formatted disk, DOS uses the first cluster and sequences through a connected series of clusters, leaving many clusters unused at the end of the FAT.

When you leave the restaurant, the hostess marks your table as being available. Likewise, when you erase or shorten a file, DOS marks the released clusters in the FAT as being available and uses them to store another file.

You may have a dining experience in which the hostess does not have enough adjacent tables to seat your entire party. Your group is fragmented across two or more tables with other parties seated at tables between the parts of your group. You can remain connected as a group by telling the waiter, "We're with those people over there," as you point to the other table.

When a DOS command or applications program asks DOS to store a file on the disk, DOS checks the FAT, finds the next available cluster, and stores a portion of the file there. If that cluster cannot accommodate the entire file, DOS finds the next available cluster and stores part of the file there. DOS does not look for the largest available block of clusters, so the entire file may not fit the first group of available clusters. If the disk has a great deal of file activity, a file may be split into many pieces, scattered around the disk. This disconnected cluster condition is known as *file fragmentation*. Even though file fragmentation can slow DOS's access to the file, this method of storing files makes efficient use of all available space.

DOS connects all clusters of a file by recording in the current cluster's entry in the FAT where the next cluster is located. When a file is allocated to more than one cluster, each cluster entry in the FAT points to the next cluster that contains more of the file, using the next cluster number as a "pointer." The result is a *chain* of clusters that comprises the map of a file's disk storage. The FAT, as a storage map, tells DOS exactly where to go on the disk to get all the parts of a file.

When you ask for a file by name, using a DOS command, DOS looks for the "who" identity of the file in the directory, which stores file names and starting clusters. To access the file from the disk, DOS needs to know the "where" identity of the file. Using the starting cluster, found in the directory, DOS then consults the FAT to identify the chain of clusters that holds the contents of the file.

Powerful utility programs also are available from several third-party software manufacturers; these utilities sometimes can repair damage to files or disks. The most popular of these disk-recovery utilities are Norton Utilities from Symantec Corporation; PC Tools Deluxe from Central Point Software, Inc.; and Mace Utilities from Fifth Generation Systems, Inc.

Note: DOS uses the directory and the FAT in a file allocation and accessing strategy. If the values in these DOS tables become corrupted due to power surges, physical damage, or media failure, DOS cannot access the files and storage areas on the disk effectively. If you have important files on a damaged disk, you may be able to reduce the damage by using certain DOS commands.

The MIRROR command makes a copy of the FAT, root directory, and boot sector and places the file in a safe place (see Chapter 15). If some calamity befalls any of these crucial tables, you can use the UNFORMAT command to recover them.

The CHKDSK command uses the directory and the FAT to check the proper tracking of each cluster and directory entry on a disk (see Chapter 6). CHKDSK detects improper relationships in the cluster chains of files and the sizes of directory entries. CHKDSK fixes a disk by adjusting improper file allocation sizes, eliminating circular references in cluster pointers, and making other technical adjustments in the FAT and directories.

The RECOVER command can reestablish a file under a new allocation chain and directory entry if the existing FAT or directory entries are damaged, but some of the recovered file's content probably will be lost (see the Command Reference). RECOVER does include a provision to recover an entire damaged disk. This full version of the command is meant for informed users only, however, and even then should be used only as a last resort, because the command sometimes can cause more harm than good.

Understanding File Attributes

The file attribute field in the directory entry is a one-byte entry that stores a number of characteristics about each file but is not displayed in a normal directory listing. Each characteristic stored in the file attribute field is referred to as a *file attribute*. Each file can have more than one file attribute. Each file attribute is represented in the attribute byte by a single bit, often called an *attribute bit*. Table 8.2 lists the attributes and their purposes in DOS. You can view and modify most attribute bits by using the DOS Shell or the ATTRIB command; DOS manages some attribute bits directly.

Table 8.2
File Attributes and Their Meanings

Attribute Bit	Meaning
Archive	This file has been created or modified since you issued the last DOS command that resets this attribute.
Hidden	This file is bypassed by most DOS file-management commands and does not appear in a directory listing. Hidden files are, however, listed by the DOS Shell in the file list area.
Read-only	This file can be accessed for information but cannot be erased or modified. (Note that a read-only file can be erased using the DOS Shell.)
Subdirectory	This attribute identifies the entry as a directory rather than data or a program.
System	This file is a DOS system file.
Volume label	This entry is the volume label for a disk. The entry does not identify an actual file.

The *archive* attribute works with certain DOS file-management commands to determine which files the commands process. XCOPY, for example, includes an optional switch that causes XCOPY to examine a file's archive attribute before copying the file to its destination. If the archive attribute is not turned on (set), XCOPY bypasses the file.

The underlying reason for having archive attributes is similar to the reason for having a small metal flag on a mailbox. The flag acts as a synchronizer of activity so that the carrier makes only necessary stops. The mail carrier passes by the mailbox each delivery day as part of the mail delivery and pick-up operation. If the mail carrier has no mail to deliver to the box on a particular day and no letters are being mailed, stopping at the box is a waste of the mail carrier's time. The owner of the mailbox can raise the red metal flag as an indicator that the box contains letters to mail, and the carrier, seeing the flag, stops to pick up the letters. After emptying the box, the carrier lowers the flag.

Likewise, the archive attribute of a file is a "flag" for the command that processes the file. When DOS adds or modifies the contents of a file, DOS sets the archive attribute, analogous to raising the mailbox flag. Commands that have the capability to use the archive attribute can "look" to see whether the flag (archive attribute) is raised and then process the file only if the archive attribute is set. When commands like XCOPY and BACKUP see that the archive attribute is turned on in a file's directory listing, the commands assume that the file is new or has changed since the last XCOPY or BACKUP command. You can use the archive attribute in these ways to make copies or backups of files that have changed since your last backup or copy using XCOPY. If only a few files have been added to or changed on a disk, only a few files are included in the backup copy operation. DOS bypasses the files whose "flags" are not raised, saving time and disk space.

Some DOS commands automatically change the archive attribute when a file is added or modified. You can use such commands as XCOPY to reset the attributes. DOS also supplies the ATTRIB command, which directly changes a file's archive attribute. ATTRIB in DOS 3.2 and later versions turns on an archive attribute (setting it) and turns it off (resetting it). With ATTRIB, you can control the files that commands like XCOPY process. (Using XCOPY's /A switch or /M switch causes XCOPY to copy only files whose archive file attribute is set. See the Command Reference for a listing of all switches available for use with XCOPY.)

A file entry with the *hidden* attribute turned on is "invisible" to most DOS file-management commands. Hidden files have file names and extensions like normal user files, but the DIR and COPY commands do not process a hidden file. The two DOS system files on the boot disk are examples, as are many copy-protection files.

You can detect the presence of hidden files with the ATTRIB or CHKDSK commands. Using ATTRIB (starting with DOS 5.0), you also can list hidden files. CHKDSK merely indicates the number of hidden files on the disk.

The *subdirectory* attribute indicates to DOS that the entry is not intended for a user file but for an additional directory called a subdirectory. (Subdirectories are explained in later sections of this chapter.) DOS knows to bypass a file with the subdirectory attribute turned on when conducting file-management commands.

The *system* attribute indicates that a file is an operating system file. The two DOS system files have this attribute in addition to the hidden attribute. You don't need to worry about the system attribute; it does not affect your DOS work.

The *volume label* attribute indicates that the directory entry involved is not for a file. This attribute tells DOS that the file name and extension fields should be combined to provide an 11-character volume label ID for the disk. Only a volume label entry can have this attribute indicated (turned on).

The archive, hidden, read-only, and system attributes are the only attributes you can change directly through DOS. DOS controls the other attributes without the need for your intervention.

Changing File Attributes Using the DOS Shell

You can change file attributes from within the DOS Shell, which enables you to change file attributes on one or more files at a time.

> *Note:* The following discussion focuses on how to change the file attributes of a selected file or files in the current directory on the logged disk. Refer to Chapter 9 for a discussion on how to use the DOS Shell to change directories and to log on to another disk. Refer also to Chapter 10 for details on how to use the mouse and keyboard to select the files whose attributes you want to change.

To change the file attributes on a single file, start the DOS Shell and follow these steps:

1. Select the file list area of the DOS Shell window.

2. In the file list area, select the file whose attributes you want to change. Use the mouse pointer to click the file name, or use the up- or down-arrow key to move the selection cursor to the desired file name.

3. Select File from the menu bar to display the File menu.

4. Choose Change Attributes to display the Change Attributes dialog box, shown in figure 8.2.

   The Shell lists four attributes in the Change Attributes dialog box: Hidden, System, Archive, and Read Only. A triangular pointer appears to the left of each attribute that is set (turned on). Figure 8.2 indicates that the Archive attribute is set for the file BUDGET.WQ1.

5. To change an attribute setting, use the mouse pointer to click the attribute name, or use the up- or down-arrow key to move the selection cursor to the attribute name and press the space bar. (*Note:* The selection cursor appears as soon as you press the up- or down-arrow key.)

Each attribute acts as a toggle switch. Select the attribute once to turn it on. Select the attribute again to turn it off.

6. After you have made all desired changes to attribute settings, choose the OK button to execute the command and set the new attributes.

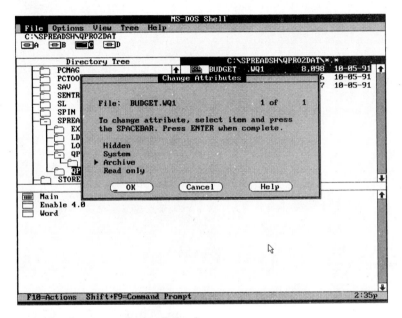

Fig. 8.2. The Change Attributes dialog box.

The Shell also enables you to change file attributes on multiple files. Follow these steps:

1. Use the mouse pointer or keyboard to select the file names of the files whose attributes you want to modify.

2. Select File on the menu bar to pull down the File menu and choose Change Attributes.

   The Shell displays another dialog box entitled Change Attributes, this time listing options to change files one at a time or to change all selected files (see fig. 8.3).

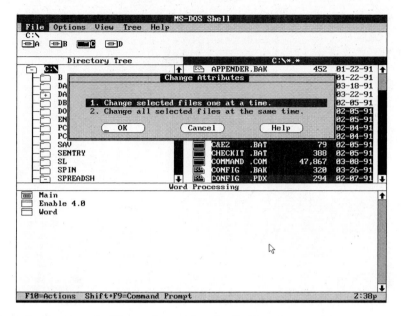

Fig. 8.3. Changing the file attributes of multiple files.

If you want to give different selected files different file attributes, choose the first option. When you want all selected files to have the same attribute settings, select the second option. The Shell then displays a Change Attributes dialog box similar to the one shown in figure 8.2.

3. To change an attribute setting, use the mouse pointer to click the attribute name, or use the up- or down-arrow key to move the selection cursor to the attribute name and press Enter. (***Note:*** The selection cursor appears as soon as you press the up- or down-arrow key.)

4. After you have made all desired changes to attribute settings, choose the OK button to execute the command and set the new attributes.

If you choose the Change Selected Files One at a Time option from the dialog box shown in figure 8.3, you must repeat steps 3 and 4 for each selected file.

Changing File Attributes with the ATTRIB Command

In addition to the DOS Shell Change Attributes command, the external DOS command ATTRIB enables you to manipulate several file attribute bits in a file's directory entry. You can issue the ATTRIB command in three ways:

- The following syntax displays on-screen a file's current attribute values:

  ATTRIB *d:path***filename.ext**/*S*

- The following syntax sets (turns on) file attributes:

  ATTRIB +*A* +*H* +*R* +*S d:path***filename.ext**/*S*

- The following syntax resets (turns off) file attributes:

  ATTRIB –*A* –*H* –*R* –*S d:path***filename.ext**/*S*

d: is an optional parameter that specifies the disk containing the files whose attributes you want to list or change.

path is an optional parameter that indicates the directory path containing the selected files. You learn about paths in the section "Understanding Path Names" in this chapter.

filename.ext is a mandatory parameter that specifies the file or files whose attributes you want to list or change. By using wild cards (* and ?), you can specify multiple files in this parameter.

The optional /*S* switch (DOS 3.3 and later versions only) instructs ATTRIB to process files that match the file parameter in all subdirectories of the path directory. You learn about subdirectories in "Expanding the File System through Subdirectories" in this chapter.

The + operator in front of each attribute letter (*A*, *H*, *R*, or *S*) instructs ATTRIB to set the respective attribute bit. Conversely, the minus (–) operator turns off the attribute.

You can specify the various attributes individually or together in the command line. You can manipulate the *H* and *S* attributes using the ATTRIB command only in DOS 5.0 or greater.

Establishing Read-Only Files

The DOS Shell and the ATTRIB command give you control over file attributes. In particular, the read-only attribute controls the capability of DOS to overwrite (change) or erase (remove) a file. Commands like COPY, ERASE, and XCOPY have the capability of removing or overwriting an existing file.

When DOS (or an application through DOS) adds a file to a directory, the read-only attribute is off, and the file can be overwritten or erased. DOS commands and applications programs are free to perform destructive operations on the file.

If you set the read-only attribute of a file, DOS commands that normally overwrite or erase files do not affect the file. Marking a file as read-only protects the file much like write-protecting a disk protects the contents of a disk. You can use the DOS Shell or the ATTRIB command to write-protect important files, ensuring that careless use of the COPY or ERASE command does not destroy the files.

For example, assume that you have created a spreadsheet file named BUDGET.WQ1, which contains the yearly budget figures for your company. You want others in your department to view this spreadsheet, but you don't want them to make any changes. Use the following command to make the BUDGET.WQ1 file read-only:

ATTRIB +R BUDGET.WQ1

Alternatively, select the file list area of the DOS Shell and select the BUDGET.WQ1 file name. Follow the steps described in the preceding "Changing File Attributes Using the DOS Shell" section to display the Change Attributes dialog box. Initially, only the archive attribute is turned on. Use the mouse or the arrow keys to select the Read Only option in the dialog box in order to turn on the read-only attribute. Finally, select OK to execute the command. The Shell returns to the DOS Shell window.

Now your colleagues can view the BUDGET.WQ1 file, but they cannot change or erase it. If someone tries to issue the command ERASE BUDGET.WQ1, for example, DOS responds as follows:

    Access Denied

DOS does not erase the file.

> *Warning:* The DOS Shell Delete command, discussed in Chapter 10, warns you if you attempt to delete a file whose read-only attribute is turned on, but the Shell permits you to delete the file if you confirm your choice.
>
> The FDISK and FORMAT commands do not observe the read-only status of a file. FDISK and FORMAT are disk-level commands; therefore, they do not look at disk directories when doing their jobs. Don't rely on the read-only attribute of a file to protect the file from a disk-level command.

After you use the ATTRIB +R command to mark a file as read-only, you can use the ATTRIB –R command to reset (turn off) the read-only attribute. For example, to reset the read-only attribute of BUDGET.WQ1, type the following command at the command prompt, and press Enter:

    ATTRIB –R BUDGET.WQ1

The file is again subject to DOS commands that can overwrite or erase the file.

To turn off the read-only attribute by using the DOS Shell, follow the same procedure, described in the preceding paragraphs, for turning on the attribute. Each attribute acts as a toggle switch, so the Shell turns the read-only attribute back off.

Making COMMAND.COM Read-Only with ATTRIB

COMMAND.COM is an important program file. To protect the file against accidental erasure or overwriting, you can make COMMAND.COM read-only by using the ATTRIB command. Assume that COMMAND.COM is in the root directory of your C disk. To determine the current attribute settings, type the following command at the command prompt, and press Enter:

    ATTRIB C:\COMMAND.COM

DOS displays the following information:

```
A        C:\COMMAND.COM
```

By default, the A (archive) attribute is set, as denoted by the letter A, which is displayed to the left of the file name. The R (read-only) attribute is not set.

To turn on the read-only attribute, issue the following command:

ATTRIB +R C:\COMMAND.COM

COMMAND.COM is now a read-only file. To verify the change, issue the following command:

ATTRIB \COMMAND.COM

DOS responds as follows:

```
A  R      C:\COMMAND.COM
```

The letter R now displays, as well as the letter A. The R indicates that the file's read-only attribute is set.

Expanding the File System through Subdirectories

The DOS designers designed one master directory with a predetermined number of file entries to limit the space occupied by the directory. Recall that FORMAT establishes one fixed-length directory for each disk. Keeping this directory small is important because the larger the directory, the less space is left on the disk for your files. The designers first established a cap on the number of entries in the directory to fix its size. This cap number was proportional to the capacity of the disk. Thus, floppies had fewer file entries in the master directory (fewer bytes) than hard disks. For most DOS users, however, one directory is not sufficient for effective file management.

The FORMAT-provided directory, called the *root directory*, is not intended to accommodate every possible file a disk can hold. DOS does not limit directory entries to those of the root directory; you also can enter files into expansion directories, or *subdirectories*. DOS provides a disk with a root directory, but you can add to the file system as many subdirectories as you require.

In the root directory or in a subdirectory, DOS still enters the name and the first cluster number of a file's FAT entry. The DOS subdirectory is a special file that DOS uses much like the root directory. Because DOS appears to work with the root directory and subdirectories in the same way, DOS users often call subdirectories "directories." Although internally DOS manages the root directory and subdirectory differently, subdirectories safely can be called directories.

DOS provides a few commands to manage the subdirectory system, including commands to create, remove, and change the current directory. You learn about these commands in detail in the next chapter, but the following paragraphs introduce them briefly.

A freshly formatted disk contains only one directory, the root directory. With the MKDIR (MAKE DIRECTORY) command, you can create a subdirectory. For example, you can create a subdirectory called LETTERS (you can use any file name DOS accepts) and keep in this new subdirectory all the letter files you create. Subdirectories have the advantage of holding files of some common type or purpose.

To change the current directory and focus DOS's attention on the LETTERS subdirectory, you can use the CHDIR (CHANGE DIRECTORY) command. DOS keeps track of the current directory in the same way it tracks the current drive. After you change to a directory, the new directory becomes the current directory for that disk. When you boot DOS, the current directory is the root directory of the boot disk.

If you want to remove the LETTERS subdirectory, you can use the RMDIR (REMOVE DIRECTORY) command, but the directory must contain no files. DOS does not enable you to delete a directory and make orphans of the files in that directory.

Subdirectories in DOS 2.0 and later versions, as well as the commands that support them, are a great advancement over the single fixed directories of DOS 1. The feature that gives the most efficiency to the DOS file system is the hierarchical relationship among the subdirectories—each subdirectory can, in turn, contain other subdirectories, which also can contain subdirectories, and so on.

Understanding the Hierarchical Directory System

You can arrange your DOS directories and subdirectories in a hierarchy. The term *hierarchy* means an organization or arrangement of entities. Entities can refer to people, objects, ideas, files, and so on. To a genealogist, entities in a hierarchy may be people in a family tree. To DOS, entities in a hierarchy are directories in a directory system. In either case, the hierarchy begins with the *root entity*. In a family tree, the root entity may be great-great-grandfather Isaac Watson. In DOS, this core entity is the root directory. In genealogy, people can trace their roots through their parents and then through their parents' generations. People know who their fore-fathers are, based on the relationships of the family tree. In DOS, subdirectories can trace their *paths* back to the root directory. DOS subdirectories and their files are identifiable by their relationships to other subdirectories.

You can create many subdirectories from the root. (Chapter 9 covers the commands for creating and deleting subdirectories.) The root is the *parent* of each subdirectory. You also can create subdirectories stemming from other subdirectories so that the new subdirectories have another subdirectory as their parent directory. Figure 8.4 illustrates how subdirectories are arranged hierarchically from the root. The arrangement looks like that of a family tree. Indeed, the DOS directory system is often called a *tree-structured* directory system.

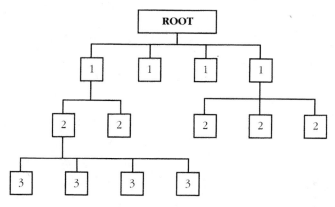

Fig. 8.4. *Hierarchical levels of a DOS directory tree.*

Figure 8.4 represents three levels of subdirectories. Because you determine the subdirectories on your disks, your directory may have more or fewer levels. Regardless of the number of levels, the relationship among the subdirectories is important.

You easily can see why the DOS hierarchical file system is called a tree-structured file system. The base of this tree structure is the root directory. In a family tree, David may be the son of Wayne, who is the son of Alex, the son of John. John is the head, or root, of the family tree for David. Another way to represent David's identity in this family tree is as follows:

John\Alex\Wayne\David

In this example, each level of the family tree is separated by a backslash character. This David is different from the following David:

Isaac\Virgil\Robert\David

Both share the name David, but their relationships to their parents are unique. DOS directories share the same kind of identity relationships as families. With DOS 2.0 and later versions, every DOS disk can have a family of directories (subdirectories) that stems from the root directory.

DOS enables you to add directories in levels like generations. The directory LETTERS is a first-level subdirectory. LETTERS (you supply the directory name) is created as an *offspring* of the root directory. The root has no name as such and is simply referenced on the command line as the backslash (\) character.

To refer to the file MEMO.DOC located in the LETTERS subdirectory, you can use the name \LETTERS\MEMO.DOC. If the MEMO.DOC file is located on a drive other than the current drive, you must specify disk, directory, and file-name parameters, such as C:\LETTERS\MEMO.DOC. The drive parameter is C:, \LETTERS is the directory parameter, and MEMO.DOC is the file parameter. The root directory of drive C is the parent directory of LETTERS, and LETTERS is the parent directory of the file MEMO.DOC.

Understanding Path Names

Each directory, including the root directory, can contain user files. Two files can have the same file name and extension as long as the files reside in different directories. When you specify a file name in a DOS command, DOS needs to know the names of the directories, starting from the root, that lead to the file. This sequence of directory names leading to a file is called the file's *directory path*, or just the file's *path*.

When specifying a file's path, use a backslash (\) to separate one directory name from another. This backslash is DOS's directory delimiter. In symbolic notation, the path for a file appears as follows:

   d:\dir1\dir2\dir3...\filename.ext

d: is the drive letter. The first \ is the DOS name for the root. *dir1\dir2\dir3...* indicates a chain of directories in which the directory to the left of another directory is the parent. The (...) indicates that more (or fewer) directory names are allowed. All characters between the first \ and the final \ comprise the file's directory path. The *filename.ext* parameter is the name of the file.

To see how the path parameter works with DOS, look again at the DIR command. Recall that issuing DIR alone on the command line causes DOS to display a list of files found in the current directory of the logged drive.

DOS supplies the drive and directory parameter for the command by using the current drive and current directory. You can, however, instruct DOS to display a list of files found in a different drive and directory by explicitly specifying the path to that drive and directory.

When you boot DOS, the current directory is the root directory of the boot disk. If you want to see the files in the \DOS subdirectory, for example, you must include the path parameter in the directory command. To see the COM extension files in \DOS from the root of the logged drive, you issue the following command:

DIR \DOS*.COM

If your current drive is A and you want to see the COM files on drive C in the \DOS directory, issue the following command:

DIR C:\DOS*.COM

You can log onto the \DOS directory by using the command CHDIR \DOS; \DOS becomes the current directory on the current disk (see Chapter 9 for a discussion of CHDIR). If you don't specify a directory parameter in a DOS command, DOS assumes that you mean to use the current directory, \DOS. Thus, to see the COM files in the \DOS directory, issue the following command:

DIR *.COM

This command produces the same list of files as the command DIR \DOS*.COM issued from the root directory. DOS supplies the \DOS path by default. Many DOS commands work with optional path parameters. When you don't supply a path, DOS uses the current drive and current directory as the default path. Check the syntax for each command to see whether you can take advantage of the default path.

Using PROMPT To Display a Full Path

While you are reading about the hierarchical directory system, you may want to confirm that your DOS prompt is displaying the current drive and current directory, referred to collectively as the *full path*. The internal command PROMPT enables you to display the full path as part of the DOS prompt. DOS 5.0 supplies the appropriate prompt command automatically in the AUTOEXEC.BAT, a special program file that runs each time you boot your computer. If your command prompt does not already show the path, issue the following command:

PROMPT pg

After you issue this prompt command, DOS shows the full path in the prompt. For example, when you are logged onto the \DOS directory on drive C, the command prompt is

```
C:\DOS>
```

The **$p** parameter in the PROMPT command tells DOS to display the full path as part of the prompt. **$g** tells DOS to display the greater-than symbol (>) as the end of the prompt. This prompt reminds you of where you are working in the hierarchical directory system.

Unless this PROMPT command is included in your system's AUTOEXEC.BAT file, the prompt returns to its former look as soon as you reboot.

Helping DOS Find External Commands

When you issue an external DOS command, DOS cannot execute the command unless the program can locate the DOS external program file. You can tell DOS where the program file is located in three ways:

- Log onto the disk and directory that contains the command.

- Supply the path in the command line.

- Establish a DOS search path to the command's directory.

So far, you have learned how to log onto the drive and directory that contain the external command file. In this case, DOS finds the command by using the default drive and path.

If you want to use an external command located on another drive or directory, you can supply the drive and path information as a part of the DOS command. For example, if drive B is the current drive and the DOS external commands are on the working DOS disk in drive A, you can issue the following command:

A:CHKDSK

DOS looks on drive A for the CHKDSK program and analyzes the disk in drive B, the current drive.

In another example, if the CHKDSK command is in a directory named \DOS on drive C, and you are logged onto drive B, you can analyze the disk in B with the following command:

C:\DOS\CHKDSK

Drive B is the current drive, so you must specify C as the drive parameter. You also must specify the directory where CHKDSK resides, \DOS. A \ separates the path from the file-name parameter. With the disk-drive parameter and path to the command given in the command line, DOS finds and executes the CHKDSK command and analyzes the disk in drive B.

The most convenient method to help DOS find external commands is to use the PATH command to establish a *search path* for DOS to use. DOS designers anticipated that you would not want to log onto the drive containing an external command or give the directory path every time you use a command. The PATH command enables you to give DOS a list of directories through which to search each time you issue an external command or type the name of a batch file or executable program file.

> *Technical Note:* The PATH command enables DOS to locate and execute program files with COM and EXE extensions. Batch files with BAT extensions also are located and executed through the search path. If you supply a path to a program on the command line, DOS does not search the path alternatives if the program is not in the directory you specify.
>
> You can include up to 127 characters in the PATH command. If you are unsure of your current PATH setting, you can issue the PATH command without parameters. DOS shows the current PATH setting.
>
> The PATH command does not help DOS find data files. A similar command, APPEND, provides a list of directories through which DOS searches for data files. The APPEND command is discussed in the Command Reference section.

The syntax of the PATH command is as follows:

PATH=*d1:path1\;d2:path2\;...*

The equal sign (=) is optional; you can simply use a space. *d1:* is the first drive and contains *path1\.* If DOS doesn't find a specified program file in the current directory, DOS looks for the program next in *path1* on disk *d1.* The semicolon (*;*) character following *path1* marks the end of the first path. *d2:path2* is a second drive and path combination for DOS to search if the desired program is not in the first path. *;...* indicates that you can add other alternative paths to the command. DOS searches for a program from left-to-right through the path alternatives. You normally should give the drive parameters with the path parameters, because you don't want DOS to search for a directory on the default drive when the directory is really on another drive.

Nearly all hard disk users take advantage of the PATH command. DOS 5's installation program, as well as the installation programs for many applications programs add to or modify the PATH statement in the AUTOEXEC.BAT file. Program instructions usually recommend which path alternative you should add. Read the documentation that comes with your application programs to determine the appropriate PATH command. For DOS use on a hard disk, you certainly want to include the directory that holds the DOS external commands. You then can issue DOS external commands from any drive or directory without specifying the drive or directory where the DOS program files reside. Thanks to the PATH command, internal and external commands are equally convenient.

For example, suppose that the DOS external program files are located in a directory named \DOS on your computer's C drive. To include the external commands in your search path, issue the following command:

PATH=C:\DOS

DOS looks in C:\DOS for any program not located in the current directory. If you have other applications programs, you can add their directories to the path. For example, to add dBASE's directory to the path, issue the following command:

PATH=C:\DOS;C:\DBASE

Notice that the semicolon separates the two directory names. When you issue the command to start dBASE at a command prompt, DOS first tries to find the program in the current directory. DOS then searches C:\DOS for the dBASE program, and failing to find it there, searches C:\DBASE, where the file is located.

TIP

Tip: You should use PATH in your AUTOEXEC.BAT file so that the desired paths are automatically established when you boot. See Chapter 13 for more information.

Summary

In this chapter, you are introduced to hierarchical directories and related concepts. You see how the FAT and directories contain the what-and-where values for a file, which DOS uses to locate data about a file. Understanding how DOS directories relate to one another is an important step toward mastering the DOS directory-level commands and using file-level commands effectively. The following key points are discussed in this chapter:

- Directories store the entries for each file. Each file has a name, time, and date of creation or modification, file attributes, and file size.

- The starting cluster stored in a file's directory entry points to a chain of clusters in the FAT that log the file's actual location on the disk.

- File attributes indicate special status for a file. Attributes are read-only (read/write), hidden, system, volume label, subdirectory, and archive.

- The ATTRIB command enables you to control the read-only, archive, system, and hidden attributes.

- DOS creates the root directory when DOS formats a disk, and you add subdirectories through the MKDIR command. You name subdirectories using any legal DOS file name and optional extension.

- The root directory and subdirectories form a hierarchical tree structure.

- You can change to a directory with the CHDIR command. That directory then becomes the current directory.

- The command PROMPT=pg causes the DOS prompt to display the current drive and directory as a part of the DOS prompt.

- The PATH command helps DOS find and execute a program file, such as an external command, when the program file is not in the current directory.

In the next chapter, you learn to use directory-management commands to manage your disks. Now that you have the information in this chapter as a background, the next chapter takes you well on your way to controlling DOS's hierarchical directory system.

Managing
Directories

This chapter explains how you can design, manage, and modify your directory system by using the directory-level commands of the DOS Shell and the DOS command line. The chapter also offers suggestions for efficiently managing the hierarchical directory system on your hard disk.

Key Terms Used in This Chapter

Relative path	The path from the current directory where the root and intervening directories are taken from DOS defaults
Absolute path	The path named from the root directory, including all intervening subdirectories
Redirection	Sending the input or output of a command to a device other than the one to which the input or output normally goes

Reviewing Directories and Subdirectories

A subdirectory is a file DOS uses in the same general way DOS uses the root directory. Recall from Chapter 8 that the root directory is a fixed-length table and resides on each disk. You can think of the root directory and subdirectories as being just "plain" directories because most of your DOS commands use the root directory and subdirectories similarly. The remainder of this book generally uses the term *directory* to refer to all directories, whether the root or subdirectories. The text uses the term *root directory* when required for clarity.

Although a disk is not physically divided into subdirectories of files—a directory's files may be spread across the disk—thinking of file data as being in a particular directory is logical because a file's data is tied to an entry in that directory. For the purpose of discussing the contents of a directory, thinking of a directory as a "place" on the disk does no harm.

> *Note:* When you are specifying a directory path in a DOS command, follow these three guidelines:
>
> - To indicate that a path begins at the root directory, begin the path with the backslash (\).
>
> - To indicate that the path begins in the current directory, do not begin with \.
>
> - When you want to use the current directory, omit the path specification from the command. DOS assumes that the path is the path of the current directory.

Working with Directories through the DOS Shell

DOS 5 provides both DOS Shell commands and internal DOS commands (for use at the command line) that manage directories. The Shell commands generally involve the directory tree area of the DOS Shell window. The following sections describe how to use the DOS Shell's directory tree area.

Understanding the Directory Tree

When you first start the DOS Shell, the DOS Shell window is divided into the drive area, at the top of the screen, and three larger areas: the directory tree area, the file list area, and the program list area (see fig. 9.1; refer to Chapter 4 for a full discussion of the DOS Shell window).

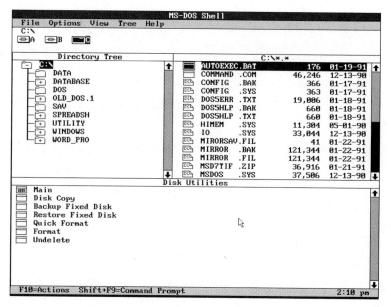

Fig. 9.1. The DOS Shell window.

The drive area at the top of the DOS Shell window indicates the selected disk by highlighting one of the drive icons. Figure 9.1, for example, shows that C is the selected drive.

As Chapter 8 explains, DOS manages files on your disks by maintaining file information in a hierarchical directory structure. The directory tree area, in the upper left quadrant of the window, graphically depicts this directory structure. At the top of this area, the root directory of the logged disk is shown as a folder-shaped icon, or as a pair of brackets ([ ]) if the DOS Shell is in text mode. All other directories are shown as folder-shaped icons (or pairs of brackets). These other directories are listed below the root icon and connected to the root icon by a vertical line. The name of each directory is listed to the right of its icon.

At any time during a session with the DOS Shell, one directory name is highlighted. This highlighted directory is referred to as the *selected directory*. When you first start the Shell, the directory that is current when you start the program is the selected directory (usually the root directory of the boot disk). The file list area of the DOS Shell window, in the upper right quadrant of the screen, lists the file names in the selected directory.

Selecting a Different Disk and Refreshing the Tree

To display the directory structure of a different disk, you must select the icon for that disk in the disk drive area of the DOS Shell window. Use one of the following methods to select a different disk:

- Move the mouse pointer to the icon for the target disk drive, and click the left mouse button.

- Press Ctrl-*d*, substituting the disk drive letter for *d*.

- Press Tab or Shift-Tab to select the disk drive area of the DOS Shell window. Use the left- or right-arrow key to highlight the drive letter of the target drive. Then press Enter to confirm your choice.

After you select a new drive, the Shell displays the selected drive's directory structure in the directory screen area. The list of files from the selected directory also displays in the file list area.

Occasionally, the Shell does not recognize that you have altered the directory or file structure on the disk and consequently displays an inaccurate list of directories, files, or both. To force the Shell to reread the directory tree and file list from the disk, press F5, or do the following:

1. Select View from the menu bar to display the View menu.

2. Choose Refresh.

The DOS Shell displays the message `Reading Disk Information` and then returns to the DOS Shell window. The directory tree and file list areas now accurately reflect the contents of the disk.

To refresh just the selected directory, press Ctrl-F5.

Occasionally, you may need to display the directory trees of two disks at the same time on one screen. At other times, you may want to see more of the directory tree than can be displayed within the standard half-screen format of the directory tree area. In either case, refer to Chapter 4 for a description of how to display a *dual file list* and a *single file list*.

Navigating the Directory Tree

Often you need to display the file names in a directory other than the currently selected directory. Use one of the following methods to select a different directory in the directory tree:

- Use the mouse to click the target directory name. If the directory tree is too long to view it entirely in the directory tree area, use the scroll bar on the right side of the directory tree area to scroll the target directory name in sight. Then click the directory name.

- Press Tab or Shift-Tab repeatedly until you select the directory tree area of the DOS Shell window. Use the up- and down-arrow keys to scroll through the directories. As you scroll up or down, the Shell displays in the file list area the names of files found in each directory in the directory tree.

Expanding and Collapsing Branches

As you recall from Chapter 8, the DOS directory structure is tree-like. The root directory is like the trunk of a tree, with all other directories growing out like branches of a tree. The DOS Shell graphically represents this tree-like nature of DOS's directory structure in the directory tree area of the DOS Shell window as an upside-down tree.

The DOS directory structure can have multiple levels, but initially the Shell shows only the first level of the tree. Each first-level directory—a directory attached directly to the root—is depicted as a *branch* of the tree. Just as branches of a real tree can have offshoot branches, each DOS directory can contain offshoot directories. The Shell indicates that a directory contains other directories by placing a plus sign (+) in the directory icon. Figure 9.1 shows plus signs in the directory icon for the following directories:

DATABASE
OLD_DOS.1
SPREADSH
UTILITY
WINDOWS
WORD_PRO

To *expand* by one level a directory tree branch that shows a + in its directory icon, use the mouse to click the + in the directory icon, or do the following:

1. Select the directory tree area that contains the target directory icon.

2. Move the selection cursor to the desired directory name.

3. Press the + key, or select E<u>x</u>pand One Level on the Tree menu.

The Shell shows the next level of directories beneath the selected directory. For example, figure 9.2 shows the expanded DATABASE directory containing four second-level directories: FOXPRO, FPDATA, FW3, and FWDATA.

Fig. 9.2. *Expanding a directory tree branch.*

> ***Note:*** Notice that the file list area in figure 9.2 indicates `No files in selected directory`. The DATABASE directory is a major division of the overall hard disk directory, used merely to hold the four subordinate directories. This approach provides an easily understandable structure for the hard disk directory. Refer to "Keeping a Clean Root Directory" in this chapter for more information on this subject.

Offshoot directories can contain more offshoots. In Chapter 8, the relationship among directory levels is described as analogous to a family tree—child, parent, grandparent, and so on. When a second-level directory contains one or more third-level directories, the Shell shows a plus sign (+) in the directory icon. For example, the directory icon of the FOXPRO directory, shown in figure 9.2, indicates that this branch of the DATABASE directory also contains at least one directory. To expand one level of the FOXPRO branch, follow the procedure you used to expand one level of the DATABASE branch.

If you do not remember precisely where a directory is located in the directory tree, expanding branches one level at a time may become tedious. When you want to expand all levels beneath a particular directory branch, use the following procedure:

1. Use the mouse to click the directory name, or use the arrow keys to move the selection cursor to the directory name.

2. Press the * key, or select Expand All from the Tree menu.

The shell expands all levels of the tree below the currently selected directory. Figure 9.3, for example, shows the fully expanded DATABASE branch of drive C's directory tree.

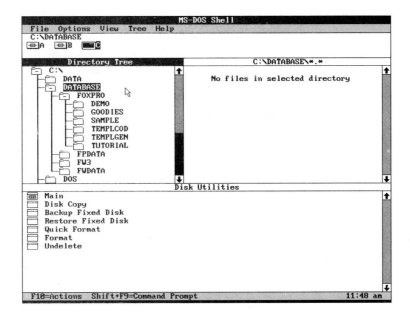

Fig. 9.3. The fully expanded DATABASE branch.

The opposite of expanding a directory branch in the directory tree area is *collapsing* a branch. When you first start the DOS Shell, you may notice that a root directory's icon contains a minus sign (–). After you expand a directory branch, the icon for the expanded branch also contains a minus sign. These minus signs are a reminder that you can collapse the branch. To collapse a branch whose icon contains a –, click the directory icon, or use the following procedure:

1. Select the directory name.

2. Press the – key, or choose Collapse Branch from the Tree menu.

To collapse the entire tree, click the root directory icon or do the following:

1. Select the root directory name, at the top of the directory tree.

2. Press the – key, or choose Collapse Branch from the Tree menu.

The Shell collapses the entire tree down to the root level and places a + in the root directory icon.

Creating Directories

Because the only automatically available directory on a DOS disk is the root, you must add any additional directories. Even after you establish a workable directory structure for your computer, you occasionally need to create new directories on your disks. DOS enables you to add directories to a disk through the DOS Shell or through the internal MKDIR (or MD) command. The following sections discuss both methods of adding directories.

Understanding the Addition of a Directory

When you instruct DOS to create a new directory, whether through the DOS Shell or through the MKDIR command, DOS does some work behind the scenes before complying.

First, DOS verifies that the given (or implied by default) parent directory exists. You cannot create two directory levels with one command. Next, DOS confirms that the new directory has a unique name. To confirm uniqueness, DOS ensures that the parent directory does not contain an entry for a file with the same name as the proposed directory's name. Because subdirectories are files, DOS has no convenient means of separating a directory from a normal file with the same name.

After confirming that the new directory name is unique in the parent directory, DOS allocates a file for the new directory and marks the new file entry in the parent directory as a subdirectory.

DOS completes two entries in the new directory. The name of the first entry is always . (pronounced "dot"). The dot entry in a directory refers, or points, to the directory that contains it. You can think of the dot entry as an *alias* for the current directory's name, analogous to the pronoun *me*.

The second entry is always named .. (pronounced "dot-dot"). DOS uses this dot-dot entry to point to the parent of the current directory. This entry is an alias for the parent directory's name and is analogous to the name *Mom* or *Dad*.

> *Note:* Every subdirectory you create automatically contains the . and .. alias entries. If you use the DIR command to view a subdirectory's file entries, you always see the . and .. entries.
>
> On the command line, COMMAND.COM accepts the alias entries . and .. as legitimate parts of path specifiers. When specifying a directory path in a DOS command, you can use the .. alias anytime as shorthand to indicate the path of the current directory's parent. Some examples of .. in commands are included in this chapter.

When you create a directory, whether through the DOS Shell or at the command line, follow these naming guidelines:

- All characters allowed in a normal file name can be used in a directory name.

- A directory name cannot be the name of a standard DOS device, such as AUX, PRN, and CON.

- A directory name cannot duplicate a file name in the intended parent directory, although you could create a directory called DAD in a directory containing the file DAD.TXT.

Creating a Directory in the Shell

To create a new directory using the DOS Shell, do the following:

1. Select the directory tree area of the DOS Shell window.

2. Select the directory to be the parent of the new directory.

3. Select <u>F</u>ile from the menu bar to display the File menu.

4. Choose Cr<u>e</u>ate Directory from the File menu.

   The Shell displays the Create Directory dialog box shown in
   figure 9.4. This dialog box indicates the name of the parent directory. In the example, C:\SPREADSH is the parent directory.

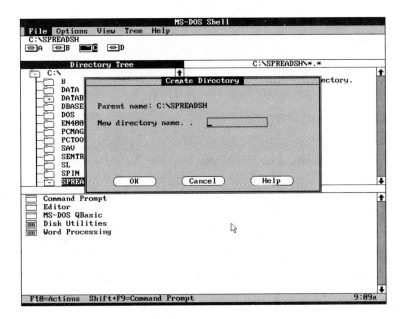

Fig. 9.4. *The Create Directory dialog box.*

5. Type the name of the new directory, and press Enter or click OK.

The Shell creates the new directory and returns to the directory tree area of
the DOS Shell window. The Shell also adds to the tree an icon for the new
directory.

TIP

Tip: Assigning directory names that in some way describe the files
they contain is often helpful, even though the name you give a
directory has no effect on the data in these files. Directory names
such as DATABASE, UTILITY, and WINDOWS, for example, are more
descriptive than DIR-ONE, FILES, or PROGRAMS.

Creating Directories with MKDIR (MD)

DOS provides the internal MKDIR, or MD, command, which you use to tell DOS to make a new directory. The MKDIR and MD names for this command are identical in operation. Anywhere you see MKDIR in the following discussions, you can substitute MD if you prefer.

When you use the MKDIR command, consider the following guidelines:

- MKDIR and MD are different names for the same DOS command (for use at the command line). Both commands produce identical results.

- The specified or implied parent directory of the intended directory must exist. MKDIR (MD) cannot make more than one directory at a time. On a disk with only a root directory, for example, the command MKDIR \PROG\DATA does not work.

- MKDIR (MD) does not change the current directory to the new directory. To change to the new directory, use CHDIR (CD).

When you issue the MKDIR command, you are instructing DOS to add a new directory to some part of the file-system tree. The following syntax and examples use the MKDIR version of the command. The syntax for the MKDIR command is as follows:

MKDIR *d:path***name**

The *d:* parameter is optional. It indicates the disk where the new directory is to be added. If *d:* is omitted, the default drive is used.

The *path*\ parameter is also optional. It indicates the directory path to which the new directory is to be added.

The **name** parameter is not optional. You must specify the name for the new directory.

The length of the full path (drive, path, and new directory name) must not exceed 63 characters, including delimiters. The full path name is the measure for length. If you are creating a directory relative to your current directory, you must count your current directory's full path length including the implied root \ character as being part of the 63-character limit.

Note: When you begin a path parameter with the \ character, you are telling DOS how to locate the directory or file from the root directory—the file's *absolute path*. If you specify a path that does not begin with \, DOS assumes that you are specifying a path *relative* to your current directory. For example, if your current directory is \DOS and you want to add the directory \DOS\DRIVERS, you can issue the command **MKDIR DRIVERS**. Notice that no leading \ appears in front of the new directory name DRIVERS. When you omit the leading \, DOS adds the current directory path to the path parameter you specified in the command in order to form the complete path parameter.

Relative path parameters also work with other DOS commands. You can see instances of relative paths as path parameters in other examples.

For this example, assume that you are currently logged onto the root directory of a formatted floppy disk in drive A. If you are using DOS on a hard disk, the examples that follow assume that you have used PATH to establish a path to the directory that contains the external DOS commands (see "Helping DOS Find External Commands" in Chapter 8). To create the directory \DATA on the disk in drive A, enter the following command:

MKDIR \DATA

DOS makes the new directory, DATA, on the disk in drive A. You can issue a DIR command to see the new directory. You also can achieve the same result by issuing the MKDIR command while logged onto the root directory of drive A. You use the relative path form of a path parameter as in the following:

MKDIR DATA

The directory is created directly from the root even though no disk name or beginning backslash is given in the command line. DOS uses the current (default) drive, A, and makes the directory relative to the current directory, the root. If you do not specify a path, DOS makes the current directory the parent directory of your new directory.

Changing the Current Directory with CHDIR (CD)

When you are working at the DOS command line, DOS remembers the current directory and the current drive name. You issue the CHDIR, or CD, command to change the current directory to a new current directory. If you omit a path parameter, in most commands, DOS searches only the current directory when looking for files or programs.

> *Note:* CHDIR and CD initiate the same command; their usage is identical.

The CHDIR command is the hierarchical directory system's navigation command. Its primary use is to change the current directory.

CHDIR alone (with no parameters) is the "Where am I?" command. If you use the CHDIR command with no path parameter, DOS reports the current directory's path name. Issuing only CHDIR tells DOS to report where commands using no drive and path parameters do their work; CHDIR alone does not change your current directory.

The syntax for CD, or CHDIR, is as follows:

CHDIR *d:path*

The *d:* parameter is optional; it indicates the disk drive where the directory is located. Using this parameter does not change the current logged drive, but this parameter enables you to change the current directory on a drive without first logging onto that drive. If you omit the drive parameter, DOS uses the current drive.

The *path* parameter is the name of the new current directory. The path parameter can begin with the .. alias, which instructs the command to begin at the parent of the current directory.

When using the CHDIR command, follow these guidelines:

- CHDIR and CD are different names for the same command. Both names produce identical results.

- The drive and path parameters in the command line must be valid.

- If the path parameter begins with \, CHDIR assumes that the directory specified in path is *absolute*—from the root.

- If the path parameter does not begin with \, CHDIR assumes that the directory given in path is *relative*—from the current directory.

- When you specify a drive parameter but no path parameter, CHDIR reports the current working directory for the specified disk.

- When the path parameter and the drive parameter are omitted from the command line, CHDIR reports the current working directory of the currently logged drive.

Tip: You can always change to the root directory of the logged disk by typing **CHDIR ** or **CD **.

Suppose, for example, that the current directory on drive A is \DIR1. To receive a report of the logged (default) directory of a disk, you issue the CHDIR command in the following form:

CHDIR A:

CHDIR reports drive A's logged directory as the following:

```
A:\DIR1
```

Suppose that the logged disk is drive C and that the current directory of C is \KEEP. To see the default directory, issue the command in the following form:

CHDIR

CHDIR reports as follows:

```
C:\KEEP
```

Tip: The easiest way to cause DOS to display the names of the current drive and directory is to use the PROMPT pg command, discussed in Chapters 8 and 13.

To change the default directory of the disk in drive A to \FILES when the logged drive is C, issue the command in the following form:

CHDIR A:\FILES

DOS changes the default directory in A to \FILES. To confirm the change, issue the command in the following form:

CHDIR A:

CHDIR replies as follows:

```
A:\FILES
```

The subdirectories \WORDS\MEMOS and \WORDS\DOCS have \WORDS as their parent directory. To change the directory in the current drive C from \WORDS\MEMOS to \WORDS\DOCS, issue the command in the following form:

CHDIR ..\DOCS

Notice that the alias for the parent directory (.. with no leading \) of the current directory acts as a shorthand substitute for the same full command:

CHDIR \WORDS\DOCS

To change from the \WORDS\DOCS directory on the current drive to \WORDS (the parent directory of \WORDS\DOCS), you issue the command in the following form:

CHDIR ..

DOS changes to \WORDS as the current directory of the logged disk. The use of the .. alias as the only parameter of the command always changes to the parent of the current directory unless the current directory is the root. The root has no parent.

Deleting Directories

Just as you occasionally need to add a directory to a disk, you may need to delete a directory. DOS enables you to remove empty directories at the end of a directory branch in the directory tree. In other words, you can remove an empty directory at the lowest level of a directory branch.

You can delete a directory from the DOS Shell or from the command line. The sections that follow describe both methods.

Deleting a Directory in the Shell

To remove a directory in the DOS Shell, use the following procedure:

1. Delete all files and other directories contained in the directory you want to delete (refer to Chapter 10).

2. Select the directory name in the Shell directory tree area.

3. Press the Del key, or choose <u>F</u>ile from the menu bar and then <u>D</u>elete from the File menu.

If you attempt to delete a directory that contains one or more files or directories, the Shell does not delete the directory. Instead, the Shell displays an error message.

Removing an Unneeded Directory with RMDIR (RD)

When you need to remove a directory from your directory tree structure, use the RMDIR, or RD, command.

> *Note:* The two command names RMDIR and RD are different names for the same command; the action of both names is identical.

RMDIR removes directories at the lowest level of a directory path. Just as you can create a directory structure with MKDIR, you can remove a directory structure with RMDIR. RMDIR enables you to rearrange your directory system if you change your mind about your current choices for directories or their names.

> *Note:* DOS does not provide a command for use at the command line to rename directories. You can use the DOS Shell to rename a directory (beginning with DOS 5.0). Alternatively, you can remove a directory and then create a new directory with the desired name.

The syntax for RMDIR is as follows:

RMDIR *d:* **path**

The *d:* parameter is optional; it specifies the disk that contains the directory to be removed. If *d:* is omitted from the command line, DOS assumes that the current (logged) disk holds the directory to be removed.

The **path** parameter is required. It specifies the directory path of the directory to be removed. If **path** begins with a backslash (\), DOS assumes that the path to the directory name is absolute from the root. If the path parameter does not begin with a backslash, DOS assumes that the path to the directory name is relative from the current directory of *d:*.

Deleting a subdirectory is similar to deleting a user file. Subdirectory entries are special files to DOS. Unlike user files, however, subdirectories may contain user files and subdirectory entries. DOS does not "orphan" a subdirectory's files and lower subdirectories by deleting the subdirectory.

When you issue the RMDIR (RD) command to delete a subdirectory, DOS checks to ensure that the subdirectory is empty.

> *Note:* An empty subdirectory contains the . and .. file entries, but DOS knows that these two entries are part of the subdirectory bookkeeping function. The presence of only the . and .. files in the directory indicates to DOS that the directory is empty.

DOS also checks to ensure that the current directory is not the directory you are deleting. You cannot delete a current directory.

TIP

> *Tip:* Hidden files that do not appear in a DIR command listing of the directory are considered user files; the directory cannot be removed if it contains hidden files. Use the ATTRIB command or the DOS Shell to uncover the presence of hidden files on a disk (DOS 5.0 or later).

After determining that the subdirectory to be deleted is empty and is not the current directory, DOS removes the directory from the file system.

When using the RMDIR command, follow these guidelines:

- The directory you remove must be empty.

- The root directory is not a subdirectory. You cannot remove a root directory.

- The number of characters in the full path name (drive, path, and directory) to be removed cannot exceed 63.

- A directory affected by a SUBST command cannot be removed.

- Do not remove directories from a drive that is affected by a JOIN or ASSIGN command.

The SUBST, JOIN, and ASSIGN commands are covered in Chapter 15, "Configuring Your Computer and Managing Devices."

When you are maintaining files, you may create a directory to contain files for a special purpose of limited duration. Perhaps you keep a few files that need to be checked in a special directory. After you check the files, you no longer need to keep the files separate, or you may not need the files at all. The directory itself may be of no further use to you, and you want to remove the directory from your disk.

As an example, assume that drive E of your system includes the directory \PROLOG\DSWORK\DONE, which contains program files that have been checked by their author. The files and the directory are no longer needed, so they can be removed. First, log onto drive E. Then, to change to the \PROLOG\DSWORK directory, use the following command:

CHDIR \PROLOG\DSWORK

You are now logged onto the parent directory of \PROLOG\DSWORK\DONE. To see the name of the directory to be deleted, type the following command:

DIR *.

DOS reports the directory on-screen as follows:

```
Volume in drive E is LOGICAL E
Directory of  E:\PROLOG\DSWORK
.         <DIR> 7-05-91       11:54a
..        <DIR> 7-05-91       11:54a
DONE    <DIR> 7-11-91        9:42a
     3 File(s)         0 bytes
                  200704 bytes free
```

DONE, the name of the directory you want to delete, is displayed in this DIR listing. The file name parameter included in the DIR command, *., causes DOS to display all file names that have no file name extensions contained in the current directory.

Now, from the parent directory of the directory to be deleted, issue the RMDIR command with no drive and path parameters as follows:

RMDIR DONE

Sometimes when you try to delete a directory, DOS responds with the following message:

```
Invalid path, not directory,
or directory not empty
```

This DOS message tells you that one of the following situations has occurred:

- The full path you specified does not exist on the disk.

- The path you specified names a file, not a directory.

- The directory you are asking DOS to delete still contains files or subdirectories.

You must determine which message applies to your situation by using a process of elimination.

First, check the current directory with the CHDIR (no path parameter) command. Use DIR to look at the parent. Finally, determine whether the DONE directory contains user files or subdirectories. Change to that directory by using the following command:

CHDIR DONE

Notice that you do not have to give an absolute path to change to DONE. DOS changes to DONE relative to the current directory. You can accomplish the same directory change by issuing the following command:

CHDIR \PROLOG\DSWORK\DONE

This second form is the absolute path form of CHDIR.

When you are logged to DONE, issue the DIR command. For this example, you see the following directory listing:

```
Volume in drive E is LOGICAL E
Directory of  E:\PROLOG\DSWORK\DONE
     .          <DIR>         8-11-91    10:23a
     ..         <DIR>         8-11-91    10:23a
DWIMDOS  PRO   3439          6-03-91    5:23p
DWIM1    PRO   5414          6-04-91    11:07a
DWIM2    PRO   11625         6-06-91    5:39p
        5 file(s)   20478 bytes
                   200704 bytes free
```

The directory listing of the DONE directory shows that the directory is not empty. You can erase all files that contain the PRO extension to empty the directory (erasing files is covered in the next chapter); then verify that the directory is empty by issuing another DIR command. The DIR command reports the following:

```
Volume in drive E is LOGICAL E
Directory of  E:\PROLOG\DSWORK\DONE
   .   <DIR>       8-11-91 10:23a
   ..  <DIR>       8-11-91 10:23a
      2 file(s)      0 bytes
                 255280 bytes free
```

Now only the . and .. alias directory entries remain. You can change to the parent directory by using the following shorthand command:

CHDIR ..

From this parent directory, you can remove the now empty DONE directory with the following command:

RMDIR DONE

The E:\PROLOG\DSWORK\DONE directory is removed.

Renaming Directories

Even if you are careful in the way you name directories, you will invariably want to change a directory name sooner or later. Suppose that you just upgraded from Quattro 2.0 to Quattro 3.0, for instance, and you want to rename a directory from QPR2DAT (for Quattro Pro 2.0 data) to QPRO3DAT (for Quattro Pro 3.0 data).

To rename a directory using the DOS Shell, do the following:

1. Select the directory name in the directory tree.

2. Choose File from the menu bar to display the File menu.

3. Select Rename from the File menu.

    The Shell displays the Rename Directory dialog box. This dialog box lists the current directory name followed by a text box labeled New Name.

4. Type the new name in the text box; then press Enter or click OK.

The Shell renames the directory and immediately registers the change in the directory tree area of the DOS Shell window.

> *Note:* DOS does not provide a command-line command to rename a directory.

Listing Directories with TREE

The files in your hierarchical directories probably are organized much the same way you physically organize floppy disks. Perhaps you keep directories for letters, applications programs, memos, and many other categories, just as you keep disks with categories of files. As the number of directories and files grows, however, your ability to remember which directory holds which file decreases. Instead of asking yourself which disk holds your file, your question becomes "Which directory holds my file?"

DOS provides an external command—TREE—that lists all the directories of a disk as a tree structure similar to the DOS Shell directory tree. The TREE command also can list the files in the directories. If you have a hard disk, you may find the TREE command especially useful.

The TREE command syntax is as follows:

> **TREE** *d:path\ /F/A*

d: is an optional parameter that indicates the drive whose directories you want to list. If you omit *d:*, TREE lists the directories on the current disk drive.

TREE with MS-DOS 3.3 and later accepts the optional *path* parameter. The path parameter names the directory where TREE starts processing the listing. If the path parameter is omitted, TREE begins processing from the root directory.

TREE in DOS 3.3 and earlier versions accepts only the single switch */F*, which directs TREE to list the files in the directories. Use this switch if you are trying to locate a file. If you do not give the switch, TREE displays only a list of the disk's directories, not the disk's files.

In DOS 4.0 and later, TREE displays the directory tree with line graphics characters. The */A* switch uses nongraphics characters to draw the tree.

Trying Hands-On Examples

The hypothetical examples given with the explanation of the directory-management commands illustrate how the commands work, but hands-on examples can be helpful as well. The exercise in this section uses a practice disk in drive A. You can try the MKDIR, CHDIR, TREE, and RMDIR commands on the practice disk. The exercise assumes that DOS is in drive C and that a PATH command tells DOS where the external FORMAT, LABEL, and TREE commands are located on drive C.

If you have two floppy disks instead of a hard disk, use DOS in drive A and perform the exercise on a disk in drive B, which should be your logged drive. You need to give the location of the drive that contains your external commands when using the FORMAT, LABEL, and TREE commands, as in **A:TREE**. Be sure that your working DOS disk is write-protected.

If you have only one floppy drive, you can use drive parameters that make DOS use the one drive as two. With DOS on a disk designated as A, start by formatting a disk with the command **FORMAT B:**. Log onto drive B. DOS asks you to insert the disk for drive B. You leave the new formatted disk in the drive. When you issue the TREE and LABEL commands, issue them as **A:TREE** and **A:LABEL**. DOS asks you to insert the disk for drive A. At that time, remove the practice disk and insert the DOS disk. Be sure that your working DOS disk is write-protected.

> *Note:* Your version of DOS may produce slightly different messages and displays from those shown. As usual, these differences are minor and don't affect the exercise.

Preparing the Exercise Disk

For this exercise, to avoid disturbing a useful disk, you should use a blank or surplus floppy disk. If you have a formatted blank disk, you can skip this part of the exercise. If you are using a previously formatted disk, use the DIR command on the disk to ensure that it is empty.

Insert the blank disk into drive A and issue the following command:

FORMAT A:

DOS responds with the following message:

```
Insert new diskette for drive A:
 press ENTER when ready...
```

Press Enter, and the formatting process begins. When FORMAT is finished, you see the following message:

```
Volume label  (11 characters, ENTER for none)?
```

Respond to this prompt by pressing Enter. (You add a volume label for the disk in a later step.) DOS reports the results of the formatting of the floppy and displays the following prompt:

```
Format another (Y/N)?
```

Press N and press Enter. FORMAT terminates, and DOS returns to the DOS prompt.

First, log onto the A drive with the command **A:**. Now, for the practice, issue the LABEL command as follows:

LABEL

DOS responds with the following prompt:

```
Volume in drive A has no label
Volume Serial Number is 394A-17EE
Volume label (11 characters, ENTER for none)?
```

Enter the volume label **PRACTICE**, and press Enter. You can use this disk for later practice sessions if you want, but for now, you use it to work with the directory commands.

Issue the DIR command on the formatted disk. You see the following:

```
Volume in drive A is PRACTICE
Volume Serial Number is 394A-17EE
Directory of A:\

File not found
```

Notice that the directory report is for A:\. You may be used to reading this report as a report for the entire disk, but the report is actually a report for the contents of drive A's root directory. The line File not found is a good indicator that the disk has no files or subdirectories, but remember that a hidden file is not listed by DIR. Because this disk is freshly formatted, it contains no files or subdirectories—just the root directory provided by FORMAT.

Issue the following command:

MKDIR \LEVEL1

DOS creates a directory named \LEVEL1, which stems from the root directory. You should see your disk light come on momentarily as DOS writes the directory entry for \LEVEL1 into the root. Now issue the DIR command again. The DIR report looks like the following:

```
Volume in drive A is PRACTICE
Volume Serial Number is 394A-17EE
Directory of A:\
LEVEL1        <DIR>   10-31-91     4:54p
     1 file(s)      0 bytes
            1457152 bytes free
```

Notice that the directory listing is still of the root of drive A. Making the new directory did not change the current directory. The new directory is listed in its parent (the root) directory. To make \LEVEL1 the current directory, issue the following command:

CHDIR LEVEL1

The DOS prompt displays as follows (assuming that the command PROMPT=pg is in your system's AUTOEXEC.BAT file):

```
A:\LEVEL1>
```

Now issue the DIR command again. You see the following directory listing:

```
Volume in drive A is PRACTICE
Volume Serial Number is 394A-17EE
Directory of A:\LEVEL1
.       <DIR>   10-31-91   4:54p
..      <DIR>   10-31-91   5:54p
    2 file(s) 0 bytes
            1457152 bytes free
```

The listing verifies that the directory being shown is of A:\LEVEL1. The two dot files are the only files in the directory. Notice that the two dot files are listed as directories. Remember that the dot directory is representative of \LEVEL1 itself. To test this representation, issue the DIR command as follows:

DIR .

You see the A:\LEVEL1 directory again.

The **..** entry is representative of a directory's parent directory. Try the following command:

DIR ..

You see the A:\ (root) directory listing again. Using **..** as a path parameter is a quick way to reference a path from a parent directory while a subdirectory is the current directory.

Now you can add a subdirectory to \LEVEL1 by issuing the following command:

MKDIR LEVEL2

Again, the path specified in the command is a relative path because no leading \ is used. DOS creates a new directory named \LEVEL1\LEVEL2 by adding the current directory, \LEVEL1, and the parameter of the MKDIR command, LEVEL2. Issue the **DIR** command now. You see the following:

```
Volume in drive A is PRACTICE
Volume Serial Number is 394A-17EE
Directory of A:\LEVEL1
.          <DIR>    10-31-91   4:54p
..         <DIR>    10-31-91   5:54p
LEVEL2     <DIR>    10-31-91   4:56p
   3 file(s)                 0 bytes
          1456640 bytes free
```

The new directory is listed in the \LEVEL1 parent directory. Now change to the new directory with the following command:

CHDIR LEVEL2

Again, the CHDIR parameter is a relative path to the new directory from its parent. Your DOS prompt should appear as A:\LEVEL1\LEVEL2>. The disk now has two subdirectories as a single branch of the root directory. Note that LEVEL2 can be reached only by passing through LEVEL1 because LEVEL1 is part of LEVEL2's path.

Now issue the **CHDIR** command to make the root the current directory. The prompt should be A:\> again. To see the directory structure you have created on drive A, issue the **TREE** command. You should see something like the following:

```
Directory PATH listing for Volume PRACTICE
Volume Serial Number is 394EA-17EE
A:.
    └───LEVEL1
        └───────LEVEL2
```

You can see that the structure is a main branch from the root to \LEVEL1 and an additional branch from \LEVEL1 to \LEVEL1\LEVEL2. DOS enables you to create directories in a branch, one level at a time. The next command tries to create two levels of a new branch. Issue the following command:

MKDIR \SUB1\SUB2

Because \SUB1 has not been created, DOS refuses to create \SUB1\SUB2. You get the following error message:

```
Unable to create directory
```

If you create SUB1 and then SUB2, you have no problem. Do so now with the following two commands:

MKDIR \SUB1

MKDIR \SUB1\SUB2

Notice that the parameters for the MKDIR commands use paths as absolute paths from the root. You can create these two directories with these two commands from any current directory on the disk. All the necessary path information is in the parameters. None of the path information comes from DOS's current directory default. To see the new structure of the disk's directory system, issue the TREE command again. The output should be as follows:

```
Directory PATH listing for Volume PRACTICE
Volume Serial Number is 394EA-17EE
A:.
├────LEVEL1
│       └─────── LEVEL2
└────SUB1
        └─────── SUB2
```

You can show the new branch in the directory tree containing \SUB1 and \SUB1\SUB2 by using the following command:

CHDIR \SUB1\SUB2

Your prompt should reflect the new current directory. To illustrate that you can manage other directories from the current directory, issue the following command:

DIR \LEVEL1\LEVEL2

DOS displays a listing of \LEVEL1\LEVEL2 even though the current directory for drive A is \SUB1\SUB2. Note that the only two files in the listing are the dot files. In other words, the \LEVEL1\LEVEL2 directory is empty. To delete \LEVEL1\LEVEL2, issue the following command:

RMDIR \LEVEL1\LEVEL2

You can delete the directory because it is empty. Notice that the path specified in the RMDIR command is absolute. You must reference another branch in the directory tree from the root when your current directory is in another branch. For now, return to the root and look at the directory tree by issuing the following commands:

**CHDIR **

TREE

The directory tree now appears as follows:

```
Directory PATH listing for Volume PRACTICE
Volume Serial Number is 394EA-17EE
A:.
LEVEL1
SUB1
    SUB2
```

Notice that \LEVEL1\LEVEL2 is now gone. You have created and then removed part of the directory structure.

You can continue to build on the \SUB1 directory branch by adding another subdirectory to \SUB1. Issue the following command:

MKDIR \SUB1\SUB_TOO

\SUB1\SUB_TOO is at the same level as \SUB1\SUB2 and stems from the same branch. Both directories have \SUB1 as their parent directory. The output of TREE should show the new relationship as follows:

```
Directory PATH listing for Volume PRACTICE
Volume Serial Number is 394EA-17EE
A:.
    ├──LEVEL1
    ┌─SUB1
    ├──────SUB2
    └──────SUB_TOO
```

Make \SUB1\SUB_TOO your current directory with the following command:

CHDIR \SUB1\SUB_TOO

The DOS prompt indicates the new current directory. You can make your current directory \SUB1\SUB2 by using the parent dot-dot alias in the current directory. Issue the following command:

CHDIR ..\SUB2

The prompt now reads A:\SUB1\SUB2>. How does the .. parameter in the CHDIR parameter work? Remember that in any subdirectory, DOS takes the .. entry to represent the parent directory. In this case, the parent directory is \SUB1. When DOS sees the .. in the path parameter, DOS assumes that \SUB1 should be substituted. The resulting parameter indicates \SUB1\SUB2 to DOS. DOS is able to change to the other second level directory in the \SUB1 branch without seeing \SUB1 as a literal part of the CHDIR command's parameter.

Reviewing the Exercise

If you have completed the exercise, you have successfully created, navigated, and modified a disk's directory structure. When you work with directory management in your daily computer activities, the directory management you use is not much different from that demonstrated in the exercise. If you observe the rules and syntax of the directory-level commands, you should be able to create a directory structure that fits your file organization categories perfectly. If you use the DOS Shell to manage your directories, you may find the process even easier.

Note: If you're still a bit uncomfortable with the concept of hierarchical directories and their management, keep the practice disk for more exercises. You may find that practice results in proficiency in just a short time. Don't be afraid to talk with other DOS users about their personal preferences for ways to arrange directories. No single best way exists.

I find that giving full, absolute path parameters in directory commands is the surest way to work with directories. An absolute path parameter tells DOS exactly which directory you intend the command to affect. You may want to develop the habit of using full path parameters to avoid copying or deleting files in relatively specified directories. Don't worry about DOS getting a relative path parameter mixed up. DOS does what you tell it to do. Telling DOS what to do through full path parameters helps to ensure that *you* aren't getting mixed up.

If you use .. and relative path parameters, always have a good sense of where you are in the directory system. Using .. and relative paths saves command keystrokes, but you should always use these convenient "shortcuts" with care.

Putting Hierarchical Directories To Work for You

DOS supplies each disk with a root directory. Beyond the root, you can use the directory-management commands to create a directory tree in any architecture you want. DOS enables you to control the external look of your directory tree, while DOS manages the internal bookkeeping tasks of the DOS hierarchical directory system. Still, some planning on your part can help make your directory system design easy to use.

Note: The following sections suggest some directory structures and tips. Each DOS user has individual tastes in creating a directory structure. You may want to consider the following suggestions for your use or as food for thought. If you already have your directories arranged, keep these suggestions in mind for the next time that you reorganize your hard disk.

Keeping a Clean Root Directory

The root directory for a 360K floppy can hold 112 file entries. Both 1.2M and 1.44M floppies hold 224 entries. If you have the DOS program files on your boot floppy, you can quickly exhaust these numbers as you add small files to the boot disk. There is no limit, however, to the number of files you can create in a subdirectory (as long as space remains on the disk for the files' contents).

If you have a hard disk, consider keeping the root directory as clean as possible. Keep in the root only the few necessary files that DOS needs to get started. With an uncluttered root directory on your hard disk, you can be a more efficient file manager.

Some files, however, need to be in the root of your boot disk. If you are using an AUTOEXEC.BAT file, it must reside in the root directory of the boot disk. The same rule applies to the CONFIG.SYS file, if you include one. If the disk is bootable, the hidden DOS system files also are located in the root directory, but the FORMAT or SYS commands put them there. The system files remain in the root unless you use special disk-editing software to change the hidden and system attributes so that you can erase or move these files. Be aware that if you erase or move the system files by using a third-party program, DOS does not boot.

COMMAND.COM is normally in the root by virtue of the /S switch of the FORMAT command. The root of a bootable disk is a good place for COMMAND.COM. You do not have to leave COMMAND.COM in the root, however, if you make some entries in the CONFIG.SYS (Chapter 15) and AUTOEXEC.BAT (Chapter 13) files. A good directory for COMMAND.COM is \DOS. In your CONFIG.SYS file, add the following line:

        SHELL=C:\DOS\COMMAND.COM C:\DOS /P

(See Chapter 15 for more information on CONFIG.SYS.)

> *Note:* If you are using DOS 5.0, you don't need to perform this fine-tuning because it is performed when you install DOS. The DOS 5.0 installation program, Setup, automatically adds the SHELL command to your CONFIG.SYS file. Setup also installs a copy of COMMAND.COM in the \DOS directory on your hard disk.

When DOS boots, it takes the assignment of the SHELL command and uses the path and file name to find the command processor. Be sure not to misspell any parts of the full path name. DOS locks up at boot time if the assignment to SHELL is an incorrect file. Of course, a working copy of DOS on a floppy disk makes any SHELL error (or any other hard disk boot failure) easier to recover from. Be sure that \DOS is present on the disk. After you put this line in CONFIG.SYS, do not reboot until you have copied COMMAND.COM to \DOS from the root with the following command:

COPY \COMMAND.COM \DOS /V

(Chapter 10 discusses the COPY command.)

With COMMAND.COM copied to \DOS, you can erase COMMAND.COM in the root. The command is as follows:

ERASE \COMMAND.COM

Note: If you get the error message `Access denied` when you attempt to erase COMMAND.COM, you may have previously used the DOS Shell or the ATTRIB command to make COMMAND.COM read-only. Refer to the discussions of setting and resetting attributes in Chapter 8 for help in turning off the read-only attribute. After the read-only attribute is reset, you can erase COMMAND.COM.

When you reboot, DOS finds COMMAND.COM in the \DOS directory of your boot disk, and your boot disk's root directory is free of the file.

Some users keep device drivers, the programs specific to the operation of input/output devices, in the root directory. If you have these types of files in your root directory, you can move them. The next section discusses driver files.

Some batch files often are located in a root directory. Batch files are ideal for relocation from the root because you can put them in another directory and use the PATH command to lead DOS to them. The next section also gives some considerations for finding a home for batch files.

When you are copying a floppy disk full of files to your hard disk, you easily can forget to use CHDIR to change the intended destination directory. If you rely on the convenience of DOS defaults instead of using the full destination path name in the COPY command, you can end up with your root full of files from the floppy because of wrong parameters in COPY.

If your root directory is fairly clean (containing only a few files), you can recover from this kind of goof by copying everything in the root to an empty temporary subdirectory. When the subdirectory contains the root's normal files and the errant files, you can erase all files in the root. The hidden DOS files remain because you cannot erase them. Now you copy the root's necessary files back to the root from the temporary directory. The root should contain only the files it contained before the goof. If you make a regular printout of the command TREE /F, you can double-check the root's content. When the root is back to normal, erase the temporary directory's contents. Now you're back where you started. Try your original COPY command again, but this time with the correct destination parameters.

Including a Directory To Store DOS Programs

The DOS external commands and other DOS programs, such as QBasic, Edlin, DEBUG, and Setup programs, have one important element in common: these programs are all files that relate directly to the functions of DOS. Including a directory to hold these programs and their associated files is a good idea. The name for this DOS directory can be \DOS, and as the name implies, the \DOS directory is a subdirectory of the root. Some users follow the UNIX operating system's convention of keeping the utility commands in a directory called \BIN. Either name works from an organizational point of view.

Note: When you use the DOS 5.0 installation program, Setup, to install DOS on a hard disk, the program automatically places all DOS external command files in the \DOS directory on your system's boot disk.

When you issue a PATH command on the command line or in an AUTOEXEC.BAT file, position the \DOS entry right after the root entry. Don't forget to include the drive parameter with each alternative search path in the PATH command line. Because all your external DOS commands are located in the second search path, you should get a good response when you are working in DOS.

Many users prefer to make a subdirectory of \DOS called \DOS\DRIVERS to keep their DOS device drivers (those files with the SYS extensions) as well as device drivers included with applications programs or hardware. Because device drivers are loaded during the processing of CONFIG.SYS at boot time, you can place the full path name to the drivers you need in the CONFIG.SYS file, eliminating the need to include a search path to the drivers with PATH. Chapter 15 covers the DEVICE configuration command and CONFIG.SYS. An example of a CONFIG.SYS line is as follows:

DEVICE=\DOS\DRIVERS\MOUSE.SYS

Separating the drivers from the DOS commands can make your tree listings from the TREE command or in the DOS Shell directory tree more indicative of the function of the file group in each subdirectory in the \DOS tree branch.

Creating a \DOS\BAT directory (or similar name) for all batch files is a good idea. Include this directory in the PATH command so that DOS can locate the batch files.

Ensuring Uniform Directories for Applications Programs

Many applications programs create directories to store sample files, tutorials, and auxiliary utilities, as well as data for the applications. Although many of these programs suggest default directory names when you install the software, often you are prompted to choose your own directory names. In most cases, you can let the package install with the default names for directories. You may not want to use the default names, however, if you have an older version of the package and want to keep the older version. dBASE III Plus and dBASE IV and Lotus 1-2-3 Releases 2.1, 2.2, and 3 are examples of programs that have several versions. When you install new software, be careful not to overwrite program or data files you want to keep. Often the best policy is to install new software in a directory different from the directory of a previous version of the program that is already installed on your system.

If you have an applications package that does not create directories during installation, you should consider how you want to structure directories for the package and its data. WordStar Release 4, for example, can be copied to a directory named \WS4. The directory or directories for your document files should be subordinate to the \WS4 directory so that all WordStar's associated files form a branch of the directory tree and are not spread across branches. You can create a \WS4\MEMOS directory for your memo documents and a \WS4\FORMS for office-form master documents.

Keeping associated files in the same branch of the directory tree also makes the job of backing up files easier. The command **BACKUP /S** backs up all files from the named directory and its subdirectories. You can make convenient partial interim backups of one branch of the directory tree if all associated files you want to back up are in that branch. (Refer to Chapter 11 for a full discussion of backing up files.)

Using a Temporary Directory

On many occasions, a temporary directory comes in handy for holding files you are preparing for another use. An example is the use of the temporary directory for recovering from an incorrect COPY command that deposited files in the wrong directory. You can create a directory called \TEMP to act as a temporary storage location for these files. A hard disk system with a single floppy disk drive is not a convenient system on which to copy floppy disks. The drive gets the job done, but the COPY command, using the same drive for the source and the target, asks for multiple disk swaps. You can use the DISKCOPY command, which may require fewer swaps, but any fragmentation of the original disk is mirrored on the copy.

If you are making multiple copies of an original, a simple and speedy way to make the copy is to copy the floppy's source files to the hard disk's \TEMP directory. You then can copy the files from the \TEMP directory to the destination floppy in the single floppy drive. This process reduces disk swapping, and the copies can be finished faster thanks to the hard disk's extra speed. When the copies are finished, you can erase the contents of \TEMP so that it is ready for your next use.

Keeping Files in \KEEP

Sometimes a file is like a favorite old shirt. You just don't know whether you want to get rid of the file. You leave it in a subdirectory like an old shirt in the corner of your closet. You may need the file again, but then again, you may not. In either case, you may be too distracted by other issues to make a decision about the file's disposition when you stumble across it yet another time. Soon, you change directories and forget about the file—that is, until your disk space gets short. Then you begin digging through the dark corners of your subdirectory closets trying to find a file or two to discard. And at "disk space running out" time, you feel less equipped to make a decision about a file's importance than ever before. In confusion, you decide to erase the old file.

If this series of events strikes a familiar chord, consider creating a \KEEP directory. When you find a file that has questionable future use, but you don't want to be bothered with making a decision about its disposition at the moment, copy it to \KEEP. As always, make sure that the file does not overwrite a different file with the same name. (You should always give your files descriptive names, avoiding generic names such as TEMP or SAVE.) You see in the next chapter that you can always rename files as a function of COPY.

Erase the copy of the file from its original subdirectory to keep that subdirectory uncluttered. When a week is up, \KEEP may have several files in it.

At this point, you may not have saved any disk space, but you have done some housecleaning in a few directories. Now comes the hard part. Before \KEEP contains more bytes of files than your floppy can hold on one disk, sit down and decide which files stay and which ones go. You may copy some back to their original directories. Some you may erase, and some you may copy to a "just in case" floppy disk for an archive copy. Before you store the floppy, issue the following command:

DIR *d:*/**W** > **PRN**

d: is the name of your floppy disk. This command with the /W switch sends a wide directory report to your printer. Put the printed copy in the disk's envelope for reference. With the floppy disk holding the \KEEP "keepers," you are free to erase the contents of \KEEP. If you use this method regularly, you develop a better sense of the files that are important; those that aren't as important, you can erase.

Summary

This chapter covers the commands used to manage the hierarchical directory structure. The hierarchical directory system is an important feature of DOS.

In this chapter, you learned the following key points:

- Subdirectories were introduced with DOS 2.0.

- All DOS disks have a root directory.

- You can use the DOS Shell to view the hierarchical directory structure in the directory tree.

- You can use the DOS Shell to create, rename, and delete directories.

- The MKDIR (MD) command creates (makes) new directories.

- The CHDIR (CD) command changes default (current) directories.

- The TREE command reports your directory tree structure.

- The RMDIR (RD) command removes empty directories.

- A DOS-specific directory gives better control of external DOS command path searches.

- Directories for applications software packages should be uniform in structure. Many applications create their own directories when you install the package.

Keeping Files in Order

After you have installed DOS on your computer, created your directories, and installed applications programs, you are ready to start your favorite program and get down to the business of computing. In a sense, you have set up housekeeping on your PC.

Most programs generate files as you work with them. You begin to accumulate files on your computer's disks in much the same way that you accumulate possessions in your home or office.

Fortunately, DOS provides useful file-management commands in the DOS Shell and at the command line. This chapter covers these file-management commands. You learn about using the Shell and the DOS command line to find, view, rename, delete, undelete, copy, move, and verify the contents of files. You also learn how to run program files and how to use the DOS Shell to associate specific file names with programs so that selecting a file causes the Shell to run the associated program. You even see how to run multiple applications programs simultaneously by using DOS 5.0's task swapper.

Key Terms Used in This Chapter

Text file	A file containing only standard ASCII characters

Binary file	A file containing instructions or data that has meaning to the PC but cannot be displayed or printed as ASCII characters
End-of-file marker	In a text file, a Control-Z (^ Z) ASCII character, which tells DOS that the end of the usable portion of a file has been reached
Character string	A series of ASCII characters
Sorting	The ordering of a list of items
Task	An applications program that DOS has loaded into memory

Using DOS To Manage Files

DOS has always provided commands for basic management of files on your computer. Beginning with DOS 4.0, however, you also can perform file-management chores through the DOS Shell. Although managing files from the DOS Shell is easy—you select options from a menu instead of typing commands at the DOS command line—you also need to understand how to perform the same tasks from the command line. Sometimes issuing a simple command from the command line is more efficient than waiting for the DOS Shell to load. At other times, you may need to use a computer on which the Shell is not loaded. The sections that follow describe how to use both the DOS Shell and the command line to manage files.

To get the most out of this chapter, you must be familiar with concepts discussed in preceding chapters. In particular, the discussions in this chapter depend heavily on concepts and techniques introduced in Chapters 4, 5, 6, 8, and 9. If you haven't yet taken a look at those chapters, you may want to read them before continuing with this one.

Selecting Files in the DOS Shell

In the DOS Shell, file-management operations are performed primarily through the File menu. The active menu options displayed in the File menu, however, vary according to which area of the window is active. Although the menu options displayed when the directory tree is active are the same as the options displayed when the file list is active, many of these menu options are dimmed (not valid) when the directory tree is active. Most of the Shell file-management operations described in this chapter are performed with the file list area active. Refer to Chapter 4 for a full discussion of how to select areas in the DOS Shell window.

The DOS Shell's file-management commands operate on all selected files. At any particular time, any number of files can be selected. The Shell displays in reverse video both the name and the file list icon of each selected file. Selected files do not have to be all from the same directory.

Selecting a Single File

To select a single file, use the following procedure:

1. Select the directory tree area.

2. Use the mouse and scroll bar or the cursor-movement keys (up arrow, down arrow, PgUp, PgDn, Home, and End) to scroll the directory tree until the name of the directory containing the files you want to select is displayed.

3. Use the mouse or the up- and down-arrow keys to move the selection cursor to the target directory.

4. Select the file list area.

5. Use the mouse and scroll bar or the cursor-movement keys to scroll the file list until the name of the file you want to select is displayed.

6. Click the name of the target file; or use the cursor-movement keys to move the selection cursor to the target file and then press the space bar.

To indicate that a file is selected, DOS displays the file name and file list icon in reverse video.

> *Note:* A file is not selected until the icon is displayed in reverse video. Simply highlighting the file name with the selection cursor is not sufficient to select the file.

Selecting Multiple Files

If you want to apply a DOS Shell command to several files, applying the command simultaneously to all the files is more efficient than doing one file at a time. After you select the first file, following the steps described in the preceding section, you can select the other files (referred to in the DOS Shell as *extending the selection*) in either of the following ways:

- While holding down the Ctrl key, use the mouse to click the name of the file you want to select.

- Press Shift-F8 to display ADD in the status line. Move the selection cursor to the name of the file you want to select. Press the space bar. Press Shift-F8 again to turn off ADD.

(Either of these methods can be used also to deselect any selected file.) The icon and file name of each selected file are displayed in reverse video (see fig. 10.1).

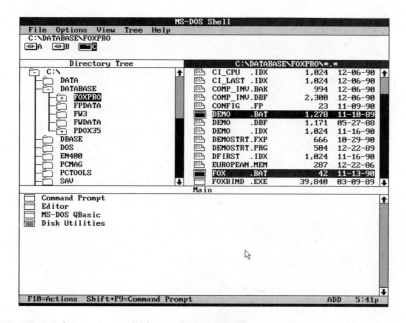

Fig. 10.1. Selecting several files in the DOS Shell.

Frequently, you may want the Shell to work on several files that are listed one after the other in the list area. To select contiguous files, you can select each file individually, using the previously discussed method. But the Shell provides an easier way to select files as a group:

1. Select the first file.

2. Use one of the following procedures to select the remaining files:

   • Use the mouse to position the pointer on the last file you want to select, press the Shift key, and click the left mouse button.

   • While holding the Shift key, use the cursor-movement keys to move the selection bar to the last file.

The Shell selects the all the files. To indicate that these files are selected, the Shell displays the file names and their icons in reverse video. In the file list area shown in figure 10.2, all files between and including DEMO.BAT and FOX.BAT are selected.

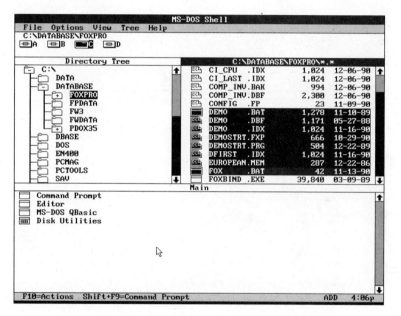

Fig. 10.2. Selecting several contiguous files in the DOS Shell.

Selecting All Files

To select all the files in a directory, do the following:

1. Select the directory in the directory tree area.

2. Select the file list area.

3. Press Ctrl-/, or choose File from the menu bar to display the File menu (see fig. 10.3). Then choose the Select All option from the File menu.

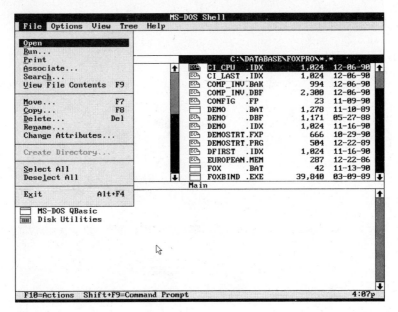

Fig. 10.3. The File menu.

The Shell displays in reverse video the file names and icons of all files in the directory.

Deselecting All Files

After you select files, you may decide that you do not want to perform a DOS Shell operation on that group of files. Perhaps you want to start a fresh selection process by *deselecting* all selected files.

To deselect all selected files in one procedure, use the mouse to click anywhere in the file area, or press the space bar, or follow these steps:

1. Select File from the menu bar to display the File menu.

2. Select Deselect All.

The Shell removes the reverse video from all file list icons and all file names except the one at which the selection cursor is located.

Normally, selecting a different directory also deselects all selected files.

Selecting Files across Directories

By default, the DOS Shell enables you to select files in only one directory at a time. By selecting a different directory, you deselect all selected files. Occasionally, however, you may want to perform a file-management operation on files from several directories. For example, you may want to copy to a floppy disk one file from each of three directories on your hard disk. You can perform this copy by using the Shell to select files across directories.

Before you can select files in several directories, you must do the following:

1. Select <u>O</u>ptions from the menu bar to display the Options menu (see fig. 10.4).

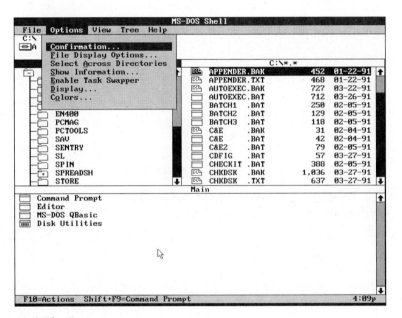

Fig. 10.4. The Options menu.

2. Choose Select <u>A</u>cross Directories.

The Shell removes the Options menu from the screen. The next time you display this menu, however, the Shell displays a small diamond (♦) to the left of the Select Across Directories menu option. This symbol indicates that the capability to select files in several directories is enabled. Now you can select a different directory without deselecting all selected files.

To copy files from three directories to a floppy disk, all in one procedure, first select the directories and then the files, one at a time. Then you can use the File menu's Copy option to copy all the selected files to the floppy disk.

Finding Files

Personal computers commonly have storage media that can hold millions of bytes of information in hundreds or even thousands of files. Ideally, you keep the files on your computer's hard disk organized and cataloged by program and by subject matter. In reality, however, you may have many files with similar-looking file names scattered throughout your hard disk. Finding a specific file may sometimes be a daunting task. DOS 5 can come to the rescue through the DOS Shell's file-finding capability.

With either the DIR command or the Shell's Search command, DOS 5 enables you quickly to scan a specific directory or an entire hard disk for all files with names fitting a particular pattern. The following sections describe how to use these DOS methods to find files.

Using the DOS Shell To Search for Files

You often have a good idea of what a file's name is but are not exactly sure how it is spelled. The DOS 5 Shell enables you to search the entire selected disk or a specific directory for every file whose file name matches given criteria.

When you want to search for a file or group of files from within the DOS Shell, use the following procedure:

1. Select the disk drive area, the directory tree area, or the file list area.

2. Choose File from the menu bar to display the File menu.

3. Select Search from the File menu.

    The Shell displays the Search File dialog box, shown in figure 10.5.

    A message in the Search File dialog box indicates which directory is currently selected in the directory tree area. Below this message is the Search For text box, which contains the default *search criterion* *.* (pronounced *star dot star*). The search criteria define the file-name pattern for which you want the Shell to search.

    The DOS wild-card character * in the search criterion tells the Shell to search for every file with any file name and any file-name extension. Clearly, the default criterion is too broad for your usual needs, and you will have to specify new criteria.

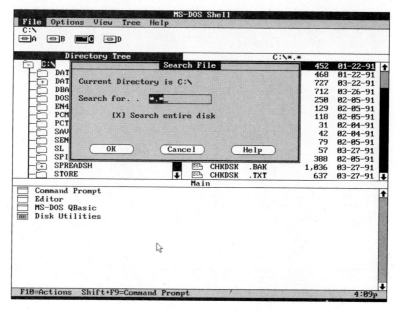

Fig. 10.5. *The Search File dialog box.*

4. Type the search criteria in the Search For text box.

   When you specify the criteria, you can use any valid file name, as
   well as the DOS wild-card characters * and *?*.

   For example, suppose that you want to search for your budget
   spreadsheet but cannot remember which directory it is in. Because
   you are not sure whether the file name is BUDGT.WQ1,
   BUDGET.WQ1, or BUDGET.WK1, you type the following search
   criterion in the text box:

   BUDG*.W?1

   The Search File dialog box also contains an option check box
   labeled Search Entire Disk, and three command buttons: OK,
   Cancel, and Help. By default, the check box contains an X.

5. Press Enter, or select the OK button.

The Shell searches the entire selected disk, clears the screen, and displays
a list of the file names that meet the criterion. For example, figure 10.6 shows
the results of the BUDG*.W?1 search.

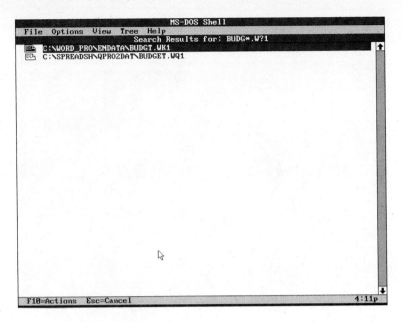

Fig. 10.6. The search results for BUDG*.W?1.

If the Shell cannot find a file name that matches the criteria, it displays the following message:

```
No files match file specifier
```

Sometimes you may want to narrow your search to a single directory. In that case, use the following procedure:

1. Select the target directory in the directory tree area.

2. Choose File from the menu bar, and then Search from the File menu.

3. In the Search File dialog box, type the search criteria in the text box.

4. Toggle off the Search Entire Disk check box (remove the X).

5. Press Enter, or select OK.

The Shell searches only the selected directory and displays a list of file names that meet the search criteria.

You can apply all the Shell's file-management commands to the file list that results from the Search command.

Searching for Files with the DIR Command

To find a file on your disk from the command line, you can use the /S switch with the DIR command. If you want to search a specific directory, first use the CHDIR command to change to that directory. To search the entire disk, change to the root directory.

At the DOS prompt, type **DIR**, followed by the search criterion. The search criterion can be a specific file name or can contain wild-card characters (* and ?). To complete the command, add the /S switch, and press Enter. The /S switch causes DOS to search the current directory and all directories lower than the current directory.

For example, to search the current disk for your budget spreadsheet (as in the example in the preceding section), change to the root directory, and then type the following command:

DIR BUDG*.W?1 /S

When you press Enter, DOS displays a listing similar to the following:

```
         Volume in drive C is QUE BRUCE
         Volume Serial Number is 1628-BA9A

    Directory of C:\SPREADSH\QPRO2DAT

    BUDGET    WQ1    4037    10-05-90    2:00A
              1 files(s)         4037 bytes

    Directory of C:\WORD_PRO\ENDATA

    BUDGET    WK1    5120    04-07-90   8:51p
              1 files(s)         5120 bytes

Total files listed:
         2 files(s)         9157 bytes
                        9400320 bytes free
```

Using the Shell To Display File Information

By default, the DOS Shell lists the file name, file size, and file date for each file in the selected directory. But the operating system stores more information about each file than just name, size, and date. The Show Information command in the DOS Shell enables you to display additional file information

If you want the Shell to display additional information about a file, follow these steps:

1. Move the selection cursor to the target file name in the DOS Shell window's file list area.

2. Choose Options from the menu bar, to display the Options menu.

3. Select Show Information from the Options menu.

The Shell displays the Show Information dialog box (see fig. 10.7).

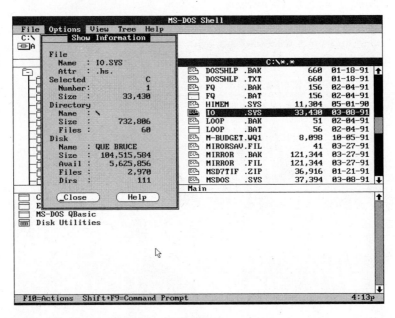

Fig. 10.7. The Show Information dialog box.

The Show Information dialog box is one of the few dialog boxes that provide information without asking you for any input. Under the headings File, Selected, Directory, and Disk, the dialog box lists information about the highlighted file.

The File section of the Show Information dialog box displays the file name (including the extension) as well as file attributes. Each currently set attribute is indicated on the Attr line by a character: r for *read-only*, h for *hidden*, s for *system*, and a for *archive*. (Refer to Chapter 8 for a discussion of file attributes.) In figure 10.7, the Show Information dialog box lists information for the file IO.SYS. Because IO.SYS is one of two hidden DOS system files, the Attr line shows the characters h (for hidden) and s (for system).

The names of the drives currently stored in the Shell's buffer appear to the right of the Selected heading in the dialog box. If you have logged onto more than one drive during the current session with the Shell, this section of the dialog box has two columns. The Selected row lists the two most recently selected drives—the first column shows the current drive; the second column, the drive you selected immediately before this one. The Number line shows the number of files currently selected on the disk. The Size row shows the total number of bytes of disk storage occupied by all the selected files (on both disks, if two disks are listed).

The Directory section of the Show Information dialog box displays the name of the currently selected directory, the total size of all files in that directory, and the total number of files in that directory. In figure 10.7, the directory name is a backslash (\ ), which indicates that the current directory is the root.

The dialog box's Disk section displays information about the disk drive. The Name row is the current drive's volume label (applied during formatting or with the LABEL command); the Size row represents the total storage space on the current disk; and the Avail entry shows how much free space is available for new files. The Files row displays the number of files stored on the disk, and the last entry, Dirs, shows the number of subdirectories on the disk.

Controlling the File List Display

When you use the Shell to display file names, it lists the names in alphabetical order. When you use the DIR command at the DOS command line, DOS normally lists files in the order the names are stored on this disk. At times, listing files in some other order is convenient. The following sections describe how to change the order in which files are displayed in the DOS Shell and how to use the DIR command to display files in a different order.

Using the Shell To Control the File List Display

Normally, the Shell displays in the file list all files in the current directory, listing them in ascending alphabetical order (A through Z). Sometimes, however, you want the program to display a more limited group of file names in the Shell window. You may want to find a particular file name or to list a certain category of files (all spreadsheets, for example). At other times, you may want the files to be listed in a different order, perhaps by date or by size. You can limit the files listed in the file list area of the DOS Shell window, and you can change the order in which the Shell lists file names. To do either, select File Display Options from the Options menu.

To limit the files listed in the file list area, select Options from the menu bar, and then choose File Display Options from the Options menu. The Shell displays the File Display Options dialog box, shown in figure 10.8.

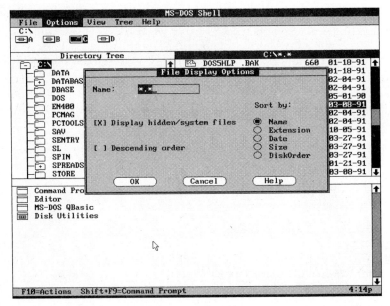

Fig. 10.8. The File Display Options dialog box.

In the File Display Options dialog box, the entry in the Name text box determines which files the Shell lists in the file list area. This text box contains the default value *.*, which causes the Shell to list all files from the selected directory. To cause the Shell to limit the files listed, type a file-name criterion. You can use either or both of the DOS wild-card characters. The asterisk (*) takes the place of any string of characters, and the question mark takes the place of any single character.

For example, assume that the currently selected directory is C:\DOS and that you want to display all files in the directory with the EXE extension. Type the following criterion in the Name text box:

*.EXE

After you type a new file-name criterion in the Name text box, press Enter, or select the OK button to execute the command. The Shell returns to the DOS Shell window and repaints the screen. The file list area now contains only file names that meet the new criterion you specified. For example, the file list area in the DOS Shell window shown in figure 10.9 lists only file names with the extension EXE.

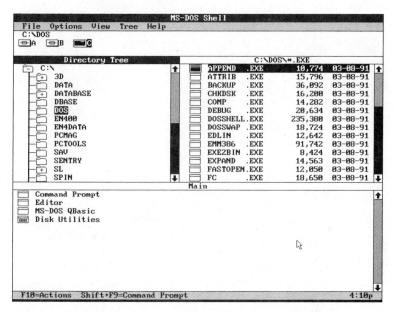

Fig. 10.9. *The file list area lists only files with the extension EXE.*

If no files meet the criterion, the Shell displays the message No files match file specifier.

As you can see from figure 10.8, the Display Options dialog box lists five option buttons (Name, Extension, Date, Size, and DiskOrder) under the heading Sort By. To change the order in which the Shell lists file information, follow these steps:

1. Display the Display Options dialog box.

2. Select one of the five option buttons to sort the file list by file name (Name), file extension (Extension), creation or modification date

(Date), file size (Size), or the order in which DOS maintains the file names in the disk directory structure (DiskOrder).

3. Press Enter, or select the OK button.

The Shell lists files in the new sort order.

The DOS Shell continues to use the new file-name criterion and the new sort order until you change either setting or exit the Shell.

> ***Tip:*** Don't forget to change the file-name criterion to *.* after you finish looking at a limited list of files. Otherwise, you may get confused and think that some of your files are missing.

Using DIR To Control the File List Display

Chapter 5 introduces you to the DIR command and two of its switches, /P and /W. Beginning with DOS 5.0, the DIR command has five additional switches that enable you to control the list of files displayed at the command line by the DIR command.

By default, DIR lists file names of all files except those with the hidden attribute or system attribute. Files are listed in no particular order. By adding certain switches to the DIR command, you can cause DOS to list only file names that have specified attributes, and you can cause DOS to list file names in a specific sorted order.

The complete syntax of the DIR command is as follows:

DIR *d:path\filename* */P/W/A:attributes/O:sortorder/S/B/L*

Refer to Chapter 5 for a discussion of the *d:*, *path*, and *filename* parameters and the */P* and */W* switches.

The */A:attributes* switch enables you to list only the files that have one or more specific file attribute set. Substitute one or more of the following codes for the *attributes* parameter:

D Directory attribute

R Read-only attribute

H Hidden attribute

A Archive attribute

S System attribute

For example, to see a listing of all hidden files in the current directory, type the following command, and press Enter:

DIR /A:H

DOS lists all files that have the hidden attribute.

Attribute codes can be included in any combination and in any order. For instance, you can list all file names with the read-only attribute and the archive attribute by issuing the following command:

DIR /A:RA

DOS lists file names that have both attributes.

To list only file names that do not have a certain attribute, insert a minus sign (–) before the attribute code. For example, to see all files that are not directories and that don't have the archive bit, type the following command at the command line, and press Enter:

DIR /A:-A-D

If you include in a DIR command the /A switch with no attributes parameter, DOS lists all file names, regardless of file attribute—even the file names of hidden files and system files.

The */O:sortorder* switch enables you to determine the order in which DOS lists file names. To cause DOS to sort the file list in a particular order, substitute for the *sortorder* parameter one of the following sort codes:

N Sorts alphabetically by name

S Sorts numerically by file size

E Sorts alphabetically by file extension

D Sorts chronologically by date and time

G Groups directories first

You can include sort codes in any combination. The order of the sort codes in the DIR command denotes the priority of each sort criterion. The command DIR /O:NE sorts the file names first by name and then by extension. The command DIR /O:EN sorts files by extension (for example, grouping all COM files together and all EXE files together) and then sorts the files by name. If you include the /O switch in a DIR command without specifying a sort code, DOS sorts the files names in alphabetic order by name.

By default, all sorting is in ascending order—A through Z, smallest to largest, earliest to latest. Precede a sort code with a minus sign (–) to reverse the sorted order—Z through A, largest to smallest, latest to earliest.

Refer to the "Searching for Files with the DIR Command" for a discussion of the /S switch.

Use the /B switch to display a "bare" file list—a list of just file names. The default file list generated by the DIR command shows the name of each file in the directory, the file name extension, the file size, and the date and time the file was last changed. Occasionally, you may want to see just the file name of each file. Perhaps you want to print a list of the files on a floppy disk. Place the disk in drive A, and issue the following command:

DIR A: /B

DOS lists on-screen all file names of files in the current directory of the disk in drive A. DOS does not list file size or file date and time. To send this list to the printer, issue the following command:

DIR A: /B >PRN

The /L switch, when used with the DIR command, causes file names to appear in lowercase letters.

TIP

Tip: If you find that you continually use one or more of the seven switches available for use with the DIR command, record the switch(es) as an environment variable named DIRCMD. Add the following command to your AUTOEXEC.BAT command:

SET DIRCMD=*switches*

Substitute for *switches* the switch or switches you want DOS to use by default. For example, if you want DOS to sort file names alphabetically and to pause scrolling after each screenful of information, include the following command in AUTOEXEC.BAT:

SET DIRCMD=/O/P

Reboot the computer. DOS creates the environment variable DIRCMD and gives it the value /O/P. Each time you issue the DIR command, DOS automatically adds these two switches.

You can override a switch that is recorded in the DIRCMD by preceding the switch with a minus sign (−). For example, to override the /P switch that is currently recorded in DIRCMD, issue the DIR command as follows:

DIR /-P

DOS lists all file names without pausing at the end of each screenful of information.

Viewing Files

As you work with files in the Shell, you occasionally need to view the contents of a file. In many applications programs, for example, a file on one of the distribution disks includes information that supplements the program's manuals. Typically, you are instructed to read this file (often named READ.ME, README.TXT, or a similar name) before you install the applications software to your system. Such files normally contain only ASCII characters; a file that contains only ASCII characters often is called an *ASCII file*.

Technical Note: To DOS, a file is simply a stream of bytes. A byte contains 8 bits (binary digits) and can represent more than one kind of value in your PC. A byte can be encoded to represent a number, a computer instruction, a table, or even an ASCII character. Usually, computer professionals represent bytes as one of two general types: ASCII and binary.

An *ASCII byte* contains a code that represents one of 256 possible ASCII characters. Files composed entirely of ASCII codes are called *ASCII files*. The DOS TYPE command and the DOS Shell's View File Contents command both work with ASCII files. Not all ASCII codes, however, represent readable text characters such as letters, numbers, and punctuation symbols.

Some ASCII codes are device-control codes; a device detects and uses a device-control code to control the device's operation. Ctrl-S is a control code; a device that detects Ctrl-S in a character stream stops sending its stream of characters. You use Ctrl-S to stop a display from scrolling off the screen, for example. When the control characters are not being used to control a device, they can represent special characters—such as a smiling face or musical notes—on-screen. Other ASCII codes make special characters on your screen but have no device-control meaning. These ASCII codes produce lines and corners of boxes and other graphical characters.

Binary files are composed of bytes that represent instructions and data. The contents of these files have no character equivalents. Only programs can read binary files and make sense of their contents. You can use the DOS TYPE command to force display of the contents of a binary file as ASCII code, but the display is gibberish—filled with random characters and graphic symbols. To view the contents of binary files expressed as hexadecimal (hex) codes, use the DOS Shell.

When you need to view the contents of an ASCII file, DOS provides two methods of doing so: the TYPE command and the DOS Shell View File Contents command. This Shell command also can be used to display the contents of any file, even of a *binary file* (one that contains non-ASCII codes). The sections that follow describe both file-viewing methods.

Using the Shell To View a File

When you want to view the contents of a file from within the DOS Shell, follow these steps:

1. Select the target file in the file list area.

2. Press F9, or display the File menu and select <u>V</u>iew File Contents.

When the file you want to view contains only ASCII characters, the Shell displays the ASCII-file viewer. For example, one of the files distributed with DOS 5 is named README.TXT and contains only ASCII text. To view the contents of README.TXT, select its file name in the file list area, display the File menu, and select <u>V</u>iew File Contents. The Shell displays the file in the ASCII viewer (see fig. 10.10).

To scroll through the file, use the cursor-movement keys (PgUp, PgDn, up arrow, and down arrow). Alternatively, you can use the mouse to click the labels.PgUp, PgDn, ↑, or ↓, which are displayed near the top of the window (again see fig. 10.10). Press Esc to return to the DOS Shell window.

When the file you want to view does not contain only ASCII characters, the Shell uses the hexadecimal (base 16, often referred to as *hex*) viewer. For instance, if you select the DOS command-processor file, COMMAND.COM, and press F9, the Shell displays the contents of the file as four columns of hexadecimal codes and one column of ASCII characters. This information has meaning only to programmers and to the computer. As in the ASCII viewer, you can scroll through the file by using the cursor-movement keys or the mouse.

Non-ASCII files, such as COMMAND.COM, frequently contain at least some ASCII text. You can switch between the ASCII and hex viewers by pressing F9.

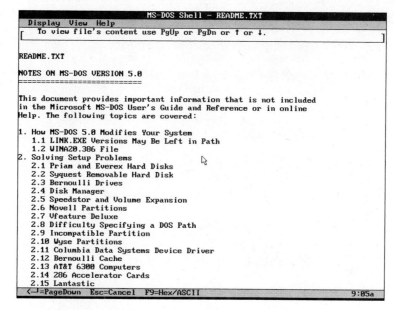

```
                       MS-DOS Shell - README.TXT
    Display  View  Help
  [      To view file's content use PgUp or PgDn or ↑ or ↓.            ]

README.TXT

NOTES ON MS-DOS VERSION 5.0
=============================

This document provides important information that is not included
in the Microsoft MS-DOS User's Guide and Reference or in online
Help. The following topics are covered:

1. How MS-DOS 5.0 Modifies Your System
      1.1 LINK.EXE Versions May Be Left in Path
      1.2 WINA20.386 File
2. Solving Setup Problems                    ⬏
      2.1 Priam and Everex Hard Disks
      2.2 Syquest Removable Hard Disk
      2.3 Bernoulli Drives
      2.4 Disk Manager
      2.5 Speedstor and Volume Expansion
      2.6 Novell Partitions
      2.7 Vfeature Deluxe
      2.8 Difficulty Specifying a DOS Path
      2.9 Incompatible Partition
      2.10 Wyse Partitions
      2.11 Columbia Data Systems Device Driver
      2.12 Bernoulli Cache
      2.13 AT&T 6300 Computers
      2.14 286 Accelerator Cards
      2.15 Lantastic
  ⬏=PageDown   Esc=Cancel   F9=Hex/ASCII                        9:05a
```

Fig. 10.10. *The ASCII viewer.*

Using the TYPE Command
To View Files

When you need to see the contents of an ASCII text file, you can use the TYPE command as well as the DOS Shell's View File Contents command. And by redirecting the output of TYPE to your printer, you can produce a hard copy of the file.

The syntax for the TYPE command is as follows:

TYPE *d:path***filename.ext**

The optional *d:* parameter is the disk that contains the file to be viewed. If you omit the drive, DOS assumes that you want the default drive.

The *path* parameter also is optional. If you omit the path, DOS assumes that you want the default directory.

Replace **filename.ext** with the name of the file you want DOS to display.

This parameter is not optional. Wild-card characters are not permitted.

TYPE is designed to display the contents of a text file that contains ASCII characters. When you issue a TYPE command, DOS opens the specified file and sends the file's contents to the screen as ASCII characters. When DOS encounters a Ctrl-Z character (ASCII decimal 26—the end-of-file character), DOS does not display any additional contents of the file but returns to the command prompt. (For more about the end-of-file character, see this chapter's explanation of the COPY command.)

When you use TYPE to view a text file, the file's contents can fill and begin to scroll off the screen faster than you can read the text. You can press Ctrl-S or the Pause key (found only on the Enhanced Keyboard) to stop scrolling, but the text you want to see may have already scrolled off the screen. MORE displays a screenful of a command's output and then pauses until you press a key. TYPE can be filtered by MORE as follows:

TYPE AUTOEXEC.BAT | MORE

The | character in this command is the DOS *pipe* character, which instructs DOS to send a command's output to the filter that follows the pipe character. Piping to MORE causes DOS to pause the scrolling of the screen when the screen fills. Press any key to display the next screenful.

TIP

Tip: An even easier way to display an ASCII file one screen at a time is to *redirect* a file into the MORE command, without using the TYPE command at all. Use the following syntax:

MORE < *d:path***filename.ext**

The < symbol causes DOS to use the specified file parameter as input to the MORE filter. DOS displays the file, one page at a time, with `-- More --` at the end of every page. For example, to display README.TXT, a file found in the C:\DOS directory, type the following command, and press Enter:

MORE < C:\DOS\README.TXT

If you want a simple printed copy of the contents of a text file, you can redirect the output of the TYPE command to the printer by using the special redirection character—the greater-than sign (>). To print the contents of README.TXT, for example, make sure that your printer is on-line, and then issue the following command:

TYPE README.TXT >PRN

Your printer prints the file. (Because TYPE does not format the text into pages, the printed output may not "break" at page boundaries.)

When you use the TYPE command, remember the following guidelines:

- The output of TYPE stops when the command encounters the first Ctrl-Z in the file.

- Because TYPE does not accept wild cards in the file name parameter, use of the command is limited to a one file at a time.

- TYPE tries to interpret any file as an ASCII text file, even if the file contains non-ASCII data. If you use a binary file, such as a COM or EXE file as the file parameter, TYPE's output may produce graphical characters, control-character sequences, and beeps. TYPE's output may even *hang* your computer (the computer does not respond to keyboard input) so that you have to reboot.

- You can pause TYPE's output by pressing Ctrl-S or Pause. Press any key to resume scrolling.

- You can terminate TYPE's output by pressing Ctrl-C or Ctrl-Break.

Printing Files from the DOS Shell

The DOS Shell has an option that uses the DOS PRINT command. You must first load PRINT.COM from the DOS prompt for the option to work, however. At the command prompt, type the following command, and press Enter:

PRINT

DOS displays the following message:

```
Name of list device [PRN]:
```

If your printer is attached to the computer's first parallel printer port (LPT1), just press Enter. Otherwise, type the appropriate printer-port device name, and press Enter. DOS displays a message similar to the following:

```
Resident part of PRINT installed
PRINT queue is empty
```

This message indicates that the PRINT program is loaded in memory as a memory-resident program. Now you can use the PRINT command (as described in the Command Reference) or the DOS Shell's Print command to print files.

Restart the DOS Shell, and then follow these steps to print a file:

1. In the DOS Shell window's file list area, select the file or files you want to print.

2. Display the File menu, and choose <u>P</u>rint.

The Shell sends all selected files to the PRINT command's *print queue*—a holding area on the disk. The print queue is controlled by the PRINT command and contains files waiting to be printed. Files are printed in the order in which they are sent to the print queue. The memory-resident portion of the PRINT command controls the flow of data to the printer. You can continue with other operations in the Shell as the selected files print.

Starting Programs

The DOS Shell provides several ways to start a program. A sophisticated capability for starting applications programs in the Shell's program list area is explained fully in Chapter 14. The following sections describe some of the other methods and the procedure for starting a program from the command line.

Running a Program in the Shell

When you want to run an applications program and you know the exact start-up command, you can use the DOS Shell's Run command to start the application. The procedure is as follows:

1. Select the disk drive area, the directory tree area, or the file list area in the DOS Shell window.

2. Display the File menu, and select the <u>R</u>un option.

The Shell displays the Run dialog box, which contains a text box labeled Command Line. Type the appropriate start-up command for the applications program, and press Enter. DOS blanks the screen and executes the command, which in turn starts the applications program.

After you finish using the application and quit the program, DOS returns you to the DOS Shell window.

Tip: The Run command works only when the program you are trying to run is located in a directory named in the current path (see the discussion of PATH in Chapter 13). The PATH command is most useful when you have created a DOS batch file for each program you routinely use. (Batch files are explained in Chapter 13.) See Chapter 14 if you are interested in an even more powerful and convenient facility for starting programs—customizing the DOS Shell's program list area.

A second way to run a program from within the Shell requires that you first locate the program file and display its name in the file list area. (The file must have the extension EXE, COM, or BAT.) Then you can start the applications program by doing one of the following:

- Use the mouse to position the mouse pointer on the program file's name. Double-click the left mouse button (press it twice in rapid succession).

- Use the cursor-movement keys to select the file name, and then press Enter, or select <u>O</u>pen on the File menu.

DOS runs the program file.

Tip: The Shell denotes program files—files with extensions EXE, COM or BAT—with the following icon:

The Shell denotes all other types of files with the following icon:

Starting Associated Programs in the Shell

Probably the most convenient way to start programs from the file list area is a procedure called *launching*—starting a program by selecting one of the program's data files. Before you can use this procedure to start a particular program, however, you must *associate*—assign or identify—at least one file extension with the applications program. Then you can start the program by selecting a file name with the associated extension.

Associating Files with Programs

Many applications programs create and work with files that have distinctive file-name extensions. For example, Lotus 1-2-3 files have the extension WKS, WK1, or WK3; Microsoft Word document files have the extension DOC; and dBASE database files have the extension DBF. The DOS Shell enables you to associate particular extensions with a specific applications program so that you easily can start the program and load a file with an associated extension in one step.

The DOS 5 Shell provides two procedures for associating an applications program with one or more file extensions. If you want to specify that all extensions be associated with a particular program, use the following procedure:

1. In the file list area, select the applications program or batch file you want to associate with specific extensions. (The program must have a COM, EXE, or BAT extension.)

2. Display the File menu, and choose the Associate option.

   The Shell displays the Associate File dialog box. This dialog box contains a message that indicates the name of the applications program. The dialog box also contains a text box, labeled Extensions.

3. In the Extensions text box, type the extension(s) you want to associate with that application or batch file. Do not type a period at the beginning of each extension. If you type more than one extension, press the space bar between entries. Finally, press Enter, or select the OK button.

For example, you may want to associate the extensions TXT and INI with the DOS Editor (the EDIT.COM program discussed in Chapter 12). Type the following in the Extensions text box (see fig. 10.11), and press Enter:

TXT INI

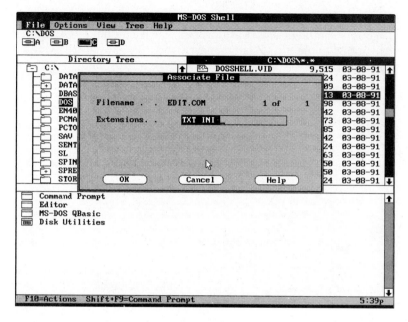

Fig. 10.11. The Associate File dialog box after file extensions are specified.

The second method of associating a file extension with an applications program starts with the data file rather than the program file. As an alternative to the preceding procedure, do the following for each file extension you want associated with a program:

1. In the file list area, select a file whose extension you want the Shell to associate with a specific applications program.

   Again using the DOS Editor as an example, you can select a file with the extension TXT, such as the file README.TXT, which is distributed with DOS 5.0.

2. Display the File menu, and choose the Associate option.

   The Shell displays another Associate File dialog box. This one contains a text box in which you can type the applications program's directory path and file name. If the current file extension already is associated with an applications program, the Shell puts the program's path and file name in the text box.

3. In the text box, type the applications program's complete file name, including the extension. If the file is in a directory not included in the PATH statement, type the directory path as well as the file name.

4. Press Enter, or select the OK button.

> *Note:* Program-to-file-extension associations are stored in an ASCII file called DOSSHELL.INI. You can use any text editor, including the DOS Editor, to edit this file.

Launching Files in the Shell

After you have associated a file extension with a program in the Shell, starting the applications program and loading an associated file in one procedure—a procedure often called launching the file—is easy. Use the following method:

1. Select the data file whose associated program you want to run.

2. Press Enter, or double-click the left mouse button, or select Open from the File menu.

The Shell starts the associated applications program and tries to load the selected data file.

For example, having associated the TXT extension with the DOS Editor (EDIT.COM), you can start the Editor and load README.TXT by double-clicking the README.TXT entry in the DOS Shell window's file list area.

> *Note:* When you launch a file using the method discussed in this section, the Shell executes a command that has the same effect as typing at the command prompt the program name followed by a space and the data file name. When you select README.TXT, for example, the Shell executes the following command:
>
> EDIT README.TXT
>
> Although this procedure is successful in many cases, not all programs can load data files that are typed as a part of the start-up command. If the Shell starts the associated program but fails to load the data file, you must issue the appropriate commands in the applications program to load the data file.

After you finish running a program you launched by using the Shell, DOS displays the following message:

```
Press any key to return to MS-DOS Shell...
```

If you press any key on the keyboard, DOS again displays the DOS Shell window.

Using the Task Swapper

Perhaps the most heralded new feature of DOS 5 is its capacity to load more than one applications program at a time. DOS 5 accomplishes this feat through a technique called *task swapping*. Before you can use this feature, you must activate it through the Options menu:

1. From any area in the DOS Shell window, select <u>O</u>ptions in the menu bar to display the Options menu.

2. Select <u>E</u>nable Task Swapper.

The Shell adds an active task list area to the window (see fig. 10.12). Initially, nothing is listed in this area because no program (other than the Shell) is active.

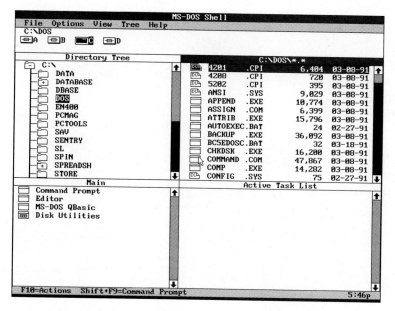

Fig. 10.12. *The DOS Shell window after the active task list area is added.*

With the task swapper enabled, you still start programs by using any of the methods described earlier in this chapter. But after you have started an applications program, you can jump back instantly to the DOS Shell without having to exit the applications program. Press Alt-Esc or Alt-Tab, and the screen returns to the DOS Shell window, where the applications program (or associated data file) is listed in the active task list area. DOS has swapped the contents of memory (RAM) to disk, freeing space in memory so that you can run another applications program.

For example, assume that you start the DOS Editor by selecting Editor from the program list area (see fig. 10.12). After you are working in the DOS Editor, you decide that you want to return to the DOS Shell in order to format a disk. Press Alt-Tab or Alt-Esc. DOS clears the screen, displays the label MS-DOS Shell at the top of the screen, and then displays the DOS Shell window. The DOS Editor is now listed as an active task in the active task list area, as shown in figure 10.13.

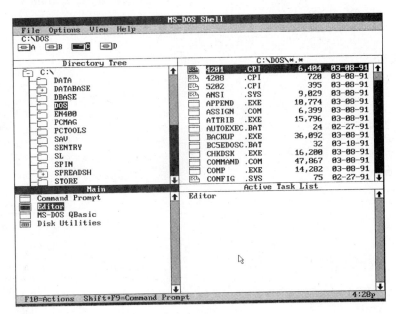

Fig. 10.13. Using the task swapper.

After you return to the DOS Shell window, you can use any DOS Shell command or load another applications program.

> *Caution:* Do not load a 3270 terminal-emulation program under the task swapper. If you do, your session with the mainframe computer may be disconnected unexpectedly, resulting in potential data loss.

After using the task swapper to load more than one applications program, you can use Alt-Tab or Alt-Esc to return to the Shell window. The Shell adds each open application (or data file) to the list in the active task list area. To jump to one of the active tasks, do the following:

1. Select the appropriate file name in the active task list.

2. Press Enter, or double-click the left mouse button.

> *Tip:* The quickest way to switch between active tasks is to use Alt-Tab. Hold the Alt key and tap the Tab key. *Do not release the Alt key.* The Shell displays the name of the task at the top of the screen. Still holding down the Alt key, press the Tab key again to see the name of the next task. Repeat this keystroke until the target task name is displayed. Finally, release the Alt key. The Shell switches to the target task.

As you quit each applications program, the Shell removes it from the active task list. When the active task list area is empty again, you can disable the task swapper by displaying the Options menu and selecting Enable Task Swapper.

Starting Programs from the Command Line

To start an applications program from the command line, you must change to the directory that contains the program and type the correct start-up command. Typically, you type the program name and press Enter. With many programs, you can select certain features or options by adding special parameters to the start-up command. Consult the documentation that comes with your software to determine the most appropriate start-up command for each of your applications programs.

Often, the most convenient practice is to include in your computer's PATH command the directory that contains an applications program. This practice normally enables you to start the program without first changing to the directory that contains the target program. When in doubt, check your software's documentation to determine whether adding the applications program to the PATH command will benefit you (see Chapter 13 for a discussion of the PATH command).

Copying and Moving Files

Probably the most common file-related function is to copy files from one disk or directory to another. Another common task for many PC users is to copy one or more files from one storage location to another location and then to delete the original files. The result is that the files are *moved* from the first location to the second. The sections that follow describe how to use DOS (from the Shell and from the command line) to copy and move files.

Copying files is a fundamental job for disk operating systems. MS-DOS provides the COPY command (for use at the command line) as well as several ways to copy files in the Shell. All these copying methods perform the same operation.

The DOS copy operation enables you to copy files as well as to copy data to and from logical devices. Figure 10.14 diagrams the copy operation used with a several possible inputs and two possible outputs. Three of the possible inputs consist of more than one file or logical device. DOS can join two or more inputs into one output in a process called *combining*. You may never need to use all these COPY inputs and outputs, but they are available with the command.

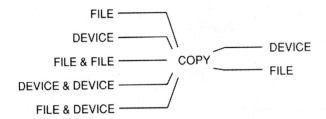

Fig. 10.14. The possible inputs and outputs of the COPY operation.

When performing a copy operation, remember the following guidelines:

- The source parameter must contain at least one of the following parameters: path, file, or device.

- If the source-file parameter is omitted, all files in the specified directory and drive are copied. This situation is equivalent to supplying *.* as the source-file parameter.

- Additional source-file parameters can be specified using the + operator to combine the files.

- If the source-file parameter contains a wild card and the destination parameter is a file name, the destination file will be the combination of source files that match the source-file parameter.

- If COPY detects an attempt to copy a single source file to itself (same drive, directory, file name, and extension), the copy operation is aborted.

- The optional destination parameter consists of a combination of drive, path, and file-name parameters. If you don't provide a drive or path, DOS uses the current drive or path for the destination. If you don't specify a destination file name, DOS uses the source file name parameter.

COPY definitely is a versatile file-management workhorse. Yet even with its versatility, an incorrect copy operation can do nearly as much damage as an incorrect ERASE command. Be sure to treat COPY with respect. Many applications programs include warning messages as part of their internal file-copying commands. The DOS COPY command gives no warning when it is about to overwrite existing files, but the Shell's Copy command does.

Copying Files in the Shell

With the DOS Shell, you can copy one or more files in a directory, between directories, or between disks, using any of several approaches. The approach described in this section—the dual file list display method—is the quickest and easiest to learn and use.

To perform the copy operation using the dual-file-lists method, complete the following steps:

1. Select the source drive and directory (those that contain the files you want to copy).

2. Use the <u>D</u>ual File Lists option on the View menu to switch to the dual file list.

Under certain specific circumstances, sometimes you can skip this step. For example, you can drag selected files to another directory on the same disk without opening a dual file list. Completing this step, however, always produces the results you want.

3. Use the mouse or the cursor-movement keys to select the target drive and directory in the second directory tree.

4. Use the mouse or keyboard to select, in the first (upper) file list, the files you want to copy. Figure 10.15 shows an example of a dual file list display. C:\SPREADSH\QPRO2DAT is displayed in the top file list area; A:\SPREADSH\BUDGET, in the bottom file list.

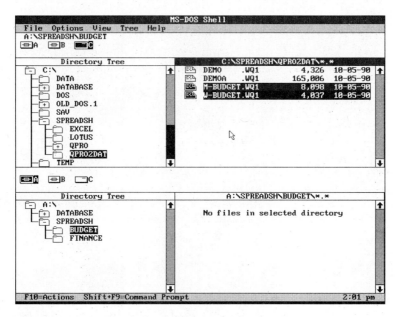

Fig. 10.15. *Using the dual file list display to copy files.*

The remaining two steps differ, depending on whether you use a mouse or keyboard. The steps that follow are for mouse users:

5. Position the mouse pointer on a selected file in the upper file list. Hold down the Ctrl key while you press and hold the left mouse button. While holding down both the Ctrl key and the mouse button, drag the mouse pointer to the target disk drive letter in the lower disk drive area, or alternatively, to the target directory's name in the lower directory tree.

When you begin to drag the mouse, the pointer changes from an arrow (a block in text mode) to a circle (two exclamation-point symbols in text mode). When the pointer enters the second directory tree, the circle becomes a file icon (a small diamond shape in text mode). If you are copying several files, the file icon resembles a stack of three files.

Note: When you are copying files to a different disk, you don't have to hold down the Ctrl key. Holding down the mouse button is enough. If you drag files to another directory on the same disk without holding down the Ctrl key, however, the Shell assumes that you want to *move* the files instead of just *copying* them.

After you release the mouse button and Ctrl key, the Shell displays the Confirm Mouse Operation dialog box, which contains the following query:

```
Are you sure you want to copy
the selected files to
d:\path\filename
```

6. To confirm that you want the Shell to copy the selected file(s) to the target directory, select the Yes button in the Confirm Mouse Operation dialog box.

If you don't have a mouse, complete the copy procedure with the following steps:

7. Press F8, or choose Copy from the File menu.

   The Shell displays the Copy File dialog box. This dialog box contains a text box labeled From and a text box labeled To. The Shell lists the source files in the From text box, but lists the source directory in the To text box.

8. To complete the copy operation, type the target drive and directory name in the To text box, and then press Enter or select the OK command button.

   As the Shell copies the files to the target directory, the Shell displays a message to that effect in the center of the screen.

If you try to copy a file into a directory that already contains a file with the same name, the Shell displays the Replace File Confirmation dialog box. This dialog box prompts you to confirm whether you want to replace the existing file with the new file. Select the Yes button to copy the file and continue with the copy procedure (if other files have yet to be copied). Select the No button to skip the file and continue the copy procedure for any remaining files. Select the Cancel button to terminate the copy operation.

Moving a File in the Shell

When the Shell moves a file, the program copies the file from one storage location to another and then deletes the file from its original location. The steps for moving one or more files with the DOS Shell are therefore nearly the same as those for copying files. When you want to move one or more files, follow steps 1 through 4 of the copy procedure (refer to the preceding section). Then perform the steps given here for mouse users or for keyboard users.

Mouse users perform the following steps:

1. Position the mouse pointer on one of the selected files in the upper file list. Hold down the Alt key while you press and hold the left mouse button. While holding both the Alt key and the mouse button, drag the mouse pointer to the target disk drive letter in the lower disk drive area, or alternatively, to the target directory's name in the lower directory tree.

> *Note:* When you are moving files to a directory on the same disk, you don't have to hold down the Alt key; holding down the mouse button is enough. But if you drag files to a directory on a different disk without holding down the Alt key, the Shell assumes that you want to *copy* the files, rather than just *move* them.

2. Select the Yes button in the Confirm Mouse Operation dialog box to confirm that you want the Shell to move the selected file(s) to the target directory.

When you start dragging the mouse, the pointer changes from an arrow (a block in text mode) to a circle (two exclamation-point symbols in text mode). When the pointer enters the second directory tree, the circle becomes a file icon (a small diamond shape in text mode). If you are copying several files, the file icon resembles a stack of three files.

After you release the mouse button and Alt key, the Shell displays the Confirm Mouse Operation dialog box, which contains the following query:

```
Are you sure you want to move
the selected files to
d:\path\filename
```

If you don't have a mouse, complete the move procedure by following these steps:

1. Press F7, or choose <u>M</u>ove from the File menu.

   The Shell displays the Move File dialog box. This dialog box contains one text box labeled From and another labeled To. The Shell lists the source files in the From text box but lists the source directory in the To text box.

2. To complete the move operation, type the target drive and directory name in the To text box, and press the Enter key, or select the OK command button.

   As the Shell moves the files to the target directory, the Shell displays a message to that effect in the center of the screen.

If you attempt to move a file into a directory that already contains a file with the same name, the Shell displays the Replace File Confirmation dialog box. This dialog box prompts you to confirm whether you want to replace the existing file with the new file. Select the Yes button to move the file and continue with the move procedure (if other files have yet to be moved). Select the No button to skip the file and continue the move procedure for any remaining files. Select the Cancel button to terminate the move operation.

> *Note:* No command equivalent to the Shell's Move command is available for use from the command line.

Setting Confirmation Preferences

By default, the Shell displays a dialog box each time you use a mouse to delete a file, replace a file, or perform a copy or move operation. In each case, you must press Enter or select the OK button to *confirm* to the Shell that you want to complete the operation.

For new DOS Shell users, having to confirm actions that may cause loss of data is good. For seasoned users, however, each confirmation dialog box may be more of a nuisance than a safeguard. The Shell therefore enables you to change your confirmation preferences so that the confirmation dialog boxes don't appear.

To change one or more confirmation preferences, select Confirmation from the Options menu. The Shell displays the File Options dialog box, which contains the following check boxes:

- Confirm on Delete. When checked, requires the Shell to ask you before the Shell deletes a file.

- Confirm on Replace. When checked, causes the Shell to prompt you for confirmation before the Shell copies a file over another file with the same name.

- Confirm on Mouse Operation. When checked, requires that you confirm each mouse operation.

Select the check box corresponding to any confirmation requirement you want to disable. Press Enter, or select OK to accept this change and return to the DOS Shell window.

Using the COPY Command

You can copy files not only by using the DOS Shell's copy procedure but also by using the COPY command at the command line. Symbolically, the COPY command says

COPY from *this source* to *this destination*

In a COPY command, the order of the parameter requirements always moves from the source to the destination, or target.

The correct syntax for the COPY command is as follows:

COPY *d1:path1***filename1.ext1** *d2:path2\filename2.ext2/V/A/B*

For combining files, the syntax is as follows:

COPY *d1:path1***filename1.ext1** */A/B* +
d2:path2\filename2.ext2 */A/B*
d0:path0\filename0.ext0

d1:, *d2:*, *d0:* are valid disk drive names. If you omit a disk drive parameter, DOS uses the current drive.

path1, *path2*, and *path0* are path parameters. If you omit a path parameter, DOS assumes that you mean the current directory.

The + character delimits source files that are to be combined.

filename1.ext1, *filename2.ext2*, and *filename0.ext0* are file-name and extension parameters. You must give a source path or file parameter.

The ellipsis (...) signifies that other drive, path, and source file-name parameters may be included in a combine operation.

The /V switch verifies that the copy has been recorded correctly.

The /A and /B switches have different effects on the source and destination files.

For the source file, /A treats the file as an ASCII file. The command copies all the information in the file up to but not including the first end-of-file marker (ASCII decimal 26). Anything after the end-of-file marker is ignored. The /B switch copies the entire file (based on its size as listed in the directory) as if the copied file were a program file (binary). Any end-of-file markers are copied.

For the destination file, /A adds an end-of file marker to the end of the ASCII file after it is copied. /B does not add the end-of-file marker to this binary file.

TIP

> *Tip:* Sometimes, you may want to change a file's date and time attribute to today's date and time. Use the following command:
>
> **COPY /B** *filename.ext* + ,,

Copying All Files in a Directory

As you add and delete files to and from a disk, the free space for new file information becomes spread physically around the surface of the disk. This phenomenon is called *fragmentation*. DOS allocates data-storage space by finding the next available disk space. If the next available space is too small to hold an entire file, DOS uses all of that space and puts the rest of the file into the next available space. Fragmented files diminish disk performance.

If you use DISKCOPY on a fragmented floppy disk, you get an exact image of the fragmented disk. To avoid copying the fragmentation, or to make an efficient copy of a fragmented floppy disk, use the copy operation (from the Shell or the command line).

For example, assume that all source files are in the source floppy's root directory. Format the destination disk, if necessary, and make sure that it has enough room to hold all the source files. Then copy the source files to the destination disk. Place the source disk in drive A, the destination disk in drive B, and then type the following:

    COPY A:*.* B:

This command copies all files on the disk in drive A to the disk in drive B, keeping the same file names. Alternatively, you can copy all the files on a floppy disk to a directory of your hard disk. For example, to copy all files on drive A to the \TEMP directory on drive C, type the following command:

COPY A:*.* C:\TEMP

Combining Text Files

Although you can use COPY to combine any two or more files, the combine operation is most effective when the files are ASCII text files. In most cases, combining binary files results in a destination file that is not usable.

For the following combine examples, assume that the current directory contains three text files, all with TXT extensions. The files and their contents are as follows:

File	Contents
INTRO.TXT	Combining is
BODY.TXT	the joining of files
ENDING.TXT	into a new file.

To join the three files into a fourth file, use the following command:

COPY INTRO.TXT+BODY.TXT+ENDING.TXT ALL.TXT

The resulting file, ALL.TXT, contains the text from the three source files. To verify ALL.TXT, issue the following command:

TYPE ALL.TXT

TYPE sends the contents of ALL.TXT to the screen; you see the following:

```
Combining is the joining of files into a new file.
```

Copying from a Device to a File

A common and handy use of the COPY command is to copy to a file keystrokes entered from the keyboard or console device. (*CON* is the device name for *console*; for all practical purposes, CON is the keyboard.) The resulting text file can be used as a batch file, a configuration file, a memo, and so on.

To practice copying from the keyboard to a file, you can create a simple batch file that changes the current directory to \123R3 and starts Lotus 1-2-3 Release 3. The command to create the batch file is as follows:

COPY CON C:\DOS\RUN123.BAT

When you press Enter, DOS displays the cursor on the next line; the DOS prompt is not displayed. Now you can start typing the file.

Type the following line, and press Enter:

C:

The cursor drops to the next line. Type the following line:

CD\123R3

Press Enter. Again, the cursor drops to the next line. Type the following:

LOTUS

The cursor drops to the next line. Press the F6 function key or the Ctrl-Z key combination to indicate the end of the file. DOS displays ^Z. Press Enter. This code then indicates to DOS that you are finished with your input into the file. DOS responds with the following message:

```
1 File(s) copied
```

To confirm that the new file is as you want it, you can use the TYPE command to review the contents of the file.

> ***Note:*** If you try this example on your system, be sure to use the appropriate directory names for DOS and Lotus 1-2-3.

Renaming Files

If copying files is the most common file-related function of DOS, renaming files probably follows close on its heels. The reasons for renaming a file are many. You may want to use the current file name for another file, or perhaps you want to create a name that better describes the contents of the current file. Whatever the reason, DOS enables you to rename a file through the Shell or from the command line.

The DOS rename operation changes the name in a file's directory entry, but the file and its physical location on the disk remain unchanged. Because two files in the same directory cannot have the same name, DOS will not change a file name if the new file name already exists.

Whether you carry out the DOS rename operation from the Shell or at the command line, remember the following guidelines:

- You can use the command names REN and RENAME interchangeably at the command line. Both command names produce identical results.

- You must supply an old file name and a new file name. Both the old file name and the new file name can contain wild cards for pattern matching.

- You cannot use the rename operation to move a file from one directory or disk to another directory or disk.

Renaming a File from the Shell

To rename a file in the Shell, follow these steps:

1. In the file list area, select the file whose name you want to change.

2. Display the File menu, and choose the Rename option.

The Shell displays the Rename File dialog box. This dialog box displays the current file name as well as a text box labeled New Name. Type the new file name in the New Name text box, and press Enter, or select the OK button. The Shell changes the name and returns the screen to the DOS Shell window.

Renaming Files from the Command Line

The internal RENAME (or REN) DOS command is your command-line tool for altering the name of an existing file. RENAME modifies a file's name without in any way changing the file's content.

> *Note:* The two command names, RENAME and REN, are equivalent. You can use either command name to rename files.

The syntax for the RENAME command is as follows:

RENAME *d:path***filename1.ext1 filename2.ext2**

The *d:* parameter is the drive that contains the file to be renamed. The *path* indicates the directory that contains the file.

The file is currently named **filename1.ext1**. Wild cards are allowed in the file name, the extension, or both.

filename2.ext2 is the new name for the file. The new file name can be a new literal name, or the new file name can contain wild cards. You cannot specify a drive or path for **filename.ext2**; both must be the same as for the original file name.

You must provide both **filename1.ext1** and **filename2.ext2**.

Suppose that you have used your word processor to prepare a sales report and that you want to give the backup file (SALES.BAK) a more descriptive name. After you log onto the appropriate disk and directory, issue the following command:

RENAME SALES.BAK SALES_08.REP

Or perhaps you want to rename the EXPENSE.YTD file, keeping the same root name but making the extension more descriptive. You can specify the entire old name and an entire new name in the command line, as in the preceding example. An easier way is to use the * wild card for the root file name and change only the extension. First, make sure that only one file with the root file name of EXPENSE is available for RENAME to process with a *.YTD specifier. Then, issue the following command:

RENAME *.YTD *._89

The new name for the EXPENSE.YTD file is EXPENSE._89. The *.YTD parameter tells DOS to "Find all files with YTD extensions." The new file-name parameter *._89 tells DOS to "Rename the found files to _89 extensions but keep their root file names the same."

TIP

Tip: If you are not sure which files a wild-card parameter will match, issue the DIR command, using the wild-card pattern you plan to use in the file name parameter. DIR lists the matching file names. Study these names carefully to see whether using the wild-card pattern with the RENAME command will produce the result you expect.

Deleting Files

Because no disk has unlimited storage space and nearly every file eventually becomes obsolete, DOS provides a way to erase or delete files from your disks. You can use DOS from the Shell or from the command line to delete files from the disk.

When you execute a delete operation, DOS locates the file in the directory and marks the directory entry with a special internal indicator. DOS considers this space available for reassignment when a new file is being added to the directory. By reclaiming a deleted file's directory entry, DOS can control the expansion of a subdirectory or reclaim one of the limited root-directory entries.

> ***Technical Note:*** The delete operation does not affect the contents of a file's allocated clusters. Deleting a file does not "record over" the file's data in the way erasing a cassette tape records over existing audio; rather, DOS alters its bookkeeping records in the directory and the file allocation table (FAT). The directory entry for the file receives a special indicator, and the FAT cluster chain for the file is deallocated. DOS marks the file's clusters as being "free."
>
> The DOS bookkeeping records for the deleted file remain relatively intact until another file is added to the directory or another file is expanded or added in any directory. Beginning with DOS 5, you can use the UNDELETE command to reverse the effect of deleting a file. The UNDELETE utility, discussed later in this chapter, takes advantage of the fact that DOS does not erase a file's content when you delete the file. UNDELETE "fixes" the deleted file's directory entry and reconstructs the deleted file's cluster chain. If another file has been added, however, the UNDELETE command may not be able to recover the deleted file. DOS may have reallocated some of or all the storage space assigned to the deleted file.

When you are executing a delete operation, remember the following guidelines:

- At the command line, the DEL (or ERASE) command does not erase files marked with the read-only attribute, the hidden attribute, or the system attribute. The Shell's Delete command deletes a file, regardless of the current attributes; but if the file is marked with the read-only attribute, the hidden attribute, or the system attribute, you first must confirm the operation.

- The DELETE operation does not remove a directory, erase a volume label, or erase a hidden or system file.

- If you type **DEL subdirectory_name**, DOS tries to delete all the files in **subdirectory_name**.

Using the DOS Shell To Delete a File

To use the DOS Shell to delete one or more files, follow these steps:

1. In the file list area, select the file(s) you want to delete.

2. Press the Del key, or display the File menu, and choose <u>D</u>elete.

DOS displays the Delete File confirmation dialog box. The Shell displays different dialog boxes, depending on whether you are deleting multiple files or only one file. When you are deleting several files, the Shell lists the selected files in a text box labeled Delete. To continue with the delete operation, press Enter, or select OK; to terminate the operation, select the Cancel command button. If you are deleting a single file, the Shell displays only the name of the file you are about to delete and asks you to confirm the operation. Press Enter, or select the Yes button to delete the file.

When several files are selected, the Shell asks you to reconfirm the deletion of each file. Select the Yes button once for each file. The Shell erases each file and then returns the screen to the Shell window.

Caution: If you have turned off the Confirm on Delete check box, by using the Confirmation command on the Options menu, the Shell does not ask you to confirm that you want to delete each file. Rather, the Shell deletes the file(s) as soon as you issue the command.

Tip: If you attempt to delete a file whose read-only attribute is set, the Shell displays the following message:

```
Warning! File is Read Only!
```

To continue with the deletion, press Enter, or select the Yes button.

Deleting Files from the Command Line

The internal DEL and ERASE commands remove files from the disk, returning to the disk the space occupied by the deleted files.

> *Note:* You can use ERASE and DEL interchangeably; both command names produce identical results.

When you erase a file with DEL or ERASE, DOS no longer can access the file; the file's directory entry and storage space are available to DOS for storage of another file.

DEL is a necessary file-management command. Unless you erase unwanted or unnecessary files from a disk, the disk eventually reaches full storage capacity. You need to erase files from a hard disk to use the disk for your primary data storage. DEL is DOS's "throw it away" command.

> *Caution:* Because DEL (or ERASE) deletes files from your disk, use the command with caution. DEL allows wild cards in the file parameter. A momentary lapse of your attention while you use DEL can eradicate important data in the blink of an eye.

The syntax for the DEL or ERASE command is as follows:

DEL *d:path***filename.ext** */P*

ERASE *d:path***filename.ext** */P*

d: is the optional drive containing the disk that holds the file(s) to be erased. If you omit the drive parameter, DOS uses the logged drive.

path is the optional directory path to the file(s) to be erased. If you omit the path parameter, DOS assumes that you mean the current directory.

filename.ext is the file-name parameter for the file(s) to be erased. Wild cards are allowed in the file name and extension. Normally, a file-name parameter is required. If you don't specify a file name, you must specify a path. DOS then assumes that you want to delete all files in the path.

The */P* switch is available with DOS 4 and later versions. Using the optional */P* switch causes DEL (or ERASE) to prompt you for confirmation before DOS deletes each file. Answer Y to cause DOS to delete a file or N to skip the file without erasing it.

Deleting Unwanted Files

For an example of how to use DEL, suppose that you have completed and delivered a series of memos composed on your word processor. Your word processor automatically creates in the C:\WP directory a backup file, with a BAK extension, for each memo. You want to keep the memo files on disk so that you can refer to them, but after the memos are safely delivered you do not need the BAK files. You can erase the files with BAK extensions one at a time, or you can issue the DEL command as follows:

DEL C:\WP*.BAK

In this command line, the *.BAK file name parameter causes DEL to delete only the files with the BAK extension. When the command completes its work, all files with BAK extensions are removed from the directory. Because this command line includes drive and path parameters, you can issue the command from any logged disk and current directory and still erase the BAK files in C:\WP.

Recovering Deleted Files with UNDELETE

Because of the way DOS deletes files, reversing the process is relatively easy—but only if you do so promptly. When DOS deletes a file, DOS changes one character in the file name recorded in the directory area of the disk so that the target file is no longer listed. As far as DOS is concerned, the file is gone. DOS does not erase the modified file name from the directory, however, nor does DOS erase any data from the disk. Eventually, as you add new files to the disk, DOS reallocates the disk space assigned to the deleted file, thus causing new data to overwrite the old data. Soon the file and its data are permanently gone. But if you use the DOS 5 UNDELETE command before DOS has a chance to overwrite a deleted file's data, DOS can reverse the DELETE operation.

Tip: If you discover that you accidentally deleted a file, immediately try to recover it. The longer you wait, the less likely your chances of recovering the file completely by using the UNDELETE command.

Using UNDELETE from the DOS Shell

DOS 5 enables you to use UNDELETE from the DOS Shell or from the command line.

> *Caution:* Using UNDELETE from the DOS Shell may not be a good practice. DOS first saves the contents of the computer's memory to a disk file and then executes the UNDELETE command. The disk file created may overwrite some of or all the data you want to recover. A safer way is to exit (press F3) from the Shell and run UNDELETE from the command line.

When you are using the Shell and want to recover an accidentally deleted file, complete the following steps:

1. Select the program list area of the DOS Shell window.

2. Select the Disk Utilities program group item to display the Disk Utilities program group in the program list area.

3. Choose the Undelete program item.

   The Shell displays the Undelete dialog box, which contains a text box labeled Parameters. The Parameters text box contains a default value of /LIST.

4. To see a list of deleted files, press Enter, or select the OK button. The section that follows describes other parameters you can type in the Parameters text box.

Using UNDELETE from the Command Line

The syntax for the UNDELETE command is as follows:

   UNDELETE *d:path\filename.ext /LIST/DT/DOS/ALL*

d: is the optional parameter that specifies the drive containing the disk that holds the deleted file(s).

path is the optional parameter that specifies path to the directory that contains the deleted file(s).

filename.ext specifies the file(s) you want to undelete. You can use wild cards to indicate multiple files. By default, if you do not specify a file name, DOS attempts to undelete all deleted files in the current directory or in the directory specified by the *path* parameter.

The */LIST* parameter causes UNDELETE to list the deleted files that can be recovered.

The */DT* switch instructs DOS to use the delete-tracking method of recovering the specified file(s). This method is described in the next section. If no delete-tracking file exists, the command will not proceed. By default, UNDELETE uses the delete-tracking method when no switch is specified; but when no delete-tracking file exists, the program uses information in the DOS directory to recover files.

/DOS causes DOS, in its attempt to undelete files, to rely on the information still stored in the DOS directory instead of using the delete-tracking method.

The */ALL* switch attempts to recover all deleted files without further input from you. When used with this switch, UNDELETE first looks in the delete-tracking file for information about the deleted files and then uses information from the DOS directory.

The UNDELETE command has two approaches to recovering a deleted file: the *delete-tracking* method and the *DOS* method. The sections that follow discuss these methods.

Using the Delete-Tracking Method To Recover a File

Ideally, your AUTOEXEC.BAT file contains a command that causes the DOS 5 MIRROR command to load its delete-tracking option, which is a memory-resident program. MIRROR's delete-tracking option constantly tracks and maintains a list of all files deleted from your computer. MIRROR saves the delete-tracking information in the *delete tracking file*. Note that this file (PCTRACKR.DEL) is assigned the system attribute and is not listed by the DIR command. Using this small but powerful program, MIRROR, is crucial if you want to provide maximum protection against accidental file deletions. (See Chapter 15 for more information about adding MIRROR to the AUTOEXEC.BAT file.)

By default, UNDELETE tries to read the MIRROR delete-tracking information. If no delete-tracking file exists, UNDELETE attempts to recover files through the DOS directory. You can also use the /DT switch to force

UNDELETE to use the delete-tracking file. When the /DT switch is used, the command terminates when no delete-tracking file can be found.

Suppose that you want to recover a file by using the delete-tracking method. If your AUTOEXEC.BAT file has loaded MIRROR's delete tracking into memory, change to the directory that contains the deleted file. Type the following command:

> **UNDELETE** *filename.ext*

Be sure to substitute *filename.ext* for the name of the file you want to recover. When you press Enter, DOS displays a message similar to the following:

```
Directory of C:\SPREADSH\QPRO2DAT
File Specs: BUDGET.WQ1

Delete Tracking file contains 1 deleted files.
Of those,    1 files have all clusters available
             0 files have some clusters available.
             0 files have no clusters available.

MS-DOS Directory contains 1 deleted files.
Of those,    1 files may be recovered.

Using the Delete Tracking file.
   BUDGET  WQ1   4037   1-29-91    4:58p    ...A Deleted 2-5-91 1:32a
All of the clusters for this file are available.

Do you want to recover this file? (Y/N)
```

This message generated by the UNDELETE command indicates first, in place of *filename.ext*, the name of the file you specified. The message then indicates the total number of deleted files by this name listed in the delete-tracking file, the number of files by this name that have all clusters available and are therefore recoverable, the number of partially recoverable files, and the number of files that are not recoverable.

Next, the DELETE command's message may indicate that the deleted file is still listed in the MS-DOS directory. Such a file may have been deleted when MIRROR's delete-tracking option was not loaded in memory as well as when delete tracking was active. The UNDELETE command's message then indicates the number of files that meet the file name criterion and may be recoverable by using information stored in the DOS directory rather than in the delete-tracking file.

Finally, the UNDELETE message lists the first file (matching *filename.ext*) found in the delete-tracking file. If this file is recoverable (that is, if the file's clusters have not yet been reallocated to another file), DOS asks you to confirm that you want to recover the file. To recover the file, press Y. DOS recovers the file and displays the following message:

```
File successfully undeleted.
```

The UNDELETE message also lists any other files by the same name found in the delete-tracking file. The files are listed one by one, starting with the most recently deleted files. For each file, UNDELETE asks whether you want to recover the file.

> *Note:* You may have created and deleted files by the same name more than once in a particular directory. So don't be alarmed or confused if UNDELETE asks you more than once whether you want to recover a particular file. Normally, you should recover the most recently deleted version of the file and discard the others.

If recovering a file will cause a duplicate file name in the directory, UNDELETE displays the following message:

```
The filename already exists. Enter a different filename.
Press "F5" to bypass this file.
```

If you want to recover this file, type a unique file name (one that does not already exist in the current directory). Otherwise, press F5 to skip this file.

Occasionally, by the time you realize that you need to recover an accidentally deleted file, other files may have reused some of the file's clusters. In this case, UNDELETE displays the message:

```
Only some of the clusters for this file are
available. Do you want to recover this file
with only the available clusters? (Y/N)
```

Press Y to recover the available bytes or N to skip the file.

If you wait too long before attempting to recover a file, the file may not be recoverable because all its clusters are being used by other files. When this is the case, UNDELETE tells you so and instructs you to `Press any key to continue`.

If you want to know which deleted files are still available to be recovered, type the following command:

UNDELETE /LIST

UNDELETE displays, from the delete-tracking file, a list of deleted files from the current directory. Partially recoverable files are listed with an asterisk (*)

to the left of the file name; unrecoverable files, with two asterisks (**) to the left of the file name.

> *Tip:* If a delete-tracking list is longer than will fit on one page, you can use Ctrl-S to pause the display. Press any key on the keyboard to resume scrolling. Do *not* use redirection or the MORE filter, because these tricks create disk files that may overwrite some of or all the data you want to recover.

> *Caution:* If you delete all the files in a directory and then remove the directory, you cannot recover any of the deleted files from that directory. UNDELETE cannot recover a directory that has been removed.
>
> The UNDELETE command is a product of Central Point Software, licensed by Microsoft for distribution as part of DOS 5. Another program from Central Point Software, PC Shell, is capable of recovering a removed directory. (PC Shell is a part of the PC Tools Deluxe utility package.)

Using the DOS Directory To Recover a File

If you were not using MIRROR's delete-tracking option when you accidentally deleted the file you want to recover, you can try to recover the file by using the information stored in the DOS directory. Type the following command:

UNDELETE *filename.ext* **/DOS**

Substitute for *filename.ext* the name of the file you want to recover.

UNDELETE displays a message similar to the following:

```
Directory of C:\SPREADSH\QPRO2DAT
File Specs: BUDGET.WQ1

        Delete Tracking file not found.
        MS-DOS Directory contains 1 deleted files.
```

```
        Of those,   1 files may be recovered.

Using the MS-DOS Directory.

   ?UDGET   WQ1   4037   1-29-91    4:58p   ...A
Do you want to undelete this file? (Y/N)
```

Press Y to recover the file or N to skip the file. After you press Y, UNDELETE displays the following prompt:

```
Enter the first character of the filename.
```

Because the DOS directory no longer has any record of this first character, you must supply the letter. Type the letter you want UNDELETE to use as the beginning letter of the file name. UNDELETE recovers the file and displays the following message:

```
File successfully undeleted.
```

Searching for Text with FIND

The FIND command, used from the command line, searches one or more files for a string of ASCII text and then displays the lines of text that contain the search string. FIND is useful for occasions when you know some of the text a desired file contains, but you can't recall which file contains the text. FIND uses the known text to help you locate the file.

The syntax for the FIND command is as follows:

FIND */C/N/V "string" d:path\filename ...*

"string" (the quotation marks are mandatory) specifies the ASCII characters you want DOS to find.

d:path\filename is the drive, path, and file name of the file to be searched. The ellipsis (. . .) indicates that more than one file can be specified.

The */C* switch causes the command to tally, or count, the number of lines that contain *string*.

The */N* switch causes the command to indicate a line number for each occurrence of *string* in a file.

The */V* switch causes the command to display all lines that do not contain *string* (rather than the lines that do).

When you use */C* and */V* together, the command counts the number of lines that do not contain *string*.

When you use /V and /N together, the command displays and numbers the lines that do not contain *string*.

When you use the FIND command, consider the following guidelines:

- Use FIND only on ASCII text files.

- The string parameter is case-sensitive. The string *LOOK* is not the same as the string *look*.

- The string parameter must be enclosed in quotation marks. If the string contains a quotation mark, type two quotation marks together (""). FIND will search for occurrences of ".

- Find looks for input from the standard input device (keyboard) if *filename* is not specified.

- Wild cards are not allowed in *filename*.

When used without switch options, the FIND command reads each specified file and displays each line that contains a particular ASCII string.

The FIND command can be used to modify or filter output from other DOS commands. FIND often is used with redirection and piping. If you need to search a text file for lines that include certain information, redirecting the output to a file or to your printer is probably more useful that displaying the information. Then you can use the list as a reference while you use a text editor or word processor to look at the entire original file.

The FIND command often is useful as a word-search utility. Consider a situation in which you forget the name of the memo you sent to your boss. You know that the memo's name is MEMO1, MEMO2, or MEMO3 and that you always use the title *Supervisor* in memos to your boss. You can use *Supervisor* as a search string. Type the following:

FIND "Supervisor" MEMO1 MEMO2 MEMO3

Each line that contains the string *Supervisor* will be listed. The form of the listing is as follows:

```
——— MEMO1
——— MEMO2
Supervisor of Communications
——— MEMO3
```

As you can see, the line that contains the word *Supervisor* is listed beneath the file name MEMO2. The file you are looking for is MEMO2. (No lines are listed under MEMO1 or MEMO3.)

Turning On Verification with VERIFY

The VERIFY command controls whether the DOS VERIFY setting is on or off. When VERIFY is on, data written to a disk by a DOS command or an applications program is *verified*—read by DOS and compared to the original. This verification is the same as that performed by DOS when you use the COPY command with the /V switch. When VERIFY is on, you do not need to use /V with COPY. When VERIFY is off, data written to disk is not verified.

When VERIFY is on and you use commands such as COPY, BACKUP, RESTORE, XCOPY, DISKCOPY, and REPLACE, you are assured that data hasn't been written to a bad sector on the disk. The verification operation can slow the execution of these commands, however. In most disk-intensive activities, a program is 20 to 40 percent slower during disk input/output than when VERIFY is off. You have to weigh the added assurance of data integrity against the inconvenience of slower execution. Many users turn on VERIFY while they work with critical files and then turn off VERIFY for normal DOS work.

The VERIFY command can be issued in any of the following three forms:

VERIFY ON

VERIFY OFF

VERIFY

When you boot the computer, the default setting of VERIFY is off. Use VERIFY ON to turn on VERIFY. Later, you can use VERIFY OFF to turn off VERIFY.

Use the VERIFY command alone, with no parameters, to see the current setting of VERIFY.

When you use VERIFY, consider the following guidelines:

- If you issue VERIFY with no parameter, DOS responds with `VERIFY is ON` or `VERIFY is OFF`.

- If VERIFY is on, specifying a /V switch in a COPY command has no additional verification effect.

- You cannot use VERIFY to cause verification of a network drive.

For example, if you plan to perform a critical backup operation on your hard disk, you can add an extra level of confidence by turning on VERIFY. During the backup procedure (see Chapter 11), DOS verifies that each sector is written without error to the backup disk(s). To turn on VERIFY, issue the command **VERIFY ON**.

To see whether VERIFY is on or off, type **VERIFY** at the DOS prompt. DOS responds as follows:

```
VERIFY is ON
```

When you no longer want verification, you can turn off the feature by typing **VERIFY OFF**.

> *Note:* Unlike PROMPT and PATH, the VERIFY setting is not stored in the DOS environment. VERIFY is an internal indicator, or flag.

Selectively Updating a Disk with REPLACE

The external command REPLACE, introduced in DOS 3.2, is a special COPY command. REPLACE enables you to update existing files in the target directory with new versions of files with the same name in the source directory. Conversely, you can use the REPLACE command to copy from the source directory only the files that don't already exist in the target directory.

When issued with no switches, REPLACE reads the source disk and directory for files matching the command line's source-file parameter. All matching files are transferred to the destination disk and path. Unlike COPY, REPLACE cannot rename the files as they are copied to the destination; therefore, no target file name is allowed (or needed).

The REPLACE command has many practical applications. For example, you can use REPLACE to collect on a floppy disk, the most recent versions of common files from a group of PCs. You can use REPLACE also to upgrade software on your hard disk to a new version.

The syntax for the REPLACE command is as follows:

> REPLACE *d1:path1***filename.ext** *d2:path2* /A/P/R/S/W/U

d1: is the optional source-drive parameter. If you omit this parameter, DOS assumes that you mean the current drive.

The optional *path1* parameter is the path of the source files. If you omit the source path parameter, DOS assumes the current directory.

The **filename.ext** parameter is the file name of the source file(s) and is required. Wild cards are allowed in the file name and extension.

d2: is the target drive parameter, where the files will be replaced. If you omit this parameter, DOS uses the current drive.

path2 is the target path name, where the files will be replaced. If the target path parameter is omitted, DOS assumes the current directory of the target disk.

The */A* switch causes REPLACE to add new files to the target disk. REPLACE copies only the source files that do not already exist in the target directory. /A may not be used with /S or /U.

The */P* switch prompts for confirmation before copying each file. To confirm the replacement, press Y. To reject the replacement, press N.

The */R* switch causes REPLACE to replace read-only files as well as other files.

The */S* switch causes REPLACE to search all subdirectories of the target directory for a file matching each source file. /S may not be used with /A.

The */W* switch causes REPLACE to wait for you to press a key before executing its copying operation.

The */U* switch causes REPLACE to copy source files with a more recent date and time than target files with the same names. /U may not be used with /A.

The */U* switch adds time selectivity to REPLACE. /U causes REPLACE to *update* destination files with source files that have a more current time and date.

When using the REPLACE command, consider the following guidelines:

- REPLACE is available with DOS 3.2 and later versions.

- You must include a source file-name parameter with REPLACE. The file-name parameter may contain wild cards.

- The destination parameters may include a drive and a path name but may not include a file name. The destination drive or path or both may be omitted. REPLACE assumes default values for omitted destination parameters.

- The /A switch cannot be used with the /U or /S switch. All other switch combinations are allowed.

Assume, for example, that you want to update the \PROGRAMS directory on your computer's hard disk in drive C. The new files are on a floppy disk in drive A. The current directory listing for C:\PROGRAMS is as follows:

```
Volume in drive C is HARD DISK
Volume Serial Number is 2F7F-16CD
Directory of  C:\PROGRAMS
  .             <DIR>        11-03-89     12:31p
  ..            <DIR>        11-03-89     12:31p
RESULT    DAT        810     08-24-90      1:32p
JUDE      DAT         56     12-12-90     10:15p
PROFILE   DAT        850     08-11-90      4:46p
RESULTS   DAT        911     08-24-90      2:46p
TESTS     DAT        488     08-26-90      3:47p
CONVERT   SYS         40     09-01-90      5:54p
GEN4SYS   BAS       6556     09-01-90      5:37p
MONITOR   BAS        993     06-22-90     12:10p
     10 File(s)    10934272 bytes free
```

A directory listing of drive A also shows several files:

```
Volume in drive A is COLLECTION
Volume Serial Number is 1B22-1ED1
Directory of  A:
PROCED    DOC      19712     10-29-91      7:34p
RESULT    DAT        810     08-25-91     11:06a
FRM_SR1   DAT        372     08-18-91     11:18a
JUDE      DAT         56     12-14-91     11:15p
FRM_PRL   DAT       9280     08-19-91      2:32p
PROFILE   DAT        850     08-11-91     10:46p
CROSS     DAT       1463     08-26-91      3:48p
RESULTS   DAT        911     08-24-91     10:55p
TESTS     DAT        488     08-28-91      2:17p
CONVERT   SYS         40     09-01-91      5:54p
GEN4SYS   BAK       6556     09-01-91      5:37p
MONITOR   BAK        993     06-22-91     12:10p
IO        BAK      22736     08-23-91     12:42p
     13 File(s)     6582 bytes free
```

Notice that some of the file names appear in both directories. You want REPLACE to copy these files from the floppy disk to the C:\PROGRAMS directory. Issue the following command:

REPLACE A:*.* C:\PROGRAMS

As REPLACE processes the files, you see the following:

```
Replacing C:\PROGRAMS\RESULT.DAT
Replacing C:\PROGRAMS\JUDE.DAT
Replacing C:\PROGRAMS\PROFILE.DAT
Replacing C:\PROGRAMS\RESULTS.DAT
Replacing C:\PROGRAMS\TESTS.DAT
Replacing C:\PROGRAMS\CONVERT.SYS
6 file(s) replaced
```

This replacement list includes all the files the two directories have in common. The files on drive A that were not in \PROGRAMS were not copied. The files in \PROGRAMS that were not on drive A remain intact. REPLACE makes the updating operation much easier than issuing a series of COPY commands.

Summary

DOS offers many useful file-management commands, both through the DOS Shell and at the command line. Use these commands to arrange your files and to keep your computer's disks well-organized and accessible. As you gain experience with file-management commands, you probably will want to incorporate additional switches or take more advantage of DOS defaults. In this chapter, you have learned the following key points:

- The names of DOS devices are reserved. If you use a reserved name for a file parameter, DOS uses the device.

- The end-of-file character ^Z marks the end of many ASCII files.

- The RENAME operation changes the name of an existing file.

- The DELETE operation removes files from a directory. Erased files are no longer available to DOS.

- The UNDELETE command can recover deleted files.

- The TYPE command displays an ASCII file's contents.

- The COPY operation copies and combines files.

- The VERIFY command manages DOS's internal VERIFY setting.

- The REPLACE command selectively updates files on the target disk with files having the same name on the source disk.

In the next chapter, you learn important ways to protect your data by making backups of your files.

Understanding
Backups and the
Care of Data

11

Desktop computers commonly contain hard disk drives that
can store thousands of pages of information. If your computer contains a hard disk, it almost certainly contains millions of
bytes of software—the programs that run your computer. The
hard disk probably also contains thousands or even millions of
bytes of data—the information you or someone else has typed into
the system. The software and data represent a significant investment in money and effort that would be lost if your hard disk were
damaged or erased.

This chapter tells you how to protect your computer files from a
variety of menaces, such as static electricity, excessive heat, and
erratic electrical power. Most important, in this chapter, you learn
how to use several DOS commands—including XCOPY, BACKUP,
and RESTORE—to back up the files on your system and then to
restore these files in the event of damage to or erasure of your disk.

> *Note:* If you have never learned how to back up your disk
> files or produce duplicates, it is time to learn! Apply this
> chapter's information, and you should never have to
> experience the sinking feeling that comes from losing a
> significant amount of hard work to a hard disk crash,
> accidental disk format, or accidental file erasure.

Key Terms Used in This Chapter

Surge protector | A protective device inserted between a power outlet and a computer's power plug. Surge protectors help block power surges that can damage the computer's circuits.

Static electricity | A high-voltage charge that builds on an object and can be discharged when another object is touched. Static electricity discharges can damage electronic circuits.

Ground | An electrical path directly to earth. Grounds can dissipate static discharges safely. A PC chassis normally is grounded.

Voltage regulator | An electrical device that keeps voltage fluctuations from reaching an electrical device. Regulators usually don't stop power surges.

Avoiding Data Loss

Today's personal computers are reliable and economical data processing machines. PCs today do the work of computers that a decade ago only a few fortunate users had access to. Like all machines, however, computers are subject to failures and operator errors.

Table 11.1 lists some hardware and software problems discussed in this chapter and suggests ways to prevent these problems.

Preventing Hardware Failures

Computers contain thousands of transistorized circuits, most of which have life expectancies of more than a century. A poor power source, excessive heat, and static discharges, however, can cause circuits to fail or operate erratically. Disk drives have precise moving parts with critical alignments. The potential always exists for hardware failures. If you follow the precautions presented in this section, you can reduce the likelihood of hardware failure.

Table 11.1
Hardware and Software Problems and Prevention Techniques

Problem	Prevention
Static electricity	Use antistatic liquid or floor mat; place a "touch pad" on desk.
Overheating	Clean clogged air vents; remove objects blocking vents; use air-conditioned room during the summer.
Damaged disks	Don't leave disks to be warped by the sun; use protective covers; avoid spilling liquids on disks; store disks in a safe place; avoid magnetic fields from appliances (TVs, microwave ovens, and so on).

Always be cautious about your computer's environment. If your power fluctuates and lights flicker, you may need to purchase a *line voltage regulator* from your computer dealer.

Is the fan on the back of your computer choked with dust? Clean the air vents and make sure that your computer has room to breathe. Your computer may perform erratically when it is too hot. Because circuits are not reliable when they overheat, you may get jumbled data.

You generate *static electricity* on your body when humidity is low, you wear synthetic fabrics, or you walk on carpet. Just by touching your keyboard while carrying a static charge, you can send an electrical shudder through your computer, causing data jumble or circuit failure. Fortunately, you can avoid static problems by touching your grounded system cabinet before touching the keyboard. If static electricity is a serious problem for you, ask your dealer about antistatic products. These products are inexpensive and easy to use.

Preventing Software Failures

A software program is a set of instructions for the microprocessor. A small minority of software packages have flawed instructions called *bugs*. Software bugs are usually minor and rarely cause greater problems than keyboard lockups or jumbled displays. The potential does exist for a software bug to cause your disk drive to operate in an erratic way, however.

Fortunately, most companies test and debug their software before marketing the packages. Performing a backup of your disks is your best insurance against bugs.

Note: Software viruses are purposely created software bugs with the potential of great file damage. Most viruses are additional program codes hidden in a COM file, such as COMMAND.COM. A virus most often does its damage by altering the disk's file allocation table (FAT) and marking clusters as bad or unavailable. A virus also has the capability of initiating a FORMAT or destroying a disk partition table.

Viruses "multiply" through the exchange of software between users. If you load an "infected" COM file onto your PC, the virus can quickly "infect" your COMMAND.COM file. Unfortunately, you can back up an infected file, and when the file is restored, the virus continues to do its dirty work. Your best defense against getting a virus on your system is to install only reputable software from a source who can attest to the program's operation. If you are hit by a virus, you may have to fall back to your write-protected master DOS disks and rebuild your system from the ground up. Many antivirus utility programs are now available; these utilities can detect and eliminate virus programs. Consult your dealer for the most up-to-date versions of these programs.

Preventing Mistakes

As you gain skill, you use DOS commands that can result in the accidental loss of files. When you use commands such as COPY, ERASE, and FORMAT, you may inadvertently remove some important data. For this reason, make a mental note to study what you type before you press Enter. Developing a typing rhythm that carries you straight through confirmation prompts into the clutches of disaster is easy.

Although you can use Ctrl-C, Ctrl-Break, and if necessary, Ctrl-Alt-Del to abandon commands, you are stopping what is already underway, and these "panic buttons" may not contain the damage. Because you are human, you are likely to make mistakes. Consequently, you should always have a backup copy of all important data.

DOS 5.0 is more forgiving than previous versions of DOS. DOS 5.0 offers a safe, reversible FORMAT command, as well as an UNDELETE command that you can use to recover from an accidental DEL or ERASE command.

Combining Copying and Directory Management with XCOPY

The external command XCOPY is an enhanced version of COPY that has, among other features, the capability to create directories on the destination disk. XCOPY is therefore handy for copying a portion of your directory tree to another disk. XCOPY is a sophisticated copy command with many uses.

The XCOPY command addresses the needs of three types of computer users: those who use more than one computer, those who have hard disks, and those who want more control over which files are copied than is provided by the standard COPY command. Almost all PC users fit into one or more of these categories, so XCOPY is an important command to know and use.

XCOPY syntax is similar to COPY syntax, but the switches are more complex. XCOPY syntax is as follows:

XCOPY *ds:paths\filenames.exts dd:pathd\filenamed.extd*
/V/P/W/S/E/A/M/D:date

In this command, *s* means source. The *source files* are the files to be copied. If you omit the source disk drive name (*ds:*), the current disk drive is used. If you omit the source path name (*paths*), the current directory on the drive is used. You can use wild cards in the source file name (*filenames.exts*). If you omit the file name, XCOPY assumes that you want to specify the wild card *.* and copies all files in the given path. You must include at least one source parameter.

With XCOPY, *d* means destination. If you do not specify a destination disk (*dd:*) or path name (*pathd*), XCOPY uses the current disk directory. If you omit the destination file name (*filenamed.extd*), files on the source disk retain their names on the destination disk.

In an XCOPY operation, DOS may not always recognize whether a particular parameter refers to a file or to a directory. When ambiguity arises, XCOPY asks you whether the destination is a file name or path name.

Consider the following command, for example:

XCOPY C:\WORDS*.* A:\WORDS

If no directory named WORDS exists on the destination disk, DOS cannot determine whether you intend to create a file or a directory named WORDS on the A disk.

XCOPY displays the following message:

```
Does WORDS specify a file name
or directory name on the target
(F = file, D = directory)?
```

Press F when the destination (target) is a file name, or D when the destination is a directory. Unlike COPY, XCOPY creates directories on the destination disk as needed.

Understanding XCOPY's Switches

XCOPY has eight switches, which are described in this section. The Command Reference section gives a complete table of XCOPY's switches.

/V is the familiar verify switch. XCOPY verifies that it has copied the files correctly.

/W causes XCOPY to prompt and wait for you to insert the source disk. This switch is particularly useful in batch files.

/P is the prompt switch. XCOPY displays the name of the file it is to copy and asks whether the file should be copied. Press Y to copy the file or N to skip it. When you answer Y, XCOPY immediately copies the file.

The /S and /E switches affect the way XCOPY handles additional subdirectories. These two switches tap the full power of XCOPY. COPY limits itself to handling the files from one directory; XCOPY starts with the named or current directory (source) and can process the files in all additional subdirectories of the source directory, all lower subdirectories of these subdirectories, and so on. XCOPY traverses the subdirectory tree and can copy complete directory branches from one disk to another.

The /S switch copies subdirectories as well as the directory specified in the command. The /S switch instructs XCOPY to copy all designated files from the current and subsequent subdirectories to a parallel set of subdirectories on the destination disk drive. Assume, for example, that you want to copy to the disk in drive A all the files in the C:\WORDS directory and all files in the two subdirectories of C:\WORDS: \WORDS\LETTERS and

\WORDS\CONTRACTS. You want XCOPY to create on the destination disk any directories necessary to hold the files from the source disks. Issue the following command:

XCOPY C:\WORDS*.* A: /S

The command executes in the following sequence:

1. XCOPY copies all files in \WORDS to the current directory on drive A.

2. If the subdirectory \LETTERS doesn't already exist on the A drive, XCOPY creates \LETTERS. XCOPY then copies all files from WORDS\LETTERS to the subdirectory \LETTERS on drive A.

3. Similarly, XCOPY creates \CONTRACTS, if necessary, on the destination disk and copies all files from the subdirectory WORDS\CONTRACTS to the corresponding subdirectory on drive A.

In essence, XCOPY lifts a copy of the directory tree starting at the source directory and transplants the copy to drive A.

Note that XCOPY does not place the copied files from the subdirectories into a single directory. XCOPY places files from one subdirectory into a parallel subdirectory. If the subdirectory does not exist on the destination, XCOPY creates the subdirectory.

The /E switch affects the operation of the /S switch. If XCOPY encounters an empty subdirectory on the source drive, XCOPY /S skips the empty subdirectory. If you give the /S and /E switches together, XCOPY also creates empty subdirectories on the destination drive. The /E switch has no effect without the /S switch.

The switches /M, /A, and /D:*date* add extra filters to the *filenames.exts* parameter. The /M and /A switches tell XCOPY to copy only files that have been modified since the last archival procedure that turned off the archive attribute. In Chapter 8, you learned about the archive attribute stored in the directory with each file name. When you create or change a file, this attribute is turned on. XCOPY, when used with the /A switch, copies only files that have their archive attribute set. The command does not affect the archive bit. When you use the /M switch, XCOPY copies only files with the archive bit set and then turns off the archive attribute for each archived file.

The BACKUP command can select files based on the archive attribute. If XCOPY has cleared this flag, however, BACKUP does not process the file. If you therefore use the commands XCOPY /M and BACKUP /M (the switches have identical meaning for the two commands), the backup you make using BACKUP may not be complete.

The */D:date* switch selects files based on their *directory date*, the date of the file's creation or modification. XCOPY copies files created or modified on or after the date specified.

Understanding the Operation of XCOPY

XCOPY is best described as a hybrid between COPY and BACKUP/RESTORE. XCOPY and COPY duplicate files between directories and disks. Unlike COPY, however, XCOPY does not copy files to a nondisk device, such as the printer (PRN) or the console (CON). Like BACKUP and RESTORE, XCOPY can copy files selectively and traverse the directory tree to copy files from more than one directory. XCOPY also can make a destination directory when one does not exist. This directory capability makes XCOPY useful for duplicating a directory branch onto another disk.

Like COPY but unlike BACKUP, XCOPY copies files that are directly usable: you cannot use files processed by BACKUP until you have processed them with RESTORE.

When using the XCOPY command, consider the following guidelines:

- XCOPY cannot copy hidden source files.

- XCOPY does not overwrite read-only destination files.

- If a file parameter is omitted in the XCOPY syntax, XCOPY assumes the *.* full wild-card pattern as the file parameter.

- If you include the /D switch, the date parameter must be entered in the format of the system's DATE command or in the format indicated by the latest COUNTRY command.

- The /V switch performs the same read-after-write checking as the SET VERIFY ON global verify flag.

- To use XCOPY to copy empty source subdirectories, you must specify both the /S and /E switches.

Using XCOPY Effectively

Using XCOPY, you can control by date or archive attribute the files copied; you can copy complete subdirectory trees; and you can confirm which files should be copied. The command has several ideal uses: copying files selectively between disks or directories, performing a "quickie" hard disk backup (backing up only a few critical files in several subdirectories), and keeping the directories of more than one computer synchronized.

With COPY, your control is limited. COPY duplicates all files that match the given name, an all-or-nothing approach. If you use the /P switch with XCOPY, DOS asks you whether you want to copy each file.

XCOPY is practical to use if you want to make backup copies of less than a diskful of files from several directories. Instead of BACKUP, you may prefer to use the command XCOPY /A to select files that have changed since the last backup.

Using XCOPY to back up a disk has two ground rules:

- If you suspect that the files cannot fit on one disk, be sure to use the /M switch. As XCOPY copies each file, the command resets the file's archive attribute bit. When the destination disk fills, XCOPY stops. Change disks and restart the XCOPY command, again using the /M switch. XCOPY copies the files whose archive bit has not yet been reset.

- XCOPY cannot break a large source file between destination disks. If you need to back up a file that doesn't fit on a single floppy disk, you must use BACKUP.

A favorite use of XCOPY is to synchronize the contents of the hard disks of two computers. Many people have one computer at work and another at home. If both computers have hard disks, keeping the copies of programs and data files current is a major task. Which files did you change today? Which machine has the more current version?

When you want to keep separate hard disks synchronized, you may find XCOPY's /A, /D:date, and /S switches especially useful. The /S switch forces XCOPY to traverse your disk's directory structure, playing a hunting game for source files. Whether you use /A or /D depends on how often you copy files between the machines. If you copy files between the machines frequently, you may prefer the /A switch. If you let many days pass between synchronizing your computers' contents, you may find that the /D switch works better. Use the /D switch if you have run BACKUP on the source machine since you last used XCOPY. BACKUP resets the archive attribute so that XCOPY's /A switch does not catch all files that have changed between XCOPY backups.

Duplicating a Directory Branch

For this example, assume that you have on your hard disk a subdirectory named \WPFILES with a few word processing files in it. \WPFILES also has two subdirectories. The first, \WPFILES\MEMOS, contains your current memos. The second, \WPFILES\DOCS, contains your document files. You want to keep a current set of the files in these three directories stored on a floppy disk. To copy all the files in this directory branch to the floppy, issue the following command:

XCOPY C:\WPFILES A:\WPFILES /S

DOS responds as follows:

```
Does WPFILES specify a filename
or directory name on the target
(F = file, D = directory)?
```

Press D, and XCOPY immediately begins to read the source directories. DOS displays the following messages:

```
Reading source file(s)...
C:\WPFILES\LET9_1.WP
C:\WPFILES\LET9_2.WP
C:\WPFILES\LET9_3.WP
C:\WPFILES\LET9_4.WP
C:\WPFILES\LET9_5.WP
C:\WPFILES\DOCS\SCHEDULE.DOC
C:\WPFILES\MEMOS\SALES.MEM
    7 File(s) copied
```

Because you included the /S switch, XCOPY copied the files in C:\WPFILES, C:\WPFILES\MEMOS, and C:\WPFILES\DOCS. The A:\WPFILES path parameter causes XCOPY to ask whether the name specifies a directory or a file. \WPFILES conceivably could be a user file in the root directory. The full path name of each file is echoed to the screen as the file is copied to drive A. When the command completes, the \WPFILES directory branch has been copied to drive A.

In another example, assume that your PC experiences a hardware failure and needs to go to the shop for repairs. You want to use your floppy disk that contains the \WPFILES directory branch to place the \WPFILES directory branch on a second computer's hard disk. Enter the following command:

XCOPY A: C: /S

XCOPY reverses the copy process described in the preceding paragraphs by copying all the files on drive A to corresponding subdirectory locations on drive C.

Comparing Files with COMP

The external command COMP compares two files or two sets of files to find differences in the files. Any differences are reported on-screen. When a copied file is extremely important, you can use COMP to compare the file with the original. If any difference exists, you know that something is wrong with the copy. (Normally, DOS detects data integrity errors while reading and writing files. But if you want to be sure that two files are the same, you can ease your mind by using COMP.)

COMP is supplied with PC DOS 1.0 and later versions and with MS-DOS 3.3 and later versions. Check your version of DOS to determine whether you have the COMP command. MS-DOS includes a similar command, FC, which is discussed in the next section.

File comparison is a useful file-management and integrity-checking tool. Unlike the DISKCOMP disk-level command, COMP reports differences at the file level. With COMP, you can determine the following information about compared files:

- Whether the files are identical in content and size

- Whether the files are identical in size but different in content

- Whether the files are different in size and content

In a practical sense, COMP is useful in determining whether a file is the same as another file on a different disk or in a different directory. If the compared files have the same name, you easily can copy an older version of the named file to another disk, not realizing that the newer version in another directory is different. You may copy a file to a file name such as TEMP to have a temporary copy. After some time, you may forget the source of TEMP. COMP can show you whether the contents of a particular file match TEMP.

The syntax for the COMP command is as follows:

COMP *d1:path1\filename1.ext1 d2:path2\filename2.ext2*
/D/A/L/N=number/C

d1: is the optional parameter for the drive that contains the first file or set of files (the primary set) to be compared. If you omit the *d1:* parameter, DOS assumes the current drive.

path1 is the optional parameter for the path to the file(s) to be compared. If you omit the *path1* parameter, DOS assumes the default directory.

filename1.ext1 is the optional file parameter for the file to be used as the basis of comparison. Wild cards are allowed for the file name and extension.

If you omit the file parameter but include a drive or a path, COMP assumes that the file parameter is *.*. To verify a copied file, you supply its name.

d2: is the optional drive parameter for the second file or set of files (the secondary set) to be used in the comparison. If you omit *d2:* but include a path or file name parameter, COMP assumes the logged disk.

path2 is the optional path parameter for the secondary set of files. If you omit the *path2* parameter, COMP assumes the default directory.

filename2.ext2 is the optional file name and extension of the secondary set of files. Wild cards are allowed in the file name and extension. If you omit the secondary set file name parameter, COMP assumes that the secondary set files have the same names as the primary set files.

DOS 5.0 has added five new switches to the COMP command.

/D causes COMP to list file differences in decimal format.

/A causes COMP to display file differences in character (ASCII) format.

/L causes COMP to display the line number of a discrepancy rather than a byte offset.

/N=number causes COMP to compare files only up to the line in the files indicated by the *number* parameter.

/C causes the comparison to ignore the case of ASCII text in the files.

If you issue COMP with no parameters, DOS prompts you for file names and switches.

Understanding the Operation of COMP

COMP reads one file and compares each byte to another file. Bytes are compared based on their relative positions in the file. COMP does not care whether the bytes represent ASCII-character data or binary data. COMP does check both files for the Ctrl-Z end-of-file markers. If an end-of-file marker is not found, COMP displays the following message:

```
EOF mark not found
```

The end-of-file marker message is informational only; it does not indicate a problem.

After the COMP program is loaded into memory, you can continue to compare files by answering Y to the following prompt:

```
Compare more files (Y/N)?
```

COMP then prompts you for parameters.

You can redirect the output of COMP to the printer (by adding **> PRN** to the end of the command). In this case, however, all prompts generated by the command also are redirected to the printer. If you use redirection, there-fore, you need to read the prompts from the device to which output has been redirected. You also can redirect the output of COMP to a file (by adding **>** *filename.ext* to the command). In this case, you must anticipate any prompting messages because you have no way to see prompts. You still must enter all responses to the prompts from the keyboard.

Consider the following guidelines when you are using COMP:

- If you do not specify parameters, COMP first prompts for the primary set parameter and then the secondary set parameter.

- As each file in the set is compared, the file names are displayed.

- If the two files being compared are different sizes, COMP issues the following report:

```
Files are different sizes
```

No further comparison of the two files is made.

- If COMP detects differences in two files of the same size, COMP reports the differences on-screen as byte offsets (positions in the file) and values of the differing bytes. By default, byte offsets and values are given in hexadecimal (base 16) notation. The /A switch causes the values of the differing bytes to display as ASCII charac-ters.

- COMP reports the first 10 differences in the two files and then gives up, generating the following message:

```
10 Mismatches - ending compare.
```

- When all sets of files are compared, COMP prompts for additional comparisons.

Comparing Two Text Files with COMP

The following simple example demonstrates the operation of COMP. Suppose that two text files identical in size, ORIGINAL.TXT and ANOTHER.TXT, are located in the default directory of the logged drive A. Assume that ORIGINAL.TXT contains the following list of numbers:

        1
        2
        3
        4
        5
        6
        7
        8
        9

Assume that ANOTHER.TXT contains the following numbers:

        9
        8
        7
        6
        5
        4
        3
        2
        1

These simple files are used here to illustrate how COMP reports the differences (mismatches) between files. Of course, your files would have more complex contents.

To compare the two files, issue the following command:

COMP ORIGINAL.TXT ANOTHER.TXT

COMP reports as follows:

```
Comparing ORIGINAL.TXT and ANOTHER.TXT...
Compare error at
File 1 = 31
File 2 = 39
Compare error at OFFSET 3
File 1 = 32
File 2 = 38
Compare error at OFFSET 6
```

```
File 1 = 33
File 2 = 37
Compare error at OFFSET 9
File 1 = 34
File 2 = 36
Compare error at OFFSET F
File 1 = 36
File 2 = 34
Compare error at OFFSET 12
File 1 = 37
File 2 = 33
Compare error at OFFSET 15
File 1 = 38
File 2 = 32
Compare error at OFFSET 18
File 1 = 39
File 2 = 31
Compare more files (Y/N)?
```

COMP found 8 mismatches in the files. You may have expected to see 9 mismatches reported. Remember, however, that the number 5 is in the same position in both files.

To compare the two files, displaying the mismatches as ASCII characters (rather than hexadecimal) and displaying the locations of the mismatches as line numbers (rather than byte offsets), issue the following command:

COMP ORIGINAL.TXT ANOTHER.TXT /A/L

COMP reports as follows:

```
Comparing ORIGINAL.TXT and ANOTHER.TXT...
Compare error at LINE 1
File 1 = 1
File 2 = 9
Compare error at LINE 2
File 1 = 2
File 2 = 8
Compare error at LINE 3
File 1 = 3
File 2 = 7
Compare error at LINE 4
File 1 = 4
File 2 = 6
Compare error at LINE 6
File 1 = 6
```

```
File 2 = 4
Compare error at LINE 7
File 1 = 7
File 2 = 3
Compare error at LINE 8
File 1 = 8
File 2 = 2
Compare error at LINE 9
File 1 = 9
File 2 = 1
Compare more files (Y/N)?
```

Performing a Full-File Comparison with FC

The external FC command is similar to the COMP command in that both compare files. FC, however, is a more versatile command than COMP. FC generally provides more information, has more options for controlling the command output, and can compare files of different lengths.

The FC command has two general syntax forms. One form uses the /B switch for a forced binary comparison; the other uses the remaining switches in an ASCII comparison. The two forms of syntax are as follows:

FC /B *d1:path1***filename1.ext1** *d2:path2***filename2.ext2**

or

FC /A/C/L/LBn/N/nnnn/T/W *d1:path1***filename1.ext1** *d2:\path2***filename2.ext2**

> *Note:* With the FC command, all switches must precede the other parameters.

d1: is an optional parameter that specifies the drive containing the first file to be compared. If the first drive parameter is omitted, FC assumes the default drive.

path1 is the path of the directory containing the first file. If the first file's path is omitted, FC assumes the default directory.

filename1.ext1 is the file name of the first file. This parameter is mandatory. Wild-card characters are not valid in this parameter.

d2: is the drive containing the second file to be compared. If the second drive parameter is omitted, FC assumes the default drive.

path2 is the path of the directory containing the second file. If the second file path is omitted, the command assumes the default directory.

filename2.ext2 is the file name of the second file. This parameter is mandatory. Wild-card characters are not valid in this parameter.

/A instructs FC to abbreviate its output (DOS 3.2 and later versions), displaying only the first line of each set of differences followed by an ellipsis (…).

/C causes FC to ignore the case of alphabetic characters when making comparisons.

/L instructs FC to compare the files in ASCII mode, even when the files have EXE, COM, SYS, OBJ, LIB, or BIN extensions (DOS 3.2 and later versions).

/LBn sets the number of lines in FC's buffer to *n*. The default number is 100 (DOS 3.2 and later versions). If the number of consecutive nonmatching lines exceeds the buffer size, FC aborts the compare operation.

/N instructs FC to include the line numbers of lines reported in the output (DOS 3.2 and later versions).

/nnnn establishes the number of lines that must match after a difference in order to resynchronize FC.

/T instructs FC to view tab characters as literal characters rather than tab-expanded spaces (DOS 3.2 and later versions).

/W instructs FC to compress *white space*—tabs, empty lines, and spaces—into a single space for purposes of file comparison.

Understanding the Operation of FC

FC works in two modes: ASCII and binary. FC defaults to ASCII mode comparison when the files to be compared do not have EXE, COM, SYS, OBJ, LIB, or BIN extensions.

In ASCII mode, FC compares two files on a line-by-line basis. Lines from both files are held in a line buffer. FC uses the lines in the buffer to compare the first file to the second.

If FC detects a difference, FC displays the first file name followed by the last matching line and the mismatching line(s) from the first file. FC then displays the next line to match in both files.

After displaying mismatch information about file 1, FC repeats the same sequence for file 2. The file 2 name is displayed first, followed by the last matching line and the mismatching lines from file 2, ending on the next line that matches in both files, thus synchronizing the two files.

FC can help you determine whether the contents of two files are different by showing you the extent and location of any mismatch FC finds. You can use this output as an alternative to a side-by-side comparison of the file contents.

In binary mode, FC compares two files byte for byte. At the first difference, the byte offset position in the first file is reported along with the value of the two files' bytes at the position. The offset as well as the byte values are reported in hexadecimal (base 16) form. This form of FC is essentially equivalent to the COMP command.

> *Tip:* If you are comparing two files that are not the same, you can quickly stop the reporting of differences with Ctrl-C or Ctrl-Break.

In binary mode, FC does not attempt to resynchronize the two files by finding an adjusted point of byte agreement. If one file has an additional byte at one place in the file, FC reports the additional byte and all subsequent bytes of the file as mismatches.

If one file is longer than its comparison file, the binary mode compares as many bytes as are present and then reports that one file is longer. When a binary file comparison results in a long listing of differences, you may want to stop the FC operation by pressing Ctrl-C.

Only one switch is available in the binary mode. The /B switch causes the comparison to be binary even if file extensions indicate that the files are not binary. You use the /B switch to compare two text files in binary mode. You may find situations in which you would rather have the binary-mode output format of FC than the ASCII mode format. Binary mode format reports differences as pairs of hexadecimal values. You then can see the values of characters, such as Ctrl-G (bell), that do not produce printed output.

Consider the following guideline when using FC:

- The default number of lines that must match in an ASCII comparison after a difference has ended is two. The files then are considered resynchronized. The number of "must match" lines can be changed using the /nnnn switch by setting *nnnn* to the desired value.

Using FC To Compare a Copied File to Its Original

Suppose that you are copying the ANSI.SYS file from your hard disk to a floppy disk to use for an important demonstration on another PC. When the copy completes, you set the disk on the edge of your desk and go to the break room to get coffee. As you return, you notice that the disk has fallen off your desk and landed against the small transformer that runs your cassette recorder. You are worried that the magnetic field from the transformer has damaged ANSI.SYS. To verify that the copied ANSI.SYS is good, you compare it to the original by using the following command:

FC A:ANSI.SYS C:\DOS\DRIVERS\ANSI.SYS

After a few seconds, FC reports as follows:

```
FC: No differences encountered
```

The copy of ANSI.SYS seems to be good.

Making Backup Sets with BACKUP

Compared to floppy disks, hard disks have many advantages. Hard disks are faster, have larger storage capacities and root directories, support multiple partitions, and never require a disk swap. A file on a hard disk can be many times the size of a file on a floppy disk. Commands like COPY and XCOPY enable you to keep a few duplicate files on a floppy for backup purposes, but DOS provides another command specifically designed for the big jobs. The external BACKUP command and its counterpart, RESTORE (discussed later in this chapter), enable users to maintain disk backup sets of a hard disk's contents.

BACKUP typically is used to copy files from a hard disk to another disk, normally a floppy disk. The "copies" of the files on the second disk are held in a modified format that can be accessed only by the RESTORE command.

Note: BACKUP does not use the normal file format on the backup disk. Only the BACKUP and RESTORE commands can use this special file format. Backed up files must be restored to a hard disk before they can be used.

Backup disks contain not only special copies of files but also directory information about each file. This information enables RESTORE to copy the backup files to their original locations in the directory tree.

BACKUP can spread a single file across more than one floppy disk. This capability enables you to copy to multiple disks files that are too big to fit on a single disk. If a BACKUP operation uses more than one disk, each disk is linked internally to the next disk to form a backup set.

During the backup operation, each disk in a set is filled to capacity before the next disk is requested. If a file is only partially written to a backup disk when the disk reaches full capacity, the remainder of the file is written to the next disk in the set.

Like XCOPY, BACKUP can copy files selectively. You can specify a directory or branch of directories, a file name, a file name patterned after a wild card, and additional selection switches. By taking advantage of BACKUP's selectivity, you can maintain more than one set of backup disks, each set having its own logical purpose.

You can, for example, keep one backup set that contains every file on your hard disk. This set is insurance against data loss resulting from a hard disk failure or crash. You may have another backup set that contains only the files that have their archive attributes turned on. With an archive set for each day of the week, you can recover a week's worth of data between complete backups. When your hard disk fails, you replace it, restore using the full set, and then update with the daily sets.

You can lose the data on your hard disk in many ways. If you have not replicated the data, you may be forced to recreate the data as much as possible and suffer the consequences of permanent data loss if you cannot recreate data. If you have never experienced a disk-related failure, don't be overconfident. With 10 million hard disk users working with their computers for an average of 8 hours per day, over 250,000 people will experience a hard-disk-related failure this year. You could be next.

Every PC user should develop a *backup policy*, a defined method of backing up data on a regular basis. Your policy may include making and keeping more than one backup set. Before you decide how to implement a backup policy, you should be familiar with the BACKUP command and its switches.

The syntax for the BACKUP command is as follows:

BACKUP d1:*path\filename.ext* **d2:** */switches*

d1: is the name of the source drive you are backing up. If you omit the source drive name, you must include a source path or file name.

path is the directory path that contains the files you are backing up. If you omit the path name, DOS assumes the current directory of the specified (or default) drive.

filename.ext is the name of the source file(s) that you are backing up. You can use wild cards in the file name parameter. If you omit the file name parameter, DOS assumes the *.* wild-card pattern.

d2: is the name of the destination drive where the backup disks are written. This parameter is mandatory.

/S includes files from the specified directory and all subsequent subdirectories of the specified directory.

/M includes files whose archive attribute is turned on.

/A adds the files to be backed up to the files existing on the backup set.

/F (DOS 3.3 or later) formats the destination disks as part of the backup operation.

/F:size (4.0 or later) causes unformatted disks to be formatted during the backup operation. The possible values for size include:

160,	160K,	160KB			
180,	180K,	180KB			
320,	320K,	320KB			
360,	360K,	360KB			
720,	720K,	720KB			
1200,	1200K,	1200KB,	1.2,	1.2M,	1.2MB
1440,	1440K,	1440KB,	1.44,	1.44M,	1.44MB
2880,	2880K,	2880KB,	2.88,	2.88M,	2.88MB

/D:date causes BACKUP to copy files created or modified on or after the *date* parameter, which must be in the form */D:mm-dd-yy* or */D:mm/dd/yy*.

/T: time (DOS 3.3 or later) includes files created or modified on or after the time specified in the form *hh:mm:ss*.

/L (DOS 3.3 or later) writes a backup log entry in the file specified as *d:path\\logfile* or in a file named \\BACKUP.LOG in the source disk when */L* with no file parameter is used.

When using BACKUP, consider the following guidelines:

- Files backed up are selected by the drive, path, and file parameters or their default values. Further selection of files is based on the optional switches.

- Unless the destination disk is a backup disk and you use the /A switch, the contents of the destination disk's root directory are lost in the backup operation.

- If the destination disk is a hard disk, BACKUP checks for a directory named \BACKUP in which to store the backed up files. The BACKUP command creates the \BACKUP directory if it does not exist.

- If \BACKUP on the destination disk contains previously backed-up files, they are erased as part of the backup operation unless you use the /A switch.

- DOS 4 and later versions automatically format the destination disk if it is not already formatted, as though the /F switch had been used.

- If BACKUP is formatting destination disks, the FORMAT command must be available in the current directory or accessible through a search path specified by the PATH command. The specified search path in the PATH command cannot be the destination drive.

- BACKUP does not format a hard disk even if the /F switch is given.

- The source disk cannot be write-protected because BACKUP resets each backed-up file's archive attribute.

- BACKUP does not back up the hidden DOS system files or COMMAND.COM in the root directory.

- You cannot use RESTORE from DOS 3.2 or earlier versions to restore files backed up by BACKUP from DOS 3.3 or later versions.

Determining a Backup Policy

The cost of performing a backup is time. The risk of not performing a backup is data loss. The gain of doing a backup is having recoverable data when original data is lost. You must weigh the cost, risk, and gains involved with backing up to determine how often to back up. The cornerstone of a good backup policy is the periodic full backup.

When you perform a full backup, you back up all your files. If disk disaster strikes, you can recover your data from your full backup set, restoring the full backup set to your existing hard disk or to a new replacement disk.

If you have DOS 3.2 or earlier, you need to format the destination disk for the full backup set. The number of disks you need is derived from the number of bytes you back up. When you run CHKDSK, DOS reports the number of bytes in various categories of files. A sample CHKDSK report looks like the following:

```
Volume LAP TOP  created Aug 17, 1990 6:41p
Volume Serial Number is 1628-BA9A
 21204992 bytes total disk space
    75776 bytes in 3 hidden files
    98304 bytes in 42 directories
19404800 bytes in 1150 user files
 1650688 bytes available on disk

    2048 bytes in each allocation unit
   10354 total allocation units on disk
     806 available allocation units on disk

  655344 bytes total memory
  598784 bytes free
```

The user files line in this report determines the disk-count calculation for BACKUP. In this example, the number of bytes to be backed up, rounded to the nearest 10,000, is 19,400,000 bytes.

Divide the rounded number by the capacity of your floppy disk drive. You can multiply your drive's capacity in K (kilobytes) by 1,024 or in M (megabytes) by 1,024,000. In this case, you need fifty-three 360K disks, twenty-seven 720K disks, fifteen 1.2M disks, or fourteen 1.44M disks. You also can use the information in table 11.2 to estimate your disk requirements.

Table 11.2
Number of Disks Required for a Full Backup

Bytes to Back Up	Diskette Capacity			
	360K	*720K*	*1.2M*	*1.44M*
10M	28	14	9	7
20M	56	28	17	14
30M	84	42	25	21
40M	112	56	34	28
70M	195	98	59	35

Issuing the Full BACKUP Command

If you are using DOS 3.3 or earlier, or if you want to speed the backup procedure, format all your backup floppies the first time you intend to use them.

Label each disk as "Full Backup Set." When you have labeled all disks, you can start the full BACKUP with the following command:

BACKUP C:\ A:/S

This command tells BACKUP to start in the root directory of the hard disk and process all subdirectories on the disk. BACKUP issues a warning message.

```
Insert backup diskette 01 in drive A:

WARNING! Files in target drive

A:\ root directory will be erased.
Strike any key to continue . . .
```

Write the words "disk 01" on the first disk's label, as indicated in the screen message. Then insert the disk into the floppy disk drive, and press a key.

DOS reports file names on-screen as they are backed up. When the first disk is filled, BACKUP repeats the message asking for the next disk. Again, mark the next disk's label with the sequential number that appears in the message.

The process repeats until the last file from the hard disk is processed by BACKUP. When you have completed the full backup, store the backup disks in order in a safe place. Be sure not to mix this set with another backup set. You may accidentally try to restore a disk from the wrong set later.

Following Up with Incremental Backups

An incremental backup copies only the files that are new or have been changed since the last full backup was performed. You use a second set of disks for the incremental backup set. The number of disks in the incremental backup set depends on the number of bytes in files that have been modified since the last BACKUP.

The key to making an incremental backup is the archive bit. As you recall, BACKUP turns off the archive attribute for any file that is backed up. When you modify or create a file, DOS turns on the new or modified file's archive attribute. If you want to back up only files that are new or that have been changed since the last full backup, you can use BACKUP with the /M switch.

TIP

> *Tip:* You can use the ATTRIB command to determine the current archive attribute setting for each file on your system. If you want to make sure that a particular file is backed up by an incremental backup procedure, use ATTRIB to turn on the archive attribute.

Two basic strategies exist for making incremental backups. Either strategy can be combined with the full backup to make your backup strategy. Either incremental backup strategy uses the /M switch, available with all versions of BACKUP.

The first incremental strategy or method—the *multiset* method—maintains several small backup sets and uses different sets over time. The second incremental backup method—the *additive* method—maintains one incremental backup set and adds files to the set over time. If your version of BACKUP supports the /A switch, the additive method is for you.

You can perform a full backup weekly, monthly, or at some other interval. The incremental backup intervals should cover your risk of data loss between full backups. The time between performing incremental backups using either method depends on the amount of risk to your data you are willing to take. In a business setting, you may reduce your risk to an acceptable level by performing an incremental backup every other day. If your PC activity level is high, you may need to perform an incremental backup daily. If your PC activity is minimal, once every two weeks may be often enough to reduce your risk to a manageable level.

If you use the multiset incremental backup method, you need to ensure that you have enough formatted backup disks on hand to complete any given incremental backup. If you always keep on hand a few spare formatted backup disks, you will not be caught short when BACKUP prompts you to insert another disk.

For each incremental backup using the multiset approach, issue the following command:

    BACKUP C:\ A:/S/M

The /S switch includes all directories on the hard disk in the operation; the /M switch selects only files with their archive attribute switch set. The backup proceeds as the full backup proceeds. Mark each disk in the set with the number and the date belonging to the increment for this backup. Store the completed set in a safe place, and avoid mixing the disks with disks from another backup set.

For example, you may perform an incremental backup every Tuesday and Friday and run a full backup every two weeks. Under this plan, you accumulate four incremental backup sets before you need to repeat the backup cycle and reuse the disks.

If you perform an incremental backup every Friday and a full backup on the last Friday of every month, you need four sets of incremental backup disks, although most months would require only three.

If you use the additive incremental backup method, you have just one incremental backup set. The first time you do an incremental backup in a backup cycle after a full backup, start with disk number 01 in your incremental backup set and issue the following command:

BACKUP C:\ A:/S/M

For the second and subsequent additive incremental backup operations, insert the last disk of your incremental backup set and issue the following command:

BACKUP C:\ A:/S/M/A

BACKUP sees the /A switch and knows to add the files to the end of the backup set. BACKUP then issues the following prompt:

```
Insert last backup diskette in drive A:
Strike any key when ready
```

If you haven't already done so, insert the final disk from the last incremental backup operation, and press a key. The operation proceeds in the same manner as the full backup proceeds.

Restoring Backup Files with RESTORE

Performing a backup operation is akin to buying an insurance policy. You hope you never have to use it, but if disaster strikes, you have a way to replace the loss. The external command RESTORE is the DOS command that enables you to reinstate lost data onto your hard disk. RESTORE is the only command that can read the files copied to the backup set by the BACKUP command. When you need to recover backup files from a backup set, you must use the RESTORE command.

Note: The DOS 5.0 version of RESTORE is capable of restoring files created by any version of BACKUP, but not all versions of RESTORE are compatible with all versions of BACKUP. Generally, files created by a newer version of DOS cannot be restored by an older version of RESTORE. To be sure that your files are properly restored, use the same version of DOS that you used to create the backup files. For example, if you use BACKUP from DOS 3.3 to create a backup set, use RESTORE from DOS 3.3 to restore the backup set. If you use DOS 5.0's BACKUP to create a backup set, use DOS 5.0's RESTORE command if you ever have to restore the files.

RESTORE puts the selection of files in your control, enabling you to restore an individual file, selected files, or an entire hard disk. Like BACKUP, the RESTORE command provides numerous switches. With RESTORE's switches, you can use time, date, presence, and absence as selection criteria for files to be restored.

The syntax of the RESTORE command is as follows:

RESTORE ds: dd:*path\filename.ext /S/P/B:date/A:date/E:time/L:time/M/N/D*

ds: is a required parameter that specifies the source drive which holds the file(s) to be restored.

dd: indicates the drive to receive the restored files. This parameter is also mandatory.

path is the path to the directory that receives the restored files. If the path parameter is omitted, DOS assumes the current directory of the destination disk.

filename.ext is the name of the file(s) to be restored. You can use wild cards in the file name root and extension.

/S causes RESTORE to restore files to the specified (or default) directory and all subdirectories.

/P prompts to confirm the restoration of a read-only file or a file modified since the last backup.

/B:date restores files created or modified before or on the date in the *date* parameter in the format *mm/dd/yy*.

/A:date restores files created or modified after or on the date in the *date* parameter in the format *mm/dd/yy*.

/L:time restores files created or modified later than or at the time given in the *time* parameter in the format *hh:mm:ss*.

/E:time restores files created or modified earlier than or at the time given in the *time* parameter as */E:hh:mm:ss*.

/M restores only files modified or deleted since the last backup.

/N restores files that no longer exist on the destination disk.

/D displays a list of the files on the backup disk(s) that meet the *path\filename.ext* specification with all switches applied.

Understanding the Operation of RESTORE

RESTORE is the only command capable of reading the files created by the BACKUP command. When you use RESTORE, you always must restore files to the directory in which they were located when the files were backed up. RESTORE cannot restore files to a directory name other than the files' original directory name.

If RESTORE is restoring a file whose original directory is no longer on the destination disk, RESTORE creates the directory before restoring the file. RESTORE makes directory entries for files that are no longer on the destination disk and allocates the next available space in the FAT for the restored file's allocation.

Like the BACKUP command, RESTORE prompts you for the disks of the backup set. If you know the disk number that contains the file(s) you want to restore, give that number. RESTORE accepts that disk as the first disk. If you used the /L switch with the BACKUP command, you can check the backup log file (BACKUP.LOG) to determine which disk contains a particular file you want to restore.

Note: Restoring a full backup set to a freshly formatted disk eliminates any file fragmentation that may have existed on the disk when you backed up the files. Restoring an additive incremental backup set, however, may result in fragmented destination files. As you recall, fragmentation doesn't affect the file's integrity, but it may slow disk performance slightly.

When using RESTORE, consider the following guidelines:

- RESTORE V3.2 or earlier cannot restore files created by BACKUP V3.3 or later.

- You must give both source and destination drive names in the command line.

- All files restored from the backup set are placed in their original directories on the destination disk. If a source directory does not exist on the destination, RESTORE creates the directory.

- Files selected for restoration are specified in the destination drive, path, and file name parameters as well as included switches.

- The destination disk must already be formatted. RESTORE, unlike BACKUP, has no provision to format the destination disk.

- Files restored to a freshly formatted disk are not fragmented.

> *Warning:* If you have copy-protected files on your hard disk when you do a backup, they may not restore properly to a destination disk. Ideally, you should uninstall copy-protected software using the manufacturer's suggested procedure prior to using BACKUP and then reinstall the copy-protected programs after restoring files using RESTORE. This practice may not be practical, however. You should simply be aware that you may have to reinstall copy-protected software after running RESTORE.

Using RESTORE after a Disk Failure

This section presents an example of using the RESTORE command. Assume that you are using a backup policy that includes a weekly full backup on Friday and an incremental backup each Wednesday. You have two backup sets. The first set from Friday contains all files. The second set contains only files modified or created after Friday, but before Thursday.

Now suppose that you are saving a worksheet file on Thursday morning when a workman begins to use a large drill next door. DOS reports the following message:

```
General Failure on drive C:
```

You abort the spreadsheet session and run CHKDSK to ensure that your FAT and directory system are in order. (Chapter 7 covers the operation of CHKDSK.) DOS reports hundreds of lost clusters.

You have had an electrical noise-induced hard disk failure. Your hard disk most likely wrote erroneous information over valid information in the FAT. If you have used the DOS 5.0 MIRROR command to create a copy of the FAT, you may be able to reconstruct the damaged file allocation table by using DOS 5.0's UNFORMAT command. (MIRROR and UNFORMAT are discussed in Chapter 7). Otherwise, you have no choice but to reformat your hard disk and then fall back to your backup disks.

You first need to reboot your computer with a DOS Startup disk in drive A because the DOS utilities on your hard disk may be corrupt. After you format your hard disk, copy the external DOS commands back to the hard disk from the DOS master disks. Use the PATH command to set a search path to the DOS directory so that DOS can locate the RESTORE command.

In case of total disk failure, restore your backup sets in chronological order. Restore your latest full backup set first. Locate the disks from your full backup set, and put them in their proper order. Then issue the following command:

RESTORE A: C:\ /S

DOS displays the following prompt:

```
Insert backup diskette 1 in drive A:
Strike any key to continue . . .
```

Put the first disk into drive A, and press a key. DOS responds as follows:

```
*** Files were backed up mm-dd-yy ***
```

DOS substitutes in place of *mm-dd-yy* the date you performed the backup procedure. DOS then prompts as follows:

```
*** Restoring files from drive A: ***
```

DOS lists the full path and file names of the files being restored. When all the files from the first disk are restored to the hard disk, DOS prompts you for the next disk in the backup set. This cycle repeats until you have completed the restore operation.

After restoring the full backup set, you must restore the incremental backup set. Because you want to restore all the files in the incremental backup set, you use the same command you used to restore the full backup set. The operation proceeds in the same fashion.

With both backup sets restored, you should run CHKDSK to ensure that the hard disk is in order. Keep both backup sets intact until you have determined that your hard disk is performing correctly. Run CHKDSK several times during the day. If all is in order, perform a full backup at the end of the day.

Performing a Selective Restoration

This section discusses how to do a selective restore operation. Assume that last week you accidentally deleted the database file PERSONL.DBF from your \DBASE directory. You discovered the error today and have already tried using the UNDELETE command to no avail. Luckily, an up-to-date version of the PERSONL.DBF file is on your most recent backup set.

To restore only the \DBASE\PERSONL.DBF file from the backup set, issue the following command:

RESTORE A: C:\DBASE\PERSONL.DBF

As in the complete restoration example, RESTORE prompts you to insert the first disk. You can insert the first disk, or if you know the disk number that holds the PERSONL.DBF file, you can insert that disk. RESTORE bypasses any files on the source disk that are not included in the destination parameter you gave in the command. When RESTORE encounters the file, \DBASE\PERSONL.DBF, the program lists the file name on-screen and copies the file to the destination disk.

Summary

This chapter covers the important DOS commands and procedures that enable you to ensure the integrity of your data and, even more important, protect yourself from data loss. Following are the key points covered in this chapter:

- You can protect your computer hardware equipment by following common-sense safety precautions.

- You can protect yourself from "computer viruses" by purchasing only tested software and using antivirus software.

- The COMP and FC commands compare a file for differences.

- XCOPY is a versatile copy command that can create subdirectories while copying.

- The BACKUP command produces special copies of your program and data files backup sets. Backup sets usually are used for recovering lost data.

- The RESTORE command reads files from backup sets and restores the files to their original directories on another disk.

- You can protect yourself from data loss by faithfully following a backup policy.

This chapter concludes Part II of this book. In Part III, you learn to tap the many expanded features available with DOS. You learn how to use the DOS Editor, customize your computer system, and customize the DOS Shell.

Part III

Getting the Most from DOS

Includes

Using the DOS Editor

Understanding Batch Files, DOSKey, and Macros

Configuring the DOS Shell

Configuring Your Computer and Managing Devices

Using the DOS Editor

12

The DOS Editor—new with DOS 5.0—is a *text processor*, a kind of mini-word processor. The Editor is the perfect tool for creating short text documents and editing text files.

By all means, try the DOS Editor. You are in for a pleasant surprise. The Editor is so simple and intuitive to use that you will likely become a regular user.

This chapter explains how to use the basic features of the DOS Editor, including how to use its menus and shortcut commands and how to create, edit, save, and print text.

Key Terms Used in This Chapter

Text file	A file that contains only ASCII text characters (without special formatting characters). The Editor works only with text files.
Editing command	One of the commands available from a pull-down menu
Shortcut key	A keystroke combination that immediately activates an editing command, bypassing the menu system

Dialog box	A window that pops open when the DOS Editor needs more information before executing a command
Highlighted option	A command or option that appears in inverse video. The highlighted option executes when you press Enter.
Location counter	The two numbers at the right end of the status bar that indicate the cursor's current row and column
Scroll bars	The two matte strips (a vertical strip along the right edge and a horizontal strip near the bottom edge) used with a mouse to control scrolling
Clipboard	An area of memory where text can be stored temporarily
Selected text	A block of text you highlight with various Shift-key combinations. Selected text can be deleted, moved, and edited as a single block.
Insert mode	The editing mode in which a typed character is inserted into the existing text at the current cursor position
Overtype mode	The editing mode in which a typed character replaces the character at the current cursor position
Place marker	A document location designated with a special keystroke combination and to which the cursor can be moved immediately by a particular keystroke combination

Understanding the DOS Editor

The DOS Editor falls into a class of programs known as text editors. As the name implies, a *text editor* works with files that contain pure text (as opposed to *binary* files, which contain programming instructions).

Here are some of the typical tasks for which the Editor is ideally suited:

- Creating, editing, and printing memos (and other text documents)

- Viewing text files whose contents are unknown

- Creating or modifying various system configuration files, such as AUTOEXEC.BAT and CONFIG.SYS

- Writing and modifying batch files (Batch files are discussed in Chapter 13.)

- Writing and saving README files. Many computer users place a README file in a hard disk subdirectory (or on a floppy disk) to explain the contents of other files in the subdirectory (or on the disk).

- Creating and viewing files that are uploaded to or downloaded from electronic bulletin boards, such as CompuServe

- Writing programs for programming-language environments that do not include a resident editor

Be aware that document files produced by some word processors are not pure text files. The files may contain special formatting or printer-control characters. Most word processors can import the pure text files created with the DOS Editor. The Editor, however, may not successfully import word processor document files that contain certain formatting characters.

Files Required To Run the DOS Editor

The DOS Editor is part of the DOS 5.0 package. The Editor is invoked by the external command EDIT, which runs the program EDIT.COM. When you run the Editor, EDIT.COM calls on two other files: QBASIC.EXE and EDIT.HLP. Only QBASIC.EXE is required. EDIT.HLP contains the text of the help messages, but the Editor works without this file.

Starting the DOS Editor

You can start the DOS Editor from the DOS Shell or from the command line.

If you're running the DOS Shell, select Editor from the Main program group in the program list area (refer to Chapter 4 for more about starting a program from the DOS Shell). After you select Editor from the DOS Shell menu, a box labeled File to Edit pops open. A message inside the box prompts you to supply a file name. To start the Editor without loading a specific file, just press Enter. But if you want to load a text file into the Editor, type the file's name, including the path if the file is not located in the default directory. Then press Enter to start the Editor with your designated file loaded and ready for editing.

If you're running the Editor from the command line, type **EDIT** at the DOS prompt, and press Enter.

Regardless of which method you choose for starting the Editor, it now initializes. A preliminary screen appears (see fig. 12.1).

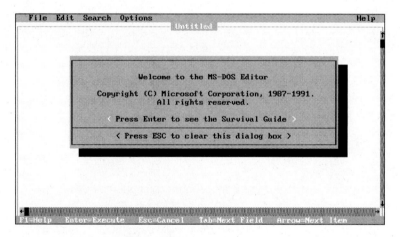

Fig. 12.1. The preliminary DOS Editor screen.

You now must press either Enter or Esc.

- Enter activates the Survival Guide. (The Survival Guide provides help about using the Editor.)

- Esc clears the box in the center of the screen and prepares the Editor for working on a text file.

Press Esc. Now the DOS Editor screen is blank, and you can begin writing a text file. Your screen should look like figure 12.2.

Getting Acquainted with the Initial Editor Screen

Take a moment to look at your screen (or at fig. 12.2). The screen is composed of several elements.

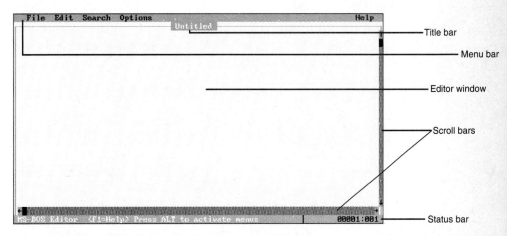

Fig. 12.2. The initial Editor screen with a blank editing area.

The *menu bar* is the line across the top of the screen that lists the available menus: File, Edit, Search, Options, and Help. The *title bar* is a short, centered bar, immediately beneath the menu bar, that contains the name of the text file being edited (it is now Untitled.) The *status bar* is the line, across the bottom of the screen, that describes the current process and shows certain shortcut key options.

Scroll bars are a vertical strip along the right edge and a horizontal strip just above the status bar. The scroll bars are used with a mouse to move through the file (Mouse techniques are described in "Using a Mouse" in this chapter.)

The *Editor window* is the large area in which the text of your file appears. The *Cursor* is the flashing underscore character that indicates where typed text will appear.

Navigating the DOS Editor

The DOS Editor provides several ways to perform most commands. The Editor has a user-friendly set of menus from which you can select options. Many of these options require you to enter further information in an on-screen box known as a dialog box.

The Editor also enables you to execute many commands by pressing special shortcut keys. You also can use a mouse.

The sections that follow describe how to use menus, dialog boxes, shortcut keys, and a mouse in the DOS Editor.

Understanding the Menu System

The DOS Editor menu system provides many editing commands. The menu bar contains the following options: File, Edit, Search, and Options. Selecting any of these options displays a pull-down menu. The File option displays a menu that enables you to load files, save files, and print files. The Edit menu is used to cut and paste text. The Search menu is used for finding and replacing specified text. The Options menu can be used to reconfigure environment options, and the Help menu provides access to on-line help.

To activate the menu bar, press Alt. The first letter of each menu name is highlighted. Then press the first letter of the menu name. For example, press Alt and then F to activate the File menu (Alt-F). Similarly, press Alt-E to activate the Edit menu, Alt-S to activate the Search menu, or Alt-O to display the Options menu.

Every time you open a main menu, the first command on the submenu is highlighted. You can move this highlight to the other commands by pressing the up- or down-arrow key. As you move the highlight, notice that the status bar displays a brief description of the highlighted command.

On a menu, one letter of each command is highlighted. On most systems, the highlighted letter appears in high-intensity white. To execute a command, move the highlight to that command and press Enter, or press the key that corresponds to the highlighted letter.

Depending on which editing commands you have executed previously, some commands in a menu may not be available. In such a case, the menu shows the command name in a dull color (usually gray), and no highlighted letter appears in the name. If you try to execute an unavailable command, the Editor sounds a beep and refuses to execute the command.

The Escape key (Esc) is the "oops" key. Pressing Esc closes the menu system and returns you to the Editor.

In the pull-down menus, an ellipsis (. . .) following the name of a command indicates that a dialog box opens when you issue that command. (Sometimes, depending on the circumstances, a command without the ellipsis also opens a dialog box.)

Understanding Dialog Boxes

When you execute a menu command, it may execute immediately, or depending on the command and the current context, a dialog box may pop up. A dialog box means that the Editor needs more information before the command can be completed. For example, if you execute the command to save a new file, the Editor first needs to know what name to give the file. A dialog box prompts you for the necessary information.

For example, if you activate the Search menu and then select Change, the Editor displays the Change dialog box shown in figure 12.3.

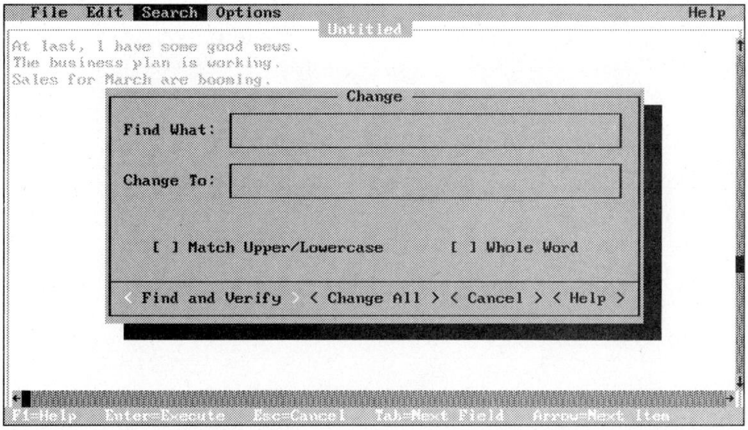

Fig. 12.3. The Change dialog box.

The DOS Editor uses dialog boxes to get a variety of information. Sometimes you must type something, such as a file name or a search string in a text box. At other times, you must choose from a list of options. And at still other times, you select from a series of command buttons (refer to Chapter 4 for a discussion of dialog boxes, text boxes, option buttons, and command buttons).

When a DOS Editor dialog box opens, the following three keys have special significance:

- Tab moves the cursor from one area of the dialog box to the next area. After you specify information in one area, use Tab to move to the next area.

- Esc aborts the menu option and returns you to the Editor. Use Esc when you change your mind and decide against issuing a particular command.

- Enter is the "go ahead" key. Press it when all options in the dialog box are as you want them and you are ready to execute the command. You press Enter only once while you are working inside a dialog box. Use Tab, not Enter, to move the cursor from one area of the dialog box to the next area. (Be careful. Most people tend to press Enter after they type information, such as a file name. Remember, when you need to specify additional information inside the dialog box, press Tab, not Enter.)

In every dialog box, one command button is enclosed in highlighted angle brackets. The highlighted brackets identify the action that takes place when you press Enter.

To highlight the angle brackets of the command you want, press Tab repeatedly. Be sure not to press Enter until you have specified everything satisfactorily.

When you are working with a dialog box, Alt is an "express" key. By pressing Alt and a highlighted letter, you activate an option even if the cursor is in another area.

Using Shortcut Keys

For convenience, many commonly used DOS Editor menu commands have an associated *shortcut key*. Pressing this shortcut key while you are working with the DOS Editor executes the command directly, bypassing the menu system. Table 12.1 provides a complete list of shortcut keys.

Using a Mouse

A mouse is an excellent pointing device for computer applications. The DOS Editor supports a mouse. You can execute menu commands and many editing tasks with a mouse. If your system is mouseless, you can get along fine; if you have a mouse, try it and see what you think.

> *Note:* The DOS Editor works with any Microsoft-compatible mouse and driver. If you have a mouse, you presumably know how to install and activate your mouse driver. Microsoft supplies a mouse driver as part of the DOS 5.0 package.

When the mouse is active, you see a special mouse cursor on-screen. The mouse cursor is a small rectangle, about the size of one text character, that moves as you move the mouse. Notice that the regular blinking cursor remains active. You can continue to use all the keyboard commands and features.

Table 12.1 also contains a comprehensive list of mouse techniques.

Table 12.1
DOS Editor Keyboard and Mouse Shortcuts

Shortcut Key	Effect	Mouse
F1	View help on menu or command	Click right button on desired item
Shift-F1	View help on getting started	Click Getting Started (Help menu)
Ctrl-F1	View next help topic	Click Next (status bar)
Alt-F1	Review preceding help screen	Click Back (status bar)
Shift-Ctrl-F1	View preceding help topic	None
F3	Repeat the last Find	Click Repeat Last Find (Search menu)
F6	Move between help and editing	Click inside desired window
Shift-F6	Make preceding window active	Click inside window
Shift-Del	Cut selected text	Click Cut (Edit menu)

continued

Table 12.1 *(continued)*

Shortcut Key	Effect	Mouse
Ctrl-Ins	Copy selected text	Click Copy (Edit menu)
Shift-Ins	Paste text from clipboard	Click Paste (Edit menu)
Del	Erase selected text	Click Clear (Edit menu)
Ctrl-Q-A	Change text	Click Change (Search menu)
Ctrl-Q-F	Search for text string	Click Find (Search menu)
Esc	Terminate Help System	Click Cancel (status bar)
Alt	Enter menu-selection mode	None
Alt-Plus	Enlarge active window	Drag title bar up
Alt-Minus	Shrink active window down	Drag title bar

Here are some additional mouse pointers:

- To open a menu, click the menu name in the menu bar.

- To execute a menu command, click the command name in the menu.

- To set an option in a dialog box, click that option.

- To abort a menu, click a location outside the menu.

- To move the cursor in the file, click the location you want.

- To select text, *drag* the mouse over the text. That is, move the mouse pointer to one end of the text to be selected; then press and hold down the mouse button while you move the mouse across the text to be selected.

- To activate the Editor window while a help screen is visible, click anywhere inside the Editor window.

- To expand or shrink the Editor window while a help screen is visible, drag the title bar of the Editor window up or down.

- To scroll the screen horizontally one character, click the left or right arrow at either end of the horizontal scroll bar.

- To scroll the screen vertically one character, click the up or down arrow at either end of the vertical scroll bar.

- To scroll text vertically to a specific position, move the mouse cursor to the *scroll box* (the inverse-video rectangle inside the vertical scroll bar). Then drag the scroll box along the scroll bar to the desired position.

- To scroll text one page at a time, click the vertical scroll bar somewhere between the scroll box and the top or bottom of the scroll bar.

- To scroll horizontally several positions at once, click the horizontal scroll bar somewhere between the scroll box and the left or right end of the scroll bar.

- To execute a dialog-box action enclosed in angle brackets, click the name between the brackets.

- To execute any keystroke action enclosed in angle brackets in the status bar, click the name inside the angle brackets.

Mastering Fundamental Editing Techniques

Editing is a skill—almost an art. Some editing techniques are simple, others more complex. Many editing tasks can be performed in more than one way.

This section discusses the fundamental editing skills, which include moving the cursor, scrolling, and inserting and deleting text.

Moving the Cursor

With text in the DOS Editor, you can move the cursor around the text in several ways. The DOS Editor provides two alternative cursor-movement interfaces:

- *Keypad interface*. The specialized IBM PC keys—the arrow keys, Ins, Del, and so on—govern most editing activities. To move the cursor up, for example, you use the up-arrow key.

- *Control-key interface*. Ctrl-key combinations govern most editing activities. To move the cursor up, for example, you press Ctrl-E. This interface is used in the word processing program WordStar.

Generally speaking, the DOS Editor accommodates both camps. Most editing techniques are available with both the keypad and Control-key (WordStar-style) sequences. A few techniques, however, can be performed with only one method. This chapter focuses on the keypad style. The Control-key combinations are mentioned only when required by a particular editing technique.

Table 12.2 summarizes the cursor-movement commands.

Table 12.2
Cursor-Movement Commands

Effect	Keypad	Control-key style
Character left	Left arrow	Ctrl-S
Character right	Right arrow	Ctrl-D
Word left	Ctrl-left arrow	Ctrl-A
Word right	Ctrl-right arrow	Ctrl-F
Line up	Up arrow	Ctrl-E
Line down	Down arrow	Ctrl-X
First indentation level	Home	None
Beginning of line	None	Ctrl-Q-S
End of line	End	Ctrl-Q-D
Beginning of next line	Ctrl-Enter	Ctrl-J
Top of window	None	Ctrl-Q-E
Bottom of window	None	Ctrl-Q-X
Beginning of text	Ctrl-Home	Ctrl-Q-R
End of text	Ctrl-End	Ctrl-Q-C
Set marker	None	Ctrl-K n
Move to marker	None	Ctrl-Q n

Look at the far right end of the status bar, in the lower right corner of the DOS Editor screen. You see two numbers, separated by a colon. The two numbers indicate the cursor's current location in your file. The first number is the current row; the second, the current column.

Use the arrow keys to move the cursor, and watch the numbers change. Press Num Lock; an uppercase N appears next to the location numbers to indicate that Num Lock is on. Press Num Lock a few more times to toggle the indicator on and off. Press Caps Lock; an uppercase C appears next to the location numbers, left of the N, to indicate that the Caps Lock key is on.

Scrolling

Scrolling is the movement of text inside the Editor window. When you scroll, you bring into view a portion of the file currently not visible in the Editor window. Scrolling, which can be horizontal as well as vertical, keeps the cursor at the same row and column number but moves the text in the window.

Table 12.3 summarizes the scrolling commands. For large-scale scrolling, you use the PgUp and PgDn keys. Try using these keys by themselves and with the Ctrl key.

Table 12.3
Scrolling Text

Effect	Keypad	Control-key style
One line up	Ctrl-up arrow	Ctrl-W
One line down	Ctrl-down arrow	Ctrl-Z
Page up	PgUp	Ctrl-R
Page down	PgDn	Ctrl-C
One window left	Ctrl-PgUp	
One window right	Ctrl-PgDn	

Inserting Text into a Line

You can insert text into an existing line. Move the cursor to the position at which you want to insert text. Type the text you want to insert. As you type, text to the right of the cursor moves right to accommodate the inserted text. You can move off the line by using any of the cursor-movement keys. Do *not* press Enter to move off the line. Pressing Enter splits the line in two.

Deleting Text from a Line

You can use one of the following two methods to delete a few characters from a line:

- Move the cursor to the character you want to delete. Press Del. To delete consecutive characters, continue pressing Del.

- Move the cursor to the character immediately to the right of the character you want to delete. Press the Backspace key.

Most people find the first method more natural. Try both methods and make your own choice.

Splitting and Joining Lines

Sometimes you need to split a line of text into two lines. Move the cursor to a position beneath the character that you want to begin the second line of text. Press Enter. The line splits in two, and the second half moves down to form a new line. Succeeding lines are pushed down to accommodate the new line.

Conversely, you can join two lines to form one line. Position the cursor in the second line and press Home to move the cursor to the left end of the line. Press Backspace. The second line moves up to the right end of the first line. Lines beneath the split line move up one line.

Inserting and Deleting an Entire Line

To insert a blank line between two lines, move the cursor to column 1 in the lower of the two lines, and then press Ctrl-N; or press Home (to move the cursor to the left end of the current line), and press Enter. Then move the cursor up to the new blank line.

To delete an entire line, place the cursor anywhere on the line, and then press Ctrl-Y.

Overtyping

By default, the DOS Editor operates in *insert* mode. If you type new text while the cursor is in the middle of a line, that new text is inserted at the cursor location.

Instead, you can *overtype*. In overtype mode, the new text replaces the former text.

To activate overtype mode, press Ins. The cursor changes from a blinking line to a blinking box. The larger cursor signifies overtype mode, in which any new character you type replaces the character at the cursor location.

To return to standard insert mode, press Ins again. The Ins key acts as a toggle switch that alternates between insert and overtype modes.

Learning Special Editing Techniques

In addition to the basic editing techniques, the DOS Editor provides several special editing features. The sections that follow describe how to use the automatic indenting, tab, and place marker features.

Using Automatic Indent

When you type a line and press Enter, the cursor drops down one line but returns to the column where you began the preceding line. This feature is convenient when you want to type a series of indented lines.

For example, assume that you type the following line and press Enter:

This line is not indented

The cursor moves to the beginning of the next line. Then press the space bar three times to move the cursor to column 4 and type the following:

But this line is

Press Enter again. Note that the second time you press Enter, the cursor moves to the next row, but remains indented at column 4. Type **So is this one** and press Enter. The cursor remains indented.

Now, press the left-arrow key until the cursor returns to column 1. Type **Back to no indentation** and press Enter.

The short text block looks like the following:

```
This line is not indented
    But this line is
    So is this one
Back to no indentation
```

Using Tab

By default, tab stops are set every eight spaces. When you press the Tab key, the cursor moves to the right to the next tab stop. All text to the right of the cursor moves right when you press Tab. Additional tabbing techniques follow.

To indent an existing line a full tab position, move the cursor to column 1 of the line, and press Tab.

To remove leading spaces and move a line to the left, move the cursor anywhere on the line, and then press Shift-Tab.

To indent or "unindent" an entire block of lines, select the lines by using one of the Shift keystrokes shown in table 12.4. Then press Tab to indent the entire block, or Shift-Tab to "unindent" the entire block.

To change the number of default tab stops, first select Display from the Options menu. Press Tab several times to move the cursor to Tab Stops; type a new value for the number of characters per tab stop, and then press Enter to close the dialog box.

Using Place Markers

A *place marker* designates a specific location—a row and column—in your text. You can set as many as four place markers. After setting a place marker, you can move the cursor instantly from anywhere in the file to that marker's location. The markers are invisible; no character displays in the text to indicate a set marker.

To set a place marker, press Ctrl-K*n*, where *n* is a number from 0 through 3. This action associates the cursor's current position with the marker numbered *n*. To move the cursor to a previously set place marker, press Ctrl-Q*n*, where *n* is marker 0 through 3.

Block Editing

You can edit blocks of text as a single unit. Block editing requires that you understand two relevant concepts: *selecting text* (which identifies the block of text to be edited) and the *clipboard* (which temporarily stores a block of text in a reserved area of memory).

This section describes the following techniques:

- Selecting text for block operations
- Using the clipboard
- Cutting and pasting blocks of text

Selecting Text

A block of selected text is always one continuous piece. The block may be one character, a few characters, a line, several lines, a paragraph, or even an entire file. Selected text appears in reverse video.

Follow these steps to select a block of text:

1. Move the cursor to one end of the block.
2. While you hold down the Shift key, use the cursor-movement keys to highlight the block.

Table 12.4 lists the keys used for selecting text. In general, the keys you use to select text are the same as those you use to move the cursor, but you also press Shift when using them to select text.

Table 12.4
Selecting Text

To select	Use this key combination
Character left	Shift-←
Character right	Shift-→
To beginning of line	Shift-Home
To end of line	Shift-End
Current line	Shift-↓
Line above	Shift-↑
Word left	Shift-Ctrl-←
Word right	Shift-Ctrl-→
Screen up	Shift-PgUp
Screen down	Shift-PgDn
To beginning of text	Shift-Ctrl-Home
To end of text	Shift-Ctrl-End

After you have selected (highlighted) a block, you can deselect it by pressing any arrow key. (Don't use Shift, however). The highlighting disappears, indicating that the entire block has been deselected.

Understanding the Clipboard

The clipboard is a text storage area in memory; the clipboard acts as a kind of halfway house for blocks of text. You can place a block of text into the clipboard and later retrieve the block. The clipboard has many uses. Its most common use is to *cut and paste*—to move or copy a block of text from one place in the file to another.

The clipboard stores only one block of text at a time. When you place text in the clipboard, the incoming text completely replaces the previous contents of the clipboard. Changing the block of text in the clipboard is always an all-or-nothing affair. You cannot add or subtract incrementally. Similarly, retrieval is all-or-nothing. You cannot move only part of the clipboard's contents into your file.

Working with Text Blocks

The DOS Editor supports four block-oriented editing techniques (see table 12.5). Each technique is available by using the Edit menu or by pressing the appropriate shortcut key. (Press Alt-E to activate the Edit menu.)

Table 12.5
Block-Editing Techniques

Menu Command	Shortcut Key	Description
Cut	Shift-Del	Deletes selected text from a file and places that text in clipboard
Copy	Ctrl-Ins	Places in clipboard a copy of selected text from file; text in file remains selected
Paste	Shift-Ins	Inserts contents of clipboard into the file at cursor; clipboard contents remain intact. If file currently has selected text, clipboard text replaces the selected text.
Clear	Del	Deletes selected text from file; contents of clipboard are not affected

For example, to select the first three lines of text in a file, press Ctrl-Home to return the cursor to the beginning of the file. While holding down the Shift key, press the down-arrow key three times. You have selected the first three lines of the file; they now are displayed in reverse video (highlighted).

After the three lines are selected, you can use one of the block-editing commands. To activate the Edit menu, press Alt-E. The Editor displays the Edit menu shown in figure 12.4. You can now use one of the menu commands. Alternatively, you can use one of the shortcut keys to operate on the selected block, even without displaying the Edit menu.

When you perform copy operations, a copy of the selected text moves to the clipboard but is not deleted from the original location. If you perform a cut command, however, the Editor places the highlighted text into the clipboard and removes the selected text from its original location.

After text has been copied or cut into the clipboard, you can use the paste operation to copy the clipboard's contents to a new location in the file. Move the cursor to the desired target location and select **P**aste from the Edit menu, or press Shift-Ins (the shortcut key for Paste). A copy of the clipboard text is inserted at the cursor's location. (The clipboard still holds a copy of the pasted text. You can insert additional copies of the clipboard text at other locations in the file.)

Pressing Del or selecting the Clear command, from the Edit menu, permanently deletes the selected text from the file without placing a copy of the text in the clipboard.

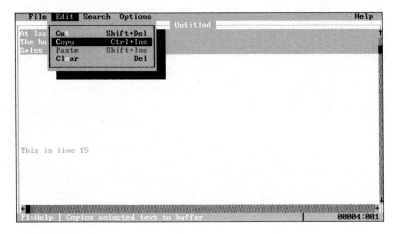

Fig. 12.4. The Edit menu.

Searching and Replacing—the Search Menu

The Search menu offers several options for searching for and replacing text. These capabilities are most useful in long files.

From the Search menu, you can perform the following actions:

- Find one or more occurrences of a designated text string

- Replace one or more occurrences of a designated text string with a second text string

A *text string* is a sequence of one or more consecutive text characters. These characters can be letters, digits, punctuation, special symbols—any characters you can type from the keyboard.

Finding or replacing text always involves a *search string*, which is simply the text string being searched for. A search string can be a single character or, more likely, a word or several consecutive characters.

You cannot search for a string that spans two or more lines. The search string is confined to a group of characters on a single line. You can place some conditions on the search string. For example, you can specify that the search not discriminate between upper- and lowercase letters.

The search begins at the cursor's location and proceeds through the file. If the end of the file is reached before the search string is found, the search wraps around to the top of the file and continues until the entire file has been traversed. Table 12.6 summarizes the three commands available from the Search menu.

Table 12.6
Search Menu Commands

Command	Shortcut Key	Description
Find...	None	Opens a dialog box in which you specify the search string; finds the search string in your file
Repeat Last Find	F3	Searches for the text specified in the last Find command
Change...	None	Replaces one text string with another

Using the Find Command

To use the Find command, first activate the Search menu by pressing Alt-S. Your screen looks similar to figure 12.5.

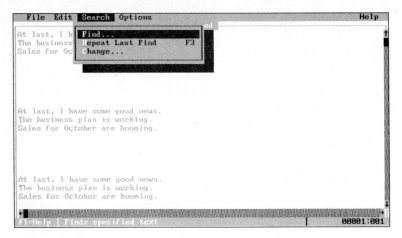

Fig. 12.5. *The Search menu.*

Select **F**ind. The Find dialog box opens, with the cursor on the Find What text box (see fig. 12.6). The word that is at the cursor's current location in the file (or the currently selected text) appears in the text box. If you want to search for this word, press Enter. Otherwise, type the correct search string, and press Enter. The Editor locates the first occurrence of the search string in your file and selects (highlights) the text found.

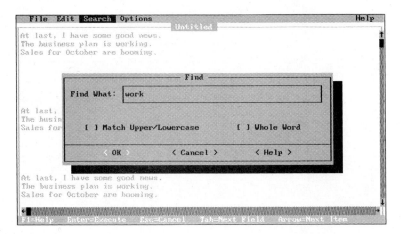

Fig. 12.6. *The Find dialog box.*

You can press F3, or select **R**epeat Last Find on the Search menu. The Editor moves to the next occurrence of the search string (if any).

As shown in figure 12.6, you can use the following check boxes in the dialog box to place conditions on the search:

- Match Upper/Lowercase. If you select this check box, a successful search occurs only when the upper- and lowercase letters in the text exactly match those in the search string. If this option is not selected, upper- and lowercase letters are considered the same.

- Whole Word. If this option is selected, the search string must exist as an independent word that cannot be embedded inside a larger word. The character that immediately precedes and immediately follows the search string must be a space, a punctuation character, or one of the special characters (such as <, *, or [).

Using the Change Command

In addition to just searching for text, you can use the Editor to search for specific text and then replace the text with other text.

Activate the Search menu by pressing Alt-S. Select the Change command. The Editor displays the Change dialog box, shown in figure 12.7.

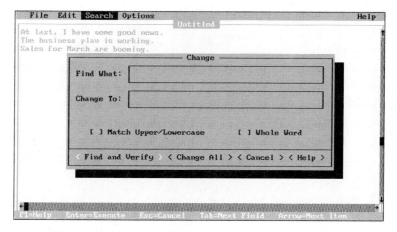

Fig. 12.7. The Change dialog box.

The first text box in the Change dialog box is labeled Find What. Type the text you want the Editor to find in this text box (the target text). The second text box is labeled Change To. Type the text you want entered. A completed Change dialog box is shown in figure 12.8.

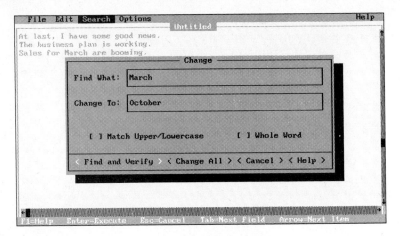

Fig. 12.8. *Performing a search-and-replace operation.*

This dialog box contains two check boxes: Match Upper/Lowercase, and Whole Word. Refer to the preceding section for a discussion of these check boxes.

After making the appropriate entries in the text boxes and selecting any desired check boxes, choose from among the following three command buttons:

- Find and Verify finds each occurrence of the target string, one after another. (You specify the target string in the Find What dialog box.) As each occurrence of the target string is found, a second dialog box opens. This second box gives you the choice of making the substitution, skipping to the next occurrence, or canceling the remaining searches. Find and Verify is the default option, which you automatically select by pressing Enter.

- Change All changes all occurrences of the target string to the string specified in the Change To box. The changes occur all at once. A dialog box informs you when the substitutions are complete.

- Cancel aborts the Change command, closing the dialog box without making any substitutions. This option is equivalent to pressing Esc.

After the Editor finishes the find-and-replace operation, it displays a second dialog box. This second box contains the message Change complete. If no matching text can be found, the box displays the message Match not found. Select the OK command button to return to the Editor window.

Managing Files

The DOS Editor closely oversees your disk files. You can manage your directories with a complete save-and-load capability.

Overview of the File Menu

The File menu is your command center for loading and saving files. Six commands are available on the File menu (see fig. 12.9).

Fig. 12.9. The File menu.

The New command clears the file currently in the Editor The result is a clean slate, as though you had just initialized the DOS Editor. This command does not affect other copies of the file. If the file previously was saved on disk, for example, the disk copy is not erased; only the working copy in the Editor is erased.

Open loads a file from disk into the DOS Editor environment. You can use this command also to see a list of file names in any directory.

Save saves the current file to disk.

Save As saves the current file to disk after prompting you for the file name.

Print prints all or part of the text in the DOS Editor environment.

Exit ends the editing session and returns to the DOS Shell or the command-line prompt.

Note: When you are working with files, keep in mind these maxims:

1. Until you name a file, the Editor displays the temporary name Untitled in the title bar.

2. When you save a file, the Editor adds the extension TXT to the file name if you do not specify another extension.

3. If you try to exit the Editor or open a new file without first saving a working file in the Editor, a dialog box opens to warn you.

Saving a File

When you save a file for the first time, you must specify two file attributes: the file path (the directory or disk on which to save the file) and the file name.

The DOS Editor stores files on disk in ASCII format. Such files are text files that can be manipulated by most text editors and word processors. You can view ASCII files directly from the DOS command line by using the TYPE command.

Using the Save As Command

Follow these steps to save the current Untitled file with a new file name:

1. Select Save **As** from the File menu. In the dialog box that opens, the current path is shown below the words File Name (see fig. 12.10). A list box, below the label Dirs/Drives, lists the directories and disk drives available on your system.

2. Type the new file name in the File Name box. You may specify any file extension as part of the file name. Typical file extensions for ASCII text files are TXT and DOC.

3. Press Enter to save the file.

The DOS Editor saves the file to disk in the directory specified by the current path.

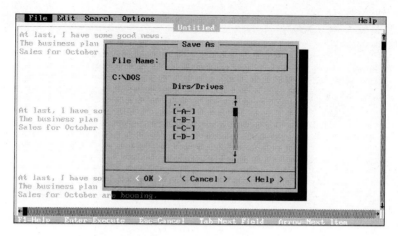

Fig. 12.10. *The Save As dialog box.*

Save As is commonly used for storing a file the first time you create it and for saving a second version of a file in a different directory or with a different name from the first version.

For example, assume that you are editing a file named MYWORK.TXT. After making a few changes, you decide to save the new version of the file under the name MEAGAIN.TXT. Display the File menu, and select Save As. The Editor displays the Save As dialog box.

The File Name text box contains the current file name, MYWORK.TXT. Type **MEAGAIN.TXT** and press Enter. The DOS Editor stores the file on disk as MEAGAIN.TXT, changing the name in the title bar accordingly. The file MYWORK.TXT remains stored on disk. Remember that if you continue editing the file on-screen, you are editing MEAGAIN.TXT (as indicated in the title bar), not MYWORK.TXT.

To store a file in a directory other than that specified by the current path, type the new directory path as part of the file name. For example, if you type the file name \MEMOS\PLAN.BID, the Editor stores the file with the name PLAN.BID in the directory \MEMOS. After you save the file, the name PLAN.BID appears in the title bar. The next time you issue the Save As command, the default directory path is specified in the dialog box as C:\MEMOS. If you save a new file without including an explicit path, the file is saved in the C:\MEMOS directory.

You can use this technique to save files on different disk drives. To save a file named MYFILE.TXT in the root directory of the disk in A drive, for example, type the file name as **A:\MYFILE.TXT**.

Using the Save Command

Use Save to store a file you have already named. No dialog box appears. The current version of the file in the Editor is saved to disk under the existing file name.

Using Save on an unnamed (untitled) file has nearly the same effect as using Save As; the Editor opens a dialog box similar to that shown in figure 12.10 so that you can enter a file name.

When you use the Save command while editing an existing file, the Editor does not prompt you for a file name. Instead, the Editor simply saves the new edited version of the file in place of the old version on disk. As you edit a file, use Save periodically to update the file on disk.

Using the Open Command To Load a File

After text files are stored on disk, you can load a file into the DOS Editor with the Open command. Because this command lists files in any directory, you also can use Open to search your directories for specific file names. When you select Open, a dialog box pops open (see fig. 12.11).

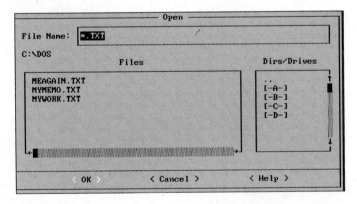

Fig. 12.11. The Open dialog box.

The Open dialog box contains the File Name text box. By default, this box contains *.TXT, the wild-card file name for all files with the extension .TXT. The current directory path (C:\DOS in fig. 12.11) is below the File Name text box. In the File Name text box, type a file name, a directory path, or a name using the * and ? wild-card characters.

To change the default path, specify a path in the File Name text box, and press Enter. Otherwise, the Editor looks in the current directory for files with the extension TXT.

The Files list box contains the names of all files that satisfy the current directory-path and file-name specification. In figure 12.10, the Files box shows all files that satisfy the path and file-name specification C:\DOS*.TXT.

The Dirs/Drives list box lists available directories and disks. You can move the cursor to the Dirs/Drives list box by pressing Tab repeatedly. Then press the up- and down-arrow keys to move the highlight to one of the directories or drives listed in the box. Press Enter to change the default path.

To load a specific file into the Editor, you can use the File Name box or the Files box. To use the File Name box, type in the box the name of the specific file, including a path (or rely on the default path shown below the box). If you do not specify an extension, the Editor assumes the TXT extension. For example, to load the file MYFILE.TXT, which is found in the current directory, type **MYFILE**, and press Enter. By default, the Editor assumes the extension TXT.

You also can select a file name from the Files list box if it contains the file name you want. First, press Tab to move the cursor to the Files list box. Then use the arrow keys to highlight the target file name. Alternatively, you can press the first letter of the file name to move the highlight. When the name you want is highlighted, press Enter.

The Editor loads the file so that you can edit or view it.

Loading a File When You First Start the DOS Editor

You can load a file when you first start the DOS Editor. The technique you use depends on whether you start the Editor from the DOS Shell or from the command line.

Use this technique if you are starting the Editor from the DOS Shell:

- After you select Editor from the DOS Shell menu, a box labeled File to Edit pops open. A message inside the box prompts you to supply a file name. When you type the file name, include the path if the file is not located in the default directory. Then press Enter to start the Editor with your designated file loaded and ready for editing.

When starting the Editor from the command line, use the following technique:

- At the DOS prompt, type **EDIT**, followed by a space and the file name. Include the path if the file is not in the current directory. For example, to start the Editor with the file \SALES\MYFILE.TXT loaded, type the following line:

  EDIT \SALES\MYFILE.TXT

The following notes apply when you load a file when starting the DOS Editor (whether you start it from the DOS Shell or from the command line):

- The Editor does not assume the extension TXT or any other extension if you don't specify an extension as part of the file name.

- The Editor initializes directly without taking the intermediate step of asking whether you want to see the help material in the on-screen Survival Guide.

- If the Editor cannot locate the specified file, the Editor assumes that you want to create a new file with that name. Accordingly, the Editor initializes with a fresh slate that includes your designated file name in the title bar. After you enter data into the file, you can save it directly with the Save command. (You don't need to use Save As and specify the file name a second time.)

Using the New Command

Use New when you want to stop work on one file and create a new file. If you haven't saved the old file, the Editor opens a dialog box for confirmation. Otherwise, the old file clears, and the screen looks as though you had just initiated the DOS Editor. You see a blank editing area with Untitled in the title bar.

Printing a File

Your computer system probably includes a printer. Whether you have a dot-matrix, daisywheel, or laser printer, follow these steps to print a copy of the file currently loaded in the Editor. You can print selected text or the complete file.

1. Activate the File option on the Main menu.

2. Select **P**rint. This command opens the Print dialog box (see fig. 12.12).

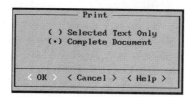

Fig. 12.12. *The Print dialog box.*

3. Choose from among the following option buttons:

   - Selected Text Only prints only selected text, which appears in reverse video in the Editor. (Selecting text is explained earlier in this chapter.) This option is the default when a block of text is selected.

   - Complete Document prints the entire file. This option is the default when no text is selected.

4. Press Enter to begin printing. Make sure that your printer is turned on and is on-line.

Exiting from the DOS Editor

When you have finished editing files you may want to leave the Editor. Display the File menu and choose the Exit command. If the file already has been saved, the Editor returns to the DOS Shell or to the command line, depending on how you started the program.

If you try to quit without first saving the document you have been editing, the Editor opens a dialog box to ask whether you want to save the file. Select the Yes command button to save the file. Select the No command button to exit from the Editor without saving any changes to the current file.

Starting the DOS Editor with Optional Switches

When you start the DOS Editor from the command line, four special parameter switches are available. These switches are listed in table 12.7.

Table 12.7
Optional Switches for the EDIT command

Switch	Description
/B	Displays the Editor in black-and-white even when a color graphics adapter is present
/G	Updates Editor screens as quickly as possible on systems with CGA (Color Graphics Adapter) video. (**Note:** Some computer systems cannot support this option. If screen flicker occurs when you choose /G, your hardware is not compatible with this option.)
/H	Displays the maximum number of lines possible with your video hardware. EGA (Enhanced Graphics Adapter) and VGA (Video Graphics Array) systems can produce more than the standard number of lines on-screen.
/NOHI	Effectively displays the Editor on monitors that do not support high intensity

To display the maximum number of lines when starting the Editor, for example, use the following command:

> **EDIT /H**

A file name can be specified with one of the command options, as in the following example:

> **EDIT \SALES\MYFILE /H**

Use the /B switch if you run the DOS Editor on a computer system with a color video adapter but a black-and-white monitor. (Many laptop computers have this configuration.) At the DOS prompt, activate the Editor as follows:

> **EDIT /B**

Customizing the DOS Editor Screen

Colors on the DOS Editor screen are preset. You can customize most of these colors and other attributes from the Options menu by using the Display command. If you have a color system, you may want different colors for the foreground and background text. If you do not use a mouse with the Editor, you may want to remove the scroll bars.

Changing Colors and Removing Scroll Bars

To change screen colors in the DOS Editor, display the Options menu and select Display. A dialog box similar to figure 12.13 opens.

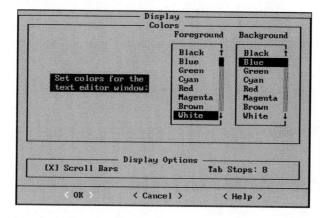

Fig. 12.13. The Display dialog box.

With the cursor on the Foreground box, you can select a new foreground text color by pressing the up- and down-arrow keys. The Foreground box cycles through the colors available with your video hardware. Note that as you press the arrow keys, the text to the left of the dialog box (Set colors for the text editor window) displays with the current foreground and background colors. Select a new foreground color by moving the highlight to the color you want. *Don't press Enter yet.* You have more selections to make before closing this dialog box.

Press Tab to move the cursor to the Background box. Select a new background color; the process is similar to the one you followed to select a new foreground color.

Now press Enter to return to the Editor screen. The new colors should be in use.

If you don't use a mouse, you may want to consider removing the scroll bars from your screen. Many users think that the screen looks less cluttered without the scroll bars. To see what you prefer, try the following exercise.

Reopen the dialog box by displaying the Options menu and selecting Display. Press Tab several times to move the cursor to the Scroll Bars check box. The X inside the brackets indicates that scroll bars are displayed.

Press the space bar or S to unselect the check box. Removing the X indicates that you wish to deselect the display of scroll bars. Press Enter, and the scroll bars are gone (see fig. 12.14).

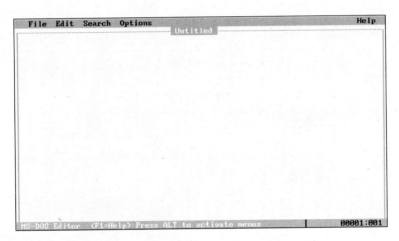

Fig. 12.14. The Editor screen with scroll bars removed.

Saving Customized Settings

If you change one or more display options, the Editor creates a file named QBASIC.INI and stores it in the directory containing the EDIT.COM and QBASIC.EXE files. (For most systems, this directory is \DOS.)

The QBASIC.INI file contains a record of the new screen configuration. When you later restart, the Editor uses QBASIC.INI to restore the screen with your customized settings.

Every time you start the Editor, it looks for QBASIC.INI in the default directory or in the directory chain established by the PATH statements in your AUTOEXEC.BAT file. If you restart from a different directory, be sure that the Editor has access to the QBASIC.INI file.

If you want to start the Editor with the original screen configuration, simply erase the QBASIC.INI file.

> *Note:* The DOS Editor "borrows" the programming editor from the QBASIC.EXE file. Thus, the DOS Editor shares the editing environment found in the QBasic programming language. Similarly, the DOS Editor and QBasic share the initial configuration file (QBASIC.INI). Whether you run the DOS Editor or QBasic, the initial configuration is saved in the QBASIC.INI file.

Using the Help System

The DOS Editor provides on-line help through the Help menu (see fig. 12.15). Help screens include information about menus and commands, shortcut keys, dialog boxes, keyboard actions, and even about the help system itself.

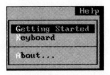

Fig. 12.15. The Help menu.

Three categories of information are available from the Help menu:

- Getting Started provides information about starting the Editor, using the menu and command system, and requesting help.

- Keyboard explains the different editing keystrokes and shortcuts for moving the cursor around your text file.

- About shows the Editor version number and copyright information.

The following are general notes on using the Help system:

- To activate the Help system at any time, press Alt-H.

- To move the cursor to the next help topic, press Tab. When the cursor is on the topic you want, press Enter to view the help screen.

- To activate the Getting Started help menu at any time, press Shift-F1.

- To close a help window and exit the help system, press Esc.

- A help screen opens in a separate window. The title bar of this window shows the help topic on display. For example, if you request help on the Save command from the File menu, the title bar of the help window reads `HELP: Save command`.

- The F1 key provides express help. To get help on any menu, command, or dialog box, press F1 when the cursor or highlight is on the desired item.

- For help when an error message occurs, move the cursor to the Help option in the error-message box, and press Enter.

- Sometime, at your leisure, consider browsing through all the help screens. To browse, press Shift-F1, and then press Ctrl-F1 repeatedly.

- To scroll any particular help screen, press PgUp or PgDn.

- When help is active, a separate help window opens in addition to the Editor window. You can move the cursor between the help and the Editor windows by pressing F6 (or Shift-F6).

- When a help window and the Editor window are open simultaneously, you can enlarge or reduce the size of the active window by pressing Alt-plus or Alt-minus. (Here, *plus* and *minus* refer to the + and – keys on the numeric keypad.)

- To cut and paste text from a help screen into your file, first use the normal editing keys to select the text on the help screen. Copy the selected lines to the clipboard. Press F6 to activate the Editor window and then, using the normal editing keys, paste the help text into your file. Now reactivate the help screen by pressing F6 again.

- When the help system is active, as in all editing contexts, the status bar at the bottom of the screen displays useful keystrokes. If you want to execute a command shown enclosed in angle brackets, press the indicated keystroke or click the mouse when the mouse cursor is on the command name in the status bar.

- The Editor keeps track of the last 20 help screens you have viewed. To cycle back through previously viewed screens, press Alt-F1.

- When you start the Editor, the initial dialog box gives you the option of seeing the Survival Guide. If you press Enter to see the Guide, the help system is activated. A help screen displays information about getting started with the Editor and using the help system.

- The Editor stores the text of the help screens in a file named EDIT.HLP. To display any help screen, the Editor must have access to this file. The Editor searches for EDIT.HLP in the current directory or in directories specified by the PATH statements of your AUTOEXEC.BAT file. Normal DOS installation automatically places this file in the default \DOS directory. If for some reason, EDIT.HLP is located outside your PATH specifications, however, you can supply the Editor with the path to EDIT.HLP by selecting the Help Path command on the Options menu.

Summary

The DOS Editor is a text processor with which you can create, edit, and save text files. Among the Editor's features are full-screen editing, pull-down menus, shortcut keys, mouse support, and on-line help.

Although not in the same class as sophisticated word processors, the Editor is a considerable improvement from Edlin, the line-oriented editor (and the only text editor) supplied with earlier versions of DOS. The new editor is simpler to use and more powerful than Edlin.

The Editor is perfectly suited for creating short text documents such as memos, README files, and batch files.

In this chapter, you have mastered the following concepts and skills:

- Navigating the menus and dialog boxes of the Editor

- Basic editing techniques in the Editor

- Editing blocks of text

- Searching for and replacing selected text

- Managing files through the DOS Editor

- Customizing your screen in the Editor

In Chapter 13, you learn how to work with batch files, use DOSKey, and create macros.

Understanding Batch Files, DOSKey, and Macros

13

When you discover that you're performing a task repeatedly on your computer, you should look for a way to get the computer to do more of the work. Your computer can perform most tasks faster than you can, and your computer doesn't make mistakes. DOS has always enabled you to automate your use of DOS commands by creating batch files. A *batch file* is a text (ASCII) file containing a series of DOS commands you want DOS to execute. When you type the batch file name, DOS executes these commands in the order you specify when you create the batch file. This chapter explains how to create and use DOS batch files.

In Chapter 12, you learned how to create text files with the Editor. In this chapter, you can put the Editor to use creating batch files. You learn about batch file commands and the AUTOEXEC.BAT file, and you see some examples of batch files you can modify to suit your needs.

In addition to batch files, DOS 5.0's DOSKey program also makes using the command line more efficient. DOSKey stores in the computer's memory the commands you type at the DOS command line, enabling you to use these commands again without retyping them. DOSKey also enables you to store a series of commands in memory and assign them to a new command name called a *macro*. You can execute the stored commands simply by typing the name of the macro. This chapter teaches you how to use these DOSKey features.

Key Terms Used in This Chapter

AUTOEXEC.BAT — A special batch file that DOS automatically executes during the booting process. The AUTOEXEC.BAT file, usually placed in the root directory, is an ideal place to include commands that initialize the operation of a PC.

Batch file — A text file containing commands that DOS executes as though the commands were entered at the DOS prompt. Batch files always have the BAT extension.

Flow control — The capability to control the order in which DOS processes lines of a batch file

Macro — A series of DOS commands stored in memory under a single name. You execute a macro by typing its name.

Meta-string — A series of characters that in DOS takes on a meaning different from the string's literal meaning. DOS displays substitute text when the program finds meta-strings in the PROMPT command.

Introducing Batch Files

The idea of getting a computer to do work in convenient, manageable batches predates the personal computer by several years. The earliest computers were large and expensive, and they could do only one job at a time. But even these early machines were fast. Making them wait for keyboard input between jobs was inefficient.

Batch processing was developed to make computers more productive. Collections of tasks to be carried out consecutively were put together off-line—that is, without using the computer's resources. The chunks, or batches, of tasks then were fed to the computer at a rate that kept the computer busy and productive.

Today, computers are less expensive than human resources. Batch processing enables the computer to carry out a series of tasks without wasting personnel time typing frequently used or complex commands.

A batch file is a text file that contains a series of DOS commands. Most commands used in batch files are familiar to you; they are explained in previous chapters of this book. Other commands, which control the flow of action in batch files, are available only in batch files. DOS executes the commands in the batch file one line at a time, treating each command as though you had issued it individually.

DOS batch files are available for your convenience. You can use batch files to automate a DOS process. Using a set of commands in a batch file, you actually create a new, more powerful command. After a few experiments, you will find this DOS facility quite handy.

Recognizing a batch file in a directory listing is easy. Batch files always have the file name extension BAT. You can execute a batch file by typing the file name at the DOS prompt and pressing Enter. For example, to execute the batch file SAFE.BAT, type **SAFE** at the command line, and press Enter.

COMMAND.COM looks in the current directory for that file name with the BAT extension, reads the file, and executes the DOS commands the file contains.

TIP

Tip: You can use the PATH command to provide DOS with alternative directories to search for the batch file you enter. PATH tells COMMAND.COM where to find BAT files as well as where to find EXE and COM files.

Batch files are useful for issuing commands that are hard to remember or that are easy to mistype at the command line. A good example would be some form of the BACKUP command. BACKUP is not a difficult command, but it is a command that you use far less frequently than the COPY and DIR commands. You may find it convenient to put properly formed backup commands in batch files that you can execute with one simple batch name.

Batch files can *echo* (display) messages you designate. This text-display capability is useful for presenting instructions or reminders on-screen. You can compose messages that describe how to execute a command or that contain syntax examples and reminders. Batch files also can use the TYPE command to display text from another file.

In some ways, batch files resemble computer programs. DOS has a host of special commands that are used primarily in batch files. Although you can type some of these commands at the DOS prompt, their main application is in batch files. These batch file commands introduce flow-control and decision-making capabilities into a batch file.

Understanding the Contents of Batch Files

Batch files are made up entirely of ASCII text characters. You can create batch files in the DOS Editor, in Edlin, as well as in nearly any text editor or word processing program. (You must use a word processor setting that omits the special formatting and control characters many word processing programs use for internal purposes.)

The easiest way to create a short batch file, however, is to use the COPY command to redirect input from the keyboard (the CON device) to a file (refer to "Copying from a Device to a File" in Chapter 10).

When you create batch files, observe the following rules:

- Batch files must be ASCII files. If you use a word processing program, be sure that it saves the file without formatting characters.

- The name of the batch file can be from one to eight characters long. The name must conform to the rules for naming files. Make batch file names meaningful so that they are easier to remember.

- The file name must end with the BAT extension.

- The batch file name should not be the same as a program file name (a file with an EXE or COM extension).

- The batch file name should not be the same as an internal DOS command (such as COPY or DATE).

- The batch file can contain any valid DOS commands that you can enter at the DOS command line. Typos cause errors.

- You can include in the batch file any program name you usually type at the DOS command line. DOS executes the program as though you had entered its name at the command line.

- Use only one command or program name per line in the batch file. DOS executes batch files one line at a time.

You start a batch file by typing its file name (excluding the extension) at the DOS prompt and pressing Enter. The following list summarizes the rules

DOS follows when it loads and executes a batch file:

- DOS looks first to the drive and directory specified in the command.

- Unless you specify the disk drive name before the batch file name, DOS uses the current drive.

- Unless you give a path, DOS searches through the current directory for the batch file.

- If the batch file is not in the current directory or the path you specified in the command, DOS searches the directories specified by the last PATH command you issued.

- When DOS encounters a syntax error in a batch file command line, DOS displays an error message, skips the incorrect command, and executes the remaining commands in the batch file.

- You can stop a batch file by pressing Ctrl-C or Ctrl-Break. DOS displays the following prompt:

```
Terminate batch job (Y/N)
```

Respond with N to skip the current command (the one being carried out) and resume execution with the next command in the batch file. Answer Y to abort execution of the batch file and return to the DOS prompt.

Creating a Simple Batch File

For practice, create a simple batch file. In this example, you use the COPY command to redirect input from the keyboard (the CON device) in order to create an ASCII text file. Remember that you also can use the DOS Editor, Edlin, another text editor, or your word processing program to create ASCII text files.

One task you may find yourself performing repetitively is copying and comparing files. Tasks consisting of the same series of commands are ideal candidates for batch files.

Suppose that you often work with two spreadsheet files called SALES.WK1 and CUSTOMER.WK1. You frequently update these files and store them in the directory \STORE on drive C. After you update the files, you normally copy them to a disk in drive A and compare the copies on the floppy disk to the originals on the hard disk.

To begin creating the batch file, type the following line at the DOS prompt, and press Enter:

COPY CON COPYCOMP.BAT

This COPY command redirects console (keyboard) input to the file COPYCOMP.BAT. After you press Enter, DOS drops the cursor to the first blank line below the DOS prompt at the left of the screen and waits. Type the following three lines, pressing Enter after each line:

ECHO OFF
COPY C:\STORE A:
COMP C:\STORE A:

After entering the last line in the file, press F6 or Ctrl-Z (both produce ^Z) to signal DOS that it has reached the end of the file. DOS displays the following message:

```
1 File(s) copied
```

DOS copies the three lines into a file named COPYCOMP.BAT.

Tip: When creating a text file with COPY CON, check each line before pressing Enter. You can use Backspace and the DOS command-line editing keys (listed in table 5.1, Chapter 5) to edit the current line. After you press Enter, DOS moves the cursor down to the next line, and you cannot correct any errors on previous lines. You can abort the process without saving the file by pressing Ctrl-C.

The first line of the COPYCOMP batch file, ECHO OFF, instructs DOS not to display the batch file's commands as the batch file executes. In other words, when you run the batch file, you do not see the command lines themselves on your display; you see only the results of their actions.

Tip: The ECHO OFF command prevents subsequent commands from displaying on-screen but does not prevent itself from displaying. When using DOS 3.3 and later versions, however, you can prevent the ECHO command from displaying by preceding the ECHO command with the @ character, as in the following command:

@ECHO OFF

The second line of COPYCOMP.BAT copies the desired files from their source location in C:\STORE to the destination root directory of drive A.

The final line of the batch file uses COMP.COM, an external DOS command that compares the copied files to the originals. Although you can use the /V (verify) switch with COPY, using COMP is more thorough.

Now that the COPYCOMP.BAT batch file is complete, you can run the file by typing the following command at the DOS prompt and pressing Enter:

COPYCOMP

DOS first copies the two files from the C:\STORE directory to drive A and then compares the copies to the original files.

Understanding the AUTOEXEC.BAT File

The batch file named AUTOEXEC.BAT has special significance to DOS. When you boot your computer, DOS searches for this file in the root directory. When an AUTOEXEC.BAT file is present, DOS executes the commands contained in the file; otherwise, DOS prompts you for the date and time (refer to Chapter 3 for a full discussion of the boot process).

The AUTOEXEC.BAT file is optional. Not every PC has this file. Most users, however, include an AUTOEXEC.BAT file of their own design on their boot disk because the file enables them automatically to establish operating parameters.

AUTOEXEC.BAT is intended as a convenience to you. You can omit this file, enter a few preliminary commands, and then start your PC work session, accomplishing the same result as an AUTOEXEC.BAT file. Unless you have a good reason not to, however, you should take advantage of this DOS feature by placing repetitive initialization commands in AUTOEXEC.BAT.

Some software packages come with installation programs that create or modify AUTOEXEC.BAT. These programs typically create AUTOEXEC.BAT if it doesn't exist or add commands to AUTOEXEC.BAT if it does exist. The installation program for DOS 5.0, for example, creates an AUTOEXEC.BAT file on your hard disk (or start-up disk, if installed on floppies).

If you have doubts about which commands you should include in your AUTOEXEC.BAT file, the following sections give you some ideas. Refer also to Chapter 15 to learn more about using AUTOEXEC.BAT to configure your computer.

Note: The AUTOEXEC.BAT file is a special batch file only in the sense that DOS executes AUTOEXEC.BAT each time you boot your computer. In every other sense, AUTOEXEC.BAT works the same way as any other batch file.

You can include any valid DOS commands in the AUTOEXEC.BAT file, subject to the following guidelines:

- The full file name must be AUTOEXEC.BAT, and the file must reside in the root directory of the boot disk.

- The contents of the AUTOEXEC.BAT file must conform to the rules for creating any batch file.

- When DOS executes AUTOEXEC.BAT after a boot, DOS does not prompt for date and time automatically. You must include the DATE and TIME commands in your AUTOEXEC.BAT file if you want to rcview the date and time every time you reboot. Most users do not use DATE and TIME in AUTOEXEC.BAT because most PCs have a battery-operated clock that correctly maintains the system's date and time.

Understanding the Contents of AUTOEXEC.BAT

Using AUTOEXEC.BAT is an excellent way for you to set up system defaults. That is, AUTOEXEC.BAT is the place to put commands you want DOS to execute every time you start your system. For example, you can use AUTOEXEC.BAT to tell your computer to change to the directory that holds your most commonly used program and start the program. Used in this way, AUTOEXEC.BAT starts your program as soon as you boot your computer. You can use this technique, for example, to cause DOS to start the DOS Shell each time you turn on your computer.

TIP

Tip: Floppy disk users often make each program disk bootable and place a different AUTOEXEC.BAT file on each disk. To start any particular program, they insert the program disk and reboot the computer. DOS does the rest.

Table 13.1 lists the commands most frequently included in simple AUTOEXEC.BAT files.

Table 13.1
AUTOEXEC.BAT File Commands

Command	Function in the AUTOEXEC.BAT File
TIME/DATE	Enables you to enter the correct time/date so that DOS can accurately "stamp" new and modified files, providing the correct time/date to applications programs that request it (not often used if your computer has a battery-operated system clock)
PATH	Establishes the directory path that DOS searches for executable files (EXE, COM, and BAT extensions)
PROMPT	Customizes the system prompt
DIR	Displays a listing of the root directory as soon as the computer boots
CD	Changes to a directory where you normally do your work
ECHO	Enables you to include a message as part of your start-up

Most of these commands are self-explanatory. The more complex commands are covered in the following sections.

Using the PATH Command

The PATH command tells DOS where to search for COM, EXE, and BAT files (see "Helping DOS Find External Commands" in Chapter 8). In this section, you learn how to use the PATH command in the AUTOEXEC.BAT file.

Suppose that you have installed the operating system files in the \DOS directory on your hard disk, C. You want to be able to issue DOS external commands from within any directory on the disk without specifying the directory that contains the operating system files. Type the following command in the AUTOEXEC.BAT file:

PATH C:\DOS

If you want DOS to search in the root directory first and the \DOS directory next, type the following PATH command in AUTOEXEC.BAT:

PATH C:\;C:\DOS

To cause DOS to search a third directory, add that directory's name to the PATH command, and so on. Notice that semicolons (;) separate the directory names.

After AUTOEXEC.BAT executes the PATH command, you can issue a command at the command line. DOS searches through the directories listed in the PATH command. If DOS cannot find the program in the current directory, the program looks to the first directory listed in the PATH command, the root directory in this example. DOS looks next in the second directory in the PATH command, then the third, and so on. DOS continues searching directories in turn until the executable file is found or until all alternatives are exhausted. If DOS cannot find an executable file by the specified name in any directory in the PATH, DOS displays the message

```
Bad command or file name
```

The path specified in AUTOEXEC.BAT becomes DOS's default search path. You can change this default path by issuing the PATH command manually at the DOS prompt or through another batch file.

Using the PROMPT Command

The default DOS prompt is rather spartan:

```
A>
```

or

```
C>
```

This DOS prompt tells you the identity of the current logged drive but nothing else (A> for the floppy disk drive A, C> for the hard disk drive C).

DOS enables you to change the look of the prompt through the PROMPT command. By using the PROMPT command, you can change the DOS prompt to a wide variety of forms that can include useful system information.

The syntax for the PROMPT command is as follows:

PROMPT *text*

The *text* parameter may be any string of characters. DOS creates the prompt from this character string. Most characters in the *text* parameter are interpreted literally. For example, if you include the word *HELLO* in the PROMPT command, DOS displays HELLO as part of the DOS prompt. Certain character strings have special meaning to DOS, however, when used in the PROMPT command. These special character strings are two-letter codes, sometimes referred to as *meta-strings*. DOS substitutes current system information or a special character for each meta-string.

Understanding Meta-Strings

A PROMPT command meta-string consists of two characters, the first of which is always the dollar sign ($). DOS interprets meta-strings to mean something other than the literal meaning of the characters.

Several PROMPT command meta-strings convey current system information. For example, including the meta-string $v in the PROMPT causes DOS to include the current system time in HH:MM:SS format.

Other meta-strings used in the PROMPT command cause DOS to display literally characters that DOS otherwise would interpret as part of a command syntax. For example, DOS normally recognizes the symbols > and < as redirection characters, and the vertical bar (|) as the pipe character. You may, however, want to include one or more of these symbols in a prompt without causing DOS to perform redirection or piping. To use one of these characters in the DOS prompt for a purpose other than redirection or piping, you must use the appropriate meta-string.

Table 13.2 lists the PROMPT command meta-strings and their meanings:

Table 13.2
Meta-Strings for Use with the PROMPT Command

Meta-string	Meaning
$_	Carriage return/line feed (moves the cursor to the beginning of the next line)
$b	The vertical bar or pipe character (|)
$d	The current system date
$e	The Esc character
$g	The greater-than sign (>)
$h	The Backspace character (moves the cursor one space to the left)
$l	The less-than sign (<)
$n	The current disk drive name
$p	The current drive and path
$q	The equal sign (=)
$t	The system time
$v	The DOS version

Customizing Your Prompt

You can use the meta-string characters with the PROMPT command to produce your own DOS prompt. Because you can use other characters in addition to meta-strings, you can experiment with different combinations of meta-strings and phrases.

Note: Issuing the PROMPT command alone with no parameters restores the prompt to the original default (A> or C>).

You may want your prompt to tell you the current DOS path, for example. Type the following command:

PROMPT THE CURRENT PATH IS $P

If the current drive is C and current directory is \DOS, the preceding PROMPT command produces the following DOS prompt:

```
THE CURRENT PATH IS C:\DOS
```

By adding the meta-string $g, you can add the greater-than symbol (>) to the prompt. The new version of the command is as follows:

PROMPT THE CURRENT PATH IS PG

Your DOS prompt appears as follows:

```
THE CURRENT PATH IS C:\DOS>
```

Using meta-strings and characters, you also can display other system information in the prompt, including the system date and time and the DOS version. For example, the following PROMPT command displays the date and time above the path and encloses the path in brackets:

PROMPT D:T$_[$P]

After you issue this command, the prompt appears similar to the following:

```
Mon 02-04-1991: 9:26:00.48
[C:\]
```

The $_ meta-string causes the prompt to move down one line before displaying the path.

You can use the $h meta-string to erase a part of the prompt. For example, in the preceding PROMPT example, the $v meta-string causes DOS to display seconds and hundredths of seconds. Using the $h meta-string several times, you can erase the seconds and hundredths of seconds, making the prompt a little less "busy." The PROMPT command is as follows:

PROMPT D:THHHHH_[$P]

After you issue this command, DOS displays a prompt similar to the following:

```
Mon 02-04-1991: 9:26
[C:\]
```

Note: The $e meta-string represents the Esc character (ASCII decimal 27). This meta-string is used with a special file named ANSI.SYS, a device driver file. Refer to Chapter 15 for a discussion of device drivers. Using the PROMPT command and ANSI.SYS codes, you can customize your system prompt further, even adding color if you want.

Examining AUTOEXEC.BAT Files

The contents of each user's AUTOEXEC.BAT file may vary, but most AUTOEXEC.BAT files contain a few of the same commands. The following sample of an AUTOEXEC.BAT file executes useful start-up commands.

```
DATE
TIME
PATH=C:\;C:\DOS;C:\KEEP;C:\;
PROMPT $P$G
CD\BATCH
DIR
ECHO Good Day, Mate!
```

The following paragraphs explain each line of the file.

DATE prompts you to enter the correct date so that DOS can accurately "date stamp" new and modified files.

TIME prompts you to enter the correct time so that DOS can accurately "time stamp" new and modified files.

PATH=C:\;C\DOS;C:\KEEP;C:\; instructs DOS to search the named directories to find files that have EXE, COM, or BAT extensions.

PROMPT PG customizes the system prompt to show the current drive and path and the greater-than (>) symbol.

CD\BATCH makes \BATCH the current directory. This directory may contain batch files that start programs on your hard disk.

DIR displays a listing of the current directory.

ECHO Good Day, Mate! displays Good Day, Mate! as part of your start-up procedure.

Note: Most computers already have an AUTOEXEC.BAT file in the root directory of the hard disk or on the bootable floppy disk. Remember that packaged software sometimes creates or adds to the AUTOEXEC.BAT file when you install the software on your hard or floppy disk. DOS 5.0 creates an AUTOEXEC.BAT file on your hard disk as a part of the installation procedure.

You easily can see whether AUTOEXEC.BAT exists in your root directory or on your logged floppy disk. Log onto your hard disk, and change to the root directory. To look at the directory listing of all files with BAT extensions, type the following command and press Enter:

DIR *.BAT

To view the contents of AUTOEXEC.BAT on-screen, type the following:

TYPE AUTOEXEC.BAT

To get a printed copy of the AUTOEXEC.BAT file, redirect output to the printer by using the following command:

TYPE AUTOEXEC.BAT >PRN

Alternatively, you can use the COPY command to copy the file to the printer:

COPY AUTOEXEC.BAT PRN

If you choose not to print a copy of your AUTOEXEC.BAT file, make sure that you write down the contents before you make any changes. Be sure that you copy the syntax correctly. This copy serves as your worksheet.

You can use your copy of AUTOEXEC.BAT to see whether a PROMPT or PATH command is contained in the batch file. If you want to add or alter PROMPT or PATH commands, jot the additions or changes on your worksheet. Use your paper copy of the AUTOEXEC.BAT file to check for proper syntax in the lines you change or add before you commit the changes to disk.

Always make a backup copy of your existing AUTOEXEC.BAT file before you make any changes in the file. To save the current version, you can copy it with a different extension. For example, to create a copy named AUTOEXEC.OLD, type the following command and press Enter:

COPY AUTOEXEC.BAT AUTOEXEC.OLD

DOS copies the contents of AUTOEXEC.BAT to the file AUTOEXEC.OLD. You now can modify your AUTOEXEC.BAT file by using the DOS Editor, Edlin, another text editor, or your word processing program. If you use the COPY CON method, you have to start from scratch and type the entire new version of the batch file.

If you find that the new AUTOEXEC.BAT file does not work or does not do what you want, you can always erase the new file. Then, using the RENAME command, you can rename the AUTOEXEC.OLD file to AUTOEXEC.BAT, and you are back where you started.

Understanding Replaceable Parameters

The batch files created so far in this chapter carry out exactly the same functions every time you use them. However, you may want a particular batch file to operate on different files each time you use it, even though the commands in the batch file are fixed. Using batch file *replaceable parameters*, you can cause the same batch file to do different things.

A *parameter* is defined in Chapter 5 as "an additional instruction that defines specifically what you want the DOS command to do." When you type the name of the batch file at the DOS prompt, you can include up to nine parameters. DOS assigns a variable name to each parameter, starting with 1 and going up to 9. (DOS always assigns the variable name 0 to the name of the batch file itself.) You can use each variable in your batch file by preceding the variable name with the percent sign (%).

The combination of the percent sign and the variable name is referred to as a *replaceable parameter*. When used in a batch file, each replaceable parameter, numbered %0 through %9, holds the place for a parameter in one or more commands of a batch file so that you can provide the actual value of the parameter at the time you execute the batch file.

Consider the COPYCOMP.BAT batch file discussed earlier in this chapter:

```
ECHO OFF
COPY C:\STORE A:
COMP C:\STORE A:
```

Each time you execute the batch file, it copies all files from the C:\STORE directory to the A disk and then compares the files. Suppose that you want to make this batch file more versatile so that you can use it to copy and compare the files in any directory. Use the DOS Editor, Edlin, another text editor, or your word processing program to revise COPYCOMP.BAT as follows:

```
ECHO OFF
COPY %1 %2
COMP %1 %2
```

Notice that *%1* and *%2* have replaced C:\STORE and A: respectively. These parameters are replaceable parameters. After making these changes to COPYCOMP.BAT you can use the batch file to copy and compare the files from any directory to any disk or directory. For example, to copy and compare the files found in the \SPREADSH\QPRO2DAT directory on the C disk to a disk in the B drive, type the following command, and press Enter:

COPYCOMP C:\SPREADSH\QPRO2DAT B:

DOS copies all files from C:\SPREADSH\QPRO2DAT to the disk in B and then compares the original files with the copies to ensure that the copy procedure was effective.

To see how DOS replaces the parameters, create a batch file called TEST1.BAT. Type the following line into this file:

@ECHO %0 %1 %2 %3 %4 %5 %6 %7 %8 %9

After you create this file, type **TEST1** followed by one space; then type your first name, last name, street address, city, state, ZIP code, and age, separated by spaces. Your screen should look similar to the following:

```
C\:>TEST1 DAVID SMITH 1234 PINE STREET ANYTOWN IN 46032 39
TEST1 DAVID SMITH 1234 PINE STREET ANYTOWN IN 46032 39
C\:>
```

The batch file command instructs DOS to display on-screen the parameters 0 through 9. These parameters worked out to be the following:

Parameter	Word
%0	TEST1
%1	DAVID
%2	SMITH
%3	1234
%4	PINE
%5	STREET
%6	ANYTOWN
%7	IN
%8	46032
%9	39

Now, try to "shortchange" DOS by not specifying a sufficient number of parameters to fill every variable marker. Run TEST1 again, but this time give only your first name. You should see something like the following:

```
C>TEST1 DAVID
TEST1 DAVID
C>
```

DOS displays the batch file name and your first name. No other information is echoed to the screen. You specified fewer parameters, and DOS replaced the unfilled markers with nothing. In this case, the empty markers did no harm.

Some commands you use in a batch file, however, may require that a replaceable parameter not be empty. For example, if you include DEL in a batch file with a replaceable parameter and the parameter is empty, you see the following error message:

```
Invalid number of parameters
```

You can use the IF command (discussed later in this chapter) to avoid such errors.

In the remainder of this section, you learn how to construct a batch file that takes advantage of replaceable parameters. Suppose that you use several computers daily, but one of the hard disk systems is your primary "work-horse," where you store all the files you want to keep.

You use floppy disks to move information between computers. After copying a file back to a hard disk, you usually delete the file from the floppy disk. Deleting the file removes it from the process so that the file is not accidentally copied to the hard disk again later. You use the following steps to transfer data from a floppy disk to a hard disk:

1. Copy file from the floppy disk to the hard disk with the verify switch on.

2. Erase the file from the floppy disk.

To simplify this process, you can create a batch file called C&E.BAT (copy and erase). Type the following commands in the file:

COPY A:%1 C:%2 /V
ERASE A:%1

To use the C&E.BAT file, type the following at the DOS prompt:

C&E oldfilename newfilename

The first parameter, *oldfilename*, represents the name of the file you want to copy from the floppy disk to the hard disk; *newfilename* is the new name for the copied file (if you want to change the file name as it is being copied).

Suppose that you put a disk containing the file NOTES.TXT into drive A and want to copy the file to the hard disk. Type the following at the DOS prompt:

C&E NOTES.TXT

The screen appears as follows:

```
C>COPY A:NOTES.TXT C: /V
1 file(s) copied
C>ERASE A:NOTES.TXT
C>
C>
```

Notice that even though you didn't type the parameter *newfilename*, DOS carried out the batch file, keeping the same file name during the copy. DOS copied NOTES.TXT from drive A to drive C and then deleted the file on the disk in drive A. The %2 parameter was dropped, and the file did not get a new name when it was copied.

One benefit of constructing a batch file that copies a file using parameters is that you can use a path name as the second parameter. By specifying a path name, you can copy the file from the floppy disk to a different directory on the hard disk. To copy NOTES.TXT to the WORDS directory, for example, type the following:

C&E NOTES.TXT \WORDS

The screen display is as follows:

```
C>COPY A:NOTES.TXT C:\WORDS /V
1 file(s) copied
C>ERASE A:NOTES.TXT
C>
```

Because \WORDS is a directory name, DOS copies the file NOTES.TXT into the directory \WORDS, following the rules of syntax for the COPY command. The batch file takes advantage of these syntax rules.

Note: Patience and persistence are important in understanding batch files. Many PC users avoid using batch files only to try one or two examples and then pick up the concept rapidly. These same users now produce batch files that anyone would be proud of. Give yourself a chance to learn batch files by practicing with the examples in this chapter. You can use the examples as templates for your own situation. After you get into the rhythm of composing batch files, you will have harnessed one of DOS's most powerful features.

Your use of batch files is not limited by your own imagination. If you pick up almost any personal computer magazine, you can find a few useful batch files introduced in a feature or an article. You can use these featured batch files as they are or as the basis for your own special situation.

Even if you don't regularly create your own batch files, you can use your knowledge of batch file principles. Many programs are started by batch files rather than the name of the actual program file. With your knowledge of batch files, you can use the TYPE command to display the contents of any batch file in order to see what the batch operation is doing.

Many applications programs install the main files through the commands included in an installation batch file. You can understand how an installation proceeds if you can read the contents of the installing batch file. Knowing what the batch file does can help you avoid installation conflicts. For example, I install 5 1/4-inch disk-based software from drive B because my drive A is a 3 1/2-inch drive. Many installation batch files, however, look for the files to be installed on drive A. To avoid this conflict, I modify a version of the installation batch file by changing all references to drive A to drive B. When I run my modified installation batch file, the new software installs without a hitch.

Working with batch files also can serve as a meaningful introduction to programming. The batch file commands covered in this chapter give batch files the kind of internal flow and decision-making that programming languages offer. Of course, you shouldn't expect batch files to equal the versatility of a full-featured programming environment. But batch files certainly can assume a programming flavor. By using batch files, you can greatly increase DOS's utility.

Using Batch File Commands

Included in DOS are special commands often used in batch files. Table 13.3 is a list of batch file commands for DOS 3.0 through 5.0.

Table 13.3
Batch File Commands for DOS 3.3 through 5

Command	Action
@	Suppresses the display of the command line on-screen (DOS 3.3 and later)
CALL	Runs another batch file and returns to the original batch file (DOS 3.3 and later)
CLS	Clears the screen and returns the cursor to the upper left corner of the screen
COMMAND /C	Invokes a second copy of the command processor, COMMAND.COM, to call another batch file (necessary in versions before 3.3)
ECHO	Turns on or off the display of batch commands as they execute; also can display a message on-screen
FOR..IN..DO	Allows the use of the same batch command for several files. The execution "loops."
GOTO	Jumps to the line following the specified label in a batch file
IF	Allows conditional execution of a command
PAUSE	Halts processing until a key is pressed. Displays the message `Press any key to continue.`
REM	Enables you to insert into a batch file comments that describe the intent of an operation
SHIFT	Shifts the command-line parameters one parameter to t

You can use any of the commands listed in table 13.3 in a batch file, and you can use some of them at the DOS system level as well. For example, you can type **ECHO** with or without an argument at the DOS prompt. DOS displays the string you type after ECHO or, if you provide no argument, tells you whether ECHO is ON or OFF. If you type **PAUSE** at the DOS prompt, DOS pauses. Although these two commands are not very useful at the DOS prompt, the FOR..IN..DO command structure can be quite useful at the operating-system level to carry out repetitive commands.

The following sections explain the batch commands and their uses.

Displaying Messages and Inserting Comments

The ECHO command does two things. ECHO ON and ECHO OFF turn on and off the display of lines from batch files as the commands are executed. ECHO also displays messages.

ECHO can display a message with a maximum length of 122 characters (the 127-character DOS command-line limit minus the length of the prompt minus a space).

You can put REM (which stands for *remark*) to good use in a batch file to remind you what the batch file does. When you review a batch file some time after you create it, you may no longer remember why you used certain commands, or why you constructed the batch file in a particular way. Leave reminders in your batch file with REM statements. Comments in REM statements don't appear on-screen when ECHO is off. The REM comments make the batch file self-documenting, a feature that you and other users will appreciate later.

If you want the batch file to display particular messages, use ECHO. Messages set with ECHO appear on-screen whether or not you set ECHO OFF.

Clearing the Screen and Suppressing Screen Display

The DOS CLS command can be used at any time at the DOS prompt to clear the screen. In batch files, CLS commonly is used after the ECHO OFF command to erase the ECHO OFF command:

```
ECHO OFF
CLS
```

Beginning with DOS 3.3, you can use the @ command-prefix feature to prevent the ECHO OFF command from appearing on-screen. Replace the preceding two command lines with the following single line:

@ECHO OFF

Because @ is the first character on the line, ECHO OFF does not appear on-screen.

You can use the @ command prefix in front of any DOS command in a batch file to prevent DOS from displaying the command, even when ECHO is on.

Branching with GOTO

Normally, when you run a batch file, DOS processes commands one line at a time, from the beginning of the batch file to the end. With the DOS GOTO command, you can change the order in which DOS executes batch commands by instructing DOS to branch to a specific line in the file.

The syntax of GOTO is as follows:

GOTO label

The DOS GOTO command uses *labels* to specify the line in the file to which DOS should send the execution of the file. A batch file label is a separate line that is not a command per se. A label consists of a colon followed by one to eight characters. The label name can be longer than eight characters, but DOS reads only the first eight characters.

When DOS encounters a GOTO command in the batch file, DOS starts at the beginning of the batch file and searches for a label matching the one specified by GOTO. DOS then jumps execution to the batch file line following the line with the label.

As an example, the batch file LOOP.BAT is listed here. This file is similar to the TEST.BAT batch file you created previously, with the addition of the GOTO and PAUSE commands.

```
:LOOP
@ECHO OFF
ECHO Hello, %1
PAUSE
GOTO LOOP
```

To test the batch file, type **LOOP DAVID**. The screen shows the following:

```
Hello, DAVID
Press any key to continue . . .
```

The batch file begins by echoing `Hello DAVID` and then pauses for you to press a key. Press a key and DOS again displays the following:

```
Hello, DAVID
Press any key to continue . . .
```

After you press a key, DOS executes the GOTO LOOP command, causing execution of the batch file to return to the line labeled :LOOP at beginning of the file. DOS again displays the messages and pauses a second time.

This batch file is an example of what programmers call an *infinite loop*. The program never stops on its own. To abort the batch file, press Ctrl-C or Ctrl-Break. DOS asks `Terminate batch job (Y/N)?` Respond Y for yes, and DOS returns to the DOS system prompt.

This simple example illustrates the operation of GOTO. You will not often create infinite loops on purpose, but you should be able to use the GOTO command to control the order that DOS executes batch file commands.

Using the IF Command

The IF command is a "test and do" command. When a given condition is true, the IF command executes a stated action. When the given condition is false, IF skips the action. If you are familiar with programming languages, such as BASIC, you should find the DOS IF command familiar.

The IF command tests three conditions:

- What the ERRORLEVEL of a program is
- Whether a string is equal to another string
- Whether a file exists

Using IF To Test ERRORLEVEL

The first condition IF can test is ERRORLEVEL. The proper syntax for IF when testing the ERRORLEVEL is as follows:

IF *NOT* ERRORLEVEL number command

ERRORLEVEL is a code left by a program when it finishes executing. A better name for this condition might be "exit level." This form of the IF command determines whether the value of ERRORLEVEL is greater than or equal to a number specified in the *number* parameter. Conversely, by adding the optional word *NOT*, you can determine whether the value of ERRORLEVEL is *not* greater than or equal to the value of the *number* parameter. If the specified condition is true, DOS executes the command specified in the *command* parameter. Otherwise, DOS skips to the next line in the batch file without executing *command*.

In DOS 3.3 and later versions, the only DOS commands that leave an ERRORLEVEL (exit) code are BACKUP, DISKCOMP, DISKCOPY, FORMAT, GRAFTABL, KEYB (DOS 4.0 and later), REPLACE, RESTORE, and XCOPY. Many other programs generate exit codes, however.

An exit code of zero (0) usually indicates that the command was successful. Any number greater than 0 usually indicates that something went wrong when the program executed. For example, the following exit codes are generated by the DISKCOPY command:

0   Successful operation

1   A read/write error occurred that did not terminate the disk-copy operation.

2   The user pressed Ctrl-C.

3   A "fatal" read/write error occurred and terminated the copy procedure before it was completed.

4   An initialization error occurred.

An IF command in a batch file enables you to test for the exit code generated by a DOS command or program to determine whether the command or program worked properly.

When you use ERRORLEVEL to test exit codes, DOS tests whether the exit code is equal to or greater than the specified *number* parameter. If the exit code is equal to or greater than the number, DOS executes the *command* parameter. If the exit code does not meet the condition, DOS skips the *command* parameter and executes the next command in the batch file. You can think of this condition as a BASIC-like statement:

IF exit code >= number THEN do command

The IF ERRORLEVEL command is most useful with noncopyrighted public-domain utilities for user keyboard input. These utilities have names like INPUT.COM, ASK.COM, GETKEY.COM and are often available from user groups or on public electronic bulletin boards. When your batch file uses these utilities, it can pause and wait for keyboard input. The utility puts a value in ERRORLEVEL related to the scan code of the key pressed. You then can make your batch file branch or perform some other task based on the key pressed. A batch file does not accept keyboard input except when the input is provided on a batch-file command line.

Suppose, for example, that you want to create a batch file named DCOPY.BAT that makes disk copies on your A drive using the DISKCOPY command and the verification switch (see Chapter 6). If the disk-copy procedure terminates before completion, you want the batch file to inform you of the cause.

Create a batch file named DCOPY.BAT containing the following lines:

```
@ECHO OFF
DISKCOPY A: A: /V
IF ERRORLEVEL 4 GOTO INIT_ERR
IF ERRORLEVEL 3 GOTO FATL_ERR
IF ERRORLEVEL 2 GOTO CTRL-C
IF ERRORLEVEL 1 GOTO NON_FATL
ECHO DISKCOPY successful and verified!
GOTO END
:INIT_ERR
ECHO Initialization error!
GOTO END
:FATL_ERR
ECHO Fatal error! DISKCOPY stopped!
GOTO END
:CTRL-C
ECHO Someone pressed Ctrl-C!
GOTO END
:NON-FATL
ECHO A non-fatal error occurred. Check data!
:END
```

To run this batch file, type **DCOPY** at the command line, and press Enter. DOS instructs you to

```
Insert SOURCE diskette in drive A:
Press any key to continue . . .
```

Press a key, and DOS begins the disk-copy procedure. After the DISKCOPY command in the batch file executes, the batch file runs through a series of IF ERRORLEVEL tests.

First, the batch file tests for an initialization error (exit code = 4). If the exit code equals (or is greater than) 4, DOS skips to the line labeled :INIT_ERR and displays the message `Initialization error!` Next, the batch file checks for exit code 3. If the exit code is 3, execution of the batch file skips to the :FATL_ERR label and displays the message `Fatal error! DISKCOPY stopped!` The batch file again tests the exit code and branches to the :CTRL_C label if an exit code of 2 is detected. The batch file also branches to the :NON_FATL label when the exit code is 1. Finally, if no errors are detected by the series of IF ERRORLEVEL commands, the batch file displays the following message:

```
DISKCOPY successful and verified!
```

Using IF To Compare Strings

The second use for the IF command is to test whether string 1 equals string 2. The syntax of the batch command is as follows:

IF *NOT* string1==string2 command

This form of the IF command determines whether the first character string, *string1*, is the same group of characters as *string2*. Usually one string is a replaceable parameter. If the two strings are exactly the same, this condition is true, so DOS executes the command specified in the *command* parameter. Otherwise, DOS skips to the next line in the batch file without executing *command*. By adding NOT to the IF command, you can test for the condition when the two strings are not the same.

Assume that you want to create a batch file named DAYBACK.BAT that backs up your hard disk each day of the week. On Fridays, you want the batch file to perform a complete backup. On Mondays through Thursdays, you want the batch file to do an additive incremental backup. Use the DOS Editor or another editor to create the following batch file:

```
@ECHO OFF
CLS
IF "%1"="" GOTO TRY_AGAIN
IF %1==FRI GOTO FULL
IF %1==MON GOTO ADD
IF %1==TUE GOTO ADD
IF %1==WED GOTO ADD
IF %1==THU GOTO ADD
:TRY_AGAIN
ECHO Try again! Type DAYBACK and day of week (MON-FRI).
GOTO END
:FULL
ECHO Insert first disk of backup set.
```

```
PAUSE
C:
CD \
BACKUP C: A: /S
GOTO END
:ADD
ECHO Insert last disk of backup set.
PAUSE
C:
CD \
BACKUP C: A: /S/M/A
:END
```

To run this batch file, type **DAYBACK**; then type the three-letter abbreviation for the day of the week (MON, TUE, WED, THU, or FRI), and press Enter.

The first IF command in DAYBACK.BAT checks to make sure that you have typed the day of the week. If you don't provide enough parameters with the IF command, DOS replaces the replaceable parameter with a null value. In batch files, null values must be enclosed in quotation marks to avoid a syntax error.

The remaining IF commands determine whether you have typed *FRI* or another day of the week. If you type *FRI*, the batch file branches to the :FULL label and does a full backup. If you type a day MON through THU, execution jumps to the :ADD label and does an additive incremental backup. Finally, if you type anything else, the batch file instructs you to try again.

> *Note:* The :END label is used often to mark the end of the batch file. In this batch file, execution branches to the :END label after a full backup, after an incremental backup, or after you are instructed to try again. Through this technique, only a portion of the batch file is executed each time you run it. DOS skips the portions of the batch file that don't apply. Because the :END label is the last line in the batch file, the batch file ends.

In this example, quotation marks are used around the replaceable parameter in the first IF command in DAYBACK.BAT because quotation marks are used commonly by programmers to delimit character strings. Actually, a comparison with any letter, number, or symbol can do the job. One common procedure is to use a single period instead of quotation marks, as the following example shows:

```
IF %1 . == . GOTO TRY_AGAIN
```

If no parameter is entered for %1, DOS interprets the line as follows:

IF . == . GOTO TRY_AGAIN

Use the syntax that is easiest for you to remember and understand.

If %1 equals nothing, DOS branches to the line following the label TRY_AGAIN and displays the message `Try again! Type DAYBACK and day of week (MON-FRI).`

If %1 equals something other than nothing, DOS does not branch to NOTHING; instead, DOS executes the second IF command in the batch file, which tests whether you typed *DAYBACK FRI*, and so on. Notice that GOTO statements are used to jump around the parts of the batch file that should not be executed.

TIP

> *Tip:* When using the IF command, DOS compares strings literally. Uppercase characters are different from lowercase characters. If you run DAYBACK by typing **DAYBACK Fri**, DOS compares Fri with the uppercase FRI and decides that the two strings are not the same. The IF test fails, and no backup operation is performed.

Using IF To Look for Files

The third type of IF command tests whether a given file is on disk. The syntax for this form of the IF command is as follows:

IF *NOT* EXIST filename command

This form of the IF command determines whether the file specified in the *filename* parameter exists on your computer's disk (or doesn't exist, if you add NOT). If the file does exist, the IF command executes the command specified in the *command* parameter.

If you want to test for a file on a drive other than the current drive, put the disk drive name in front of *filename* (for example, IF EXIST B:CHKDSK.COM).

You can use IF EXIST when starting your word processing program. Perhaps you use a file called TEMP.TXT to store temporary files or to write blocks to be read into other documents. You can use IF EXIST to test for the existence of the file and erase the file if it does exist.

Your batch file, called WORD.BAT, looks like the following:

```
@ECHO OFF
CLS
CD \DOCUMENT
IF EXIST TEMP.TXT DEL TEMP.TXT
\WORDS\WP
CD \
```

In this batch file, ECHO is turned off, and the screen is cleared. The current directory is changed to \DOCUMENT, the directory where you store your word processing documents.

Next, the IF command tests for the existence of TEMP.TXT. If the file does exist, DOS deletes the file. Next, DOS starts your word processing program from the \WORDS subdirectory.

TIP

> ***Tip:*** Notice the last line of the batch file: CD \. When your word processing program starts, the batch file is suspended temporarily. After you quit your word processing program, control is given back to the batch file. The batch file then executes its last line, CD \, which changes back to the root directory. The batch file ends.

Using FOR..IN..DO

FOR..IN..DO is an unusual and extremely powerful batch command. The command's syntax is as follows:

FOR %%variable IN (set) DO command

variable is a one-letter name that takes on the value of each item in *set*. You can use this command on the DOS command line as well as from within a batch file; however, when using the command on the command line, use only a single percent sign (%) instead of the double percent sign (%%) in front of the variable. You must use two percent signs in a batch file so that DOS does not confuse *variable* with a replaceable parameter.

The *set* parameter is the list of items, commands, or disk files whose value you want *variable* to take. You can use wild-card file names with this parameter. You also can use drive names and paths with any file names you specify. If you have more than one item in the set, use a space or a comma between the names.

The *command* parameter is any valid DOS command you want to perform for each item in *set*.

Using a FOR..IN..DO Batch File

An interesting example of the use of FOR..IN..DO is a batch file that compares file names found on a disk in drive A with the file names found on another disk and produces a list of the files on both. Create the batch file CHECKIT.BAT with the following content:

```
@ECHO OFF
CLS
IF "%1"=="" GOTO END
FOR %%a IN (B: C: D: E: b: c: d: e:) DO IF =="%1" GOTO COMPARE
ECHO Syntax error: You must specify a disk to compare.
ECHO      Be sure to leave a space before directory.
GOTO END
:COMPARE
%1
IF "%2"=="" GOTO SKIP
CD %2
:SKIP
ECHO The following files are on both disks:
FOR %%a IN (*.*) DO IF EXIST A:%%a ECHO %%a
:END
```

Put the disk you want to compare into drive A and then type the following:

CHECKIT drive *directory*

where *drive* is the drive that contains the other disk you want to compare, and *directory* is the directory you want to compare. This batch file substitutes the drive you specify in place of %1 in the batch file commands and substitutes any directory you specify in place of %2. The directory is optional; if you specify a drive and directory, separate their names with a space. Otherwise, the batch file treats the drive and directory together as one replaceable parameter—%1. If you don't specify a directory name, the current directory of the drive you specify is compared with the current directory of the disk in A.

For example, suppose that you want to compare the list of files on A with the list of files found in the \GAMES directory on drive B. Type the following at the command line:

CHECKIT B: \GAMES

The batch file determines which files in the \GAMES directory of the disk in drive B are also on the current directory of the disk in drive A.

When the CHECKIT batch file is called, DOS first checks whether %1 is empty (%1 is empty if you typed no drive letter or directory after CHECKIT in the command line). If %1 is empty, the batch file displays an error message, branches to the end of the file, and quits without performing a comparison.

If you specify a disk drive, DOS goes to the third line of the batch file and checks whether the drive letter is a valid drive letter; valid drive letters are B, C, D, E, b, c, d, or e. (If your system has more or fewer drives, this list changes to reflect your configuration.) If no valid drive letter is found, or if you don't include a colon (:) and space after the drive letter, the batch file displays a message and branches to the end of the batch file.

When you have specified a valid drive, CHECKIT branches to the :COMPARE section of the program. When executing the first line in this section, DOS logs onto the drive you specified in the command line (the drive designation replaces %1 in the batch file). The batch file determines whether you included a directory parameter, and if so, DOS changes to that directory.

Finally, the batch file displays a message and then looks at all the files in the current directory to see whether a file with the same name exists on drive A. For every match found, the batch file lists the file name.

Using FOR..IN..DO at the DOS Prompt

You may find that you want to issue commands such as the ones in CHECKIT at the DOS prompt. Instead of using the batch file for the preceding example, you can change subdirectories manually and then type the FOR..IN..DO line (the line that does all the work in the batch file) at the DOS prompt. If you do use FOR..IN..DO outside a batch file, DOS requires that you enter only one percent sign.

Another use for FOR..IN..DO can occur if you have copied files from a disk to the wrong subdirectory on a hard disk. You can delete the files from the hard disk by using FOR..IN..DO.

Using FOR..IN..DO with Other Commands

FOR..IN..DO works equally well with commands and file names. Instead of naming a set of files, you can name a series of commands you want DOS to carry out. Consider the following example:

FOR %%a IN (COPY DEL) DO %%a C:*.*

In a batch file, this line first copies all the files on drive C to the current directory and then erases the files from drive C. You can put a replaceable parameter in the line instead of naming the drive and file specifications:

FOR %%a IN (COPY ERASE) DO %%a %1

To use this batch file, you first must change to the destination directory (for example, D:\BAK). When you invoke this version of the batch file, you type the names of the files you want copied and removed. If you name the batch file MOVER.BAT, you can type the following to invoke the file:

MOVER C:\WP

MOVER.BAT copies all the files in the subdirectory C:\WP to D:\BAK and then erases the files in C:\WP. This file works much like the C&E.BAT file created earlier in this chapter.

Moving Parameters with SHIFT

The SHIFT command moves the parameters in the command line that invoked the batch file; each parameter moves one parameter to the left. SHIFT tricks DOS into accepting more than 9 replaceable parameters (10 if you include the batch file name, which is %0). The diagram of SHIFT is as follows:

```
%0 ←%1 ←%2 ←%3 ←%4 ←%5 . . .
↓
bit bucket
```

In this diagram, parameter 0 is dropped. The old parameter 1 becomes parameter 0. The old parameter 2 becomes parameter 1; parameter 3 becomes 2; parameter 4 becomes 3; and so on. A command line parameter that previously was 11th in line and not assigned a parameter number now becomes parameter 9.

The following batch file, SHIFTIT.BAT, is a simple example of the use of the SHIFT command:

```
@ECHO OFF
CLS
:START
ECHO %0 %1 %2 %3 %4 %5 %6 %7 %8 %9
SHIFT
```

```
PAUSE
GOTO START
```

Suppose that you type the following:

SHIFTIT A B C D E F G H I J K L M N O P Q R S T U V W X Y Z

The screen shows the following:

```
SHIFTIT A B C D E F G H I
Press any key to continue . . .
```

Notice that the batch file name is displayed because %0 holds the name of the batch file. Press a key to continue; ECHO now shows the following:

```
A B C D E F G H I J
Press any key to continue . . .
```

In this case, the file name has been dropped into the bit bucket. %0 now equals A. All the parameters have shifted one to the left. Each time you press a key to continue, SHIFT continues moving down the list of parameters you typed. Press Ctrl-C when you want to stop.

SHIFT has many uses. You can use it to build a new version of the C&E.BAT file created earlier in the chapter. The following modified version of the copy-and-erase batch file, called MOVE.BAT, shows a use for SHIFT:

```
@ECHO OFF
CLS
:LOOP
COPY %1 /V
ERASE %1
SHIFT
IF NOT %1. == . GOTO LOOP
```

This batch file copies and erases the specified file or files. The batch file assumes nothing about the files to be copied; you can specify a disk drive, a path, and a file name. The batch file copies the files to the current directory and then erases the files from the original disk or directory.

The last two lines shift the parameters to the left, test whether any parameters remain, and then repeat the operation if necessary.

Running Batch Files from Other Batch Files

On some occasions, you may want to run a batch file from another batch file. Running batch files from within batch files is particularly useful when you want to create a menu batch file that can start several different applications programs. This section discusses three ways to run batch files from other batch files. One method is a one-way transfer of control. The other two ways show you how to run a second batch file and return control to the first batch file. These techniques are useful if you want to build menus with batch files or use one batch file to set up and start another batch file.

Shifting Control Permanently to Another Batch File

The first method of calling a second batch file is simple. Include the root name of the second batch file as a line in the first batch file. The first batch file runs the second batch file as if you had typed the second batch file's root name at the DOS prompt. To run BATCH2.BAT, for example, include in BATCH1.BAT the following line:

    BATCH2

DOS loads and executes BATCH2.BAT. Control passes in only one direction—from the first batch file to the second. When BATCH2.BAT finishes executing, DOS displays the system prompt. You can consider this technique an interbatch-file GOTO. Control goes to the second file but doesn't come back to the first file.

Calling a Batch File and Returning Using CALL

In all versions of DOS, you can call a second batch file from the first, execute the second batch file, and return to the first batch file. With DOS 3.0 through 3.2, you use COMMAND /C (discussed in the next section). With DOS 3.3 and later versions, you use the CALL command.

The syntax of the CALL command is as follows:

CALL *d:path***filename** *parameters*

d:path is the optional disk drive and path name of the batch file you want to execute. *filename* is the root name of the batch file. When you type the CALL command, you can specify any parameters you want to pass to the batch file you are calling. You can place the CALL command anywhere in the first batch file.

When DOS executes a CALL command, it shifts execution temporarily to the called batch file. As soon as the called batch file stops, DOS returns to the first batch file and continues execution with the line immediately after the CALL command.

The following three batch files demonstrate how CALL works:

BATCH1.BAT

```
@ECHO OFF
CLS
REM This file does the setup work for demonstrating
REM the CALL command or COMMAND /C.
ECHO This is the STARTUP batch file
ECHO The command parameters are %%0-%0 %%1-%1
CALL batch2 second
ECHO MEM from %0
MEM
ECHO Done!
```

BATCH2.BAT

```
ECHO This is the SECOND batch file
ECHO The command parameters are %%0-%0 %%1-%1
CALL batch3 third
ECHO MEM from %0
MEM
```

BATCH3.BAT

```
ECHO This is the THIRD batch file
ECHO The command parameters are %%0-%0 %%1-%1
ECHO MEM from %0
MEM
```

The first line of BATCH1.BAT sets ECHO OFF. The second line clears the screen. The next two lines in BATCH1 are remarks intended only to document the purpose of the batch file.

The two ECHO lines are similar for all three batch files. The first of the two lines identifies the batch file being used. The second ECHO line shows the 0 parameter (the name by which the batch file was invoked) and the first parameter (the first argument) for the batch file. Notice that to display the strings %0 and %1, you must use two percent signs (%%0 and %%1). If you use a single percent sign, DOS interprets the string as a replaceable parameter and does not display the actual symbol %.

Each CALL statement in the first and second batch files invokes another batch file. BATCH1.BAT calls BATCH2.BAT, and BATCH2.BAT in turn calls BATCH3.BAT. In each case, a single argument passes to the batch file being called: *second* to BATCH2.BAT and *third* to BATCH3.BAT. Each batch file then displays its name (by using the %0 variable) and runs MEM. When DOS encounters the end of each called batch file, DOS returns to the calling batch file.

Note: MEM is new in DOS 5.0. Use CHKDSK instead of MEM if you are using an earlier version of DOS.

After you type the batch files explained in the preceding paragraphs, make sure that your printer is ready. (The power is on, paper and ribbon loaded, and so on.) Press Ctrl-PrtSc to activate the printer, and then type **BATCH1 FIRST**.

When the printer is finished, turn off the printer's capability to print echoed lines by pressing Ctrl-PrtSc again (you don't need to turn off the printer's power). If you do not have a printer to record the information displayed on-screen, press Ctrl-S to pause the screen as needed. When you have viewed the screen, press any key to "unpause" the screen display.

Check the printout or the screen display for the largest executable program size provided by the MEM command (in other words, the largest block of memory available for use by an executable program). This number grows larger after each batch file is executed and removed from memory. The following is output from a PS/2 computer when BATCH1 FIRST is typed:

```
This is the STARTUP batch file
The command line parameters are %0-BATCH1 %1-FIRST
This is the SECOND batch file
The command line parameters are %0-batch2 %1-second
This is the THIRD batch file
The command line parameters are %0-batch3 %1-third
MEM from batch3
```

```
     655360 bytes total conventional memory
     655360 bytes available to MS-DOS
     442640 largest executable program size

    3145728 bytes total contiguous extended memory
          0 bytes available contiguous extended memory
    2632704 bytes available XMS memory
            MS-DOS resident in High Memory Area
MEM from batch2

     655360 bytes total conventional memory
     655360 bytes available to MS-DOS
     442720 largest executable program size

    3145728 bytes total contiguous extended memory
          0 bytes available contiguous extended memory
    2632704 bytes available XMS memory
            MS-DOS resident in High Memory Area
MEM from batch2

     655360 bytes total conventional memory
     655360 bytes available to MS-DOS
     442800 largest executable program size

    3145728 bytes total contiguous extended memory
          0 bytes available contiguous extended memory
    2632704 bytes available XMS memory
            MS-DOS resident in High Memory Area
Done!
```

Each time you use the CALL command, DOS temporarily uses 80 bytes of RAM until the called batch file finishes running. Because DOS uses that much memory for each nested CALL command, you may run out of memory. (A *nested* CALL command is a CALL command from a called batch file.) Not many people nest CALL commands very deeply in batch files. The accumulated memory-usage problem does not occur when a single batch file calls multiple other batch files. In that case, you can use the CALL command as many times as desired and use only the same 80 bytes of RAM for each call.

You can use batch files like the ones described in this section with all versions of DOS by making three changes. First, delete the @ character in the first line of BATCH1.BAT. The @ feature is not available with versions of DOS earlier than 3.3. Second, change the CALL commands to COMMAND /C. The CALL command was also introduced in DOS 3.3. Finally, for DOS versions prior to DOS 5, substitute CHKDSK for MEM.

Calling a Batch File with COMMAND /C

If you use a version of DOS earlier than 3.3, you cannot use the CALL command, but you can use COMMAND.COM, the command interpreter, to call other batch files. The syntax of COMMAND, when used in a batch file to call another batch file, is as follows:

COMMAND /C *d:path***filename** *parameters*

The main difference between the syntaxes of CALL and COMMAND is that you must use the /C switch. As with the CALL command, *d:path* is the optional disk drive and path name of the batch file you want to execute, and *filename* is the name of the batch file. Similarly, you also can specify any parameters you want to pass to the batch file you are calling. You can place the COMMAND /C command anywhere in the first batch file.

When COMMAND.COM executes the called batch file, two copies of COMMAND.COM are in memory. When the called batch file is finished executing, the second copy of COMMAND.COM is removed from memory, and the original copy regains control.

If you use COMMAND /C in the example batch files, the results are almost identical to the results when CALL is used. Each copy of COMMAND.COM, however, uses more memory than the CALL command. The amount of memory used by COMMAND.COM varies among versions of DOS, particularly DOS 5.0, which uses approximately 1K less memory than COMMAND.COM of previous versions.

Another difference between CALL and COMMAND /C is worth noting. Because COMMAND loads a new version of COMMAND.COM, any changes you make to the environment while the second batch file is being processed are lost when you return to the calling batch file. If you use CALL, however, environment changes made during execution of the called batch file are "permanent" during the current DOS session or until they are changed again by some other command. These changes are available to the calling batch file as well as to subsequent programs run by the same command processor.

To better understand this process, consider the following example. Because these batch files use both the CALL command and COMMAND /C, you must use DOS 3.3 or a later version to test them:

TEST1.BAT

```
@ECHO OFF
SET VAR1=ONE
SET VAR2=
SET VAR3=
ECHO The environment before calling TEST2.BAT:
SET
PAUSE
COMMAND /C TEST2
ECHO The environment after returning from TEST2.BAT:
SET
PAUSE
CALL TEST3
ECHO The environment after returning from TEST3.BAT:
SET
```

TEST2.BAT

```
@ECHO OFF
SET VAR2=TWO
ECHO The environment while TEST2.BAT is executing:
SET
PAUSE
```

TEST3.BAT

```
SET VAR3=THREE
ECHO The environment while TEST3.BAT is executing:
SET
PAUSE
```

To run these batch files, type **TEST1**, and press Enter. A message similar to the following appears on your screen:

```
The environment before calling TEST2.BAT:
COMSPEC=C:\DOS\COMMAND.COM
PROMPT=$P$G
PATH=C:\;C:\DOS
TEMP=C:\DOS
VAR1=ONE
Press any key to continue . . .
```

This message indicates the DOS environment before calling TEST2.BAT. Notice that the environment variable VAR1 is set to the value ONE. Press any key, and nearly the same message appears, but with the following line added:

```
VAR2=TWO
```

TEST1.BAT called TEST2.BAT by using the COMMAND /C method. While TEST2.BAT is executing, a second copy of COMMAND.COM is loaded into memory. TEST2.BAT creates the environment variable VAR2 and gives it the value TWO. Press any key to display a third message:

```
The environment after returning from TEST2.BAT:
COMSPEC=C:\DOS\COMMAND.COM
PROMPT=$P$G
PATH=C:\;C:\DOS
TEMP=C:\DOS
VAR1=ONE
Press any key to continue . . .
```

After returning from TEST2.BAT, the second copy of COMMAND.COM is no longer in memory, and the environment variable VAR2 has disappeared. Press any key to display a fourth message:

```
The environment while TEST3.BAT is executing:
COMSPEC=C:\DOS\COMMAND.COM
PROMPT=$P$G
PATH=C:\;C:\DOS
TEMP=C:\DOS
VAR1=ONE
VAR3=THREE
Press any key to continue . . .
```

Notice that the new environment variable VAR3 has a value of THREE. Again, press any key. The final message appears:

```
The environment after returning from TEST3.BAT
COMSPEC=C:\DOS\COMMAND.COM
PROMPT=$P$G
PATH=C:\;C:\DOS
TEMP=C:\DOS
VAR1=ONE
VAR3=THREE
Press any key to continue . . .
```

Because TEST3.BAT was called using the CALL command, the environment is still intact on return to TEST1.BAT. The environment variable VAR3 still exists.

Using DOSKey

A welcome new feature of DOS 5.0 is the keyboard utility program DOSKey. DOSKey is a memory-resident program that enables you to edit and reuse DOS commands without having to retype them. The program also enables you to create new commands, referred to as *macros*, that can take the place of several DOS commands. The following sections explain how to load DOSKey into your computer's memory and how to use the program's capabilities.

Loading DOSKey

DOSKey is a memory-resident (terminate-and-stay resident, or TSR) program, first available in DOS 5.0. This program enables you to edit easily commands on the DOS command line. DOSKey also stores in a buffer in memory a running history of the commands you issue at the command. DOSKey then enables you to reuse commands without having to retype them.

Before you can use DOSKey's features, you must load the program into memory. To load DOSKey from the command line, type the following command and press Enter:

DOSKEY

The following message appears on the screen:

```
DOSKey installed.
```

After you see this message, all DOSKey's features are available; yet DOSKey occupies only about 4K of memory.

The most convenient way to load DOSKey is in AUTOEXEC.BAT. Simply include the command DOSKEY somewhere in your AUTOEXEC.BAT, and DOSKey loads each time you turn on your computer.

> **Tip:** Refer to Chapter 15 for instructions on loading DOSKey into Upper Memory Blocks (UMBs). This technique makes DOSKey available without using any conventional (below 640K) memory but is available only on 80386 (DX or SX) or 80486 systems.

As is true with most DOS commands, DOSKey has several available switches. The full syntax of the command to install DOSKey is as follows:

DOSKEY */REINSTALL/BUFSIZE=size/MACROS/HISTORY/INSERT*

/OVERSTRIKE

The */REINSTALL* switch installs another copy of DOSKey and clears the command-history buffer. This command does not, however, remove existing copies of DOSKey already in memory.

/BUFSIZE sets the size of the command buffer. The *size* parameter represents the number of bytes the buffer occupies in memory. The default size is 512 bytes; the minimum size is 256 bytes.

/MACROS displays a list of all the currently defined DOSKey macros.

/HISTORY displays the contents of the command-history buffer.

/INSERT causes new text to be inserted into the existing text at the cursor. This switch cannot be used with */OVERSTRIKE*.

/OVERSTRIKE, the default condition, causes new text to replace existing text at the cursor. Do not use this switch with the */INSERT* switch.

As with all DOS 5.0 commands, you can display a listing of available switches by typing either of the following commands and pressing Enter:

DOSKEY /?

HELP DOSKEY

Editing the Command Line

A primary purpose of DOSKey is to facilitate editing of DOS commands. If you are a typical PC user, you find yourself issuing the same or similar commands frequently, and you don't always type each command correctly the first time you enter it. DOSKey can save you typing by enabling you to edit commands without having to type them from scratch every time you notice an error.

Suppose, for example, that you want to see a directory listing of all files with the WQ1 extension in the \SPREADSH\QPRO2DAT directory on the C drive. In your haste, however, you type the DIR command as follows:

DIT C:\SPREADSH\QPRO2DAT*.WQ1

Before you press Enter, you realize you have mistyped the DIR command, but you don't want to start over. With DOSKey loaded, you can use the following procedure to correct the mistake:

1. Press the Home key to move the cursor to the left end of the command line.

2. Use the right-arrow key to move the cursor to the *T* in the word *DIT*.

3. Type **R** to correct the error.

4. Press Enter.

DOS displays the directory listing as you requested.

Even before you load DOSKey, DOS provides some command-line editing capability. Table 13.4 lists the normal DOS command-line editing keys, which are available whether or not you make DOSKey memory resident. DOSKey's command-line editing keys, listed in table 13.5, supplement the normal DOS keys.

Table 13.4
DOS Command-Line Editing Keys

Key	Action
\ ←	Moves the cursor to the next tab stop
→\	
Esc	Cancels the current line and does not change the buffer
Ins	Enables you to insert characters into the line
Del	Deletes a character from the line
F1 or →	Copies one character from the preceding command line
F2	Copies all characters from the preceding command line up to but not including the next character you type
F3	Copies all remaining characters from the preceding command line
F4	Deletes all characters from the preceding command line up to but not including the next character typed (opposite of F2)
F5	Moves the current line into the buffer but does not allow DOS to execute the line
F6	Produces an end-of-file marker ($^\wedge$Z) when you copy from the console to a disk file

Table 13.5
DOSKey Command-Line Editing Keys

Key	Action
←	Moves the cursor one character to the left
→	Moves the cursor one character to the right
Backspace	Moves the cursor one character to the left; in insert mode, also erases character to the left
Ctrl-←	Moves the cursor one word to the left
Ctrl-→	Moves the cursor one word to the right
Ins	Toggles between replace mode (the default) and insert mode
Home	Moves the cursor to the left end of the command line
End	Moves the cursor to the space after the last character in the command line
Esc	Erases the contents of the command line

Reusing Commands

In addition to enhancing DOS's command-line editing capabilities, DOSKey adds a capacity not previously found in DOS. DOSKey enables you to redisplay a command you have issued earlier during the current DOS session. You then can execute the command without changing it, or you can use the DOS and DOSKey editing keys to make modifications before executing the command.

After you load DOSKey into memory, the program maintains in memory a buffer that contains a history of DOS commands issued at the command prompt during the current DOS session. DOSKey enables you to reuse the commands in this command-history buffer.

For example, assume that earlier during the current DOS session you issued the following COPY command:

COPY C:\DATABASE\FOXPRO\MAIL.DBF C:\WORD_PRO\WP

Now you want to issue the following similar command without retyping the entire command:

COPY C:\DATABASE\DBASE\MAIL.DBF C:\WORD_PRO\WP

Use the following procedure:

1. Press the up-arrow key repeatedly until the original COPY command displays in the command line.

2. Use the DOS and DOSKey editing keys to change the command.

3. Press Enter.

In addition to the up-arrow key, DOSKey provides the keys listed in table 13.6 for use in retrieving commands from the command-history buffer.

Table 13.6
DOSKey Command Buffer History Keys

Key	Action
↑	Displays the preceding DOS command
↓	Displays the DOS command issued after the one currently displayed, or displays a blank line when you are already at the end of the list
PgUp	Displays the earliest command issued that is still stored in the DOSKey command buffer
PgDn	Displays the last command stored in the DOSKey command buffer
F7	Displays the contents of the command-history buffer in a numbered list
Alt-F7	Clears the command-history buffer
F8	Searches for the command that most closely matches characters typed at the command line
F9	Prompts for a line number, where line number refers to the number displayed next to a command in the command-history listing generated by pressing F7. Press the number to display the corresponding command.

To view the entire list of commands currently stored in the command-history buffer, press F7. DOSKey lists all commands contained in the buffer, one on each line, with a number at the left end of each line. The oldest command—the command issued earliest in this DOS session—is number 1. Successive commands are listed in the order you issued them.

DOSKey provides another way to see the entire list of commands in the command-history buffer. Type the following command, and press Enter:

DOSKEY /HISTORY

DOSKey provides the same list of commands as the F7 command, without line numbers.

TIP

> *Tip:* To create a batch file that contains all commands in the current command-history buffer, use the following command syntax:
>
> **DOSKEY /HISTORY > filename.BAT**
>
> Substitute for *filename* the name you want to give the batch file. After you issue this command, the new batch file contains all the commands from the command-history buffer, including the command that created the batch file itself. Use the DOS Editor, Edlin, or some other editor to delete the last command and any other commands you don't want included in the batch file.

You can use the up-arrow key to display previously issued commands. Each time you press the up arrow, DOSKey displays the preceding command. After you have displayed one or more previous commands by using the up arrow, you can use the down arrow to move back down through the commands to the most recent command. Sometimes, however, selecting from the command-history list generated by pressing F7 may be easier. Press F9; DOSKey displays the message:

```
Line number:
```

Type the number that corresponds to the desired command in the list of commands generated by pressing F7. DOSKey displays the selected command in the command line for you to edit or execute.

When you want to move quickly to the first command in the buffer, press PgUp. To go to the last command in the buffer, press PgDn.

If you want to clear the command-history buffer, press Alt-F7. DOSKey abandons the contents of the command-history buffer.

DOSKey also can help you locate a command quickly. Type the first several characters of the command you need to find, and press F8. Suppose that you want to locate the following command:

COPY C:\DATABASE\FOXPRO\MAIL.DBF C:\WORD_PRO\WP

Type **COPY** and press F8. Each time you press F8, DOSKey shows you the next command that contains the COPY command. When the desired command is displayed, you easily can edit and reuse the command with a minimum of typing.

Creating and Using Macros

In addition to providing command-line editing capabilities and the command-history buffer, DOSKey also enables you to create your own DOS commands, referred to as *macros*. A DOSKey macro is similar to a batch file but is contained in memory rather than on disk. Each macro can contain one or more DOS commands, up to a maximum of 127 characters.

DOSKey macros are similar to batch files in the following ways:

- Macros can contain multiple DOS commands.

- Macros are invoked by typing a name at the DOS prompt.

- Macros can use replaceable parameters.

Macros differ from batch files in the following ways:

- Macros are stored in memory (RAM); batch files are stored on disk.

- Macros are limited to 127 characters; batch files have unlimited maximum length.

- Ctrl-C or Ctrl-Break stops a single command in a DOSKey macro; Ctrl-C or Ctrl-Break stops an entire batch file.

- The GOTO command is not available in macros.

- One macro cannot call another macro, and you cannot call a macro from within a batch file.

- Macros can define environment variables but cannot use them.

The sections that follow explain how to create and run DOSKey macros.

Creating Macros

DOSKey enables you to create macros at the command line or through a batch file. The syntax for creating a macro is as follows:

DOSKEY macroname=*command(s)*

The *macroname* parameter is the name you want to give the macro. Use any keyboard characters in the name, except < > | or =. Do not include a space in the macro name. Use an underscore instead if you want the macro name to have the appearance of two words.

The *command* parameter can include any number of DOS commands, subject to the following rules:

- The entire command cannot exceed 127 characters (the DOS command-line limit).

- Each pair of commands must be separated by the characters *$t*.

- Instead of using the redirection/piping operators < > or |, use *$l*, *$g*, or *$b*, respectively.

- The ECHO OFF command is not effective in macros. Commands always display.

When you want to use replaceable parameters in a macro, use the codes $1 through $9 rather than %1 through %9. For example, you can create a macro that duplicates the effect of the C&E.BAT batch file, discussed several times in this chapter. Type the following at the command line and press Enter:

DOSKEY MOVE=COPY $1 $2 /V $T ERASE $1

DOSKey has a special type of replaceable parameter not found in batch files. The characters *$** represent not just one parameter, but all the characters you type in the command line to the right of the macro name. This type of replaceable parameter is useful when you don't know ahead of time how many parameters or switches you may type when you execute the macro.

For example, suppose that you want to create a macro to help you format floppy disks in drive A, a 3 1/2-inch high-density drive. You want to be able to type **FA 720** to format a 720K disk and **FA 1.44** to format a 1.44M disk. Occasionally, however, you may want to use one or more of FORMAT's switches, such as the /S switch to create a system disk, the /Q Quick Format switch, or the /U unconditional format switch. To create the FA macro, type the following command:

DOSKEY FA=FORMAT A: /F:$*

To confirm that DOSKey has stored the macros you have defined, type the following command, and press Enter:

DOSKEY /MACROS

DOSKey lists all macros currently stored in the DOSKey macro buffer. Assuming that you have defined the MOVE and FA macros, the preceding command should display the following lines:

```
MOVE=COPY $1 $2 /V $T ERASE $1
FA=FORMAT A: /F:$*
```

TIP

Tip: You easily can save a copy of the entire contents of the macro buffer by using redirection. To create a file named MACROS.BAT containing all the current macros, type the following command and press Enter:

DOSKEY /MACROS > MACROS.BAT

If you want to use this batch file later to recreate the macros during a future session, edit the file, and add DOSKEY to the beginning of each line.

Because DOSKey macros reside in memory rather than on disk, all macros are erased when you turn off or reboot the computer. One disadvantage of DOSKey macros is that you need to reenter commonly used macros each time you turn on your computer. This drawback is easily overcome, however, by using AUTOEXEC.BAT to define the macros you use most often. For example, to make the MOVE and FA macros routinely available, include the following commands in AUTOEXEC.BAT:

```
DOSKEY MOVE=COPY $1 $2 /V $T ERASE $1
DOSKEY FA=FORMAT A: /F:$*
```

Every time you turn on or reboot your computer, the preceding commands create the MOVE and FA macros in the DOSKey macro buffer.

TIP

Tip: The first DOSKEY command in AUTOEXEC.BAT loads the program as memory resident even if the command also is defining a macro.

Running Macros

Using a DOSKey macro is as easy as using any DOS command. Just type the macro name at the command line, and press Enter. If the macro has any replaceable parameters, include appropriate values on the command line.

Suppose that you want to use the new MOVE macro to move all WK3 files from your C:\LOTUS directory to your C:\LDATA directory. Type the following at the command line, and press Enter:

MOVE C:\LOTUS*.WK3 C:\LDATA

DOS executes the COPY and ERASE commands and displays the command output.

Perhaps you want to use the FA macro created in the preceding section to format a 1.44M disk. You want to use Quick Format, make this disk bootable, and assign the volume label BOOT_DISK. Type the following command at the DOS prompt, and press Enter:

FA 1.44 /Q /S /V:BOOT_DISK

DOS first displays the command:

```
FORMAT A: /F:1.44 /Q /S /V:BOOT_DISK
```

Then DOS prompts as follows:

```
Insert new diskette for drive A:
and press ENTER when ready...
```

Press Enter to proceed with the formatting operation. DOS displays messages indicating the progress and successful completion of the procedure. Finally, DOS asks:

```
QuickFormat another (Y/N)?
```

Respond Y if you want to format another disk using the same switch settings, or press N to return to the DOS prompt.

Summary

Batch files and macros can make your computer do the hard work for you. They can replace repetitive typing with commands that execute automatically. As you work with batch files and macros, remember the following key points:

- You must give batch files the BAT extension.

- You invoke batch files by typing the name of the batch file (without the extension) and pressing Enter. You can specify an optional disk drive name and path name before the batch file name.

- You can use any command you can type at the DOS prompt in a batch file.

- AUTOEXEC.BAT is a special batch file that DOS calls when booting.

- Each word (or set of characters) in a command separated by a delimiter is a parameter. When you use a batch file, DOS substitutes the appropriate parameters for the variable markers (%0 through %9) in the file.

- You can use the ECHO command to turn on or off the display of DOS commands being executed by the batch file.

- The PAUSE command causes the batch file to suspend execution and then displays a message on-screen.

- Use the REM command to leave comments and reminders in your batch file; the comments do not display (when ECHO is off).

- Use the CLS command to clear the screen completely.

- You can use the GOTO command to create a loop in the batch file.

- IF tests for a given condition.

- FOR..IN..DO can repeat a batch-file command for one or more files or commands.

- SHIFT shifts command parameters to the left.

- The @ character suppresses the display of a single line from a batch file.

- COMMAND /C and CALL invoke a second batch file and then return control of the computer to the first batch file.

- DOSKey enables you to redisplay a command that you have issued earlier during the current DOS session.

- DOSKey macros are stored in memory (RAM).

- Macros can contain multiple DOS commands but are limited to 127 characters.

- The GOTO command is not available in macros.

In the next two chapters, you learn about configuring your computer system. Chapter 14 describes how to configure the DOS Shell, and Chapter 15 explains how to take full advantage of your computer's memory and peripheral devices.

Configuring the DOS Shell

14

This chapter shows you how to fine-tune DOS 5.0's DOS Shell to best meet your requirements. The discussions here follow up on topics introduced in Chapter 4, "Using the DOS Shell."

In Chapter 4, you learned how to switch among dual file lists, a single file list, and the program list, and how to change the Shell screen mode. This chapter teaches you how to change screen colors in the Shell.

Chapter 4 also teaches you how to use the program list area to start an applications program. Now that you are more familiar with the Shell and with DOS in general, you are ready to learn how to customize the program list. This chapter explains how to build a menu system by adding program groups and program items to the program list area of the DOS Shell window, as well as how to tailor these elements to your exact specifications.

Key Terms Used in This Chapter

Color scheme
A collection of color settings that are applied as a group to the DOS Shell

Program group
A collection of program items and other program groups, displayed as a group in the program list area of the DOS Shell window

Program item
An option, listed in the DOS Shell program list area, that enables you to start a particular applications program or DOS utility program

Setting Screen Colors

When you start the DOS Shell for the first time, the program sets screen colors according to its default settings. If you are happy with the default color scheme, you can skip this section of the chapter.

In an effort to make color selection quick and easy, the designers of the DOS Shell provided eight predefined color schemes. Each color scheme sets the colors the Shell uses to display the various components in the DOS Shell window—background color, text color, menu color, and so on. Instead of requiring you to set the color for each component separately, you simply choose one of the ready-made color schemes.

To choose a different color scheme for the Shell, do the following:

1. Display the DOS Shell window, and select <u>O</u>ptions from the menu bar to display the Options menu.

2. Choose C<u>o</u>lors from the Options menu.

The Shell displays the Color Scheme dialog box shown in figure 14.1. This dialog box contains a list box and three command buttons. The title bar of the list box indicates the name of the current color scheme. For example, the list box in figure 14.1 indicates that the current color scheme is named Ocean.

3. To choose a different color scheme, use the mouse and scroll bar to display and select your new choice, or use the cursor-movement keys to move the selection cursor to the new color scheme name. Click OK, or press Enter.

After you select a new color scheme, the Shell returns to the DOS Shell window, repainting the screen with the new colors.

You may want to experiment with the color schemes without permanently changing the settings. The Shell provides a way for you to preview a color scheme before actually adding it to the DOS Shell configuration. Move the selection cursor to a different color setting in the Color Scheme dialog box, and then select the Preview command button. The Shell changes the screen colors to the new scheme but does not remove the Color Scheme dialog box from the screen. If you like the new colors, choose the OK button to accept the change and return to the Shell window. Otherwise, move the selection cursor to another color scheme and choose Preview, or select the Cancel command button to revert to the original color scheme.

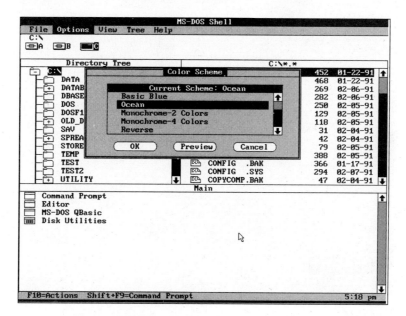

Fig. 14.1. The Color Scheme dialog box.

Note: In addition to the predefined color schemes, you can create custom color schemes by editing the DOS Shell configuration file, DOSSHELL.INI.

Locate the file DOSSHELL.INI in the directory that contains your operating system files (usually C:\DOS). Load DOSSHELL.INI into the DOS Editor (discussed in Chapter 12) or into another text editor that can handle lines more than 256 characters in length without truncating or splitting the lines.

Without making any changes to the file, scroll through DOSSHELL.INI until you see the following lines:

```
color=
{
        selection =
```

These lines mark the beginning of the color scheme section of DOSSHELL.INI. Use your text editor's block copy feature to make a duplicate of the lines, beginning with selection and ending with the right brace (}) that appears in the line above the second occurrence of selection. Use the editor to change the name in the color = line to the name you want to give the new color scheme. Finally, use the editor to change the color settings within the copied lines. For example, if you want the menu bar to have a cyan background color, edit the menubar line in the background = section so that it reads as follows:

```
menubar = cyan
```

Working with Program Groups

The program list area of the DOS Shell window provides a convenient method for running the programs stored on your computer. The Shell enables you to create any number of menus, referred to as *program groups*, on which you can list all the programs stored on your computer.

When you start the Shell for the first time, the program list area of the Shell window displays the Main program group. This program group consists of three program items and one program group, as shown in figure 14.2.

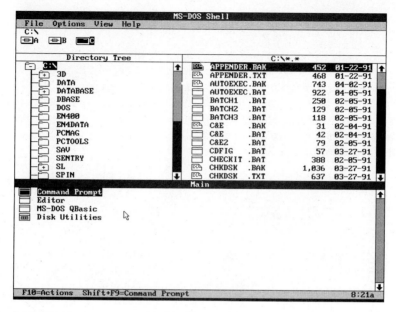

Fig. 14.2. The Main program group.

By default, the Main program group includes the following program items:

Command Prompt

Editor

MS-DOS QBasic

The Main group also includes the Disk Utilities program group, which in turn consists of six external DOS commands, used primarily for disk management: DISKCOPY, BACKUP, RESTORE, QUICK FORMAT, FORMAT, and UNDELETE.

By creating your own program groups within the Main group, you easily can organize your computer programs according to your personal work habits. You might, for instance, divide your programs according to software type, creating a word processing group, a database group, a spreadsheet group, and a graphics group. Or you might decide to split programs into groups according to subject matter, establishing a Business Productivity group, a Personal Management group, and a Rest and Relaxation group.

Adding a Program Group

To add a new program group, make the program list area the active area of the DOS Shell window, and display the program group to which the new group is to be added. For example, if you want to add a new program group to the Main program group, press Esc until the title area of the program list area displays the title *Main*. When you want to add a program group to another program group, use the mouse or cursor-movement keys to select this "parent" group in the program list area.

When the program group you want is displayed, complete the following steps:

1. Select File from the menu bar to display the File menu, and choose New.

   The Shell displays the New Program Object dialog box shown in figure 14.3. The New Program Object dialog box contains two option buttons: Program Group and Program Item.

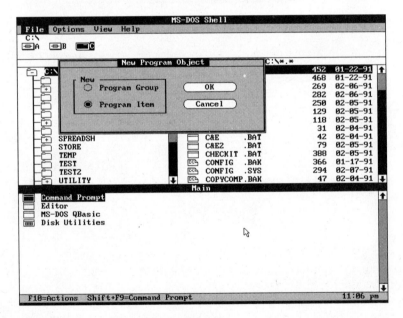

Fig. 14.3. The New Program Object dialog box.

2. Select the Program Group option button in the New Program Object dialog box, and press Enter or click the OK command button.

The Add Group dialog box appears, as shown in figure 14.4.
This dialog box contains three text boxes: Title, Help Text, and
Password. You must type an entry in the Title text box, but entries
in the Help Text and Password text boxes are optional.

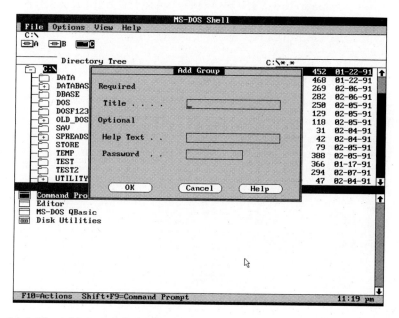

Fig. 14.4. The Add Group dialog box.

3. Type a program group title consisting of up to 23 characters,
    including spaces, in the Title text box.

    The program group title is the name, or menu option, that appears
    in the program list area when the parent program group is dis-
    played. If you are creating a program group for your database
    applications, for example, you might type **Database Applications**
    in the Title text box. The title not only appears in the program list
    area, but when a program group is activated, its title appears in the
    program list area title bar also.

4. Type a help message, if you choose, in the Help Text text box. The
    message can be up to 255 characters in length, even though only
    20 characters can be viewed at once in the text box. The text in the
    text box scrolls to the left as you type past the 20th character.

    For the Database Applications group, for example, you might type
    the following help message:

    Displays list of database applications.

Afterward, when someone using the program list presses F1 while the Database Applications item is highlighted, the help message displays. The Shell displays help messages in the Shell Help dialog box and formats the help message to fit in the dialog box. If you want a line to break at a particular point, insert the characters ^m (or ^M). Any following text starts on the next line when the help message is displayed in the Help dialog box.

5. Type a password, if you choose, in the Password text box, up to 20 characters in length, including spaces.

> **Warning:** Using a password to limit access to a DOS Shell program group provides only minimal security. Any user with access to your computer easily can bypass the Shell and start programs from the DOS command line.

6. Press Enter, or select the OK command button.

The Shell adds the new program group item to the selected program group. Now, if you select the new program group item, the Shell opens an empty file list area so that you can add program items.

TIP

> **Tip:** The Shell enables you to build links to the built-in DOS Shell help messages from your custom help messages. These links provide more ways for users to get help when they are confused or want to do something new. When you are typing a help message in the Add Group dialog box, enclose in double quotation marks a word or words you want displayed as a link to another help message. Type the help message reference number, enclosed in tildes (~), just to the right of the link word(s). You can determine the help message reference number by displaying or printing the DOS Shell help file, DOSSHELL.HLP. For example, to include a link that displays a help screen discussing the program list, include the following text in the Help Text text box of the Add Group dialog box:
>
> ^m^mRelated Topic^m   "The Program List"~S120~
>
> When the user presses F1 while the program list selection cursor is resting on Database Applications, the Shell displays a help message similar to the one shown in figure 14.5. The user can then click The Program List to display the help message shown in figure 14.6.

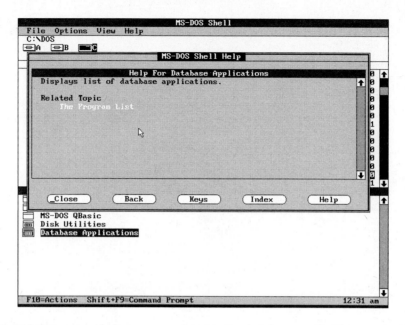

Fig. 14.5. *A custom help message related to the database applications program item in the program list area.*

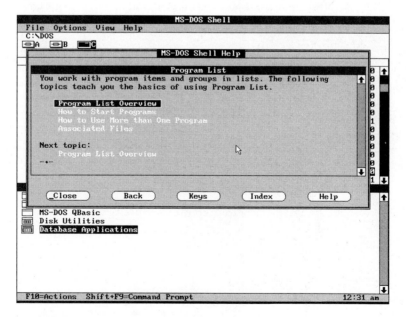

Fig. 14.6. *The built-in Program List help message.*

Modifying Program Group Properties

After you have created a program group, you can change the parameters used to define it—its *properties*—through the Shell File menu. Use the following procedures:

1. Select the program list area. If the group that contains the properties you want to change is not included in the Main group, select the program group that includes the target group.

2. Use the mouse or cursor-movement keys to move the selection bar to the name of the program group that contains the properties you want to modify.

3. Select File from the menu bar, and choose Properties from the File menu.

   The Shell displays the Program Group Properties dialog box. This dialog box is essentially a copy of the Add Group dialog box shown in figure 14.4, except that the title, help message, and password for the selected group are already in the text boxes.

4. Make any desired changes to the title, help message, and password, and press Enter or select the OK command button. Select Cancel to return to the Shell window without changing any of the program group's properties.

Deleting a Program Group

Through the File menu, you also can remove a program group. Before deleting a program group, make sure that all items in the group are deleted (see "Deleting a Program Item" later in this chapter). Use the following steps to delete a program group:

1. Move the selection cursor to the name of the group to be deleted.

2. Press Del, or choose Delete from the File menu.

   The Shell displays the Delete Item dialog box.

3. Select 1. Delete this item. Press Enter, or choose the OK command button.

The program group is removed from the selected program group list.

> **Note:** If you attempt to delete a program group before it is empty, the Shell displays an error message box.

Changing the Order of a Group's Listings

Placing your most frequently used groups near the top of the group listing is convenient; then you can find these groups more quickly. You can place groups in any order you want. To move a group from one place to another in the menu list, follow these steps:

1. Move the selection bar to the group to be moved.

2. Display the File menu, and choose Reorder.

    The Shell displays the following message in the status line:

    ```
    Select location to move to, then press ENTER. ESC to
    cancel.
    ```

3. Use the cursor-movement keys to move the selection bar to the desired new location for the selected group, and press Enter.

The Shell moves the group to the new position. You can repeat these steps as often as necessary to produce the order you want for your groups.

Working with Program Items

After you have created program groups, the next step in building your menu system is to add program items. The following sections describe how to add new program items, as well as how to modify, copy, and delete program items in the program group. To reorder program items, follow the procedure described in the preceding section.

Adding a Program Item

Adding a program item is similar to adding a program group. When you want to add a new program item to a particular group, make the program list area the active area of the DOS Shell window, and display the program group to which the new program item is to be added. For example, if you want to add a new program item to the Database Applications program group, press Esc until the title area of the program list displays the title *Main*. Then use the mouse or cursor-movement keys to choose Database Applications.

After the program group is selected, complete the following steps:

1. Select File from the menu bar to display the File menu, and choose New.

   The Shell displays the New Program Object dialog box (again see fig. 14.3).

2. Select the Program Item option button in the New Program Object dialog box. Press Enter, or click the OK command button.

   The Add Program dialog box appears, as shown in figure 14.7. This dialog box contains five text boxes: Program Title, Commands, Startup Directory, Application Shortcut Key, and Password. You must type an entry in the Program Title and Commands text boxes, but entries in the Startup Directory, Application Shortcut Key, and Password text boxes are optional. All entries in the Add Program dialog box are referred to collectively as the program item's properties.

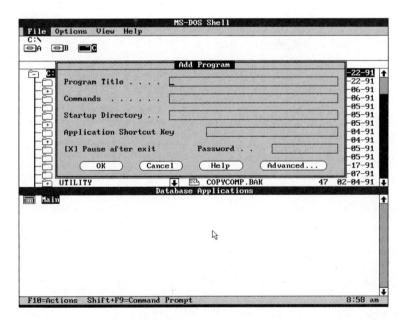

Fig. 14.7. The Add Program dialog box.

3. Type a program item title consisting of up to 23 characters, including spaces, in the Program Title text box.

   The title is the name, or menu option, that you select from the program group when you want to run the program. For example, if you are creating a program item to start the database program Paradox 3.5, you might type **Paradox 3.5** in the Program Title text box.

4. Type the applications program's start-up command in the Commands text box.

   A start-up command can be as simple as the applications program's name. For example, the start-up command for Paradox 3.5 is PARADOX.

   (Refer to the sections that follow for discussion of more complex options available for use in the Commands text box, including the capabilities to issue multiple commands and to use replaceable parameters.)

5. Specify a start-up directory, if you choose, in the optional Startup Directory text box. The start-up directory is the name of the directory that should be current when the Shell issues the specified start-up command.

   For example, if you are specifying a start-up directory for Paradox 3.5, you might type **C:\DATABASE\PDOX35\P35DATA** in the Startup Directory text box. (The program file that is to be started by the start-up command must be located in the start-up directory or listed in the PATH command.)

   If you don't specify a start-up directory, the directory that is currently selected on the logged disk is the start-up directory.

6. Specify a shortcut key for the applications program, if you choose, in the Application Shortcut Key text box. Press and hold Ctrl, Alt, Shift, or any combination of these keys, and then press another key on the keyboard. The Shell displays the keystroke combination in the Application Shortcut Key text box. (For more information about shortcut keys, refer to the Tip at the end of these steps.)

7. Type a password, if you choose, in the Password text box. The password can be up to 20 characters in length, including spaces.

   In addition to the five text boxes, the Add Program dialog box also contains a Pause after Exit check box. When you leave an applications program that you started from the program list area, the

Pause after Exit check box determines whether the screen returns immediately to the DOS Shell window. By default, this check box is selected, and the Shell clears the screen and displays the following message:

```
Press any key to return to MS-DOS Shell.
```

The Shell window reappears on the screen after you press a key.

8. Disable the Pause after Exit check box (remove the X) if you prefer that the Shell window immediately reappear when you leave the applications program.

9. Choose the Advanced command button to add a help message, to specify special memory or video requirements, or to select other advanced options. For more about this option, refer to "Specifying Advanced Program Item Properties" in this chapter.

10. After making all desired entries in the Add Program dialog box, press Enter or select the OK command button to save the settings and return to the DOS Shell Window.

The Shell adds the new program item to the program list area. For example, figure 14.8 lists Paradox 3.5 as a program item in the Database Applications program group.

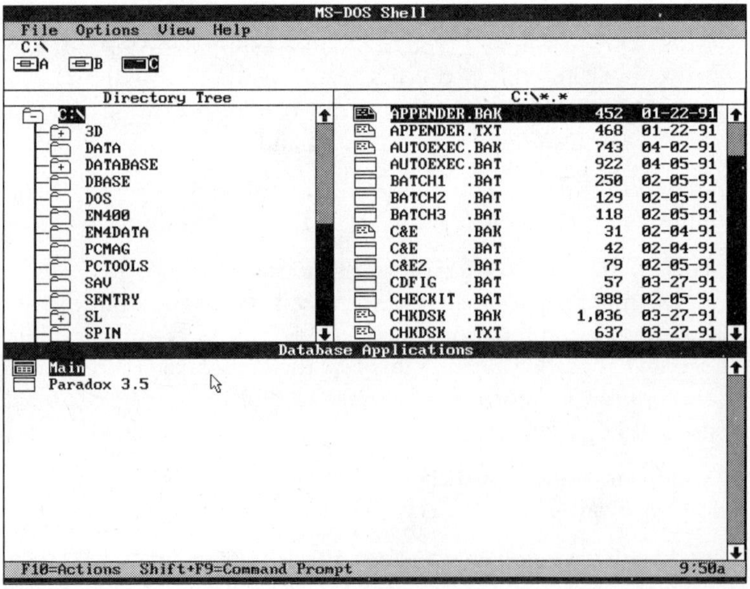

Fig. 14.8. The Database Applications program group after adding Paradox 3.5.

TIP

Tip: You can specify shortcut keys to start applications. When you specify these key combinations, the Shell displays them in the Application Shortcut Key text box. For example, if you press and hold Ctrl and Alt simultaneously and press P, the Shell displays ALT+CTRL+P in the text box.

The specified shortcut key displays the applications program only if all the following three conditions are met:

- The DOS 5.0 task swapper is enabled.

- You have started the applications program through the DOS Shell program list area.

- You have used one of the task swapper keystrokes (Alt-Tab, Alt-Esc, or Ctrl-Esc) to switch to another program or back to the Shell.

For example, suppose that you first enable the DOS Shell task swapper, then you start Paradox 3.5 from the program item in the Database Applications program group, switch back to the Shell by pressing Alt-Tab, and then start Microsoft Word. To return quickly to Paradox 3.5, you simply press the shortcut key you defined: Ctrl-Alt-P. The task swapper quickly swaps Word to disk and displays the Paradox 3.5 screen.

When you return to the DOS Shell window while the applications program is swapped out to disk, the Shell lists the shortcut in parentheses to the right of the program item title in the active task list area.

Using Multiple Start-Up Commands

Often a single command is sufficient to load an applications program, but sometimes you need to perform several operations before, after, or before and after running a program.

The DOS Shell enables you to specify multiple DOS commands in the Commands text box of the Add Program dialog box. Multiple commands in the Commands text box act essentially as a batch file, with all the commands typed on a single line, one after the other. Separate each pair of commands with a semicolon (;) preceded and followed by a space. The total number of characters and spaces in the Commands text box cannot exceed 255.

Consider again the Paradox 3.5 example. Suppose that you want the Shell to issue a PATH command before issuing the PARADOX command so that DOS can find the Paradox 3.5 start-up command. In addition, you want the directory containing the Paradox 3.5 program files to be the first directory listed in the path in order to speed access to Paradox 3.5 program files.

Type the following text into the Commands text box in the Add Program dialog box:

PATH=C:\DATABASE\PDOX35;C:\DOS ; PARADOX

In the command, the first semicolon is a part of the PATH command. The second semicolon, preceded and followed by a space, separates the PATH command from the start-up command.

If you select Paradox 3.5 from the Database Applications program group after entering the preceding commands, the Shell clears the screen and executes the two DOS commands in order.

In addition to including multiple commands in the Commands text box, you also can call batch files from the Commands text box. Use the CALL batch file command. Using the preceding example, you can create a batch file named PDOX35.BAT that contains the following lines:

```
PATH=C:\DATABASE\PDOX35;C:\DOS
PARADOX
```

In the Commands text box, include only the single command CALL PDOX35. The result is the same as placing the two preceding commands in the Commands text box.

> **Note:** A batch file called from the Commands text box must be located either in the directory specified in the Startup Directory text box or in a directory that is in the current PATH statement. Otherwise, DOS may not be capable of finding the batch file, and the program item fails to load the intended software.

TIP

> **Tip:** When you load an applications program through the DOS Shell, DOS loads a copy of COMMAND.COM, the command interpreter. DOS also loads a copy of the DOS environment, which includes the PATH statement (if any was issued). The PATH commands discussed in the preceding examples change the PATH value in the copy of the DOS environment but have no effect on the original environment. After you exit from the applications program, DOS removes the copy of COMMAND.COM from memory and reverts to the original environment, including the original PATH statement.

Providing Information through Replaceable Parameters

Often, you may want to supply certain information to an applications program before loading and running it. You learned in Chapter 13 how to use replaceable parameters in batch files and macros. The DOS Shell provides a similar capability for use in program items. This section describes how to provide additional start-up information through use of replaceable parameters.

Specify replaceable parameters in the Commands text box of the Add Program dialog box the same way you specify them in batch files. Type a percent sign (%) followed by a single numeral (1 through 9). You can have up to nine different replaceable parameters and can use any of the nine replaceable parameters multiple times in the same Commands text box.

For example, if you want Paradox 3.5 to run a specified Paradox Application Language (PAL) script at start-up, add %1 to the commands, making the full entry in the Commands text box as follows:

PATH=C:\DATABASE\PDOX35;C:\DOS ; PARADOX %1

After making any other desired entries in the Add Program dialog box, press Enter, or select the OK command button. The Shell displays a second Add Program dialog box, as shown in figure 14.9. A message at the top of the dialog box prompts you to `Fill in information for %1 prompt dialog.` The information you type in this dialog box defines the dialog box displayed when you execute the program item you are defining.

For example, in this second Add Program dialog box, you can define a custom dialog box that displays each time you start Paradox 3.5 from the DOS Shell program list. The Shell enables you to create a custom dialog box for each replaceable parameter specified in the Commands text box. After adding the replaceable parameter in the preceding example, you can cause the custom dialog box to prompt the user to enter the name of a PAL script for Paradox to run at start-up.

The Add Program dialog box shown in figure 14.9 contains four text boxes: Window Title, Program Information, Prompt Message, and Default Parameters. Making entries to these text boxes is optional.

In the Window Title text box, enter the title you want displayed at the top of the custom dialog box. Using the Paradox example, you enter **Paradox 3.5** in the Window Title text box.

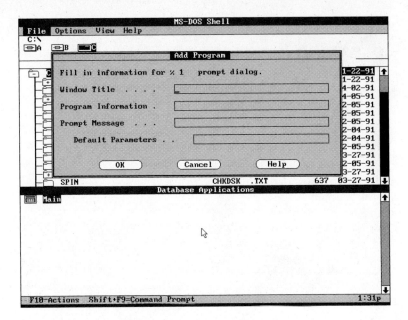

Fig. 14.9. Adding information through a replaceable parameter.

> *Note:* If you don't specify a window title, the Shell displays the first 25 characters from the Commands text box as the window title.

In the Program Information text box, type any general instructions you want to appear at the top of the custom dialog box, just below the title. Your message can have a maximum length of 106 characters. Using the Paradox example, you might type the following instructions:

Type the name of an optional script and press Enter.

If you choose to type a prompt in the Prompt Message text box, this prompt appears to the left of the text box into which the replaceable parameter is typed. You could, for example, type the following prompt in the Prompt Message text box:

PAL script...

In the Default Parameters text box, you can type a value you want the Shell to use when no entry is made in the dialog box that displays when you execute the program. You also can use either of the following two special parameters in the Default Parameters text box to provide a default parameter:

%F   This replaceable parameter automatically is replaced by the file name currently selected in the Shell's file list area.

%L   This parameter automatically reverts the Shell to the preceding entry in the custom dialog box.

Use the %F parameter to cause the Shell to use a selected file as the default entry. Use the %L parameter when you expect constantly to reuse the same parameter value. When you use the %L parameter, the replaceable parameter is given the value you used the last time you selected this item from the program list. For example, use the %F parameter to cause the Paradox 3.5 program item to remember the last script name you entered.

> *Note:* The Shell remembers parameters entered during only the current DOS Shell session.

After you have made all desired entries in the second Add Program dialog box, press Enter or select the OK command button to save the entries and return to the Shell window. The Shell adds the program item to the program group.

When you execute the new program item, the Shell displays the custom dialog box that you defined for the purpose of entering a start-up parameter. Figure 14.10 shows the custom Paradox 3.5 dialog box that displays when you select Paradox 3.5 from the Main program group.

Specifying Advanced Program Item Properties

In addition to the properties described in the preceding sections, the DOS Shell enables you to specify the following properties for a program item:

- A help message
- The amount of conventional memory required by the applications program
- The amount of XMS (Lotus/Intel/Microsoft/AST Extended Memory Specification) memory required
- Video mode—text or graphics—used by the applications program
- Reserved shortcut keys
- Task swapping disabled or enabled

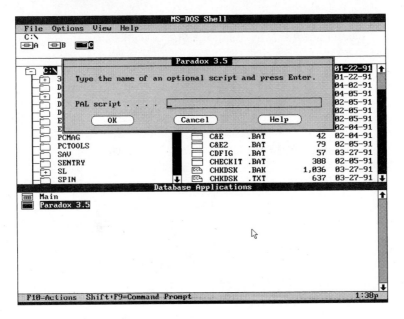

Fig. 14.10. *The custom Paradox 3.5 dialog box.*

When you want to specify any of these properties for a program item, choose the Advanced command button in the Add Program dialog box. The Shell displays the Advanced dialog box, shown in figure 14.11.

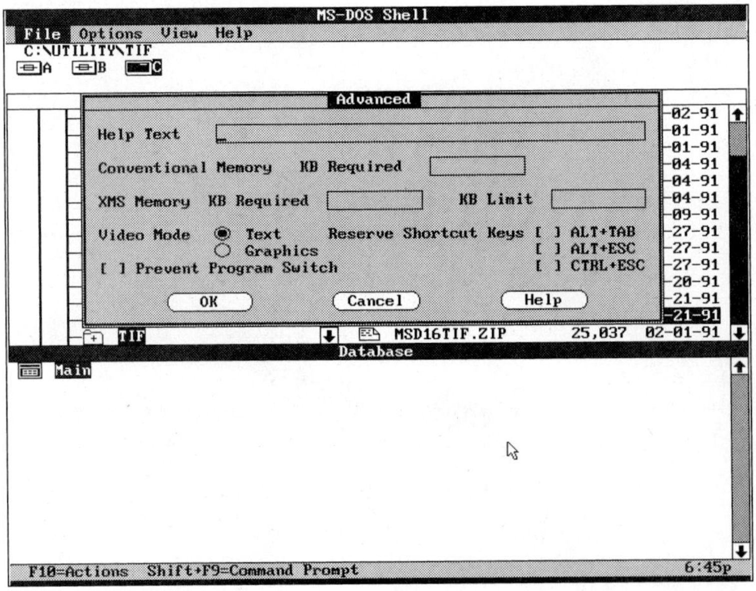

Fig. 14.11. *The Advanced dialog box.*

The Advanced dialog box contains four text boxes: Help Text, Conventional Memory KB Required, XMS Memory KB Required, and XMS Memory KB Limit. The dialog box also contains two Video Mode option buttons, three Reserve Shortcut Keys check boxes, and a Prevent Program Switch check box.

Use the following procedures to specify properties in the Advanced dialog box:

1. Type a help message, if you choose, in the optional Help Text text box. The message can be up to 255 characters in length, but only 20 characters can be viewed at once in the text box. The text in the text box scrolls to the left as you type past the 20th character.

   If you are using the Paradox 3.5 program item, for example, you might type the following help message in the Help Text text box:

   Starts the database program Paradox 3.5. You also can specify a script for Paradox to run at start-up.

   Afterward, pressing F1 while the Paradox 3.5 item is highlighted in the program list area displays the help message. The Shell displays help messages in its standard Shell Help dialog box. The Shell formats the help message to fit within the Help dialog box. If you want a line to break at a particular point, insert the characters ^**m** (or ^**M**). Any additional text starts on the next line when the help message is displayed in the Help dialog box. (See "Adding a Program Group" in this chapter for a tip on linking your custom help message to the built-in DOS Shell help message system.)

2. Enter, if you choose, in the optional Conventional Memory KB Required text box, the minimum number of kilobytes (KB) of conventional memory required to run the applications program. (Refer to the applications program's documentation for this number.)

   The Shell uses this information only when the task swapper is enabled. If insufficient conventional memory (below 640K) is available in memory when you attempt to execute this program item, the Shell does not attempt to run the program at all. This property does not limit the amount of memory DOS makes available to the application; the property simply determines whether sufficient memory is available to run the program before the Shell instructs DOS to do so.

If insufficient memory is available to run the applications program, the Shell displays a message to that effect. This property provides a much cleaner method of handling insufficient memory than merely waiting for the applications program to load, only to have it "bomb out" from lack of memory.

3. Enter, if you choose, in the XMS Memory KB Required text box the minimum amount of Lotus/Intel/Microsoft/AST Extended Memory Specification (XMS) memory (refer to Chapter 15 for more about XMS memory), in kilobytes (KB), required to run the applications program.

   The Shell uses this information only when the task swapper is enabled. If insufficient XMS memory is free when you attempt to execute this program item, the Shell does not attempt to run the program. By default, the Shell does not require any XMS memory to be free before it attempts to run an application.

Warning: Using the XMS Memory KB Required text box can increase significantly the time required to swap between programs. Use this property only if the applications program causes your system to "freeze up" in the event that insufficient XMS memory is available.

---

4. Enter, if you choose, in the XMS Memory KB Limit text box, the maximum amount of Lotus/Intel/Microsoft/AST Extended Memory Specification (XMS) memory, in kilobytes (KB), that you want DOS to allocate to the applications program, even if more XMS memory is free.

   The Shell uses this information only when the task swapper is enabled. By default, the Shell allocates a maximum of 384K of XMS memory to an application. Some applications may need more or less XMS memory. Specify a larger number if the applications program requires more than 384K. You can type **-1** in the KB Limit text box to instruct the Shell to allocate all free XMS memory to the application.

5. Select the Text option button (the default Video Mode setting) for all program items when you have a VGA, EGA, or monochrome monitor. Choose the Graphics option button if you have a CGA monitor and experience problems switching to a program that uses graphics.

The Graphics option button reserves more memory for a program that employs the graphics mode of your display adapter. This option button is used only when the task swapper is active and is not necessary when you are using a VGA or an EGA monitor.

6. Check any Reserve Shortcut Keys check box to disable the specified task swapper shortcut key. Disable a shortcut key only if it is used in the applications program.

Using the DOS 5.0 task swapper is discussed in Chapter 10. The task swapper uses the keystroke combinations Alt-Tab, Alt-Esc, and Ctrl-Esc to switch between applications programs and the DOS Shell window. If an applications program uses one or more of these keystroke combinations (shortcut keys), you can use the appropriate check box in the Advanced dialog box to disable the shortcut key with regard to the task swapper. Otherwise, the task swapper shortcuts override the applications program's shortcuts.

7. Enable the Prevent Program Switch check box to prevent the Shell's task swapper from switching to another program without quitting the program you are using. As a result, you have to quit the applications program to return to the Shell to select another program.

8. Press Enter or select the OK command button to close the Advanced dialog box and return to the Add Program dialog box.

Modifying Program Item Properties

Now that you understand how to use the New option from the File menu to add a program item to a program group, modifying the properties of an existing program item should be easy.

Follow these steps to modify the properties of an existing program item:

1. Select the program list area. If the group that contains the program item you want to modify is not included in the selected group, select the program group that includes that item.

2. Use the mouse or cursor-movement keys to move the selection bar to the name of the program item that contains the properties you want to modify.

3. Select File on the menu bar, and choose Properties from the File menu.

The Shell displays the Program Item Properties dialog box. This dialog box is essentially a duplicate of the Add Program dialog box shown in figure 14.7, except that the title, commands, start-up directory, application shortcut key, and password for the selected program item are already in the text boxes.

4. Make your desired changes to the values in the text boxes (including changes to values in any dialog boxes associated with replaceable parameters and any changes to values in the Advanced dialog box if you are using any advanced options), and press Enter or select the OK command button. Select Cancel to return to the Shell window without changing any of the program item's properties.

Deleting a Program Item

You may want to delete a program item you no longer use. The program itself is not removed, only the program item. To remove a program from your computer, you must delete its files from the disk.

To delete a program item, follow these steps:

1. Move the selection cursor to the name of the item to be deleted.

2. Press Del, or select Delete from the File menu.

   The Shell displays the Delete Item dialog box.

3. Select 1. Delete this item, and press Enter or choose the OK command button.

The program item is removed from the selected program group list.

Copying a Program Item

You also can place a duplicate of the current program item in the current program group or in a different program group.

Note: The DOS Shell has no prohibition against having two programs in the same group with the same name; but such an arrangement would be confusing to the user.

Use the following procedure to copy a program item:

1. Select the program item you want to copy.

2. Select File from the menu bar, and choose Copy from the File menu.

   The Shell displays the following message in the status line:

   ```
   Display Group to Copy To, then press F2. ESC to cancel.
   ```

3. Select the program group to which you want the Shell to copy the item.

4. Press the F2 key to copy the program item to the new group.

Summary

You now know how to customize the DOS Shell by changing its color settings and by adding and modifying program groups and program items. Important points covered in this chapter include the following:

- You can change the screen colors in which the Shell appears.

- You can add or change the program groups and program items that appear in the Shell program list area.

- You can add custom help messages to program groups and program items in the program list area.

Turn now to Chapter 15 to learn how to fine-tune DOS 5.0 to get the most from your computer and its peripheral devices.

Configuring Your Computer and Managing Devices

15

Your computer's operating system, DOS, provides you with the means to do more than just manage disks and files. DOS gives you the tools to fine-tune the operation of every element of your computer system, an exercise often called *configuring* your system.

The default configuration of DOS may be adequate for many users, but it is designed as a "lowest-common-denominator," intended to work with the greatest number of systems. As PC technology advances, DOS also must enable users of the most up-to-date systems to take full advantage of the computers' most powerful features. This chapter describes how to use DOS to create the optimum configuration for your computer system, whether your system is a plain-vanilla PC or a banana split with all the toppings.

In this chapter, you learn how to use the two files CONFIG.SYS and AUTOEXEC.BAT to configure your system. After examining the default DOS 5.0 configuration, the chapter gives you an overview of how to customize your system configuration with DOS 5.0 and with earlier versions of DOS. The remainder of the chapter then explains in detail how to optimize your system's memory resources, enhance disk performance, protect your disk files with the utility program MIRROR, and use several other handy configuration commands and techniques. After you master the information presented in this chapter, you can fine-tune your PC until it provides all the power you expected when you bought it.

Key Terms Used in This Chapter

CONFIG.SYS	A special text file that DOS reads during booting to find and execute configuration commands
Device driver	A special program file, usually with a SYS extension, that DOS can load through a configuration command. Device drivers control how DOS and applications programs interact with specific items of hardware.
Disk cache	A specialized intelligent buffer that DOS can use to increase disk efficiency
Expanded memory	Also referred to as EMS—Expanded Memory Specification—special RAM that DOS accesses as a device. Expanded memory conforms to the Lotus/Intel/Microsoft (LIM) EMS 3.2 or 4.0 standards.
Extended memory	Memory at addresses above 1M on 80286, 80386, and 80486 PCs. Most DOS applications are not equipped to use extended memory, but DOS 5.0 can load part of the operating system into the first 64K of extended memory.
High memory area	The first 64K of extended memory. DOS 5.0 can load a part of the operating system files into this area of memory.
Upper memory area	A 384K area of memory (in 80286, 80386, and 80486 PCs) between 640K and 1M, usually reserved for use by certain system devices, such as your monitor. On a 80386 or 80486 PC, DOS 5.0 can use a portion of this upper memory area, referred to as *upper memory blocks*, for memory-resident programs and device drivers.

XMS

The Lotus/Intel/Microsoft/AST Extended Memory Specification, a standard that specifies a set of rules by which several programs can use extended memory cooperatively by means of a device driver.

RAM disk

An emulation of disk storage in RAM through a device driver. DOS accesses a RAM disk as it accesses a standard disk.

Getting the Most from Your Computer Resources

Whether you use your own computer or a computer owned by your employer, someone has invested a significant sum of money in the system. This chapter helps you discover how to configure your computer to operate most efficiently—how to get the "most bang for the buck."

You generally can improve the performance of software running on your PC in two ways:

- Increase the amount of memory available to the software.

- Increase the speed at which your system or its components operate.

You can tackle these efficiency-oriented goals in two general ways:

- Add or replace hardware.

- Use software to attain an optimal configuration for your existing hardware resources.

DOS fits into the software category. This chapter teaches you how to use DOS 5.0 and its CONFIG.SYS and AUTOEXEC.BAT files to increase the amount of memory available to applications. The chapter also explains how to use special device drivers and utility programs to enhance the performance of your hard disk, which in turn enhances software performance.

Reviewing AUTOEXEC.BAT

Chapter 13 introduces you to batch files and to the special batch file AUTOEXEC.BAT. Each time you turn on or reboot your computer, DOS executes AUTOEXEC.BAT (if it exists where DOS can find it on your computer's boot disk). AUTOEXEC.BAT is therefore a natural place to put configuration-related commands you want DOS to execute every time you start your system. Chapter 13 describes several examples of configuration-related commands, including TIME, DATE, PATH, and PROMPT.

This chapter introduces you to several more commands that are prime candidates for inclusion in your AUTOEXEC.BAT file. For example, the SET command is used often in AUTOEXEC.BAT to assign a value to an environment variable. And the new (in DOS 5.0) utility MIRROR, which helps protect you from loss of data, is usually run from AUTOEXEC.BAT. This chapter also discusses the LOADHIGH command, which you can use in AUTOEXEC.BAT to load memory-resident applications programs into a special reserved memory area, where they don't use up precious conventional (below 640K) memory.

Understanding CONFIG.SYS

After DOS starts—but before it runs AUTOEXEC.BAT—DOS looks in the root directory of the boot disk for a file called CONFIG.SYS. If DOS finds CONFIG.SYS, DOS attempts to carry out the commands in the file. This file is intended specifically to *configure* your *system*, hence its name: CONFIG.SYS.

Similar in nature to AUTOEXEC.BAT, CONFIG.SYS is an ASCII text file consisting of a series of one-line commands. You can view the contents of CONFIG.SYS by issuing the following command at the DOS prompt:

  TYPE CONFIG.SYS

Because CONFIG.SYS is an ASCII text file, you can create it using the command COPY CON CONFIG.SYS. You also can create or edit CONFIG.SYS by using the DOS editor Edlin, a text editor, or any word processing program that can output ASCII text files.

The commands you can include in CONFIG.SYS are not the same as those available in batch files. These commands are intended solely to configure your system at start-up and therefore, in this book, are referred to as *configuration commands*. (Some books refer to these commands as *directives*.) Table 15.1 lists the configuration commands you can use in your CONFIG.SYS file and describes the action each command performs.

Table 15.1
Configuration Commands

Command	Action
BREAK	Determines when DOS recognizes the Ctrl-C or Ctrl-Break key combination
BUFFERS	Sets the number of file buffers DOS reserves for transferring information to and from the disk
COUNTRY	Sets country-dependent information
DEVICE	Loads a driver that enables a particular device to be used with your system
DEVICEHIGH*	Loads a device driver into an upper memory block (reserved memory)
DOS*	Determines whether DOS is loaded into the high memory area and whether upper memory blocks are allocated
DRIVPARM	Sets disk drive characteristics
FCBS	Determines the number of file control blocks that can be opened simultaneously
FILES	Sets the number of files that can be open at one time
INSTALL	Installs a memory-resident program
LASTDRIVE	Specifies the highest valid disk drive letter
REM	Causes a line not to be executed so that you can insert a remark
SHELL	Informs DOS what command processor should be used and where the processor is located
STACKS	Sets the number of stacks that DOS uses to process hardware interrupts
SWITCHES	Disables extended keyboard functions

New in DOS 5.0

This chapter discusses the most important configuration commands listed in table 15.1. The most frequently used configuration commands are probably FILES, BUFFERS, and DEVICE; you may want to pay special attention to the discussions of these commands. You also may find the DEVICEHIGH command interesting. CONFIG.SYS's counterpart to LOADHIGH, DEVICEHIGH can load a device driver into reserved memory, leaving more conventional memory available for your applications programs. Configuration commands not discussed in this chapter are explained in the Command Reference in Part IV of this book.

> *Note:* The documentation for most applications software packages and peripheral hardware devices recommends that you include particular commands in CONFIG.SYS. Read these recommendations carefully to determine whether you need to alter your CONFIG.SYS. Otherwise, a new software or hardware device you install may not operate the way you expect.

Examining the Default Configuration

In the strictest sense, DOS has no standard, or default, configuration. DOS doesn't require that you have CONFIG.SYS or AUTOEXEC.BAT on your boot disk in order to start your computer, but you nearly always have these files on any boot disk you use. Moreover, when you use the Setup installation program to install DOS 5.0 on your computer, Setup creates CONFIG.SYS and AUTOEXEC.BAT files. Therefore, thinking of these two files created by Setup as the default configuration is convenient and logical, at least with regard to DOS 5.0. If you are using an earlier version of DOS, you also can think of these files as a starting point for configuring your system, but remember to remove any commands that are new in DOS 5.0.

The default CONFIG.SYS for DOS 5.0, when installed on a hard disk, is as follows (assuming that you instructed Setup to install DOS 5.0 on your C drive in the \DOS directory):

```
DEVICE=C:\DOS\SETVER.EXE
DEVICE=C:\DOS\HIMEM.SYS
DOS=HIGH
FILES=10
SHELL=C:\DOS\COMMAND.COM C:\DOS\ /P
STACKS=0,0
```

If you install DOS on a floppy disk system, Setup creates the following slightly different version of CONFIG.SYS (assuming that you have installed DOS on the A drive):

```
DEVICE=A:\SETVER.EXE
DEVICE=A:\HIMEM.SYS
DOS=HIGH
FILES=10
STACKS=0,0
```

The first command in each version of CONFIG.SYS is useful in maintaining compatibility between DOS and older versions of applications programs. The second and third CONFIG.SYS commands relate to how your computer uses extended memory, a type of memory available only in PCs that contain an 80286, 80386 (DX or SX), or 80486 CPU. These two commands therefore are not included in your CONFIG.SYS file if your PC uses an Intel 8088 or 8086 CPU.

All the commands in these two files are discussed later in this chapter.

Note: The first three commands in the preceding CONFIG.SYS files relate to features that are new in DOS 5.0; they should not be used with earlier versions of DOS.

Setup also creates the following AUTOEXEC.BAT file on hard disk systems (assuming that you have installed DOS in the \DOS directory on C):

```
@ECHO OFF
PROMPT $P$G
PATH C:\DOS
SET TEMP=C:\DOS
```

The equivalent AUTOEXEC.BAT file for floppy disk systems is as follows:

```
@ECHO OFF
PROMPT $P$G
```

The remainder of this chapter explains the meaning of the commands in these configuration files and introduces you to other commands you may want to add to CONFIG.SYS and AUTOEXEC.BAT.

Note: The preceding AUTOEXEC.BAT file examples work with earlier versions of DOS as well as with DOS 5.0.

Installing Device Drivers with DEVICE

Device drivers are special software additions to DOS's basic input/output system. DOS is supplied with a wealth of device drivers you can use to get the most from your computer hardware equipment. Some add-on hardware comes with a device driver file that enables your system to recognize and use the hardware. For example, if you buy a mouse to use with your computer, you also must load the appropriate device driver.

To make DOS aware of the device drivers you want to use, include the DEVICE command in the CONFIG.SYS file. The syntax for the DEVICE command is as follows:

DEVICE = *d:path***filename.ext** */switches*

d: is the disk drive where the device driver file resides, *path*\\ is the directory path to the device driver file, and **filename.ext** is the name of the device driver file. */switches* are any switches the device driver software needs.

To use a Microsoft mouse, for example, you can load a mouse device driver named MOUSE.SYS, located on drive C, with the following command:

DEVICE = C:\\MOUSE.SYS

> *Note:* The spaces around the equal sign in this syntax are optional. For example, if you have a Microsoft mouse, you can load a mouse device driver with the following command:
>
> **DEVICE=C:\\MOUSE.SYS**

You can load as many device drivers as you need, but you must use a separate DEVICE line for each driver you install. As each device driver is loaded, DOS extends its control to that device.

The device driver must be accessible when DOS starts. For convenience, floppy disk users should place device driver files in the root directory. Hard disk users can make a special subdirectory called \\DRIVERS or \\SYS and put the driver files in this directory, out of the way of daily files. (You can give the directory containing your device drivers any valid file name.) If you put the driver files in a separate subdirectory, add the directory path name to the device driver file name, as in the following examples:

DEVICE = C:\\DRIVERS\\MOUSE.SYS

DEVICE = C:\\SYS\\MOUSE.SYS

Table 15.2 lists the device driver files included with DOS 5.0.

Table 15.2
DOS 5.0 Device Drivers

Device Driver	Description
EGA.SYS	Saves and restores an EGA screen when using DOSSHELL and the task swapper
DISPLAY.SYS	Provides support for code-page switching to the screen
PRINTER.SYS	Provides code-page switching to change characters printed by the printer
HIMEM.SYS	Manages extended memory
ANSI.SYS	Enables control of display using ANSI control sequences
RAMDRIVE.SYS	Uses a portion of random-access memory (RAM) to simulate a hard disk—often called a RAM disk
SMARTDRV.SYS	Uses extended or expanded memory to buffer disk reads
DRIVER.SYS	Sets parameters for physical and logical disk drives
SETVER.EXE	Establishes a version table that lists the version number DOS 5.0 reports to named programs
EMM386.EXE	Uses XMS memory in an 80386 or 80486 computer to emulate EMS memory and provide upper memory blocks

The most commonly used device drivers are discussed in this chapter. Refer to the Command Reference for the syntax of the drivers not covered here.

Optimizing Memory Resources

A requirement for running most applications software is to have sufficient memory resources in your computer system. Often, a program refuses to run at all if sufficient memory is not available. At other times, you may be able to run the program, but you may not be able to access all its features.

The most pervasive limitation to the memory available to a program traditionally has been imposed by DOS. Even though PCs with 80286, 80386, or 80486 CPUs can have megabytes of memory chips physically installed—usually referred to as extended memory—DOS enables software to access no more than 640K of memory. PC manufacturers and programmers have come up with several different approaches to getting around this so-called "640K barrier" erected by DOS. The most popular approach—EMS, or expanded memory—can supply up to 32M of memory to applications but normally requires special hardware and software.

Versions of DOS before 5.0 do not address directly the issue of providing more memory for applications programs. DOS 5.0, however, provides several techniques that usually can free some of the first 640K of memory; in some cases, these techniques provide access to your computer's extended memory by converting it to expanded memory. The following sections explain how you can take advantage of these DOS 5.0 enhancements.

Using Extended Memory and HIMEM.SYS

The most significant improvement offered by DOS 5.0, in terms of optimizing the use of your computer, is the capacity to load most of the operating system software into extended memory. *Extended memory* is the portion of your computer's random-access memory (RAM) that is above the 1 megabyte (1,024K) mark. Only PCs based on an 80286, 80386 (DX or SX), or 80486 CPU can have extended memory. Not all PCs in this category have extended memory installed.

Most currently available applications programs don't use extended memory, but they often do need as much *conventional* (below 640K) memory as they can get. By loading most of the operating system software into extended memory, DOS 5.0 provides more conventional memory for applications, ultimately improving the performance of your system.

Before DOS or applications software can use extended memory, you must add to your CONFIG.SYS file an *extended memory manager*—a driver that provides a standard way for applications to address extended memory so that no two programs use the same portion of extended memory at the same time. DOS 4.0 and later versions include the extended memory manager HIMEM.SYS.

HIMEM.SYS manages memory according to the rules set out in the Extended Memory Specification (XMS) Version 2.0. According to this specification, three areas of memory above the conventional 640K barrier can be made available for programs to use:

- *Upper Memory Area*—also known as *upper memory, upper memory blocks,* or *reserved memory*—consists of the memory between 640K and 1,024K. The PC's video adapter uses a portion of this area of memory. Upper memory also may be used to place a copy of the computer's ROM (read-only memory) into RAM (random-access memory, referred to in this book simply as memory). DOS 5.0 has the capability of loading device drivers and memory-resident programs into the upper memory area. Upper memory is sometimes referred to as *high memory*.

- *High Memory Area* (*HMA*) is the first 64K of memory above 1,024K. DOS 5.0 has the capability of loading a portion of the operating system into the HMA.

- *Extended Memory Blocks* (*XMS memory*) include all memory above 1,024K. In essence, when extended memory is managed by an extended memory manager, you refer to the memory as XMS memory.

When used on an 80286, 80386, or 80486 PC, HIMEM.SYS provides HMA and XMS memory to programs that "know" how to use it. To access upper memory, however, the PC must contain an 80386 or 80486 CPU, and you must include one of the following device driver commands in CONFIG.SYS:

DEVICE=EMM386.EXE RAM

DEVICE=EMM386.EXE NOEMS

Refer to the next section for a full discussion of EMM386.EXE.

The syntax for using HIMEM.SYS is as follows:

DEVICE=*d:path***\HIMEM.SYS** */HMAMIN=m /NUMHANDLES=n /INT15=xxxx /MACHINE:xx /SHADOWRAM:ON|OFF /CPUCLOCK:ON|OFF*

d: is the disk drive where the HIMEM.SYS resides, and *path* is the directory containing the device driver file.

For example, if HIMEM.SYS is contained in the \DOS directory on your C drive, you include the following command in CONFIG.SYS:

DEVICE=C:\DOS\HIMEM.SYS

In most cases, you need only this command to activate the extended memory manager. In special cases, however, you may need to use one of the available switches described in the following paragraphs. The next section continues the discussion of loading DOS into upper memory.

According to the XMS specification, only one program at a time can use the high memory area. The switch /HMAMIN=n sets the minimum amount of memory that must be requested by an application before the application is permitted to use HMA. If you load DOS into HMA, you can omit this switch (see discussion of the DOS=HIGH command later in this chapter).

When the extended memory manager assigns memory to a particular program, the extended memory manager assigns one or more *extended memory block handles* to the program. The /numhandles=n switch indicates the maximum number of handles available. The number n must be from 1 through 128. The default is 32 handles, usually a sufficient number. Each reserved handle requires an additional 6 bytes of memory.

Most current versions of commercial software support the XMS specification for addressing extended memory. Some older versions of programs, however, use a different method of addressing extended memory, known as the *Interrupt 15h* (*INT15h*) interface. Add the /INT15=xxxx switch if you want to load DOS into HMA and you work with software that uses the INT15h interface. The number *xxxx* indicates the amount of extended memory you want HIMEM.SYS to assign to the INT15h interface; this number must be from 64 through 65,535 (kilobytes). The default is 0. This memory is not available to programs that expect XMS memory.

DOS uses the A20 memory address line to access the high memory area. Not all brands of PCs, however, handle the A20 line in the same way. Normally, HIMEM.SYS can detect your computer's A20 handler. If not, HIMEM.SYS displays the following error message:

```
Unable to control A20
```

If you see this message, use the /MACHINE:xx switch in the HIMEM.SYS command to specify which type of A20 handler is being used. Insert for *xx* in the /MACHINE switch the code that matches your computer. You will find the text codes in the Code column and the number codes in the Number column in table 15.3. If you see the error message but your computer is not listed in table 15.3, try the switch /MACHINE:1.

You may have listed in CONFIG.SYS before DEVICE=HIMEM.SYS a device driver that also uses the A20 line. By default, HIMEM.SYS takes control of A20 even though the line is turned on when HIMEM.SYS loads. HIMEM.SYS warns you when this condition occurs by displaying the following message:

```
Warning: The A20 Line was already enabled!
```

Table 15.3
A20 Handler Codes

Code	Number	Computer
at	1	IBM PC/AT
ps2	2	IBM PS/2
pt1cascade	3	Phoenix Cascade BIOS
hpvectra	4	HP Vectra (A and A+)
att6300plus	5	AT&T 6300 Plus
acer1100	6	Acer 1100
toshiba	7	Toshiba 1600 and 1200XE
wyse	8	Wyse 12.5 MHz 286
tulip	9	Tulip SX
zenith	10	Zenith ZBIOS
at1	11	IBM PC/AT
at2	12	IBM PC/AT (alternative delay)
css	12	CSS Labs
at3	13	IBM PC/AT (alternative delay)
philips	13	Philips
fasthp	14	HP Vectra

Determine whether you really intend to have both drivers installed at once. If so, you can prevent HIMEM.SYS from taking control of A20 by adding the switch */A20CONTROL:OFF* (the default setting is */A20CONTROL:ON*).

Many 80386 computers offer a feature known as *shadow RAM*, which places a copy of the system's read-only memory (ROM) into the computer's upper memory (RAM). The purpose of this trick is to make the software stored in ROM more responsive, increasing the computer's overall performance. If you prefer to increase the amount of upper memory available for device drivers and memory-resident programs, use the */SHADOWRAM:OFF* switch. As HIMEM.SYS loads, it displays the message `Shadow RAM disabled`.

In some cases, DOS cannot turn off shadow RAM. Instead, DOS displays the message `Shadow RAM disable not supported on this system` or `Shadow RAM is in use and can't be disabled`. (Check your hardware documentation for other methods of disabling shadow RAM.)

The */CPUCLOCK:ON* switch ensures that HIMEM.SYS does not slow your computer's *clock speed*, the speed at which your computer processes instructions. (Any change in clock speed does not affect your computer's real-time clock, which keeps time of day.) Many PCs have on the front panel an LED or other indicator that indicates the current clock speed. To prevent the clock speed from slowing, add the */CPUCLOCK:ON* switch to the DEVICE=HIMEM.SYS command in CONFIG.SYS.

Loading DOS into High Memory

DOS 5.0 enables you to load most of the operating system into an area of extended memory known as the high memory area (HMA), or just high memory (the first 64K of extended memory). After the device driver HIMEM.SYS is loaded into the computer's memory, the following command in CONFIG.SYS loads DOS into high memory:

> DOS=HIGH

The next time you boot the computer, DOS uses about 14K of space in conventional memory and loads the remainder of the operating system in upper memory. If you don't use this command in CONFIG.SYS, however, or don't have extended memory installed in your computer, DOS 5.0 occupies more than 62K of memory. By loading the operating system into high memory, DOS 5.0 can free about 48K of conventional memory.

Using Expanded Memory and EMM386.EXE

Expanded memory is memory that meets a published specification known as the Lotus-Intel-Microsoft Expanded Memory Specification, LIM/EMS, or just EMS. The purpose of the EMS specification is to enable DOS applications to access memory above the 640K limit.

The first version of the EMS specification, published in 1985, was numbered EMS Version 3.0 because it was compatible with DOS 3.0. The second revision was numbered EMS Version 3.2. Both EMS 3.0 and EMS 3.2

provided up to 8 megabytes of additional memory to applications written to take advantage of this specification. The most recent EMS revision, Version 4.0, announced in August 1987, can address up to 32 megabytes of expanded memory.

Even though many PCs can contain megabytes of extended memory—memory above 1,024K—most DOS applications software cannot use extended memory. A large number of applications programs are available, however, that can use expanded memory.

The EMS specification normally requires special hardware and software to operate. EMS does not use the generally less expensive extended memory; EMS requires memory boards designed specifically for use as expanded memory. The EMS standard also requires a special device driver called an *expanded memory manager*.

DOS does not provide an expanded memory manager per se because each expanded memory board manufacturer supplies a driver. DOS 5.0 does, however, provide the device driver EMM386.EXE, which can be used in 80386 and 80486 PCs to take the place of an expanded memory manager. EMM386.EXE uses extended memory to *emulate* (act like) expanded memory. EMM386.EXE therefore most accurately can be called an *expanded memory emulator*, even though EMM386.EXE fills the role of an expanded memory manager.

> *Note:* The device driver HIMEM.SYS, discussed in this section, must be loaded before EMM386.EXE. In other words, list DEVICE=HIMEM.SYS before DEVICE=EMM386.EXE in the CONFIG.SYS file. Do not use EMM386.EXE as an expanded memory emulator if you are already using another driver as an expanded memory manager.

In addition to its role as an expanded memory emulator, EMM386.EXE also is a *UMB provider*, working with HIMEM.SYS to provide upper memory blocks (UMBs), into which you can load device drivers and memory-resident programs. Refer to the next section for further discussion of providing UMBs.

The syntax of the command for EMM386.EXE, used as a device driver, is as follows:

DEVICE=c:\path**EMM386.EXE** ON|OFF|AUTO MEMORY
W=ON|OFF MIX|FRAME=address /Pmmmm Pn=address
X=mmmm-nnn I=mmmm-nnn B=address L=minxms A=altregs
H=handles D=nnn RAM NOEMS

In many cases, the following command is sufficient:

    DEVICE=EMM386.EXE RAM

This command loads the expanded memory emulator and allocates 256K of EMS memory. The *RAM* switch enables upper memory.

The remaining switches for the EM386.EXE device driver are sometimes needed to customize your computer for use with particularly demanding software or hardware.

You can specify ON, OFF, or AUTO in the EMM386.EXE device driver command to indicate whether your computer starts in the EMM386.EXE active, inactive, or automatic mode, respectively. By default, the device driver is active, and EMM386.EXE makes extended memory available. However, some applications programs may not run properly when EMM386.EXE is active because EMM386.EXE places the computer in a mode known as virtual 8086 mode. When you use EMM386.EXE as a device driver, the driver loads in memory and remains active (ON) unless you specify otherwise with the OFF switch.

The OFF switch starts the computer with EMM386.EXE loaded in memory but inactive. The XMS memory allocated as EMS memory is unavailable for any purpose. You can activate the driver with the following command at the DOS command prompt:

    EMM386 ON

The OFF switch is not compatible, however, with the RAM or NOEMS switches, discussed later in this section.

Use AUTO if you want EMM386.EXE to activate only when an application requests EMS memory. This setting provides maximum compatibility with software that may not work properly in virtual 8086 mode. Like the OFF switch, AUTO is not compatible with the *RAM* or *NOEMS* switches.

> *Note:* Even though EMM386.EXE activates when an applications program requests EMS memory, the driver does not automatically deactivate when the applications program terminates. To turn off the driver, you have to issue the following command at the command prompt:
>
>   EMM386 OFF

The *memory* parameter enables you to specify the amount of XMS memory you want EMM386.EXE to allocate as EMS memory. Type the number of kilobytes in the range 16 through 32,768. EMM386.EXE rounds any number you type down to the nearest multiple of 16. All unallocated memory remains available as XMS memory. The default EMS memory allocated is 256K.

TIP

> *Tip:* As a general rule, allocate only as much EMS memory as is required by your applications programs. Any memory allocated as EMS memory is no longer available as XMS memory. Some of the most powerful applications programs currently available, such as Microsoft Windows 3.0, work best with the maximum amount of XMS memory available.

Use the *L=minxms* switch, in which *minxms* is the number of kilobytes, to indicate the minimum XMS memory that EMM386.EXE should allocate. This parameter overrides the *memory* parameter.

If you have installed a Weitek math coprocessor chip—a special computer chip that improves the performance of computation-intensive software such as computer-aided design (CAD) software—use the *W=ON* switch. By default, the device driver does not support this type of coprocessor. You also can turn on or off support for the Weitek coprocessor with one of the following commands at the DOS prompt:

    EMM386 W=ON

    EMM386 W=OFF

In some circumstances, you may want to use upper memory for device drivers and memory-resident programs, but you don't need EMS memory. Use the *NOEMS* switch with the EMM386.EXE driver to free the maximum amount of upper memory and to provide no EMS memory. For example, you may intend to run Windows 3.0 on your computer. Windows can use all your XMS memory, so this software doesn't need EMS memory.

The *NOEMS* switch has two disadvantages:

- Windows 3.0 cannot provide EMS to an application running in a DOS session.

- Applications that support the Virtual Control Program Interface (VCPI) for use of XMS memory in protected mode do not run in protected mode when the *NOEMS* switch is used with EMM386.EXE.

Use the *RAM* switch instead of *NOEMS* if you want to have access to upper memory and you intend to run a program that requires EMS memory in a Windows 3.0 DOS session, or if you expect to use a program that requires VCPI support.

The remaining switches available for use with EMM386.EXE are highly technical and therefore beyond the scope of this book. Refer to Que's *DOS Programmer's Reference*, 3rd Edition, or to your DOS User's Guide or Technical Reference Manual for more information.

Loading Device Drivers and TSRs into Upper Memory

In addition to enabling you to run DOS in high memory, DOS 5.0 provides the capability of loading memory-resident programs and device drivers into an area of memory between 640K and 1,024K, freeing more conventional memory for other applications programs. DOS can access this area of memory—called the *upper memory area*, *upper memory*, *upper memory blocks*, or *reserved memory*—in 80386 and 80486 PCs that have 1M or more of memory.

The PC's video adapter uses a portion of upper memory. Sometimes upper memory also is used to store a copy of the computer's ROM—a technique often called shadow RAM.

> *Note:* The upper memory area is sometimes also referred to as *high memory*, but DOS 5.0 uses the term *high memory* to refer to the first 64K of extended memory.

To load device drivers or memory-resident programs, also called *terminate-and-stay-resident (TSR) programs*, into upper memory, all the following conditions must be met:

- Your computer has an 80386 or 80486 CPU.

- HIMEM.SYS is loaded as a device driver.

- EMM386.EXE is loaded as a device driver with the RAM or NOEMS switch.

- The following command appears in the CONFIG.SYS file:

  DOS=UMB

If you also want to use the command DOS=HIGH to load DOS into high memory, combine the two commands as follows:

DOS=HIGH, UMB

You can load two types of programs into upper memory: device drivers and memory-resident programs (TSRs). You already know that device drivers normally are loaded using the DEVICE command. When you want to load a device driver into upper memory, however, use the DEVICEHIGH command. The syntax for this configuration command is as follows:

DEVICEHIGH=*c:path***filename.ext** */switches*

For example, to load into upper memory the screen driver ANSI.SYS, you need the following command in CONFIG.SYS:

DEVICEHIGH=C:\DOS\ANSI.SYS

When you boot the computer, DOS attempts to load ANSI.SYS into the upper memory area.

To load a memory-resident program into upper memory, precede the program's start-up command with LOADHIGH. (You can use LH in place of LOADHIGH.) The syntax for the command for LOADHIGH is as follows:

LOADHIGH *c:path***programname** */switches*

For example, to load DOSKey (discussed in Chapter 13) into upper memory each time you start your computer, add the following command to your AUTOEXEC.BAT file:

LOADHIGH DOSKEY

The next time you reboot the computer, DOS attempts to load DOSKey into upper memory.

DOS does not load a program into upper memory if the program requests that DOS allocate more memory during initialization than is available in the largest available upper memory block. If DOS is not successful when it tries to load device drivers or TSRs into the upper memory area, DOS loads the program into conventional memory instead.

DOS may successfully load a device driver into upper memory only to have the driver allocate more memory some time after initialization, potentially causing the system to "lock up." To prevent this occurrence, insert the following parameter in place of the equal sign in the DEVICEHIGH command:

SIZE=*hhhh*

For *hhhh*, insert a hexadecimal number (base 16) that specifies the maximum amount of upper memory required to run the program. (You can use DOS 5.0's MEM command, discussed in the next section, to determine the amount of memory allocated by a program.) If DOS cannot find the amount of upper memory indicated by the SIZE parameter, DOS loads the driver into conventional memory.

Use the MEM command to determine whether a driver or program has loaded into upper memory.

Displaying the Amount of Free and Used Memory

To enable you to make the most efficient use of DOS 5.0's memory management utilities, discussed in the preceding sections, DOS also enables you to display the amount of free and used memory at any point during a DOS session. Use DOS 5.0's MEM command for this purpose.

The syntax for the MEM command is as follows:

MEM */PROGRAM /DEBUG /CLASSIFY*

You can abbreviate each switch by typing just the first letter (/P, /D, or /C).

To see a "short" version of the memory report that indicates the amount of free conventional memory, EMS memory, and XMS memory, type **MEM** with no switch. DOS displays a report similar to the following:

```
 655360   bytes total conventional memory
 655360   bytes available to MS-DOS
 623776   largest executable program size

 655360   bytes EMS memory
 262144   free EMS memory

3145728   bytes total contiguous extended memory
      0   bytes available contiguous extended memory
2686976   bytes available XMS memory
          MS-DOS resident in High Memory Area
```

This report tells you the following information about the conventional memory: the total amount of conventional memory (640K, where 1K = 1,024 bytes); the amount of conventional memory available to DOS (usually the same as the preceding number); and the largest program you can run in conventional memory. In this example, 623,776 bytes of the original 655,360 bytes are available to any applications program you may decide to run.

The MEM report then shows the total amount of EMS memory and the amount free for use by an applications program. The first number includes the 384K reserved (upper) memory area between 640K and 1,024K. In the example, 262,144 bytes (256K) of EMS memory are free.

Next, MEM tells you the total amount of extended memory installed in your computer and the amount of extended memory that has been mapped (converted) to XMS memory and is available for use. In the example, 2,686,976 bytes of XMS memory of the original 3,145,728 bytes (3,072K, or 3M) are available.

If you are not using an extended memory manager (such as HIMEM.SYS), MEM also indicates the amount of available extended (non-XMS) memory; otherwise, this number is 0.

Finally, MEM indicates whether MS-DOS is currently loaded in the high memory area.

Sometimes, MEM's short report doesn't provide enough information to meet your needs. The three available switches produce longer versions of the report. Because these reports do not fit on a single DOS screen, you usually use the pipe feature with the MORE command to display one screen of the report at a time.

The reports generated by MEM's /PROGRAM (/P) and /DEBUG (/D) switches are highly technical in content and therefore are not discussed here. However, the report produced by /CLASSIFY (/C) is useful in determining whether device drivers and TSRs can be loaded into upper memory.

To see a listing of programs, drivers, and free space in conventional and upper memory, type the following command and press Enter:

MEM /C

DOS scrolls a report similar to the following down the screen:

```
Conventional Memory :

    Name          Size in Decimal        Size in Hex
 ----------      ----------------       -------------
    MSDOS         12016   ( 11.7K)          2EF0
    HIMEM          1184   (  1.2K)           4A0
    EMM386         8208   (  8.0K)          2010
    SETVER          384   (  0.4K)           180
    COMMAND        2624   (  2.6K)           A40
    MIRROR         6528   (  6.4K)          1980
    FREE             64   (  0.1K)            40
    FREE            144   (  0.1K)            90
    FREE         623968   (609.3K)          8560

  Total  FREE :  624176     (609.5K)
```

```
Upper Memory :

    Name         Size in Decimal              Size in Hex
    ----------   -----------------            ----------
    SYSTEM       163840  (160.0K)                28000
    ANSI           4192  (  4.1K)                 1060
    MOUSE         12784  ( 12.5K)                 31F0
    DOSKEY         4160  (  4.1K)                 1040
    FREE            144  (  0.1K)                   90
    FREE          11376  ( 11.1K)                 2C70

    Total  FREE :        11520        ( 11.3K)
Total bytes available to programs (Conventional+Upper) :635696 (620.8K)
Largest executable program size:                        623776 (609.2K)
Largest available upper memoryblock :                    11376 ( 11.1K)

   655360  bytes total EMS memory
   262144  bytes free EMS memory
  3145728  bytes total contiguous extended memory
        0  bytes available contiguous extended memory
  2686976  bytes available XMS memory
           MS-DOS resident in High Memory Area
```

Because some of the report scrolls off the screen before you can read it, you may want to use the following variation of the same command:

MEM /C | MORE

DOS pipes the report through the MORE filter and displays the first screen of the report followed by the message `-- MORE --`. Press any key when you are ready to display the next screen.

You also can send the MEM report to your printer by using the following command:

MEM /C > PRN

This command redirects the report to the DOS device PRN, your computer's first printer port.

The top portion of the report, titled `Conventional Memory`, shows you how much memory is allocated to any particular driver or program. Use the section of the report titled `Upper Memory` to determine whether any drivers or programs are loaded in upper memory and how much upper memory is still free.

Before attempting to move a driver or program from conventional to upper memory (using DEVICEHIGH or LOADHIGH), compare the driver/program's size (in the Conventional Memory Size column) to the available upper memory block (UMB) sizes (indicated by FREE in the Upper Memory Name column). The available UMB must be at least as big as the driver or program before you can load the driver or program into upper memory.

After you identify a driver or memory-resident program that appears to be the right size to fit in the available UMB, edit CONFIG.SYS or AUTOEXEC.BAT to add DEVICEHIGH or LOADHIGH to the appropriate command. Reboot your computer, and issue the MEM /C command again to see whether the driver or program loaded.

TIP

> *Tip:* Arriving at the optimal combination of device drivers and memory-resident programs loaded into upper memory may require some experimentation. DOS loads programs in the largest available UMB first, so try loading the largest drivers and programs first by placing their start-up commands earliest in CONFIG.SYS or AUTOEXEC.BAT.

Enhancing Disk Performance

Often the most dramatic way to increase your computer's performance is to purchase a faster hard disk. Because fast hard disks are not inexpensive, you should make sure that you are getting the best performance available from your present hard disk.

DOS offers several techniques for enhancing disk performance. The sections that follow describe the BUFFERS command, the SMARTDRV.SYS disk cache, and the FASTOPEN command. You also learn about one technique that doesn't use a disk at all but configures a portion of your computer's memory as a virtual disk.

Using BUFFERS To Increase
Disk Performance

The BUFFERS command is used in CONFIG.SYS to tell DOS how much memory to reserve for file transfers. DOS sets aside an area of RAM called a *buffer* for temporary storage of data being transferred between the disk and an applications program.

When DOS is asked to retrieve information from a disk, DOS reads the information in increments of whole sectors (512 bytes). Excess data not required from that sector is left in the buffer. If this data is needed later, DOS does not need to perform another disk access to retrieve the data. Similarly, DOS tries to reduce disk activity when DOS writes information to the disk. If less than a full sector is to be written to the disk, DOS accumulates the information in a disk buffer. When the buffer is full, DOS writes the information to the disk. This action is called *flushing the buffer*. To make sure that all pertinent information is placed into a file, DOS also flushes the buffers when a program closes a disk file.

When a disk buffer becomes full or empty, DOS marks the buffer to indicate that it has been used recently. When DOS needs to reuse the buffers for new information, DOS takes the buffer that has not been used for the longest time.

The net effect of DOS's use of buffers is to reduce the number of disk accesses by reading and writing only full sectors. By reusing the least recently used buffers, DOS retains information more likely to be needed next. Your programs and DOS run faster.

The syntax for the BUFFERS command is as follows:

BUFFERS = n, *m*

The **n** parameter is the number of disk buffers you want DOS to assign. A single buffer is about 512 bytes long (plus 16 bytes used by DOS). Use a number from 1 through 99. If you do not give the BUFFERS command, DOS uses a default value from 2 through 15, depending on the size of your disk drives, the amount of memory in your system, and the version of DOS you are using. Table 15.4 lists the different default buffer configurations.

The *m* parameter is a number in the range 1 through 8, that specifies the number of sectors DOS reads each time it is instructed to read a file. This feature is sometimes called a *secondary cache* or a *look-ahead buffer* and is available only in DOS 4.0 or later. When files most often are read sequentially, this type of buffer increases performance. Do not use this secondary cache feature if you are using or you plan to use a disk caching program such as SMARTDRV.SYS.

Table 15.4
Default Number of Disk Buffers

DOS Version	Number of BUFFERS	Hardware
DOS pre-3.3	2	Floppy disk drives
	3	Hard disk
DOS 3.3/4	2	360K floppy disk drive
	3	Any other hard or floppy disk drive
	5	More than 128K of RAM
	10	More than 256K of RAM
	15	More than 512K of RAM

Increasing the number of buffers—up to a point—generally improves disk performance. The recommended number of buffers increases with the size of your hard disk. Consider the suggested buffer numbers listed in table 15.5 when adding a BUFFERS command to CONFIG.SYS. Using a number higher than the recommended number of buffers probably uses more memory without further improving speed.

Table 15.5
Default Number of Disk Buffers

Hard Disk	Number of BUFFERS
Less than 40M	20
40M to 79M	30
80M to 119M	40
120M or more	50

For example, if you have an 85M hard disk and are not using a hard-disk caching program, you may include the following BUFFERS command in CONFIG.SYS:

    BUFFERS=40,8

Using a Disk Cache

Another way to enhance the performance of your hard disk is to use a *disk-caching* program. You can think of a disk cache as a large, smart buffer. Like a buffer, a disk cache operates from a section of your computer's memory set aside specifically to handle data being read from your computer's disks. The disk-caching program that comes with DOS 5.0, Windows, and some earlier versions of DOS is a device driver named SMARTDRV.SYS. (The version of SMARTDRV.SYS supplied with DOS 5.0 is an improved version of previous editions; use the new SMARTDRV.SYS instead of older versions.) SMARTDRV.SYS builds its buffer area in XMS or EMS memory using very little conventional memory.

When information is read from the disk, the information is placed in the cache, and requested information is sent to the program. SMARTDRV.SYS, however, reads more information than is requested by the program and stores this information in memory. If the program later requests information already in memory, the cache can supply the information faster than if the disk had to be read again. SMARTDRV.SYS also eliminates redundant writes by putting information on disk only when the data is different from what is there already.

A disk cache like SMARTDRV.SYS remembers which sections of the disk have been used most frequently. When the cache must be recycled, the program keeps the more frequently used areas and discards those less frequently used.

In an absolutely random disk access in which program and data files are scattered uniformly across the disk, the cache method of recycling the least frequently used area is more efficient than the buffer method of recycling the oldest area. A cache tends to keep in memory the most heavily used areas of the disk.

MS-DOS 5.0 and some versions of DOS 4.0 and 4.01 include a disk-cache program called SMARTDRV.SYS. (SMARTDRV.SYS also comes with Microsoft Windows.) The DOS 5.0 version of SMARTDRV.SYS supersedes all previous versions. This section explains how to install and use SMARTDRV.SYS.

The syntax for the command to install SMARTDRV.SYS is as follows:

DEVICE = *d:path***SMARTDRV.SYS** *initsize minsize* /A

d:path\\ is the optional disk drive and path name for the SMARTDRV.SYS program.

The *initsize* parameter specifies how much memory you want SMARTDRV to use when it initializes. The default size is 256K; you can specify any size between 128 and 8,192 (kilobytes). The larger the cache, the more performance improvement you see, up to a maximum size of about 2M (2,048K). A cache any larger than 2M is probably just wasting memory.

Use the *minsize* parameter only if you may run an applications program that can reduce the cache size (such as Microsoft Windows) This parameter prevents the program from reducing the cache size below the specified minimum.

The /A switch tells SMARTDRV to use EMS memory if it is available. If you do not use this switch, SMARTDRV uses XMS memory.

> *Tip:* For best performance, when you have a choice, allocate SMARTDRV.SYS to XMS memory rather than to EMS memory. The DEVICE=SMARTDRV.SYS line must be listed after the DEVICE=HIMEM.SYS command in CONFIG.SYS.

A typical SMARTDRV.SYS command looks like the following:

        DEVICE=SMARTDRV.SYS 1024 512

This CONFIG.SYS command initializes a disk cache in XMS memory with space for 1,024K (1M) of data. Applications programs can reduce the size of the cache, in an effort to use some of the XMS memory the cache is using, to a minimum cache size of 512K.

The next time you boot your computer after inserting the example SMARTDRV.SYS command into CONFIG.SYS, a message similar to the following appears during initialization:

```
Microsoft SMARTDrive Disk Cache version 3.13
   Cache Size: 1,024K in Extended Memory
   Room for 62 tracks of 33 sectors each
   Minimum cache size will be 512K
```

The operation of a disk cache is invisible after you install the cache; however, you should notice that your disk drive works faster.

> *Warning:* Do not run a disk compacting (optimizing, unfragmenting) program while SMARTDRV.SYS is loaded, or you may lose data from your hard disk. To unload SMARTDRV.SYS, remove DEVICE=SMARTDRV.SYS from CONFIG.SYS, and reboot the computer.

Using RAMDRIVE To Make a RAM Disk

Another way to speed disk operation doesn't use a disk at all. A *RAM disk* is a device driver that uses a portion of your computer's memory to emulate a disk drive. Because this "imitation," or *virtual*, disk is located in RAM, a RAM disk is extremely fast compared to a real disk drive. The major limitation of a RAM disk is that its contents disappear when you turn off or reboot your computer.

TIP

Tip: As a general rule, a disk cache, such as SMARTDRV.SYS, provides more overall performance gains than a RAM disk. RAM disks are used most often to enhance the performance of one or two specific programs that read and write to the disk frequently or that use overlays (see the accompanying Technical Note). A disk cache, on the other hand, improves the performance of all programs that read and write to disk. When your computer's memory resources are limited, you should allocate more memory to your disk cache than to a RAM disk.

Technical Note: Some programs are too large to fit in your PC's memory. These programs load a core part into memory and access additional parts from overlay files, as needed. When a new section of the program is needed, the appropriate overlay for that section is read from the disk into the area occupied by the current overlay. The term *overlay* comes from this process of overlaying sections of program space in memory with new sections. RAM disks enable rapid switching of active overlays because the overlay disk files are actually in memory, not on disk. You must copy any needed overlay files to the RAM disk before starting the application. Of course, you must configure the application to look for its overlays on the RAM disk.

The RAM disk driver that comes with DOS 5.0 (and with some earlier versions of DOS) is named RAMDRIVE.SYS. To install RAMDRIVE and create a virtual disk, include RAMDRIVE.SYS as a device driver in CONFIG.SYS. The syntax for including RAMDRIVE.SYS is as follows:

DEVICE = *d:path***RAMDRIVE.SYS** *disksize sectorsize entries* /E /A *d:* is the disk drive, and *path* is the directory path for RAMDRIVE.SYS. The options for RAMDRIVE are described in the following sections.

The *disksize* parameter indicates the size of the RAM disk in kilobytes. This number can range from 16 through 4,096. The default value is 64.

The *sectorsize* parameter sets the size of the sectors used in the virtual disk. You can specify one of three sector sizes: 128, 256, or 512 bytes. The default sector size is 512 bytes in DOS 5.0 and 128 bytes in earlier versions. (DOS usually uses a sector size of 512 bytes for real disks.) You normally should not change this parameter, but if you do, you also must specify the *disksize* parameter.

The *entries* parameter determines the maximum number of directory entries permitted in the RAM disk's root directory. This parameter can have a value from 2 through 1,024. The default value is 64. You normally don't need to change this parameter. If you do specify the *entries* parameter, you also must enter the *disksize* and *sectorsize* parameters. Set the number of directories based on the size of the RAM disk and the size of the files you are storing.

By default, DOS creates a RAM disk in conventional memory. You can, however, include the /E switch to cause the RAM disk to be created in XMS memory (the DEVICE=RAMDRIVE command must follow the DEVICE=HIMEM.SYS command). Even with this switch, RAMDRIVE uses some conventional memory (1,184 bytes). You therefore may want to try loading the RAMDRIVE.SYS device driver into upper memory. For example, the following command creates a 1,024K RAM disk in XMS memory and loads the device driver into upper memory:

```
DEVICEHIGH=C:\DOS\RAMDRIVE.SYS 1024 /E
```

The /A switch, available in DOS 4.0 and higher, creates the RAM disk in EMS memory. To use this switch, you must load an expanded memory manager (such as EMM386.EXE) before loading RAMDRIVE.SYS. You cannot use the /A and /E switches for the same RAM disk. You can create different RAM disks, however, some using EMS memory and others using XMS memory. Given a choice, use XMS memory.

After you insert the DEVICE=RAMDRIVE.SYS command into CONFIG.SYS and reboot your computer, DOS displays a message similar to the following during initialization of your computer:

```
Microsoft RAMDrive version .3.06 virtual disk D:
   Disk size: 1024
   Sector size: 512 bytes
   Allocation unit: 1 sectors
   Directory entries: 64
```

This message tells you the name DOS has assigned to the virtual disk (see the following Note), the disk size, sector size, allocation unit (cluster) size, and maximum number of root directory entries.

Note: The logical disk drive names (the drive letters) that DOS assigns to disks created by RAMDRIVE.SYS and DRIVER.SYS (see the Command Reference) depend on the placement of the commands in the CONFIG.SYS file. You may try to use the wrong disk drive name if you do not know how DOS assigns drive names.

When DOS encounters a block device driver (that is, any device that transfers data in blocks rather than in bytes), DOS assigns the next highest drive letter to that device. The order is first come, first assigned.

The potential for confusion comes when several block device drivers are loaded. The order of loading, determined by the order of the commands in the CONFIG.SYS file, determines the names assigned by DOS.

If you load RAMDRIVE.SYS first and DRIVER.SYS second, the RAM disk may be named D and the DRIVER.SYS disk one letter higher (E). If you switch the lines so that DRIVER.SYS is loaded first, the disk drive names also are switched. The DRIVER.SYS disk is named D, and the RAM disk is named E.

The amount of RAM in your computer, the programs you use, and the convenience of a RAM disk play a part in determining what size RAM disk you use or whether you should use a RAM disk.

Warning: Because RAM disks are memory-based devices, they lose their contents when you reboot or turn off your PC. To prevent loss, you must copy the contents of a RAM disk to a conventional disk file before rebooting or turning off the power. If you (or your applications program) are creating or modifying RAM disk files, you should regularly copy the files to an actual disk in case an unexpected power failure occurs.

One excellent way to use a RAM disk is to assign the TEMP environment variable to this virtual drive. Certain applications programs use an environment variable named TEMP to determine where to create various temporary files. These temporary files usually are written and read frequently during the operation of the program; their temporary nature makes them good candidates for storing in a RAM disk. The DOS 5.0 Shell, for example, stores swap files in the directory specified by the TEMP environment variable. Indeed, the default AUTOEXEC.BAT file discussed earlier in this chapter includes the following command:

    SET TEMP=C:\DOS

To assign TEMP to a RAM disk, you first have to determine a name for the virtual disk and then use the SET command (see the Command Reference). You should assign the TEMP variable to a subdirectory rather than to the RAM disk's root directory in order to avoid the 64-file-name limit. Assuming that the RAM disk becomes drive D, use the following commands in AUTOEXEC.BAT to create a directory on the virtual disk and to cause temporary files to be written to that directory:

    MD D:\TEMPDATA
    SET TEMP = D:\TEMPDATA

Some programs use an environment variable named TMP instead of TEMP for the same purpose. In such a case, substitute TMP for TEMP in the preceding command.

TIP

> *Tip:* When you use a RAM disk and then run the DOS Shell in the graphics display mode, the virtual disk is labeled with a special RAM icon.

Gaining More Speed with FASTOPEN

Yet another way to improve hard disk performance is through the FASTOPEN program. FASTOPEN is not a device driver per se; FASTOPEN is an executable program that can be included in AUTOEXEC.BAT. But you also can load the program through CONFIG.SYS using the special INSTALL command (available in DOS 4.0 and covered in this chapter). FASTOPEN, introduced with DOS 3.3, can be used only with hard drives. FASTOPEN caches directory information, holding in memory the locations of frequently used files and directories.

Directories are a type of file not accessible by users. DOS reads and writes directories in a manner similar to the way DOS handles other files. A part of the directory entry for a file or subdirectory holds the starting point for the file in the file allocation table (FAT). Because DOS typically holds the FAT in the disk buffers, FASTOPEN was developed to hold directory entries in memory.

FASTOPEN is not a complex command, but you must do a little work before you can use it effectively. FASTOPEN's syntax is as follows:

INSTALL *d:path***FASTOPEN.EXE d:** = *(n, m)* /X

or

d:path**FASTOPEN.EXE d:** = *n* /X

The first version of the FASTOPEN command uses INSTALL to load the program from CONFIG.SYS. If you issue the FASTOPEN command at the DOS prompt (or in your AUTOEXEC.BAT file), you must use the second version of the command.

TIP

> *Tip:* To load FASTOPEN into upper memory, use LOADHIGH in AUTOEXEC.BAT. For example, the following command loads FASTOPEN into upper memory and tracks file names and directories on drive C:
>
> LOADHIGH C:\DOS\FASTOPEN C:

The *d:path*\\ parameters are the disk drive and path to the FASTOPEN.EXE file. The **d:** following the file name is the name of the first hard drive you want FASTOPEN to track; you can specify up to 24 hard disks or hard disk partitions at once.

The *n* parameter is the number of directory entries that FASTOPEN should cache. Each file or subdirectory requires one directory entry, and you can enter a value from 10 through 999. If you do not specify a value for *n*, DOS defaults to 48 (10 in DOS 3.3 and 4).

The /X switch is similar to the /X switches of other commands. It enables FASTOPEN information to reside in EMS. By default, FASTOPEN uses conventional memory.

You can use FASTOPEN on as many disks as you want. Note, however, that the total number of directory entries or fragmented entries FASTOPEN can handle is 999. If you issue the command for several disk drives, the sum of the *n* values cannot exceed 999.

The practical limit of *n* is between 100 and 200 per disk. If you specify a value much higher, DOS wades through the internal directory entries more slowly than it reads information from disk. Additionally, each directory entry stored in memory takes 35 bytes. Considering this speed and memory trade-off, the 100 to 200 limit yields adequate performance.

Using too small a number for *n* also can be a disadvantage. When directory entries are recycled, the least recently used entry is discarded if a new entry is needed. If the *n* value is too small, DOS discards entries it may still need. The object is to have enough entries in memory so that FASTOPEN operates efficiently but not so many that FASTOPEN wastes time wading through directory entries.

At the least, *n* must exceed the number of subdirectories you travel to get to the "deepest" subdirectory. The minimum value for *n* is 48; this value nearly always exceeds the number of levels in your directory organization. Suppose that you have a directory structure such as \DOS\BASIC\TEST. The deepest level is 3 down from the root, much less than DOS's default of 48.

> **Note:** The disk drive you name cannot be one on which you use JOIN, SUBST, or ASSIGN because these commands do not create real drives. If you load a disk drive device driver through AUTOEXEC.BAT rather than through CONFIG.SYS, you must use FASTOPEN after you have defined all disk drives. FASTOPEN can get confused if you add additional disk drives after invoking it.

Protecting Your Files with MIRROR

The utility program MIRROR, included for the first time in DOS 5.0, has three functions; MIRROR can

- Recover an accidentally formatted hard disk or incorrect use of the RECOVER command

- Undelete an accidentally erased file

- Save a copy of each hard drive's partition table to a floppy disk for safe keeping

You can use MIRROR to make a copy of your hard disk's FAT, root directory, and boot record. MIRROR saves this information to disk in the file MIRROR.FIL, the *mirror image file*. DOS 5.0's UNFORMAT command can recover from an accidental format or an ill-advised use of RECOVER by restoring the FAT, root directory, and boot record from the mirror image file.

You also can use MIRROR to track files that you delete from any disk. MIRROR saves to disk a list of deleted files along with information about where the data for the deleted files was located. This information is saved to the file PCTRACKR.DEL, which enables the UNDELETE command (discussed in Chapter 10) to undelete many accidentally deleted files. This method is easier and more reliable than the DOS directory method (also discussed in Chapter 10).

The sections that follow describe these uses of MIRROR.

The syntax of the MIRROR start-up command is as follows:

> **MIRROR** *d:* ... */1 /Td -entries* ... */U /PARTN*

The *d:* parameter is the disk drive you want MIRROR to process. MIRROR processes the current logged drive if you don't specify a drive. You can list multiple disk drives (shown in the syntax by the first ellipsis [...]) and normally should include all the hard disk drives in your system. You also use this parameter with the */PARTN* switch.

The */1* switch causes MIRROR to save only the most recent information about the disk instead of maintaining the previous version of the mirror image file as a backup.

The */Td* switch, in which *d* denotes a disk drive, loads DOS 5.0's delete-tracking memory-resident program and starts tracking the drive denoted by the *d* parameter. You can cause MIRROR to track multiple disks by including a /T switch for each drive (shown by the second ellipsis in the syntax).

The *-entries* parameter is a number from 1 through 999 preceded by a hyphen (-). This parameter sets a maximum on the number of deleted files you want to track and indirectly determines the maximum size of the mirror image file.

The */U* switch unloads the delete-tracking program from memory.

The */PARTN* switch saves information about the specified hard disk to a floppy disk.

MIRROR's parameters and switches are explained more fully in the sections that follow.

Creating a Mirror Image File

To create a mirror image file on drive D, type the following command at the DOS prompt, and press Enter:

> **MIRROR D:**

MIRROR makes a copy of the hard disk's FAT, root directory, and boot record and saves this information to disk in the file MIRROR.FIL. The following message appears on-screen:

```
MIRROR, UNDELETE, and UNFORMAT Copyright (C) 1987-1991
Central Point Software, Inc.

Creates an image of the system area.

Drive D being processed.

The MIRROR process was successful.
```

The UNFORMAT command can use the mirror image file, MIRROR.FIL, to recover from an accidental FORMAT or RECOVER command (refer to Chapter 7 for a discussion of UNFORMAT).

For MIRROR to be most effective, you should run MIRROR at least every time you turn on the computer. UNFORMAT cannot recover files added since the last time you ran MIRROR. The easiest way to run MIRROR is to add the command to your AUTOEXEC.BAT file. For example, if your system has two hard disk drives, C and D, add the following command to AUTOEXEC.BAT:

```
MIRROR C: D:
```

Every time you turn on your computer, MIRROR creates a mirror image file on each drive.

The parameter /1 in MIRROR'S start-up command enables you to turn off the default feature that normally causes MIRROR to keep two copies of MIRROR.FIL. By default, when you run MIRROR, it renames the most recent copy of MIRROR.FIL to MIRROR.BAK and deletes any previous copy of MIRROR.BAK. Unless you are running severely short on disk space, do not use the /1 parameter. The earlier copy of MIRROR.FIL, stored as MIRROR.BAK, provides additional insurance that you can restore the hard disk after an accidental erasure.

Warning: If you accidentally format a hard disk, do not run MIRROR again before using UNFORMAT to recover the deleted files. However, if you do run MIRROR, you still can run UNFORMAT using MIRROR.BAK (see Chapter 7).

Fortunately, DOS 5.0's FORMAT command poses less danger than previous versions of FORMAT because DOS 5.0 performs a safe format by default, creating its own mirror image file (see Chapter 7). This mirror image file enables DOS 5.0's UNFORMAT command to recover your files and directories if you format the disk by mistake.

Note: When you perform a safe format with DOS 5.0's FORMAT command, FORMAT creates a mirror image file that contains the same type of information as the MIRROR.FIL. Unlike MIRROR.FIL, the mirror image file created by FORMAT is not listed in the disk's directory. UNFORMAT can use either mirror image file to recover data on a formatted disk.

DOS 5.0, however, provides an unconditional format option that can render UNFORMAT ineffective, depending on whether you accidentally format a floppy disk or a hard disk.

If you mistakenly format a floppy disk using DOS 5.0's unconditional format switch (/U), you cannot recover the files and directories on the formatted floppy disk even if you ran MIRROR just before formatting the disk. When FORMAT unconditionally formats a floppy disk, the command writes the hexadecimal value F6 to every byte on the disk, erasing all data on the disk. Nothing remains for UNFORMAT to recover.

The unconditional format option does not, however, erase data from a hard disk. When DOS 5.0'S FORMAT command performs an unconditional format of a hard disk, the command does not destroy existing data. Rather, FORMAT clears the FAT, root directory, and boot record, leaving all data intact, and then does a surface scan of the hard disk, looking for bad sectors. The only difference between this procedure and the unconditional format procedure is the absence of a mirror image file. In other words, if you run MIRROR immediately before doing an unconditional format of your hard disk, you have in effect performed the safe format operation. UNFORMAT can successfully recover your hard disk if you decide you didn't want to format the hard disk after all.

Performing Delete Tracking

Adding the optional /Td switch causes MIRROR to load the delete-tracking memory-resident program. Replace *d* in this switch with the drive to be monitored.

The *-entries* parameter is a number from 1 through 999 preceded by a hyphen (-). This parameter sets a maximum on the number of deleted files you want to track and indirectly determines the maximum size of the delete-tracking file (PCTRACKR.DEL). The default number of files tracked varies depending on the size of the disk MIRROR is tracking. Table 15.6 lists the default number of files tracked for each disk size and the resulting maximum delete-tracking file size.

Table 15.6
Default Number of Files Tracked
and Maximum Delete-Tracking File Sizes

Disk Size Tracked	Number of Files Size	Maximum File
360K	25	5K
720K	50	9K
1.2M	75	14K
1.44M	75	14K
20M	101	18K
32M	202	36K
Larger	303	55K

To cause MIRROR to start delete tracking for drives C and D each time you turn on the computer, include the following command in AUTOEXEC.BAT:

MIRROR /TC /TD

If you want to start delete tracking and create a mirror image file for both drives, add the following command to AUTOEXEC.BAT file instead:

MIRROR C: D: /TC /TD

This command creates a mirror image file for drives C and D and causes MIRROR to load the memory-resident delete-tracking program. The delete-tracking program then saves separate PCTRACKR.DEL files for drives C and D, tracking deletions on both disks.

At times, you may want to unload all memory-resident programs from your computer's memory. To unload MIRROR's delete-tracking feature, type the following command at the command line and press Enter:

MIRROR /U

Saving the Partition Table

As a part of the initial setup of your computer, the DOS program FDISK creates one or more partitions on your hard disk. A *partition* is a section of the hard disk set aside for use as a unit. You must have at least one DOS partition on your hard disk. You can have one or more partitions set up for use with another operating system, such as UNIX. DOS stores partition information in a file called the *partition table*. If this table is damaged, DOS cannot locate any files on the disk. The third purpose for MIRROR, therefore, is to save a copy of the partition table to a file on a floppy disk for safekeeping. The UNFORMAT command can restore the contents of the file to the hard disk in case of damage to the partition table.

> *Note:* MIRROR saves standard DOS partition tables only. Some hard disk manufacturers distribute with large hard disks special setup programs that create nonstandard partitions. The programs Disk Manager by On-Track and SpeedStor by Storage Dimensions are examples of programs that create partitions that MIRROR cannot save to a floppy.

To save partition information to a floppy disk, type the following command at the DOS command line, and press Enter:

MIRROR /PARTN

When you execute this command, MIRROR displays the following messages:

```
MIRROR, UNDELETE, and UNFORMAT Copyright (C) 1987-1991
Central Point Software, Inc.

Disk Partition Table saver.

The partition information from your hard drive(s) has
been read.

Next, the file PARTNSAV.FIL will be written to a floppy
disk. Please insert a formatted diskette and type the
name of the diskette drive.

What drive? A
```

Place a formatted disk in a floppy disk drive, type the letter of the floppy drive, and press Enter (for drive A, just press Enter). Mirror saves the partition table to the floppy disk in the file PARTNSAV.FIL and displays the following message:

```
Successful
```

Put this disk in a safe place so that it will be available if the hard disk partition table is damaged.

You need to repeat this partition-saving routine only if you later use FDISK to change your hard disk's partition information.

Refer to "Rebuilding a Partition Table" in Chapter 7 for instructions on using UNFORMAT to restore a damaged partition table from the file PARTNSAV.FIL.

Fine-Tuning Your Computer with CONFIG.SYS and AUTOEXEC.BAT

In addition to the commands already covered in this chapter, you can use many other commands in CONFIG.SYS or AUTOEXEC.BAT to customize your computer configuration. The following sections discuss other useful commands: SETVER, FCBS, FILES, LASTDRIVE, SHELL, INSTALL, REM, and SWITCHES.

Setting the Version with SETVER

When a new version of DOS is introduced, some time passes before popular applications programs are upgraded to take full advantage of DOS's new features. Many programs query the operating system to determine which version of DOS is loaded. If an unsupported version of DOS is in memory, these programs may refuse to run. Therefore, one or more of your applications programs may refuse to run because they have not been certified by the manufacturer to run properly with DOS 5.0.

You can get a reluctant program to run in DOS 5.0 in two ways:

- Contact the software manufacturer or your vendor to determine whether you need to obtain an upgrade.

- Use the SETVER command to add the name of the applications program to DOS 5.0's *version table*, a list of applications programs with a corresponding DOS version number. When a program listed in the version table loads into memory and queries DOS for its version number, DOS reports the version number listed in the version table rather than reporting the actual version number—5.0. The application is fooled into running in DOS 5.0.

The first option is preferable. By checking with the manufacturer, you can determine whether the applications program has been tested in DOS 5.0. If you use the second option, you run the risk, however slight, that data may be corrupted if the program turns out to be incompatible with DOS 5.0. Assuming that you choose to throw caution to the wind and modify the version table, follow the procedure set out in this section.

The SETVER command operates as a device driver and an executable command. Before DOS can use the version table, you must load SETVER.EXE as a device driver. Use the following syntax:

DEVICE=*d:path***\SETVER.EXE**

The parameters *d:* and *path* are the disk and directory that contain the SETVER.EXE external program file. The default CONFIG.SYS file, for example, discussed at the beginning of the chapter, includes the following command:

DEVICE=\DOS\SETVER.EXE\

After the device driver SETVER.EXE is loaded into memory, DOS uses the version table automatically to report the DOS version to listed applications programs.

You can use SETVER from the command line to display the current version table as well as add or delete program names. The syntax for using SETVER at the command line is as follows:

SETVER *d:path\filename.ext n.nn /DELETE /QUIET*

To display the version table, use SETVER with no switches or parameters. DOS displays a two-column listing with applications program names in the first column and the DOS version number in the second column. Microsoft has already tested the programs listed in the initial version table and determined that they operate properly in DOS 5.0. The version list that displays on your screen should look similar to the following:

```
WIN200.BIN        3.40
WIN100.BIN        3.40
WINWORD.EXE       4.10
EXCEL.EXE         4.10
HITACHI.SYS       4.00
MSCDEX.EXE        4.00
REDIR4.EXE        4.00
NET.EXE           4.00
NET.COM           3.30
NETWKSTA.EXE      4.00
DXMA0MOD.SYS      3.30
BAN.EXE           4.00
BAN.COM           4.00
MSREDIR.EXE       4.00
METRO.EXE         3.31
IBMCACHE.SYS      3.40
REDIR40.EXE       4.00
DD.EXE            4.01
```

```
DD.BIN              4.01
LL3.EXE             4.01
REDIR.EXE           4.00
SYQ55.SYS           4.00
SSTDRIVE.SYS        4.00
ZDRV.SYS            4.01
ZFMT.SYS            4.01
TOPSCR.EXE          4.00
```

When you run one of the programs listed in the first column of the version table, DOS reports to the program the DOS version number listed in the second column.

If you have trouble running a program and the application displays an error message indicating that you are trying to execute the program with an incompatible version of DOS, you may want to try adding the program to the version table. Type the SETVER command as follows:

SETVER *c:path***filename.ext n.nn**

The *c:path* parameter indicates the disk and drive where the SETVER.EXE file is located on your system.

The **filename.ext** parameter is the name and extension of the command that starts the applications program in question.

The **n.nn** parameter is a DOS version number recognized by the applications program. Consult the program's documentation to determine the versions of DOS supported.

For example, assume that you want to run the program KILLERAP.EXE, but the program supports only DOS Versions 3.0 to 3.3. To add KILLERAP.EXE to the version table, type the following command at the command prompt, and press Enter:

SETVER KILLERAP.EXE 3.30

DOS displays the following series of messages, including an initial warning:

```
WARNING - The application you are adding to the MS-DOS
version table may not have been verified by Microsoft
on this version of MS-DOS. Please contact your software
vendor for information on whether this application will
operate properly under this version of MS-DOS. If you
execute this application by instructing MS-DOS to
report a different MS-DOS version number, you may lose
or corrupt data, or cause system instabilities. In that
circumstance, Microsoft is not responsible for any loss
or damage.
```

```
Version table successfully updated
The version change will take effect the next time you
restart your system
```

To verify that the application has been added to the version table, execute SETVER again without switches or parameters. The added application is listed at the end of the list. The modified table takes effect, however, only after you restart or reboot your computer.

If you later decide to delete a program from the version list, use the /DELETE (/D) switch and the *filename* parameter. For example, to delete KILLERAP.EXE from the version table, type one of the following commands at the command line, and press Enter:

SETVER KILLERAP.EXE /DELETE

or

SETVER KILLERAP.EXE /D

DOS deletes the application name from the version table and displays the following message:

```
Version table successfully updated
The version change will take effect the next time you
restart your system.
```

If you are using a batch file to delete an applications program name from the version table, you may want to suppress the preceding message. To prevent this message from displaying, add the /QUIET switch in addition to the /DELETE switch.

Accessing Files through FCBS

The FCBS configuration command enables you to use programs written for DOS 1.1; some DOS users find FCBS indispensable.

FCB is an acronym for *file control block*. FCBs serve as one way a program can access a file. This method of file access was used by DOS 1.1 to communicate with programs. Later versions of DOS borrow a UNIX-like method for controlling files, called handles (discussed in "Using the FILES Command" in this chapter). Although FCBs can be used with any version of DOS, handles can be used only with DOS 2.0 and higher.

The syntax for the FCBS command in the CONFIG.SYS file is as follows:

FCBS = maxopen

The **maxopen** parameter is a number from 1 through 255 that sets the maximum number of unique FCBs programs can open at one time. The default number is 4. You don't need to use this command in CONFIG.SYS unless you have a program that was designed to work with DOS 1.1 and the program cannot open all the required files (a message to this effect appears). In that case, use the FCBS command to increase the number of FCBs that can be open at one time.

You pay a small price in RAM to use the FCBS command. For each number above 4 that *maxopen* exceeds, DOS uses about 40 bytes.

Using the FILES Command

FILES is the configuration command used in DOS 2.0 and higher to enable UNIX-like file handling. UNIX and later versions of DOS use a *file handle* (a number corresponding to the file name) instead of file control blocks to access files. You never have to deal with file handles directly. Each applications program gives the operating system the name of the file or device you want to use. The operating system gives back to your program a handle—a two-byte number—and your program uses the handle to manipulate the file or device.

To include the FILES command in CONFIG.SYS, use the following syntax:

FILES = n

The n parameter is a number from 8 (the default) through 255 that determines the number of files which can be open at any time during a DOS session. Each additional file over 8 increases the size of DOS by 39 bytes.

If you do not specify the FILES command, DOS starts with eight file handles and immediately takes five handles for the standard devices, leaving only three handles for your programs. The default CONFIG.SYS file, listed earlier in the chapter, includes the following FILES command:

FILES = 10

This command establishes 10 file handles, which should be enough for most programs. If a program displays an error message about file handles, edit CONFIG.SYS, and increase the number of handles to 20 or 30.

> *Note:* Many installation programs for full-featured applications edit CONFIG.SYS for you and increase the number of files when necessary to run the software efficiently.

Using LASTDRIVE To Change the Number of Disk Drives

The LASTDRIVE configuration command informs DOS of the maximum number of disk drives on your system. Generally, LASTDRIVE is a command used with networked computers or with the pretender commands (such as SUBST).

If you do not use the LASTDRIVE command, DOS assumes that the last disk drive on your system is one more than the number of physical drives and RAM disks you are using. If you give DOS a letter corresponding to fewer drives than you are using—physically attached to your computer or created as RAM disks—DOS ignores the command. The LASTDRIVE command enables you to tell DOS how many disk drives, real or apparent, are on your system, including network drives and directories (if any) and drives created with the SUBST command, discussed later in this chapter.

If you want to use the LASTDRIVE command in CONFIG.SYS, use the following syntax:

LASTDRIVE = *x*

The *x* parameter is the letter for the last disk drive on your system. The letters A through Z in upper- or lowercase are acceptable.

A typical reason you may want to use LASTDRIVE is to establish logical disk drives. A *logical* disk drive can be a nickname for another disk drive (see the SUBST command in this chapter and in the Command Reference). A logical disk drive also may be another partition of the hard disk. A logical disk drive is just a name. DOS "thinks" that the logical disk drive is real.

Using the SHELL Command

The SHELL command was originally implemented to enable programmers to replace the DOS command interpreter (COMMAND.COM) with other command interpreters. The SHELL command is more commonly used, however, to perform two other functions:

- Inform DOS that the command interpreter is in another directory, not in the boot disk's root directory.

- Expand the size of the *environment*—an area of RAM that stores named variables used by DOS and applications programs. Commands such as PATH and PROMPT store their current settings as environment variables. To display the contents of the environment, type **SET** at the command prompt, and press Enter.

> *Warning:* SHELL is a tricky command, which you should use cautiously. Used incorrectly, the SHELL command can lock up your system. Keep a bootable floppy disk handy for restarting your computer should you run into a problem.

The syntax for the SHELL command is as follows:

SHELL = *d:path***filename.ext** *parameters*

The *d:path* parameter specifies the disk drive and path that contain the command processor you want to use. **filename.ext** is the name of the command processor.

The SHELL command itself doesn't take any other parameters or switches, but you can add command-line parameters or switches available for use with the command processor.

When used from the command line, COMMAND loads a copy of the command processor into memory. A common use of COMMAND is as a parameter of the SHELL command.

The syntax for COMMAND is as follows:

COMMAND *d:path\ device /E:size /P /C string /MSG*

The *d:path* parameter specifies the disk drive and path that contain the command processor if it is not located in the root directory. Always use this parameter when including COMMAND in the SHELL configuration command. This parameter has the additional effect of setting an environment variable named *COMSPEC*, which informs DOS and other programs of the location and name of the current command processor.

/E:size is an optional switch that sets the environment space. The *size* parameter is a number from 160 through 32,768 that denotes the amount of memory reserved for the environment. (If you do not specify a multiple of 16, DOS rounds the *size* parameter up to the next highest multiple of 16). By default, DOS 5.0 reserves 256 bytes for the environment (160 bytes in DOS 3.2 through 4.0).

The */P* switch instructs DOS to load the command processor permanently. Without the /P switch, DOS loads COMMAND.COM only temporarily into memory. When you are using COMMAND with the SHELL command in CONFIG.SYS, be sure to use the /P switch. Otherwise, you cannot access the command line until you reboot the system using a disk that doesn't contain the inappropriate SHELL command.

The /C switch and *string* parameter work together. This combination causes DOS to load the command processor, execute any command represented by *string*, and then unload the command processor. Chapter 13 discusses how to use COMMAND with /C *string* to call a batch file from within a batch file. Do not use this switch-parameter combination with SHELL.

The /MSG switch tells DOS to store all its error messages in memory rather than read them from the disk. This feature can speed operation somewhat. More important, when you are running a floppy disk system, you sometimes remove from the disk drive the disk that contains COMMAND.COM. Without the /MSG switch, DOS cannot access error messages contained on disk within the COMMAND.COM file itself. You normally should use this switch only if running DOS from floppy disks. You also must use the /P switch any time you use the /MSG switch.

The DOS 5.0 Setup program adds the following command to the default CONFIG.SYS file, listed earlier in the chapter:

    SHELL=C:\DOS\COMMAND.COM C:\DOS\ /P

This configuration command tells DOS that COMMAND.COM is the command interpreter and that it is located in the \DOS directory on the C drive. The /P switch causes the command interpreter to be loaded permanently, not temporarily, in memory.

The preceding SHELL command enables you to place a copy of COMMAND.COM in C:\DOS and delete the copy in the root directory. This practice helps you maintain a clean root directory (discussed in Chapter 9) and protects COMMAND.COM from being replaced by an older version that may be on a floppy disk you are copying. If you accidentally copy the disk to the root directory, you don't overwrite the current version of COMMAND.COM.

Sometimes you create such a long PATH command in AUTOEXEC.BAT that you fill the available environment space, causing DOS to display the message Out of environment space. If you see this message, use COMMAND with the SHELL command and the /E switch to specify a larger environment space. For example, the following command, used in CONFIG.SYS, increases the environment to 384 bytes:

    SHELL=C:\DOS\COMMAND.COM /E:384

If you already have a SHELL command in CONFIG.SYS, you can add the /E switch. For example, combining the two preceding SHELL commands, you can include the following command in CONFIG.SYS:

    SHELL=C:\DOS\COMMAND.COM C:\DOS\ /P /E:384

Note: The SHELL command itself doesn't use any memory, but by increasing the environment space, you are reducing the amount of free conventional memory by an equal amount. In other words, increasing the environment space from 256 bytes to 384 bytes reduces free memory by 128 bytes.

Using the INSTALL Command

The INSTALL configuration command (new in DOS 4.0) enables you to load certain utility programs that remain in memory from the CONFIG.SYS file. In versions of DOS before 4.0, you had to load these programs from the DOS prompt or through a batch file, such as AUTOEXEC.BAT. You can save several kilobytes of memory by loading a program from CONFIG.SYS with INSTALL rather than from the command line or a batch file as an executable program. DOS 4.0 and later versions support loading any of the following programs by using INSTALL:

FASTOPEN.EXE
KEYB.COM
NLSFUNC.EXE
SHARE.EXE

The Command Reference provides more information about these programs.

The syntax for using INSTALL in CONFIG.SYS is as follows:

INSTALL = *d:path***filename** *parameters*

The *d:path* parameter is the disk and path information, and **filename** is the name of the utility you want to load. The *parameters* parameter specifies parameters and switches that may be available for use with the utility you want DOS to load.

You may be able to use INSTALL with some memory-resident non-DOS programs. Do not use INSTALL to load a memory-resident program that uses environment variables or shortcut keys or that uses COMMAND.COM. The program you install with this command must have the extension COM or EXE.

Using the REM Command

The REM configuration command (new in DOS 4.0) is equivalent to the REM batch file command (discussed in Chapter 13). This command enables you to insert remarks into your CONFIG.SYS file. You can leave notes to yourself (or others) explaining what particular lines do. Such documentation in a CONFIG.SYS file is especially helpful if you use non-DOS device drivers for your hardware. You also can temporarily remove a CONFIG.SYS statement by prefacing it with a REM command. After you test the new configuration, you can return easily to the old configuration by simply removing the REM command.

The syntax for the REM command is as follows:

> **REM** *remarks*

The *remarks* parameter can be any string of characters that fits on a single line in the CONFIG.SYS file.

Using the SWITCHES Command

The SWITCHES configuration command (new in DOS 4.0) turns off the Enhanced Keyboard functions. This command works like the ANSI.SYS /K switch. The syntax for this command is as follows:

> **SWITCHES = /K**

Some software cannot work with the Enhanced Keyboard. Use this command to disable the Enhanced Keyboard, and the software should function properly.

If you use the SWITCHES=/K command in CONFIG.SYS and also install ANSI.SYS as a device driver, add the /K switch to the DEVICE=ANSI.SYS line as well.

Telling DOS When To Break

You have learned that Ctrl-Break and Ctrl-C are helpful but not foolproof panic buttons you use to stop commands. The response to a Ctrl-Break or Ctrl-C is not instantaneous. Only an "oh-no" second may have passed from the time you pressed the panic button until DOS responded, but you still had time to wonder what took so long for DOS to pay attention. The reason is that DOS is busy doing other things most of the time and looks for

Ctrl-Break only at intervals. You can use the BREAK command in CONFIG.SYS to tell DOS when to check for this key sequence. BREAK does not enable or disable this feature.

The syntax for the BREAK command is as follows:

> **BREAK=ON**

or

> **BREAK=OFF**

The default setting for this command is OFF.

If you use the command BREAK=ON in CONFIG.SYS, DOS checks to see whether you have pressed Ctrl-Break whenever a program requests some activity from DOS (performs a DOS function call). If you use the command BREAK=OFF, DOS checks for a Ctrl-Break only when DOS is working with the video display, keyboard, printer, or asynchronous serial adapters (the ports at the back of the computer).

If you use programs that do a great deal of disk accessing but little keyboard or screen work, you may want to set BREAK=ON. This setting enables you to break out of the program if something goes awry or if you simply want to stop DOS.

Using the DOS Pretender Commands

Because DOS manages disks in a logical rather than a strictly physical way, DOS can "pretend" that a disk's identity is different from the disk's name. DOS provides three commands that pretend that a disk's identity has changed. ASSIGN redirects disk operations from one disk to another. JOIN attaches an entire disk as a subdirectory to the directory structure of another disk. SUBST makes a directory of a disk appear to commands as a separate disk. The following sections examine these commands.

Reassigning Drive Names with the ASSIGN Command

Some older versions of software still expect files to be on floppy disk drives. Such assumptions by your software may not match your system's disk drive resources. Most users place their software on a hard disk, so software that wants to work from floppy disk drives sometimes refuses to work properly.

Installation programs for some newer programs occasionally "insist" that you place the installation disk in drive A. But the new software you purchased may contain only 3 1/2-inch disks, and your 3 1/2-inch drive is drive B. You may not be able to install the program if its installation procedure requires you to insert the first disk into drive A.

You can use the external command ASSIGN to solve problems of this sort. This command redirects all DOS read and write requests from one drive designation to another. By using the ASSIGN command, DOS can work with a disk different from the one actually specified by an applications program or on the command line.

> **Tip:** The DOS 5.0 documentation indicates that future versions of DOS may not support the ASSIGN command. You may want to consider using the SUBST command instead of ASSIGN.

The syntax for the ASSIGN command is as follows:

ASSIGN d1=d2 ... */STATUS*

d1 is the drive letter from which you want to redirect read and write operations, the drive letter your software "thinks" it is working with.

d2 is the drive letter of the drive you actually want the program to use.

The ellipsis (...) indicates that more than one drive assignment can be made through a single ASSIGN command.

Use the */STATUS* switch with no other parameters to display a listing of current disk drive assignments (DOS 5.0 only).

When you issue the ASSIGN command, DOS redirects all read and write requests for d1 to d2. If you assign drive A to drive B, all commands referring to drive A are actually sent to drive B. The command to make this assignment is as follows:

ASSIGN A=B

If you later cannot remember what disk assignment you made, issue the following command:

ASSIGN /STATUS

DOS displays the following message:

```
Original A: set to B:
```

To revert to all original disk assignments, issue the ASSIGN command with no parameters, as follows:

    ASSIGN

The ASSIGN command should be used sparingly. If it is not required for a particular purpose, do not use it. Certain programs may require disk information that is not available from the reassigned drive.

When using ASSIGN, consider the following guidelines:

- Do not assign the drive letter of a hard disk to another drive.

- Do not reassign a drive that is currently in use by a program.

- You can use an optional colon after the drive letter with DOS 4.0 and later.

- Remove any ASSIGN settings before running BACKUP, FDISK, LABEL, or RESTORE.

- Do not use ASSIGN if JOIN or SUBST is being used.

- Do not use ASSIGN before using the APPEND command.

- DISKCOPY, DISKCOMP, and FORMAT do not recognize any drive reassignments.

- d1 and d2 must physically exist in the computer.

Joining Two Disk Drives with JOIN

The ASSIGN command makes an entire disk drive appear to have a drive letter different from its real value. The JOIN command is used to add a disk drive to the directory structure of another disk. This command can be used from the command line or from within a batch file, including AUTOEXEC.BAT.

The external command JOIN enables you to have a floppy disk that appears to be part of a hard disk. The directory structure on the floppy disk is added to the directory structure of the hard disk. You also can use JOIN to attach one hard drive to a subdirectory on another hard drive.

The syntax for JOIN is as follows:

    JOIN d1: *d2:path* /D

The **d1:** parameter indicates the disk drive you want DOS to join to another drive. You can think of this drive as the *guest* disk drive.

The *d2:* parameter is the disk drive to which **d1:** is to be joined. You can think of this second drive as the *host* disk drive.

The *path* is the path of the directory to which you want to join the guest disk drive. You can think of this directory as the *host* directory.

Use the /D switch to disconnect, or "unjoin," a specified guest disk drive from its host.

To show currently connected drives, use the JOIN command alone, as follows:

JOIN

For example, to join drive B to the \DATA directory on your C drive, issue the following command:

JOIN B: C:\DATA

If you later are not sure to which directory you assigned drive B, issue the JOIN command without parameters to display the following message:

```
B: => C:\DATA
```

Chapters 8 and 9 discuss hierarchical directories and associated commands. The JOIN command connects or joins a guest drive to a directory position on a host disk drive. Any directory hierarchy on the guest drive becomes a part of the other disk drive's hierarchical structure.

Using the terminology of a directory tree, you can think of the JOIN command as grafting a second tree onto the first. The second tree is positioned at least one level down the structure. The grafting point must be assigned a name so that DOS can refer to it. In this way, the root directory of the guest disk is given a new name. All directories below the root directory on this reassigned drive have this new name as part of their path.

DOS internally converts all read and write requests to this new subdirectory—and all layers below the subdirectory—into a drive assignment with the appropriate path.

When you use JOIN, consider the following guidelines:

- The directory specified by the *path* parameter must be empty or nonexistent.

- You cannot join a disk to the current directory.

- You cannot join a disk to the root directory of any drive.

- While a guest drive is joined to a host drive, you cannot access the guest drive by its original name.

- The entire guest drive is joined with the JOIN command.

- You cannot specify a networked drive as d1: or d2:.

- Do not use JOIN with SUBST or ASSIGN.

- Remove any JOIN settings before running DISKCOPY, DISKCOMP, FDISK, FORMAT, BACKUP, or RESTORE.

Substituting a Drive Name for a Path with SUBST

The external command SUBST is an opposite of the JOIN command. Instead of grafting a second disk onto the tree structure of another disk, the SUBST command splits a disk's directory structure into two. In effect, the SUBST command creates an alias disk drive name for a subdirectory—a *virtual drive*. You can use this command from the command line or from within a batch file, such as AUTOEXEC.BAT.

The syntax for the SUBST command is as follows:

SUBST d1: *d2:***path** */D*

The **d1:** parameter indicates the disk drive name you want DOS to assign as a virtual drive. d1 normally is not the name of a drive that exists in your system; however, d1 must be within the range specified by the LASTDRIVE command in CONFIG.SYS.

The *d2:* parameter is the disk drive that contains the path to which you want to assign the virtual drive, d1.

The **path** is the path of the directory you want to be able to access as if it were a disk named d1.

Use the */D* switch to delete the virtual drive.

To see the current virtual drives (created by SUBST), use the SUBST command without any parameters.

The SUBST command replaces a path name for a subdirectory with a drive letter. When a SUBST command is in effect, DOS translates all I/O requests to a particular drive letter to the correct path name.

The virtual drive "created" by the SUBST command inherits the directory tree structure of the subdirectory reassigned to a drive letter.

When using SUBST, consider the following guidelines:

- d1: and d2: must be different drive letters.

- You cannot specify a networked drive as d1: or d2:.

- d1: cannot be the current drive.

- d1: must have a designator smaller than the value in the LASTDRIVE statement of CONFIG.SYS.

- Do not use SUBST with ASSIGN or JOIN.

- Remove any SUBST settings before running BACKUP, CHKDSK, DISKCOPY, DISKCOMP, FDISK, FORMAT, LABEL, MIRROR, RECOVER, RESTORE, or SYS.

SUBST is commonly used in two different situations. If you are using a program that does not support path names, you can use the SUBST command to assign a drive letter to a directory. The program then refers to the drive letter, and DOS translates the request into a path. If, for example, the data for a program is stored in C:\WORDPROC, you can type the following:

SUBST E: C:\WORDPROC

You tell the program that the data is stored in drive E.

When the substitution has been made, you can issue the following command:

SUBST

The following message appears:

```
E: => C:\WORDPROC
```

To disconnect the substitution of drive E for the C:\WORDPROC directory, type the following command, and press Enter:

SUBST E: /D

The second common use for SUBST is to reduce typing long path names. Typing long path names can be a tedious process when more than one person uses a PC. Each user may have a separate section of the hard disk for storing data files, but common areas of the disk are used to store the programs. If the paths \USER1\WORDDATA and \USER1\SPREDATA exist on drive C, the typing needed to reach files in the directories can be reduced by entering the following command:

SUBST E: C:\USER1

Using Other Device Control Commands

DOS provides other commands to control devices and report system information. All these other commands are explained in the Command Reference. The following are brief descriptions of some commands you may want to use.

The SET command displays the current environment settings and enables you to make new variable assignments.

The PRINT command enables you to print text files on your printer while you continue to do other PC work. This "background" printing can be a great time-saver if your applications programs don't have a similar feature.

The MODE command is a multifaceted device-control command. MODE can establish the height and width of your screen's lines and characters and control the speed of your serial ports. MODE can redirect the output from a parallel printer port to a serial port. MODE also can be used in association with code page support for international character sets on the PC. You may want to browse through the MODE section of the Command Reference.

Summary

In this chapter, you have learned the following important points:

- DOS can alter your system's configuration through instructions in the CONFIG.SYS and AUTOEXEC.BAT files.

- The CONFIG.SYS file must be in the root directory of the boot disk. When you alter CONFIG.SYS, configuration changes do not occur until DOS is rebooted.

- Disk buffers make DOS work faster by placing requested information in RAM.

- DOS 5.0 provides several new memory management features that can free significant portions of conventional memory as well as speed the operation of your system.

- Disk caches, such as the SMARTDRV.SYS program, can speed certain disk operations.

- RAMDRIVE.SYS, the DOS RAM disk software, can speed disk operations if your computer has sufficient random-access memory.

- The FILES command sets the number of files DOS can open at any one time.

- The LASTDRIVE command specifies the last disk drive letter you want to use in your system.

- You can tell DOS when to look for the Ctrl-Break key sequence.

- You can cause DOS to pretend that a drive's identity is different than it really is through the JOIN, SUBST, and ASSIGN commands.

The next part of the book, Part IV, contains the comprehensive Command Reference. The Command Reference lists, in alphabetical order, the commands available with DOS. The commands are shown with syntax, applicable rules, and examples. You can use the information in the Command Reference both as a reference when you have problems and as a source of practical advice and tips.

Part IV

Command Reference

Command Reference

This command reference indexes and describes the DOS commands. The commands are presented with the command name appearing first, followed by the versions of DOS to which the command applies.

Next, the terms *internal* and *external* indicate whether the command is built into DOS or is disk-resident. A brief description of the command's purpose immediately follows the title line. Each command entry illustrates the syntax in one or more syntax lines showing how to invoke the command. Occasionally, a command may have a long and a short form, equally valid as command terms in a syntactical structure. In these instances, both forms are given. When switches can be used in the command line, these are listed and defined.

Notes give further information about the command, amplifying the purpose, giving insight into its efficient use, or otherwise acquainting you with the scope of the command. As appropriate, cautionary notes are included to help you avoid particular pitfalls associated with a command. A reference may be given directing you to a chapter within the book that treats the command at greater length. Finally, in some cases, an example of how to use the command is given.

Command Reference Conventions

Great effort has been taken to make the DOS Command Reference as easy as possible to use. Yet to understand fully the syntax lines discussed, you must be familiar with a few conventions. These conventions indicate what is mandatory or optional and what components of the syntax line are variable. Conventional substitute forms also stand in place of the variable terms.

To represent a file name, you see the following:

> *d:path***filename.ext**

The *d:* represents a drive designation and can be any valid drive letter that is available on your computer.

path\ represents a single subdirectory or a path of subdirectories on a valid drive.

filename.ext represents the full file name and its extension. When specifying a file name, you must give the extension if one exists. The **.ext** is always shown in the syntax line as a reminder.

When the syntax specifies an external command, you see a command line that resembles the following:

> *dc:pathc***command_name**

The *dc:* represents the drive that contains the command. Again, this entry can be any valid drive letter that is on your computer.

pathc\ represents the subdirectory or path of subdirectories that leads to the command.

command_name is any valid DOS command. When entering the command name, you do not need to specify the extension.

If FORMAT.COM resides in drive C in the subdirectory path \DOS\DISK, the syntax line

> *dc:pathc***FORMAT**

means that you can type

> **C:\DOS\DISK\FORMAT**

to start formatting a disk.

In this Command Reference, any literal text that you type in a syntax line is shown in uppercase letters. Any text that you replace with other text (variable text) is shown in lowercase letters.

As an example, the syntax line

> **FORMAT d:**

means that you must type **FORMAT** to format a disk. The **d** is replaced by any valid disk drive letter. To format a disk in drive A, you type

> **FORMAT A:**

Any mandatory portions of a syntax line are shown in **boldface**; optional elements are shown in *italic*.

For example, if FORMAT.COM is in the \DOS directory on drive C and your current directory is C:\DOS, you do not have to type the drive and path to start FORMAT.COM. The following syntax form shows that the drive and path information can be omitted:

> *C:\DOS***FORMAT**

If you have FORMAT.COM residing on a drive and directory other than those shown in this example, the syntax is represented as follows:

> *dc:pathc***FORMAT**

where *dc:pathc* is variable text and optional, and **FORMAT** is literal text and mandatory.

Look at this sample syntax line:

> *dc:pathc***FORMAT** **d:**/*S*/*1*/*8*/*V*/*B*/*4*/*N:ss*/*T:tt*/*V:label*;/*F:size*

The drive and path pointing to the command are both optional and variable (indicated by the italic, lowercase type). All the switches are optional. The switches are shown in uppercase, to signify literal text. A few options for the /N, /T, /V, and /F switches are variable.

The only mandatory items in the syntax line are the command, **FORMAT**, and the drive to format, **d:**.

> *Note:* DOS 5.0 includes an on-line help facility not found in earlier versions of DOS. To see a screen of information describing the syntax for a particular DOS command, type the command followed by /?. For example, to see a help screen for the DIR command type **DIR** /? and press Enter.

APPEND   V3.3, V4, V5—External

Instructs DOS to search for nonprogram/nonbatch files in the directories on the disks you specify

Syntax

> *dc:pathc***APPEND** /*X* /*E d1:path1;d1:path2;d2:path1;...*

or

> *dc:pathc***APPEND;**

DOS 4 or DOS 5 additional switches are as follows:

*dc:pathc***APPEND** */X:ON /X:OFF /PATH:ON /PATH:OFF*

dc:pathc is the disk drive and directory that hold the command.

d1:path1, *d1:path2*, *d2:path1* are valid disk drive names and paths to the directories you want DOS to search for nonprogram/nonbatch files. The ellipsis (...) represents additional disk drive and path names.

; cancels any paths APPEND searches.

Switches

/X	Redirects programs that use the DOS function calls SEARCH FIRST, FIND FIRST, and EXEC
/X:ON	Same as /X (DOS 4 and 5 only)
/X:OFF	Turns off this feature (DOS 4 and 5 only)
/E	Places the disk drive paths in the environment
/PATH:ON	Turns on the search for files that have a drive or path specified (DOS 4 and 5 only)
/PATH:OFF	Turns off the search for files that have a drive or path specified (DOS 4 and 5 only)

Notes

The first time you execute APPEND, the program loads from the disk and installs itself in DOS. APPEND then becomes an internal command and is not reloaded from the disk until you restart DOS. You can give the /X and /E switches only when you first invoke APPEND. You cannot specify any path names when you issue these two switches.

If DOS encounters an invalid path (one that is misspelled or that no longer exists, for example), DOS skips the path and does not display a message.

Do not use APPEND with RESTORE. The RESTORE command searches for files in the directories on which you have used APPEND. If you use the /N or /M switch with RESTORE, the correct files may not be processed. Before using RESTORE, be sure to deactivate APPEND.

Examples

APPEND is the complement of PATH. PATH searches for program and batch files (COM, EXE, or BAT), and APPEND searches for all other files.

Before using APPEND to set search paths, use the following form:

APPEND /E /X

(DOS stores append path in environment; SEARCH FIRST, FIND FIRST, and EXEC are enabled.)

or use this form:

APPEND /E

(DOS stores append path in environment only.)

After you run APPEND with the switches, you can tell APPEND which directories to search. For example, to search the directories C:\DOS and C:\DOS\UTILS, use the following form:

APPEND C:\DOS;C:\DOS\UTILS

To disable the APPEND command, type this form:

APPEND;

ASSIGN   V2,V3, V4, V5—External

Instructs DOS to use a disk drive other than one specified by a program or command

Syntax

To reroute drive activity, use the following form:

*dc:pathc***ASSIGN d1=d2 ...** */STATUS*

dc:pathc is the disk drive and directory that hold the command.

d1 is the letter of the disk drive the program or DOS normally uses.

d2 is the letter of the disk drive you want the program or DOS to use instead of the usual drive.

The ellipsis (...) represents additional disk drive assignments.

Switches

/STATUS   Displays all current drive assignments

Notes

ASSIGN reroutes a program, causing it to use a disk drive other than the one the program intends. A program "thinks" it is using a certain disk drive, when in fact the program is using another. You should use ASSIGN primarily for programs that are written to work only with drives A and B but that you want to load and run from your hard disk.

Do not use a colon after the disk drive letter for **d1** or **d2**. You can use a space on either side or both sides of the equal sign.

You can give more than one assignment on the same line. Use a space between each set of assignments, as in the following example:

ASSIGN B=C A=C

ASSIGN was added to DOS for compatibility with programs that do not support drive letters other than A and B. Using ASSIGN, a program can be placed on drive C, and any calls to drive A or B are redirected to drive C. For compatibility with future versions of DOS, however, use SUBST. SUBST performs the same type of reassigning ASSIGN does; however, you can substitute a subdirectory name with a drive letter.

ATTRIB   V3, V4, V5—External

Displays, sets, or clears the read-only or archive attributes of a file

Syntax

*dc:pathc***ATTRIB** *+R -R +A -A d:path***filename.ext** */s*

In DOS 5, additional parameters are as follows:

*dc:pathc***ATTRIB** *+S -S +H -H d:path***filename.ext** */s*

dc:pathc is the disk drive and directory that hold the command.

+R turns on a file's read-only attribute.

+A turns on a file's archive attribute.

+*S* turns on a file's system file attribute.

+*H* turns on a file's hidden attribute.

-*R* turns off a file's read-only attribute.

-*A* turns off a file's archive attribute.

-*S* turns off a file's system file attribute.

-*H* turns off a file's hidden attribute.

d:path is the disk drive and directory holding the files for which the attribute will be displayed or changed.

filename.ext is the name of the file(s) for which the attributes will be displayed or changed. Wild cards are permitted.

Switches

/S   Sets or clears the attributes of the specified files in the specified directory and all subdirectories to that directory

Notes

With the addition of ATTRIB in DOS 3, users gained greater control over the DOS read-only and archive file attributes. ATTRIB sets or clears these attributes.

DOS 5 enables you to have even more control over a file's attributes. You can make a file a system file or hide the file.

For more information, see Chapter 8.

BACKUP   V2, V3, V4, V5—External

Backs up one or more files from a hard disk or floppy disk onto another disk

Syntax

*dc:pathc***BACKUP d1:***path\filename.ext* **d2:** */S /M /A /D:date /T:time /F /L:dl:pathl\filenamel.extl*

dc:pathc is the disk drive and directory that hold the command.

d1:*path* is the hard disk or floppy disk drive and the directory to be backed up.

filename.ext specifies the file you want to back up. Wild cards are allowed.

d2: is the hard or floppy disk drive that receives the backup files.

Switches

/S	Backs up all subdirectories, starting with the specified or current directory on the source disk and working downward
/M	Backs up all files modified since their last backup
/A	Adds to files already on the specified floppy disk drive, the file(s) to be backed up
/D:date	Backs up any file that was created or changed on or after the specified date
/T:time	Backs up any file that was created or changed on or after the specified time on the specified date (used only with the /D switch)
/F	Formats the target floppy disk if the floppy disk is not formatted. DOS 4 and 5 automatically format the target floppy disks (without use of this switch).
/F:size	With DOS 4 or 5, formats the destination floppy disk according to the size specified. If you have a 1.2M disk drive, but only 360K floppy disks, you can specify /F:360 to format the 360K disk in the 1.2M drive.
/L:dl:pathl\ filenamel.ext	Creates a log file

Notes

At completion, BACKUP produces exit codes. An exit code is a number telling DOS the status of BACKUP when it stopped. You can test for exit codes in a batch file using IF. Depending on the exit code you test for, you can change the outcome of the batch file. The following is a list of exit codes that BACKUP produces:

Exit Code	Meaning
0	Backup was successful
1	No files found

Exit Code	Meaning
2	File-sharing conflict caused some files not to be backed up
3	Ctrl-C or Ctrl-Break stopped back up
4	An error stopped the back up

For more information, see Chapter 15.

Batch Program   V1, V2, V3, V4, V5—Internal

Executes one or more commands contained in a disk file

Syntax

*dc:pathc***filename** *parameters*

dc:pathc is the disk drive and directory that hold the command.

filename is the root name of the batch file.

parameters are the parameters to be used by the batch file.

Notes

A batch file is an ASCII text file that contains DOS commands and the special batch commands. A batch file is useful for performing repetitive tasks, such as issuing commands to start programs.

For more information, see Chapter 13.

Batch Command
CALL   V3.3, V4, V5

Runs a second batch file, then returns control to the first batch file

Syntax

CALL *dc:pathc***filename** *parameters*

dc:pathc is the drive and directory that hold the command.

filename is the name of the batch file called.

parameters are the parameters to be used by the batch file.

Notes

Use the CALL command to run one batch file from another. When the second file is finished, DOS resumes processing the remaining commands in the first file.

For more information, see Chapter 13.

Batch Command
ECHO   V2, V3, V4, V5

Controls the display of batch commands and other messages as DOS executes batch subcommands

Syntax

To display a message, use the following form:

ECHO *message*

To display a blank line, use the form:

ECHO.

To turn off the display of commands and batch-command messages, use the form:

ECHO OFF

To turn on the display of commands and messages, use the form:

ECHO ON

To check the status of ECHO, use the form:

ECHO

message is the text of the message to be displayed.

Notes

To display a message regardless of whether ECHO is on or off, use the command **ECHO message**. To display a blank line, as when you want to separate text on the screen, place a period directly after ECHO on a line. (This command may be used from the command line and in a batch program.)

For more information, see Chapter 13.

Batch Command
FOR..IN..DO
V2, V3, V4, V5

Allows iterative processing of a DOS command

Syntax

FOR %%variable IN (set) DO command

variable is a single letter.

set is one or more words or file specifications. The file specification is in the form *d:path***filename.ext**. Wild cards are allowed.

command is the DOS command to be performed for each word or file in the set.

Notes

You can use more than one word or a full file specification in the set. You must separate words or file specifications by spaces or by commas.

%%variable becomes each literal word or full file specification in the set. If you use wild-card characters, FOR..IN..DO executes once for each file that matches the wild-card file specification. (You can use this command from the command line and in a batch file. Use only a single percent symbol with variable on the command line, however.)

For more information, see Chapter 13.

Batch Command
GOTO
V2, V3, V4, V5

Transfers control to the line following a label in the batch file

Syntax

GOTO label

label is the name used for a marker in a batch file. Although more than eight characters can be used, DOS reads only the first eight characters.

Notes

When the command **GOTO label** is executed, DOS jumps to the line following **label** and continues execution of the batch file. **label** is used as a marker in a batch file and must be preceded by a colon. You do not use a colon in the GOTO statement, however.

For more information, see Chapter 13.

Batch Command
IF   V2, V3, V4, V5

Allows conditional execution of a DOS command

Syntax

IF *NOT* **condition command**

NOT tests for the opposite of **condition** and executes the command when the condition is false.

condition is the basis of the test and can be any of the following:

ERRORLEVEL number	DOS tests the program's exit code (0 to 255). If the exit code is greater than or equal to the number, the condition is true.
string1 == string2	DOS compares these two alphanumeric strings to determine whether they are identical.
EXIST *d:path***filename.ext**	DOS tests whether *d:path***filename.ext** is in the specified drive or path (if given) or on the current disk drive and directory.

command is any valid DOS command.

Notes

For the IF subcommand, if **condition** is true, **command** is executed. If **condition** is false, **command** is skipped, and the next, line of the batch file is executed. For the IF NOT command, if **condition** is false, **command** is executed. If **condition** is true, **command** is skipped, and the next line of the batch file is executed.

For **string1 == string2**, DOS makes a literal, character-by-character comparison of the two strings. The comparison is based on the ASCII character set; however, an uppercase A is not the same as a lowercase a.

When you are using **string1 == string2** with the parameter markers (%0–%9), neither string may be null (empty or nonexistent). If either string is null, DOS displays a syntax error message and aborts the batch file.

For more information, see Chapter 13.

Batch Command
PAUSE
V1, V2, V3, V4, V5

Suspends batch-file processing until a key is pressed; optionally, displays a message

Syntax

PAUSE *message*

message is any text message of up to 121 characters.

Notes

Regardless of the ECHO setting, DOS displays the following message:

```
Strike a key when ready
```

DOS suspends processing of the batch file until you press a key. Afterward, DOS continues processing the batch-file lines. To end processing of a batch file, press Ctrl-Break or Ctrl-C.

The optional message is displayed only if ECHO is on. If ECHO is off, the message is treated as part of the command and is not displayed.

For more information, see Chapter 13.

Batch Command
REM   V1, V2, V3, V4, V5

Enables you to place a message in a batch file

Syntax

REM *message*

message is a string of up to 123 characters.

Notes

The message can contain up to 123 characters and must follow the word REM. When REM is used in a batch file, if ECHO is off, DOS does not display the message. REM normally is used to place notes in batch files.

For more information, see Chapter 13.

Batch Command
SHIFT   V2, V3, V4, V5

Shifts command-line parameters one position to the left when a batch file is invoked

Syntax

SHIFT

Notes

When you use SHIFT, DOS moves the command-line parameters one position to the left. DOS discards the former first parameter (%0).

For more information, see Chapter 13.

BREAK   V2, V3, V4, V5—Internal

Determines when DOS looks for a Ctrl-Break sequence to stop a program

Syntax

To turn on BREAK, use the following form:

BREAK ON

To turn off BREAK, use the following form:

BREAK OFF

To determine whether BREAK is on or off, use the following form:

BREAK

Notes

The setting of BREAK controls when DOS checks for Ctrl-Break. When BREAK is on, DOS checks for a Ctrl-Break sequence whenever a program uses a DOS device. The Ctrl-Break key then causes the program to halt.

With BREAK turned off, the default setting, DOS checks for a Ctrl-Break key sequence only when the program writes to the screen or the printer, reads the keyboard, or reads or writes from the serial adapter.

CHCP   V3.3, V4, V5—Internal

Changes or displays the code page (foreign-language character set) used by DOS

Syntax

CHCP *codepage*

codepage is a valid three-digit code-page number.

Notes

Before issuing this command, you must use the NLSFUNC command.

For more information, see Chapter 15.

CHDIR or CD V2, V3, V4, V5—Internal

Changes or shows the path of the current directory

Syntax

CHDIR *d:path*

or

CD *d:path*

d:path is a valid disk drive name and a valid directory name.

For more information, see Chapter 8.

CHKDSK V1, V2, V3, V4, V5—External

Checks the disk's directory and file allocation table (FAT) and reports disk and memory status. CHKDSK also can correct errors in the directories or in the FAT.

Syntax

*dc:pathc***CHKDSK** *d:path\filename.ext /F /V*

dc:pathc is the disk drive and directory that hold the command.

d: is the disk drive to be analyzed.

Switches

/F   Fixes the file allocation table and other problems if errors are found

/V   Shows CHKDSK's progress and displays more detailed information about the errors the program finds; known as the verbose switch

For more information, see Chapter 7.

CLS

Erases the display from the screen

Syntax

CLS

Notes

This command clears all information from the screen and places the cursor at the home position in the upper left corner. This command affects only the active video display, not memory.

For more information, see Chapter 6.

COMMAND

Starts an additional copy of COMMAND.COM, the command processor

Syntax

For DOS versions through 3.3, use the form:

*dc:pathc***COMMAND** *d:path\\ /E:size /P /C string*

For DOS 4 or 5, use the form:

*dc:pathc***COMMAND** *d:path\\ cttydevice /E:size /P /C string /MSG*

dc:pathc is the disk drive and directory that hold the command.

d:path is the disk drive and directory to assign to the COMSPEC environment variable. DOS looks for COMMAND.COM in this disk drive and directory.

cttydevice is the device to be used for input and output. (See the CTTY command.)

string is the set of characters you pass to the new copy of the command processor.

Switches

/E:size	Sets the size of the environment. Size is a decimal number from 160 to 32,768 bytes, rounded up to the nearest multiple of 16.
/P	Keeps this copy "permanently" in memory (until the next system reset)
/C	Passes the string of commands (shown as *string*) to the new copy of COMMAND.COM and returns control to primary processor
/MSG	Loads all error messages into memory; doesn't work without /P

Notes

COMMAND is used most often with the SHELL directive. This combination allows you to relocate COMMAND.COM from the root directory of a disk to a subdirectory.

If you are using DOS 5 with a floppy-disk-only system, you can specify the */MSG* switch in the SHELL directive of CONFIG.SYS. This switch loads all error messages into memory. If an error occurs, the disk with COMMAND.COM does not have to reside in the drive. An additional 1K of RAM is required to use this switch.

For more information, see Chapters 13 and 15.

COMP   V1, V2, V3, V4, V5—External

Compares two sets of disk files. This command is not available with some versions of DOS. If COMP is not available with your version of DOS, see the FC command.

Syntax

For versions of DOS through V4, use the form:

>*dc:pathc***COMP** *d1:path1\\filename1.ext1*
>*d2:path2\\filename2.ext2*

For DOS 5, use the form:

>*dc:pathc***COMP** *d1:path1\\filename1.ext1*
>*d2:path2\\filename2.ext2 /d /a /l /n:line /c*

dc:pathc is the disk drive and directory that hold the command.

d1:path1 is the drive and the directory containing the first set of files to be compared.

filename1.ext1 is the file name for the first set of files. Wild cards are allowed.

d2:path2 is the drive and the directory containing the second set of files to be compared.

filename2.ext2 is the file name for the second set of files. Wild cards are allowed.

d1:path1\filename1.ext1 is the *primary* file set.

d2:path2\filename2.ext2 is the *secondary* file set.

Switches

/D	Displays the hexadecimal values of the differing characters
/A	Displays the differing characters
/L	Displays the line number of the differing characters
/N:line	Compares the specifed number of lines in one file to the same number of lines in another; line is the number of lines to compare
/C	Makes the comparison of the files not case-sensitve

For more information, see Chapter 11.

Configuration Command
BREAK
V3, V4, V5—Internal

Determines when DOS looks for a Ctrl-Break or Ctrl-C to stop a program

Syntax

BREAK = ON

or

BREAK = OFF

Notes

The process and purpose of setting BREAK in the CONFIG.SYS file are the same as the process and purpose of setting BREAK from the DOS prompt.

For more information, see Chapter 15.

Configuration Command
BUFFERS   V2, V3, V4, V5—Internal

Sets the number of disk buffers DOS reserves in memory

Syntax

BUFFERS = nn

If you are using DOS 4, use this form:

BUFFERS = nn,*m* /X

If you are using DOS 5, use this form:

BUFFERS = nn,*m*

nn is the number of buffers to set, in the range of 1 to 99. If you have DOS 4, you can use the /X switch to set a maximum of 10,000 buffers.

m is the number of sectors, from 1 to 8, that can be read or written at a time. The default is 1.

Switches

/X   Uses expanded memory for buffer storage

For more information, see Chapter 15.

Configuration Command
COUNTRY   V3, V4, V5—Internal

Instructs DOS to modify the input and display of date, time, and field-divider information

Syntax

COUNTRY = nnn

If you are using DOS 3.3 or later, use the following form:

COUNTRY = nnn,*mmm,d:path\filenamef.extf*

nnn is the country code.

mmm is the code page.

d:path is the drive and directory that contain *filenamef.extf*

filenamef.extf is the file (COUNTRY.SYS) that contains the country information.

Notes

You cannot mix code-page codes with country codes. If you use the country code 001 for the United States, for example, you cannot use the code-page code for another country, for example, 863 for French Canada.

For more information, see Chapter 15.

Configuration Command
DEVICE
V2, V3, V4, V5—Internal

Instructs DOS to load, link, and use a special device driver

Syntax

DEVICE = *d:path***filename.ext** *options*

d:path is the disk drive and directory that hold the device driver.

filename.ext is the file name and optional extension of the device driver.

options are any parameters or switches that may be used with a device driver.

For more information, see Chapter 15.

Configuration Command
DEVICEHIGH   V5—Internal

Instructs DOS to load device drivers into reserved memory on 80386sx, 80386, and 80486 computers

Syntax

DEVICEHIGH *SIZE=hexbyte dd:pathd\filenamed.extd*

SIZE = hexbyte is the amount of reserved memory that must be available for the device driver to be loaded into memory. *hexbyte* is the size in bytes, expressed as a hexadecimal value.

dd:pathd is the disk drive and path that hold the device driver.

filenamed.extd is the file name and extension of the device driver.

Notes

Before you can use DEVICEHIGH, you must install HIMEM.SYS and EMM386.EXE (using the RAM or NOEMS parameter) as device drivers. These device drivers must precede the DEVICEHIGH command in your CONFIG.SYS file. In addition, you must use the DOS=UMB CONFIG.SYS command to link conventional memory and upper memory blocks.

For more information, see Chapter 15.

Configuration Command
DOS   V5—Internal

Loads DOS into the high-memory area or controls a link between conventional and reserved memory

Syntax

DOS = HIGH | LOW

or

DOS = UMB | NOUMB

or

DOS = HIGH | LOW, UMB | NOUMB

HIGH is used to remap a portion of DOS in the high-memory area.

LOW, the default setting, causes DOS to reside entirely in conventional memory.

UMB establishes and maintains a link between conventional memory and the upper memory blocks in reserved memory.

NOUMB, the default setting, disconnects a link between conventional memory and the upper memory blocks in reserved memory.

For more information, see Chapter 15.

Configuration Command DRIVPARM
V4, V5—Internal

Defines or changes the parameters of a block device, such as a disk drive

Syntax

DRIVPARM = /D:num */C /F:type /H:hds /I /N /S:sec /T:trk*

Switches

/D:num — Specifies the drive number, *num*, ranging from 0 through 255, where drive A = 0, drive B = 1, drive C = 2, and so on.

/C — Specifies that the drive supports change-line and can sense that the drive door is open. When the drive door is open, the drive is sensed as empty.

/F:type — Determines the type of drive. *type* is one of the following:

Type	Drive specification
0	160K/320K/180K/360K
1	1.2M
2	720K (3 1/2-inch disk)
3	Single-density 8-inch disk

Type	Drive specification
4	Double-density 8-inch disk
5	Hard disk
6	Tape drive
7	1.44M (3 1/2-inch disk)
8	Read/write optical disk
9	2.88M (3 1/2-inch disk)

Type 2 is the default if you do not specify /F.

/H:hds   Specifies the total number of drive heads, where *hds* is a number from 1 through 99. The default for *hds* is 2.

/I   Used if you have a 3 1/2-inch drive connected internally to your floppy drive controller, but your ROM BIOS does not support a 3 1/2-inch drive

/N   Specifies that your drive or other block device is not removable—a hard disk, for example

/S:sec   Specifies the total number of sectors per side on the drive. *sec* can be a number from 1 through 999.

/T:trk   Specifies the number of tracks per side of a disk or the total number of tracks per tape. *trk* can be a number from 1 through 99.

Notes

Make sure that you specify the correct type of device and the correct number of heads and sectors. Incorrect values will cause the device to work incorrectly or not at all.

For more information, see Chapter 15.

Example

To specify an internal 3 1/2-inch, 1.44M drive to be drive B and to support change-line, use the following form:

DRIVPARM /D:1 /C /F:7 /I

Configuration Command
FCBS
V2, V3, V4, V5—Internal

Specifies the number of DOS file-control blocks that can be open simultaneously and how many always remain open

Syntax

FCBS = maxopen, *neverclose*

maxopen is the number of FCBs that can be open at any given time. The default is 4.

neverclose is the number of FCBs that are always open. The default value is 0. (This parameter is not used by DOS 5.)

For more information, see Chapter 15.

Configuration Command
FILES
V2, V3, V4, V5—Internal

Specifies the number of file handles open at any given time

Syntax

FILES = nnn

nnn is the number, from 8 through 255, of file handles that may be open at any given time. The default value is 8.

For more information, see Chapter 15.

Configuration Command
INSTALL
V4, V5—Internal

Starts program from CONFIG.SYS. Valid programs to start with INSTALL are FASTOPEN, KEYB, NLSFUNC, and SHARE.

Syntax

INSTALL = *dc:pathc***filename.ext** *options*

dc:pathc is the disk drive and directory that hold the command.

filename.ext is the name of the file, which may be FASTOPEN.EXE, KEYB.EXE, NLSFUNC.EXE, SHARE.EXE, or another valid terminate-and-stay-resident (TSR) program.

options are any parameters the command used or required by **filename.ext**.

For more information, see Chapter 15.

Configuration Command
LASTDRIVE

Sets the last valid drive letter acceptable to DOS

Syntax

LASTDRIVE = x

x is the letter for the highest system drive. Without using LASTDRIVE, the highest default drive is E.

Notes

If you use the SUBST command to assign drive letters to subdirectories, use the LASTDRIVE statement to increase the number of usable drive letters. Local area network (LAN) users can use the LASTDRIVE statement to identify the highest letter that can be assigned as a drive letter to a subdirectory. For example, the CONFIG.SYS command LASTDRIVE=G enables drives A through G to exist or be created; however, drive H cannot exist or be created. G is the highest letter.

For more information, see Chapter 15.

Example

If you want to use J as a drive letter, type (in your CONFIG.SYS file) the form:

LASTDRIVE = J

Configuration Command
REM

Places remarks or hidden statements in the CONFIG.SYS file

Syntax

REM *remark*

Notes

You may find REM useful in the CONFIG.SYS file to document commands in the file.

For more information, see Chapter 15.

Configuration Command
SHELL

Changes the default DOS command processor

Syntax

SHELL = *d:path***filename.ext** *parameters*

d:path is the drive and directory that hold the command processor to be used.

filename.ext is the command processor's file name and optional extension.

parameters are the optional parameters the command processor uses.

Notes

Although most users will not replace COMMAND.COM with another command processor, many users like to move COMMAND.COM to a subdirectory. The SHELL command can help accomplish this task.

For more information, see Chapter 15; also see COMMAND, in this Command Reference.

Configuration Command
STACKS
V3.2, V3.3, V4, V5—Internal

Allots memory storage when a hardware interrupt occurs

Syntax

STACKS = n,m

n is the number of stacks to allot. For computers using the 8088/8086 microprocessor, the default is 0; for computers that use the 80286, 80386sx, 80386, and 80486 microprocessor, the default is 9.

m is the size in bytes of each stack. The default for computers using the 8088/8086 microprocessor is 0; for those using the 80286, 80386sx, 80386, and 80486, the default is 128.

Notes

The default stacks are adequate for normal use, but if you start receiving the `Fatal: Internal Stack Failure, System Halted` error message, you should increase the number of stacks. If the error persists after you increase the number of stacks, increase the size of each stack.

For more information, see Chapter 15.

COPY
V1, V2, V3, V4, V5—Internal

Copies files between disk drives and/or devices, either keeping or changing the file name

Syntax

To copy a file, use the following form:

COPY */A /B d1:path1***filename1.ext1***/A /B d0:path0***filename0.ext0** */A /B /V*

To join several files into one, use the following form:

COPY */A /B d1:path1***filename1.ext1***/A /B + d2:path2***filename2.ext2** */A /B + #d0:path0***filename0.ext0#*

d1:path1 and *d2:path2* are valid disk drive names and directories.

filename1.ext1 and **filename2.ext2** are valid file names. Wild cards are allowed.

The ellipsis (...) represents additional files in the form *dx:pathx/***filenamex.extx**.

The file being copied *from* is the *source file*. The names containing 1 and 2 are the source files.

The file being copied *to* is the *destination file*. This file is represented by a 0.

Switches

/V   Verifies that the copy has been recorded correctly

The following switches have different effects on the source and the destination.

For the source file:

/A   Treats the file as an ASCII file. The command copies all the information in the file up to but not including the end-of-file marker (^ Z). Anything after the end-of-file marker is ignored.

/B   Copies the entire file (based on its size as listed in the directory) as if the source file were a program file (binary1). Any end-of-file markers (^ Z) are treated as normal characters, and the EOF characters are copied.

For the destination file:

/A   Adds an end-of-file marker (^ Z) to the end of the ASCII text file after the file is copied.

/B   Does not add the end-of-file marker to this binary file.

For more information, see Chapter 10.

CTTY   V2, V3, V4, V5—Internal

Changes the standard input and output device to an auxiliary console, or changes an auxiliary console to the keyboard and video display

Syntax

CTTY device

device is the device you choose as the new standard input and output device. This name must be a valid DOS device name.

Notes

The CTTY command was designed so that a terminal or teleprinter, rather than the normal keyboard and video display, can be used for console input and output. This added versatility has little effect on most personal computer users.

Example

To change the standard input and standard output from the default console to the first communications port, type the form:

CTTY COM1

DATE   V1, V2, V3, V4, V5—Internal

Displays and/or changes the system date

Syntax

DATE *date_string*

date_string is in one of the following forms:

mm-dd-yy or *mm-dd-yyyy* for North America

dd-mm-yy or *dd-mm-yyyy* for Europe

yy-mm-dd or *yyyy-mm-dd* for East Asia

mm is a one- or two-digit number for the month (1 through 12).

dd is a one- or two-digit number for the day (1 through 31).

yy is a one- or two-digit number for the year (80 through 99). The 19 is assumed.

yyyy is a four-digit number for the year (1980 through 2099).

The delimiters between the day, month, and year can be hyphens, periods, or slashes. The result displayed varies according to the country code set in the CONFIG.SYS file.

For more information, see Chapter 3.

DEBUG
V2, V3, V4, V5—External

Tests and edits programs

Syntax

*dc:pathc***DEBUG** *de:pathe\\filenamee.exte*

dc:pathc is the disk drive and directory that hold the command.

de:pathe is the disk drive and directory that hold the file to edit.

filenamee.exte is the file to load into memory for editing.

Notes

DEBUG is a utility that enables you to load a program into memory, edit the program, test it, and save the edited program to the disk. With DEBUG, you can create small machine-language programs; you even can use assembly language to create the small programs.

Examples

To start DEBUG, type the following:

DEBUG

To start DEBUG and load PROGRAM.EXE from C:\UTILS, so that you can edit the program, type the following:

DEBUG C:\UTILS\PROGRAM.EXE

DEL
V1, V2, V3, V4, V5—Internal

Deletes files from the disk

DEL is an alternative form of the ERASE command and performs the same functions. See ERASE for a complete description.

DELOLDOS
V5—External

Removes from the hard disk all DOS files of versions earlier than DOS 5

Syntax

*dc:pathc***DELOLDOS** */B*

dc:pathc is the drive and directory that hold the command.

Switches

/B   Forces a black-and-white screen display rather than color display

Examples

To remove the old version of DOS from your disk, use the form:

DELOLDOS

DIR   V1, V2, V3, V4, V5—Internal

Lists any or all files and subdirectories in a directory

Syntax

For DOS versions earlier than V5, use the form:

DIR *d:path\\filename.ext* */P* */W*

For DOS 5, use the form:

DIR *d:path\\filename.ext* */P* */W* */A:attrib* */O:sort* */S* */B* */L*

d: is the drive holding the disk you want to examine.

path is the path to the directory you want to examine.

filename.ext is a valid file name. Wild cards are permitted.

Switches

/P   Pauses when the screen is full and waits for you to press any key

/W   Provides a wide (80-column) display of the file names. Information about file size, date, and time is not displayed.

/A:attrib   Displays only the files that have the attribute you specify. The following table lists the settings for attrib:

Attribute	Description
(/A only)	Displays all directory entries, including system and hidden
H	Displays hidden files
-H	Displays files that are not hidden
S	Displays system files
-S	Displays files that are not system files
D	Displays subdirectories
-D	Displays files only (no subdirectory names)
A	Displays files for archiving
-A	Displays archived files
R	Displays read-only files
-R	Displays files that can be read and written to

/O:sort Displays the directory in sorted order. The following table lists the settings for *sort*:

Sort	Description
(/O only)	Directory entries sorted alphabetically, listing subdirectories before files (0–9, A–Z)
N	Sorts alphabetically by name (0–9, A–Z)
-N	Sorts reverse-alphabetically by name (Z–A, 9–0)
E	Sorts alphabetically by extension (0–9, A–Z)
-E	Sorts reverse-alphabetically by extension (Z–A, 9–0)
D	Sorts by date and time, earliest to latest

Sort	Description
-D	Sorts by date and time, latest to earliest
S	Sorts by size, smallest to largest
-S	Sorts by size, largest to smallest
G	Lists subdirectories before files
-G	Lists subdirectories after files

/S	Lists all files in the current directory and all subsequent directories
/B	Lists only file name and extension, separated by a period (FILENAME.EXT); lists no other information (such as size, date, and time created)
/L	Lists file and subdirectory names in lowercase

For more information, see Chapter 10.

DISKCOMP   V1, V2, V3, V4, V5—External

Compares two floppy disks, track-for-track and sector-for-sector

Syntax

*dc:pathc***DISKCOMP d1:** *d2: /1 /8*

dc:pathc is the disk drive and directory that hold the command.

d1: and *d2:* are the disk drives that hold the disks to be compared. These drives may be the same or different.

Switches

/1	Compares only the first side of the disk, even if the disk or disk drive is double-sided
/8	Compares only 8 sectors per track, even if the first disk has a different number of sectors per track

For more information, see Chapter 6.

Examples

If you want to compare the disk in drive A with the disk in drive B, type the form:

DISKCOMP A: B:

If you have only one floppy disk drive and must compare two disks, type the form:

DISKCOMP A: A:

or the form:

DISKCOMP A:

DISKCOPY V1, V2, V3, V4, V5—External

Copies the entire contents of one floppy disk to another floppy disk, track-by-track, making an exact duplicate. DISKCOPY works only with floppy disks.

Syntax

*dc:pathc***DISKCOPY d1:** *d2: /1*

If you are using DOS 5, you can use the additional switch in this form:

*dc:pathc***DISKCOPY d1:** *d2: /V*

dc:pathc is the disk drive and directory that holds command.

d1: is the floppy disk drive that holds the source disk.

d2: is the floppy disk drive that holds the destination disk.

The disk you are copying from is the *source* (or first) disk.

The disk you are copying to is the *destination* (or second) disk.

Switches

/1   Copies only the first side of the disk

/V   Verifies the copy. Even though this switch slows the copy procedure, you should use it when you copy important disks.

For more information, see Chapter 6.

DOSKEY

Enables you to recall a history of DOS commands, edit DOS command lines, and create macros

Syntax

*dc:pathc***DOSKEY** */REINSTALL /BUFSIZE=bytes /MACROS /HISTORY /INSERT\|OVERSTRIKE macroname=macrotext*

dc:pathc is the disk drive and directory that hold DOSKEY.

macroname is the name of the macro to create.

macrotext is the command(s) contained by the macro name *macroname*.

Switches

/REINSTALL	Starts a second copy of DOSKEY, disabling any previous settings or macros
/BUFSIZE=bytes	Used to set aside memory in which DOSKey can store commands and macros; the value of *bytes* is the amount of memory to set aside (The default is 1,024 bytes, or 1K.)
/MACRO	Lists all the macros created with DOSKey
/HISTORY	Lists all commands stored in memory, from earliest to latest
/INSERT|OVERSTRIKE	Enables insert mode or overstrike mode; when you edit a command line in insert mode, you insert characters instead of typing over characters in the line. Use the switch by typing **/INSERT** or **/OVERSTRIKE**. When editing a command, you can switch between insert and overstrike mode by pressing the Ins key.

Notes

Ordinarily, DOS remembers the last command typed at the command line. With DOSKey, however, a history of commands can be stored in memory. The number of commands retained in memory depends on the size of the buffer (normally 512 bytes). When the buffer is full, the oldest command is eliminated to make room for the new command. The buffer contains macros as well as a history of commands.

For more information about DOSKey, see Chapter 13.

DOSSHELL   V4, V5—External

Starts the Shell that comes with DOS

Syntax

To start DOS Shell in text mode, use the form:

> *dc:pathc***DOSSHELL** */T:screen* */B*

To start DOS Shell in graphics mode, use the form:

> *dc:pathc***DOSSHELL** */G:screen* */B*

To start DOS Shell in the default screen mode, type the form:

> *dc:pathc***DOSSHELL**

dc:pathc is the disk drive and directory that hold DOSSHELL.

Switches

/T:screen	Displays DOS Shell in text mode, using the resolution described by *screen*
/G:screen	Displays DOS Shell in graphics mode, using the resolution described by *screen*

The following table lists the switches that you may use when starting the DOS Shell. These switches alter the screen mode.

Switch	*Monochome/CGA*	*EGA*	*VGA*
/T:L	25 lines	25 lines	25 lines
/T:M	x	43 lines	43 lines

Switch	Monochome/CGA	EGA	VGA
/T:M1	x	43 lines	43 lines
/T:M2	x	43 lines	50 lines
/T:H	x	43 lines	43 lines
/T:H1	x	43 lines	43 lines
/T:H2	x	43 lines	50 lines
/G:L	25 lines	25 lines	25 lines
/G:M	x	43 lines	30 lines
/G:M1	x	43 lines	30 lines
/G:M2	x	43 lines	34 lines
/G:H	x	43 lines	43 lines
/G:H1	x	43 lines	43 lines
/G:H2	x	43 lines	60 lines
/B	Starts DOS Shell in black-and-white rather than color		

For more information, see Chapters 4, 7, 8, 9, 10, 11, and 14.

Example

To start the shell, use the form:

DOSSHELL

EDIT   V5—External

A full-screen editor, included with DOS for creating ASCII files, such as batch files

Syntax

*dc:pathc***EDIT** *d:path\\filename.ext /B /G /H /NOHI*

dc:pathc is the disk drive and directory that hold EDIT.

d:path\\filename.ext is the location and name of the file to load into EDIT when EDIT starts.

Switches

/B	Displays the DOS Editor in black-and-white
/G	Quickly writes to a CGA monitor (may cause "snow" on some monitors)
/H	Editor displays in the maximum number of lines that your screen supports (43 for EGA, 50 for VGA)
/NOHI	Uses reverse video rather than high-intensity characters (for LCD screens)

Notes

The DOS Editor, a full-screen editor, works like the Editor in QBasic, the BASIC interpreter included with DOS 5. The Editor performs many of the tasks Edlin performs but is much easier to use than Edlin. The Editor not only enables you to print an open file and to cut and paste text but also offers on-line help and supports a mouse.

For more information, see Chapter 12.

EDLIN   V1, V2, V3, V4, V5—External

A line-by-line editor, included with DOS for creating ASCII files, such as batch files

Syntax

*dc:pathc***EDLIN** *d:path***filename.ext** */B*

dc:pathc is the disk drive and directory that hold Edlin.

*d:path***filename.ext** are the location and name of the file to edit with Edlin. You must give a file name when you start Edlin.

Switches

/B	Makes Edlin ignore end-of-file characters that may be in a file. The file to be edited is read based on the size in the directory rather than the location of an end-of-file character.

EMM386 V5—External

Enables an 80386sx, 80386, or 80486 computer to convert extended memory into EMS 4.0 expanded memory, and control that expanded memory; also remaps some extended memory to reserved memory

Syntax

As a device driver:

DEVICE = *dc:pathc***EMM386.EXE** *ramval w=ON|OFF Ms FRAME=xxxx /Pn=xxxx X=xxxx-xxxx B=xxxx L=xms A=regs H=bbb RAM|NOEMS*

ramval is the amount of RAM in 1K bytes to assign as EMS 4.0 memory. Enter a value (from 16 through 32,768) as a multiple of 16. Any number you enter is rounded to the nearest 16. The default is 256.

w=ON|OFF enables or disables support for the Weitek coprocessor. The default is w=OFF.

Ms is used to specify the segment base address. *s* is a number used to represent the address. The segment base address is the beginning address of the EMS page frame. The numbers and associated addresses (listed in hexadecimal) are as follows:

s	Address
1	C000
2	C400
3	C800
4	CC00
5	D000
6	D400
7	D800
8	DC00
9	E000
10	8000
11	8400
12	8800
13	8C00
14	9000

FRAME=xxxx specifies the beginning address of the EMS page frame. *xxxx* may be one of the addresses listed under *Ms*.

/Pxxxx specifies the beginning address (same as *FRAME=xxxx*).

Pn=xxxx defines an address for a page segment. *n* can be any of the numbers 0, 1, 2, 3, 254, 255. To remain compatible with programs that support EMS 3.2 but not EMS 4.0, P0 through P3 must be contiguous addresses. You cannot use this option if you use Ms, FRAME=xxxx, or /Pxxxx.

X=xxxx-xxxx specifies that a range of memory should not be used for the EMS page frame. *xxxx-xxxx* are the ranges to keep free.

B=xxxx specifies the lowest address to use for bank switching. The default is 4000.

L=xmsmem specifies the number of 1K bytes that will remain as extended memory instead of being converted to EMS memory. *xmsmem* is the value of 1K of memory. For 1M to remain as extended memory, use the parameters L=1024.

A=regs is used to allocate the number of alternative registers EMM386 may use. Although the default number is 7, you can specify a number from 0 through 254 for *regs*.

H=hhh enables you to change the number of handles (EMM386 uses a default number of 64). *hhh* may be a number from 2 through 255.

RAM|NOEMS is used to allocate reserved memory (to place some extended memory in open areas in the 640K to 1M address space). *RAM* leaves room in the reserved area for an EMS page frame, whereas *NOEMS* does not leave room for the EMS page frame.

Syntax

As a command:

   *dc:pathc***EMM386** *ON | OFF | AUTO W=ON | OFF*

dc:pathc is the disk drive and directory that hold EMM386.

ON enables expanded memory.

OFF disables expanded memory.

AUTO enables expanded Weitek coprocessor support when a program requests it.

W=ON | OFF enables (or disables) Weitek coprocessor support.

For more information, see Chapter 15.

ERASE   V1, V2, V3, V4, V5—Internal

Removes one or more files from the directory

Syntax

You can use the command form:

ERASE *d:path***filename.ext**

or the form:

DEL *d:path***filename.ext**

With DOS 4 or 5, you can add the /P switch in the form:

ERASE *d:path***filename.ext** */P*

or with its alternative command:

DEL *d:path***filename.ext** */P*

d:path is the disk drive and directory that hold the file(s) to be erased.

filename.ext is the name of the file(s) to be erased. Wild cards are allowed.

Switches

/P   With DOS 4 or 5, this switch prompts you with the message `filename.ext, Delete (Y/N)?` **before** erasing the file.

For more information, see Chapter 10.

EXE2BIN
V1.1. V2, V3, V4, V5—External

Changes suitably formatted EXE files into BIN or COM files

Syntax

dc:pathc**EXE2BIN** *d1:path1***filename1.ext1**
d2:path2*filename2.ext2*

dc:pathc\\ is the disk drive and directory that hold the command.

d1:path1\\ is the disk drive and the directory holding the file to be converted.

filename1.ext1 is the name and extension of the file to be converted.

d2:path2\\ is the disk drive and the directory for the output file.

filename2.ext2 is the name and extension of the output file.

The file to be converted is the *source* file.

The output file is the *destination* file.

Notes

EXE2BIN is a programming utility that converts EXE (executable) program files to COM or BIN (binary image) files. The resulting program takes less disk space and loads faster. But this conversion may be a disadvantage in future versions of DOS. Unless you use a compiler-based language, you may never use this command.

EXIT
V2, V3, V4, V5—Internal

Leaves a secondary command processor and returns to the primary command processor

Syntax

EXIT

Notes

This command has no effect if a secondary command processor was loaded with the /P switch or is not loaded.

EXPAND

Copies a compressed, unusable file from the original DOS disks to an uncompressed, usable form

Syntax

*dc:pathc***EXPAND** *d1:path1***filename.ext** ...
dd:*pathd\\filenamed.extd*

dc:pathc is the disk drive and directory that hold the command.

d1:path1 is the disk drive and path that hold the compressed file.

filename.ext is the name of the compressed file.

The ellipsis (...) represents additional compressed file specifications.

dd:*pathd\\filenamed.extd* is the drive, path, or new file name to which the compressed file should be expanded.

Notes

Files on the original DOS 5 disks are stored as compressed files; more data can be stored on fewer disks than if the files were not compressed. Before you can use a compressed file, however, you must decompress it.

When you use Setup to install DOS, the files are decompressed as they are transferred to the correct disks. But suppose that you delete a file accidentally or that for some reason a file gets corrupted. To replace the lost or corrupted file, you must transfer the file from the original DOS disk. To transfer the file, decompressing it as you transfer it, use EXPAND. Think of EXPAND as another form of COPY—but EXPAND is a "one-way" copy.

Examples

To expand FORMAT.COM from the 5 1/4-inch Disk 1 to C:\\DOS\\, type the following:

EXPAND A:FORMAT.CO_ C:\\DOS\\FORMAT.COM

FASTOPEN

V3.3, V4, V5—External

Keeps directory information in memory so that DOS can quickly find frequently needed files

Syntax

*dc:pathc***FASTOPEN d:**=*nnn* ...

For DOS 4, additional syntax is as follows:

*dc:pathc***FASTOPEN d:**=*(nnn,mmm)* ... */X*

For DOS 5, the syntax is as follows:

*dc:pathc***FASTOPEN d:**=*nnn* ... */X*

dc:pathc is the disk drive and directory that hold the command.

d: is the name of the disk drive containing directory information to be held in memory.

nnn is the number of directory entries to be held in memory (10 through 999).

mmm is the number of fragmented entries for the drive (1 through 999).

The ellipsis (...) designates additional disk drives in the forms *d:*=*nnn* or *d:*=*(nnn,mmm)*.

Switches

/X   Tells DOS to use expanded memory to store the information buffered by FASTOPEN

For more information, see Chapter 15.

FC

V2, V3, V4, V5—External

Compares two sets of files

Syntax

*dc:pathc***FC** */A /B /C /L /LBx /N /T /W /x*
*d1:path1***filename1.ext1** *d2:path2***filename2.ext2**

dc:pathc is the disk drive and directory that hold the command.

d1:path1 is the drive and the directory containing the first set of files to be compared.

filename1.ext1 is the file name for the first set of files. Wild cards are allowed.

d2:path2 is the drive and the directory containing the second set of files to be compared.

filename2.ext2 is the file name for the second set of files. Wild cards are allowed.

d1:path1\filename1.ext1 is the *primary* file set.

d2:path2\filename2.ext2 is the *secondary* file set.

Switches

/A	Abbreviates ASCII comparison displays
/B	Forces a binary file comparison
/C	Causes DOS to disregard case of letters
/L	Compares files in ASCII mode
/LBx	Sets internal buffer to *x* lines
/N	Displays line numbers for ASCII comparisons
/T	Suppresses expansion of tabs to spaces
/W	Compresses tabs and spaces
/x	Sets the number of lines (1 through 9,999) to match; the default is 2

Notes

The FC file-comparison program is similar to but more powerful than COMP (refer to COMP in this Command Reference). With FC, you can compare source or binary files.

For more information, see Chapter 11.

FDISK
V2, V3, V4, V5—External

Readies a hard disk to accept an operating system

Syntax

dc:pathc**FDISK**

dc:pathc\ is the disk drive and directory that hold the command.

Notes

Before you can format a hard disk with DOS, you must use FDISK. You use FDISK to partition a hard disk into different drives. In versions of DOS earlier than V4, DOS could recognize only a hard disk of 32M or less. Thus, a 40M hard disk was partitioned into two drives—drives C and D, for example. However, starting with DOS 4, FDISK can partition a disk larger than 32M into one drive.

If you plan to use more than one operating system, use FDISK to partition part of the hard disk for DOS and another part of the hard disk for the other operating system.

For more information, see Chapter 7.

> *Caution:* Do not use FDISK to remove or change a partition unless you have all data on the partition safely backed up. Removing or changing a partition causes all data on that partition to be lost.

FIND
V2, V3, V4, V5—External

Displays from the designated files all the lines that match or do not match (depending on the switches used) the specified string. This command also can display the line numbers.

Syntax

*dc:pathc***FIND** */V/C/N* "**string**"
d:path\\filename.ext...

If you are using DOS 5, you can use the additional switches in the form:

*dc:pathc***FIND** */I* "**string**" *d:path\\filename.ext...*

dc:pathc is the disk drive and directory that hold the command.

string is the set of characters you want to find. Note that **string** must be enclosed in double quotation marks, as shown in the syntax line.

d:path is the disk drive and directory that hold the file.

filename.ext is the file you want to search.

Switches

/V	Displays all lines that do *not* contain *string*
/C	Counts the number of times *string* occurs and displays that number
/N	Displays the line that contains *string*, preceded by the number of that line
/I	Enables a search that is not case-sensitive

For more information, see Chapter 10.

FORMAT V1, V2, V3, V4, V5—External

Initializes a disk to accept DOS information and files; also checks the disk for defective tracks and optionally places DOS on the floppy or hard disk

Syntax

*dc:pathc***FORMAT d:** */S/1/8/V/B/4/N:ss/T:tt*

With DOS 4, you can add the */V:label* and */F:size* switches, as follows:

*dc:pathc***FORMAT d:** */S/1/8/V/B/4/N:ss/T:tt /V:label /F:size*

With DOS 5, you can use the following additional switches:

*dc:pathc***FORMAT d:** */Q /U*

dc:pathc is the disk drive and directory that hold the command.

d: is a valid disk drive name.

Switches

/S	Places a copy of the operating system on the disk so that it can be booted
/1	Formats only one side of a floppy disk
/8	Formats an eight-sector floppy disk (V1)
/V	Writes a volume label on the disk
/B	With V4 and earlier versions of DOS: formats an eight-sector, 5 1/2-inch floppy disk, leaving the proper places in the directory for any operating system version, but does not place the operating system on the disk. With V4 and V5 of DOS: formats any disk, leaving ample room on the disk to copy the operating system files to the disk so that it can be booted, but does not place the operating system on the disk.
/4	Formats a floppy disk in a 1.2M disk drive for double-density (320K/360K) use
/N:ss	Formats the disk with *ss* number of sectors (*ss* can range from 1 through 99)
/T:ttt	Formats the disk with *ttt* number of tracks per side (*ttt* can range from 1 through 999)
/F:size	Formats the disk to less than maximum capacity, with *size* designating one of the following values:

Drive	Allowable Values for size
160K, 180K	160, 160K, 160KB, 180, 180K, 180KB
320K, 360K	All of above, plus 320, 320K, 320KB, 360, 360K, 360KB
1.2M	All of above, plus 1200, 1200K, 1200KB, 1.2, 1.2M, 1.2MB
720K	720, 720K, 720KB
1.44M	All values for 720K, plus 1440, 1440K, 1440KB, 1.44, 1.44M, 1.44MB

Drive	Allowable Values for size
2.88M	2880, 2880K, 2880KB, 2.88, 2.88M, 2.88MB (DOS 5 only)
/V:label	Transfers volume label to formatted disk; replaces *label* with 11-character name for new disk
/U	Formats a disk unconditionally; erases any data from disk (data cannot be recovered)
/Q	Performs a quick format on the disk, erasing only the file allocation table and root directory; does not recheck disk for bad sectors

For more information, see Chapter 7.

GRAFTABL   V3, V4, V5—External

Loads into memory the tables of additional character sets to be displayed on the Color Graphics Adapter (CGA)

Syntax

For versions of DOS earlier than V5, use the form:

> *dc:pathc***GRAFTABL** *codepage /STATUS ?*

For DOS 5, use the form:

> *dc:pathc***GRAFTABL** *codepage /STATUS*

dc:pathc is the disk drive and directory that hold the command.

codepage is the three-digit number of the code page for the display.

Switches

/STATUS   Shows the current active code page

Notes

In graphics mode, the IBM Color Graphics Adapter and compatible color/graphics adapters smear characters with ASCII codes ranging from 128 through 255. This range includes language-specific characters and many graphics characters. GRAFTABL produces a legible display of these ASCII characters.

GRAFTABL does not affect characters in text mode. GRAFTABL should be used only on systems that have the Color Graphics Adapter.

Please note that with DOS versions earlier than V5, you type just a question mark to get instructions for using GRAFTABL (**GRAFTABL ?**). Beginning with V5 of DOS, however, you use the question mark as a switch (**GRAFTABL /?**).

On completion, GRAFTABL produces exit codes. An exit code is a number that tells DOS the status of GRAFTABL when it stopped. You can test for exit codes in a batch file using IF, and you can change the outcome of the batch file accordingly. The following is a list of exit codes GRAFTABL produces:

Exit Code	Meaning
0	Character set loaded successfully
1	Character set replaced previously loaded table
2	File error
3	Incorrect parameter; no action
4	Incorrect DOS version

Examples

To load a table of graphics characters in memory, type the form:

GRAFTABL

To display the code-page table currently in memory, type the form:

GRAFTABL /STATUS

or the shorter form:

GRAFTABL /STA

GRAPHICS   V2, V3, V4, V5—External

Prints the contents of a graphics screen on a suitable printer

Syntax

*dc:pathc***GRAPHICS** *printer* /R /B /LCD

With DOS 4 or 5, you can add the name of a file containing printer information, as follows:

*dc:pathc***GRAPHICS** *printer filename* /R /B /LCD

/PRINTBOX:x

dc:pathc is the disk drive and directory that hold the command.

printer is the type of personal computer printer you are using. The printer can be one of the following:

COLOR1	Color printer with a black ribbon
COLOR4	Color printer with an RGB (red, green, blue, and black) ribbon, which produces four colors
COLOR8	Color printer with a CMY (cyan, magenta, yellow, and black) ribbon, which produces eight colors
COMPACT	Compact printer (not an option with V4 or V5)
GRAPHICS	Graphics printer and IBM ProPrinter
THERMAL	Convertible printer

With DOS 4 or 5, you may specify the following printer also:

GRAPHICSWIDE	Graphics printer and IBM ProPrinter with 11-inch wide carriage

With DOS 5, the list also includes the following printers:

HPDEFAULT	Any Hewlett-Packard PCC printer
DESKJET	Hewlett-Packard DeskJet printer
LASERJETII	Hewlett-Packard LaserJet Series II III, IIP, IID) printer
PAINTJET	Hewlett-Packard PaintJet printer
QUIETJET	Hewlett-Packard QuietJet printer
QUIETJET PLUS	Hewlett-Packard QuietJet Plus printer
RUGGED WRITER	Hewlett-Packard Rugged Writer printer

| RUGGED WRITERWIDE | Hewlett-Packard Rugged Writer Wide printer |
| THINKJET | Hewlett-Packard ThinkJet printer |

filename is the name of the file that contains printer information (DOS 4 or 5 only). If no file name is specified, DOS uses the name GRAPHICS.PRO.

Switches

/R	Reverses colors so that the image on the paper matches the screen—a white image on black background
/B	Prints the background color of the screen; use only when printer type is COLOR4 or COLOR8
/LCD	Prints image as displayed on a PC Convertible's LCD display
/PRINTBOX:x	Prints image and uses print box size *id* represented by *x*. This value (*lcd* or *std*) must match the first entry of a Printbox statement in the printer profile (DOS 4 or 5 only).

Notes

The GRAPHICS command enhances your print-screen capability. Normally, you can send a copy of the screen to your printer by pressing Shift-PrtSc or Print Screen. If graphics are displayed, you cannot send a copy of the screen to the printer unless you have GRAPHICS loaded in memory. The GRAPHICS command enables you to send graphics screens to the printer by pressing Print Screen or Shift-PrtSc.

Examples

To load GRAPHICS in memory so that you can print a graphics screen on a printer, type the command:

GRAPHICS

JOIN
V3.1, V3.2, V3.3, V4, V5—External

Produces a single directory structure by connecting one disk drive to a subdirectory of another disk drive

Syntax

To connect disk drives, use the following form:

*dc:pathc***JOIN d1:** *d2:***dirname**

To disconnect disk drives, use this form of the command:

*dc:pathc***JOIN d1:** **/D**

To show currently connected drives, use the following form:

*dc:pathc***JOIN**

dc:pathc is the disk drive and directory that hold the command.

d1: is the disk drive to be connected. DOS calls this drive the *guest disk drive*.

d2: is the disk drive to which **d1:** is to be connected. DOS calls d2: the *host disk drive*.

\\dirname is a subdirectory in the root directory of *d2:*, the host drive. DOS calls \\dirname the *host subdirectory*. \\dirname holds the connection to d1:, the guest drive.

Switches

/D   Disconnects the specified guest drive from its host

For more information, see Chapter 15.

KEYB
V2, V3, V4, V5—External

Changes the keyboard layout and characters to one of five languages other than American English

Syntax

With versions of DOS earlier than DOS 3.3, you can change the current keyboard layout by using the following form:

*dc:pathc***KEYB/c**

To change the current keyboard layout with DOS 3.3, use the

following form:

> *dc:pathc***KEYB** *keycode, codepage, d:path***KEYBOARD.SYS**

To specify a particular keyboard identification code using DOS 4, use this form:

> *dc:pathc***KEYB** *keycode, codepage, d:path***KEYBOARD.SYS**
> **/ID:***code*

With DOS 5, an additional switch is added to the preceding form, as follows:

> *dc:pathc***KEYB** *keycode, codepage, d:path***KEYBOARD.SYS**
> **/ID:***code* **/E**

To display the current values for KEYB using V3.3 through V5 of DOS, use the form:

> *dc:pathc***KEYB**

dc:pathc is the disk drive and directory that hold the command.

/c is a two-letter code that specifies a country. The codes (before V3) are as follows:

/c	Country
UK	United Kingdom
GR	Germany
FR	France
IT	Italy
SP	Spain

keycode is the two-character keyboard code for the country (see following table).

codepage is the three-digit code page (437, 850, 860, 863, or 865) that will be used (see the following table).

d:path is the drive and the path to the KEYBOARD.SYS file.

Country	Keycode	Code Page	Code
Australia	us	850, 437	(none)
Belgium	be	850, 437	(none)
Brazil	br	850, 437	(none)
Canadian-French	cf	850, 863	(none)
Denmark	dk	850, 865	(none)

Country	Keycode	Code Page	Code
Finland	su	850, 437	(none)
France	fr	850, 437	129, 189
Germany	gr	850, 437	(none)
Italy	it	850, 437	141, 142
Latin America	la	850, 437	(none)
Netherlands	nl	850, 437	(none)
Norway	no	850, 865	(none)
Portugal	po	850, 860	(none)
Spain	sp	850, 437	(none)
Sweden	sv	850, 437	(none)
Swiss-French	sf	850, 437	(none)
Swiss-German	sg	850, 437	(none)
United Kingdom	uk	850, 437	166, 168
United States	us	850, 437	(none)

Switches

/ID:code	The code for the Enhanced Keyboard you want (see the preceding table)
/E	Used to specify that you are using an Enhanced Keyboard (useful for 8088/8086 computers)

Notes

Previously, KEYB was a set of five programs, one for each of the five national languages DOS supported. DOS 3.3 codified the five programs into one program.

When KEYB is active, it reassigns some alphanumeric characters to different keys and introduces new characters. The new layout and characters vary among the supported languages.

If you do not specify a code page, DOS uses the default code page for your country. The default code page is established by the COUNTRY command in CONFIG.SYS or, if the COUNTRY command is not used, by the DOS default code page. KEYB attempts to activate the default code page.

If you plan to use the KEYB command regularly, you should start the command from the CONFIG.SYS file, using the INSTALL command. Starting KEYB this way uses less memory than starting KEYB from the command line (refer to Configuration Command—INSTALL in this Command Reference).

On completion, KEYB produces exit codes. An exit code is a number that tells DOS the status of KEYB when it stopped. You can test for exit codes in a batch file using IF and change the outcome of the batch file accordingly. The following is a list of exit codes that KEYB produces:

Exit Code	Meaning
0	Keyboard definition loaded successfully
1	Invalid syntax, keyboard code, or code page
2	Corrupt or missing keyboard definition file
4	Error occurred while communicating with CON
5	Code page not prepared

Example

To display the current keyboard code and code page, type the command:

KEYB

LABEL   V3, V4, V5—External

Creates, changes, or deletes a volume label for a disk

Syntax

*dc:pathc***LABEL** *d:volume_label*

dc:pathc is the disk drive and directory that hold the command.

d: is the disk drive whose label will be changed.

volume_label is the disk's new volume label.

For more information, see Chapter 7.

LOADFIX

Loads and executes a program that gives the `Packed file corrupt` error message when the file is executed from the command line without LOADFIX

Syntax

*dc:pathc***LOADFIX** *d:path***filename.ext**

dc:pathc is the disk drive and directory that hold the command.

filename.ext is the name of the file to execute.

Notes

Some files expand when loaded into memory. When loaded into the first 64K of RAM, these files give the error message `Packed file corrupt` and return the computer to the DOS prompt. LOADFIX can be used to load *filename.ext* into memory above the first 64K of RAM.

For more information, see Chapter 15.

Examples

To execute the MESSAGE.EXE program that gave the `Packed file corrupt` error message, type the following:

LOADFIX MESSAGE.EXE

LOADHIGH

Loads device drivers or memory-resident programs into memory beyond conventional memory

Syntax

LOADHIGH *d:path***filename.ext** *prog_options*

or

LH *d:path***filename.ext** *prog_options*

d:path is the disk drive and directory that hold the device driver or memory-resident program to load into reserved memory.

filename.ext is the name of the device driver or memory-resident program to load into reserved memory.

prog_options are any options required by **filename.ext**.

For more information, see Chapter 15.

MEM   V4, V5—External

Displays the amount of used and unused memory, allocated and open memory areas, and all programs currently in the system

Syntax

*dc:pathc***MEM** */PROGRAM* */DEBUG* */CLASSIFY*

dc:pathc is the disk drive and directory that hold the command.

Switches

/PROGRAM	Displays names of programs loaded into memory, including the address, name, size, and type of each file for every program; also shows the amount of memory currently free. You also may use the short form /P.
/DEBUG	Displays names of programs loaded into memory, including the address, name, size, and type of each file for every program. Also displays system device drivers and installed device drivers, as well as all unused memory. You also may use the short form /D.
/CLASSIFY	Displays names of programs loaded into memory, including the program's name and its size in bytes (decimal and hexadecimal). Programs are shown loaded into conventional memory and, if available, reserved memory (upper memory blocks). Displays the total bytes free (conventional memory plus reserved memory) and the size of the largest executable program. You also may use the short form /C.

Notes

You can use MEM to display information about how memory is used. MEM displays statistics for conventional memory, as well as for upper, extended, and expanded memory if available. You cannot specify /PROGRAM, /DEBUG, and /CLASSIFY at the same time.

For more information, see Chapter 15.

MIRROR   V5—External

Saves information about a disk drive so that you can recover accidentally lost data

Syntax

To save information about a drive and files, in case they are deleted, use the form:

> *dc:pathc***MIRROR** *d1: d2: dn: /Tdrive-entries /1*

To save information about a drive partition, use the form:

> *dc:pathc***MIRROR** *d1: d2: dn: /***PARTN**

To stop tracking deleted files, use the form:

> *dc:pathc***MIRROR** /U

dc:pathc is the disk drive and directory that hold the command.

d1:, *d2:*, and *dn:* are disk drives about which you want to save information.

Switches

/Tdrive-entries	Loads as memory-resident a portion of MIRROR to keep track of files you delete. *drive* is the mandatory disk drive for which deleted files are tracked. *entries* is an optional value (from 1 through 999) that specifies the maximum number of deleted files remembered.

/1	Keeps MIRROR from making a backup of the mirror-image file when it is updated
/PARTN	Makes a copy of the drive's partition table
/U	Removes from memory the memory-resident portion of MIRROR that keeps track of deleted files

For more information, see Chapters 7 and 15.

> *Caution:* The MIRROR and UNFORMAT commands do not take the place of proper backups of your hard disk!

MKDIR or MD   V2, V3, V4, V5—Internal

Creates a subdirectory

Syntax

> **MKDIR** *d:path***dirname**

or

> **MD** *d:path***dirname**

d: is the disk drive for the subdirectory.

path\ indicates the path to the directory that will hold the subdirectory.

dirname is the subdirectory you are creating.

For more information, see Chapter 9.

MODE   V1, V2, V3, V4, V5—External

In this reference, this command's many forms are treated as separate commands. Generally, MODE sets the printer characteristics, keyboard rate, the video display, the Asynchronous

Communications Adapter, and code pages for international characters. MODE controls redirection of printing between parallel and serial printers, as well as code-page switching for the console and printer. Other functions differ according to DOS implementation.

MODE
CODEPAGE PREPARE   V3.3, V4, V5—External

Determines the code pages to be used with a device

Syntax

*dc:pathc***MODE device CODEPAGE PREPARE=((codepage,** *codepage, ...***)** *dp:pathp***pagefile.ext)**

or

*dc:pathc***MODE device CP**
PREP = **((codepage,** *codepage, ...***)** *dc:pathp***pagefile**.*ext*)

dc:pathc is the disk drive and directory that hold the command.

device is the device for which code page(s) will be chosen. You can select one of the following devices:

CON:	The console
PRN:	The first parallel printer
LPTx:	The first, second, or third parallel printer (x is 1, 2, or 3)

codepage is the number of the code page(s) to be used with the device. The following are valid numbers:

437 United States

850 Multilingual

860 Portugal

863 French Canadian

865 Denmark/Norway

The ellipsis (...) represents additional code pages.

dp:pathp is the disk drive and directory holding the code-page information.

pagefile.*ext* is the file holding the code-page (font) information. DOS currently provides the following code-page files:

4201.CPI	IBM ProPrinter
4208.CPI	IBM ProPrinter X24 and XL24
5202.CPI	IBM Quietwriter III Printer
EGA.CPI	EGA/VGA type displays
LCD.CPI	IBM Convertible LCD display

Notes

MODE CODEPAGE PREPARE is used to prepare code pages (fonts) for the console (keyboard and display) and the printers. You should issue this command before issuing the MODE CODEPAGE SELECT command, except for the IBM Quietwriter III printer, which holds font information in cartridges. If the code page needed is in a cartridge and has been specified to the PRINTER.SYS driver, no PREPARE command is needed.

Examples

To prepare code pages 850, 863, and 865 for use with an EGA or VGA display, type the form:

MODE CON CODEPAGE PREPARE = (850, 863, 865) C:\EGA.CPI

To prepare code pages 850 and 863 for an IBM ProPrinter Model 4201 attached to LPT1, type the form:

MODE LPT1 CP PREP = (850, 863) C:\4201.CPI

MODE
CODEPAGE REFRESH   V3.3, V4, V5—External

Reloads and reactivates the code page used with a device

Syntax

*dc:pathc***MODE device CODEPAGE REFRESH**

or

*dc:pathc***MODE device CP REF**

dc:pathc is the disk drive and directory that hold the command.

device is the device for which code page(s) will be chosen. You can select one of the following devices:

CON:	The console
PRN:	The first parallel printer
LPTx:	The first, second, or third parallel printer (x is 1, 2, or 3)

Notes

MODE CODEPAGE REFRESH sends the code page to the device, if necessary, and reactivates the currently selected code page on a device. Use this command after you turn on your printer or after a program makes a mess of the video display and leaves the console code page unusable. You do not provide a code page for MODE CODEPAGE REFRESH—the command uses the last selected code page for the device.

Examples

To reactivate the code page for the video display, type the form:

MODE CON: CODEPAGE REFRESH

or

MODE CON: CP REF

MODE
CODEPAGE SELECT   V3.3, V4, V5—External

Activates the code page used with a device

Syntax

*dc:pathc***MODE device CODEPAGE SELECT = codepage**

or

*dc:pathc***MODE device CP SEL = codepage**

dc:pathc is the disk drive and directory that hold the command.

device is the device for which code page(s) will be chosen. You can select one of the following devices:

CON:	The console
PRN:	The first parallel printer
LPTx:	The first, second, or third parallel printer (x is 1, 2, or 3)

codepage is the number of the code page(s) to be used with the device. The valid numbers are as follows:

437 United States

850 Multilingual

860 Portugal

863 French Canadian

865 Denmark/Norway

Notes

MODE CODEPAGE SELECT activates a prepared code page or reactivates a hardware code page. You can use MODE CODEPAGE SELECT only on these two types of code pages.

Examples

To activate the prepared 863 font for use with an EGA or VGA display, type the form:

MODE CON CODEPAGE SELECT = 863

To activate the prepared 850 font for use with the printer attached to LPT1, type the form:

MODE LPT1 CP SEL = 850

MODE
CODEPAGE STATUS   V3.3, V4, V5—External

Displays a device's code-page status

Syntax

*dc:pathc***MODE device CODEPAGE** */STATUS*

or

*dc:pathc***MODE device CP** */STA*

dc:pathc is the disk drive and directory that hold the command.

device is the device for which code pages are chosen. You can select one of the following devices:

CON:	The console
PRN:	The first parallel printer
LPTx:	The first, second, or third parallel printer (x is 1, 2, or 3)

Switches

/STATUS   Displays the status of the device's code pages; abbreviated form is /STA

Notes

MODE CODEPAGE /STATUS displays the following information about the device:

- The selected (active) code page, if one has been selected
- The hardware code page(s)
- Any prepared code pages
- Any positions available for additional prepared code pages

Here is a sample output for the command:

```
Active codepage for device CON is 437
hardware codepages:
    Codepage 437
prepared codepages:
    Codepage 850
    Codepage not prepared
MODE Status Codepage function completed
```

Examples

To display the status of the console's code page, type the form:

MODE CON CODEPAGE /STATUS

or

MODE CON CP

MODE
COMMUNICATIONS V1.1, V2, V3, V4, V5—

External

Controls the protocol characteristics of the Asynchronous Communications Adapter

Syntax

*dc:pathc***MODE COMy**: **baud**, *parity, databits, stopbits, P*

With DOS 4 or 5, you can use the following form:

*dc:pathc***MODE COMy: BAUD=baud** *PARITY=parity*
DATA=databits STOP=stopbits RETRY=ret

dc:pathc is the disk drive and directory that hold the command.

y: is the port number (1, 2, 3, or 4); the colon after the number is optional.

baud is the baud rate (110, 150, 300, 600, 1200, 2400, 4800, 9600, or 19200).

parity is the parity checking (None, Odd, or Even; in versions of DOS earlier than V4.0, use N, O, or E, respectively).

databits is the number of data bits (7 or 8).

stopbits is the number of stop bits (1 or 2).

P represents continual retries on time-out errors.

ret tells DOS what to do when a time-out error occurs. You can choose from the following options:

ret	*Action*
E	Return the error when port is busy (default)
B	Return busy when port is busy
P	Continue retry until port is ready
R	Return ready when port is busy
NONE	Take no action

Notes

You must enter the port's number, followed by a space and a baud rate. If you type the optional colon, it must immediately follow the port number. All other parameters are optional.

If you do not want to change a parameter, enter a comma for that value.

If you try to use the 19200-baud rate on a PC or compatible (computers that do not support 19200 baud), DOS displays the message `Invalid parameter` and takes no further action.

If the adapter is set for continual retries and the device is not ready, the computer seems to be locked up. You can abort this loop by pressing Ctrl-Break.

Examples

To set up your communications port for 9600 baud, even parity, 8 data bits, 1 stop bit, and continual retry, use the following form:

MODE COM1:9600,E,8,1,P

or

MODE COM1:96,E,8,1,P

With DOS 4 or 5, you can use the form:

MODE COM1 BAUD=9600 PARITY=EVEN DATA=8 STOP=1 RETRY=B

MODE
CONSOLE RATE/DELAY   V4, V5—External

Adjusts the rate at which the keyboard repeats a character when a key is held down

Syntax

*dc:pathc***MODE CON***:* **RATE=x DELAY=y**

dc:pathc is the disk drive and directory that hold the command.

x is a value that specifies the character-repeat rate. You can select a value between 1 and 32.

y is a value that specifies the delay between the initial pressing of the key and the start of automatic character repetition. This value can be 1, 2, 3, or 4, representing delays of 1/4 second, 1/2 second, 3/4 second, and one full second, respectively.

Notes

On some keyboards, you may want characters to repeat faster when you hold down a key; on others, the keys may cause characters to repeat too fast or may start repeating before you want them to. Use this command to vary the speed and delay of key repeat.

Examples

To set the keyboard rate to 10 and the delay to 2, enter the following form:

MODE CON RATE=10 DELAY=2

MODE DISPLAY TYPE
                                                    V3, V4, V5—External

Switches the active display adapter between the monochrome display and a graphics adapter/array (Color Graphics Adapter, Enhanced Color Graphics Adapter, or Video Graphics Array) on a two-display system, and sets the graphics adapter/array characteristics on a one- or two-display system

Syntax

*dc:pathc***MODE dt**,*y*

or

*dc:pathc***MODE** *dt*, **s**, *T*

With DOS 4 or 5, you can use the following form:

*dc:pathc***MODE CON: COLS**=*x* **LINES**=*y*

dc:pathc is the disk drive and directory that hold the command.

dt is the display type, which may be one of the following:

40	Sets the display to 40 characters per line for the graphics display
80	Sets the display to 80 characters per line for the graphics display

BW40	Makes the graphics display the active display and sets the mode to 40 characters per line, black-and-white (color disabled)
BW80	Makes the graphics display the active display and sets the mode to 80 characters per line, black-and-white (color disabled)
CO40	Makes the graphics display the active display and sets the mode to 40 characters per line (color enabled)
CO80	Makes the graphics display the active display and sets the mode to 80 characters per line (color enabled)
MONO	Makes the monochrome display the active display

s shifts the graphics display right (**R**) or left (**L**) one character.

T requests alignment of the graphics-display screen with a one-line test pattern.

x specifies the number of columns to display; 40 or 80 columns are possible.

y specifies the number of lines on the display, used only for EGA and VGA displays. EGA values are 25 and 80; VGA adds the value 50.

Notes

For the first form of the command, you must enter the display type (*dt*); all other parameters are optional. For the second form of the command, you must enter the shift parameter *s* (an *R* for *right* or an *L* for *left*); the display type (*dt*) and test pattern (*T*) are optional.

The *s* (*R* or *L*) parameter works only with the Color Graphics Adapter; the display does not shift if you use this command with any other adapter. Conversely, the *T* parameter causes the test pattern to be displayed with any graphics adapter (Convertible, EGA, or VGA). If you use the *R* or *L* parameter with the Monochrome Adapter, DOS responds with an error message.

Although color is not displayed automatically when you use the CO40 or CO80 parameter for the display type, programs that use color can be displayed in color.

Examples

To set an 80-column color monitor to black-and-white mode, type the form:

MODE BW80

If you have a VGA display and want to display color, 80 columns, and 50 lines of text, type the form:

MODE CO80,50

If you have DOS 4 or 5, type the form:

MODE CON COLS=80 LINES=50

MODE
PRINTER

V1, V2, V3, V4, V5—External

Sets IBM-compatible printer characteristics

Syntax

*dc:pathc***MODE LPTx:***cpl,lpi,P*

With DOS 4 or 5, you can use the following form:

*dc:pathc***MODE LPTx** *COLS=cpl LINES=lpi RETRY=ret*

dc:pathc is the disk drive and directory that hold the command.

x: is the printer port number (1, 2, or 3). The colon is optional.

cpl is the number of characters per line (80, 132).

lpi is the number of lines per inch (6 or 8).

P specifies continual retries on time-out errors.

ret tells DOS what to do when a time-out error occurs. You can choose from the following options:

ret	Action
E	Return the error when port is busy (default)
B	Return busy when port is busy
P	Continue retrying until port is ready
R	Return ready when port is busy (infinite retry)
NONE	Take no action

Notes

You must specify a printer number, but all other parameters are optional, including the colon after the printer number.

If you do not want to change a parameter, enter a comma for that parameter.

The characters-per-line and lines-per-inch portions of the command affect only IBM and Epson printers and others that use IBM/Epson-compatible control codes.

Examples

To set the printer on LPT1 to 132 characters per line with 8 lines per inch, and to keep checking for the printer's busy condition, type the form:

MODE LPT1:132,8,P

With DOS 4 or 5, you can use the following form:

MODE LPT1 COLS=132 LINES=8 RETRY=B

MODE
SERIAL PRINTER   V2, V3, V4, V5—External

Forces DOS to print to a serial printer rather than to a parallel printer

Syntax

*dc:pathc***MODE LPTx: = COMy:**

dc:pathc is the disk drive and directory that hold the command.

x: is the parallel printer number (1, 2, or 3). The colon is optional.

y: is the Asynchronous Communications Adapter number (1, 2, 3, or 4).

Notes

This form of MODE is useful for systems that have only a serial printer. When rerouting is used, the serial printer receives all the output usually sent to the system printer (assuming that the serial printer is connected to the first Asynchronous Communications Adapter). This output includes the print-screen (Shift-PrtSc) function.

Before you issue the MODE LPT=COMy command, use the MODE COMn: command to set up the serial adapter used for the serial printer.

Examples

To redirect to COM1: all output meant for LPT1:, you must first initialize COM1: with the MODE command. Then type the form:

MODE LPT1 = COM1

MODE
STATUS
V4, V5—External

Displays the status of a specified device or of all devices that can be set by MODE

Syntax

*dc:pathc***MODE device /STATUS**

dc:pathc is the disk drive and directory that hold the command.

device is the optional device to be checked by MODE.

Switches

/STATUS   Mandatory switch for checking the status of a device or devices; you can type /STA or /STATUS

Notes

Use this command to see the status of any device you normally set with MODE. For example, type **MODE LPT1 /STA** to display the status of the first parallel port.

Examples

To display the current status of the console, type the form:

MODE CON /STATUS

MORE

V2, V3, V4, V5—External

Displays one screenful of information from the standard input device and pauses while displaying the message —More—. When you press any key, MORE displays the next screenful of information.

Syntax

> *dc:pathc***MORE**

dc:pathc is the disk drive and directory that hold the command.

Notes

MORE is a DOS filter that enables you to display information one screenful at a time. Because MORE is a filter, you must pass information to MORE, rather than start MORE from the command line like a program. You pass information to MORE using the redirection character (<) or the pipe character (|).

One screenful of information is normally 40 or 80 characters per line and 23 lines per screen. But MORE does not always display 23 lines from the file; rather, the command wraps long lines that exceed the display width (40 or 80 characters). If one of the file's lines takes 3 lines to display, MORE displays a maximum of 21 lines from the file, pauses, and shows the next screenful of lines. MORE also follows the number of display lines set by MODE CON LINES=n. If you set the number of lines on your EGA or VGA display to 43, MORE displays 41 lines of the file. If you set your VGA display to show 50 lines, MORE displays 48 lines of the file at a time.

For more information, see Chapter 10.

Examples

To use redirection to display TEST.TXT one screenful at a time, type the following form:

> **MORE < TEST.TXT**

To display a sorted directory one screenful at a time, type the following form:

> **DIR | SORT | MORE**

NLSFUNC

V3.3, V4, V5—External

Supports extended country information and allows use of CHCP

Syntax

*dc:pathc***NLSFUNC** *d:path\filename.ext*

dc:pathc is the disk drive and directory that hold the command.

d:path is the disk drive and directory that hold the country-information file.

filename.ext is the country-information file. This country information is contained in the default file COUNTRY.SYS.

Notes

NLSFUNC loads support for extended country information and enables you to use the CHCP (Change Code Page) command. When you load NLSFUNC, DOS increases in size by 2,672 bytes.

Load NLSFUNC only if your programs use the extended country information available from DOS, or if you want to use the CHCP command to change code pages. Your program's documentation should tell you whether NLSFUNC is required.

If you use NLSFUNC regularly, use the INSTALL directive to start NLSFUNC from the CONFIG.SYS file. (See Configuration Command—INSTALL, in this command reference.)

Examples

To load NLSFUNC, assuming that the file COUNTRY.SYS is in the root directory of your disk, type the command:

NLSFUNC

To load NLSFUNC when COUNTRY.SYS is in the directory C:\DOS, type the form:

NLSFUNC C:\DOS\COUNTRY.SYS

PATH

V2, V3, V4, V5—Internal

Tells DOS to search specific directories on specified drives if a program or batch file is not found in the current directory

Syntax

> **PATH** *d1:path1;d2:path2;d3:path3;...*

or

> **PATH;**

d1:, *d2:*, and *d3:* are valid disk drive names.

path1, *path2*, and *path3* are valid path names to the commands you want to run while in any directory.

The ellipsis (...) represents additional disk drives and path names.

A semicolon (;) used directly after the PATH command disables all search paths.

For more information, see Chapters 9 and 13.

PRINT   V2, V3, V4, V5—External

Prints a list of files while the computer performs other tasks

Syntax

> *dc:pathc***PRINT** */D:device /B:bufsiz /M:maxtick /Q:maxfiles /S:timeslice /U:busytick d1:path1\\filename1.ext1 /T*

or

> *dc:pathc***PRINT** *d2:path2\\filename2.ext2/P /C ...*

dc:pathc is the disk drive and directory that hold the command.

d1: and *d2:* are valid disk drive names.

path1 and *path2* are valid path names to the files you want to print.

filename1.ext1 and *filename2.ext2* are the files you want to print. Wild cards are allowed.

The ellipsis (...) represents additional file names in the form *x:pathx\\filenamex.extx.*

Switches

You can specify any one of the following switches, but only the first time you start PRINT:

/D:device	Specifies the device to be used for printing. *device* is the name of any valid DOS device. (You must list this switch first when you use it.)
/B:bufsiz	Specifies the size of the memory buffer to be used while the files are printing. *bufsiz* can be any number from 1 to 16,386.
/M:maxtick	Specifies, in clock ticks, the maximum amount of time PRINT has for sending characters to the printer, when PRINT gets a turn. (A tick is the smallest measure of time used on PCs. A tick happens every 1/18.2 [0.0549] seconds.) *maxtick* can be any number from 1 through 255; the default is 2.
/Q:maxfiles	Specifies the number of files that can be in the queue (line) for printing. *maxfiles* can be any number from 4 through 32; the default is 10.
/S:timeslice	Specifies the number of slices (ticks of the clock) in each second. *timeslice* can be a number from 1 through 255; the default is 10.
/U:busytick	Specifies, in clock ticks, the maximum amount of time for the program to wait for a busy or unavailable printer. *busytick* can be any number from 1 through 255.

You can specify any one of the following switches whenever you use PRINT:

/P	Places in line (queues up) the files for printing
/T	Terminates background printing of any or all files, including any file currently being printed
/C	Cancels background printing of file(s)

Notes

PRINT controls the background-printing feature of DOS. During *background printing*, DOS orders a specified printer to print a text file while the computer performs a separate task, such as running a program. The computer must devote most of its resources to the separate task, which is said to be in the *foreground;* because PRINT gets less attention from the computer, printing is called a *background* task. When the cursor sits at the system prompt (C>), fewer resources are required of the computer; PRINT receives most of the computer's time.

You can specify any of the switches from the first set (/D, /B, /M, /Q, /S, and /U) only when PRINT is first used. If you specify the /D switch, it must be the first switch on the line. You can type the remaining five switches in any sequence before you specify a file name.

Examples

To enable background printing to the LPT1 device, type the form:

PRINT /D:LPT1

After PRINT is enabled, you can start printing the files MEMO.TXT, LETTER.TXT, and REPORT.PRN by typing the following form:

PRINT MEMO.TXT /P LETTER.TXT REPORT.PRN

If the three files begin printing, and you want to cancel LETTER.TXT, type the form:

PRINT LETTER.TXT /C

To cancel all the jobs queued for printing, type this form:

PRINT /T

PROMPT   V2, V3, V4, V5—Internal

Customizes the DOS system prompt (C>, the C prompt)

Syntax

PROMPT *promptstring*

promptstring is the text to be used for the new system prompt.

A *meta-string* produces a special character or prompt. The meta-string is made up of a $ character, followed by another character. To use special characters (for example, the < or > I/O redirection symbols), you must enter the appropriate meta-string to place the desired characters in the *promptstring*. Otherwise, DOS immediately attempts to interpret the special character.

All meta-strings begin with the dollar sign ($) and include a second character. The following list contains meta-string characters and their meanings:

Meta-String	Meaning
$$	$, the dollar sign
$_	Newline (moves to the first position of the next line)
$b	|, the vertical bar
$e	The Escape character, CHR$(27)
$d	The date
$h	The backspace character, CHR$(8), which erases the preceding character
$g	>, the greater-than character
$l	<, the less-than character
$n	The current disk drive
$p	The current disk drive and path, including the current directory
$q	=, the equal sign
$t	The time
$v	The DOS version number
Any other	Nothing or null; the character is ignored

For more information, see Chapter 13.

QBASIC   V5—External

Loads the BASIC interpreter into memory for BASIC programming

Syntax

*dc:pathc***QBASIC** *d:path\\filename.ext /H /NOHI /B /EDITOR /G /MBF /RUN d:pathc\\filename.ext*

dc:pathc is the drive and directory that hold the command.

d:path is the disk drive and directory that hold the BASIC program to be loaded into memory.

filename.ext is the name of the BASIC program.

Switches

/H	Changes display mode so that QBasic displays the maximum number of lines on-screen for your display adapter (43 for EGA, 50 for VGA)
/NOHI	Causes QBasic to work with monitors that do not support high-intensity video
/B	Puts QBasic in black-and-white mode
/EDITOR	Starts Editor in nonprogramming mode
/G	Causes CGA monitors to update quickly; do not use this switch if "snow" appears on-screen
/MBF	Enables the QBASIC statements CVS, CVD, MKS$, and MKD$ to use the Microsoft Binary Format for numbers
/RUN d:path\\filename.ext	Loads *filename.ext* into memory and starts execution

Notes

QBasic is a comprehensive development environment for interpreted BASIC. A subset of Microsoft QuickBASIC, QBasic replaces BASIC, BASICA, and GW-BASIC from earlier versions of DOS.

For more information, see Chapter 12.

Examples

To start QBasic, use the form:

QBASIC

To start QBasic on a black-and-white monitor, and load the program INVNTRY.BAS, use the form:

QBASIC INVNTRY /B

To start QBasic, and load and execute the program TRANSFER, use the form:

QBASIC /RUN TRANSFER

RECOVER   V2, V3, V4, V5—External

Recovers a file with bad sectors or a file from a disk with a damaged directory

Syntax

To recover a file, use the following form:

*dc:pathc***RECOVER** *d:path***filename.ext**

To recover a disk with a damaged directory, use this form:

*dc:pathc***RECOVER d:**

dc:pathc is the disk drive and directory that hold the command.

d:path is the disk drive and directory holding the damaged file or floppy disk.

filename.ext is the file to be recovered.

Notes

RECOVER tries to recover a file with a bad sector or a disk with a directory that contains a bad sector. If a file has bad sectors, DOS displays a disk-error message when you try to use the file. To recover a file with one or more bad sectors, type **RECOVER d:filename.ext**.

If the damaged file is a program file, the program probably cannot be used. If the file is a data or text file, some information can be recovered. Because RECOVER reads the entire file, make sure that you use a text editor or word processor to eliminate any garbage at the end of the file, after using RECOVER.

Example

To recover the file MEMO.TXT, which contains a few bad sectors, type the form:

RECOVER MEMO.TXT

RENAME or REN   V1, V2, V3, V4, V5—Internal

Changes the name(s) of file(s)

Syntax

RENAME *d:path***filename1.ext1 filename2.ext2**

or

REN *d:path***filename1.ext1 filename2.ext2**

d:path is the disk drive and directory that hold the file(s) to be renamed.

filename1.ext1 is the file's current name. Wild cards are allowed.

filename2.ext2 is the file's new name. Wild cards are allowed.

For more information, see Chapter 10.

REPLACE   V3.2, V3.3, V4, V5—External

Replaces files on one disk with files of the same name from another disk; adds files to a disk by copying them from another disk

Syntax

*dc:pathc***REPLACE** *ds:paths***filenames.***exts dd:pathd*
/A /P /R /S /W

With DOS 4 or 5, you can use the form:

*dc:pathc***REPLACE** *ds:paths***filenames.***exts dd:pathd*
/A /P /R /S /W /U

dc:pathc is the disk drive and directory that hold the command.

ds:paths is the disk drive and directory that hold the replacement file(s); the source drive and directory.

filenames.exts are the replacement files. Wild cards are allowed.

dd:pathd are the disk drive and directory whose file(s) will be replaced; the destination drive and directory.

Switches

/A	Adds, from the source disk, files that do not exist on the destination disk
/P	Displays a prompt asking whether the file should be replaced or added to the destination
/R	Replaces files on the destination disk even though the files' read-only attribute is on
/S	Replaces all files with matching names in the current directory and its subdirectories; does not work with the /A switch
/W	Causes REPLACE to wait for the source floppy disk to be inserted, prompting you with the message `Press any key to continue`
/U	Replaces only those files created or modified at an earlier date and time than the source files (DOS 4 or 5)

Notes

The following is a list of exit codes that REPLACE produces:

Exit Code	Meaning
0	Replace successful
2	Source files not found
3	Source or destination path not found
5	Files to replace not accessible by user
8	Not enough memory
11	Incorrect syntax used

For more information, see Chapter 10.

RESTORE   V2, V3, V4, V5—External

Restores one or more backup files from one disk onto another; complements BACKUP

Syntax

*dc:pathc***RESTORE** *d1: d2:path***filename.ext** */S /P /M /N /B:date /A:date /L:time /E:time /D*

dc:pathc is the disk drive and directory that hold the command.

d1: is the disk drive that holds the backup files.

d2: is the disk drive that will receive the restored files.

path is the path to the directory that will receive the restored files.

filename.ext is the file you want to restore. Wild cards are allowed.

Switches

/S	Restores files in the current directory and all its subdirectories. When this switch is given, RESTORE re-creates any necessary subdirectories that have been removed and then restores the files in the re-created subdirectories.
/P	Causes RESTORE to prompt for your approval before restoring a file that has changed since the last backup or is marked as read-only
/M	Restores all files modified or deleted since the backup set was made
/N	Restores all files that no longer exist on the destination drive and directory
/B:date	Restores all files created or modified on or before the date you specify
/A:date	Restores all files created or modified on or after the date you specify
/L:time	Restores all files created or modified at or later than the time you specify
/E:time	Restores all files created or modified at or earlier than the time you specify
/D	Lists files that will be restored; does not perform the restoration (DOS 5 only)

Notes

In DOS 3.3, 4, and 5, BACKUP and RESTORE differ radically from earlier versions. In 3.3 and later versions, BACKUP places all backed-up files in one large file and maintains a separate information file on the same disk. In 3.3 and later versions, RESTORE handles the new and old backup-file formats; these later versions will restore backups created by any version of BACKUP.

You can use the RESTORE command only on files saved with the BACKUP command.

RESTORE prompts you to insert the backup disks in order. If you insert a disk out of order, RESTORE prompts you to insert the correct disk.

To view the files that will be restored, issue the /D switch. This switch simulates a restoration based on the source file specification and other switches you have used. By using the /D switch, you ensure that the correct files will be restored.

Be careful when you restore files that were backed up while an ASSIGN, SUBST, or JOIN command was in effect. When you use RESTORE, clear any existing APPEND, ASSIGN, SUBST, or JOIN commands. Do not use RESTORE /M or RESTORE /N while APPEND /X is in effect. RESTORE attempts to search the directories for modified or missing files. APPEND tricks RESTORE into finding files in the paths specified to the APPEND command. RESTORE then might act on the wrong files and fail to restore files as you want. To disable APPEND, issue the APPEND command.

On completion, RESTORE produces exit codes. An exit code is a number that tells DOS the status of RESTORE when it stopped. You can test for exit codes in a batch file using IF and change the outcome of the batch file accordingly. The following is a list of exit codes that RESTORE produces:

Exit Code	Meaning
0	Restore successful
1	Files not found to restore
3	Ctrl-C or Ctrl-Break stopped restoration
4	An error stopped restoration

For more information, see Chapter 11.

Examples

To restore an entire backup set of disks from drive A to drive C, type the form:

RESTORE A: C:\ /S

To restore the file MEMO.TXT from the backup disks in drive A to C:\LETTERS, type the form:

RESTORE A: C:\LETTERS\MEMO.TXT

To restore all files from the disks in drive B to C:\REPORTS, type this form:

RESTORE B: C:\REPORTS

To view the files that will be restored from the backup disks in the preceding example, without performing the restoration, type the form:

RESTORE B: C:\REPORTS\ /D

RMDIR or RD   V2, V3, V4, V5—Internal

Removes a subdirectory

Syntax

RMDIR *d:***path**

or

RD *d:***path**

d: is the drive that holds the directory.

path is the path to the directory. The last path name is the directory you want to delete.

Notes

RMDIR, or the short form, RD, removes subdirectories from the disk. RMDIR is the opposite of MKDIR (make directory).

If you want to remove a subdirectory, it must be empty except for the current directory file (.) and any parent directory files (..). You cannot remove the current directory. If the directory you want to remove is the current directory, you must first move to another directory (such as the parent directory) and then use RMDIR to remove what *was* the current directory. If you try to remove a subdirectory that is not empty or is the current directory, DOS displays an error message and does not delete the directory.

For more information, see Chapter 9.

Examples

To remove the directory C:\LETTERS when drive C is the current drive, type the form:

RD \LETTERS

To remove the same directory when drive A is the current drive, type the form:

RD C:\LETTERS

To remove the directory REPORTS from the path C:\DATA\REPORTS, type the form:

RD C:\DATA\REPORTS

The directory REPORTS is removed; DATA is not removed. Note that the directory being removed must be empty before it can be removed.

SELECT
V3, V4—External

Creates a disk to hold the DOS files, and configures the CONFIG.SYS and AUTOEXEC.BAT files for your country. For DOS 4, SELECT was expanded to a full-featured, menu-oriented DOS installation utility. SELECT does not exist in DOS 5.

Syntax

For DOS 3, use the following form:

*dc:pathc***SELECT** *ds: dd:pathd* **countrycode keycode**

For DOS 4, use the following form:

*dc:pathc***SELECT**

dc:pathc is the disk drive and directory that hold the command.

ds: is the source disk drive.

dd:pathd is the destination disk drive and directory.

countrycode is a valid country code from the COUNTRY.SYS device driver.

keycode is a valid key code that can be set with KEYB.

Notes

The SELECT program helps you set up DOS on a new disk. SELECT 3.3, which is different from earlier versions, works with any hard or floppy disk. SELECT 3.2 and earlier versions work with floppy disks only.

For V4.0 and V4.01, SELECT has been modified even further. With these versions, SELECT is the program that starts when you boot your computer from the DOS Install disk. SELECT 4 enables you to configure and format your hard disk, install the DOS Shell, and set up the CONFIG.SYS and AUTOEXEC.BAT files. SELECT does not exist in DOS 5.

Example

From your hard disk (drive C), you can prepare a disk in drive A for use with a French country code by typing the following:

SELECT C: A: 437 FR

SET
V2, V3, V4, V5—Internal

Sets or shows the system environment

Syntax

To display the environment, type the command:

SET

To add to or alter the environment, use this form:

SET name=*string*

name is the string you want to add to the environment.

string is the information you want to store in the environment.

The *environment* is the portion of RAM that can be examined and used by DOS commands or user programs. The environment contains alphanumeric information. For example, the environment usually contains the following:

- COMSPEC, the location of COMMAND.COM
- PATH, the additional paths for finding programs and batch files
- PROMPT, the string defining the DOS system prompt

Notes

SET places information in memory so that the data can be used later by batch files or programs. The command is most commonly used to store the directory path to data files or program overlays. When a program is invoked, it examines the part of RAM in which the SET information is stored; then the program issues the necessary commands to find the data or program overlays you need.

Examples

To set an environment variable, WPPATH, so that it is equal to C:\WORDS\LETTERS, type the form:

SET WPPATH=C:\WORDS\LETTERS

To delete the environment variable WPPATH from the environment, type the form:

SET WPPATH=

SETVER   *V5—External*

Enables DOS to report specific version numbers to different programs for compatibility of the program with DOS 5

Syntax

To load the DOS version table into memory, in CONFIG.SYS use the form:

DEVICE=*dc:pathc***\SETVER.EXE**

The following are syntax examples typed from the command line.

To add a program to the version table, use the form:

*dc:pathc***\SETVER** *d:* **filename.ext dosver**

To remove a program from the version table, use the form:

*dc:pathc***\SETVER filename.ext /DELETE** */QUIET*

To view the version table, use the form:

> *dc:pathc***SETVER**

dc:pathc is the disk drive and directory that hold SETVER.

d: is the drive that contains the DOS system files.

filename.ext is the program file to add to the version table.

dosver is a valid version of DOS earlier than 5 (4.01, 4.00, 3.30, 3.20, etc.).

Switches

/DELETE	Removes a program and its associated DOS version from the version table
/QUIET	Suppresses information sent to the screen when a program is removed from the version table

Notes

Use SETVER if you want to use with DOS 5 programs that require specific early versions of DOS. To enable SETVER capabilities, you must first install SETVER.EXE as a device through CONFIG.SYS.

The following is a list of exit codes SETVER produces:

Exit Code	*Meaning*
0	SETVER successful
1	Invalid switch used
2	Invalid file name specified
3	Not enough memory
4	Invalid version number format
5	Entry not found in version table
6	System files not found
7	Invalid drive specified
8	Too many parameters specified
9	Missing parameter
10	Error reading system files
11	Version table corrupted

Exit Code	Meaning
12	System files do not support version table
13	Not enough space for an entry in version table
14	Error occurred while writing system files

For more information, see Chapter 15.

SHARE

Enables DOS support for file and record locking; not available in the Epson Equity implementation of DOS

Syntax

*dc:pathc***SHARE** */F:name_space /L:numlocks*

dc:pathc is the disk drive and directory that hold the command.

Switches

/F:name_space	Sets the amount of memory space (*name_space* bytes large) used for file sharing
/L:numlocks	Sets the maximum number (*numlocks*) of file/record locks to use

Notes

SHARE is the DOS 3 through 5 program for file and record locking.

You use SHARE when two or more programs or processes share a single computer's files. After SHARE is loaded, DOS checks each file for locks whenever it is opened, read, or written. If a file is opened for exclusive use, any subsequent attempt to open the file causes an error message. If one program locks a portion of a file, an error message results if another program attempts to read or write the locked portion.

You must use SHARE if you use DOS 4.0 and 4.01 and a hard disk formatted larger than 32M. But if you are using DOS 5 with a hard disk formatted larger than 32M, you do not need to use SHARE.

For convenience, you can use INSTALL in the CONFIG.SYS file to activate SHARE (see Configuration Command—INSTALL in this command reference).

SORT   V2, V3, V4—External

Reads lines from the standard input device, performs an ASCII sort of the lines, and then writes the lines to the standard output device; sorting may be in ascending or descending order and may start at any column in the line.

Syntax

*dc:pathc***SORT** */R /+c*

dc:pathc is the disk drive and directory that hold the command.

Switches

/R	Sorts in reverse order (from Z through A)
/+c	Starts sorting with column number *c*

Notes

SORT is a general-purpose program that sorts ASCII text. SORT is a powerful filter, but it does have some limitations. One limitation, for example, is that SORT cannot sort a file larger than 63K (64K, in DOS 5).

SORT uses the ASCII sequence of characters for sorting. For example, special characters are sorted as follows: ! " # $ % & ' ( ) * + , - . /. SORT treats numbers as characters. The following table shows how the numbers 1 through 10 are sorted. SORT arranges text by the column in the file.

Unsorted	Sorted	
1	1	
2	1	0
3	2	
4	3	
5	4	

Unsorted	Sorted
6	5
7	6
8	7
9	8
10	9

With DOS 3 through 5, SORT correctly handles alphabetic characters, giving upper- and lowercase characters the same treatment. SORT V2 treats these characters differently. In the ASCII characters, the uppercase *A* precedes the uppercase *Z*, but the lowercase *a* comes after the uppercase *Z*.

With V3 through V5, SORT also correctly sorts certain ASCII characters in the range of 128 through 225; this range includes foreign-language characters and symbols. SORT V3 through V5 can handle most files that contain non-English text.

Examples

To sort the lines in the file WORDS.TXT and display the result, type the form:

SORT < WORDS.TXT

To sort the lines in the file WORDS.TXT and place the result of the sort in the file WORDS.SRT, type the form:

SORT < WORDS.TXT > WORDS.SRT

To produce a sorted directory listing, type the form:

DIR | SORT

To produce a directory listing sorted by extension, type this form:

DIR | SORT /+10

SUBST   V3.1, V3.2, V3.3, V4, V5—External

Creates an alias disk drive name for a subdirectory; used principally with programs that do not use path names (not available in Epson Equity implementation of DOS)

Syntax

To establish an alias, use the following form:

*dc:pathc***SUBST d1:** *d2:***pathname**

To delete an alias, use this form:

*dc:pathc***SUBST d1:** **/D**

To see the current aliases, use this form:

*dc:pathc***SUBST**

dc:pathc is the disk drive and directory that hold the command.

d1: is a valid disk drive name that becomes the alias or nickname. **d1:** may be a nonexistent disk drive.

*d2:***pathname** is the valid disk drive name and directory path to be nicknamed **d1:**.

For more information, see Chapter 15.

Switches

/D   Deletes the alias

Examples

To assign the drive designation E: to the directory path C:\WORDS\LETTERS, type the form:

SUBST E: C:\WORDS\LETTERS

To display all current substitutions, type the command:

SUBST

For the preceding substitution, for example, you would see the following message:

```
E: => C:\WORDS\LETTERS
```

To deactivate the preceding substitution, type the form:

SUBST E: /D

SYS   V1, V2, V3, V4, V5—External

Places a copy of DOS on the specified disk

Syntax

For versions of DOS earlier than V4, use the form:

*dc:pathc***SYS d:**

For DOS 4 and 5, use the form:

*dc:pathc***SYS** *d1:* **d:**

dc:pathc is the disk drive and directory that hold the command.

d: is the *destination* drive, the disk drive that will receive the copy of DOS.

d1: is the *source* drive, the disk drive that contains the DOS system files to copy.

For more information, see Chapter 7.

TIME   V1.1, V2, V3, V4, V5—Internal

Sets and shows the system time

Syntax

To enter the time, use the form:

TIME *hh:mm:ss.xx*

With DOS 4 or 5, use the form:

TIME *hh:mm:ss.xxA|P*

hh is the one- or two-digit number for hours (0 through 23).

mm is the one- or two-digit number for minutes (0 through 59).

ss is the one- or two-digit number for seconds (0 through 59).

xx is the one- or two-digit number for hundredths of a second (0 through 99).

A|P may be typed to designate A.M. or P.M. Include *A* if the time you enter is in the A.M., and *P* if the time you enter is in the P.M. If you do not use *A* or *P*, you must enter the time as military time.

> *Note:* Depending on the country code setting in your CONFIG.SYS file, you may have to use a comma rather than a period as the separator between seconds and hundredths of seconds.

For more information, see Chapter 3.

TREE   V2, V3, V4, V5—External

Displays all subdirectories on a disk; optionally, displays all files in each directory

Syntax

   *dc:pathc***TREE** *d: /F*

With DOS 4 or 5, you may add the /A switch, as follows:

   *dc:pathc***TREE** *d: /F /A*

dc:pathc is the disk drive and directory that hold the command.

d: is the disk drive that holds the disk you want to examine.

Switches

/F   Displays all files in the directories

/A   Graphically displays the connection of subdirectories

For more information, see Chapters 5 and 10.

TYPE   V1, V2, V3, V4, V5—Internal

Displays a file's contents

Syntax

   TYPE *d:path***filename.ext**

d:path is the disk drive and directory that hold the file to be displayed.

filename.ext is the file that will be displayed. Wild cards are not permitted.

For more information, see Chapter 10.

UNDELETE

V5—External

Restores files that have been deleted

Syntax

To restore deleted files using the delete-tracking file created with MIRROR, use the form:

*dc:pathc***UNDELETE** *dd:pathd\filenamed.extd /LIST /DT /DOS /ALL*

dc:pathc is the disk drive and directory that hold the command.

dd:pathd is the disk drive and directory that hold the file(s) to be restored.

filenamed.extd is the file name and extension of the file(s) to be restored.

Switches

/LIST — Displays the files that can be recovered. If you specify files to be recovered using wild cards, the list is limited to the files that match the wild-card specifications.

/DT — Tells UNDELETE to restore files based on the information of the deleted files stored in the delete-tracking file created by the MIRROR command

/DOS — Tells UNDELETE to restore files based on the files marked as deleted in the directory. You must confirm each file before it is restored by typing **Y** or **N** when prompted `Undelete (Y/N)?` If a delete-tracking file exists, it is ignored.

/ALL — Recovers all files without prompting. UNDELETE uses the delete-tracking file if one exists; otherwise, UNDELETE uses the standard DOS directory. If the DOS directory is used, the missing first character will be replaced by the pound sign (#). If a second file name conflicts with a file that already is restored, the # is replaced by another character.

For more information, see Chapter 10.

UNFORMAT

V5—External

Reconstructs a formatted hard disk

Syntax

To test or recover erased files on a formatted disk, use the form:

*dc:pathc*__UNFORMAT__ *d1:* */J /P /L /TEST*

To recover a disk whose partition has been lost, use the form:

*dc:pathc*__UNFORMAT /PARTN__

dc:pathc is the disk drive and directory that hold the command.

d1: is the drive in which UNFORMAT should act.

Switches

/J	Tests files created by MIRROR to see whether they are up-to-date with information on the disk; does not unformat the disk
/L	Lists on-screen all files and subdirectories UNFORMAT finds; used with the /PARTN switch, displays the partition table
/P	Prints list of all files and subdirectories UNFORMAT finds; used with the /PARTN switch, prints the partition table
/TEST	Simulates unformatting of the disk
/PARTN	Uses the PARTNSAV.FIL created by MIRROR to restore the hard disk's partition table

For more information, see Chapter 7.

> *Caution:* The MIRROR and UNFORMAT commands do not replace proper backups of your hard disk.

Examples

If you want to use disk information to evaluate the mirror files on drive A, use the form:

__UNFORMAT A: /J__

To perform a simulated UNFORMAT on the disk in drive A, use the form:

UNFORMAT A: /TEST

To UNFORMAT drive D, use the form:

UNFORMAT D:

VER   V2, V3, V4, V5—Internal

Displays the DOS version number

Syntax

VER

For more information, see Chapter 6.

VERIFY   V2, V3, V4, V5—Internal

Sets the computer to check the accuracy of data written to a disk to ensure that information is recorded properly; then shows whether the data has been checked

Syntax

To show the verify status, type the command:

VERIFY

To set the verify status, use this form:

VERIFY ON

or

VERIFY OFF

For more information, see Chapter 10.

VOL   V2, V3, V4, V5—Internal

Displays the disk's volume label, if a label exists

Syntax

> **VOL** *d:*

d: is the disk drive whose label you want to display.

For more information, see Chapter 7.

XCOPY   V3.2, V3.3, V4, V5—External

Selectively copies files from one or more subdirectories

Syntax

> *dc:pathc***XCOPY** *ds:paths***filenames.exts**
> *dd:pathd***filenamed.extd** */A /D:date /E /M /P /S /V /W*

dc:pathc is the disk drive and directory that hold the command.

ds:path is the source disk drive and the directory that holds the file(s) to be copied.

filenames.exts is the file to be copied. Wild cards are allowed.

dd:pathd is the destination disk drive and directory, which will receive the copied file(s).

filenamed.extd is the new name of the file that is copied. Wild cards are allowed.

Switches

/A	Copies files whose archive flag is on but does not turn off the archive flag (similar to the /M switch)
/E	Creates parallel subdirectories on the destination disk even if a subdirectory on the source disk is empty
/D:date	Copies files that were changed or created on or after the date you specify. The date's form depends on the setting of the COUNTRY command in CONFIG.SYS.

/M	Copies files whose archive flag is on (modified files) and turns off the archive flag (similar to the /A switch)
/P	Causes XCOPY to prompt you for approval before copying a file
/S	Copies files from this directory and all subsequent subdirectories
/V	Verifies that the copy has been recorded correctly
/W	Causes XCOPY to prompt you and wait for the correct source floppy disk to be inserted (This switch works exactly as the /W switch works in REPLACE.)

Notes

The following is a list of exit codes that XCOPY produces:

Exit Code	Meaning
0	Copy successful
1	Files not found to copy
2	Ctrl-C or Ctrl-Break stopped XCOPY
4	Not enough memory or disk space, invalid drive or invalid syntax
5	Error writing disk

For more information, see Chapter 11.

Part V

Appendixes

Includes

DOS Messages

Changes between Versions of DOS

DOS Control and Editing Keys

Using Edlin

DOS Messages

DOS messages can be divided into two groups: *general* and *device error* messages. The larger group of general messages is listed first, followed by the device error messages. Both lists are organized alphabetically.

General DOS Messages

General DOS messages fall into three groups: error messages, warning messages, and informational messages. Error messages indicate that DOS has encountered a problem with a command or with the syntax you used. Execution stops when DOS displays an error message. Warning messages tell you in advance that the next action you take may cause unwanted changes to files or to your system. Informational messages display needed information about your system's operation or your DOS version's performance. Informational and warning messages often include prompts, which enable you to select an action.

The following messages may appear when you are starting DOS or any time when you are using your computer. Messages that occur only when you are starting DOS are marked "start-up." With most start-up errors, DOS did not start; you must reboot the system.

Other error messages occur when DOS aborts a program and returns to the system prompt, such as A> or C>.

```
10 Mismatches - ending compare
```

INFORMATION: You compared two different files with COMP. After 10 mismatches, DOS considers the files too different and ends the compare operation.

641

`Abort edit (Y/N)?`

PROMPT: You ended an edit session in Edlin with Q (Quit). This message gives you one last chance to cancel the command before leaving without saving any changes. To cancel and return to Edlin, press N. Otherwise, press Y to quit.

`Access denied`

ERROR: You or a program attempted to change or erase a file that is marked as read-only or that is in use. If the file is marked as read-only, you can change the read-only attribute with the ATTRIB command.

`Active Code Page: xxx`

INFORMATION: You issued CHCP, which displayed *xxx*, the code page currently in use by the system.

`Active Code Page for device ddd is xxx`

INFORMATION: You issued MODE, which lists the code page currently in use for device *ddd*. To display a single screen at a time, pipe this command into MORE (MODE|MORE).

`Active Code Page not available from con device`

ERROR: You used KEYB with a code page not supported on the CON device (screen).

`Add filename? (Y/N)`

PROMPT: You issued REPLACE /W; DOS asks whether you want to add the file to the disk.

`Adding filename`

INFORMATION: REPLACE displays this message while adding *filename* to your disk.

`All available space in the Extended DOS Partition is assigned to logical drives.`

ERROR: No room remains for logical drives in the extended partition. Use FDISK to change the size of the extended partition.

```
All files canceled by operator
```

INFORMATION: You issued PRINT /T, which removes all files from the print queue.

```
All files in directory will be deleted!
Are you sure (Y/N)?
```

WARNING: You issued DEL or ERASE with the *.* wild card. To continue, press Y; to cancel, press N.

```
All logical drives deleted in the Extended DOS Partition
```

INFORMATION: While using FDISK, you removed all logical drives associated with the extended DOS partition.

```
Allocation error, size adjusted
```

WARNING: The contents of a file have been truncated because the size indicated in the directory is not consistent with the amount of data allocated to the file. Use CHKDSK /F to correct the discrepancy.

```
All specified files are contiguous
```

INFORMATION: All files are written sequentially to disk. This message may display when you are using CHKDSK.

```
ANSI.SYS must be installed to perform requested function
```

WARNING: While using MODE, you requested a screen function that cannot be performed until you load ANSI.SYS.

```
An incompatible DOSKey is already installed.
```

ERROR: The current version of DOSKey is not compatible with the version of DOS your computer is running. Delete DOSKEY.COM from your disk and copy the DOSKEY file from a backup of your original DOS System disk.

```
APPEND already installed
```

INFORMATION: You tried to issue APPEND with /X or /E after previously using APPEND. The /X and /E switches can be used only the first time you type **APPEND** after starting your system. To change the APPEND switch, you must reboot your computer.

APPEND/ASSIGN Conflict

> WARNING: You cannot use APPEND on an assigned drive. Cancel the drive assignment before using APPEND with this drive.

Attempted write-protect violation

> WARNING: The floppy disk you are trying to format is write-protected. If you want to format this disk, remove the write-protect tab (for minifloppies), or move the write-protect shutter down (for microfloppies). If the floppy disk in the drive is the wrong floppy disk, insert the correct floppy disk into the drive, and try the command again.

Attempting to recover allocation unit

> INFORMATION, WARNING: A bad allocation unit was found when the FORMAT command executed.

/B invalid with black and white printer

> ERROR: You tried to print the background color by using GRAPHICS /B, but you do not have a color printer connected to your computer.

Backing up files to drive x:
Disk Number:n

> INFORMATION: This message displays while you are backing up files to the specified drive.

Bad command or filename

> ERROR: You entered an invalid name for invoking a command, program, or batch file. The most frequent causes are the following: you misspelled a name, you omitted a required disk drive or path name, or you omitted the command name when giving parameters (for example, omitting the WordStar command, WS, by typing **MYFILE** instead of **WS MYFILE**).

> Check the spelling on the command line, and make sure that the command, program, or batch file is in the location specified. Then try the command again.

Bad or Missing Command Interpreter

ERROR (start-up): DOS does not start because it cannot find COMMAND.COM, the command interpreter.

If this message appears during start-up, COMMAND.COM is not on the start-up disk, or a COMMAND.COM file from a previous version of DOS is on the disk. If you have used the SHELL command in CONFIG.SYS, the message means that the SHELL command is improperly phrased or that COMMAND.COM is not where you specified. Place another disk that contains the operating system (IBMBIO.COM, IBMDOS.COM, and COMMAND.COM) in the floppy disk drive, and reset the system. After DOS has started, copy COMMAND.COM to the original start-up disk so that you can boot DOS in the future.

If this message appears while you are running DOS, several explanations are possible. COMMAND.COM has been erased from the disk and directory you used when starting DOS; a version of COMMAND.COM from a previous version of DOS has overwritten the good version; or the COMSPEC entry in the environment has been changed. You must restart DOS by resetting the system.

If resetting the system does not solve your problem, restart the computer from a copy of your DOS master disk. Copy COMMAND.COM from this disk to the offending disk.

Bad or missing filename

WARNING (start-up): This message means that the device driver file name was not found, that an error occurred when the device driver was loaded, that a break address for the device driver was beyond the RAM available to the computer, or that DOS detected an error while loading the driver into memory. DOS continues booting without the device driver file name.

If DOS loads, check your CONFIG.SYS file for the line DEVICE=filename. Make sure that the line is typed correctly and that the device driver is at the specified location; then reboot the system. If the message reappears, copy the file from its original disk to the boot disk and try starting DOS again. If the error persists, the device driver is bad, and you should contact the dealer or publisher who sold it to you.

Bad or Missing Keyboard definition file

WARNING: DOS cannot find KEYBOARD.SYS as specified by the KEYB command. Solving this problem may take several steps. First, check to make sure that KEYBOARD.SYS exists and is in the correct path; then retype the KEYB command. If you get the same message, KEYB.COM or KEYBOARD.SYS may be corrupted.

Bad Partition Table

ERROR: While using FORMAT, DOS was unable to find a DOS partition on the fixed disk you specified. Run FDISK and create a DOS partition on this fixed-disk drive.

Batch file missing

ERROR: DOS could not find the batch file it was processing. The batch file may have been erased or renamed. With DOS 3.0 only, the disk containing the batch file may have been changed, causing DOS to abort processing the batch file.

If you are using DOS 3.0 and you changed the disk that contains the batch file, restart the batch file without changing the disk. You may need to edit the batch file so that you do not need to change disks. This procedure applies only to DOS 3.0.

If the batch file includes a RENAME command that causes the originating batch file name to change, edit the batch file to prevent renaming when the batch file is processed again. If the file was erased, re-create the batch file from its backup file if possible. Edit the file to ensure that the batch file does not erase itself.

Baud rate required

ERROR: When using MODE COMx commands at minimum, you must indicate the baud rate for MODE to initialize the COM port.

BREAK is off (or on)

INFORMATION: When you use BREAK by itself, this message displays the current BREAK setting. You can set BREAK at the command line or in CONFIG.SYS.

Cannot change BUFSIZE

> ERROR: You cannot change the DOSKey buffer.

Cannot CHDIR to path - tree past this point not processed

> ERROR: CHKDSK was unable to go to the specified directory. No subdirectories below this directory are verified. Run CHKDSK /F to correct this error.

Cannot CHDIR to root

> ERROR: CHKDSK was checking the tree structure of the directory and was unable to return to the root directory. Remaining subdirectories were not checked. Restart DOS. If the message continues to display, the disk is unusable and must be reformatted.

Cannot Chkdsk a Network drive

> WARNING: You cannot use CHKDSK to check drives that are redirected over the network.

Cannot Chkdsk a SUBSTed or ASSIGNed drive

> WARNING: You cannot use CHKDSK to check substituted or assigned drives.

Cannot create a zero size partition

> ERROR: While using FDISK, you tried to create a partition of zero percent (0 megabytes). To correct this error, you must allocate one percent (or a minimum of 1M) of hard disk space to any partition you create.

Cannot create extended DOS partition without primary DOS partition on disk *x*

> ERROR: While using FDISK, you tried to create an extended DOS partition before giving your first fixed-disk drive a primary DOS partition. To correct this problem, simply create a DOS partition on your first fixed-disk drive. When this operation is complete, you can create an extended DOS partition if you have room on this disk or if you have a second fixed disk.

Cannot create Logical DOS drive without an Extended DOS
Partition on the current drive

> ERROR: When using FDISK, you must create an extended DOS
> partition before you can create a logical drive.

Cannot DISKCOMP to or from a network drive

> ERROR: You cannot compare disks on any disk drive that has been
> reassigned to a network.

Cannot delete Extended DOS Partition while logical drives
exist

> ERROR: When using FDISK to delete an extended DOS partition, you
> first must remove any logical drives.

Cannot DISKCOMP to or from an ASSIGNed or SUBSTed drive

> ERROR: You specified a drive created with the ASSIGN or the SUBST
> command.

Cannot DISKCOMP to or from a network drive

> ERROR: You specified a drive redirected over the network.

Cannot DISKCOPY to or from a network drive

> ERROR: You attempted to copy a floppy disk to a drive that was
> redirected to a computer network. DISKCOPY does not copy disks
> directly to a networked disk drive. Use COPY to copy the disk.

Cannot do binary reads from a device

> ERROR: You tried to copy from a device by using the /B switch. To
> complete the copy process, use the ASCII (/A) switch to create an ASCII
> copy, or you can use the COPY command without the /B switch.

Cannot edit BAK file—rename file

> ERROR: Files that have a BAK extension cannot be altered in Edlin.
> Rename the file by changing the extension to any name other than
> BAK.

Cannot find file QBASIC.EXE

ERROR: DOS 5.0 cannot find the QBASIC program for one of the following reasons: QBASIC.EXE is in another subdirectory, not on the path; QBASIC.EXE is on a disk in another drive or is otherwise unavailable. Insert a disk containing QBASIC.EXE into a floppy disk drive to continue.

Cannot find FORMAT.EXE

ERROR: While running BACKUP, you provided an unformatted floppy disk, and BACKUP could not find the FORMAT command.

Cannot find GRAPHICS profile

ERROR: You did not give the path of the GRAPHICS.PRO file; DOS could not find it in the current directory.

Cannot find System Files

ERROR: While running FORMAT, you specified a drive that did not have the system files in the root directory.

Cannot format an ASSIGNed or SUBSTed drive.

ERROR: You attempted to format a drive that was mapped to another drive with ASSIGN or SUBST. To perform a successful format, you must run ASSIGN or SUBST again to clear the drive assignments.

Cannot FORMAT a network drive

ERROR: You tried to format a disk in a drive being used by a network.

Cannot FORMAT nonremovable drive x:

ERROR: You attempted to use FORMAT /F on a fixed-disk drive. First, make sure that you want to back up files to a fixed-disk drive. If you do, format the fixed-disk first. The /F switch works only with floppy disks.

Cannot JOIN a Network drive
Cannot LABEL a Network drive

ERROR: You cannot use JOIN or LABEL with drives redirected over the network.

`Cannot LABEL a SUBSTed or ASSIGNed drive`

ERROR: You attempted to label a drive created with SUBST or ASSIGN.

`Cannot load COMMAND, system halted`

ERROR: DOS attempted to reload COMMAND.COM, but the area where DOS keeps track of memory was destroyed, or the command processor was not found in the directory specified by the COMSPEC= entry. The system halts.

This message may indicate that COMMAND.COM was erased from the disk and directory you used when starting DOS, or that the COMSPEC= entry in the environment has been changed. Restart DOS from your usual start-up disk. If DOS does not start, the copy of COMMAND.COM has been erased. Restart DOS from the DOS start-up or master disk, and copy COMMAND.COM onto your usual start-up disk.

Alternatively, an errant program may have corrupted the memory allocation table where DOS tracks available memory. Try running the same program that was in the computer when the system halted. If the problem occurs again, the program is defective. Contact the dealer or publisher who sold you the program.

`Cannot perform a cyclic copy`

ERROR: When using XCOPY /S, you cannot specify a target that is a subdirectory of the source. You may use a temporary disk or file to bypass this limitation if the directory tree structure allows a temporary disk or file.

`Cannot read file allocation table`

ERROR: The file allocation table (FAT) resides in a bad sector of a defective disk. Recovering your data from the bad sectors may be impossible.

`Cannot recover . entry, processing continued`

WARNING: The . entry (the working directory) is defective and cannot be recovered.

```
Cannot recover .. entry,
Entry has a bad attribute (or link or size)
```

ERROR, WARNING: The .. entry (the parent directory) is defective and cannot be recovered. If you have specified the /F switch, CHKDSK tries to correct the error.

```
Cannot RECOVER a Network drive
```

ERROR: You cannot recover files from drives redirected over a network.

```
Cannot setup expanded memory
```

ERROR: Your expanded memory (EMS) card is not functioning properly and should be serviced.

```
Cannot specify default drive
```

ERROR: You entered identical drive letters with SYS (for example, SYS A: A:). You must enter different letters.

```
Cannot start COMMAND, exiting
```

ERROR: You or one of your programs directed DOS to load another copy of COMMAND.COM, but DOS could not load it. Your CONFIG.SYS FILES command is set too low, or you do not have enough free memory for another copy of COMMAND.COM.

If your system has 256K or more and FILES is less than 10, edit the CONFIG.SYS file on your start-up disk, using FILES=15 or FILES=20. Then restart DOS.

If the problem recurs, you do not have enough memory in your computer, or you have too many resident or background programs competing for memory space. Restart DOS, loading only the essential programs. If necessary, eliminate unneeded device drivers or RAM disk software. You also can obtain additional RAM for your system.

```
Cannot SUBST a Network drive
```

ERROR: You cannot substitute drives redirected over the network.

Cannot SYS to a Network drive

ERROR: You cannot transfer system files to drives that are redirected over the network.

Cannot use FASTOPEN for drive x:

ERROR: You attempted to use FASTOPEN over a network, with a floppy disk drive, or with more than four disks at one time.

Cannot use PRINT - Use NET PRINT

ERROR: You tried to use PRINT over the network. Use NET PRINT, or consult your system administrator for the correct procedure for printing files over the network.

Cannot XCOPY to a reserved device

ERROR: The specified XCOPY target is a character device (printer), an asynchronous communication device, or NULL. You must specify a file or block device as your target.

CHDIR .. failed, trying alternate method

WARNING: CHKDSK was unable to return to a parent directory while checking the tree structure. CHKDSK attempts to return to the parent directory by starting over at the root and repeating the search.

CHKDSK not available on drive x

INFORMATION: The alternate file system you attempted to CHKDSK cannot be found.

xxxxxxx code page cannot be initialized

ERROR (start-up): Either PRINTER.SYS or DISPLAY.SYS did not start. Check your CONFIG.SYS file's DEVICE command line and look for illegal parameters.

Code page not prepared

ERROR: While using MODE, you selected a code page not yet prepared for the system or without the correct font to support the current video mode. To correct this error, prepare a code page using the MODE PREPARE command. If you have installed the DISPLAY.SYS installable device driver, make sure that the DEVICE command line in your CONFIG.SYS file allows for additional subfonts.

Code page *xxx* not prepared for all devices

ERROR: While using CHCP, you selected a code page not currently supported by a device. To correct this error, first make sure that your device supports code-page switching and that it is on-line. Then issue the MODE PREPARE command to ready the device for the code page. You are ready to retry CHCP.

Code page *xxx* not prepared for system

ERROR: CHCP is unable to select a code page for the system. If NLSFUNC is installed and your CONFIG.SYS file does not install device drivers, you can retry CHCP. If CONFIG.SYS installs device drivers, you must issue the MODE PREPARE command to prepare the specific code page for each device before retrying the CHCP command.

Code page operation not supported on this device

ERROR: While using MODE, you selected a device and code page combination not recognized by DOS. Make sure that you specified a valid device and code page and that the code page you selected is supported on the device.

Code page requested *xxx* is not valid for given keyboard code

ERROR: You selected an incompatible keyboard code and code page combination. Reenter the KEYB command with a valid keyboard code and code page.

Code page specified has not been designated

ERROR: You issued the KEYB command with an unrecognized code page. Prepare the code page for your CON (your console screen device) using the MODE PREPARE command; then retry KEYB.

Code page specified has not been prepared

> ERROR: You issued the KEYB command with an unrecognized code page. Prepare the code page for your CON (your console screen device) by using the MODE PREPARE command; then retry KEYB.

Code page specified is inconsistent with invoked code page

> WARNING: You invoked a KEYB option not compatible with the code page for your console screen device. Specify a compatible option, or issue the MODE select command to change the code page for your console screen device.

Code page specified is inconsistent with selected code page

> WARNING: You used KEYB with an option not compatible with the code page for your console screen device. Specify a compatible option, or issue the MODE select command to change the code page for your console screen device.

Code page *xxx*

> INFORMATION: This message displays the code page currently in use by the specified device. For example, if you type **MODE CON**, the message returns the code page in use for your screen.

Code pages cannot be prepared

> ERROR: You attempted to use a duplicate code page for the specified device; or with MODE PREPARE, you specified more code pages than DOS supports for that device. Check CONFIG.SYS to see how many prepared code pages your device command line allows, or issue MODE /STATUS at the command line (for example, MODE /STATUS CON) to view the code pages already prepared for the device.

Compare error at offset *xxxxxxxx*

> INFORMATION: The files you are comparing are not the same. The difference occurs at *xxxxxxxx* bytes from the beginning of the file. The number of bytes as well as the values for the differing bytes are given in hexadecimal format, base 16.

`Compare error on side s, track t`

> INFORMATION: DISKCOMP has located a difference on the disk in the specified drive on side *s*, at track *t*.

`Compare process ended`

> ERROR: A fatal error occurred during the comparison operation.

`Comparing t tracks n sectors per track, s side(s)`

> INFORMATION: This message confirms the format of the disks you are comparing.

`X contains n non-contiguous blocks`

> ERROR: CHKDSK found noncontiguous blocks on drive *X*. Use a defragmenter to eliminate the fragmentation, or use COPY or XCOPY to transfer the fragmented files to a freshly formatted floppy disk in a sequential form.

`Configuration too large`

> ERROR (start-up): DOS could not load because you set too many FILES or BUFFERS in your CONFIG.SYS file or specified too large an environment area (/E) with the SHELL command. This problem should occur only on systems with less than 256K.
>
> Restart DOS with a different disk; then edit the CONFIG.SYS file on your boot disk, lowering the number of FILES, BUFFERS, or both. You also can edit CONFIG.SYS to reduce the size of the environment in addition to or as an alternative to lowering the number of FILES and BUFFERS. Restart DOS with the edited disk.
>
> Another alternative is to increase the RAM in your system.

`Content of destination lost before copy`

> ERROR: The original contents of the destination file for the COPY operation were overwritten because the destination and source files had the same name. You may be able to recover the file with UNDELETE; if not, you can restore the destination file from your backup disk.

Copy process ended

ERROR: The DISKCOPY process ended before completion. Copy the remaining files onto the disk with COPY or XCOPY.

Current code page settings

INFORMATION: You issued the MODE command with a specified device. If you want to see code settings for all devices, type **MODE** without listing a device.

Current CON code page: *xxx*

INFORMATION: This message displays the current keyboard code and code page along with the current code page used by the console screen device (CON).

Current drive is no longer valid

WARNING: You have set the system prompt to PROMPT $p. At the DOS system level, DOS attempted to read the current directory for the disk drive and found the drive no longer valid.

If the current disk drive is set for a floppy disk, this warning appears when you do not have a disk in the disk drive; DOS reports Drive not ready. Press F to fail or I to ignore the error. Then insert a floppy disk into the disk drive or type another drive designation.

The invalid drive error also occurs when a current networked or SUBST disk drive is deleted or disconnected. Simply change the current drive to a valid disk drive.

Current keyboard does not support this code page

ERROR: You selected a code page incompatible with the current keyboard code. First, check the selected code page. If the code page is correct, change the keyboard code with KEYB.

Device *ddd* not prepared

ERROR: No code page is present for this device.

Disk boot failure

ERROR (start-up): An error occurred when DOS tried to load into memory. The disk contained IBMBIO.COM and IBMDOS.COM, but one of the two files could not be loaded.

Try starting DOS from the disk again. If the error recurs, try starting DOS from a disk you know is good, such as a copy of your DOS start-up or master disk. If DOS still fails to boot, you have a disk drive problem. Contact your dealer.

Disk full. Edits lost.

ERROR: Edlin cannot save your work to disk because the designated disk is full. Always make sure that you have a disk with plenty of room to save your files.

Disk unsuitable for system disk

WARNING: FORMAT detected one or more bad sectors on the floppy disk in the area where DOS normally resides. Because the portion of the disk where DOS must reside is unusable, you cannot boot DOS from this disk.

Try reformatting the disk. Some floppy disks format successfully the second time. If FORMAT gives this message again, you cannot boot from the disk.

Divide overflow

ERROR: DOS aborted a program that attempted to divide by zero. The program was incorrectly entered, or it contains a logic flaw. A well-written program should never have this problem. If you wrote the program, correct the error and try the program again. If you purchased the program, report the problem to the dealer or publisher.

This message also may appear when you attempt to format a RAM disk with DOS 3.0 or 3.1. Make sure that you are formatting the correct disk and try again.

Do not specify filename(s) Command format: DISKCOMP drive1: drive2: [/1] [/8]

ERROR: You typed an incorrect switch or added one or more file names with the DISKCOMP command. DISKCOMP syntax does not accept file names on the command line.

`Do not specify filename(s) Command Format: DISKCOPY drive1:`
`drive2: [/1] [/v]`

> ERROR: You added an incorrect switch to the command or placed a file name in the command string. Retype the command, and press Enter.

`DOS memory-arena error`

> ERROR: When you are using the DOS Editor, this message indicates a serious memory error. If possible, save your work to different file, and reboot your computer.

`Drive or diskette types not compatible`

> ERROR: When using DISKCOMP or DISKCOPY, you specified two drives of different capacities. You cannot, for example, DISKCOMP or DISKCOPY from a 1.2M drive to a 360K drive. Retype the command using compatible drives.

`Duplicate filename or File not found`

> ERROR: While using RENAME (or REN), you attempted to change a file name to a name that already exists, or the file to be renamed did not exist in the directory. Check the directory to make sure that the file name exists and that you have spelled it correctly. Then try again.

`Enter current Volume Label for drive d:`

> WARNING: You are attempting to format a hard disk that has a volume label. Enter the exact volume label to proceed with the format; if you do not want to enter a volume label, press Enter.

`EOF mark not found`

> INFORMATION, WARNING: You may see this message when you compare files with COMP. This message is informational if you are comparing program files. If you are comparing text files, the message, a warning, indicates that COMP could not find the customary end-of-file marker (Ctrl-Z or 1A hex). That is, COMP reached the end of the file before it found the EOF marker.

Error in COUNTRY command

WARNING (start-up): The COUNTRY command in CONFIG.SYS is improperly phrased or has an incorrect country code or code page number. DOS continues to load but uses the default information for the COUNTRY command.

After DOS has started, check the COUNTRY line in your CONFIG.SYS file (see Chapter 15). Make sure that the command is correctly phrased (with commas between country code, code page, and COUNTRY.SYS file) and that any given information is correct. If you detect an error in the line, edit the line, save the file, and restart DOS.

If you do not find an error, restart DOS. If the same message appears, edit CONFIG.SYS. Reenter the COUNTRY command and delete the old COUNTRY line. The old line may contain some nonsense characters that DOS can see but that are not apparent to your text-editing program.

Error in EXE file

ERROR: DOS detected an error while attempting to load a program stored in an EXE file. The problem, which is in the relocation information DOS needs to load the program, may occur if the EXE file has been altered.

Restart DOS and try the program again, this time using a backup copy of the program. If the message appears again, the program is flawed. If you are using a purchased program, contact the dealer or publisher. If you wrote the program, issue LINK to produce another copy of the program.

Error loading operating system

ERROR (start-up): A disk error occurred when DOS was loading from the hard disk. DOS does not start.

Restart the computer. If the error occurs after several tries, restart DOS from the floppy disk drive. If the hard disk does not respond (that is, you cannot run DIR or CHKDSK without getting an error), you have a problem with the hard disk. Contact your dealer. If the hard disk does respond, place another copy of DOS on your hard disk by using SYS. You also may need to copy COMMAND.COM to the hard disk.

Increase to 15 or 20 the number of FILES in the CONFIG.SYS file of your start-up disk. Restart DOS. If the error recurs, you may have a problem with the disk. Try a backup copy of the program. If the backup works, copy it over the offending file.

If an error occurs in the copying process, you have a flawed disk. If the problem is a floppy disk, copy the files from the flawed disk to another disk and reformat or discard the original disk. If the problem is the hard disk, immediately back up your files and run RECOVER on the offending file. If the problem persists, your hard disk may be damaged.

Error reading directory

ERROR: During a FORMAT procedure, DOS was unable to read the directory; bad sectors may have developed in the file allocation table (FAT) structure.

If the message occurs when DOS is reading a floppy disk, the disk is unusable and should be thrown away. If DOS cannot read your hard disk, however, the problem is more serious, and you may have to reformat your disk. Remember to back up your data files regularly in order to prevent major losses.

Error reading (or writing) partition table

ERROR: DOS could not read from (or write to) the disk's partition table during the FORMAT operation because the partition table is corrupted. Run FDISK on the disk, and reformat the disk.

File allocation table bad, drive *d*
Abort, Retry, Fail?

WARNING: DOS encountered a problem in the file allocation table of the disk in drive *d*. Press R to retry several times; if the message recurs, press A to abort.

If you are using a floppy disk, try to copy all the files to another disk, and then reformat or discard the original disk. If you are using a hard disk, back up files on the disk, and then reformat it. You cannot use the disk until you have reformatted it.

File cannot be copied onto itself

ERROR: You attempted to copy a file to a disk and directory containing the same file name. This error often occurs when you misspell or omit parts of the source or destination drive, path, or file name; this error also may occur when you are using wild-card characters for file names. Check your spelling and the source and destination names, and then try the command again.

File creation error

ERROR: A program or DOS failed to add a new file to the directory or to replace an existing file.

If the file already exists, issue the ATTRIB command to check whether the file is marked as read-only. If the read-only flag is set and you want to change or erase the file, remove the read-only flag with ATTRIB; then try again. If the problem occurs when the read-only flag is not set, run CHKDSK without the /F switch to determine whether the directory is full, the disk is full, or some other problem exists with the disk.

File not found

ERROR: DOS could not find the specified file. The file is not on the current disk or directory, or you specified the disk drive name, path name, or file name incorrectly. Check these possibilities and try the command again.

filename device driver cannot be initialized

WARNING (start-up): In CONFIG.SYS, the parameters in the device driver file name or the syntax of the DEVICE line is incorrect. Check for incorrect parameters and phrasing errors in the DEVICE line. Edit the DEVICE line in the CONFIG.SYS file, save the file, and restart DOS.

FIRST diskette bad or incompatible

or

SECOND diskette bad or incompatible

ERROR: One of these messages may appear when you issue DISKCOMP. The messages indicate that the FIRST (source) or the SECOND (target) floppy disk is unreadable, or that the disks you are attempting to compare have different format densities.

`Format not supported on drive x:`

> ERROR: You cannot use the FORMAT command on the specified drive. If you entered device driver parameters that your computer cannot support, DOS displays this message. Check CONFIG.SYS for bad DEVICE or DRIVPARM commands.

`Formatting while copying`

> INFORMATION: DISKCOPY displays this message as it copies data to an unformatted disk.

`Illegal device name`

> ERROR: DOS does not recognize the device name you entered with the MODE command.

`Incorrect DOS Version`

> ERROR: The copy of the file holding the command you just entered is from a different version of DOS.

> Get a copy of the command from the correct version of DOS (usually from your copy of the DOS start-up or master disk), and try the command again. If the disk you are using has been updated to hold new versions of DOS, copy the new versions over the old ones.

`Insert disk with batch file`
`and strike any key when ready`

> PROMPT: DOS attempted to execute the next command from a batch file, but the disk holding the batch file is not in the disk drive. This message occurs for DOS 3.1 and later versions. DOS 3.0 gives a fatal error when the disk is changed.

> Insert the disk with the batch file into the disk drive, and press a key to continue.

`Insert disk with \COMMAND.COM in drive d`
`and strike any key when ready`

> PROMPT: DOS needs to reload COMMAND.COM but cannot find it on the start-up disk. If you are using floppy disks, the disk in drive d (usually A) most likely has been changed. Place a disk with a good copy of COMMAND.COM in drive d, and press a key.

`Insert diskette for drive x and strike`
`any key when ready`

> PROMPT: On a system with one floppy disk drive or a system in which DRIVER.SYS creates more than one logical disk drive from a physical disk drive, you or one of your programs specified a tandem disk drive *x* (such as A or B) that is different from the current disk drive.

> If the correct disk is in the disk drive, press a key. Otherwise, insert the correct disk into the floppy disk drive, and then press a key.

`Insufficient disk space`

> WARNING, ERROR: The disk does not have enough free space to hold the file being written. All DOS programs terminate when this problem occurs, but some non-DOS programs continue.

> If you think that the disk should have enough room to hold the file, run CHKDSK to determine whether the disk has a problem. When you terminate programs early by pressing Ctrl-Break, DOS may not be able to do the necessary clean-up work, leaving some disk space temporarily trapped. CHKDSK can free these areas.

> If you simply have run out of disk space, free some disk space, or insert a different disk; then try the command again.

> If you loaded a resident program, such as PRINT, GRAPHICS, SideKick, or ProKey, restart DOS; and before you load any resident program, again try the command that caused the message to appear. If this method fails, remove all nonessential device drivers and RAM disk software from CONFIG.SYS, and restart DOS. If this action fails, your computer does not have enough memory to run this command.

`Insufficient memory to store macro. Use the DOSKEY command`
`with the /BUFSIZE switch to increase available memory.`

> WARNING: Your DOSKey macros have filled the total space set aside for them. You must enlarge the memory area for macros (the default is 1,024 bytes) by using the BUFSIZE switch before you can enter any new macros.

`Intermediate file error during pipe`

> ERROR: DOS cannot create or write to one or both of the intermediate files it uses when piping information between programs because the disk is full, the root directory of the current disk is full, or DOS cannot find the files. The most frequent cause is insufficient disk space.

Run DIR on the root directory of the current disk drive to make sure that you have enough room in the root directory for two additional files. If you do not have enough room, make room by deleting or copying and deleting files. You also can copy the necessary files to a different disk with sufficient room.

This error also may occur if a program is deleting files, including the temporary files DOS creates. In this case, you should correct the program, contact the dealer or program publisher, or avoid using the program with piping.

```
Internal stack over flow
System halted
```

ERROR: Your programs and DOS have exhausted the stack, the memory space reserved for temporary use. This problem is usually caused by a rapid succession of hardware devices demanding attention. DOS stops, and the system must be turned off and on again to restart DOS.

The circumstances that cause this message are generally infrequent and erratic, and they may not recur. If you want to prevent this error from occurring, add the STACKS command to your CONFIG.SYS file. If the command is already in your CONFIG.SYS file, increase the number of stacks specified.

```
Invalid characters in volume label
```

ERROR: You attempted to enter more than 11 alphanumeric characters, or you entered illegal characters (+, =, /, \, and |, for example) when you typed the disk's volume label (the disk name). Retype the volume label with valid characters.

```
Invalid COMMAND.COM in drive d:
```

WARNING: DOS tried to reload COMMAND.COM from the disk in drive *d* and found that the file was from a different version of DOS. Follow the instructions for inserting a disk with the correct version.

If you frequently use the disk that generated this warning message, copy the correct version of COMMAND.COM to that disk.

```
Invalid COMMAND.COM, system halted
```

ERROR: DOS could not find COMMAND.COM on the hard disk. DOS halts and must be restarted.

COMMAND.COM may have been erased, or the COMSPEC variable in the environment may have been changed. Restart the computer from the hard disk. If a message indicates that COMMAND.COM is missing, the file was erased. Restart DOS from a floppy disk, and copy COMMAND.COM to the root directory of the hard disk or to the location your SHELL command indicates, if you have placed this command in your CONFIG.SYS file.

If you restart DOS and this message appears later, a program or batch file is erasing COMMAND.COM or altering the COMSPEC variable. If a program is erasing COMMAND.COM, contact the dealer or publisher who sold you the program. If a batch file is erasing COMMAND.COM, edit the batch file. If COMSPEC is being altered, edit the offending batch file or program, or place COMMAND.COM in the subdirectory your program or batch file expects.

Invalid COUNTRY code or code page

WARNING (start-up): The COUNTRY code number or the code page number given to the COUNTRY command in CONFIG.SYS is incorrect or incompatible. DOS ignores the COUNTRY command and continues the start-up process.

Check the COUNTRY command in your CONFIG.SYS file (see Chapter 15) to determine whether the correct and compatible country code and code page numbers are specified. If you detect an error, edit and save the file. Then restart DOS.

Invalid date

ERROR: You gave an impossible date or an invalid character to separate the month, day, and year. This message also displays if you enter the date from the keypad when it is not in numeric mode.

Invalid device parameters from device driver

ERROR: The partition did not fall on a track boundary. You may have set the DEVICE drivers incorrectly in CONFIG.SYS or attempted to format a hard disk formatted with DOS 2.x so that the total number of hidden sectors is not evenly divisible by the number of sectors on a track. Therefore, the partition may not start on a track boundary.

To correct the error, run FDISK before performing a format, or check CONFIG.SYS for a bad DEVICE or DRIVPARM command.

Invalid directory

> ERROR: One of the following occurred: you specified a directory name that does not exist, you misspelled the directory name, the directory path is on a different disk, you did not give the path character (\) at the beginning of the name, or you did not separate the directory names with the path character. Check your directory names to make sure that the directory exists, and try the command again.

Invalid disk change

> WARNING: The disk in the 720K, 1.2M, or 1.44M disk drive was changed while a program had open files to be written to the disk. You see the message Abort, Retry, Fail. Place the correct disk in the disk drive, and press R to retry.

Invalid drive in search path

> WARNING: You specified an invalid disk drive name in the PATH command, or a disk drive you named is nonexistent or hidden temporarily by a SUBST or JOIN command.

> Use PATH to check the paths you instructed DOS to search. If you gave a nonexistent disk drive name, issue the PATH command again with the correct search paths. If the problem is temporary because of a SUBST or JOIN command, you can run PATH, leaving out or correcting the wrong entry. Or you can just ignore the warning message.

Invalid drive or file name

> ERROR: You gave the name of a nonexistent disk drive, or you mistyped the disk drive or file name.

> Remember that certain DOS commands (such as SUBST and JOIN) temporarily hide disk drive names while the command is in effect. Check the disk drive name you gave, and try the command again.

Invalid drive specification

> ERROR: One of the following occurred: you entered an invalid or nonexistent disk drive as a parameter to a command; you specified the same disk drive for the source and destination; or by not giving a parameter, you defaulted to the same disk drive for the source and the destination.

Remember that some DOS commands (such as SUBST and JOIN) temporarily hide disk drive names while the command is in effect. Check the disk drive names. If the command is objecting to a missing parameter and defaulting to the wrong disk drive, name the correct disk drive explicitly.

```
Invalid drive specification
Specified drive does not exist
or is non-removable
```

ERROR: One of the following occurred: you gave the name of a nonexistent disk drive, you named the hard disk drive when using commands for floppy disks only, you did not give a disk drive name and defaulted to the hard disk when using commands for floppy disks only, or you named or defaulted to a RAM disk drive when using commands for an actual floppy disk.

Remember that certain DOS commands (such as SUBST and JOIN) temporarily hide disk drive names while the command is in effect. Check the disk drive name you gave, and try the command again.

```
Invalid environment size specified
```

WARNING: You gave an invalid SHELL command in CONFIG.SYS. The environment-size switch (</E:*size*) contains nonnumeric characters or a number less than 160 or greater than 32,768.

Check the form of your CONFIG.SYS SHELL command; it must be exact. You need a colon (:) between /E and *size*, no comma or space should occur, and *size* should be from 160 through 32,768.

```
Invalid keyboard code specified
```

ERROR: You selected an invalid code. Enter the KEYB command again with the correct keyboard code.

```
Invalid macro definition
```

ERROR: You entered an illegal character or command with DOSKey or attempted to create a DOSKey macro with an illegal definition. For example, this message displays if you use a GOTO command in a DOSKey macro. Correct any errors, and carefully retype the macro.

```
Invalid media or Track 0 bad - disk unusable
```

ERROR: A disk you are trying to format may be damaged. A disk may not format the first time. Try to format again; if the same message appears, the disk is bad and should be discarded.

```
Invalid number of parameters
```

ERROR: You have given too few or too many parameters to a command. One of the following occurred: you omitted required information, you omitted a colon immediately after the disk drive name, you inserted an extra space, you omitted a required space, or you omitted a slash (/) in front of a switch.

```
Invalid parameter
```

or

```
Incorrect parameter
```

ERROR: At least one parameter you entered for the command is not valid. One of the following occurred: you omitted required information, you omitted a colon immediately after the disk drive name, you inserted an extra space, you omitted a required space, you omitted a slash (/) in front of a switch, or you used a switch the command does not recognize. For more information, check the explanation of this message in the Command Reference for the command you issued.

```
Invalid parameter combination
```

You typed conflicting parameters with a DOS command. Retype the command with only one of the conflicting switches.

```
Invalid partition table
```

ERROR (start-up): DOS has detected a problem in the hard disk's partition information. Restart DOS from a floppy disk. Back up all files from the hard disk, if possible, and run FDISK to correct the problem. If you change the partition information, you must reformat the hard disk and restore all its files.

Invalid path

ERROR: One of the following problems exists: the path name contains illegal characters, the name has more than 63 characters, or a directory name within the path is misspelled or does not exist.

Check the spelling of the path name. If necessary, check the disk directory with DIR to make sure that the directory you have specified exists and that you have specified the correct path name. Make sure that the path name contains no more than 63 characters. If necessary, change the current directory to a directory "closer" to the file to shorten the path name.

Invalid path or file name

ERROR: You gave a directory name or file name that does not exist, specified the wrong directory name (a directory not on the path), or mistyped a name. COPY aborts when it encounters an invalid path or file name. If you specified a wild card for a file name, COPY transfers all valid files before it issues the error message.

Check to see which files already are transferred. Determine whether the directory and file names are spelled correctly and whether the path is correct. Then try again.

Invalid STACK parameter

WARNING (start-up): One of the following problems exists with the STACKS command in your CONFIG.SYS file: a comma is missing between the number of stacks and the size of the stack, the number of stack frames is not in the range of 8 through 64, the stack size is not in the range of 32 through 512, you have omitted the number of stack frames or the stack size, or the stack frame or the stack size (but not both) is 0. DOS continues to start but ignores the STACKS command.

Check the STACKS command in your CONFIG.SYS file. Edit and save the file; then restart DOS.

Invalid switch character

WARNING: DOS loaded VDISK, located in your CONFIG.SYS file, attempting to install VDISK in low (nonextended) memory, but DOS encountered a switch other than the /E extended memory switch. You misspelled the /E switch, or you left a space between the / and the E. Edit and save your CONFIG.SYS file, and then restart DOS.

Invalid time

ERROR: You gave an impossible time or invalid character to separate the hour, minute, and second. This message also displays if you enter the time from the keypad when it is not in numeric mode.

Invalid Volume ID

ERROR: When formatting a fixed (or hard) disk, you entered an incorrect volume label, and DOS aborted the format attempt. Type **VOL** at the C prompt and press Enter to view the volume label of the disk, and try the command again.

Memory allocation error
Cannot load COMMAND, system halted

ERROR: A program destroyed the area where DOS keeps track of memory. You must restart DOS. If this error occurs again with the same program, the program has a flaw. Try a backup copy of the program. If the problem persists, contact the dealer or program publisher.

MIRROR cannot operate with a network.

WARNING: MIRROR cannot save file reconstruction information when your computer's hard disk is redirected to a network.

Missing operating system

ERROR (start-up): The DOS hard disk partition entry is marked as bootable (capable of starting DOS), but the DOS partition does not contain a copy of DOS. DOS does not start.

Start DOS from a floppy disk. Issue the SYS C: command to place DOS on the hard disk, and then copy COMMAND.COM to the disk. If this command fails to solve the problem, you must back up the existing files, if any, from the hard disk; then issue FORMAT /S to place a copy of the operating system on the hard disk. If necessary, restore the files you backed up.

Must enter both /T and /N parameters

ERROR: You must specify /T (number of tracks per side) and /N (number of sectors per disk) on the same command line.

```
No free file handles
Cannot start COMMAND, exiting
```

ERROR: DOS could not load an additional copy of COMMAND.COM because no file handles were available. Edit the CONFIG.SYS file on your start-up disk to increase by five the number of file handles (using the FILES command). Restart DOS, and try the command again.

```
No room for system on destination disk
```

ERROR: The floppy or hard disk was not formatted with the necessary reserved space for DOS. You cannot put the system on this floppy disk without first copying all data to another disk and then reformatting the disk. You must reformat your hard disk to place the system files, or you must continue to boot from a system floppy disk

```
Non-System disk or disk error
Replace and strike any key when ready
```

ERROR (start-up): Your disk does not contain IBMBIO.COM and IBMDOS.COM (or IO.SYS and MSDOS.SYS for MS-DOS), or a read error occurred when you started the system. DOS does not start.

If you are using a floppy disk system, insert a bootable disk into drive A, and press a key. The most frequent cause of this message on hard disk systems is leaving a nonbootable disk in drive A with the door closed. Open the door to disk drive A, and press a key. DOS boots from the hard disk.

```
No system on default drive
```

ERROR: SYS cannot find the system files. Insert a disk containing the system files, such as the DOS disk, and type the command again.

```
No target drive specified
```

ERROR: You did not specify a target drive when you typed a backup command. Retype the command, using first a source and then a target disk drive.

Not enough memory

or

Insufficient memory

ERROR: The computer does not have enough free RAM to execute the program or command. If you loaded a resident program, such as PRINT, GRAPHICS, SideKick, or ProKey, restart DOS, and try the command again before loading any resident program. If this method fails to solve the problem, remove any nonessential device drivers or RAM disk software from CONFIG.SYS, and restart DOS. If this option also fails, your computer does not have enough memory for this command. You must increase your RAM memory to run the command.

Out of environment space

WARNING: DOS cannot add additional strings to the environment from the SET command because the environment cannot be expanded. This error occurs when you are loading a resident program, such as MODE, PRINT, GRAPHICS, SideKick, or ProKey.

If you are running DOS 3.1 or later, refer to the SHELL command in Chapter 15 (on customizing DOS) for information about expanding the default space for the environment. DOS 3.0 has no method for expanding the environment.

Out of memory

ERROR: The amount of memory is insufficient to perform the operation you requested. This error occurs in the DOS 5.0 Editor.

Packed File Corrupt

ERROR: A program file could not load into the first 64K of memory. This error may occur when a packed executable file is loaded into memory. Use the LOADFIX command to load the offending program above 64K.

Parameters not supported

> or

Parameters not supported on drive

> ERROR: You entered parameters that do not exist, that are not supported by the DOS version you are running, or that are incompatible with the specified disk drive. Run VER to determine whether the current DOS version supports the parameters (or switches) you specified.

Parameters not compatible
with fixed disk

> ERROR: A device driver for a hard disk does not support generic IOCtl functions.

Path not found

> ERROR: A specified file or directory path does not exist. You may have misspelled the file name or directory name, or you may have omitted a path character (\) between directory names or between the final directory name and the file name. Another possibility is that the file or directory does not exist in the place specified. Check these possibilities, and try again.

Path too long

> ERROR: You have given a path name that exceeds the DOS 63-character limit, or you omitted a space between file names. Check the command line. If the phrasing is correct, you must change to a directory "closer" to the file you want and try the command again.

Program too big to fit in memory

> ERROR: The computer does not have enough memory to load the program or the command you invoked. If you have any resident programs loaded (such as PRINT, GRAPHICS, or SideKick), restart DOS, and try the command again without loading the resident programs. If this message appears again, reduce the number of buffers (BUFFERS) in the CONFIG.SYS file, eliminate nonessential device drivers or RAM disk software, and restart DOS. If the problem persists, your computer does not have enough RAM for the program or command. You must increase the amount of RAM in your computer to run the program.

`Same parameter entered twice`

> ERROR: You duplicated a switch when you typed a command. Retype the command using the parameter only once.

`Sector size too large in file` *filename*

> WARNING: The device driver *filename* is inconsistent. The device driver defined a particular sector size for DOS but attempted to use a different size. The copy of the device driver is bad, or the device driver is incorrect. Make a backup copy of the device driver on the boot disk, and then reboot DOS. If the message appears again, the device driver is incorrect. If you wrote the driver, correct the error. If you purchased the program, contact the dealer or software publisher.

`SOURCE diskette bad or incompatible`

> ERROR: The disk you attempted to read during a copy process was damaged or in the wrong format (for example, a high-density disk in a double-density disk drive). DOS cannot read the disk.

`Syntax error`

> ERROR: You phrased a command improperly by omitting needed information, giving extraneous information, inserting an extra space into a file or path name, or using an incorrect switch. Check the command line for these possibilities, and try the command again.

`TARGET diskette bad or incompatible`

> or

`Target diskette may be unusable`

> or

`Target diskette unusable`

> ERROR: A problem exists with the target disk. DOS does not recognize the format of the target disk in the drive, or the disk is defective. Make sure that the target disk is the same density as the source disk, run CHKDSK on the target disk to determine the problem, or try to reformat the disk before proceeding with the disk copy operation.

```
TARGET media has lower capacity than SOURCE
Continue anyway (Y/N)?
```

WARNING: The target disk can hold fewer bytes of data than the source disk. The most likely cause is bad sectors on the target disk. If you press Y, some data on the source disk may not fit onto the target disk.

To avoid the possibility of an incomplete transfer of data, type N, and insert a disk with the same capacity as the source disk. If you are not copying "hidden" files, you also can issue the COPY *.* command to transfer files.

```
Too many block devices
```

WARNING (start-up): Your CONFIG.SYS file contains too many DEVICE commands. DOS continues to start but does not install additional device drivers.

DOS can handle only 26 block devices. The block devices created by the DEVICE commands plus the number of block devices automatically created by DOS exceed this number. Remove any unnecessary DEVICE commands from your CONFIG.SYS file, and restart DOS.

```
Top level process aborted, cannot continue
```

ERROR (start-up): COMMAND.COM or another DOS command detected a disk error, and you chose the A (Abort) option. DOS cannot finish starting itself, and the system halts.

Try to start DOS again. If the error recurs, start DOS from a floppy disk (if starting from the hard disk) or from a different floppy disk (if starting from a floppy disk). After DOS has started, issue the SYS command to place another copy of the operating system on the disk, and copy COMMAND.COM to the disk. If DOS reports an error while copying, the disk is bad. Reformat or discard the floppy disk, or back up and reformat the hard disk.

```
There is not enough room to create a restore file
You will not be able to use the unformat utility
Proceed with Format (Y/N)?
```

WARNING: The disk lacks sufficient room to create a restore file. Without this file, you cannot use UNFORMAT to reverse the format you are attempting.

Unable to create directory

ERROR: You or a program could not create a directory for one of the following reasons: a directory by the same name already exists; a file by the same name already exists; you are adding a directory to the root directory, and the root directory is full; or the directory name has illegal characters or is a device name.

Issue DIR to make sure that no file or directory already exists with the same name. If you are adding the directory to the root directory, remove or move (copy, then erase) any nonessential files or directories. Check the spelling of the directory name, and make sure that the command is properly phrased.

Unable to load MS-DOS Shell, Retry (y/n)?

ERROR, PROMPT: DOS could not load the Shell. You may be using a DOS command-line feature of a program, and the Shell does not fit into memory. The DOS Shell program also may be corrupted.

Exit the program, and try to load the Shell. If the Shell still doesn't load, it probably is corrupt. Reboot your system, and load the Shell. If the same error message appears, copy the Shell from a backup disk to your hard disk.

Unable to write BOOT

ERROR: FORMAT cannot write to the BOOT track or DOS partition of the disk that is being formatted because one of these areas is bad. Discard the bad disk, insert another unformatted disk, and try the FORMAT command again.

Unrecognized command in CONFIG.SYS

WARNING (start-up): DOS detected an improperly phrased command in CONFIG.SYS. The command is ignored, and DOS continues to start, but DOS does not indicate the incorrect line. Examine the CONFIG.SYS file, looking for improperly phrased or incorrect commands. Edit the line, save the file, and restart DOS.

Unrecoverable read error on drive x side n, track n

ERROR: DOS was unable to read the data at the specified location on the disk. DOS makes four attempts before generating this message.

Copy all files on the questionable disk to another disk, and try the command again, first with a new disk and then with the backup disk. If the original disk cannot be reformatted, discard it.

`Unrecoverable write error on drive x side n, track n`

ERROR: DOS was unable to write to a disk at the location specified. Try the command again; if the error recurs, the target disk is damaged at that location. If the damaged disk contains important data, copy the files to an empty, freshly formatted disk, and try to reformat the damaged disk. If the disk is bad, discard it.

`Write failure, diskette unusable`

ERROR: DOS found bad sectors in the boot or FAT areas of the target disk. Discard the disk, and use another to create a System disk.

`Wrong DOS`

ERROR: The version of DOS is incompatible with UNFORMAT.

DOS Device Error Messages

When DOS detects an error while reading or writing to disk drives or other devices, one of the following messages appears:

`type error reading device`

`type error writing device`

type is the type of error, and *device* is the device at fault. If the device is a floppy disk drive, do not remove the disk from the drive. Refer to the possible causes and corrective actions described in this section, which lists the types of error messages that may appear.

`/B invalid with a black and white printer`

You issued the GRAPHICS command with the /B switch, which indicates a background color. You cannot print a background color on a black-and-white printer.

Bad call format

A device driver was given a requested header with an incorrect length. The problem is the applications software making the call.

Bad command

The device driver issued an invalid or unsupported command to the device. The problem may be with the device driver software or with other software trying to use the device driver. If you wrote the program, correct it. For a purchased program, contact the dealer or publisher who sold you the program.

Bad format call

The device driver at fault passed an incorrect header length to DOS. If you wrote this device driver, you must rewrite it to correct the problem. For a purchased program, contact the dealer or publisher who sold you the driver.

Bad unit

An invalid subunit number was passed to the device driver. The problem may be with the device driver software or with other software trying to use the device driver. Contact the dealer who sold you the device driver.

Data

DOS could not correctly read or write the data. The disk most likely has developed a defective spot.

Drive not ready

An error occurred when DOS tried to read or write to the disk drive. For floppy disk drives, the drive door may be open, the floppy disk may not have been inserted, or the disk may not be formatted. For hard disk drives, the drive may not be prepared properly; that is, you may have a hardware problem.

FCB unavailable

With the file-sharing program (SHARE.EXE) loaded, a program using the DOS 1 method of file handling attempted to open concurrently more file control blocks than were specified with the FCBS command.

Select the Abort option (see the end of this section). Increase the value of the FCBS CONFIG.SYS command (usually by four), and reboot the system. If the message appears again, increase the value again, and reboot.

General failure

This message is a catchall for errors not covered elsewhere. The error usually occurs for one of the following reasons: you are using an unformatted disk; the disk drive door is open; the floppy disk is not seated properly; or you are using the wrong type of disk in a disk drive, such as a 360K disk in a 1.2M disk drive.

Lock violation

With the file-sharing program (SHARE.EXE) or the network software loaded, a program attempted to access a locked file. Your best choice is Retry. Then try Abort. If you press A, however, any data in memory is lost.

Must specify COM1, COM2, COM3 or COM4

You must specify the COM port in the MODE command.

No paper

The printer is out of paper or not turned on.

Non-DOS disk

The FAT has invalid information, making the disk unusable. You can abort and run CHKDSK to determine whether corrective action is possible. If CHKDSK fails, you can reformat the disk. Reformatting, however, destroys any remaining information on the disk.

If you use more than one operating system, the disk has probably been formatted under the other operating system and should not be reformatted.

Not ready

The device is not ready and cannot receive or transmit data. Check the connections, making sure that the power is on and the device is ready. For floppy disk drives, make sure that the disk is formatted and properly seated in the disk drive.

`Read fault`

DOS was unable to read the data, probably from a disk. Check the disk drive doors to make sure that the disk is inserted properly.

`Sector not found`

The disk drive was unable to find the sector on the disk. This error is usually the result of a defective spot on the disk or of defective drive electronics. Some copy-protection schemes also use a defective spot to prevent unauthorized duplication of the disk.

`Seek`

The disk drive could not find the proper track on the disk. This error is usually the result of a defective spot on the disk, an unformatted disk, or drive electronics problems.

`Write fault`

DOS could not write the data to this device. You may have inserted the disk improperly or left the disk drive door open. Another possibility is an electronics failure in the floppy or hard disk drive. The most frequent cause is a bad spot on the disk.

`Write protect`

The disk is write-protected.

> *Note:* One of the previously listed messages (usually `Data`, `Read fault`, or `Write fault`) appears when you are using a double-sided disk in a single-sided disk drive or a 9-sector disk (DOS 2 and later) with a version of DOS 1.
>
> DOS displays one of these error messages and the `Abort,Retry,Fail?` prompt for DOS 3.3, 4.x, and 5.0 or `Abort,Retry,Ignore?` for versions of DOS before 3.3.

If you press A for Abort, DOS ends the program that requested the read or write condition. Pressing R for Retry causes DOS to try the operation again. If you press F for Fail or I for Ignore, DOS skips the operation, and the program continues. Some data may be lost, however, when you select Fail or Ignore.

The order of preference, unless stated differently under the message, is R, A, and F or I. You should retry the operation at least twice. If the condition persists, you must decide whether to abort the program or ignore the error. If you ignore the error, data may be lost. If you abort, data still being processed by the program and not yet written to the disk is lost.

Changes between Versions of DOS

B

Several major changes occurred between DOS 2.0 and 3.0. Additional revisions occurred between DOS 3.0 and 3.3, between DOS 3.3 and 4.0, and between DOS 4.0 and 5.0. This appendix briefly describes all these changes.

Changes between DOS 2.0 and DOS 3.0

DOS 3.0 offers several new commands, changed commands, and changed features.

New Configuration Commands

The following CONFIG.SYS commands are new in DOS 3.0:

COUNTRY	Enables DOS to change the way it displays date, time, and other characteristics for international use
FCBS	Controls DOS's reactions to a program's use of DOS 1 file handling
LASTDRIVE	Sets the last disk drive letter that DOS uses
VDISK.SYS	Provides a RAM (virtual) disk

Other New Commands

The following commands were added in DOS 3.0:

ATTRIB	Enables you to set the read-only attribute of a file
GRAFTABL	Provides legible display of some graphics characters when you use the Color/ Graphics Adapter in medium-resolution graphics mode
KEYBxx	Changes the keyboard layout for international character sets
LABEL	Enables you to add, change, or delete a disk's volume label
SELECT	Enables you to customize the start-up disk for use with international character sets other than English
SHARE	Provides file sharing (file and record locking)

Changed Commands

The following commands were changed between DOS 2.0 and DOS 3.0:

BACKUP/RESTORE	Backs up floppy disks; enables backups to be placed on another hard disk
DATE/TIME	Supports international date and time formats
FORMAT	Includes the /4 switch to format 360K floppy disks on 1.2M disk drives; warns you when you are about to format a hard disk
GRAPHICS	Enables you to print graphics screens on some dot-matrix and color printers

Changed Features

With DOS 3.0, you can specify drive and path names before an external command or program name. Using this command format enables you to run programs that do not reside in the current directory or in a directory specified in the PATH command.

Changes between DOS 3.0 and DOS 3.1

The following changes were made between DOS 3.0 and 3.1.

New Commands

The following commands are new under DOS 3.1:

JOIN	Enables the user to connect the directory structures of two disk drives, creating "one" disk drive
SUBST	Enables a subdirectory to be used as a disk drive

DOS 3.1 supports the IBM PC Network.

Changed Commands

The following commands were changed between DOS 3.0 and DOS 3.1:

LABEL	Prompts before deleting a volume label
TREE	/F displays file names with the directory tree

Changes between DOS 3.1 and DOS 3.2

The following changes were made between DOS 3.1 and DOS 3.2.

New Configuration Commands

DRIVER.SYS	Supports different sizes of floppy disks, particularly 720K microfloppy drives on personal computers
STACKS	Sets the number and size of the DOS internal stacks

Other New Commands

The following commands were added in DOS 3.2:

REPLACE	Selectively updates files in one or many directories; adds missing files to a directory
XCOPY	Copies files from one or more directories to another; selectively copies files

Changed Commands

The following commands were changed between DOS 3.1 and DOS 3.2:

ATTRIB	+A/–A switch controls the archive attribute
COMMAND	/E supports the environment size (often used with the SHELL configuration command)
DISKCOPY /DISKCOMP	Supports 720K floppy disks
FORMAT	Supports formatting of 720K floppy disks; requests verification before formatting a nonremovable disk that has a volume label; disk drive name required
SELECT	Formats the hard disk and copies DOS files

New Feature

DOS 3.2 supports the IBM Token Ring.

Changes between DOS 3.2 and DOS 3.3

The following changes were made between DOS 3.2 and DOS 3.3.

New Configuration Commands

The following device drivers for use with the DEVICE configuration command are new in DOS 3.3:

DISPLAY.SYS	Supports code pages (multiple fonts) on EGA, VGA, and PC Convertible displays
PRINTER.SYS	Supports code pages (multiple fonts) on the IBM ProPrinter and Quietwriter III

DOS 3.3 supports 1.44M microfloppy disks, COM4, 19200-baud rates, and switchable code pages (international character fonts).

Other New Commands

The following commands are new with DOS 3.3:

APPEND	Performs PATH-like function for data files
CHCP	Provides code-page changing
FASTOPEN	Provides a directory-caching program for hard disks
NLSFUNC	Provides support for additional international character sets (code pages)

Changed Commands

The following commands were changed between DOS 3.2 and DOS 3.3:

ATTRIB	/S changes the attributes of files in subdirectories

BACKUP	Places all backed-up files into a single file on each backup disk; /F formats floppy disks; /T backs up files based on their time; /L produces a log file
Batch files	Support the environment variable (%variable%); @ suppresses display of a line; CALL runs a second batch file, returning control to the first batch file
BUFFERS	Bases default buffers on random-access memory in the computer
COMMAND	Changes default environment size from 128 to 160 byte
COUNTRY	Supports code pages and a separate country information file (COUNTRY.SYS)
DATE/TIME	Sets the computer's clock/calendar
DISKCOPY /DISKCOMP	Support 1.44M floppy disks
FDISK	Supports multiple logical disks on a large hard disk
FORMAT	Adds the /N switch for number of sectors and /T for number of tracks
GRAFTABL	Supports code pages as well as additional devices and higher baud rates
KEYB	Replaces KEYBxx programs; supports additional layouts
MODE	Supports code pages as well as additional devices and higher baud rates
RESTORE	/N restores erased or modified files; /B restores files modified before a given date; /L and /E restore files modified after or before a given time

Changes between DOS 3.3 and DOS 4.0

The following changes were made between DOS 3.3 and DOS 4.0.

New Configuration Commands

The following configuration commands are new with DOS 4.0:

INSTALL	Enables loading of terminate-and-stay-resident programs previously loaded from the DOS command prompt or in the AUTOEXEC.BAT file. Installable programs include FASTOPEN.EXE, KEYB.COM, NLSFUNC.EXE, and SHARE.EXE.
REM	Enables you to insert into a CONFIG.SYS file remarks, which DOS ignores when the computer is booted
SWITCHES	Disables Enhanced Keyboard functions for compatibility with software that does not recognize the Enhanced Keyboard
XMA2EMS.SYS	An expanded memory manager (DOS 4.0 only)
XMAEM.SYS	Uses extended memory to emulate an expanded memory adapter on 80386 machines (DOS 4.0 only)

Other New Commands

The following commands are new in DOS 4.0:

MEM	Provides a report on available conventional, extended, and expanded memory; lists how much of each is unused
TRUENAME	Lists the actual name of a drive or directory affected by a JOIN or SUBST command

Changed Commands

The following commands were changed between DOS 3.3 and DOS 4.0:

ANSI.SYS	/X redefines keys added to Enhanced Keyboards; /L overrides applications programs that reset the number of screen rows to 25; /K turns off extended keyboard functions for compatibility with older software
APPEND	Ignores file operations that already include a drive or path in the original specification
BACKUP	Formats destination floppy disks automatically if necessary
BUFFERS	/X tells DOS to use expanded memory; specifies up to 10,000 buffers and 1 through 8 look-ahead buffers
CHKDSK	Shows the disk's serial number and lists the size and number of allocation units
COUNTRY	Provides support for Japanese, Korean, and Chinese characters—on special Asian hardware only
DEL/ERASE	/P prompts for confirmation before each file is deleted
DIR	Shows the disk's serial number
DISPLAY.SYS	Checks hardware and chooses the most appropriate type of active display if you don't specify an adapter type
FASTOPEN	/X tells DOS to use expanded memory
FDISK	Supports larger disk partitions and has easier-to-use menus and displays
FORMAT	/V:label specifies the volume label; /F:size indicates the size of a floppy disk
GRAFTABL	Supports code page 850
GRAPHICS	Supports EGA and VGA adapters; can support more printers

KEYB	/ID.nnn chooses a specific keyboard for countries, such as France, Italy, and Great Britain, that have more than one Enhanced Keyboard
MODE	Specifies the keyboard rate and number of lines displayed on-screen; has parameters for COM ports
PRINTER.SYS	Supports additional features of the IBM ProPrinter
REPLACE	/U updates files that have a more recent date and time
SELECT	Installs DOS
SYS	Enables specification of an optional source drive
TIME	Enables a 12- or 24-hour clock depending on the country code in use
TREE	Creates a graphic depiction of the directory tree
VDISK.SYS	/X tells DOS to use expanded memory; /E tells DOS to use extended memory

New User Interface

A new user interface, the DOS Shell, enables you to run programs and manage files using a visually oriented menu system. Many error messages are different, and error checking is refined.

Changes between DOS 4.0 and DOS 5.0

The following changes were made between DOS 4.0 and DOS 5.0.

New Configuration Commands

The following configuration commands are new with DOS 5.0:

DEVICEHIGH	Loads device drivers into reserved memory

DOS	Loads the operating system into the high memory area; supports loading of device drivers into upper memory blocks
EMM386.EXE	Provides expanded memory management; uses XMS memory to emulate expanded memory in 80386 and 80486 PCs; provides upper memory block (UMB) support in 80386 and 80486 PCs; includes VCPI and busmaster support
HIMEM.SYS	Manages extended memory in compliance with the extended memory specification (XMS)
SETVER	Enables you to control the DOS version reported to an application

Other New Commands

The following commands are new in DOS 5.0:

DOSKEY	Stores command-line statements into memory for later editing and use
EDIT	Invokes a a full-screen, mouse-compatible ASCII-file editor that has on-line documentation with hypertext links
LOADHIGH (LH)	Loads programs into upper (reserved) memory
MIRROR	Saves FAT (file allocation table) information; loads delete-tracking memory-resident program
QBASIC	Invokes an improved BASIC programming language interpreter and a full-screen programming environment
SETUP	Installs DOS 5.0
UNDELETE	Recovers a deleted file
UNFORMAT	Recovers data after an accidental format

Changed Commands

The following commands were changed between DOS 4.0 and DOS 5.0

ATTRIB	+S/–S sets and clears the system attribute; +H/–H sets and clears the hidden attribute.
DIR	/S searches multiple subdirectories for files; /O sorts the directory listing by file size, file name, type of file and date and time of file creation; /A displays file attributes; the DIRCMD environment variable stores DIR settings; /B displays file name only; /L displays file names in lowercase
DOSSHELL	Enables you to view the file list area and program list area simultaneously, rename directories, search for files, and switch between active programs; provides full mouse support
FDISK	Creates a single partition up to 2G (gigabytes); SHARE is no longer needed to access partitions larger than 32M
FIND	Ignores case during a search for a character string
FORMAT	Runs MIRROR automatically in anticipation of a possible need to unformat a disk; /Q quick-formats a previously formatted disk; /U performs unconditional format; supports 2.88M 3.5-inch floppy disks
MEM	/Program and /Debug display the status of programs and drivers as well as information regarding RAM availability; /Classify lists program size, summarizes memory in use, and lists the largest blocks of RAM available in conventional and upper memory
MODE	Sets typematic rate and delay

On-line help

/? after or HELP before any command-line command displays the command syntax with a short description of the command's purpose

DOS Control and Editing Keys

C

T his appendix lists the functions of various keystrokes for control and editing when used at the command line and within the DOS Shell.

Command-Line Control Keys

Enter, ↵	Tells DOS to act on the line you just typed
Backspace, ←	Moves left and deletes one character from the line
Ctrl-C, Ctrl-Break	Stops a command
Ctrl-Num Lock, Ctrl-S	Freezes the video display; pressing any other key restarts the display
PrtSc, Print Screen	Prints the contents of the video display
Ctrl-PrtSc, Ctrl-Print Screen, Ctrl-P,	Echoes lines sent to the screen to the printer also; giving this sequence a second time turns off the printer echo feature
Ctrl-Alt-Del	Restarts (reboots) DOS

Command-Line Editing Keys

When you type a line at the DOS prompt and press Enter, DOS copies the line into an input buffer. By using certain keys, you can use the same line over and over again. The following keys enable you to edit the input buffer line. When you press Enter, the new line is placed into the primary input buffer as DOS executes the line:

←| →|	Moves the cursor to the next tab stop
Esc	Cancels the current line without changing the buffer
Ins	Enables you to insert characters into the line
Del	Deletes a character from the line
F1 or →	Copies one character from the preceding command line
F2	Copies all characters from the preceding command line up to but not including the next character you type
F3	Copies all remaining characters from the preceding command line
F4	Deletes all characters from the preceding command line up to but not including the next character you type (opposite of F2)
F5	Moves the current line into the buffer but does not enable DOS to execute the line
F6	Produces an end-of-file marker ($^\wedge$Z) when you copy from the console to a disk file

Note: If you have DOSKey loaded, the following keys are also available:

←	Moves the cursor one character to the left
→	Moves the cursor one character to the right
Backspace	Moves the cursor one character to the left; in insert mode, also erases character to the left
Ctrl-←	Moves the cursor one word to the left
Ctrl-→	Moves the cursor one word to the right
Home	Moves the cursor to the left end of the command line

End	Moves the cursor to the space after the last character in the command line
Esc	Erases the contents of the command line
Del	Deletes the character positioned directly above the cursor
Ctrl-End	Removes all characters from the cursor to the end of the line
Ctrl-Home	Removes all characters from the cursor to the beginning of the line
Ins	Toggles between replace mode (the default) and insert mode
↑	Displays the preceding DOS command
↓	Displays the DOS command issued after the one currently displayed, or displays a blank line when you are at the end of the list
PgUp	Displays the earliest command issued that is still stored in the DOSKey command buffer
PgDn	Displays the last command stored in the DOSKey command buffer
F7	Displays contents of the command-history buffer in a numbered list
Alt-F7	Clears the command-history buffer
F8	Searches for the command(s) that most closely match characters typed at the command line
F9	Prompts for a line number, where *line number* refers to the number displayed next to a command in the command-history listing generated by pressing F7. Press the number to display the corresponding command.

Keystroke Commands within the DOS Shell

DOS 5.0 assigns special functions to some keys when used within the DOS Shell:

F1	Displays context-sensitive help
F3	Exits the DOS Shell to the command line and removes the DOS Shell from memory (same as Alt-F4)
Alt-F4	Exits the DOS Shell to the command line and removes the DOS Shell from memory (same as F3)
F5	Refreshes the file list(s)
Shift-F5	Repaints the screen
F7	Moves selected file(s)
F8	Copies selected file(s)
Shift-F8	Toggles add mode for extending selection of nonconsecutive files—select files by pressing the space bar
F9	Views file contents
Shift-F9	Accesses the command line without removing the DOS Shell from memory
F10	Activates the menu bar (same as Alt)
Alt	Activates the menu bar (same as F10)
Del	Deletes selected file(s)
+	Expands one level the current branch in the directory tree
*	Expands all levels of the current branch in the directory tree
Ctrl-*	Expands all branches in the directory tree
–	Collapses the current branch in the directory tree
Tab	Cycles through areas of the DOS Shell window in clockwise direction

Shift-Tab	Cycles through areas of the DOS Shell window in counterclockwise direction
Alt-Tab	Switches between active task and DOS Shell if task swapper is enabled
Esc	Cancels the current function
Alt-Esc	Cycles through active tasks
↑ or →	Moves selection cursor in the direction of the arrow
Shift-↑ or Shift-↓	While in the file list area, extends selection in the direction of the arrow
PgUp	Scrolls up through the selected area one screen at a time
PgDn	Scrolls down through the selected area one screen at a time
Home, Ctrl-Home	Moves to the top of the selected area
End, Ctrl-End	Moves to the bottom of the selected area
Ctrl-/	Selects all files in the selected directory
Ctrl-\	Deselects all files in the selected directory

Using Edlin

Y ou use Edlin to create and edit ASCII files. Edlin, unlike most text editors, is a *line editor*. A line editor is a program that enables you to edit a file one line at a time. Rather than moving freely and easily from line to line, as with a word processor, you must designate the line you want to edit.

When Edlin creates a file, the program assigns to each line a number for editing purposes. When editing a file, you specify the number of the line you want to edit. When you save the file after you finish editing it, Edlin does not save the line numbers with the file.

Creating a file with Edlin is easy. The syntax for Edlin is as follows:

> *dc:pathc***EDLIN** *df:pathf***filename.ext** */B*

If Edlin is not in your search path (designated in the PATH statement in your AUTOEXEC.BAT file), you must specify the optional drive and subdirectory where Edlin is located, as shown by *dc:pathc*. When you start Edlin, you must specify the name of the file you want to edit. You optionally can specify the drive and subdirectory where this file is located, shown by *df:pathf*. You also have the option to include Edlin's only switch, */B*, to load a file and ignore the end-of-file characters ($^\wedge$Z).

To create a batch file called MOVE.BAT that includes Edlin in your search path, type the following:

> **Edlin MOVE.BAT**

After Edlin starts, you see the following:

```
New file
*
```

The asterisk is Edlin's command prompt. You can issue any of Edlin's commands from this prompt. The following table lists Edlin's commands and an example and description of each command:

Command	Example	Description
n	7	Displays a line to edit
nA	4A	Specifies the number of lines to read into memory. Use when a file is too large to load into memory.
n1,n2,n3,n4C	4,6,15,2C	Copies a line or lines to any other position in the file. n1,n2 is the range of lines to copy. n3 is the line where Edlin inserts the copy. n4 is the number of copies inserted. If n1, n2, and n4 are omitted, Edlin copies the current line one time (,,15C).
n1,n2D	3,5D	Deletes a range of lines. n1,n2 is the beginning and ending line to delete. You can omit n1 and n2. If both are omitted, Edlin deletes the current line (D).
E	E	Ends and saves the current file
nI	4I	Begins inserting new lines before the current line number n. If n is omitted, Edlin begins inserting before the current line (I).
n1,n2L	4,10L	Lists lines in the file. The lines listed are from n1 through n2. If n1 and n2 are omitted, Edlin displays up to 23 lines of the file (L).

Command	Example	Description
*n1,n2,*n3M	**3,6,15M**	Moves a range of lines to another location in the file. You can move lines *n1* through *n2* to precede the location line *n3*. If *n1* and *n2* are omitted, Edlin moves the current line to precede line n3 (**,,15M**).
*n1,+n,n3*M	**5,+5,21M**	Moves a range of lines to another location in the file. You can move line *n1* and the next *+n* lines to precede the location line *n3*. If *n1* and *+n* are omitted, Edlin moves the current line to precede line n3 (**,,21M**).
*n1,n2*P	**6,16P**	Displays lines *n1* through *n2*. The last line displayed becomes the current line. If *n1* and *n2* are omitted, Edlin displays 23 lines from the current line (**P**).
*n1,n2?*Rs1^Zs2	**5,10?Rme^zI**	Replaces the occurrence of s1 with the new string s2. The search and replace takes place from *n1* through *n2*. If you include *?*, Edlin prompts you before s1 is replaced. You create the separator, ^Z, by pressing F6 or the key combination Ctrl+Z.
*n1,n2?*Ss	**5,10?SJohn**	Searches for the occurrence of s in the file. The search takes place from line *n1* through line *n2*. If you include *?*, Edlin prompts you when s is found, before the search continues.

Command	Example	Description
*n*T*d:path*\filename	**15TMEMO.TXT**	Transfers the file specified to precede the line *n*. This combines the file filename.ext with the current file being edited. If *n* is omitted, Edlin transfers the file to precede the current line.
*n*W	**25W**	Specifies the number of lines to write to disk. Use when a file is too large to load into memory.

An additional feature of Edlin is the capability to use redirection. You can save Edlin commands in an ASCII file and, using redirection, can modify other ASCII files.

To use Edlin with redirection, type the following command:

EDLIN \BATCH\REPAIR.BAT < \DOS\MODIFY.FIL

This command starts Edlin and loads REPAIR.BAT into memory for editing. Edlin uses the file MODIFY.FIL as the *command* file, where the program stores commands. Be sure to remember that the last command in the command file (for example, MODIFY.FIL) must be E, the command to save and quit Edlin.

Index

Computer Books From Que Mean PC Performance!

Free Catalog!

Mail us this registration form today, and we'll send you a free catalog featuring Que's complete line of best-selling books.

Name of Book _____

Name _____

Title _____

Phone (___) _____

Company _____

Address _____

City _____

State _____ ZIP _____

Please check the appropriate answers:

1. Where did you buy your Que book?
   - ☐ Bookstore (name: _____)
   - ☐ Computer store (name: _____)
   - ☐ Catalog (name: _____)
   - ☐ Direct from Que
   - ☐ Other: _____

2. How many computer books do you buy a year?
   - ☐ 1 or less
   - ☐ 2-5
   - ☐ 6-10
   - ☐ More than 10

3. How many Que books do you own?
   - ☐ 1
   - ☐ 2-5
   - ☐ 6-10
   - ☐ More than 10

4. How long have you been using this software?
   - ☐ Less than 6 months
   - ☐ 6 months to 1 year
   - ☐ 1-3 years
   - ☐ More than 3 years

5. What influenced your purchase of this Que book?
   - ☐ Personal recommendation
   - ☐ Advertisement
   - ☐ In-store display
   - ☐ Price
   - ☐ Que catalog
   - ☐ Que mailing
   - ☐ Que's reputation
   - ☐ Other: _____

6. How would you rate the overall content of the book?
   - ☐ Very good
   - ☐ Good
   - ☐ Satisfactory
   - ☐ Poor

7. What do you like *best* about this Que book?
   _____
   _____

8. What do you like *least* about this Que book?
   _____
   _____

9. Did you buy this book with your personal funds?
   - ☐ Yes   ☐ No

10. Please feel free to list any other comments you may have about this Que book.
    _____
    _____
    _____

que

Order Your Que Books Today!

Name _____

Title _____

Company _____

City _____

State _____ ZIP _____

Phone No. (___) _____

Method of Payment:

Check ☐ (Please enclose in envelope.)

Charge My: VISA ☐   MasterCard ☐

American Express ☐

Charge # _____

Expiration Date _____

Order No.	Title	Qty.	Price	Total

You can **FAX** your order to **1-317-573-2583**. Or call **1-800-428-5331, ext. ORDR** to order direct.
Please add $2.50 per title for shipping and handling.

Subtotal _____

Shipping & Handling _____

Total _____

que

NO POSTAGE
NECESSARY
IF MAILED
IN THE
UNITED STATES

BUSINESS REPLY MAIL
First Class Permit No. 9918   Indianapolis, IN

Postage will be paid by addressee

11711 N. College
Carmel, IN 46032

NO POSTAGE
NECESSARY
IF MAILED
IN THE
UNITED STATES

BUSINESS REPLY MAIL
First Class Permit No. 9918   Indianapolis, IN

Postage will be paid by addressee

11711 N. College
Carmel, IN 46032